The Modern School Movement

The Modern School Movement

Anarchism and Education in the United States

Paul Avrich

Princeton University Press
Princeton, New Jersey

PUBLISHED BY PRINCETON UNIVERSITY PRESS,
PRINCETON, NEW JERSEY
IN THE UNITED KINGDOM: PRINCETON UNIVERSITY PRESS,
GUILDFORD, SURREY

CLOTHBOUND EDITIONS OF PRINCETON UNIVERSITY PRESS BOOKS
ARE PRINTED ON ACID-FREE PAPER, AND BINDING MATERIALS ARE
CHOSEN FOR STRENGTH AND DURABILITY

PRINTED IN THE UNITED STATES OF AMERICA BY PRINCETON
UNIVERSITY PRESS, PRINCETON, NEW JERSEY

LIBRARY OF CONGRESS CATALOGING IN PUBLICATION DATA

Avrich, Paul.
The modern school movement.

Bibliography: p.
Includes index.
1. Education—United States—Philosophy—History—20th century. 2. Education—United States—Experimental methods—History—20th century. 3. Ferrer Guardia, Francisco, 1859-1909. 4. Educators—United States—Political activity—History—20th century. 5. Anarchism and anarchists—United States—History—20th century.
I. Title.
LA216.A78 370′.973 79-3188
ISBN 0-691-04669-7
ISBN 0-691-10094-1 pbk.

In Memory of Agnes Inglis
1870-1952

Contents

Illustrations

(following page 240)

The initial letters in this volume are reproduced from the decorative alphabet designed by Rockwell Kent for *The Modern School* magazine.

Preface

BETWEEN 1910 and 1960 a remarkable educational experiment took place in the United States under the aegis of the anarchist movement. For half a century anarchists from New York to Los Angeles carried on a venture in learning that was unique in American history. Inspired by the execution of Francisco Ferrer, the Spanish educator and martyr, more than twenty schools were established in different parts of the country where children might study in an atmosphere of freedom and self-reliance, in contrast to the formality and discipline of the traditional classroom. These Modern Schools, as they were called, differed from other educational experiments of the same period in being schools for children of workers and directed by the workers themselves. Their founders, moreover, were anarchists, whose prophets were Bakunin, Kropotkin, and Tolstoy as well as Rousseau, Pestalozzi, and Froebel, and who sought to abolish all forms of authority, political and economic as well as educational, and to usher in a new society based on the voluntary cooperation of free individuals.

To prepare men and women for this new society, the anarchists pinned their hopes on education. No other movement assigned education a more prominent place in its writings and activities. It is surprising, therefore, that the Modern Schools have never received a comprehensive historical treatment. Apart from a handful of works on specific aspects of the subject, notably *The Communal Experience* by Laurence Veysey and *The Modern School of Stelton* by Joseph Cohen and Alexis Ferm, the Ferrer movement has remained an uncharted region of American history, another reminder of how many gaps there are in our knowledge of even the recent past.

In view of these circumstances, I began, in the early 1970s, to examine the available source materials in an effort to unravel the entire story. The present volume is the result. Its purpose is to narrate the history of the Modern School movement, to analyze its successes and failures, and to assess its place in American life. It was a rich and diverse movement, involving experiments in art and communal living as well as in education, and I hope that the reader will tolerate the complexity of the narrative as inherent in the subject itself. Among the participants were many famous figures in the radical and artistic world, including Emma Goldman and Alexander Berkman, Margaret Sanger and Carlo Tresca, Robert Henri and George Bellows, Man Ray and Rockwell Kent. Their object, during an era of war, social ferment, and government repression, was to create not only a new type of school but also a new culture, a new life, a new world.

In attempting to bring together in a single volume the evidence bearing on events at once so complex and controversial, I have preferred to err on the side of explicitness and completeness, rather than to run the risk of leaving serious gaps or of inviting the suspicion of partiality in the selection of material. Besides, the more I studied the documents the more I realized that an understanding of the issues demanded the kind of treatment that only a detailed exposition and analysis could provide. For similar reasons, I have adhered as closely as possible to the primary sources, quoting extensively from the statements of the participants, both published and unpublished.

As in my previous volume on anarchism in the United States, *An American Anarchist: The Life of Voltairine de Cleyre* (Princeton, 1978), my approach has been largely biographical, focusing on individual men and women in actual situations. I have tried, moreover, to convey not only what they said and did but also what they meant and felt, though the theoretical premises on which they acted are not neglected. As Leonard Abbott, one of the central figures in my narrative, observed, "Nothing in the world is more fundamental and more fascinating than the questions: Why are we as we are? Why do we act as we do? What is it that we really desire? Why is one man a conservative and another a radical? Why is one man religious and another a freethinker? And so on."[1] Such are the questions this book will try to answer with regard to the Modern School movement.

After half a dozen years spent working on this book, I am pleased to acknowledge the help and generosity of those who made its completion possible. Above all, it has been my good fortune to have enjoyed the friendship of many of the surviving participants—students, teachers, colonists—without whose cooperation I could not have embarked upon a study that depended so heavily upon personal testimony. Though their names are too numerous to be listed here, most are acknowledged in the footnotes. Some, however, have gone to special lengths in supplying me with materials and information, and I owe them particular thanks: William Morris Abbott, Suzanne Hotkine Avins, Sally Axelrod, Eva Bein, Abe Bluestein, Eva Brandes, Jo Ann Wheeler Burbank, James Dick, Jr., Nellie Dick, Gussie Denenberg, Emma Cohen Gilbert, Maurice Hollod, Anatole Freeman Ishill, Moritz Jagendorf, Dora Keyser, Manuel Komroff, David Lawson, Ben Lieberman, Rose Lowensohn, Crystal Ishill Mendelsohn, Charles Robert Plunkett, Mary Schwartz Rappaport, Jack Rudome, Magda Boris Schoenwetter, and Ray Miller Shedlovsky.

Others who have aided me in important ways, including the furnishing of information and the reading of the manuscript, are Marion Bell, Senya and Mollie Fleshin, Ann Hutchinson Guest, Harry Lawton, Elaine Sproat, and Ahrne Thorne. My thanks are due also to Sanford Thatcher, Gail Filion, and Judith May of Princeton University Press for their valuable suggestions and their unfailing kindness and encouragement.

The search for material has taken me to many libraries and archives, in Europe as well as in America. To the staffs of these institutions, the most important of which are listed in the Bibliography, I am much indebted for assistance. I am especially grateful in this regard to Rudolf de Jong of the International Institute of Social History, Hillel Kempinski of the Bund Archives, Gerd Muehsam of the Queens College Art Library, Donald Sinclair of the Rutgers University Library, Dorothy Swanson of the Tamiment Library, and Edward Weber of the Labadie Collection.

My exploration of the relevant archival and printed sources was facilitated by a grant from the Research Foundation of the City University of New York and by a National Endowment for the Humanities Senior Fellowship, for which I am deeply grateful. The responsibility for this volume, however, is entirely my own.

P.H.A.

New York City
September 1978

PART I
New York

CHAPTER 1

The Martyrdom of Ferrer

ON OCTOBER 13, 1909, Francisco Ferrer y Guardia, a Spanish educator and freethinker, was shot in the trenches of Barcelona's Montjuich fortress. Following a mock trial, at which no solid evidence against him was brought forward, a military court had found him guilty of fomenting a popular insurrection, which had raged for a week—the "Tragic Week," it was called—before being crushed by government forces. The execution of Ferrer, the founder of rationalist schools, provoked an international outcry. A little-known figure outside radical circles, he was catapulted into sudden prominence. On both sides of the Atlantic there were meetings and demonstrations of protest. In a number of European cities, streets were renamed after him and statues erected in his memory. Most important, however, a movement for libertarian education, inspired by his example, quickly spread throughout the world.

Who then was Ferrer? Why did he become an international martyr? Was he or was he not an anarchist? Did his schools teach social rebellion? Was he involved in a plot to assassinate the king? After seventy years his name remains the subject of controversy. It is still not easy to disentangle fact from fantasy, truth from lies and half-lies. Yet we know enough about Ferrer and his work to understand why his name became synonymous with modern education, and why, as a result, the Spanish authorities were determined to get rid of him.

FRANCISCO FERRER Y GUARDIA

Francisco Ferrer was born on January 10, 1859, on a farm near Barcelona, where his mother was still living at the time of his execution. Although his parents were devout Catholics, one of his uncles was a freethinker, and his first employer, a grain merchant, was a militant atheist. The spirit of revolt seems to have been in Ferrer's blood. He grew into a young man of independent character, with violently anti-clerical views and a taste for conspiratorial adventure. By 1883 he was a Freemason and radical Republican, a follower of Manuel Ruíz Zorilla, who was living in Parisian exile. As a conductor on the railroad between Barcelona and the French frontier, Ferrer was able to act as a courier for Ruíz and to help political refugees find sanctuary across the border. In 1885 he himself was involved in an abortive republican rising and compelled to take refuge in France.[1]

Ferrer and his family spent the next sixteen years in Paris. Married and the father of three daughters, he earned a living by teaching Spanish and by selling wine on commission. At the same time, he served as unpaid secretary to Ruíz until the latter's death in 1895. Ferrer threw himself into various radical causes, becoming an ardent defender of Dreyfus and a delegate to the 1896 Congress of the Second International, held in London. His years in Paris, moreover, saw a hardening of his lifelong hostility to the Church. Active in rationalist circles, he taught at the Masonic school of the Grand Orient Lodge and attended the International Free Thought Congress at Prague in 1897.[2]

While engaged in these activities, Ferrer met many people and was exposed to new ideas. As Emma Goldman noted, he "learned, absorbed, and grew."[3] Cast adrift by the death of Ruíz, he moved from radical republicanism to the extreme left. Studying anarchist literature and frequenting anarchist clubs, he encountered such prominent French anarchists as Louise Michel, Elisée Reclus, and Sébastien Faure, as well as Charles Malato and Jean Grave, with whom he became close friends. He also formed ties with exiled Spanish anarchists, above all Anselmo Lorenzo and Fernando Tarrida del Mármol. Impressed by their personal qualities and attracted by their ideas, he came to regard himself as their comrade. By the end of the 1890s he had developed a philosophy based on "the sovereignty of the individual, free from institutional restraints."[4]

Ferrer, as a teacher, conceived a special interest in education, a subject of intense discussion in both anarchist and rationalist circles. In 1900 Jean Grave, editor of *Les Temps Nouveaux*, published a widely read brochure contrasting "bourgeois" with "libertarian" education,[5] and a spate of similar works appeared in print. Ferrer's appetite for such literature was insatiable. His imagination, moreover, was captured by Paul Robin's school at Cempuis, which became a model for his own Escuela Moderna.

Robin, a leading pioneer in the movement for libertarian education, had been named director of the Prévost Orphanage at

Cempuis, near Paris, in December 1880. Remaining in this post for fourteen years, he laid the groundwork for an "integral" education, of girls as well as boys, designed to develop both the physical and intellectual capacities of the pupils in a noncoercive atmosphere. "He believed," said Emma Goldman, who made a pilgrimage to Cempuis, "that whatever part heredity may play, there are other factors equally great, if not greater, that may and will eradicate or minimize the so-called first cause. Proper economic and social environment, the breath and freedom of nature, healthy exercise, love and sympathy, and, above all, a deep understanding for the needs of the child—these would destroy the cruel, unjust, and criminal stigma imposed on the ignorant child."[6]

Because of his unconventional methods of education and other radical activities (he was also a pioneer of the birth-control movement in France) Robin became the target of conservative critics, both secular and religious. Finally, in 1894, he was removed from his position. The reason, as Benjamin Tucker wryly put it, was that he had "refused to teach the orphans that France is bigger than the world or that God is bigger than man."[7]

But Robin had left an enduring example. After his departure, the school at Cempuis continued to function; and in 1897 two of his disciples, Manuel Degalvès and Emile Janvion, formed a League for Libertarian Education which aimed to start a school in Paris on the lines of Robin's experiment. Supported by such luminaries as Jean Grave, Louise Michel, and Elisée Reclus, as well as Kropotkin and Tolstoy, the Libertarian School, as it was to be called, was to offer an active, outdoor education as opposed to instruction primarily from books. According to the League's prospectus, entitled *Freedom Through Education*, "the sciences will be studied at the same time as letters, by practical illustration, even before reading is learned. The children will be brought face to face with Nature, and excursions will be made into the fields and Zoological Gardens to promote this end."[8]

Tolstoy offered his personal help in the project. "I started my social activity with the school and teaching," he wrote to *Les Temps Nouveaux*, "and after forty years I am more convinced that only by education, free education, can we ever manage to rid ourselves of the existing horrible order of things and to replace it with a rational organization."[9] For lack of funds, however, the school was unable to open. Only a summer school was established, which lasted but a single season.

Although Ferrer apparently never visited Cempuis, we know that he met Paul Robin and corresponded with him, and that he was deeply influenced by his ideas. Furthermore, he became an active member of the League for Human Regeneration, of which Robin was the founder. By the beginning of the new century, Ferrer had begun to dream of founding a libertarian school in Spain similar to that at Cempuis, a school where instruction would be based on rational principles and where children of both sexes could study in freedom and harmony. "I intend," he wrote to his friend José Prat, "to form a school of emancipation, which will be concerned with banning from the mind whatever divides men, the false concepts of property, country, and family, so as to attain the liberty and well-being which all desire and none completely realizes."[10]

Ferrer's dream soon became a reality. For in March 1900 he inherited a large sum of money—almost a million francs—from Ernestine Meunié, a middle-aged French lady to whom he had given lessons in Spanish. Mlle. Meunié had been a woman of conventional outlook until Ferrer, a persuasive teacher, succeeded in converting her to his ideas, and when she died she left him half of her estate. This unexpected legacy enabled him to return to Spain and found a Modern School in Barcelona.

FREEDOM IN EDUCATION

Ferrer returned to Barcelona in 1901, after sixteen years of exile in France. It was a time of widespread unrest, a moment when, as a result of the defeat in the war with the United States and the loss of almost all the remaining Spanish empire, many intellectuals were discussing and criticizing the conditions of Spanish life. Among the areas of greatest neglect was education. The need for educational reform was acutely felt by all social elements. Two-thirds of the Spanish population were unable to read or write. Only 15,000 of the nation's 45,000 towns had a public school; and most schools, whether lay or ecclesiastical, were grossly inadequate both in equipment and in the quality of the teachers, who were sworn to uphold Catholic dogma and were under the supervision of parish priests and diocesan inspectors.[11]

The decade of the 1890s had seen a rising tide of revolt against the old ways in Spain, in education as in industry and government. A spontaneous movement for secular instruction had sprung up in different parts of the country, in which efforts had been made by liberals and radicals to incorporate new ideas of science, history, and sociology into the educational curriculum. The impulse toward national regeneration after the defeat of 1898 gave these reformers a new audience, and the debate sharpened over how best to educate the illiterate masses.

In this debate Ferrer became an active participant. Starting from his deep hatred of the church and its domination over education, he called for a rational school in which pupils would not be stifled by religious dogma but would be free to organize their own lessons without compulsion. Ferrer, as we have seen, was one of a succession of European educators who aimed at bringing literacy and enlightenment to the laboring classes. In Spain itself, a tradition of rationalist education can be traced back to a scattering of republican and Fourierist schools in the 1840s and '50s, and to a larger number of anarchist and secularist schools in the 1870s and '80s, all of them makeshift affairs organized in the teeth of government opposition. Although Ferrer may have been the first to call his enterprise a "Modern School" (Escuela Moderna), he was following in the footsteps not only of Paul Robin at Cempuis but also of Elías Puig in Catalonia and José Sanchez Rosa in Andalusia, who had responded earlier to the yearning of Spanish workmen for independent secular schools.[12]

As to his pedagogical theories, Ferrer drew heavily on both precursors and contemporaries, from Rousseau, Pestalozzi, and Froebel to Kropotkin, Tolstoy, and Robin. He was in the direct line of an educational tradition which, rooted in eighteenth-century rationalism and nineteenth-century romanticism, involved a shift from emphasis on instruction to emphasis on the process of learning, from teaching by rote and memorization to teaching by example and experience, from education as a preparation for life to education as life itself. With "freedom in education" as its watchword, this tradition aimed to do away with the formality and discipline of the conventional classroom, the restrictions and regulations that suppressed individual development and divided education from play. It cultivated physical as well as mental development, crafts and arts as well as books. Hostile to dogma and superstition, it emphasized reason, observation, and science, as well as independence, autonomy, and self-reliance. Anticoercive and antiauthoritarian, it stressed the dignity and rights of the child, encouraging warmth, love, and affection in place of conformity and regimentation. Among the key words of its vocabulary were "freedom," "spontaneity," "creativity," "individuality," and "self-realization."

For the conventional school the proponents of libertarian education wished to substitute a "free" school—free, that is, from religious and political domination, indeed from authority of any sort. To Ferrer and his predecessors, the church presented the greatest obstacle to public enlightenment. They held that children should be given a "rational" education in a freethinking, nonreligious atmosphere. As Bakunin declared, education "must be founded wholly upon the scientific development of reason and not upon faith; upon the development of personal dignity and independence, not upon piety and obedience; upon the cult of truth and justice at any cost; and above all, upon respect for humanity, which must replace in everything the divine cult." Schools, Bakunin added, must be rid of "this fiction of God, the eternal absolute enslaver."[13] Ferrer, a militant atheist, thought in similar terms. Education, he wrote, must be antireligious because "science has shown that the story of the creation is a myth and the gods legendary." His aim, in Emma Goldman's words, was "to free the child from superstition and bigotry, from the darkness of dogma and authority."[14]

To Ferrer, however, state education was as noxious as that of the church. For state and church alike sought to keep out new ideas that might undermine the status quo. "Rulers have always taken care to control the education of the people," he declared. "They know better than anyone else that their power is based almost entirely on the school, and they therefore insist on retaining their monopoly on it."[15]

In these phrases Ferrer was echoing the views of libertarian thinkers since William Godwin, whose *Enquiry Concerning Political Justice* (1793) is considered the first modern anarchist attack on the state. To Godwin government education was an instrument of political control, stunting "the progress of knowledge and illumination" while endeavoring "to form all minds upon one model." He saw the public schools as a weapon wielded by the state to shape the will and character of its citizens and to condition children to docility and obedience, rather than stimulate independent judgment and a critical attitude towards authority. "Government by its very nature counteracts the improvement of the individual mind," he wrote. "Before we put so powerful a machine under the direction of so ambiguous an agent, it behooves us to consider well what it is that we do. Government will not fail to employ it to strengthen its hands and perpetuate its institutions."[16]

For Ferrer, as for Godwin, the school was "an instrument of domination in the hands of the ruling class." The government used the schools to produce loyal citizens; the church, faithful parishioners; the manufacturers, obedient workers. Those in charge of education had "never wanted the uplift of the individual, but his enslavement." Ferrer believed that the emancipation of the people could not be accomplished so long as they remained in ignorance. The central problem was therefore to break the stranglehold of church and state over education and to inaugurate a system of schools in which "the child will develop freely without subjection to any dogmatic patron." What was needed, he insisted, was "the establishment of new schools, in which, as far as possible, there shall rule the spirit of freedom which, we feel, will color the whole education of the future."[17]

"Freedom in education" meant freedom from the authority of the teacher as well as of the church and state. Under the prevailing system, argued Ferrer, the teacher was merely an agent of the ruling classes, training his charges "to obey, to believe, to think according to the social dogmas which govern us." Like the soldier and policeman, he was "always imposing, compelling, and using violence; the true educator is the man who does not impose his own ideas and will on the child, but appeals to its own energies."[18]

For thinkers like Godwin and Bakunin, learning could flourish only in a libertarian environment.[19] Reacting sharply against the barracks tradition of drilling lessons into students through a combination of repetition and punishment, they saw education as a spontaneous process rather than something to be imposed on the child. Rote, memorization, routine, the staples of conventional learning, destroyed the imagination and inhibited the natural development of children. Under the existing system, where originality and individuality were suppressed and conformity and mediocrity were at a premium, where children were taught *what* to believe, not *how* to think, even the most flexible student might be drained of all creativity and initiative.

Accordingly, the true function of the teacher was to encourage self-learning, to allow each child to develop in his own way, rather than force a predetermined program of study on him. Nor should the teacher smother the pupils under the weight of formal instruction. The emphasis, rather, must be on improvisation and experiment. Rigid programs, curricula, and timetables must be banished from the classroom, and instruction given in a manner that will cause the least interference with the pupil's freedom. For if a child is not compelled to learn, his own curiosity will draw him to the subjects that interest him, and his education will be more natural and pleasant, more enduring and meaningful.

Such was the credo of Ferrer and his precursors. It marked a radical departure from the old formula of cramming the memory with facts learned by rote in an atmosphere of rigorous discipline. Yet its elements are traceable to the late seventeenth century. As early as 1693, John Locke attacked the "orthodox methods of education," which he defined as the "charging of children's memories with rules and principles." The real job of the teacher, Locke said, was "to give them a liking or inclination to what you propose to them to be learned, and that will engage their industry and application." As far as possible, he suggested, pupils should have the freedom to develop their own capacities and to work at projects of their own selection.[20]

In his celebrated novel *Emile*, published in 1762, Rousseau expounded a similar method of education that would let pupils follow their inclinations. But it was Godwin, more than any previous thinker, who emancipated the child from the shackles of authority and placed him at the center of the learning process. Godwin firmly rejected the idea of education by means of compulsion. "Man is a creature that loves to act for himself, and actions performed in this way have infinitely more sound health and vigour in them than the actions to which he is prompted by a will foreign to his own," he wrote in *The Enquirer*,[21] perhaps the most advanced educational treatise of his time. Therefore, instead of forcing a child to learn what he is unwilling or unable to understand, the teacher should seek to gain his interest by aiding and encouraging and by giving him the greatest possible independence of action. "No creature in human form," he declared, "will be expected to learn anything but because he desires it and has some conception of its utility and value."[22]

The ideas of Godwin and Rousseau were taken up and elaborated by a whole succession of nineteenth-century thinkers, both famous and obscure, who shared a set of common assumptions. Pestalozzi and Froebel, Fourier and Owen, Proudhon and Stirner, Bakunin and Spencer, Kropotkin and Tolstoy—all believed that conventional education restrained the spontaneous development of the child, stunted his growth, and brutalized his character. All were agreed that freedom must be the cornerstone of education, that education was a process of self-development, a drawing out rather than a driving in, a means by which the child's unique spirit was nurtured rather than shaped or suppressed. They held that the pupils themselves must decide what to learn and how to learn it, that the function of the teacher was to allow them free scope, to encourage their self-reliance and independence. A favorite metaphor in their writing was that of a tree or a flower, growing, unfolding, blossoming, with nature alone to sustain it.

Froebel, the noted founder of the kindergarten system, warned against using the child as you would use a piece of wax, to be molded into a shape that others desired. In *The Education of Man* he called for a method of learning that was "not directive and interfering" but that "would have each human being develop from within, self-active and free, in accordance with the eternal law."[23] Fourier, in a similar vein, favored the full and unrestrained development of all aspects of the child's personality, regarding "absolute liberty" as indispensable for individual growth and happiness.[24] And Stirner, the German apostle of individualism, whose *Ego and His Own* has been called the most revolutionary book ever written, demanded "an education for freedom, not for subservience." Condemning the "false principle" of existing pedagogy, Stirner maintained that the imparting of facts or beliefs by the teacher established a master-slave relationship in which "freedom is not allowed to put a word in edgewise." The purpose of education, he insisted, was to produce not "useful citizens" but "free men," autonomous, independent, and self-sufficient.[25]

In a comparable spirit, Proudhon, Bakunin, and Kropotkin lashed out at the sterility of conventional education which produced, in Kropotkin's words, "superficiality, parrot-like repetition, slavishness, and inertia of mind."[26] Tolstoy's school at Yasnaya Polyana provided an alternative system. There Tolstoy tried to put into practice the methods advocated by previous libertarian theorists. Inspecting schools in Western Europe in 1861, he saw everywhere "rigid discipline, a constant demand for silence and obedience, the refusal to allow pupils to criticize, an utter lack of initiative." Rejecting this "compulsory structure," he saw learning as a creative and liberating process, enriching the child's unique spirit rather than molding him to suit the teacher's preconceptions. For Tolstoy the role of the teacher was not to inculcate or indoctrinate, but to suggest and encourage, to listen and modify what he hears. Like Pestalozzi and Froebel, like Godwin and Stirner, he wished to stimulate the pupil to think and act for himself. He favored an "unconscious education," a natural process in which the children are not even aware that they are being educated. All aspects of education were to be directed towards the pupil's emancipation. "Let it be established that there is only one criterion in teaching: freedom!" he wrote in his pedagogical review *Yasnaya Polyana*. For the whole object of education was "the free child."[27]

Libertarians were perhaps the first educational theorists to defend the rights of children, whom they regarded as fundamentally equal to adults, with the same need for freedom and dignity. "Children," wrote Bakunin in 1866, "belong neither to their parents nor to society. They belong to themselves and their future liberty." Accordingly, they must not be looked down upon as inferior beings, but treated with respect—treated as "creators," not "creatures," as Stirner put it.[28]

This attitude stemmed from a faith in the essential goodness of human nature which was shared by all libertarian thinkers. Rejecting the notion of original sin, they insisted that children are innocent at birth and that evil is rooted in a corrupt environment, in repressive institutions. We bring "neither virtue nor vice with us at our entrance into the world," wrote Godwin, so that "depravity in children is always learned." Given this premise, a libertarian education acquired critical importance. For if a child's character was shaped by his environment, it was necessary to provide conditions, not least in the school, in which his nobler qualities would prosper. Education, in other words, must be based on freedom and love rather than on tyranny and fear. "There is not in the world a truer object of pity," said Godwin, "than a child terrified at every glance, and watching, with anxious uncertainty, the caprices of a pedagogue."[29]

In keeping with this philosophy, students at libertarian schools were treated with patience and affection. Self-discipline was encouraged, and teachers were instructed to be kind and considerate, abjuring, as Godwin put it, "a harsh tone and peremptory manner." By the same token, rewards and punishments were done away with, arbitrary rules abolished, and there were no marks or examinations which might engender hypocrisy and dissimulation or arouse feelings of envy among the pupils. Children, it was held, must be free to learn without fear and without the pressure of rivalry and competition. At New Harmony, for example, Owen adopted Pestalozzi's view that "intercourse between educator and pupil, and school discipline especially, must be based on and controlled by love."[30] The situation at Yasnaya Polyana was similar. Pupils sat where they pleased—on bench or table, on window-sill or floor—and came and went without restraint. Attendance was optional. Only those came who wanted to learn. A "class" was adjourned when the pupils lost interest in it, and if they did not feel like working, nobody forced them. There were no lessons to memorize at home, no written assignments to prepare in advance, no report cards or grades, no surprise quizzes or other examinations to dread. "I am convinced," said Tolstoy, "that the school has no right and ought not to reward or punish; that the best police and administration of a school consists in giving full liberty to the pupils to study and settle their disputes as they know best."[31]

In a free school, moreover, noise was considered part of the natural order of things. Attempts to restrain the child's exuberant impulses only resulted in unhappiness and frustration. Godwin, who recognized that boisterous activity was often a mere outlet for energy, criticized teachers who favored "the sober, the dull, the obedient, lads that have no will and no understanding of their own." For Stirner, too, a certain amount of disorder was inevitable in the school. He believed that the qualities of obstinacy and intractability in a pupil were mere expressions of the "natural strength of the will," from which conventional teachers defended themselves with "the convenient rampart of authority."[32]

In the ideal school, wrote Godwin, "no such characters are left upon the scene as either preceptor or pupil. The boy, like the man, studies, because he desires it. He proceeds upon a plan of his own invention, or which by adopting, he has made his own. Everything bespeaks independence and equality." Treating the child with respect, the teacher would establish a personal relationship with him, a relationship of confidence and reciprocity in which the teacher might learn as much from the pupil as the pupil from the teacher. "In the little world of the classroom, teacher and pupil are not to assume the parts of tyrant and slave: the child's natural dignity and candour are precious and ought not to be undermined."[33]

By displacing the teacher from his position of superiority, by making the desire of the pupil rather than the will of the instructor the motive element in learning, Godwin and his successors made a truly revolutionary departure in educational method. Herbert Read captured the essentials when he wrote that the teacher must be "primarily a person and not a pedagogue, a friend rather than a master or mistress, an infinitely patient collaborator."[34] This role does not, however, come easily. It demands unusual ability on the part of the instructor, a sensitivity and responsiveness to the needs of each child. Often it is the teacher's personality, his moral qualities, that count the most. Such was the case with Tolstoy. He had unusual rapport with the children of his Yasnaya Polyana school, who called him Lev Nikolaevich while he in turn called them by their first names. His favorite pupil, Fedka, looking back over fifty years, thus recalled his childhood days: "There I am a ten-year-old schoolboy, there is young, jolly Lev Nikolaevich, there I am sliding down the steep hill, romping with Lev Nikolaevich, covering him with snow, playing ball, walking in the woods and fields and having conversations on the terrace, telling our tales about the wizards. . . . The remembrances of those happy bright days of my life I have never lost and never will. The love for Lev Nikolaevich that burned within me then still burns brightly in my soul and illumines my life."[35]

Such was the kind of education of which the dreams of libertarians were made. Bakunin's Swiss disciple James Guillaume summed it up as follows: "No longer will there be schools, arbitrarily governed by a pedagogue, where the children wait impatiently for the moment of their deliverance when they can enjoy a little freedom outside. In their gatherings the children will be entirely free. They will organize their own games, their talks, systematize their own work, arbitrate disputes, etc. They will easily become accustomed to public life, to responsibility, to mutual trust and aid. The teacher whom they have themselves chosen to give them lessons will no longer be detested as a tyrant but a friend to whom they will listen with pleasure."[36]

To the theorists of libertarian education, individuality was a positive trait, as opposed to conformity and standardization. Godwin and his successors believed that children are too diverse to be squeezed into a preconceived mold. Diversity, moreover, was essential to the evolution of freedom. A good teacher, accordingly, would minister to the unique personality of each student and encourage the development of all his potentialities. "To the educator," Pestalozzi declared, "the individuality of the child must be sacred." Education, said Froebel, must be adapted to each pupil's "nature and needs."[37]

At the same time, however, libertarian educators recognized

that all children have much in common. Anticipating the theories of Piaget and Erikson, they maintained that there are natural stages of development, from the simple to the complex, through which all children must pass, whatever their individual differences. These stages, moreover, must not be breached or circumvented, lest the child become frustrated and unhappy. This meant that different skills must be learned at different periods. If this principle were followed, it was argued, education would be enjoyable and efficient.

With regard to stages of development, reading was the primary cause for concern. Premature exposure to books was to be avoided at all costs. With the single exception of Godwin, opinion on this point was unanimous. Rousseau, insisting that education be tied to concrete experience, regarded books as the bane of childhood. So too did his disciples, some of whom argued that, quite apart from problems of comprehension, the eyes of young children are insufficiently developed for the physical task of reading. Instead of being taught from books, therefore, pupils should receive an active education, amid natural outdoor surroundings, and learn by doing and observing at first hand. Rousseau's Emile, the prototype of the liberated student, confronted the world directly, learning geography by tramping through the woods, agriculture by working in the fields, and so on. He was not taught to read until his teens.

Following Rousseau, nineteenth-century libertarians recoiled from the intellectualization of life and regarded action rather than verbalism as the groundwork of education. "The first rule," wrote Pestalozzi, "is to teach always by THINGS rather than by WORDS." Through learning by doing and applying, children would derive knowledge from direct experience with the practical and concrete. As Kropotkin argued: "By compelling our children to study real things from mere graphical representations, instead of *making* these things themselves, we compel them to waste the most precious time; we uselessly worry their minds; we accustom them to the worst methods of learning; we kill independent thought in the bud; and very seldom we succeed in conveying a real knowledge of what we are teaching."[38]

This is not to say that anarchists and libertarians scorned books. On the contrary, they had a deep respect for the printed word, for literature, history, and science; and in many free schools of the nineteenth and twentieth centuries children learned the arts of printing and binding and enjoyed the pleasures of a well-stocked library. The question was one of timing and priorities. At what age should reading be taught? And how much should reading be emphasized? What they rejected was early reading, premature reading, to the neglect of physical pursuits. For Pestalozzi, Fourier, and Owen, book-learning was to be deferred until the age of ten. Emphasis, meanwhile, was to be placed on such activities as woodworking, drawing, and weaving, through which both mental and manual skills might be acquired.

The notion of an "integral" education that would cultivate physical as well as mental skills and develop all aspects of the child's personality appears to have originated with Fourier, the French "utopian" socialist, whose theories exerted a powerful influence on the anarchist movement. Taking his cue from Fourier, the French anarchist Proudhon advocated a combination of physical and intellectual training whose elements would both complement and reinforce each other. "Labor and study," he wrote, "which have for so long and so foolishly been kept apart, will finally emerge side by side in their natural state of union. Instead of being confined to narrow, specialized fields, vocational education will include a variety of different types of work which, taken as a whole, will ensure that each student becomes an all-around worker." By this method, Proudhon maintained, "the industrial worker, the man of action, and the intellectual will all be rolled into one."[39]

After Proudhon, the same idea was taken up by many radical thinkers, socialist and anarchist alike. Thus Marx, in volume one of *Capital* (1867), called for an "integral education" as the "way of producing full human beings." Bakunin, too, in 1869, called for "a full integral education" which would prepare children of both sexes for "a life of thought as well as of work, so that all will become complete and integrated individuals."[40] The same year, Paul Robin, whose influence on Ferrer has been noted, published an essay "On Integral Education," setting forth the ideas that he later tried to implement at Cempuis. And in 1876, the year of Bakunin's death, his disciple James Guillaume wrote that "the education of children must be integrated; that is, it must at the same time develop both the physical and mental faculties and make the child into a whole man."[41]

Influenced by Proudhon and Bakunin, the leaders of the Paris Commune of 1871 sought to inaugurate an "integral" education so as to remedy the overspecialization caused by the emergence of large-scale industry and the division of labor. During its brief life, the Commune launched a number of educational experiments—schools of industrial arts, workshop schools, schools for orphans, schools for women—with the result that, according to its educational commissioner, "the main lines of an egalitarian education had been sufficiently mapped out for the idea to start to spread."[42] And spread it did, penetrating the ranks of the International Working Men's Association (the famous First International). In 1870 the Spanish section of the International had already passed a resolution calling for a program of "integral education" (*ensenañza integral*) at its Barcelona Congress. Thereafter, the idea was invoked repeatedly in anarchist pamphlets, journals, and manifestoes, and in 1872 the Second Workers' Congress of the Spanish Region, held at Zaragoza, endorsed it in an elaborated form.

Nor was that all. In 1898 Jean Grave's *Temps Nouveaux* printed an International Manifesto on "Integral Instruction," signed by Tolstoy, Kropotkin, Louise Michel, Charles Malato, and Grave himself.[43] The following year, Kropotkin further popularized the idea in his celebrated book, *Fields, Factories and Workshops*, which called for "industry combined with agriculture, and brain work with manual work," as its subtitle proclaimed. Like Fourier and Proudhon, Kropotkin sought an end to the invidious separation between work with brain and with hand, and between labor in field and factory. What he envisioned was a thoroughly "integrated" society "where each individual is a producer of both manual and intellectual work; where each able-bodied human being is a worker, and where each worker works in both the field and the industrial workshop." How was this to be realized? The answer, he wrote to Ferrer, lay in "integral instruction—i.e., teaching which, by the practice of hand on wood, stone, metal, will speak to the brain and develop it." In this way, asserted Kropotkin, we shall achieve "the merging of manual with mental labor preached by Fourier and the International."[44]

While setting a high value on education, libertarians were deeply suspicious of philosophical and sociological systems and of the intellectuals who spun them. Bakunin, in particular, assailed the theorists and system-builders who claimed to possess superior wisdom but who, in his eyes, were sacrificing real life on the altar of scholastic abstractions. He held that life cannot be reduced to a set of formulas and that efforts in this direction will lead to tyranny. Some anarchists, Bakunin among them, went so far as to argue that intellectuals are a special breed who have nothing in common with manual laborers but try to lure them with high-flown theories in order to catapult themselves into power. The workers, they warned, must not rely on "professional revolutionaries" who are cut off from the life of the masses by their special knowledge and training and who might substitute a new yoke for the old, a despotic oligarchy of "experts" in place of aristocrats and capitalists. Bakunin, more than anyone else, warned against the emergence of a "new class" of intellectuals who would keep the masses in ignorance in order to rule over them.

Bakunin, however, did not reject all forms of expertise. "In the matter of boots," he declared, "I defer to the authority of the bootmaker; concerning houses, canals, or railroads, I consult that of the architect or engineer."[45] Yet everyone, including architect and engineer, must work with his hands as well as his brain. For those who do not perform their share of physical labor will be parasites who live off the toil of industrial and agricultural workers. This would be particularly true of clergymen, bureaucrats, lawyers, and nonproducing holders of property, who batten on the misery of the poor. It was for this reason, if nothing else, that anarchists favored an integral education that stressed the acquisition of practical knowledge and upheld activity over theory, crafts over books.

This form of anti-intellectualism runs like a scarlet thread through the libertarian tradition. As far back as the Puritan Revolution, Gerrard Winstanley, the leader of a radical group called the Diggers, emphasized the need for shared physical labor as the basis of an equitable society. In such a society, he maintained, there would be no place for idlers or parasites. Everyone would work with his hands, and "one sort of children shall not be trained up only to book-learning, and to no other employment, called scholars, as they are in the government of monarchy. For then through idleness they spend their time to find out policies to advance themselves to be lords and masters over their laboring brethren, which occasions all the troubles in the world." For Fourier, too, the schools of the future must cease to produce a class of professional scholars, educated from books alone and incapable of any craft or trade: "No attempt will be made, as in the case of existing educational methods, to create precocious little *savants*, intellectual primary school beginners, initiated from the sixth year in scientific subtleties."[46]

What was more, as Bakunin insisted, education must be wrested from the monopolistic grasp of the wealthier classes and made available equally to everyone. "Can the emancipation of the workers be complete," he asked, "so long as the education received by the masses is inferior to that given to the bourgeoisie, or so long as there is in general any class whatever, large or small in numbers, enjoying by virtue of birth the privileges of superior and more thoroughgoing instruction?" Like capital, said Bakunin, learning must cease to be the patrimony of the few and become the patrimony of all men. "Everyone must work," he declared, "and everyone must be educated," so that there will be "neither workers nor scientists, but only men."[47]

For libertarians, finally, education was a continuous, never-ending process extending from cradle to grave. In libertarian schools adult education invariably held an important place, and parents as well as children took an active part in the day-to-day administration. The school, indeed, was viewed as a model of what was desirable in human relations. In its structure and operations, in the behavior of its participants toward one another, it provided a foretaste of the libertarian future, of what life could be like once the restraints imposed by authority had been removed. For some it was also a vehicle of rebellion, a means of altering social foundations by removing the fetters of ignorance, dogmatism, and convention. Its central aim, however, was to free the child. From this the rest would follow.

THE ESCUELA MODERNA OF BARCELONA

If the principles of libertarian education did not originate with Ferrer, it was he who implanted them in Barcelona, the main stronghold of Spanish anarchism. Ferrer was not a theorist, not a conceiver of new ideas. Nor was he a charismatic figure, although respected by his colleagues in both the anarchist and free thought movements. Simple, direct, unpretentious, he never assumed an air of intellectual superiority and was utterly indifferent about his appearance. His voice was uninspiring, and he was a mediocre orator, yet when he spoke his audience listened with attention, won over by his manifest sincerity. "Ferrer made a tremendous impression on me," recalled the German anarchist Rudolf Rocker, who met him in London in 1909. "Every word he spoke breathed sincerity. He had no pose. There was a warmth about him." Ferrer, moreover, had a "positive genius" for organization,[48] and brought to his work an immense store of energy and a passionate dedication to the system of learning that came to be associated with his name. It was in this sense, primarily, that he was a pioneer of libertarian education, becoming a figure of considerable importance.

With Mlle. Meunié's inheritance, Ferrer was able to launch his educational experiment on a secure financial footing. Finding quarters in the Calle de las Cortes, he opened the Escuela Moderna on September 8, 1901, with a class of thirty pupils. The pupils, eighteen boys and twelve girls, were divided into three sections, primary, intermediate, and advanced. The school had a workshop and laboratory and was well equipped with maps, charts, and other teaching aids. A tuition fee was charged, but on a sliding scale according to the economic condition of each family. As Ferrer's ideas appealed to both working-class and middle-class parents, the school was coeducational in terms of the social position as well as the sex of its students. Enrollment grew steadily, from 70 boys and girls at the end of the first year to 114 in 1904 and 126 in 1905. The figure was still rising when the school was closed by the authorities in 1906.[49]

During the five years of its existence, the Escuela Moderna attempted to put into practice the philosophy of education outlined in the preceding pages: learning by doing in a natural environment, cultivation of manual as well as intellectual skills, recognition of the rights and dignity of the child, give and take between pupil and teacher, participation of children and parents in the administration of the school. Like his predecessors, Ferrer was determined to free the child from the stultifying effects of the formal classroom, with its fixation on order and discipline, its rigid and often irrelevant curriculum, its pressure for conformity and denial of originality and independence. "I am convinced," he declared, "that constraint arises from ignorance, and that the educator who is really worthy of the name will obtain his results through the spontaneous response of the child, whose desires he will learn to know, and whose development he will try to further by giving it every possible gratification."[50]

Against the dogmas of conventional education Ferrer set a system based on reason, science, and observation: "I will teach them only the simple truth. I will not ram a dogma into their heads. I will not conceal from them one iota of fact. I will teach them not what to think but how to think." Furthermore, he wrote, "the whole value of education consists in respect for the physical, intellectual, and moral faculties of the child. Education is not worthy of the name unless it is stripped of all dogmatism, and unless it leaves to the child the direction of its powers and is content to support them in their manifestations."[51]

Ferrer had no use for motivation induced by fear or by competition for grades or prizes. Invidious distinctions he viewed as psychologically harmful to children, encouraging deception rather than sincerity among them. Rewards and punishments were therefore excluded from the Escuela Moderna. Nor were there examinations or marks "to puff up some children with the flattering title of 'excellent,' to give others the title of 'good,' and make others unhappy with a consciousness of incapacity or failure." Examinations, Ferrer believed, were "torture" for the students and in no way furthered their education.[52]

Ferrer, moreover, gave clear priority to the acquisition of practical over theoretical knowledge. He wished to place the child in a "natural environment" where vital impressions would replace "the wearisome reading of books."[53] No one is really educated, he believed, whose knowledge is acquired at second hand. Accordingly, a lesson in the Escuela Moderna often consisted of a visit to a factory or laboratory, where things were demonstrated and explained, or to a museum where art was displayed, or to a park or the hills or the sea, where geological conditions were studied, botanical specimens collected, and individual observation encouraged.

In short, what Ferrer created was the kind of school that had been contemplated by his colleagues in France, a school in which pupils were not subjected to discipline but were allowed to come and go freely and to plan and organize their own work. But the Escuela Moderna was more than a day school for children. To Ferrer education was a process that never stopped. Thus parents were encouraged not only to take a direct part in the operation of the school, but also to attend evening and Sunday afternoon lectures delivered by prominent scholars on such subjects as hygiene, physiology, geography, and natural science. These lectures, open to the general public and attended by many "workers who were anxious to learn," evolved into regular evening courses during the second school year. Their success led Ferrer to consult with professors at Barcelona University on the possibility of creating a popular university in conjunction with the Escuela Moderna. Higher learning, he said, which was then confined to "a privileged few," should be "given gratuitously to the general public, by way of restitution, as every human being has a right to know, and science, which is produced by observers and workers of all ages and countries, ought not to be restricted to a class."[54]

Thirty years earlier, Bakunin had called for adult schools "in which neither pupils nor masters will be known, but where the people will come freely to receive, if they like, free instruction, and in which, rich in experience, they will teach many things to their professors, who shall bring them the knowledge that they lack."[55] Ferrer, no doubt, was familiar with these phrases. More directly, however, he was influenced by a French example, the Universités Populaires, begun in Paris at the turn of the century and attracting the support of scholars in every field of learning, who offered lectures to large, mostly working-class audiences. By 1902 the movement of Universités Populaires had spread throughout France, with forty-seven in Paris alone, forty-eight in its suburbs, and an equal number in the provinces.[56] Similar institutions had also been started in Belgium and Italy, while in Spain itself cultural centers for workers had been established as early as the 1870s by anarchists of the First International, and afterwards by freethinkers and radical Republicans.

Beyond the Sunday and evening lectures, however, Ferrer's adult university did not materialize. What he did start, on the premises of the Escuela Moderna, was a rationalist normal school for the training of libertarian teachers. In the same building, moreover, he established a radical publishing house which turned out a steady stream of literature for readers of all ages. For while Ferrer objected to learning from books alone, he was not an opponent of reading per se, a fact to which his publishing venture bears witness. When he set about organizing the Escuela Moderna, he searched in vain for appropriate materials, and the school opened before a single volume could be chosen for the library. To repair this deficiency he equipped a modern printing plant, collected a staff of translators, and enlisted the cooperation of some of the most celebrated minds of Europe in preparing a series of textbooks that would embody the latest scientific discoveries and yet be couched in a language comprehensible to the untrained intellect.

More than forty such textbooks were issued, compact, red-covered volumes ranging from primers of arithmetic and grammar to popular introductions to the natural and social sciences and serious treatises on geography, sociology, and anthropology. There were also collections of writings on the mythology of religion and "the injustices connected with patriotism, the horrors of war, and the iniquity of conquest." Mostly translated from the French, these works were regarded with intense disfavor by the Spanish authorities as tending to undermine the established order, cultural as well as political. Some of the titles were these: *Survey of Spanish History* by Nicolás Estévanez, *Compendium of Universal History* by Clémence Jacquinet, *Physical Geography* by Odón de Buen, *First Stages of Humanity* by Georges Engerrand, *The Origins of Christianity* by Malvert, *Ethnic Psychology* by Charles Letourneau, *Man and the Earth* (abridged edition) by Elisée Reclus, *Poverty: Its Cause and Cure* by Léon Martin, and *Social Classes* by Charles Malato.[57]

The most popular of the children's texts was *The Adventures of Nono* by Jean Grave, a utopian fairy tale in which "the happier future is ingeniously and dramatically contrasted with the sordid realities of the present order," to quote Ferrer's description.[58] The publishing house, in addition, issued miscellaneous educational materials as well as a monthly review, the *Boletín de la Escuela Moderna*, which served as the school's official organ and carried articles by Ferrer, Kropotkin, Tolstoy, Robin, and other well-known libertarian writers.[59]

Ferrer saw the Escuela Moderna not only as an educational institution but as a center of propaganda and agitation, a training ground for revolutionary activity. Basic to his philosophy was the belief that education should develop individuals who were equipped, mentally, morally, and physically, to build the future libertarian society. To quote his own words: "We do not hesitate to say that we want men who will continue unceasingly to develop; men who are capable of constantly destroying and renewing their surroundings and renewing themselves; men whose intellectual independence is their supreme power, which they will yield to none; men always disposed for things that are better, eager for the triumph of new ideas, anxious to crowd many lives into the life they have."[60]

The school, in other words, was at once an instrument of self-development and a lever of social regeneration. With this lever, Ferrer believed, the revolution was destined to triumph, "first among individuals, and finally in society as a whole."[61] In the meantime, it would serve as a libertarian alternative to the existing regime, an embryo of the coming millennium, an enclave of freedom within the larger authoritarian society, providing a model for others to emulate. Ferrer, in effect, was applying the principles of syndicalism to educational practice, with the school, the counterpart of the union, acting as a vehicle of social transformation. (The Industrial Workers of the World would have described this as "building the new society within the shell of the old.") Ferrer, moreover, hoped that rational education would serve as a means of liberating not only Spanish children but the children of all lands. He dreamed that Spain would become the vanguard and that the entire world would follow its example.

Insofar as the Escuela Moderna actively preached specific social values, its pupils were subjected to indoctrination. "Moral" education, indeed, had always been a goal of libertarian pedagogy, to supplement physical and intellectual training. As Bakunin had written: "Reason, truth, justice, respect for fellow men, the sense of personal dignity which is inseparable from the dignity of others, love of personal freedom and the freedom of others, the conviction that work is the base and condition for rights—these must be the fundamental principles of all public education. . . . The essence of all moral education is this: inculcate children with respect for humanity and you will make good men."[62]

In the Escuela Moderna, accordingly, children were educated to believe in liberty, equality, and social justice. They were imbued with the ideals of brotherhood and cooperation and with a sympathy for the downtrodden and oppressed. They were taught that war is a crime against humanity, that the capitalist system is evil, that government is slavery, that freedom is essential for human development. "It must be the aim of the rationalist school," wrote Ferrer, "to show the children that there will be tyranny and slavery as long as one man depends on another."[63] In keeping with this approach, the textbooks of the Escuela Moderna—Kropotkin's *Anarchist Morality*, Charles Malato's *War*, Jean Grave's *A Free World*, Anselmo Lorenzo's *The Feast of Life*—were heavily anticapitalist, antistatist, and antimilitarist in orientation. In addition, Esperanto was taught as an international language, promoting solidarity among the different nationalities. Lessons were illustrated with examples of patriotism, superstition, and exploitation, and the suffering they produce. A field trip to a chemical factory was followed with a lecture by Anselmo Lorenzo on the evils of capitalism. Student essays (excerpts from which appeared in the *Boletín de la Escuela Moderna*) were likely to dwell on themes of religious and economic oppression.

Ferrer, however, denied any personal connection with the anarchist movement, professing to have repudiated entirely his former belief in violence and revolution. In an address at the opening of the Escuela Moderna he emphasized his nonpolitical role: "I am not a speaker, not a propagandist, not a fighter. I am a teacher; I love children above everything. I think I understand them. I want my contribution to the cause of liberty to be a young generation ready to meet a new era."[64] In succeeding years, when his life was endangered by government prosecution, he repeated these denials in stronger terms. But in truth, Ferrer's anarchist credentials are beyond dispute. He was not a "Rousseauian idealist rather than a revolutionary," as a British historian has described him. Neither was he a Tolstoyan pacifist, as some of his defenders maintained, nor had he "renounced all idea of militant Anarchism in order to devote himself to educational work."[65] Until his death in 1909, he was deeply involved in anarchist causes and activities. He published anarchist books, financed anarchist periodicals, and subsidized a whole range of anarchist undertakings, in France and other countries as well as Spain. In organizing and operating the Escuela Moderna, he worked hand in hand with the anarchist movement of Barcelona. José Prat, editor of the anarchist journal *Natura*, was administrator of the school. The veteran anarchist Anselmo Lorenzo, one of Ferrer's closest collaborators, lectured at the school and served as a translator in its publishing house. And other local anarchists and sympathizers fulfilled similar functions.

Ferrer, moreover, was on intimate terms with anarchist leaders throughout Europe, including Kropotkin, Reclus, and Malatesta, who gave him advice and contributed to his publications. Attracted in particular by the doctrines of Anarcho-Syndicalism, a rapidly emerging force at the beginning of the century, Ferrer devoted himself to the organization of a revolutionary labor movement in Catalonia and to the propaganda of direct action. Between 1901 and 1903 he published a syndicalist journal, *La Huelga General* (The General Strike), which was suppressed by the Spanish government. He was, in short, a "virilely rebellious warrior," not a "spineless thing of text-books and village primers."[66] Indeed, as we shall see, he may even have been party to terrorist intrigues against the Spanish king.

Such were the principal features of the Escuela Moderna. It was an active and varied enterprise: a children's school, an adult educational center, a radical publishing house, and a center to prepare the workers for revolution. Its manifold character bore witness to Ferrer's administrative talents. Only a methodical organizer, as Emma Goldman noted, could have accomplished so much in so short a time.[67] For nearly a decade Ferrer dominated the movement for libertarian education in Barcelona. His experiment won favor not only among workers but also among middle-class liberals and reformers, impressed by his anticlerical views and by the respectability of the intellectuals who delivered his Sunday lectures.

In October 1905 Ferrer opened a branch of the Escuela Moderna in Villanueva y Gettrú, a neighboring textile center, the rector of Barcelona University presiding at the inaugural ceremony. Other schools adopted his textbooks and methods of instruction. In this way, his influence was felt in Seville and Málaga, in Tarragona and Córdoba, as well as in smaller villages and towns. By the end of 1905 there were fourteen Ferrer-type schools in Barcelona alone and thirty-four in Catalonia, Valencia, and Andalusia. Though more modest in scope and equipment, they patterned themselves after the Escuela Moderna, offering a libertarian education for children of both sexes as well as adult classes in which working people were taught to read and to abjure religion and militarism.

In addition, Ferrer helped radical Republican leaders organize classes in their party centers, for which his publishing house provided textbooks and other materials. These materials were used also in secular schools started by the League of Freethinkers in the early years of the century. The total number of such schools in Barcelona province ultimately surpassed 120, bringing literacy to adults and a rationalist education to their children. The zenith of the movement was reached on Good Friday, April 12, 1906, when Ferrer led 1,700 children in a procession and picnic on behalf of secular education. Less than two months later, the whole edifice collapsed under the burden of government repression.

PROPAGANDA BY THE DEED

By 1906 five years had elapsed since Ferrer's return from exile. During this time, the Spanish authorities had been viewing his activities with increasing alarm. His influence had spread rapidly. His talent for organization, combined with his substantial fortune, had made him a powerful enemy of the established order. To the defenders of the status quo he represented a dangerous subversive force, a challenge to accepted social and religious ideas. As one Madrid journal put it, he was the enemy of "all social foundation: Religion, Family, Property, Authority, and Army."[68]

As an anarchist and former republican conspirator, Ferrer had earned the undying hatred of the government, to whom his school and those like it were merely a subterfuge for teaching revolutionary doctrines, a network of sedition and violence. And Ferrer was a freethinker as well as an anarchist, so that the church too was bitterly hostile to the Escuela Moderna, which questioned its dogmas and threatened its monopoly of education. (As Emma Goldman put it, Ferrer had "dared to strike her in her most vulnerable spot.") To the Catholic hierarchy his school was a "nursery of atheism," "in league with the devil," and "worse than a brothel."[69]

It was only natural that a school which taught antireligious, antigovernmental, and antimilitarist ideas should have incurred the loathing of conservative minds. Coeducation, moreover, a conspicuous feature of the school, aroused deep-seated religious and social prejudices. In a short time, then, Ferrer had become an evil monster in the eyes of the ruling authorities, who feared the further spread of his influence. To the state he was a dangerous revolutionary, to the church a blasphemer and heretic. Both were determined to eliminate him.

From the very opening of the Escuela Moderna Ferrer had become a marked man. He was followed by the police. His house was raided in a futile effort to incriminate him in some kind of plot. The weapons of slander, innuendo, and rumor were used to discredit him and his ideas. He was depicted as a gambler and financial speculator, a voluptuary and practitioner of "free love." His relations with women—he had separated from his wife, Teresa Sanmartí, taken up with Léopoldine Bonnard, companion to Mlle. Meunié, then fallen in love with Soledad Villafranca, a teacher in the Escuela Moderna—were cited as an example of what the children were being taught in his school.

In the spring of 1906, six weeks after the Good Friday procession, the authorities almost succeeded in removing Ferrer. A year before, on the night of May 31, 1905, Alfonso XIII had been returning from the opera during a visit to Paris when two bombs were thrown at his carriage. One of them exploded, wounding seventeen bystanders and damaging a number of vehicles. But the king was unhurt. Exactly one year later, on May 31, 1906, Alfonso and his bride were returning to the palace after their wedding in Madrid when again someone threw a bomb at his car.

Though 24 onlookers were killed and 107 more injured, the royal couple escaped unharmed.

The assassin, Mateo Morral, was a young anarchist of twenty-five, the son of a wealthy cotton manufacturer in the industrial town of Sabadell. Well educated, with a command of several languages, he worked in the publishing house of the Escuela Moderna and had been a friend of Ferrer's since 1903. Morral, it appears, had also been involved in the first attempt, along with several other anarchists, but had not been apprehended. After the second attempt he again succeeded in escaping, but two days later, sighted at a railroad station near Madrid, he shot a policeman and then took his own life to avoid capture.[70]

The authorities seized on Morral's act as a pretext to get rid of Ferrer. On June 4, 1906, he was arrested on charges of planning the assassination and inducing Morral to carry it out. For a year he was kept in prison while the prosecutor sought evidence against him. When finally brought to trial, he was acquitted for lack of proof, though the police remained convinced of his complicity.

The Escuela Moderna was not so fortunate. Morral's association with the enterprise reinforced the government's conviction that it was nothing more than a bomb factory. On June 15, 1906, it was forcibly closed, to the delight of clerical and conservative elements, who had long denounced it as a nest of subversion. In the Cortes, six conservative deputies petitioned for the closing of all secular and anarchist schools, including the branches of the Escuela Moderna, but without success. As one right-wing journal declared, "these crimes will continue as long as Spaniards maintain the freedom to read, to teach, and to think, from which come all these antisocial monsters."[71]

Was Ferrer in fact involved in the attacks on King Alfonso? He himself, of course, maintained his innocence, denying any connection with revolutionary conspiracies. This contention was supported by Emma Goldman, who wrote: "It was known throughout Spain that Ferrer was opposed to acts of political violence, that he firmly believed in and preached modern education as against force."[72] A major cause of his release was an international campaign, mounted by anarchist and rationalist groups, portraying him as the victim of a new Spanish Inquisition.

Yet others have disagreed. According to Joaquín Romero Maura, a historian at Oxford University, Ferrer was indeed "the master-mind behind the 1905 and 1906 attempts," supplying the bombs and the money with which the plot, designed to signal a general insurrection, was made possible.[73] Maura bases his conclusions on documents in the archives of the French police and of the Spanish ministry of foreign affairs, buttressing these with other materials, including the personal papers of Spanish officials. These same materials, however, and much additional documentation since lost or destroyed, had been insufficient at the time of Ferrer's arrest and trial to connect him with the conspiracy. Moreover, the evidence unearthed by Maura is largely circumstantial in nature. Police files, which he accepts at face value, are notorious for the unfounded denunciations and sheer nonsense they contain, inspired by the personal vindictiveness of informers and the tendency of police agents to see plots in every corner, if only to show how effective they are in combating them.

On at least two occasions prior to 1905-1906 the Spanish police had tried, and failed, to implicate Ferrer in assassination attempts. This is not to say that he was innocent of any involvement in the 1905 and 1906 incidents. For, despite his repeated denials, he was indeed a militant anarchist, a champion of "direct action," who did not shrink from the necessity of violence. In his younger years, he had exhibited a strong taste for conspiratorial adventure, which had never been satisfied. Barring the discovery of conclusive evidence, Ferrer's role in the Morral affair must remain an open question.

Ferrer was released from prison on June 12, 1907. On July 22nd he embarked on a tour of France, Belgium, and England, lecturing on education, seeing old friends, and making new contacts. Returning to Barcelona in September, although barred from reopening the Escuela Moderna, he revived his rationalist publishing house, issuing new textbooks, pamphlets, and translations of libertarian classics.[74] At the same time, he supported the new syndicalist labor federation, Solidaridad Obrera, subsidizing its journal of the same name launched in 1907.

The following year, undeterred by official harassment, Ferrer began a campaign to promote libertarian education throughout Europe. In April 1908 he founded in Paris the International League for the Rational Education of Children, an organization of freethinkers, radicals, and reformers, with himself as president. Anatole France served as honorary president, with an international committee made up of Ernst Haeckel of Jena, William Heaford of Surrey, Lorenzo Portet of Liverpool, Charles Malato of Paris, Sébastien Faure of Rambouillet, and Ferdinand Domela

Nieuwenhuis of Amsterdam. Also affiliated with the League was the writer Maurice Maeterlinck, whose plays were often performed by the children of libertarian schools. Under Ferrer's editorship, the journal of the League, *L'Ecole Renovée*, made its debut in Brussels on April 15, 1908 (it was moved to Paris nine months later). This was a serious educational review featuring articles by Kropotkin, Paul Robin, James Guillaume, Tarrida del Mármol, and Ferrer himself. The League supported two other periodicals, *La Scuola Laica* in Rome and *El Boletín de la Escuela Moderna* in Barcelona, which, together with *L'Ecole Renovée*, served as media of communication among progressive educators and intellectuals throughout Europe.

The first number of *L'Ecole Renovée* contained the League's official program, "The Rational Education of Children." Labeling "neutral" instruction a myth, it openly acknowledged its own bias: "We should not, in the school, hide the fact that we would awaken in the children the desire for a society . . . without violence, without hierarchies, without privilege of any sort." It hastened to add, however, that "we have no right to impose this ideal on the child," but merely to arouse his sense of justice, which would spur him to work for human emancipation.[75] A second manifesto, issued by the Paris Group of the League, lashed out at the regimentation of existing schools, in which pupils were "kept motionless for hours, and walks, museums, scenes of human activity—all these marvelous natural factors of education are ignored." Nothing was being done, the manifesto added, "towards rendering the child capable of assimilating what is taught or towards discovering the child's inclinations and possibilities. The ideal is to fill up the brain as one fills a sack of corn."[76]

Through its journals and manifestoes, combined with the prestige of its executive committee, the International League for the Rational Education of Children attracted an active multinational membership which spread its ideas throughout Europe. During its first year of operations, before Ferrer's execution, the League gave the impulse to the formation of libertarian schools in such cities as Amsterdam, Brussels, and Milan, each of which adapted the methods of the Escuela Moderna to local conditions. The League also won the cooperation of several previously established free schools, including Sébastien Faure's La Ruche (The Beehive) and Madeleine Vernet's L'Avenir Social (The Social Future), both located in the vicinity of Paris. La Ruche, started in 1904, became one of the most famous experiments of its type, on a par with Robin's Cempuis and Ferrer's own Escuela Moderna. "No one has yet fully realized the wealth of sympathy, kindness and generosity hidden in the soul of the child," Faure told Emma Goldman, who visited the school in 1907. "The effort of every true educator should be to unlock that treasure—to stimulate the child's impulses and call forth the best and noblest tendencies. What greater reward can there be for one whose life-work is to watch over the growth of the human plant, than to see its nature unfold its petals and observe it develop into a true individuality?"[77]

THE TRAGIC WEEK

In August 1909 the International League for the Rational Education of Children lost its guiding spirit when Ferrer was arrested in Barcelona. The previous month disturbances had broken out when the Spanish army called up the reserves to fight in an unsuccessful colonial war in Morocco. This was too much for a population that had suffered enough from corrupt and oppressive government and for whom the disasters of the War of 1898 were still fresh. Antiwar rallies and demonstrations culminated in a general strike, called on July 26th by the Solidaridad Obrera federation. The following day martial law was proclaimed throughout Catalonia. This triggered the so-called Tragic Week, in which the general strike developed into open insurrection. Incendiarism and street-fighting claimed hundreds of lives in Barcelona and nearby towns before the government succeeded in quelling the uprising. Mass arrests were followed by tortures, deportations, and executions. Ferrer was the most celebrated victim.[78]

Arrested on August 31, 1909, Ferrer was charged with being the "author and chief" of the rebellion. This he certainly was not, even if he was not a complete innocent as his defenders maintained. From all reliable accounts the rising was a spontaneous affair, not part of an "anarchist plot." As Anselmo Lorenzo wrote to Tarrida on July 31st: "What is happening here is amazing. A social revolution has broken out in Barcelona, and it has been started by the people. No one has instigated it. No one has led it. Neither Liberals, nor Catalan Nationalists, nor Republicans, nor Socialists, nor Anarchists."[79]

There can be little doubt that Ferrer, like many others, was actively involved in the disorders. But his role appears to have been marginal. At his trial before a military court on October 9th, nothing was brought to light to show that he had engineered or directed the insurrection. For his own part, he flatly denied the charges against him. "All the evidence presented to the investigating judge of the police is nothing but a tissue of lies and calumnious insinuations," he wrote to a friend.[80] What evidence there was, apart from his old writings dredged up to prove his subversive intentions, came mainly from political enemies, while those who might have testified in his favor were not allowed to appear. The government, as Voltairine de Cleyre put it, did all in its power to show that Ferrer was "a believer in violence, a teacher of the principles of violence, a doer of acts of violence, and an instigator of widespread violence perpetrated by a mass of people."[81]

After a mock trial, Ferrer was found guilty and condemned to death by firing squad. It was a case of judicial murder, a deliberate attempt by the authorities to get rid of one of their most troublesome opponents, who for eight years had been a thorn in their flesh. "Had Ferrer actually organized the riots," wrote Emma Goldman, "had he fought on the barricades, had he hurled a hundred bombs, he could not have been so dangerous to the Catholic Church and to despotism as his opposition to discipline and restraint."[82] Insofar as he had devoted his energies and resources to undermining established values, they held him morally if not actually responsible for the rising. In any case, they were making good their failure to convict him in the 1906 conspiracy against the king. This time he would not escape.

On October 13, 1909, Ferrer's death sentence was carried out. He was fifty years old, in the full vigor of life, when led to the trenches of Montjuich fortress, the scene of mass tortures and executions of anarchists a dozen years before. Reportedly his last words to the firing squad were: "Aim well, my friends. You are not responsible. I am innocent. Long live the Modern School!"

The execution of Ferrer, like that of Sacco and Vanzetti two decades later, aroused a storm of protest all over the world. In Europe, in America, even in Asia, hundreds of meetings took place to denounce what was regarded as a monstrous miscarriage of justice. There were demonstrations in London, Rome, Berlin, Vienna, Amsterdam, Brussels, Geneva, and many other cities. A crowd of 15,000 stormed the Spanish embassy in Paris, while in Milan a group of anarchists ran the black flag from a spire of the great cathedral. But the protests were not only by anarchists. They came from all sections of liberal society, for whom Ferrer was a martyr of free thought, done to death by a vindictive clericalism in league with a reactionary state. Maeterlinck, Gorky, Jaurès, and Anatole France were among the notables who vented their indignation. In Great Britain, George Bernard Shaw, H. G. Wells, and Arthur Conan Doyle protested side by side with Kropotkin, Malatesta, and Tarrida.[84]

It was because of his execution that Ferrer, rather than Paul Robin or Sébastien Faure, became the most celebrated representative of the movement for libertarian education. Instantly, the comparatively obscure pedagogue became a universal figure, the victim of priest-ridden Spain, condemned, like Socrates, for corrupting the morals of youth and challenging accepted conventions. In August 1910 a marble slab commemorating Ferrer was unveiled in the Grand Place of Brussels before a delegation of Belgian freethinkers. Similar memorials appeared in Italy and France, where streets and squares were named after him. On November 5, 1911, the first statue in his honor was dedicated in the Place de Sainte-Catherine, Brussels, showing a nude male figure upholding a torch, the symbol of enlightenment triumphant over obscurantism and reaction. Pulled down by the Germans in 1915, it was restored in 1926 by the international free-thought movement.[85]

The martyrdom of Ferrer kindled a widespread interest in his educational ideas. His writings were translated into many languages, and a spate of publications appeared describing his life and work. From Spain and Western Europe a movement for rationalist education spread all over the world. In Brazil and Argentina, in Poland and Czechoslovakia, in China and Japan, schools were started on the Barcelona model, bearing Ferrer's name and promoting his concept of education. During the Bavarian Revolution of 1919, Gustav Landauer drew up an educational program based on the methods of Ferrer, whose works he had translated into German. And during the Russian Revolution of 1917-1921, the anarchist leader Makhno was planning a Ferrer school in the Ukraine before his movement was dispersed by the Bolsheviks. In the three decades between Ferrer's death and the Second World War, Modern Schools were founded in Britain, France, Belgium, Holland, Italy, Germany, Switzerland, Poland, Czechoslovakia, Yugoslavia, Argentina, Brazil, Mexico, China, and Japan. The most extensive Ferrer movement, however, arose in the United States, where it endured for more than fifty years.

CHAPTER 2

The Francisco Ferrer Association

In the United States, as in Europe, the martyrdom of Ferrer inspired a vigorous movement to establish schools on the model of the Escuela Moderna. His execution, a major story in the American press, dominated the headlines of *The New York Times* and other leading newspapers, lifting his name from obscurity and arousing curiosity about his ideas. "Paradoxical as it may sound," wrote a participant in the New York Ferrer School, "the volley of shots fired into the body of Francisco Ferrer on October 13, 1909, at Montjuich prison in Barcelona did more to stir up interest in modern education than all the strivings of the founder of the Escuela Moderna and his followers."[1]

News of Ferrer's arrest on August 31st touched off the first wave of protests, mounted by both anarchist and rationalist groups. His trial in early October provoked a wider response because of the obvious bias displayed by the prosecution. But the anarchists carried the lead. "Meetings, conferences, *Mother Earth*, and a constant stream of people kept us busy from early morning until late hours of the night," recalled Emma Goldman, who was at the center of the agitation.[2] When the death sentence was announced, anarchists protested in midtown Manhattan and cabled objections to the Spanish government. All to no avail. When Ferrer was shot their sense of defeat was overwhelming. "Ferrer has been murdered," wrote Emma Goldman to her companion Ben Reitman on the day of the execution. "I am broken in spirit and body, I feel weary, just weary. My struggle never seemed more useless, a lone voice against a multitude."[3]

The protests, however, continued. In all parts of the country freethinkers and anarchists mourned the death of their Spanish comrade as that of "another victim of the Black Terror."[4] In New York Emma Goldman herself took the initiative in organizing a mass meeting on October 17th, the Sunday following the execution, and similar meetings were held in other cities, winning a good deal of public sympathy. "Everyone felt, and felt rightly, that a crime had been committed against civilization," wrote Leonard Abbott. As Jack London put it: "It were as if New England had, in the twentieth century, resumed her ancient practice of burning witches."[5]

Apart from the rallies and demonstrations, the execution brought a flood of tributes, in poetry and prose, to Ferrer's role in the service of enlightenment. Professor Lester F. Ward, the distinguished Brown University sociologist, declared: "Ferrer was a martyr to the principle of education. There have been martyrs to religion and to science, but never before was there a martyr to education." Even the ordinary citizen, Voltairine de Cleyre noted, could "not believe it possible that any group of persons calling themselves a government, be it of the worst and most despotic, could slay a man for being a teacher, a teacher of modern sciences, a builder of hygienic schools, a publisher of text-books."[6]

LAUNCHING AN ORGANIZATION

"The execution of Ferrer," wrote Leonard Abbott a month after the event, "made my blood *boil*! The one redeeming feature was the way it electrified the radical movement in all countries."[7] This was especially true of the United States. From coast to coast anarchist and free-thought groups marshaled their resources in an effort to spread Ferrer's teachings. By the spring of 1910 these activities had crystallized into a national association dedicated to perpetuating his work.

The idea of forming such an organization was first discussed on May 20, 1910, at the Lexington Avenue home of Dr. Edward Bond Foote, a New York freethinker and sex reformer, who, together with his father, had been an early pioneer of birth control and contraception and a liberal donor to radical causes. After the discussion at Dr. Foote's, an open meeting was scheduled for Friday evening, June 3, 1910, to which all with an interest in modern education were invited. It was at this meeting, held at the Harlem Liberal Alliance on West 116th Street, that the Francisco Ferrer Association was founded.[8]

To a packed hall of "Ferrer enthusiasts"[9] the chairman, Harry Kelly, explained the general aims of the proposed organization. Kelly was followed by Jaime Vidal, a personal friend of Ferrer's, who described the workings of the Barcelona Escuela Moderna. Next came Leonard Abbott, associate editor of *Current Literature*, who linked Ferrer's name with those of earlier martyrs to the cause of human freedom, from Socrates and Christ to Jan Hus and Giordano Bruno. Abbott then told of the efforts being made in other countries to perpetuate the legacy of Ferrer, announcing that a monument was to be unveiled in Brussels. "It was a crime against civilization in an era when such things were supposed impossible," said Abbott of Ferrer's execution. "The world stood aghast, and the world protested."

The last speaker of the evening was Alexander Berkman, editor of Emma Goldman's *Mother Earth*, who had already started a Modern Sunday School with a group of fellow New York anarchists, the first Ferrer school in America. To a man of action like Berkman, monuments and tributes were not enough. The best way to honor their fallen comrade, he argued, was to continue Ferrer's work with the same ardor and dedication as Ferrer himself had brought to it. "Ferrer," said Berkman, "would wish no granite or marble shaft as a monument to perpetuate his name." A more fitting memorial would be the creation of Modern Schools, in which no knowledge would be forced upon the children, "no ideas crammed into their heads," but where they would be encouraged to educate themselves on their own initiative, "forming their own ideas and imbibing natural notions of everything about them."[10]

When the speeches were over, the meeting got down to the business for which it was assembled. The Francisco Ferrer Association was formally inaugurated, and an election of officers took place for a one-year term. Of those present, twenty-two signed up as charter members and paid the initiation fee of one dollar. (An annual membership fee of the same amount was also agreed upon.) The object of the association was declared to be "to perpetuate the work and memory of Francisco Ferrer." At Emma Goldman's suggestion, it was decided to commemorate the anniversary of Ferrer's death on October 13, 1910, with a dinner similar to the annual banquet of the Thomas Paine National Historical Association, with which many of the charter members were affiliated. It was decided also to gather material for a memorial volume on Ferrer's life and work.

Apart from these, no further plans were mapped out. The organization adopted no constitution or bylaws. Yet enough of a start had been made for Leonard Abbott, the newly elected president of the association, to declare that Ferrer's influence was "more vital and far-reaching in America today than ever before."[11] It was the beginning, in fact, of the most impressive and long-lived among the many movements around the world inspired by Ferrer's execution.

Who were the originators of this movement? Although liberals and socialists played an important part, pride of place must go to the anarchists as the most active organizers and supporters of the Ferrer Association. Of the twenty-two charter members, as many as half were active anarchists, among them all four speakers at the June 3rd meeting, Harry Kelly, Leonard Abbott, Alexander Berkman, and Jaime Vidal. Included, besides, were Michel Dumas, a key figure among French-speaking anarchist immigrants, Anyuta Krimont, Harry Kelly's sister-in-law and one of four anarchist siblings of a Russian-Jewish family, Margaret Perle McLeod, a close associate of Voltairine de Cleyre's in Philadelphia, and Dr. Charles L. Andrews, a sixty-year-old New York dentist whose father, Stephen Pearl Andrews, had been a celebrated pioneer of the nineteenth-century anarchist movement.

The best-known figure, however, was Emma Goldman, the most famous and articulate anarchist in America. Indeed, with her exuberant and overpowering vitality, her audacity and physical courage, and her passionate advocacy of unpopular causes, from feminism and syndicalism to free speech and free love, she was one of the most vital and influential women of her time. "She was a square little solid block of blue-eyed belligerent energy," wrote Max Eastman, "and had, besides a fiery hate, a warmly human kindness in her."[12] Through her writing, lecturing, and publishing, she campaigned vigorously in support of birth control, the labor movement, and artistic and cultural freedom. Strong in her opinions, hot in her sympathies, she was a powerful orator who toured the country restlessly, incessantly, selling vast quantities of anarchist literature and raising funds for the anarchist coffers. Her function, said Floyd Dell, was "that of holding before our eyes the ideal of freedom. She is licensed to taunt us with our moral cowardice, to plant in our soul the nettles of remorse at having acquiesced so tamely in the brutal artifice of present day society."[13]

It was Emma, said Harry Kelly, who "vitalized" the Ferrer Association and started it on the road to whatever success it was to achieve. At the center of the initial protests against Ferrer's execution, she was tireless in her efforts to publicize his ideas. On November 7, 1909, she addressed a Harlem audience on "Ferrer and the Modern School," and three weeks later she spoke on "Francisco Ferrer: His Life and Work" at the Woman's Trades

Union Hall on East 22nd Street. Ferrer, furthermore, was the featured subject of a coast-to-coast lecture tour on which she embarked in February 1910. "Genuine interest in the life and works of that great man [is] manifested at every meeting dedicated to him," she reported while on the road. And in response to her appeals, audiences in San Francisco, Portland, Seattle, and other western cities made substantial financial contributions toward the memorial volume to Ferrer, the project contemplated by her associates in New York. Leonard Abbott did not exaggerate when he wrote, in June 1910, that "Emma Goldman has done more than anyone else to keep alive American interest in the martyred founder of the Modern Schools."[14]

As early as 1899 Emma had told an audience of Italian miners in Illinois of "the necessity of the unhampered development of the child."[15] But her real interest in educational reform dated from her visit to Cempuis in 1900; and among the early contributors to her journal *Mother Earth* was Robin's disciple Emile Janvion, who published an article on "Libertarian Instruction" in the June 1906 issue. Emma herself wrote on education in the journal's second issue, and subsequent numbers, both before and after Ferrer's execution, contained important material on pedagogical reform, including Ferrer's essay "The Modern School" and the program of his International League for the Rational Education of Children. Other contributors were Froebel's American translator, W. N. Hailmann (of the Normal Training School of Cleveland) and Elizabeth Ferm, whose role as a pioneer of American libertarian education will be discussed in a later chapter. Emma Goldman, it might be added, was a friend of John Dewey's and "had a high regard for his ideas." Dewey, for his part, insisted that Goldman's "reputation as a dangerous woman was built up entirely by a conjunction of yellow journalism and ill-advised police raids. She is a romantic idealistic person with a highly attractive personality."[16]

To Emma Goldman the ordinary public school was a "veritable barrack, where the human mind is drilled and manipulated into submission to various social and moral spooks, and thus fitted to continue our system of exploitation and oppression," as she told an international anarchist congress at Amsterdam in 1907. Visiting Sébastien Faure's Beehive school after the congress, she beheld a completely different picture. Instead of authority and competition there were freedom, understanding, and love. Like a colony of bees, in which each works for the good of all, the Beehive children worked together, yet without neglecting individual needs. Having discarded "the old methods of education," she wrote, Faure "established understanding for the needs of the child, confidence and trust in its possibilities, and respect for its personality." Her imagination caught fire, and she vowed to start such schools in the United States: "My visit to La Ruche was a valuable experience that made me realize how much could be done, even under the present system, in the way of libertarian education. To build the man and woman of the future, to unshackle the soul of the child—what grander task for those who, like Sébastien Faure, are pedagogues, not by the mere grace of a college degree, but innately, born with a gift to create, as the poet or artist is?"[17]

Berkman, too, who worked closely with Emma Goldman throughout his life, played a vital role in the movement for libertarian education, especially in its formative stage. A man of courage and intelligence, he was, like Emma herself, one of the best known anarchists in the country, passionately devoted to the cause of social justice. Released from prison in 1906, after serving fourteen years for shooting Henry Clay Frick during the Homestead strike of 1892, he resumed his life as an agitator, taking up the editorship of *Mother Earth*. A magnetic personality, he was a powerful speaker, a capable writer, and an effective organizer.

Apart from Emma Goldman, Berkman did more than anyone else to spread the ideas of Ferrer in the wake of his execution. He started, as we have seen, the first Modern Sunday School in the United States and was a founder of the Ferrer Association. Like his fellow anarchists, he had great confidence in the power of education to bring about a new social order. "Just in proportion that the young generation grows more enlightened and libertarian, will we approach a freer society," he insisted. "Can we indeed expect a generation reared in the atmosphere of a suppressive, authoritarian educational regime to form the cornerstone of a free, self-reliant humanity?"[18]

For all the importance of Goldman and Berkman, the Ferrer Association was not an exclusively anarchist endeavor. The role of freethinkers, still a force to be reckoned with in the United States, was almost as prominent, at least in the early stages. Thus the founding meeting of the association took place at the hall of a free-thought organization, the Harlem Liberal Alliance; and the officers elected at that meeting, Leonard Abbott as president, William van der Weyde as secretary, and Dr. E. B. Foote as treasurer, held identical positions within the Thomas Paine National Historical Association, another free-thought group. It was at Dr. Foote's home, one recalls, that the idea of forming the association had first been discussed, and van der Weyde, a professional photographer, offered his studio at 241 Fifth Avenue as offices of the association until a permanent headquarters could be secured. Both men had strong libertarian sympathies, while Abbott was active in the anarchist as well as the free-thought movement. Nor was this uncommon, Dr. Andrews being another case in point, to say nothing of Ferrer himself. For between anarchism and free thought there was a close and longstanding affinity, both sharing a common antiauthoritarian outlook and a common tradition of secularist radicalism stretching back to Paine and Robert Owen, heroes to atheists and anarchists alike.

In addition to anarchists and freethinkers, the founders of the Ferrer Association included socialists, syndicalists, single-taxers, civil libertarians, and others of progressive persuasion. Of the nine members elected to the Advisory Board at the June 3rd meeting, no fewer than five were socialists, among them some of the most prominent names in the party, which was then at the peak of its influence in the United States. Two others were anarchists, Emma Goldman and Jaime Vidal. The remaining two, Alden Freeman and Hutchins Hapgood, defy categorization, combining elements of anarchism, liberalism, and conservatism.

The five socialists on the Advisory Board were Jack London, Upton Sinclair, Charles Edward Russell, J. G. Phelps Stokes, and his wife Rose Pastor Stokes. Russell, a muckraking journalist of some repute (though not as well known as London or Sinclair), was the socialist candidate that year for governor of New York state. Leonard Abbott, it might be added, had been an active socialist before converting to anarchism in 1908. A member of the Socialist Party since its formation in 1900, he was a founder of both the Inter-Collegiate Socialist Society and the Rand School of Social Science, and it was he who had introduced Upton Sinclair to the socialist movement.[19]

Apart from Abbott, both Hapgood and Freeman harbored anarchist sympathies, and it was largely the magnetism of Emma Goldman that had attracted them to the association. A professional writer who had taught English composition at Harvard and the University of Chicago and served as drama critic for *The Chicago Evening Post*, Hapgood had published a number of widely acclaimed books on offbeat subjects, including *The Spirit of the Ghetto* (1902), *The Spirit of Labor* (1907), and *An Anarchist Woman* (1909), the last inspired in part by Emma Goldman herself. A defender of "the insurgent and unconventional," he had been drawn into the cultural underworld of immigrants, anarchists, and feminists which flourished in Chicago and New York before the First World War, and was a friend not only of Emma Goldman, Alexander Berkman, and Leonard Abbott, but also of Alfred Stieglitz, Theodore Dreiser, and Eugene O'Neill, all of whom will figure in our story.

Alden Freeman, son of the treasurer of the Standard Oil Company, was to become the financial "angel" of the association. Born in Cleveland in 1862, he received both a bachelor's and a master's degree at New York University and was a member of the Society of Mayflower Descendants and of the Society of Colonial Wars. In May 1909 he attended an Emma Goldman lecture on Ibsen which was broken up by the New York police. Outraged by this suppression of fundamental liberties, he invited her to his estate in East Orange, New Jersey, where she spoke on the modern drama before an overflow crowd.[20] Thus began a friendship which involved him with the Modern Schools and other libertarian causes over the next five years.

Insofar as they believed in free thought and expression, all of the original members of the Ferrer Association were civil libertarians. Some, however, went further, taking a prominent part in civil rights campaigns and organizations. One finds a striking overlap between the membership of the Ferrer Association and that of the Free Speech League (an early forerunner of the American Civil Liberties Union), organized during the antiradical hysteria that followed the assassination of President McKinley in 1901 by a self-proclaimed anarchist named Czolgosz. Leonard Abbott and Dr. Foote were president and treasurer of both the Ferrer Association and the Free Speech League (as well as of the Thomas Paine Association), and among the rank and file of the League, Emma Goldman, Harry Kelly, Alden Freeman, and Voltairine de Cleyre played important roles in the Ferrer movement during its formative period.

The same was true of three of the League's most distinguished attorneys, Gilbert E. Roe, Theodore Schroeder, and Bolton Hall. Roe, a former law partner of Senator Robert La Follette of Wisconsin and an "aging deacon of the Single Tax church," was, in

Emma Goldman's words, "an anarchist by feeling and one of the kindest men it has been my good fortune to know."[21] Schroeder, too, was a single-taxer, with a deep interest in advanced ideas in anthropology, psychology, and sociology, especially as they pertained to religion and sex. On these subjects he wrote and spoke incessantly (he published articles in 170 periodicals), a practitioner of the freedoms he advocated. His "wild swooning desire to talk, in season and out, about the obscenity of religion" caused Lincoln Steffens to remark, "I believe in Free Speech for everybody except Schroeder."[22]

Bolton Hall, a highly respected figure in New York legal circles, was Henry George's foremost disciple in the east and a founder of the single-tax colony of Free Acres, New Jersey. An indefatigable writer, he published a dozen books on land reform and corresponded with Theodore Roosevelt, Woodrow Wilson, William Jennings Bryan, and Jacob Riis. Hall, in the description of Konrad Bercovici, was "a mixture of practical idealist, businessman, lawyer, banker, artist, real estate dealer, theorist, philosopher, and flirt."[23] He was also a bit of an anarchist, at least in the philosophical sense. ("Of course I am an anarchist; and a Land Rent man, only as the best method of getting anarchy," he wrote to Joseph Cohen.) An admirer of Peter Kropotkin and a friend of Emma Goldman, he presented her with a farm in Westchester County as a retreat from police harassment after the slaying of McKinley. Goldman said of him: "An unconditional libertarian and single-taxer, he had entirely emancipated himself from his highly respectable background except for his conventional dress. His frock-coat, high silk hat, gloves, and cane make him a conspicuous figure in our ranks."[24]

One can see from the foregoing sketches how widely these "Ferrer enthusiasts" differed in background, wealth, and occupation. The anarchists among them tended to be younger (in their thirties as a rule) and poorer (of working-class or lower-middle-class origin) than the rest. They were mostly foreign-born (many of them East European Jews), collectivist in economics, and revolutionary in temperament, favoring terrorism in some cases. The freethinkers and civil libertarians tended to be older (Bolton Hall and Dr. Foote were born in 1854, Theodore Schroeder in 1864, Gilbert Roe in 1865), of Anglo-Saxon stock, individualist in economics, socially less militant (often with Tolstoyan inclinations), and more deeply rooted in the nineteenth century than their anarchist and socialist colleagues. The native Americans, whether individualist, socialist, or anarchist, were invariably more affluent and better educated than the immigrants (Bolton Hall, Princeton '77, Alden Freeman, NYU '82, Hutchins Hapgood, Harvard '92), earning their living in the main as authors or professionals (Hall, Schroeder, and Roe were lawyers, Foote a physician, Andrews a dentist, van der Weyde a photographer, Abbott, London, Sinclair, Hapgood, Russell all writers). Few could be described as businessmen, though some possessed considerable fortunes: Freeman, with his estate in East Orange; Roe, with his lavish home at Pelham Manor; and Hall, with his New York town house and extensive landholdings. All of them rubbed shoulders with tenement dwellers from the Lower East Side ghetto. The millionaire Phelps Stokes and his immigrant Jewish wife were symbolic of the movement's diversity.

There were, of course, wide variations in the amount of labor members devoted to the association. Some, like Berkman and Goldman, plunged into the day-to-day work of raising funds, publishing literature, starting schools, and securing pupils and teachers. Others were merely notables who lent the prestige of their names to the organization and occasionally chaired a dinner, delivered a lecture, served on the Advisory Board, or sat on the platform at the annual meeting. Upton Sinclair, Jack London, and Charles Edward Russell were particularly suited to this role.

What then held them together? The strongest bond, according to Harry Kelly, was "a deep, underlying protest against the shooting of Ferrer, a broad general understanding as to the desirability of a school such as he had started in Spain." All—whether pacifist or revolutionary, prosperous or indigent, native or foreign-born—shared a faith in education as an instrument of reform, a conviction, as one of them put it, that "the best way to make the world a better place to live in was to start with children." All were libertarians of one sort or another, and each, said Kelly, "was able to read into [Ferrer's] teachings some of his own ideas."[25]

Many, even if not social militants, were philosophical anarchists who believed with Thomas Jefferson that "that government is best which governs least," as Hutchins Hapgood noted.[26] Hapgood himself belonged to this category, together with Bolton Hall, Theodore Schroeder, Gilbert Roe, and Dr. Foote. So too did the association's secretary, William van der Weyde, who considered Thomas Paine "perhaps the earliest apostle of what today we call

Anarchism," citing Paine's dictum that "government, like dress, is the badge of lost innocence."[27] They shared, finally, an optimistic view of the world, rooted in an Enlightenment faith in reason and progress and in a nineteenth-century belief in the ability of science to cure the ills of society. "Our faith," declared Leonard Abbott, "is in the forces of life itself and in the perfectibility of human nature. We believe that humanity is rapidly outgrowing government and militarism and coercion. All about us we see the germs of a future that shall be very different from the present. . . . The new movement towards industrial unionism, the movement towards free thought in religion, the increasing disposition to face the problems of sex and to try to understand them—all are carrying us forward in the right direction."[28]

The immediate tasks confronting the Ferrer Association were threefold: (1) to publish literature on Ferrer and his ideas; (2) to organize memorial meetings on the first anniversary of his execution; and (3) to establish Ferrer schools and centers in American cities.

The first two publications to bear the association's imprint were *The Modern School* by Ferrer (translated by Voltairine de Cleyre) and *The Rational Education of Children*, the program of the International League for the Rational Education of Children, both reprinted from *Mother Earth* during the summer of 1910. To gather material for the third, a memorial volume on Ferrer's life and work, a committee was established consisting of Leonard Abbott, Jaime Vidal, and Helen Tufts Bailie of Boston, wife of the biographer of Josiah Warren. Articles were contributed by Emma Goldman, William van der Weyde, and William Heaford, among others. There were also poems by Bayard Boyesen and J. William Lloyd, and tributes by Anatole France, Ernst Haeckel, Maxim Gorky, Havelock Ellis, Edward Carpenter, Jack London, Upton Sinclair, and Hutchins Hapgood. In response to an appeal from Vidal, Anselmo Lorenzo sent further material from Barcelona. The result was *Francisco Ferrer: His Life, Work and Martyrdom*, a 94-page booklet edited by Abbott, of which 5,000 copies were printed and distributed.

Beyond this, the association issued a prospectus and other materials. A monthly *News Letter*, edited by Harry Kelly and Stewart Kerr, was started in the fall of 1910 and maintained through the following summer, to enable friends and members outside New York to know what was being done. Like Ferrer's *Boletín de la Escuela Moderna*, it served as a vehicle for radical criticism of existing educational methods, with articles by such capable writers as Abbott, Hapgood, and Boyesen. The association also contemplated the publication in English of the complete set of textbooks used in Ferrer's Escuela Moderna, a project that never materialized.

In addition to its own publications, the association distributed other literature on modern education that appeared during the next few years. Of particular importance was *The Origin and Ideals of the Modern School*, a collection of Ferrer's essays which, apart from a Spanish grammar, was his only published book. And there were two English biographies of Ferrer, one by Joseph McCabe, a former monk turned atheist who had spent twelve years in a Franciscan monastery, and the other by William Archer, a well-known literary critic and translator of Ibsen who went to Barcelona after the execution to gather materials at first hand.[29]

The second task before the association was to organize meetings throughout the country to commemorate the first anniversary of Ferrer's death, an idea suggested by Emma Goldman at the founding convention. On October 13, 1910, memorial meetings were held in some twenty-five cities, from Boston to San Francisco. In Buffalo, for example, a crowded gathering heard Voltairine de Cleyre lash out at the obscurantists, secular and ecclesiastical, who had "laid in the ditch of Montjuich a human being who but a moment before had been the personification of manhood, in the flower of life, in the strength and pride of a balanced intellect, full of the purpose of a great and growing undertaking—that of the Modern Schools." The largest meeting took place in New York City, where a crowd of 5,000 packed the Great Hall of Cooper Union to pay tribute to the Spanish martyr.[30]

The object of these meetings, apart from honoring Ferrer, was to raise the funds necessary for the creation of Modern Schools, in accordance with the Spaniard's last wish ("Long live the Modern School!"). The sum of $500 was collected at the Cooper Union meeting, augmented by pledges from Alden Freeman and Edward Foote. To raise additional money, Leonard Abbott and William van der Weyde sent an appeal to groups and individuals around the country,[31] and contributions began to trickle in. By the end of the year, sufficient means had been secured to open a Ferrer Center in New York. Elsewhere the pattern was the same. Bit by bit, a nationwide movement was taking shape.

THE MODERN SCHOOL MOVEMENT

During the next five years the Ferrer Association prospered. Branches were started in all parts of the country, except the deep south. Membership grew with a rapidity that surpassed the most optimistic forecasts. Colonies were founded at Stelton, New Jersey, and later at Mohegan, New York. Schools were opened in a dozen locations, more than anywhere else in the world. Classes were conducted in German, Italian, Yiddish, Czech, and Esperanto, in addition to English. Near the larger cities, such as New York and Philadelphia, summer camps were established as retreats from the squalor of ghetto life.

Although the movement was centered in New York, the first Ferrer schools, apart from the short-lived Sunday School organized by Alexander Berkman, sprang up in other cities. By the end of 1910 schools had been started in Philadelphia, Chicago, Salt Lake City, and Seattle. It was not until October 1911 that a school was opened in New York (and another in Portland, Oregon). Still other Modern Schools appeared in Detroit in 1912 and in Brooklyn in 1913. Afterwards, as we shall see, schools were opened in San Francisco, Los Angeles, Paterson, Stelton, Lakewood, and Mohegan, and planned in a dozen other locations, including Denver, St. Louis, Cleveland, Buffalo, Pittsburgh, and the Bronx.

The following chart contains a list of these schools, as far as one can recover them from the oblivion into which they have sunk. Under the heading of "Modern Schools" are listed only those which called themselves "Ferrer" or "Modern" Schools or which belonged to the Francisco Ferrer Association or its successor (from 1916), the Modern School Association of North America. "Related Schools" includes libertarian schools which were closely connected to the Ferrer schools in ideology, method, and personnel.

How much do we know about these schools? A great deal, in the case of New York, Stelton, and Mohegan, rather less of Philadelphia and Lakewood. Of the remainder we know very little. A glance at the chart will show that most were ephemeral ventures, seldom lasting more than three years, though the Stelton school continued for four decades and the Mohegan school for nearly two. While the ultimate goal of the Ferrer Association was to organize a hierarchy of schools, including Modern High Schools and Colleges, it rarely got beyond the lowest stage. Most, that is to say, remained merely Sunday Schools. Of the twenty-two Modern Schools listed, only five were Day Schools—in New York, Los Angeles, Portland, Mohegan, and Stelton. There were no higher schools or universities, though adult classes in such subjects as literature, science, history, anthropology, and art were everywhere offered, and most schools had adult libraries or reading rooms.

Improvisation remained the rule, and there was considerable variation, depending on location, resources, and staff. The founders, as in the parent body, were an assortment of anarchists, atheists, socialists, syndicalists, and single-taxers. Principals and teachers were predominantly native Americans of Anglo-Saxon origin, whereas the pupils, especially in industrial cities with large immigrant populations, were heavily Jewish, and nearly all were of working-class parents. Among the teachers, qualifications differed widely in terms of both training and experience; and some, while well educated in a general sense (William Thurston Brown at Yale, Bayard Boyesen and Will Durant at Columbia, James F. Morton and Henry Schnittkind at Harvard), had little previous knowledge of pedagogical technique.

Yet, for all the variation, the schools had much in common. All were administered by local branches of the Ferrer Association. In every case Ferrer's Escuela Moderna provided the model, adapted to local needs and conditions. Instruction, as in Barcelona, was based on libertarian and rationalist principles, with emphasis on learning by doing, crafts rather than books, and hygiene and physical health. All pursued the dual aim of children's and adult education, with lectures on a broad range of scientific and literary subjects. Several had classes in Esperanto, the international language. All served as radical centers, involved not only with education but with a variety of social causes, from industrial unionism and freedom of speech to sexual liberation and antimilitarist propaganda. The prevailing ideology was a mixture of anarchism, socialism, and syndicalism, with Kropotkin as the most influential theorist (there was a Kropotkin Library at Stelton). Apart from the association's *News Letter*, a number of anarchist publications, especially *Mother Earth* in the east and *The Agitator* in the west, carried news of the different schools

Modern Schools in North America, 1909-1961

Name	*Address*	*Dates*	*Day/Sunday*	*Staff*	*Remarks*
Modern School	New York City	1910	Sunday	Alexander Berkman	First Modern School in U.S.
Ferrer School	New York City	1910-1920s	Sunday	Josef Jülich	A German Modern School.
Modern School	424 Pine St., Philadelphia	1910-c.1930	Sunday	Joseph Cohen, Abe Grosner	Organized by the Radical Library. Had Camp Germinal, summers, 1925-c.1930.
Chicago Modern School	Twelfth St., Chicago	1910-1911	Sunday	William Nathanson, Voltairine de Cleyre	
Modern School	146 S.W. Temple St., Salt Lake City	1910-1911?	Sunday	William Thurston Brown, Virginia Snow Stephens	
Seattle Modern School	601 Columbia St., Seattle	1910-1912?	Sunday?	Bruce Rogers, Anna Falcoff	
Ferrer Modern School	6 St. Mark's Place,	1911	Adult Ctr.	Bayard Boyesen	Day School moved to Stelton, May 1915. Adult Center continued in New York till 1918.
	104 E. 12th St.,	1911-1912	Day	John and Abby Coryell,	
	63 E. 107th St., New York City	1912-1915	Day	Will Durant, Cora Bennett Stephenson, Robert and Delia Hutchinson	
Modern School	167 Fourth St., Portland	1911-1912?	Day	William Thurston Brown, Louise Olivereau	N.Y. and Portland were first Modern Day Schools in U.S.
Detroit Modern School	257 Beaubien St., Detroit	1912-1917?	Sunday	Dr. Tobias Sigel, Carl Nold, Yetta Bienenfeld	
Modern School	Brownsville district, Brooklyn, N.Y.	1913-1915?	Sunday	Dr. Solomon Bauch	
Modern School	Toronto	1913-1914?	Sunday	Rudolf Rocker, Jr.	
Ferrer Modern School	Stelton, Piscataway Twp., N.J.	1915-1953	Day	Alexis and Elizabeth Ferm, James and Nellie Dick *et al.*	The longest-lived Modern School in America.
Francisco Ferrer School	Paterson, N.J.	1915-1917?	Sunday		An Italian Modern School.
Francisco Ferrer School	Philadelphia	1916-1917	Sunday	Erasmo Abate *et al.*	An Italian Modern School.
Ferrer Modern School	New York City	1917-1923	Sunday		A Czech Modern School.

Walt Whitman School	517 S. Boyle Ave., Los Angeles	1919-1924	Day	William Thurston Brown	
William Morris School	409 Ashbury St., San Francisco	1921-1924?	Sunday	Benjamin Ellisberg	
Ferrer Modern School	Gary, Ind.	1920s-1930s	Sunday		A Spanish Modern School.
Mohegan Modern School	Crompond, N.Y.	1924-1941	Day	Harry Kelly, James and Nellie Dick *et al.*	
Weekend Modern School	230 E. 15th St., New York City	c. 1932-1935	Weekend	Abraham L. Goldman	
Lakewood Modern School	115 Carey St., Lakewood, N.J.	1933-1958	Day	James and Nellie Dick	
RELATED SCHOOLS					
Home Colony School	Lakebay, Wash.	1896-1930s	Day	George H. Allen James F. Morton *et al.*	
Children's Playhouse	New Rochelle, N.Y.	1901-1902	Day	Alexis & Elizabeth Ferm	
Children's Playhouse	Dyker Heights, Brooklyn, N.Y.	1902-1906	Day	Alexis & Elizabeth Ferm	
Children's Playhouse	Madison St., New York City	1906-1913	Day	Alexis & Elizabeth Ferm	
The Birds	Lower East Side, New York City	1907-1908?	Nursery	Naomi Bercovici	During World War I she ran a libertarian school in Hewlett, Long Island.
Boy Land	Santa Barbara, Calif.	1912-1918	Day	Pryns Hopkins	He established a similar school near Paris in the 1920s.
Stony Ford School	Goshen, N.Y.	1915-1918	Day	Robert and Delia Hutchinson	
Free Workers' College	Los Angeles	c. 1923-1927	Adult	Thomas Bell, Joseph Spivak *et al.*	
Sunrise Colony School	Alicia, Mich.	1933-1940	Day	Joseph Cohen, Philip Trupin	
University of the Free Life	Camp Germinal, Jamison, Pa.	1935	Adult	John G. Scott	
Modern Piano School	New York City	1940s	Music	Edwina Behr, Suzanne Avins, Clara Freedman	
Walden School	Berkeley, Calif.	1950s-1960s	Day	David Koven and Audrey Goodfriend	

(and of similar experiments overseas), keeping them abreast of each other's activities. Contacts between them were frequent, including exchanges of teachers and equipment, and they shared a sense of a common mission in their quest for educational freedom.

Still another similarity might be mentioned. Like their counterparts in Spain, the Modern Schools in America incurred the hostility of the authorities, and especially of the Catholic church. At a Ferrer memorial lecture in Cleveland delivered by Voltairine de Cleyre, a priest in the audience became so infuriated that he went out to get a policeman to arrest her. When the Ferrer School opened in New York, the neighborhood priest expressed his displeasure by casting dark looks in its direction whenever he passed. It was precisely this attitude, observed the school's teacher, that compelled America to "carry on the work of Ferrer. This is a land of pseudo liberty only, and we are dominated by the same soul-destroying superstitions and traditions to which he was sacrificed."[32]

Not that conditions in the two countries were the same. Even the most ardent supporters of the Modern School recognized that in America the church did not oversee educational and cultural life as in Spain. Nor was there a comparable rate of illiteracy or so reactionary and militaristic a government. And the system of public schools was far more efficient and widespread. Yet the broader problems for both remained the same: how to develop a well-rounded, thinking individual, independent of reigning dogmas and prejudices; how to establish schools that would stimulate pupils to rely on their own initiative and judgment and have the courage of their convictions; how to raise a generation of children free from subservience to authority and capable of working for the freedom of others. As William Thurston Brown put it in the prospectus of the Salt Lake City Modern School: "The problems of America are as critical for America as those of Spain are for Spain. At bottom they are the same. And here, as there, the only road to justice and freedom is through popular knowledge of evolutionary science."[33]

Earlier Experimental Schools

The idea of educating children in an atmosphere of freedom and spontaneity was by no means new to America. As in Spain, there had been a long history of alternative schools which antedated the Ferrer movement and which drew upon the theories of

Froebel, Pestalozzi, and other educational innovators. This is not the place for a comprehensive survey of radical educational experiments in the United States. But a brief account is needed to set the Ferrer schools in historical perspective.

At the New Harmony community in Indiana, established in the 1820s, Robert Owen and his disciples introduced many of the ideas and methods that were employed nearly a century later in the Modern Schools. Most important, the New Harmony school followed Pestalozzi's principle that "the individuality of the child must be sacred" and that relations between teacher and pupil "must be based on and controlled by love."[34] Furthermore, crafts and games received particular emphasis, and adult education held an important place.

In charge of education at New Harmony was the "father of American geology," William Maclure, president of the Philadelphia Academy of Sciences and America's leading pioneer of the Pestalozzian system of instruction. At New Harmony Maclure established the first trade school, the first kindergarten, the first school offering the same educational advantages to both sexes, and the first self-governing or "free" school in the United States. Vocational as well as academic, it was "the last word in progressive pedagogy," with its workshops, experimental farm, and scientific museum.[35]

For Maclure, society was divided into two distinct categories, the productive majority, on the one hand, and the exploiting minority, on the other. The latter, he believed, controlled not only the instruments of wealth and of coercion, including the army and the police, but also the educational system, with which they conditioned the minds of the workers to acquiesce in their subjugation. The schools were "poison," he maintained, when "misapplied by the rich and powerful to stupefy the poor." Like Godwin, Bakunin, and Kropotkin, Maclure espoused the cause of "equality of education, property, and power among men." Through the acquisition of knowledge, he said, the poor would achieve independence, for "KNOWLEDGE IS POWER in political societies, and it is, perhaps, as impossible to keep a well informed people in slavery as it is to make an ignorant people enjoy the blessings of freedom." In short, "the division of property divides knowledge, and the division of property and knowledge divides power. The nearly equal division of knowledge will equalize both property and power."[36]

Maclure's chief aim at New Harmony was to establish a school, after the manner of Pestalozzi, in which manual and mental training would be combined, so as to encourage "a habit of working and thinking conjointly."[37] To this end he brought to the colony a distinguished group of Pestalozzian educators and scientists, among them Joseph Neef, who had started the first Pestalozzian school in America at Schuylkill Falls, near Philadelphia. Like Maclure, Pestalozzi, and Owen, Neef believed that education should concentrate on practical rather than theoretical learning. "Books," he wrote, "shall be the last fountain from which we shall endeavor to draw our knowledge. . . . It is irrevocably decided and determined that my pupils shall pry into no book, turn over no book, read no book, till they are able not only to comprehend what they read, but also to distinguish perfectly well good from bad, truth from falsehood, reality from chimera, and probabilities from absurdities. God's beauteous and prolific creation—all nature—shall be their book, and facts their instructors. But as soon as they shall have reached the necessary maturity, then, and only then, shall they read; then their reading will be really useful, and both instructive and pleasing to them."[38]

Book learning, accordingly, was deferred until the age of ten. In its place Neef conducted nature walks, took the children on long hikes in the country, and taught them such subjects as botany and geology amid the actual specimens to be studied. He also encouraged vigorous exercise, gymnastics, and play. "My pupils," he said, "shall run, jump, climb, slide, skate, bathe, swim and exert their adroitness, display their dexterity and exercise their bodily force, just as much as they please, or at least as it is rational to allow them."[39]

Devoted to the principle of self-education, Neef sought, like Tolstoy, to remain on an equal footing with his pupils. "Instead of crowding into their heads an infinity of half-understood, misunderstood, and very frequently not-at-all understood rules and precepts," he wrote, "I shall, on the contrary, act the mere part of a disciple. The teacher's part will entirely devolve on them. My only task will be to present, in their successive order, the theorems to be demonstrated and the problems to be solved." The children, moreover, were to be free from coercion and punishment: "The grave, doctorial, magisterial, and dictatorial tone shall never insult their ears; they shall probably never hear of cat-o'nine-tails. I shall be nothing else but their friend and guide, their school-fellow, play-fellow, and messmate." And Neef agreed with Maclure and Owen that religious dogma had no place in the school, though all three believed in a moral instruction, based on the Golden Rule, which would "acquaint the children with their inalienable rights and immutable duties in a moral world."[40]

A similar educational philosophy was evolved by Josiah Warren, who, leaving New Harmony in 1827, embarked on a career of social reform that earned him the title of "the first American anarchist." After his departure, Warren corresponded with Maclure and visited Neef's Pestalozzian school at Schuylkill Falls. Like them, he was determined to save the child from dependence on adults, teachers and employers as well as parents. At Spring Hill, Ohio, in the early 1830s, he instructed boys in a variety of trades in an effort to make them self-supporting. Leaving them to their own resources, he gave them full responsibility over their activities and treated them according to the principles of "equity" and "self-sovereignty." According to his biographer, William Bailie, Warren "taught them more in one week, when all their interests were aroused and their innate capacities called forth, than they would have learned in a year by the common method of enforced instruction." The result, said Warren, was that they quickly formed habits of "thinking and deciding for themselves."[41]

In a like manner, Warren trained his own children in habits of industry and self-reliance. "I would throw them upon their own resources," he declared, "and enable them to learn by experience the responsibilities of life." At the age of four his son George was taught the use of carpenter's tools, and at seven he learned typesetting and composed a small book. Said Warren: "I shall act as their friend rather than as their master; or, as one member of society should act towards another, strictly respecting their individual rights and thus teaching them *by example* to respect those of other people."[42]

Warren, who published a brochure entitled *Modern Education*, wrote often of the need to recognize the "rights of children." "If we would have them practice equity towards each other in adult life, we must surround them with equitable practice and treat them equitably," he insisted. "If we would have them respect the individual peculiarities and the personal liberty of others, then we must respect their individual peculiarities and their personal liberty. . . . If we would have them capable of self-government in adult age, they should practice the rights of self-government in childhood." Since lawmakers are "the last to learn and respect these rights," Warren cautioned, to place the schooling of children in government hands would be like asking "the fox to take care of the chickens." In fact, he added, "I think that the power of educating the rising generation is of too much importance to be trusted in a manageable shape in the hands of *any* small body of men, as society is now constituted."[43]

New Harmony, of course, was not the only cooperative community to boast an experimental school. Indeed, utopian colonies in general, whatever their particular philosophy, tended to place education at the center of their endeavors and to regard the school as a laboratory for social improvement. Thus at Brook Farm in Massachusetts, the most famous Fourierist colony in America, the members vowed "to secure for our children, and to those who may be entrusted to our care, the benefits of the highest physical, intellectual, and moral education which, in the present state of human knowledge, the resources at our command will permit." A relationship of informality and mutual respect existed between pupils and teachers, with little discipline imposed, apart from an effort "to arouse a sense of personal responsibility, to communicate a passion for intellectual work." Each child, however, was expected to work a few hours every day at some form of manual labor, in keeping with Fourier's doctrine of integral instruction. Evening lectures and discussions, as well as concerts, plays, and a well-stocked library, all testify to a lively interest in adult education and culture.[44]

A similar outlook prevailed at the Skaneateles community in New York state, one of the earliest anarchist colonies in America, where children were instructed "in facts more than words, and in principles more than dogmas." As in New Harmony and Brook Farm, priority went to crafts over books, and lectures for adults had an important place. Its founder, John A. Collins, declared in 1844: "Our present education is as false as our religion—as barbarous and inhumane as our governments. The mind and body are not properly educated together. Their equilibrium is not sustained. Education is not confined to schools. It does not commence at four and terminate at twenty. It commences with our first breath, and terminates with our life." Like William Maclure and Josiah Warren, Collins distinguishesd sharply between the laboring majority and the parasitical elite who enjoyed a monopoly on learning. Scorning those who did not perform manual labor, especially lawyers and "hireling clergy," he regarded an equal education for all as the lever of fundamental reform.[45]

Alternative schools, however, were not confined to utopian

communities. During the antebellum decades, free schools were launched in New York and other cities by the abolitionist followers of William Lloyd Garrison. A particularly noteworthy experiment was the Temple School in Boston, started by A. Bronson Alcott in September 1834. Jo Ann Wheeler, a teacher at Stelton and Mohegan, rightly considers Alcott's venture a direct forebear of the Modern Schools.[46] Alcott was a well-known New England transcendentalist and libertarian. ("Why should I employ a church to write my creed or a state to govern me?" he asked. "Why not write my own creed? Why not govern myself?") Convinced of the importance of teaching and sure of his own love for children, he early decided to devote himself to education. He read Rousseau and Pestalozzi, Owen and Neef, and corresponded with Maclure at New Harmony. He also read *Political Justice* by Godwin, whose ideas "flashed upon his brain. They seemed to be spoken inside him."[47] For five years, assisted by Elizabeth Peabody, he endeavored to put them into practice.

The Temple School boasted a varied program of activities, both intellectual and physical, with emphasis on self-analysis and self-development. The children learned as individuals, each making progress at his own rate of speed. Play and gymnastics occupied an important place in the curriculum. Pupils were allowed to sing, dance, and make noise without fear of corporal punishment. Abandoning the birch rod, Alcott gave the children love.

Alcott believed that every child, even the youngest, had a mind, an imagination, of his own, and should be encouraged to use it. His admiration for the Pestalozzian system stemmed from its insistence that "children are the best judges of what meets their views and feelings." "We need schools," he wrote in October 1834, "not for the inculcation of knowledge, merely, but for the development of genius." In his own experiment he drew out the pupil's ideas rather than pour in instruction by mechanical or compulsory techniques. For Alcott, according to Ralph Waldo Emerson, "a teacher is one who can assist the child in obeying his own mind." By following this precept, Emerson added, "he made the schoolroom beautiful."[48]

Emerson himself exerted a powerful influence on the founders of the Modern Schools, who quoted his writings with enthusiastic approval. A friend of Alcott's, he admired the Temple School and shared many of the assumptions on which it was organized. He personally felt that conventional schooling had done him little good. "We teach boys to be such men as we are," he once complained. "We do not teach them to aspire to be all they can. We do not give them a training as if we believed in their noble nature. We scarce educate their bodies. We do not train the eye and the hand. We exercise their understandings to the apprehension and comparison of some facts, to a skill in numbers, in words; we aim to make accountants, attorneys, engineers; but not to make ably earnest, great-hearted men." "We are students of words," Emma Goldman quoted him as saying. "We are shut up in schools and colleges for ten or fifteen years and come out a bag of wind, a memory of words, and do not know a thing."[49]

For Emerson, life itself educated as the classroom did not. He held that the difficulties of learning would be solved as soon as "we leave institutions and address individuals," for the mind cannot be opened by any "mechanical or military method." Like Alcott, he thought of education as a process of unfolding, of development from within. The secret of good teaching thus lay in respecting the pupil and his self-reliance. "It is not for you to choose what he shall know, what he shall do," Emerson advised the would-be instructor. "It is chosen and foreordained, and he only holds the key to his own secret. By your tampering and thwarting and too much governing he may be hindered from his end and kept out of his own. Respect the child. Wait and see the new product of Nature. Nature loves analogies, but not repetitions. Respect the child. Be not too much his parent. Trespass not on his solitude."[50]

Another partisan of Alcott's methods was Henry David Thoreau, like Emerson a venerated figure among the proponents of libertarian education. An advocate of nature studies and learning by doing, Thoreau resigned his position in the Concord public schools rather than use physical force against his students. He believed that children were innately good and that the school was meant to stimulate their inner development. He was also a champion of adult education, taking part in evening lectures and other cultural activities.[51]

A more immediate precursor of the American Modern Schools was Marietta Pierce Johnson's School of Organic Education, founded in 1907 at the single-tax colony of Fairhope, Alabama. The concept of "organic" education, designed to meet the "whole needs of children as individuals," bore a close resemblance to that of "integral" education, as conceived by the Fourierists and anarchists. To Marietta Johnson the child was a "unit organism," constantly growing and changing. She was as much concerned with the moral and physical development of the child as with his intellectual development. "Education is life," "education is growth," were the maxims which guided her work. As in New Harmony and other early experiments, reading and writing gave place to "occupational" or "activity" programs, and examinations and report cards were done away with, so that no child would ever feel the "stigma of failure."[52]

The Organic School had no desks, and classes were often held out of doors. Singing, dancing, and story-telling were daily activities. "It is very thrilling to contemplate what society might be in a few years if our educational system could accept and apply this point of view," Mrs. Johnson wrote. "No examinations, no tests, no failures, no rewards, no self-consciousness; the development of sincerity, the freedom of children to live their lives straight out, no double motives, children never subjected to the temptation to cheat, even to appear to know when they do not know; the development of fundamental sincerity, which is the basis of all morality."[53] The school's innovations aroused the interest of many progressive educators, among them John Dewey, who came to Fairhope for a firsthand look and devoted a chapter of his *Schools of Tomorrow* to Mrs. Johnson's experiment. Alexis Ferm, it is worth noting, spent his last years at Fairhope, and two of his ablest teachers at Stelton, Lillian Rifkin and Sherwood Trask, had previously taught at the Organic School.

THE FIRST MODERN SCHOOLS

It must be clear from the above that the initiators of the Ferrer schools could draw upon a rich legacy of dissenting education, American as well as European. How much of it they were familiar with is open to speculation, but they surely knew of the writings of Emerson and Thoreau, if not of Warren and Collins, and of the experiments at Brook Farm and New Harmony, if not at Skaneateles and Spring Hill. It is not surprising, then, that a glimpse at the first Modern Schools should reveal a marked continuity with their predecessors.

Take the case of the Modern Sunday School started in October 1910 by the Radical Library of Philadelphia, an anarchist branch of the Workmen's Circle, the Jewish fraternal society. Its driving spirit, a young cigar worker named Joseph Cohen, was to play a major role in the Ferrer movement over the next four decades, becoming the custodian of the Ferrer Center in New York and a founder of the Ferrer colony in New Jersey, in addition to his labors in Philadelphia. Located at 424 Pine Street, in the heart of the Jewish ghetto, the Radical Library school was one of the largest and most active in the movement. By the spring of 1911 nearly sixty children, aged five to sixteen, were enrolled under the care of Cohen and his wife Sophie, assisted by two non-Jewish anarchists, an English shoemaker named George Brown and his Danish-born companion Mary Hansen, whose daughter Heloise, like little Emma Cohen, was one of the brightest pupils.

By 1916 the enrollment at the Philadelphia school had nearly doubled, with more than one hundred children in attendance. Classes met every Sunday at 2 P.M. There was singing, dancing, story-telling, and arts and crafts. Emma Cohen recalls that an effort was made to indoctrinate the children with revolutionary and antimilitarist beliefs. This is confirmed by interviews with other pupils and by documentary evidence. At one Sunday session, in June 1911, the children sang the *Internationale* and recited Herwegh's "Freedom," Hood's "Song of the Shirt," and other radical poems. The adults were very pleased with the results: "It is interesting as well as greatly encouraging to watch the youngsters gradually learn to respect the views and opinions of others. Freedom, Reason, Broad-mindedness—these are the cornerstones of the Modern School."[54]

The Philadelphia Modern School was also an adult educational center, with lectures almost every evening on a wide variety of subjects, both topical and academic. Local speakers included Scott Nearing of the University of Pennsylvania and Dr. Uvarov, a member of the Radical Library, who lectured on hygiene and physiology. From Chicago came Lucy Parsons to speak on the Haymarket tragedy, and Leonard Abbott and Will Durant of New York held forth on literature and philosophy respectively. Once a year the members organized a Russian Tea Party, or *vecherinka*, to raise money to meet expenses.[55]

When Cohen departed at the end of 1913 to manage the Ferrer Center in New York, Abe Grosner, a graduate student in philosophy at the University of Pennsylvania, took charge of the Philadelphia school. Running it with the same energy as his predecessor, he increased the number of concerts and of evening lectures and discussions, the dominant question being that of the world war, "to which we were all opposed."[56] At the same time, Grosner's younger brother Ellis added astronomy and general science to the Sunday curriculum, with the aid of a slide lantern.

Unlike its counterpart in New York, the Philadelphia Modern School never became a "yeasting place" of avant-garde culture and art, as Emma Cohen has noted. But it had its share of intellectual stimulation, and "we all became good friends, teachers, parents, and students."[57] Many of the participants were afterwards associated with the Modern Schools in New York, Stelton, and Mohegan, among them Abe Grosner and the Cohens.

To the members of the Radical Library, the Sunday School was but a first step. What they wanted more than anything else was to establish a Day School, such as that in New York or in Portland, both opened in 1911. This aim was never realized. In the fall of 1924, however, land was acquired at Jamison, Pennsylvania, thirty miles above Philadelphia, as the site of a children's camp and adult colony. The following summer Camp Germinal was started, with Joseph Cohen at the helm. Named after Zola's novel, which made a powerful impression on anarchists of Cohen's generation, it endured until the early 1930s, as did the Sunday School in Philadelphia.[58] Camp Germinal continued as an informal bungalow colony, shorn of its anarchist character, until the end of the Second World War, while the Radical Library survived as a branch of the Workmen's Circle into the 1960s. Both maintained close relations with the Ferrer colony at Stelton, New Jersey, less than a two-hour journey away.

In Chicago, as in Philadelphia, the Modern School movement got off to an early start. During the summer of 1910 a Francisco Ferrer Club, with a free library and reading room, was established at 1015 South Halsted Street, followed by a branch of the Ferrer Association. October 1910 saw the opening of a Chicago Modern School, organized by William Nathanson and a group of fellow anarchists in the house of Nathanson's mother-in-law on Twelfth Street. Like the venture in Philadelphia, which began at the same time, it was a Sunday School for children with evening lectures for adults. In contrast to Philadelphia, however, it lasted only one year.

Of the participants in this short-lived enterprise, the best known was Voltairine de Cleyre, a gifted writer and speaker and one of the most interesting personalities in the annals of American radicalism. Although born in rural Michigan and educated in a Catholic convent, she became the apostle of anarchism to the Jewish immigrants of Philadelphia, learning the Yiddish language while teaching English to her working-class comrades (Joseph Cohen was among her pupils). For twenty-five years she was an active agitator and propagandist, one of the movement's most admired representatives. Emma Goldman called her "the poet-rebel, the liberty-loving artist, the greatest woman Anarchist of America."[59]

Like Ferrer himself, Voltairine de Cleyre was a freethinker as well as an anarchist, and she translated his essay "The Modern School" for *Mother Earth*. Having been educated in a convent, she shared Ferrer's hatred for the Catholic church and its authoritarian methods of instruction. With Ferrer she also rejected the public school, which she considered an agent of government indoctrination bent on instilling a blind obedience and "revolting patriotism" in the minds of children. Her ideal, rather, was "a boarding school built in the country, having a farm attached, and workshop where useful crafts might be learned in daily connection with intellectual training,"[60] a vision which anticipated the experiment begun at Stelton in 1915, three years after her death. It was fitting, then, that the main thoroughfare of the Stelton community should have been christened Voltairine de Cleyre Street in her memory.

Voltairine de Cleyre moved to Chicago in October 1910. Until January 1911 she taught on Sunday afternoons at the Modern School and delivered evening lectures for adults, "an intense speaker, overflowing with sympathy," as one of her pupils remembers.[61] Declining health, however, compelled her to withdraw. The school itself did not survive beyond the spring, owing to a lack of funds. Attempts to revive it came to nothing. In 1914 a Modern School League was formed by Robert McConochie, a socialist, and Dr. J. H. Greer, an anarchist, together with William Thurston Brown, among others. Dr. Rudolf von Liebich, later active in the Los Angeles movement, offered his house as quarters for a new Sunday School. But financial difficulties and the sudden death of McConochie in May 1915 cooled the ardor of the group, and their plans failed to bear fruit.[62]

In October 1910 a third Sunday School was started at Salt Lake City, simultaneously with those in Philadelphia and Chicago. Its founder, William Thurston Brown, had a veritable passion for organizing Modern Schools. One of the most active figures in the movement, he also started Day Schools in Portland and Los Angeles in 1911 and 1919. In between, he sought without success to revive the Sunday School in Chicago and directed the Day School at Stelton. He was thus associated with five Ferrer-type ventures in less than ten years, each in a different part of the country. Never staying long in one place, he was at Salt Lake City and Portland for a single year each, at Stelton and Los Angeles for three.

Brown's entire career was marked by a series of rapid changes. Beginning as a "moral idealist," he ran the political gamut from Christian socialism to Soviet communism, moving steadily to the left between the 1890s and 1920s, with a momentary lapse during the First World War, when he defended American military involvement. Born in 1861, the son of an upstate New York clergyman, Brown was descended from the seventeenth-century founders of Rhode Island. He himself prepared for the ministry at Yale, occupying the pulpit of the Congregational Church of Madison, Connecticut, from 1893 until 1896, when some of the more conservative parishioners, upset by his unorthodox sermons, brought charges of heresy against him. Although acquitted by an ecclesiastical council, Brown left Madison in 1898. By then he had become a Christian socialist and a vigorous opponent of the Spanish-American War, editing *The Social Gospel* with Bolton Hall and Ernest Howard Crosby, America's leading apostle of Tolstoyan nonresistance.

An effective preacher, Brown secured a new pulpit in Rochester, New York, at the fashionable Plymouth Congregational Church. While serving in this post he attended socialist lectures at the Labor Lyceum and found them "always convincing and instructive." Dropping the "Christian" prefix, he became a socialist pure and simple, the author of anticapitalist pamphlets, and a contributor to *The Comrade* and other leading socialist periodicals of the day. In May 1901 Brown presided at the "socialist" wedding of George Herron and Carrie Rand, and the following year he started his own socialist journal, *Here and Now*.[63]

That these activities should have antagonized Brown's congregation is not surprising. Matters came to a head after the assassination of President McKinley in September 1901, when Brown sought to explain Czolgosz's motives and defended the right of Emma Goldman and her comrades to do the same. In May 1902 Brown was ousted from the pulpit. As Emma Goldman put it, he "lost a fat church because he dared, as few did, give reasons for Czolgosz's act."[64]

Abandoning Congregationalism for the more liberal Unitarian church, Brown at the same time became an organizer for the Socialist Party and ran for lieutenant-governor of New York on the Socialist ticket. Over the next few years he traveled the length and breadth of the country, denouncing the evils of capitalism and upholding the rights of labor, free speech, and free sex. A prolific writer, he contributed to anarchist as well as socialist papers, although he never joined the anarchist movement.[65]

The formation of the Ferrer Association found Brown in Salt Lake City. Embracing the new cause with characteristic fervor, he bent his energies toward the creation of a Modern School, the first with which he was to be associated. His plan called for four departments: the Sunday Evening Lecture, the School of Social Science, the Literature and Modern Drama Club, and the Civic Survey. How much of this was realized is unclear from our meager sources. Since Brown left Salt Lake City less than a year later, he probably did not get much beyond the usual Sunday afternoon sessions for children and evening lectures and discussions for adults. One notable feature, however, was a class in art offered by Virginia Snow Stephens, an instructor at the University of Utah, whom Emma Goldman called "a very courageous and able woman."[66] The daughter of Lorenzo Snow, a former president of the Mormon church, she had abandoned her conservative surroundings to join the socialist movement. "Do you believe there is justice for the poor working factory girl, or for the ill-paid person in other employment?" she asked a friend. "If you knew and had seen right here in Salt Lake City what I have seen with my own eyes, you might change your view."[67]

As a Mormon stronghold, Salt Lake City provided unfruitful soil for libertarian ideas, and the Modern School closed not long after Brown's departure in 1911. Three years later, Mrs. Stephens threw herself into the struggle to save Joe Hill, the Wobbly songster who had been charged with the murder of a Salt Lake City merchant. After his execution in 1916, she was fired from her position at the university.[68]

A fourth Modern Sunday School opened its doors at Seattle in December 1910. Its director, Bruce Rogers, was an active anarchist who often spoke at radical gatherings and contributed to *The Agitator* and other journals. Apart from Rogers himself, the school had a capable teacher in Anna Falcoff, formerly of the Home Colony near Tacoma, the west-coast equivalent of Stelton. An anarchist of Russian-Jewish origin and Tolstoyan cast, she liked to walk barefoot in her garden in the university district of Seattle, an exotic spectacle in those days. Local patriots accused her of indoctrinating the children with Marxist principles. "I am no Marxist and I have never studied Marxist economics," she protested. "And anyway, I doubt if it would be worthwhile to teach Marxist economics to such young children." But certainly some indoctrination was going on in her school, they insisted. "Yes," she replied. "I try to teach them to be free."[69]

The Seattle Modern School, like its Chicago and Salt Lake City counterparts, was a short-lived endeavor, closing in 1912 or 1913. Yet the movement as a whole continued to expand, with branches springing up in many cities. By the fall of 1911 Leonard Abbott could report that "the Ferrer movement is now national in its scope and activities."[70] As these words were being written, the first Modern Day Schools were taking shape in New York City and Portland, Oregon, opening simultaneously in October 1911, the second anniversary of Ferrer's death. The New York school, which moved to Stelton in 1915, maintained a continuous existence for forty-two years, by far the longest such venture on record. The school at Portland, by contrast, lasted no more than two years, yet another ephemeral creation of William Thurston Brown, who departed for Chicago in 1912. Offering daily classes for children and evening and weekend classes for adults, it served as an outlet for Brown's seemingly inexhaustible energies. In the course of a single year, it issued a whole series of his pamphlets, including *Love's Freedom and Fulfilment, The Moral Basis of the Demand for Free Divorce,* and *Walt Whitman: Poet of the Human Whole*.[71]

Two additional schools are worthy of mention at this point, the Modern Schools of Brooklyn and Detroit. The Brooklyn school was started in October 1913 in the Brownsville section of the borough, inhabited predominantly by Jewish immigrants. Its founder, Dr. Solomon Bauch, had previously taught in the Sunday School of the Ferrer Center in Harlem, which will be treated in the next chapter.[72] The Detroit Modern School, likewise a Sunday affair, opened in November 1912 with eleven boys and girls, children of German and Jewish anarchists. By the spring of 1914 more than thirty were enrolled, ranging from five to thirteen in age. Classes met on Sunday morning from ten to twelve, the subjects including science, history, and music. (There was also a class in Esperanto for adults.) At the end of the first year, the children were rewarded with a week's vacation on Lake St. Clair. Of the seven teachers at the school, all of whom served without pay, three were German-born physicians: Paul Sigel (hygiene), Tobias Sigel (Esperanto and physical training), and Victor Stutzke (anatomy and physiology). Tobias Sigel, a colleague of Robert Reitzel and Johann Most, the foremost German anarchists in America, published an Esperanto translation of Most's antireligious tract, *The God Pestilence*. Another instructor, Carl Nold, was a close friend of Alexander Berkman, with whom he served in prison for alleged complicity in the attempt upon Frick. The remaining teachers were Albert Gluck (history and music), Alexander Schwarzingen (Esperanto), and Yetta Bienenfeld (natural history), whose children were among the first pupils.[73]

Of the later schools, Stelton, Mohegan, and Lakewood will be treated in subsequent chapters. Elsewhere, a Los Angeles branch of the Ferrer Association had been founded at the outset, but a school was not started until 1919, when William Thurston Brown, fresh from three years at Stelton, launched the Walt Whitman School with the aim of attracting parents who refused "to submit their children to the poisoning, degrading, dwarfing influence of the public school."[74] In San Francisco, as in Los Angeles, interest in the Ferrer movement was awakened at an early date, yet a decade elapsed before a Modern School was established. This occurred in 1921 with the opening of the William Morris School on Ashbury Street. The principal, Benjamin Ellisberg, was a communist who had served on the Mooney-Billings Defense Committee, while Mildred Rebac, the wife of a San Francisco Wobbly, acted as secretary. A Sunday School and adult center, it sponsored monthly entertainments, with music, dancing, and refreshments.[75]

In a number of other cities, Modern Schools were contemplated but did not get off the ground. In Denver, St. Louis, and the Bronx, plans were far advanced before being abandoned for lack of support. As early as 1911 a Denver branch of the Ferrer Association had been formed by Dr. J. H. Ward and Julia May Courtney, with the intention of opening a school. Dr. Ward, a libertarian socialist, had edited a journal called *Up the Divide* with the peripatetic Thurston Brown, who had spent some months in Denver in 1909. He was also acquainted with Emma Goldman, and helped arrange her lectures when she passed through on her coast-to-coast tours. She thought him a "loveable and broad-minded man" and "an Anarchist by nature and intellect, though still a Socialist by habit."[76] For all his efforts, however, the Denver school did not materialize.

Preparations went even farther in the Bronx, where Harry Kelly and George Seldes resolved to start a school in 1921. To raise a building fund a ball was held in November of that year. A few months later suitable premises were found at 1327 Clinton Street, and a prospectus was published in *The Modern School* magazine. For unknown reasons, however, the school failed to open.[77] Kelly and Seldes had better luck the following year when they founded the Mohegan colony and school, which survived until the Second World War.

So far we have spoken only of schools in which classes were conducted in English. From the outset, however, Modern Schools were also founded by immigrant anarchists who employed their native languages: German, Yiddish, Czech, Italian, and Spanish. All appear to have been Sunday Schools, and again there had been forerunners. As early as 1883, Johann Most had drafted a manifesto for the Pittsburgh Congress of the International Working People's Association, calling for the "organization of education on a secular, scientific, and equal basis for both sexes."[78] Inspired by Most and by the Haymarket martyrs, German anarchists sponsored Sunday Schools in different parts of Chicago toward the end of the 1880s.

During the summer of 1888, a reporter for *The Chicago Herald* visited one of these schools and, under the caption "How to Throw Bombs," described what he saw and heard. "After reading such a hair-lifting head-line," remarked a leading Chicago anarchist, "one would expect to learn of schools where children are taught to make and hurl bombs, but the dynamite dispensed at the school was, it seems, of quite a different kind. The children were taught scientific theories as to the formation of the earth, and the presence of animal life thereon, and were told that the lot of labor had always been to receive crusts, bones, and water, while the lords of the earth revelled in fine meats and rich wines. A dangerous doctrine, no doubt, but we can all say heartily, success to such good work."[79] When Jane Addams, founder of the Hull House settlement, visited a German Sunday School the following spring, it is hardly surprising that she should have been greeted with suspicion and told that " 'Americans' never came up there except the reporters of the capitalist newspapers and they always exaggerated." She found some two hundred children in a hall in back of a saloon, with a young man "trying to teach them free thought without any religion or politics. The entire affair was very innocent."[80]

At the turn of the century, similar schools were started in New York by German socialists and (beginning in 1906) by the Jewish

Workmen's Circle. According to Harry Kelly, he and Alexander Berkman taught in the Workmen's Circle schools before the Ferrer movement was launched. In 1908 the Socialist Party began to organize Sunday Schools in a number of American cities because the public school system glorified "the competitive idea." The Socialist schools, by contrast, were designed to teach "the value of the Socialist spirit of cooperative effort."[81]

During the first years of the century, German anarchists in New York formed the Free Educational League (Freier Entwicklungs-Verein), which sponsored lectures and Sunday classes for adults. And in 1910 the first German Modern School was established in New York by Josef Jülich, a contributor to Johann Most's *Freiheit*. A Sunday and evening school, it remained in existence for several years after Jülich's death in 1918. From 1917 to 1923 there was also a Czech Ferrer School in New York, and it is probable that Czech and German schools were founded in other large cities.[82]

Beyond this, there were at least two Italian Ferrer schools in America during the early years of the movement. In Paterson, New Jersey, a stronghold of immigrant anarchism before the First World War, the Young Men's Ferrer Club opened a street-front Sunday School near the great mills where its members worked. The following year another Sunday School was founded by the Francisco Ferrer Circle of Philadelphia, whose secretary, Erasmo Abate, later served on the executive board of the Modern School Association of North America.[83]

Oddly, there seems to have been only a scattering of Spanish Modern Schools in the United States, despite the existence of a sizable Spanish anarchist movement in the country. During the interwar decades, Spanish anarchist steelworkers conducted a Sunday School in Gary, Indiana, offering such subjects as geography, natural history, and astronomy, in addition to lectures for adults.[84] Similar schools emerged in other locations with Spanish working-class inhabitants, but detailed information is lacking.

Finally, a word about the Home Colony is in order. The school of this Pacific coast anarchist community, founded in 1896, did not call itself a Modern School, nor was it directly affiliated with the Ferrer Association. Accordingly, it has not been listed among the Modern Schools in the chart provided above. On the other hand, Anna Falcoff, a resident of Home, became a teacher at the Seattle Modern School, and James F. Morton, who conducted the colony's school for several years, afterwards taught at the Ferrer

School in New York. More important, the school itself was run on the same principles as those evolved by Ferrer and his precursors. The birthday of Froebel, the German educational innovator, was regularly celebrated by the community with children's singing and games and addresses by teachers and parents. The death of Ferrer, by the same token, was an occasion for mourning. One colonist, Nathan Levin, named his infant son after Ferrer and kept a bust of the Spanish educator on his mantelpiece.[85]

The Agitator, a journal published at the colony, called itself "A Semi-Monthly Advocate of the Modern School, Industrial Unionism, and Individual Liberty," and carried articles on "The Martyrdom of Ferrer" and the "Necessity for the Modern School," as well as contributions by Bruce Rogers, director of the Seattle Modern School, and Aristide Pratelle, secretary of the International League for the Rational Education of Children. "We want a school," declared the journal's editor, Jay Fox, at a memorial meeting for Ferrer, "that will teach the truth about everything; nothing more, nothing less. A school where no subject will be tabooed. A school where science, not sophistry, will be taught; where no fetish rag will obscure the child's view of the heavens and confine the scope of humanity within the radius of imaginary geographical lines. An education that will teach the children how to think. Such an education Ferrer taught, and died for his daring deed, and the gilded lie is exposed."[86]

Fox and his fellow colonists held no brief for the existing educational system. Public schools, they argued, educated children in the spirit of capitalism and crammed them with facts and dates about blood-spilling "heroes"—statesmen, generals, captains of industry—but never a word about the workers. Discouraging freedom of thought, they paralyzed the mind with blind patriotism and exaltation of government, preached "my country right or wrong," waved the flag above the schoolhouse and taught the pupils to worship it. George H. Allen, one of the community's original settlers, contrasted public education with the "liberty of thought and action allowed in our school," in which he himself was the first teacher. Opposed to the needless formality and discipline of the conventional classroom, he argued against placing a lot of "foolish restrictions" on the children. "A pupil who does not wish to take part in any of the exercises is allowed to remain in his seat," he declared, "the teacher depending on the interest she can awaken in him to cause him to join the class." According to one visitor, Allen himself gave his pupils "Mill, Huxley, Darwin,

Josiah Warren, and those parts of Henry Thoreau dealing with the necessity for civil disobedience."[87]

As the children grew older, the colonists hoped, they would become "the best possible advertisements of Anarchist principles and methods of training." This, they held, could be accomplished only under a system of libertarian education. As in the Modern Schools, crafts, play, field trips, and sex education had an important place in the Home curriculum. Nor was adult education neglected, with lectures, classes, and study groups on a wide range of subjects, from Esperanto and German to eugenics and Oriental philosophy. (Guest lecturers included Emma Goldman, who visited the colony several times.) And plans were begun for the creation of a "Liberty University of the Northwest," a project, however, which remained unrealized.[88]

By the time of the First World War, then, a network of Modern Schools, of varying scope and duration, had taken shape throughout the country. And a number of related experiments, such as the one at Home Colony, were pursuing the same principles and objectives. On the fourth anniversary of Ferrer's death in October 1913, Leonard Abbott was able to report that libertarian ideas in education and other fields were becoming "almost commonplace."[89] What was more, the question of education occupied a position of growing importance within the libertarian movement itself. This was reflected in the extensive space devoted to it in *The Agitator, Mother Earth*, and other publications. "Education must be integral, rational, varied, and free," proclaimed an anarchist journal in Tacoma, which publicized the innovations of Montessori as well as of Tolstoy and Ferrer.[90] In Indiana, similarly, Bruce Calvert called for an education that would "preserve the intellectual freedom of the child" and "develop his initiative and spontaneity in every direction." Hailing Ferrer as "the greatest educator of modern times," Calvert pointed to the Barcelona Escuela Moderna as a model for America to emulate. "The Rational School," he declared, "must be the corner stone of the new free society."[91]

Calvert wrote these words in 1911. That year the most important Ferrer school in the United States was started in New York City. Enduring for more than four decades, during which it underwent many changes, it was the longest-lived experiment of its kind anywhere in the world. Its early years are the subject of the following chapter.

CHAPTER 3

The Ferrer School of New York

AT ITS PUBLIC MEETING of October 13, 1910, held to commemorate the first anniversary of Ferrer's death, the Ferrer Association pledged itself to establish a Day School in New York on the lines of the Barcelona Escuela Moderna. Toward this end, the sum of five hundred dollars was collected, augmented by contributions from Alden Freeman and E. B. Foote. Quarters were found at 6 St. Mark's Place, half a block east of Cooper Union, where the memorial had taken place. A small, old brownstone on the south side of the street, the building still stands, with a plaque near the door announcing that James Fenimore Cooper lived there from 1834 to 1836. Freeman was the main financial "angel" of the venture. Preferring to remain in the background, he seldom came to meetings or took part in the work of the school, but thanks to Emma Goldman's powers of persuasion, he contributed fifty dollars a month, which covered two-thirds of the rent. Goldman herself took part in the inaugural ceremony, along with Alexander Berkman, Leonard Abbott, and Harry Kelly. It was mainly through her efforts, said Kelly, that the New York Ferrer School was opened.[1]

It was Emma Goldman, too, who secured Bayard Boyesen as the school's director. The son of Hjalmar Hjorth Boyesen, a distinguished Norwegian scholar and professor of Germanic languages at Columbia University, Boyesen had attended Groton and Columbia College where, despite his comparatively short stature, he had starred on the football team. His mother was a beautiful woman of old American stock, and the family, both well-to-do and respected, was listed in the Social Register.

Following in his father's footsteps, Boyesen became an instructor in the Department of English and Comparative Literature at Columbia. Carl Zigrosser, one of his students in freshman English, found him a stimulating teacher who aroused a strong interest in the art of writing.[2] His tenure, however, was brief. For, in spite of his upper-class background, he found himself, like Leonard Abbott and Hutchins Hapgood, drawn irresistibly into the bohemian world of anarchism, feminism, and avant-garde literature and art. As a result, he was "always at sword's point" with Columbia's president, Nicholas Murray Butler, who censured him for contributing a poem to the memorial volume of the Ferrer Association and for hobnobbing with Emma Goldman and other "dangerous" anarchists at the Ferrer meeting in Cooper Union.[3]

Under continuous pressure from President Butler, Boyesen resigned from the university and accepted Emma Goldman's invitation to direct the Ferrer School. It was a capacity, Emma remarked, in which he could expect "neither salary nor glory."[4] Having a private income, however, he was able to assume his new duties while taking up residence in fashionable Gramercy Park. To everyone he seemed a happy choice. Well educated and from a prominent family, a former instructor at an ivy-league university, he conferred a measure of respectability upon the fledgling institution which, despite the participation of several noted professionals, it might otherwise have lacked.

While "aristocratic in bearing,"[5] Boyesen displayed neither snobbishness nor condescension toward the working-class immigrants who came under his tutelage. As the son of America's leading Ibsen specialist, he held a special attraction for Emma Goldman, Margaret Sanger, and other devotees of the Norwegian playwright, whose works were immensely popular among the men and women of advanced social views who made up the Ferrer Association's membership. John Sloan, the artist, thought Boyesen "a very intelligent and well educated young man." He was also a "handsome young man," recalls Gussie Denenberg, who lived next door to the school and often attended its functions.[6]

The Ferrer School opened its doors on New Year's Day, 1911. Owing to cramped quarters and insufficient funds, plans for a children's Day School were deferred. What was established, rather, was a center for adults, "class-room, committee-room, check-room, lecture-hall and library, all in one," as Leonard Abbott described it.[7] The premises, moreover, served as headquarters of the Ferrer Association, of which Boyesen, replacing William van der Weyde, was now the secretary, with Bolton Hall as treasurer, succeeding the ailing Edward Foote, and Leonard Abbott remaining as president.[8] A new office, that of organizer of the association, was filled by Paul Luttinger, a young New York physician, whose chief tasks were to raise money, attract new members, and expand the organization's activities.

Boyesen began his work by arranging a series of Sunday afternoon lectures on social questions, like those at Ferrer's Escuela Moderna. Leonard Abbott, Theodore Schroeder, William Thurston Brown, James F. Morton, John R. Coryell, and Boyesen himself were among the speakers. He also organized three evening classes: principles of American government, conducted by Gilbert E. Roe, contemporary history by Dr. Luttinger, and contemporary literature by himself, including discussions of Ibsen, Tolstoy, Gorky, and Anatole France. To help cover expenses, a tuition of fifteen cents a week was imposed. Soon afterwards, two additional courses, in English and in Esperanto, were introduced by James Morton, an energetic and versatile figure who had taught for several years at the Home Colony school on Puget Sound.

Morton, the scion of an old New England family (his grandfather, the Reverend Samuel Francis Smith, wrote the hymn *America*), was a Phi Beta Kappa graduate of Harvard, where he had been a classmate of Hutchins Hapgood and a friend of W.E.B. DuBois, the black leader. Himself an ardent champion of Negro rights, he was an early member of the N.A.A.C.P. and the author of several works on civil liberties. In *The Curse of Race Prejudice*, published in 1906, he indicted racial bigotry in the United States as a national rather than a strictly southern problem, and also showed concern for the rights of Indians, Orientals, and Jews. When Harry Kelly met him in the 1890s, he found him "a brilliant young fellow with a good grasp of natural science, and he is a splendid speaker and writer."[9]

Like Leonard Abbott and William van der Weyde, Morton served as president of the Thomas Paine National Historical Association and was at this time a lecturer for the American Secular Union, a leading free-thought organization, and associate editor of its journal, *The Truth Seeker*. He was also a member of the New York bar, and spoke and wrote on behalf of free speech, birth control, and the single tax ("the application of ethics to economics," he called it). A lover of words and languages, he was vice-president of the Esperanto Association of North America and, in later years, a mainstay of the Riddlers' Club and the National Puzzlers' League. On the west coast, he had edited two important anarchist journals, *Free Society* and *The Demonstrator*, and was also a contributor to *Mother Earth*.[10]

With teachers of Morton's ability, the school got off to an encouraging start. Apart from the Sunday and evening lectures, there were occasional Sunday classes for children, conducted by Alexander Berkman among others. "The subjects discussed were of an economic nature," wrote Leonard Abbott after attending one of the sessions. "The method pursued was absolutely libertarian. Mr. Berkman guided the pupils, but he did not dogmatize. He concentrated all his efforts on stimulating the thoughts of the children, and on leading them to express themselves as clearly as possible. Every child was keenly alive, and every child had something to say. The study, instead of being drudgery, was a pleasure and a fascination to all. I was deeply impressed by the possibilities of the libertarian method. It requires a kind of genius to be a good teacher in the libertarian sense. All one's faculties and intuitions must be on the alert. One must learn to respond instantly, and with the artist's sensitiveness, to the different temperaments of the children. The whole purpose of education becomes one of vitalizing the child-nature, of getting at the *true* nature beneath the appearances that so often cloud it."[11]

The Ferrer School also featured musicales, dances, and dramatic entertainment, as well as lively debates on the burning questions of the day, from industrial unionism and sexual freedom to psychoanalysis and modern art. A social club and radical center combined, equipped with a library and reading-room, the school was "a beehive of activity," as one of its visitors described it. It became, like its Barcelona predecessor, a focal point of intellectual and social ferment, with a monthly *News Letter* patterned after Ferrer's *Boletín de la Escuela Moderna*. Soon after it opened, according to one participant, "liberals of every shade of thought began to frequent the 'center.' Lectures, debates and discussions were held in those small quarters almost nightly. The place became a rendezvous for intellectuals in New York."[12]

In November 1910 Alexander Berkman had written that Ferrer's death would not have been in vain if his admirers embarked on "the creation of libertarian centers which shall radiate the atmosphere of the dawn into the life of humanity."[13] Such, in rather grandiloquent terms, was the object of the St. Mark's Place endeavor. Yet a major ingredient was lacking: the premises were unsuitable for children. Hastily secured in the anxiety of the association to get a center started, the building was too small to house workshops and playrooms, nor was there an outdoor yard or access to a neighborhood park. A move was therefore unavoidable if the chief goal of the association, the creation of a Day School, was to be realized.

Pending the discovery of proper quarters, Bayard Boyesen drew up a prospectus for the school. The underlying idea, he wrote, was that "education is a process of drawing out, not of driving in; that the child must be left free to develop spontaneously, directing his own efforts and choosing the branches of knowledge which he desires to study; that, therefore, the teacher, instead of imposing or presenting as authoritative his own opinions, predilections, or beliefs, should be a sensitive instrument responding to the needs of the child as they are at any time manifested—a channel through which the child may obtain so much of the ordered knowledge of the world as he shows himself ready to receive or assimilate. Scientific, demonstrable facts will be presented as facts; but no interpretation or theory—social, political, or religious—will be presented as having in itself such sanction or intellectual sovereignty as precludes the right to criticize or disbelieve." Choosing the adjective "libertarian" to describe the type of education to be offered, Boyesen stressed that coercion would not be employed. "Each pupil will be free to be his true self," he asserted. "The main object of the [school] is the promotion of the harmonious development of all the faculties latent in the child."[14]

The creation of such a school required money, substantially more money than had been needed to maintain the adult center on St. Mark's Place. The first anniversary of the formation of the Ferrer Association provided the occasion for a new fund-raising drive. On June 30, 1911, a banquet was held at the Café Boulevard on Tenth Street and Second Avenue to celebrate a successful year of life and "to crystallize into reality the main object of the Association: the first Modern Day School for Children in America."[15] With 163 people in attendance, Leonard Abbott began the proceedings with a review of the year's achievements. Following this, Emma Goldman, fresh from a six-month lecture tour during which she had started new branches and gathered contributions, spoke of the interest which the association had awakened throughout the country, an interest, she said, shared by teachers and educators as well as by citizens at large. Then came short addresses by Alexander Berkman, Hippolyte Havel, Eugene Randolph Smith (a future president of the Progressive Education Association), Henrietta Rodman, Dr. Cecile Greil, Moses Oppenheimer, and Amy Mali Hicks. Harry Kelly acted as chairman, as at the previous year's meeting.

The appeal for funds met with a gratifying response. Kelly announced that an anonymous donor (probably Alden Freeman) had pledged $2,500 toward the establishment of the Day School, and that $700 more was assured in amounts ranging from $25 to $200. The collection at the dinner itself netted an additional $73, and pledges of $127 more, a total of $3,400 toward the $5,000 deemed necessary to open the school on a solid footing. In addition, a gift of $1,000 came from Pryns Hopkins of Santa Barbara, California, who himself was to open a libertarian school the following year. And Alden Freeman supplemented his gift with regular contributions, which were to continue for three more years. "The method of education appeals most strongly to me," he wrote to Emma Goldman, "and I have decided to concentrate in that direction."[16]

Assured of the necessary support, Leonard Abbott and Harry Kelly went looking for suitable premises. After a brief search, they found an old-style building four blocks away at 104 East Twelfth Street between Third and Fourth Avenues, a few doors west of St. Ann's Church. The dark red structure, with columns in front, had a basement and three stories with a yard in the rear. The stout lady from whom they rented it occupied the top floor.[17]

On October 1, 1911, the Ferrer Center moved from St. Mark's Place to its new location. Tended by Frank, "our silent, moody Lithuanian janitor," who once decapitated a cat in front of the children to show them "what life was really like,"[18] the Day School opened on October 13th, the second anniversary of Ferrer's execution. The first to arrive that morning was Dr. Benzion Liber, with his six-year-old son Amour. Before long, the "youthful and enthusiastic" Leonard Abbott appeared, all smiles. "Great, isn't it?" were his first words. That evening, in conjunction with the annual Ferrer memorial, an inaugural celebration was held at the Murray Hill Lyceum on 34th Street and Third Avenue. Despite the seriousness of the occasion, there was general jubilation. A Day School had been started at last![19]

EAST TWELFTH STREET

When the move took place, Bayard Boyesen remained in his dual capacity as director of the school and secretary of the Ferrer Association. (Leonard Abbott continued as president and Bolton Hall as treasurer, while Harry Kelly had replaced Dr. Luttinger as organizer.) Under the association's imprint, Boyesen issued a pamphlet entitled *The Modern School in New York*, in which he elaborated upon his previously published prospectus. An important document in the history of the Ferrer movement, it focused on the independence and self-development of children. "It is our purpose to have all study develop directly out of the lives of the pupils, instead of being imposed from without," Boyesen declared. "The personality of the child, during the sensitive and hazardous years of early youth, must be kept free from the intrusive hands of those who would mould and fashion it according to preconceived models, who would thwart this quality and divert that, in order to fit the child into the ideals of the teacher. We take the centre of gravity, which has lain hitherto in the teacher, and put it firmly in the child itself, for it is our aim not to lead, but to follow the activities of the child, using its natural interests as points upon which it can be allowed to fasten knowledge and aiding the child always to draw out and develop its native qualities."[20]

Like his predecessors from Fourier to Ferrer, Boyesen called for an integral education "which combines the training of the senses and of the mind, skill of hand and skill of brain." This education, moreover, must take place in an atmosphere of freedom. We must rid ourselves, he insisted, of the notion that "examinations are necessary to a school and that children must be ranked, punished and rewarded." And we must do away with "all coercive discipline and all the rules and paraphernalia of such discipline: the raised desk of the teacher, the rigid rows of seats for the children, and the idea that every class should be conducted according to particular preconceived codes of order. We prefer the 'free order' which is developed by the class itself." Discussion, too, must be organized by the pupils, the teacher's role being "simply to keep the ideas from dancing too far afield, to hold them coherent to a central point, and to restrain himself from supplying the conclusions which the children are working out for themselves."[21]

On a particularly interesting note, Boyesen maintained that shyness in youth was not a defect that needed correction. "On the contrary, shyness is often wrapped up and intimately commingled with all the burgeonings of emotions and ideas which in later life one cherishes as having been most valuable in his development, most ennobling, most refining, most individualizing." Individuality, autonomy, self-realization—such were the precepts to observe, concluded Boyesen, if children were to be "kept free of the cramping influences of the old education, and to become, instead of neat and narrow little figures in a definite and circumscribing scheme, young men and women buoyant and able before the world, valuable to themselves and to mankind."[22]

At the new school, however, Boyesen did not himself assume the duties of teacher. These fell, rather, to John and Abby Coryell, a couple highly regarded on the libertarian scene. An immensely prolific writer, the sixty-year-old Coryell was the originator of the famous "Nick Carter" detective stories and "Bertha M. Clay" romances, which made him a key figure in the Bernarr Macfadden publishing empire and the director of Macfadden's Physical Culture College. "He was one of the most generous persons I had ever met," recalled Emma Goldman, who was instrumental in bringing him to the Ferrer movement. "His writings had brought him a fortune, of which he had kept almost nothing, having given lavishly to those in need. His greatest charm lay in his rich sense of humor, no less incisive because of his polished manners."[23]

Born in 1851, Coryell (accent on last syllable) was descended from a family of Huguenots driven out of France in the seventeenth century. (There was also Irish, Dutch, and old American blood in his veins, and one Coryell had been a pallbearer to George Washington.) As a young man, Coryell had traveled extensively, developing a wide outlook on life and a deep understanding of human nature. Abandoning the study of law, he left college at seventeen and sailed to China to join his family (his father was building warships for the Chinese government). His life in the Orient was "varied and colorful," his son informs us, "an ideal background for a writer."[24] At twenty he became American vice-consul in Shanghai. In his spare time, he trained wild Manchurian ponies and learned to shoot with bow and arrow.

Returning to the United States, Coryell worked as a newspaperman in California before settling down to write the mystery and love stories which made his fortune. "Intellectually an Anarchist but not a revolutionist," to quote Harry Kelly's description, he also wrote plays on social themes and numerous articles for the anarchist press on such subjects as "Love and Passion," "Sex Union and Parenthood," and "What Is Seduction?" A contributor to *Mother Earth* from its earliest days, he was arrested with Emma Goldman and Alexander Berkman at an unemployment demonstration in 1907.[25]

A short man with greying hair and heavy brows, clear blue eyes and square chin, Coryell stood very erect, with a quick, muscular way of walking and an air of quiet self-confidence that concealed an inner shyness. His wife, Abby Hedge Coryell, was "a dignified, high-principled woman" of old New England stock. An impressive pair, they set themselves the task of making the East Twelfth Street school "a place of joy and interest to the children."[26]

Coryell was sharply critical of the public school system. "Our public schools," he wrote in *Mother Earth*, "cultivate superstition and impose belief in the worst and most cruel of our traditions. They fail to teach children to reason; they teach them to accept statements as truths. They exist for the specific purpose of making good citizens of our children. A good citizen is naturally one who submits to exploitation in the proud hope of being an exploiter himself some day; one who takes off his hat to the flag and stands reverently on his feet when the national song is being played, but who believes in a jail for anyone who says anything is wrong in the land. . . . Our schools deliberately set about making imitators and automatons of our children; and a creative and original child is called a bad or difficult one." The Modern School must be the opposite of all this: "No doctrine, radical or otherwise, will be taught there. Such a course would bring the Modern School down to the level of the public school. The one controlling idea is to teach the child to reason and to let him develop into himself. To pump opinions into the child's brain is to clog it and render it useless."[27]

The Coryells' first pupil was Amour Liber, the son of a thirty-six-year-old anarchist physician who himself was to play an active part in the school, lecturing on physiology and sexual hygiene. A socialist in his native Rumania, Dr. Liber was educated in Paris, where his child was born in 1905. Having converted to anarchism, he named the boy Amour (*amour libre*—free love) as an expression of his libertarian faith. (He himself had a brother called Liberty Liber, and he persuaded his friends Jack and Mollie Albert to name their infant son Freethought.)[28]

Emigrating to the United States, Dr. Liber became a single-taxer, a friend of Bolton Hall's and a member of the Free Acres colony in New Jersey, where he and his family spent the summers. At the same time, he belonged to the Jewish anarchist group, "Solidarity," and served as treasurer of the Anarchist Red Cross, which aided political prisoners in tsarist Russia. Anarchism, however, was "too utopian and impractical" for him to accept without reservation. "I belong a little to all of the radical movements," he later wrote, his allegiance having shifted to Soviet communism.[29] A voluminous writer, he published a dozen books and edited magazines in English and Yiddish. He was also a good amateur artist, having studied with Robert Henri. He wrote frequently for the anarchist press on a variety of subjects, but especially on hygiene and health. A strict vegetarian, he won more than a few admirers in progressive circles who followed his dietary prescriptions.

A pedagogue in his own right (he had been a teacher before entering medical school), Liber had very definite ideas about education, which agreed in most respects with those of the Ferrer Association. He was therefore delighted to enroll his little boy in the Modern Day School when it opened—so much so, that he arrived early and had to wait for the Coryells to appear. Convinced of the desirability of a natural and informal learning environment, he was pleased to find, besides a piano and large work table, "small movable tables and folding chairs, so that the room can change its form according to the work of the class."[30]

Liber was equally impressed with the methods of instruction, conforming as they did with his own ideas on the subject. "The teacher," as he wrote in the Ferrer Association *News Letter*, "must be a free man, free thinking and free acting, and must be a lover of truth. He will never consider himself an authority for the children, he will always be their equal and friend and will never claim to have more rights than they have. He will try never to impose his views or his conclusions on them, although it must be borne in mind that this is not always possible; but whenever he gives the children an opinion of his own, he shall always give them his reasons for holding it, so that they may be duly warned and not believe blindly. He will interfere with the children's work and research as little as possible, will follow them rather than lead them, will always answer their questions and answer them at the time when asked, or, where this is possible, will look, together with them, for the answer. He will have respect for the children's personality and will always have in mind the idea that any of his conclusions, even those in which he believes the most and for which he always fights, may be wrong, and that the child, in its simple and largely unbiased way, may be right. . . . He will never forget that the development of a character in the child, the future man, is more important than the acquirement of any knowledge. He will know that he himself can learn something from every child and that that will make his task much easier."[31]

Such also was the attitude of the Coryells toward their pupils, eight of whom, aged four to ten, were in regular attendance before the end of the year. (A ninth, Stuart Sanger, was enrolled soon after.) All appear to have been children of anarchist parents. Three, Hyperion, Gorky, and Révolte Bercovici, were cousins of Amour Liber, being the offspring of Dr. Liber's younger sister, Naomi, who herself, in 1907, had opened a libertarian nursery on the Lower East Side. She and her husband Konrad Bercovici, a fellow Rumanian Jew, had met in Paris, where they attended the Université Populaire in the Faubourg St. Antoine, a product of the movement for libertarian education pioneered by Paul Robin and Sébastien Faure. There, in the evenings, they heard lectures by Anatole France, Peter Kropotkin, and Jean Jaurès, while Konrad, "a kind of amateur Nietzsche, mustachioed and braggadocious, scorning morals, forgetting debts, and sprouting a flowing black tie,"[32] worked by day in a furniture factory.

Emigrating to New York, the Bercovicis settled on the Lower East Side. Life was hard, with Konrad laboring in a succession of sweatshops and teaching piano to make ends meet. "The only ray of light in this bleakness," he tells us, "was the 'Free School' on Madison Street near the East River, established by Alexis and Elizabeth Ferm."[33] Sharing her brother's radical convictions ("atheism, anarchism, and vegetarianism were the Holy Trinity of my childhood," Hyperion Bercovici recalled), Naomi and Konrad joined the Free Acres colony and enrolled their children in the Modern School, where they themselves took part on Sundays and evenings. They wanted a libertarian education for their youngsters, free, Hyperion writes, from contamination by the "capitalist virus of public schools." "Our little ones who have gone to school because they joyed in the work done there and loved their teacher," said Konrad in 1912, "they—and only they—will make the Revolution. Raised in liberty they will not live as slaves."[34]

Another of the original pupils, along with Amour Liber and his cousins, was five-year-old Magda Boris, a daughter of the Russian actor Paul Orleneff, whose troupe had been managed by Emma Goldman when it toured the United States in 1905 and 1906. Magda's mother, a nurse of Russian-Jewish origin, was a close friend of the Bercovicis, and it was at their recommendation that she entered her child in the school.[35] Of the rest, there was a boy named Oscar and a pretty girl named Ruth (called "Root the Beaut" by the boys). And in early 1912 came Stuart Sanger, whose parents, having moved to New York and plunged into Greenwich Village radicalism, were looking for just such a school for their oldest child.

Like the Libers and Bercovicis, by whom they were quickly befriended, the thirty-two-year-old Margaret Sanger and her architect husband William were then confirmed anarchists and single-taxers, for whom freedom in education was a primary concern. Strongly influenced by Emma Goldman, her chief ideological mentor during this period, Sanger, a professional nurse, was on the threshold of achieving public notoriety as a birth-control propagandist and feminist. Taking "No Gods No Masters" for its battle cry, her journal *The Woman Rebel*, published in 1914, proclaimed that women were enslaved "by the machine, by wage slavery, by bourgeois morality, by customs, laws and superstitions." The first issue featured excerpts from Emma Goldman's "Love and Marriage" and Voltairine de Cleyre's "Direct Action," as well as an article on Mary Wollstonecraft and the preamble to the I.W.W. constitution. "She made love into a serious undertaking," said Mabel Dodge of Mrs. Sanger. "She was the first person I ever knew who was openly an ardent propagandist for the joys of the flesh."[36]

In due course the Sangers were to separate, both abandoning their anarchist affiliations. "My own personal feelings drew me towards the individualist anarchist philosophy," Margaret wrote in her autobiography, "and I read Kropotkin, Bakunin, and Fourier, but it seemed to me necessary to approach the ideal by way of Socialism."[37] For five years, however, they were intensely involved in the Ferrer movement. All of their children attended Modern Schools, Grant and Peggy as well as Stuart. Margaret, moreover, lectured on birth control at the Ferrer Center and wrote for *Mother Earth* and *The Modern School* magazine.

"Gentle souls, and cogenial," in Harry Kelly's description, John and Abby Coryell were well liked by the children. Révolte Bercovici remembers them with affection, and Amour Liber, who recalls visiting their home after school, told his father that he wanted to marry Mrs. Coryell.[38] For the aging couple, however, the children were difficult to manage. "We were wild," says Révolte Bercovici, "and very badly behaved." Magda Boris tells of wearing long stocking caps that stretched, "and it was fun to pull another child's cap and run."[39] Unnerved by the children's antics, John Coryell remained only a few weeks, departing after one of the Bercovici boys climbed onto a window sill and threatened to jump out. His wife stayed on a few months longer before she too had to give up.

To replace the Coryells was no easy task. Emma Goldman invited the Ferms, who were running their own libertarian school on the Lower East Side, and they came up to have a look. But Elizabeth Ferm, of Irish Catholic background and educated in a convent, was disturbed to find anticlerical pictures on the wall. Education, she insisted, should have nothing to do with religion, either for or against, and the children should be left to grow in freedom, independent of the prejudices of adults. The Ferms, accordingly, declined the invitation. It is ironic, then, that the Coryells' eventual successor, William J. Durant, should himself have been the product of a seminary, trained for the Catholic priesthood.

WILL DURANT

At first glance, Will Durant might seem an odd choice for a teacher in an anarchist school. The son of French-Canadian parents, he was born in North Adams, Massachusetts, on November 5, 1885. His father, a factory worker, never learned to read or write, and his mother, a devout Catholic, pushed him toward the priesthood. When Will was a child the family moved to Arlington, New Jersey, where his father became a foreman in a chemical factory. An excellent student, Will won a scholarship to St. Peter's College in Jersey City, across the Hudson from Manhattan. "I came from an institution," he remarked, "where the mere mention of Ferrer would have been rebuked with holy horror."[40]

During his years at St. Peter's, the inquisitive youth read Darwin and Spencer and Bellamy, who "first fanned in him the smoldering fire of radical thought."[41] Although increasingly skeptical of religious dogma, he completed both his B.A. and M.A. and, in September 1908, entered the seminary of Seton Hall College at South Orange to prepare for the priesthood. Appointed the college librarian, he picked up a copy of Spinoza's *Ethics*. "As soon as I opened it," he recalled, "I realized I was reading one of the great books of the world." With growing excitement he came upon a passage proclaiming that "desire is the essence of life." The idea gripped his imagination. It was "pretty injurious stuff for a simple boy in a seminary," he told an interviewer nearly seventy years later. "I haven't gotten over it yet."[42]

In June 1909 Durant attended Emma Goldman's lecture on

drama at Alden Freeman's estate in East Orange. "I did not relish her dogmatism," he remembers, "but I respected in her the energy and courage that inspired hundreds of followers with unquestioning devotion." By now, at any rate, he realized that theology was not his calling. Recoiling from the confining atmosphere of the seminary, he abandoned the notion of pursuing a clerical career. "The old lust of living and of literature burned in me again," he writes. "I wanted to know. I longed for every stimulating contact, every educative environment, every deepening experience. I wanted to read every good book ever written, see every good play, hear every good composition. I wanted to feel the feverish flux of a varied life around me."[43]

In June 1910, to his mother's chagrin and disappointment, Durant withdrew from the seminary and resolved to devote himself to education. He had already taught French and Latin at Seton Hall, and now he secured an appointment, at ten dollars a week, as a substitute teacher in the Newark public schools. In 1911, having come to regard socialism as "the hope of the world,"[44] Durant and a Newark bookseller founded a Social Science Club where a circle of young men and women discussed economics and sociology, literature and history. It was here that he began his lecturing career. In spite of his diffident nature, he was a gifted popularizer with the knack of making complicated ideas accessible to the ordinary layman. At one meeting he read a paper on "The Bondage of Tradition." Seated in the audience was Alden Freeman, "a homosexual, ill at ease in the heterosexual society that gathered about him as the son of a Standard Oil millionaire," Durant recollects. Impressed by the young man's lecture, Freeman invited him to his home. Durant accepted, "with no harm to my morals," he says, but "with powerful influence upon my life."[45]

It was at this time that John and Abby Coryell resigned from the Day School on East Twelfth Street. Freeman, convinced of Durant's ability, recommended him to the Ferrer Association, which invited him to deliver a lecture. Eager to earn extra money, Durant accepted, holding forth on "The Origins of Religion" one Sunday afternoon in January 1912, shortly after the Coryells' departure. The people he met at the school differed completely from his expectations. Anarchists were then among the most hated groups in America. No movement had been more abused by the authorities or more feared by the public, for the association of anarchism with terrorism was deeply embedded in the popular imagination. As a result, Durant recalls, "I was prepared to find my new acquaintances a rather wild lot. I looked for long whiskers, disheveled hair, flowing ties, unwashed necks, and unpaid debts. I had been led to believe that most of these men and women were criminals, enemies of all social order, given to punctuating their arguments with dynamite. I was amazed to find myself, for the most part, among philosophers and saints."[46]

Durant's lecture was a great success. His heavily sexual interpretation, inspired by the theories of Krafft-Ebing and Havelock Ellis, pleased his avant-garde listeners who, intrigued by the spectacle of a young man out of the seminary standing up to renounce his faith, gave him a friendly reception. His audience, Durant thought, was "delighted to hear that almost every symbol in religious history, from the serpent of paradise to the steeples of churches in nearby Fifth Avenue, had a phallic origin."[47]

The same lecture caused Durant's excommunication. But he had found a new niche for his talents. Young, attractive, enthusiastic, he seemed an ideal candidate for the vacant teaching position at the school. Unlike the Coryells, he had had some prior experience as an educator, of adults as well as of children. And, only twenty-six years old, he was more malleable than they and better able to cope with active youngsters. It is not surprising, then, that shortly after the lecture he should have been asked to become the teacher of the Day School.

The invitation was delivered by David Lawson, a member of the Ferrer Association, who went to New Jersey to see him. Though "a bit scared," Durant agreed to return to the school for a closer look. There he was received by Lawson's companion, Lola Ridge, who had succeeded Harry Kelly as organizer of the association. An "intense rebel from Australia," as Margaret Sanger described her, Lola was a tall, fragile-looking poet with dark hair and eyes that matched her plain black dress. Emma Goldman regarded her as a "sweet and lovely spirit," and Leonard Abbott said that no one who took part in the early years of the school could forget "her vivid personality and her tireless energy." Durant fell in love with her at first sight. As she tried to persuade him to take the job, he remembered how many times he had felt "the absurdity and the inhumanity" of the discipline that he had been forced to impose upon his pupils in Newark, and he was inclined to accept. But he hesitated. "You are all Anarchists here," he remarked. "Are you sure that you want a Socialist to come to take charge of your school?" "I'm sure," Lola replied, "that when you get to know more about anarchism you will become an Anarchist too."[48]

Her prediction, to some extent, came true. Durant accepted the position and, throughout his association with the school, applied himself to the study of anarchist theory. In discussions with his new colleagues he was struck by the similarities between the anarchist ideal of peace, love, and brotherhood and his own discarded faith. The result was that he developed a new tolerance for anarchism and "began to read the literature with sympathy." He read everything "from Zeno to Kropotkin," as he put it, and reveled in the "exhilarating iconoclasm of Stirner and Nietzsche, Tolstoi and Whitman."[49]

At the same time, he came into contact with numerous practicing anarchists and found them, with few exceptions, "actuated by such honest revolutionary ardor as went straight to my heart (not my head)." The founders of the school—Abbott, Kelly, and the rest—he regarded as "a group of splendid dreamers," and though he shrank from embracing their anarchism completely, he was "passionately interested in its theories and its hopes" and "admired without restraint the moral heroism of its leaders," above all Kropotkin, whom he visited the following summer. Durant, then, remained a socialist, but with strong anarchist leanings. He accepted Nietzsche's dictum that "the State is the coldest of all monsters" and upheld individual freedom as the highest of human ideals. "Liberty," he wrote, "is no mere 'ideological' abstraction with me; it is something whose need I feel as I feel the need of air and food. It is the vital medium of the soul; without it we are not souls but cogs."[50]

For young Durant, the warmth and fellowship he found at the Ferrer School filled the spiritual and emotional void created by his abandonment of the church. The salary, too, was hard to resist, being twenty-five dollars a week, more than twice what he was earning at Newark and a handsome income in those days. But what appealed to him more than anything else was the idea of providing a libertarian education for children and adults. "To teach the people to be free," he wrote, "to let them know the happiness of a natural and spontaneous existence: what better program could there be for any school?" It was through education alone, through the rearing of a new generation in the spirit of freedom, that Durant could conceive the possibility of anarchism as an attainable ideal. "Doubtless the adults of our generation were too violent and insensitive a lot to get along without policemen and magistrates and jails," he asserted, "but why should we not take the virgin soil of childhood and sow in it the love of liberty? And then would it not be a delight to see children freed from the hundred compulsions of class-room discipline? Too long the underpaid and overworked teacher has solaced himself with the practice of absolute monarchy; democracy had shaken every citadel but that. What if the best school, like the best government, was that which governed least? To be a guide, philosopher and friend, and never a disciplinarian; to be a comrade and fellow-student rather than a teacher; to let children grow up freely without artificial pedantry or unnatural constraints: surely that would be a delight to the soul, and perhaps an illuminating test? We would try education by happiness."[51]

By happiness, which he considered essential to the development of intellect and character, Durant meant the "free play" of the child's initiative and instincts, as he explained in a pamphlet issued by the Ferrer Association in 1912. There must be no external compulsion, he insisted, or indoctrination with political ideas. The association had pledged itself "to keep all isms out of the school, and though I am a Socialist, I have made it a point never to impress my views upon the children, but rather to let them arrive at original views upon the basis of their own observations."[52]

All questions, however, must be fully aired, not least the question of sex: " 'Where do I come from?' asks the child, puzzling at once both theology and science; 'who made me?' We lie to it as well as we can; we mutter infantile futility about storks and Indians and doctors with a whim for bringing babies to unwilling parents; but we know, every one of us, that it were better to tell the truth at once than to wait for it to come later from sources that defile it in the giving. But we are so morally corrupt that we look upon sex as an indecent thing; we forget that to the mind of the child, undefiled by the horrible absurdities of our immoral moral code, the truth about the body will seem indeed a beautiful truth—that its body was once part of its mother's body, flesh of her flesh and bone of her bone."[53]

Durant showed equal candor on the question of militarism and war, expressing a view from which many of the Ferrer school parents would have dissented: "To ask the boy to repress his interest in war and battle is to ask him to be untrue to himself; it is to fly in the face of the libertarian principle; it is to confess at the outset that the libertarian principle is not sound. Let that wholesome barbarian instinct take its part in the moulding of the child; it will work itself out sooner in our children than it did in ourselves—if it has worked itself out in ourselves. And after all, we do not want our children to be too soft, too weak; there are times when it is not virtue to keep the peace; there are times when a little of the Nietzschean spirit would serve us well and bring us nearer to liberation. That does not mean violence, fistic or other; it means strength of character, force of personality, and the readiness to suffer all things for principle's sake."[54]

But it was not the function of education to produce obedient servants of authority, whether in military or civilian dress. Ferrer had argued that the ruling powers misused the schools to fashion disciplined workmen, "perfected instruments of labor to make their industrial enterprises and the capital employed in them profitable." Echoing this view, Durant resolved that the Modern School was "not going to turn out human cogs for the wheels of the capitalistic machine. The Modern School product is going to be *different*; he is going to be imbued with the idea, and accustomed to the full enjoyment of Liberty." "Free the child," Durant concluded, "and the child will free the race."[55]

Will Durant thus cast his lot with the Ferrer movement, becoming, in his own description, "the principal, sole teacher, and chief learner" of the New York Modern School. It was less than a year, he tells us, since he had "escaped from [the] Catholic seminary (I had almost said cemetery—which would have been a very trivial error),"[56] and he felt an exhilaration, a sense of freedom and adventure, that he had never known before. Assisted by Lola Ridge, who raised funds, arranged adult activities, and edited the association journal, not to mention "frying bananas and telling charming stories" to the children,[57] he plunged into the work of educating the nine pupils in his care. During his tenure, school hours were from 9:30 A.M. to 3 P.M. But they were not adhered to with any rigidity. Freedom, rather, remained the keynote, the pupils coming and leaving when they desired. "Last Monday," noted Durant in the spring of 1912, "Gorky came at 7:30, Stuart at 8, Oscar at 9, Rion at 9:30, Amour at 9:45, Magda and Sophie at 10, Ruth and Révolte at 11. That day was exceptional in its demonstration of the 'liberty of assemblage'; on most days we are all together before 10." As in Tolstoy's Yasnaya Polyana, moreover, the children sat or stood where they wished, talked, played, or read according to their own inclination. Attendance was not required, and there was no enforced discipline, but only "patient reasoning" when necessary.[58]

At first, however, matters did not proceed as smoothly as Durant might have wished. For the children missed the Coryells, who had won their respect and affection, and regarded their new teacher with suspicion. "He was more interested in lecturing to the adults," recalls Révolte Bercovici, "than in teaching children. 'There comes the faker,' we said. We wanted to kill him. So we danced around him in a circle, like Indians on the warpath, drawing closer and closer. And that frightened him a little." Amour Liber remembers him as a good teacher, "but to succeed the Coryells was an unenviable fate. The children all loved the Coryells. So at first he had a hard time. We played pranks on him, and he didn't know why."[59]

One little girl insisted on skipping rope noisily while Durant expounded on the evolution of man. When he suggested that she play in another room she refused, so that (applying the method of "patient reasoning") he had to take her by the arm and escort her into the street. By April 1912 Amour had stopped attending. "They only fight," he complained to his father. "Nothing else happens. I don't want to go there." Durant wrote to Liber in the hope that he might persuade his son to change his mind ("Tell Amour that I miss him very much"). But Amour refused. He preferred to study at home under his father's supervision and in libraries and museums. He never returned to the school.[60]

As for the others, Durant managed to overcome their hostility, except for Révolte Bercovici, who continued to view him with intense disfavor until, following her cousin's example, she left towards the end of the term. Among the adults, opinion was more charitable. Margaret Sanger considered him "extraordinarily effective," and Lola Ridge judged him "the best teacher the Modern School ever had."[61] To Joseph Cohen he seemed "quite successful with the children and even more so with the adults," although his pedagogical ideas were "vague and undefined, his methods amateurish and unconvincing." At the end of the school year, Durant admitted that he had made mistakes and that he had learned more from the pupils than they had from him. "I think, " he wrote in *Mother Earth*, "this lack of an experienced teacher was the greatest difficulty besetting us."[62]

All the same, nearly everyone agreed that Durant's presence had breathed new life into the day-to-day activities of the school. Under his administration, the children received lessons in crafts, writing, singing, piano, and drawing, the last conducted by Amy Londoner, a pupil of Robert Henri, who himself gave an adult art class in the evening. "Here perhaps more than in any other field the initiative of the pupils is brought out," thought Durant. "There is no copying of other pictures, nor any direction to draw this and not that; the pupil is given full liberty to draw whatever it wishes to draw, to use pencil or ink or crayon, to draw on paper or on the blackboard."[63]

Mornings at the school were usually devoted to academic work. Each pupil had a notebook in which Durant would enter problems in reading and arithmetic. But whether they were completed in the morning or the afternoon, or indeed done at all, was up to each child. To Durant's delight, the children not only did the assignments but often asked for more. "You would be surprised to see how readily you can get a thing done by a child if you ask, and do not command," he observed. "Try to force a child to do a thing and he will either refuse to do it or will do it ill; ask him to do it, give him the reason and let him see that it is entirely his concern, not yours, as to whether or not he is to do it, and you will find him not only doing it, but doing it well."[64]

Every effort was made by Durant to link academic subjects to the pupil's direct experience. Thus geography was studied in conjunction with history and current events, so that when the children read about Leif Ericsson or Columbus, they traced the course on the map. When they discussed the textile strike at Lawrence or a trip of suffragettes to Albany, they found the location on the map and traced the routes from New York City, learning something about the transportation facilities between the places. In history, moreover, the boys and girls put themselves into the place of the characters, and scenes were sometimes enacted in the yard. More than once they played the drama of John Smith and Pocahontas, with Durant as the English captain and the class as Indians bent on destroying him. (This, no doubt, was what Révolte Bercovici recollected, though some of the children really meant it!) With history they read stories illustrating the lives and customs of the peoples who lived in North America before the arrival of the Europeans, and they went to the Museum of Natural History to see exhibits that helped them in this study.

Afternoons were generally spent in the little carpentry shop that had been fitted up for the class, the children "hammering and sawing and planing away with all the creative earnestness in the world." At three o'clock, Durant tried to send them home, with only occasional success: "they want to stay, and do stay, sometimes till five o'clock. Did you ever hear of a school where the children came too early and stayed too late?" Weather permitting, Durant would take his charges to Stuyvesant Park at Second Avenue and Fifteenth Street. "Astounded passers-by wondered what manner of man this was who, hatless and coatless, tumbled about with a dozen children on top of him, and then suddenly subsided into science or history," he recalled. "Occasionally those who came to scoff remained to listen to these tales. Parents too would join us when they could; simple, timid mothers who had had little time for education amid the poverty and oppression of their native lands. What happy hours we had together, we big and little children, on those sunny afternoons!"[65]

The children did not call him "Mr. Durant" or "teacher," a word that "reeked of prim authority and indigestible erudition." They called him "Will" and looked upon him as "a big brother who knew incomparable stories. When we parted at three they clung to my coat-tails till I had to shake them off and take to my heels. Many of them gave me their affection with a trustful abandon which made their parents jealous. All in all that first half-year was a bright rosary of happy days. I shall never forget them, nor those natural little anarchists, my pupils."[66]

As Durant's position became more secure, Bayard Boyesen, still nominal director of the Day School, faded out of the picture, and Durant, with the title of Principal and Teacher, took effective charge of the enterprise. Under his supervision, a Sunday School was started for children who, for one reason or another, were unable to attend the Day School. From 4 to 11 P.M. daily, a radical reading-room was opened to which the general public was invited. A tea and lunchroom was also established ("good food at popular prices") which, while not successful from a financial point of view, drew additional friends to the school. And a Ferrer Dining Club was organized, with short talks on topics of current interest, followed by group discussion after dinner. To raise money for the school, a "concert and fancy dress ball" was held during the winter at the Terrace Lyceum on the Lower East Side, and another at the Lenox Casino in Harlem during the spring. Meetings of one sort or another took place at the school almost nightly. Dramatic performances were put on throughout the year, and there were picnics and excursions during the warmer months.

Adult education, for which Durant had a special talent, continued to occupy a central place in the curriculum. The evening classes in literature, physiology, Esperanto, and English, which had been organized at St. Mark's Place, were all renewed, as were the Sunday afternoon lectures on social questions, with Emma Goldman, Leonard Abbott, Harry Kelly, and Dr. Liber among the speakers. Durant himself, having read Krafft-Ebing and Havelock Ellis, was "prepared to acquaint New York with the facts of sex psychology," as Margaret Sanger put it,[67] presenting a series of well-attended Sunday lectures on prostitution, homosexuality, the phallic origin of religion, and the connection between sexual and religious psychosis. On Monday evenings a new class was started in music appreciation, at which Manuel Komroff played "selections from the great masters" on the piano. In addition, an art class ("with living model") was offered by Robert Henri and a course on sexual hygiene by Dr. Cecile Greil, who had spoken at the Ferrer Association anniversary the previous June. Before the end of the school year, additional evening classes were introduced in such subjects as drama, science, and economics.[68]

The Ferrer School, as Rion Bercovici remarked, was more than a radical educational institution. It was also a center of propaganda for anarchists and socialists, I.W.W.'s and syndicalists.[69] In February 1912, children of the Lawrence strikers, escorted to New York by Margaret Sanger, were given temporary homes with families of the school, who also gave the strikers financial support. (A second group of children was received and cared for by the Radical Library in Philadelphia.) The school, in addition, raised funds for the Mexican Revolution, and especially for the movement led by the Mexican anarchists Ricardo and Enrique Flores Magón in southern California. In January 1911 the school protested against the execution of Denjiro Kotoku and a group of Japanese anarchists in Tokyo. And on June 14, 1912, when the Ferrer Association held its second anniversary dinner, the subject for discussion was revolutionary syndicalism, then very much in the public eye with the growth of the I.W.W. and the upsurge of militant unionism at Lawrence and other industrial cities. Attended by 240 people, the dinner was a resounding success, with speeches by Alexander Berkman, Leonard Abbott, Hippolyte Havel, William English Walling, and Louis Levine, a young anarchist scholar whose doctoral thesis on French syndicalism was to appear in 1914.[70]

The June 1912 banquet also marked the end of the first year of the Ferrer Day School, "grown," said *Mother Earth*, "from such a tiny spark, blown from that trampled flame in Barcelona."[71] Despite the small number of pupils and the change of teachers in mid-course, it had been a successful and an encouraging year, with a varied program of child and adult education which drew correspondence from such far-flung places as Norway, Australia, and the Dutch West Indies. It was a year which saw the appearance of two important publications of the Ferrer Association, *The Modern School in New York* by Bayard Boyesen and *The Ferrer Modern School* by Will Durant, and the birth of *The Modern School* magazine ("To Retain the World for the Masters They Cripple the Souls of the Children," proclaimed its masthead), conceived by Lola Ridge, who served as its first editor. For the children it had been a year of adventure, after which the public school to which Rion Bercovici was sent could only be a disappointment. "The banality of the place disgusted me," he complained. "No discussions on sex and the revolution, no rioting, no excitement."[72]

The Ferrer School, however, had its drawbacks. Although an enclosed outdoor area did exist, which made things pleasant for the adults as well as the children during the warmer months, there was little in the way of equipment. And the physical accommodations, as Harry Kelly acknowledged, were "far inferior to those provided by the public and parochial schools of the city."[73] An even greater disadvantage was that few radical families lived within walking distance, so that it was hard to get new pupils. Another problem was the hostility shown by some of the local residents. When the priest of St. Ann's Church walked past the building, his eyes were invariably drawn to the sign above the front door, identifying it as "The Modern School," and he would look at the place darkly. "We were always amused by that," wrote Harry Kelly, "and now and then, when Leonard Abbott and I had reason to walk over to Third Avenue, we would inspect the front of St. Ann's Church and the adjacent rectory with the same seeming intensity, and turn some dark looks toward those edifices, for the benefit of anybody who might be behind the curtains of the rectory windows."[74]

Beyond this, there were problems of a more fundamental nature. Dependent on the nominal dues and fees imposed on its mostly working-class participants and on the generosity of a small number of benefactors, the school was in chronic financial difficulty. More than that, it lacked not only trained and experienced teachers but also a clear direction and program. Its founders, as Joseph Cohen noted, were not themselves educators of children. "Their interests and capabilities inclined them towards the education of adult workers. They were what may be more properly termed agitators. Some of them were gifted with pen or word of mouth, many were well instructed in the wisdom of our age, yet none of them was qualified or by nature inclined for the work of a teacher in the ordinary school room."[75]

Another difficulty lay within the Ferrer organization itself, with its libertarian theories and practices. A meeting for members took place each week, during which, said Lola Ridge, "every new measure had to be put to the vote, and I had to fight hostile forces inside that mob of three hundred—mostly foreigners and all wild unkempt spirits, haling from one another by its hair that new, wonderful doll, Liberty." Joseph Cohen too noted a tendency on the part of the adults "to interfere in the classrooms, though doubtless with a desire to be helpful, and many wordy battles over this practice took place at the Association's meetings."[76]

Voltairine de Cleyre leveled similar criticisms at the Philadelphia Modern School, of which Cohen himself was the originator. There was, she wrote to Cohen, a "strong desire to accomplish something with no definite idea of *what* it is nor *how* to do it. *What* should a child learn? And *how* should he learn it? Can you answer? Does he need arithmetic? How much? Geography? How much? History? What kind? Gardening? Manual training? In what lines? What should we throw away and what add to the present system? I would want clear systematic replies."[77]

After teaching at the Chicago Modern School, de Cleyre was left with the same reservations. There was "too much 'liberty' and too little orderly idea of work," she complained to Cohen, and so she decided to withdraw. In February 1911, moreover, she declined an invitation from Alexander Berkman and Leonard Abbott to become organizer of the Ferrer Association, Dr. Luttinger having vacated the position. What do people like Emma Goldman and Hutchins Hapgood know about running a school? she asked. Bayard Boyesen was "the only teacher in the bunch," and he was probably good only at his college-level specialty, comparative literature. Two months later, in April 1911, Leonard Abbott asked her for a copy of a lecture she had delivered on "Modern Educational Reform," explaining that everyone at the association seemed to be "misty" on the subject. "I told him that six months ago," wrote de Cleyre to Cohen, "but he didn't seem to feel the force of it then. I really think that he, like a good many others, got swept off their feet by Ferrer's death, and began to holler 'Modern Ed.' without knowing what they were hollering about."[78]

Faced with these criticisms, Harry Kelly admitted that the association's ideas on education were "rather vague." Yet its members were familiar enough with Ferrer's teachings, he insisted, to know that they possessed the "vital glow of reality and truth."[79] Paul Luttinger disagreed. A socialist who had lectured at St. Mark's Place on contemporary history, he resigned as organizer after serving only a few weeks and formed his own Rational Education League in the Bronx. In a scathing attack on his former colleagues, he declared that the association had been founded in the home of a "well-known quack doctor" (i.e., E. B. Foote) and had fallen under the control of "the worst specimens of American anarchism," namely Emma Goldman and her coterie, who were using the school as "an instrument for anarchist agitation of the worst sort, under the cloak of rational education." According to Luttinger, the most serious problem confronting the association was that of attracting competent teachers. "The reason for the chronic dearth is obvious," he wrote. "The majority of the schools pay no salary at all or offer a minimal compensation."[80]

Though Will Durant was getting a comfortable twenty-five dollars a week, Dr. Luttinger was right about the rapid turnover of teachers, who seldom remained for more than a year or two, a pattern which continued at Stelton until the arrival of the Ferms in 1920. In the case of the Coryells, they dropped out of the movement entirely, apart from an occasional contribution to *Mother Earth* or *The Modern School*. In July 1924 John Coryell died at his summer home in Maine at the age of 73. Abby lived to be nearly 100, surviving into the 1950s.

Bayard Boyesen too drifted away from the movement. His last poem in *Mother Earth* appeared in March 1912 and his last article (a tribute to Kropotkin) in December of that year. Though he continued to serve on the advisory board of the Ferrer Association, he gave up his position as director of the Day School and, in the summer of 1912, retired to his farm at Royalston, Massachusetts, to raise horses and dogs. Laboring over an unfinished novel, he drank heavily and became subject to fits of melancholy and ennui. "Nothing, except my writing, can hold my interest for any length of time," he wrote to Hutchins Hapgood in August 1913. "It doesn't matter whether it's teaching, horse-racing, farming, 'anarchising,' or what-not. After the first excitement, after I have extracted whatever is for me its essence, I am done with it, bored. I sometimes wonder whether this is due to an inherent weakness of character in me or whether it is due simply to the necessity for certain types of people to go through as many different kinds of experiences as possible. I wish I could decide, but I am honestly in doubt."[81]

Some years later, having lost his inheritance on the stock market, Boyesen settled down to breeding Norwegian elkhounds. For a time, like many of his former Ferrer associates, he became a convert to Bolshevism. But this too proved only a passing enthusiasm. "Boyesen is a tragedy, and has been that for years," wrote Leonard Abbott to Lola Ridge in 1920. "Of no man that I know was more expected, and no man that I know has so pitifully failed to make good his promise."[82]

Boyesen had no further connection with the Modern Schools, apart from occasional correspondence with old acquaintances like Emma Goldman. "I see that you are engaged in breeding dogs," she wrote him in 1925. "I am sure it must be more interesting and pleasant than breeding the students at Columbia. I hope it is also more profitable for you. I have often wondered whether you ever harbored resentment against me for being the indirect cause of the loss of your position at Columbia. Have you?"[83]

Will Durant stayed on at the school, completing the spring 1912 term. His most serious deficiency, he felt, had been the lack of the experience of travel: "I feel that the man who has never traveled can hardly be inspired by geography, or inspire others thereby. I wish I could get people who have traveled, and who have interesting stories to tell, to come and tell those stories to my boys and girls; I picture some old sea-captain recounting his exploits, with the children hanging upon his neck and arms as they hung on mine yesterday when I told them of George Washington's trip to Fort Duquesne. And though it is too late for me to remedy my own defect now, I think I should see to it, were the world run to suit me, that all teachers of geography should be well-traveled men and women."[84]

But it was not in fact too late to remedy the defect. During the summer of 1912, Alden Freeman, agreeing that Durant needed to broaden his horizons, took him on a tour of Europe. For Durant it was the experience of a lifetime: "Had I not dreamed for years of the day when, after long stinting and saving, I might sail off to see England and France and Spain and Italy and Germany, and perhaps even Greece; dreamed how I might at last murmur a prayer in the Acropolis like Renan, and worship in the Sistine Chapel like the pagan Goethe, and bask like Nietzsche in the sunshine of St. Mark's? I could scarcely believe that I was about to see those sacred monuments to man's creative passion."[85]

But see them he did: London, Brussels, Paris, Berlin, Vienna, Rome, Florence, Venice, even Athens. And Russia too: St. Petersburg, Moscow, Kiev, then down the Volga to Sevastopol and Odessa. In Brussels he made a pilgrimage to the Ferrer monument, erected the previous year. "I doubt if there is a finer conception, more beautifully executed, among all the public monuments of Europe," he wrote in a letter to *Mother Earth*. "A bronze figure, life-size, absolutely nude, holding aloft a blazing torch, and standing tip-toe—every muscle tense—that the light may shine the farther; could there be any fitter form for a monument to Ferrer?"[86]

In England, Durant called on Peter Kropotkin, whose *Mutual Aid*, he believed, provided "an answer to Darwin and Spencer, and a biological basis for a socialist philosophy." He found Kropotkin a "gentle, fatherly old man whom I learned to love even while he was scolding me for lecturing too much about sex." Having known Ferrer personally and supported his work, Kropotkin was interested to hear about the school in New York that bore his name. Praising Ferrer, he urged Durant to learn Spanish in order to translate the writings of the martyred educator. "You felt at once that this man was both a philosopher and a saint," said Durant of his host. "I have never met a finer man."[87]

After a "long and splendid vacation," Durant, armed with a rich store of new experiences, was eager to return to his pupils. "What stories I shall be able to tell the boys and girls who come to me," he wrote to his comrades in New York, "what pictures I shall be able to show them! I understand that you have all been working hard while I have been playing with Baedeker and Kodak; but I hope to do a little work myself when I get back."[88]

EAST 107TH STREET

Durant's New York comrades had indeed been working hard during his absence. Above all they were arranging to move the school to a new location. The building on East Twelfth Street, cramped for space and remote from the homes of most Ferrer Association members and potential members, had proved inadequate to the needs of both the Day School and the adult center. When Durant returned to New York toward the end of September, preparations for the move were in their final stages. On October 1, 1912, exactly a year after the transfer from St. Mark's Place to East Twelfth Street, the school moved to its third and final New York location, an old brownstone at 63 East 107th Street, situated on the north side of the street between Madison and Park Avenues, a section of Harlem then inhabited by Jews, Italians, and other working-class immigrants, many of them with radical sympathies. There the Day School remained until its removal to Stelton in 1915, and the adult center until its demise three years after.

The building on East 107th Street (for which Alden Freeman continued to pay the rent) was three stories high, with a basement and a yard in the rear. In the basement were a kitchen and dining room where the children ate lunch and which served as a tea room for adults after school hours. The main floor, consisting of one large room, was converted into an auditorium for lectures, concerts, and plays. On its walls were hung pictures of Darwin, Spencer, William Morris, and other radical thinkers, with a life-size portrait of Ferrer at the front. The second floor contained two classrooms and a bathroom, while the rooms on the upper floor were used as apartments. (Joseph Cohen and his family lived there after coming from Philadelphia in 1913.)

Will Durant remained in charge of the Day School in its new quarters. But few of his pupils from East Twelfth Street could be expected to make the trek to Harlem unless their families moved into the neighborhood, as was the case with Magda Boris. Thus the Bercovici children dropped out (no doubt to Durant's relief), as had Amour Liber, who was taught at home by his father until ready for high school.[89] Before long, however, the school attracted a new crop of students from the surrounding area, so that sixteen boys and girls were under Durant's care before the end of the autumn term.

Mornings at the school were devoted to lessons. There were reading and arithmetic, geography and history, writing and music; and there was arts and crafts, or what Durant called "industry lessons," based on information gleaned mostly from *The Book of Knowledge*, a set of which Margaret Sanger had donated to the class. "What do I teach them?" wrote Durant in *The Modern School* magazine. "Everything under the sun, from match-making to French. One of my children is beginning algebra, and is rewriting Shakespeare and Charles Lamb; another is struggling with that regrettable institution called interest; another is flirting with improper fractions; and the youngest of them is grappling with the mysterious fact that two and two make four." At the end of three months, though there were inevitable disappointments, Durant concluded that "we have been immensely more successful this year than last. Immensely more successful." More than the year before, he said, the children were showing "an intense desire to learn."[90]

After lunch the children would play games and tell stories, "sometimes making more noise, I fear, than is good for the nerves of those who live above us, and who forgive us because they understand," wrote Durant. "After all, a certain degree of noise is as essential to a child as water to a fish; it is the vital medium, without which either would suffocate." One of the pupils later recalled what it was like. "I was only four," she said, "but remember pandemonium, noise. It wasn't restrictive, but spontaneous, easy-going, permissive."[91] Many of the afternoon activities took place in the back yard, where the children tinkered with little tools or walked on stilts and climbed the fence. Benjamin Greenstein, the eleven-year-old son of a Russian-Jewish anarchist who had been a disciple of Kropotkin in London, was particularly fond of the art class, conducted every Thursday afternoon by Adolf Wolff. The boy had previously attended the local public school but, unable to adjust to the routine, had been exceedingly unhappy. In the fall of 1912 he was transferred to the Ferrer School. "I liked it at once," he recalls. "There I was at home! I could draw, scribble, and model with clay."[92]

In good weather, after morning lessons, Durant might take his charges to Central Park, only a block and a half from the school. Dispensing with "theoreticals," they would worship Pan for three or four hours. "I feel profoundly grateful for that advantage," wrote Durant of the park's proximity. "To go there after a hard morning's conflict with the three R's, to eat our lunch like little happy picknickers, to chase each other over the splendid fields and around the rocks and the trees till the whole wild troop of us is breathless, and then to lie on our backs—the children all huddled about me, their heads on my breast or on my outstretched arms—and feast on the wealth of the summer sun; I say that is a glorious thing for the body, and a glorious thing for the soul."[93]

It was a scene out of Yasnaya Polyana, Durant, like Tolstoy, cavorting with his pupils. On winter afternoons they pelted him with snowballs and clambered onto his back in an effort to pull him down into the snow. The mood was one of gaiety and freedom. "I loved Will Durant," Magda Boris recalls. "He was my first love, my favorite teacher. He used to take us to Central Park. We had games, picnics, and nature study there. And he told us stories and sang 'Way Down Upon the Swanee River.' After I got home I would nag my mother to take me to the park—maybe Will would be there!"[94]

Durant, for his own part, reciprocated the feelings of the children. He was delighted with his job, with the new building, and especially with his pupils. "I thank whatever gods there be for sending me such children," he wrote in early 1913. "Clean children, bright, reasonable, generous, affectionate; children of the sort that overwhelm the bachelor with remorse; children whom it is an honor and a high privilege to teach. I owe an immense debt to these children: they have given me the spiritual ecstasies of fatherhood without its burdens; they have taught me a thousand wonderful lessons that only children can teach; and they have given me that for which one hungers—not admiration, but affection. I dare intrude this personal note here because I have no respect for the conventions of print, and because it is perhaps my only chance to acknowledge a debt which I can never repay. A debt to the parents for their generous understanding of our disadvantages and our limitations, and for their sympathy with our work; but above all a debt to the children for their love."[95]

Nor were the needs of the parents neglected. Under Durant's leadership, as Leonard Abbott remarked, the Ferrer Center became "a real factor in the radical movement in New York."[96] Evening classes for adults were opened in literature, art, physiology, and psychology, as well as in English, French, Spanish, and Esperanto. The most successful of these, the art class conducted by Robert Henri and George Bellows, will be described in the next chapter. Another popular course was the weekly forum on "Radical Literature and the Great Libertarians," organized by Leonard Abbott, who arranged for guest speakers or who lectured himself on Blake, Maeterlinck, Shaw, and other writers of advanced views. Also successful were the lessons in Esperanto offered by James Morton, "as excitable and enthusiastic as the rest,"[97] and the English class for foreigners taught by Robert Allerton Parker, biographer of John Humphrey Noyes, and by young Carl Zigrosser, for whom the Ferrer Center had the "potentiality of a genuine people's university."[98]

Lectures and classes were held every night of the week, mostly in the auditorium, equipped with a fireplace, a piano, and "rows and rows of folding chairs." A portrait of Ferrer hung on the wall, Magda Boris recalls, and the children sang the *Internationale* from the platform "at the top of our lungs."[99] It was here that Dr. Liber held forth on hygiene and sex, Dr. Bauch on physiology and psychology, Emma Goldman on theater, Alexander Berkman on revolution, and Louis Levine on syndicalism and the general strike. Beginning in November 1912, Will Durant gave a course of ten lectures on the history of philosophy from Plato to Nietzsche, and in early 1913 William Thurston Brown came from Chicago to speak on "The New Education, Its Principles and Progress." Additional lectures were offered on Sunday afternoons, including a well-attended series by Durant on "Five Great Rebels" (Socrates, Jesus, Spinoza, Darwin, and Walt Whitman). Furthermore, every Saturday evening the Ferrer Dining Club gathered in the yard or in the tea room to deal with artistic and social questions, beginning with the modern drama.

Apart from the lectures and discussions, violin and piano instruction was offered to both children and adults, and a variety of musical and dramatic entertainments took place under the auspices of the Ferrer Association. On October 13, 1912, the third anniversary of Ferrer's death was commemorated in Clinton Hall on the Lower East Side, while on June 2, 1913, the association held its third annual dinner (one dollar, tips included) at the Café Boulevard, with Alexander Berkman, Harry Kelly, and Hutchins Hapgood among the speakers. All in all it was a successful year, with an expanding program of activities. A good part of this success may be attributed to Will Durant, who was regarded as a model director. Then suddenly the mild young teacher conceived a passion for one of his students, which became "the scandal of a season."[100]

WILL AND ARIEL

In a report on the progress of the school, written at the beginning of 1913, Will Durant describes the warm relationship that had grown up between himself and his pupils. "So the day passes," he writes, "and when the time comes to separate you hear touchingly affectionate good-byes from everybody to everybody else. One little fellow persists in coming to me before he goes and putting his hand upon my face; others expect me to put an arm around them and give them a parting paternal touch; and still others demand that they be allowed the holy rite of the kiss. To have permitted this last is, possibly, one of my blunders, since in the case of the older girls it is quite probably, however unconsciously, tinged with their sweetly-budding sex; but tho I recognize the danger of unnecessarily accelerating sexual development, I cannot for the life of me muster up the courage to refuse these tenderly proffered delicacies of affection."[101]

In this seemingly innocent observation one discovers the first hint of a relationship that had begun to develop between Durant and his oldest pupil, Ida Kaufman. The child of a broken marriage, Ida, who had been born in a Russian ghetto fourteen years before, lived with her anarchist mother at 64 East 107th Street, directly opposite the Ferrer Center. A lively and mischievous girl, she was a truant from public school, which had proved too confining for her restless energy. One day, in October 1912, she was playing hookey when she saw a woman with a group of Modern School children in Central Park. They were playing games on the grass, and the woman seemed so kind and understanding toward the children that Ida went over and joined them. She said that she wanted to go to their school.[102]

Thus, just after the beginning of the school year, Ida Kaufman became Will Durant's pupil. From the first moment, he recalls, there was something about her untamed nature that "captured my eyes and possessed my memory. I was attracted by her high spirit; she romped and babbled and laughed and sang with the innocence of a girl who had never known theology." As strong as a boy, as swift as an elf, on outings in the park Ida ran the fastest, jumped the highest, and tired the last or not at all. Her schoolmates called her "Puck," and the name stuck. Years later, Durant vividly remembered "how that wild fairy of a girl would leap like a spirit over the earth and race to victory." In his novel *Transition*, where the names of real people appear in altered form, "Puck" of *A Midsummer Night's Dream* became "Ariel" of *The Tempest*, the forename by which she became known as her husband's literary collaborator, though old friends still address her as Puck. Will, however, preferred Ariel, "because she seemed to be light and heavenward. I pictured her always ready to fly off."[103]

At fourteen Puck was physically mature, "a buxom and ebullient lass," in her own description. Man Ray, who attended the Ferrer Center art class in 1913, says that she posed in the nude and possessed a well-developed body.[104] She also had an intensely affectionate nature. Instead of shaking your hand, recalls a friend, she would give you a hug and a kiss; and Durant's youngest pupil, four-year-old Eva Bein, remembers how she was the first "to hold my hand and wipe away the tears if I fell down and got hurt."[105]

Puck fell in love with the school and its unrestricted freedom. "No child had to listen to the teacher if he wanted to do something else," she later recalled. "He might at any time leave the room and go out into the yard and play, though he was not free to go into the street. There were no punishments, no examinations, no report cards. Here, for a natural anarchist like me, was a sudden paradise." During morning lessons, however, Puck found it hard to remain quiet. She was not made for sedentary study, Durant notes, "and her vibrant body was like a string stretched taut and waiting for release." In the afternoons, by contrast, she was always the last to go. "Many times I looked through the window to see her darting across the street to her home," Durant remarks, "her brown arms swinging, her perfect body singing aloud with health. I called her my 'Whitman' girl, for surely she personified the *Song of the Body Electric*, and the spirit of the open road, as no other girl that I have ever known."[106]

The ex-seminarian of twenty-seven and the Jewish girl of fourteen presented a study in contrasts, the one shy, subdued, immaculate, the other outgoing, boisterous, ebullient. "I was all learning," says Durant, "and she was all life; I knew ten thousand books, and she knew only what nature and hardship had taught her." Yet if opposites attract, this was a case in point. For before long Will found himself "concerned in no impersonal way with her looks, her clothing, her language, her body." She, for her part, found him awkward and "not at all handsome." He was "unimpressively short—five feet five and a half inches. He had nice black hair, but his pink face was blotched." Yet she sensed a certain courage behind his timid nature and was struck by the simple directness with which he answered the pupils' questions, particularly about sex. She soon came to admire him: "I noticed so many instances of his patience, kindness, and sensitivity that I, who had long resented the rough men of our neighborhood, warmed to him with every new experience until, not quite knowing it, I was in love. All the hidden forces of youth and growth coursed in my excited blood."[107]

And then the inevitable happened. One day, as Durant describes it, "the tide came to a flood, and all the moorings were torn away. It was after three o'clock, and the children had gone. Ariel had stayed to help me put things in order. By some fated accident our bodies touched, and my whole being was swept electrically with a current of desire. . . . I should have paused and weighed circumstances. I should have considered that this was my pupil, that I was her teacher, that here was the last place in the world for love. But I caught her wildly in my arms, and kissed her hair, and her eyes, and her mouth."[108]

Only then did he consider the consequences: "the break-up of the school; the clash of hostile races, families, and creeds; the surrender of my freedom and the end of my solitude; the assumption of new tasks and new responsibilities in the world." He was unsure, he remarked to a friend, whether to marry her or to adopt her. But love prevailed, and Durant chose the former course. To the Ferrer Association he proceeded to tender his resignation. Writing to its president, Leonard Abbott, he confessed to having fallen in love with one of the pupils and offered to relinquish his post as soon as a replacement could be found. Without recrimination, the executive board of the association replied by asking him to stay until the end of the school year, to which Durant readily agreed.[109]

At the close of the spring term in May 1913, Durant ended his year-and-a-half association with the Modern School. On October 31, 1913, he and Ariel were married. She was fifteen and he nearly twenty-eight. Arriving at City Hall on roller-skates from the secretarial school where she was now studying, the young bride, her hair wild and stocking torn from a spill she had had on the way, was joined in wedlock with her former instructor. The judge, according to Manuel Komroff, shook his finger at Durant and said: "Remember, you're not to sleep with her till she's sixteen!"[110]

The couple found an apartment on West 136th Street, not far from Columbia University, where Durant enrolled as a graduate student in philosophy. Financially, this would not have been possible but for the generosity of Alden Freeman who, having paid Durant's Ferrer School salary and having taken him on a tour of Europe, now contributed to his support until his studies were completed. Durant expressed his gratitude in *The Story of Philosophy*, published in 1926, the book which brought him fame and fortune. "The author," he wrote in the Acknowledgments, "would like to record here a debt which he can never repay to Alden

Freeman, who gave him education, travel, and the inspiration of a noble and enlightened life."

The four years spent by Durant at Columbia—he received the Ph.D. in 1917—were among the happiest of his life. During the day he and his bride would study together in the library, beginning an intellectual partnership that has endured for more than sixty years. "I thrill even now," he wrote ten years after graduating, "at the sight of its great domed library, and that quiet, vaulted reading room where for many golden years, with Ariel beside me, I explored the treasures of our race." Perhaps, he mused, when he and Ariel were old, they would sit once more in the library and feel those treasures "passing down to unstained generations, giving them the light and the power to make America again a land brave enough to be free."[111]

The Ferrer Center was now behind him, though from time to time he would lecture there or contribute to *The Modern School* magazine, and Ariel would visit the school to see her friends and play on the seesaw. Studying at Columbia, Durant recalls, "undid me as a radical." Coming to the university from a center of American anarchism, he passed "from the clash of controversy to the calm of study and research, from the discussion of discordant hopes to the analysis of impartial facts."[112] For all his success as a teacher, Durant had never been fully at home in anarchist circles. The dust of the seminary, the appeals of religion, clung to him for the rest of his life. In a lecture delivered in 1940, after the outbreak of the Second World War, he declared that only a revival of religion could cure the world's accumulating ills. And in a television interview in 1974 he remarked that, if he had it to do over again, instead of a simple City Hall ceremony he would have an elaborate church wedding. "I still have a certain priestly unction about me that you mustn't take too seriously," he said.[113]

Emma Goldman would not have been surprised. For she had predicted it all. "I was not mistaken in Durant," she wrote in 1927, after the appearance of *Transition*. "I had no faith in him from the very beginning when he came to the Ferrer school. I had a feeling that he will use the movement as a stepping stone to fame and material success. I see I was correct, but then America is the country, the gold mine for the Durants. It is only when one can write as superficially as he does, yet making it appear very profound, that he will be accepted by the multitude. But then he is welcome to his success. I confess that I am grateful to the Gods that he did not find the Anarchist movement lucrative. I prefer that our movement should be sustained by the few who have quality and conviction, than by the many who make use of it as a means to an end."[114]

After he left the Ferrer movement, Durant's political evolution traced a course, in his own words, "from Utopian aspiration through a cynical despondency to some measure of reconciliation and good cheer."[115] By 1916 he was voting for Woodrow Wilson, who had promised to keep America out of war, though the government entered the conflict in April 1917. Durant's vocal opposition to American involvement cost him an instructorship at Columbia. After that, he settled down to the career of writing and lecturing that made him wealthy and famous.

His first book, *Philosophy and the Social Problem*, was not a success. Of the thousand copies printed by Macmillan in 1916, only a hundred were sold. At the publisher's request, Durant fetched the unsold copies and carted them back to his apartment. The books covered two walls, from floor to ceiling, and Will, quoting Thoreau, told his friends that "I am now the proud possessor of a library of 1,000 volumes, 900 of which I have written myself."[116]

Undeterred, Durant continued to write while earning a living from his lectures, popularizing the ideas of philosophy and history for adult audiences, as he had done at the Ferrer Center. He was much in demand as a lecturer. At the Labor Temple School on East Fourteenth Street, of which he was made director in 1914, he spoke twice a week for fourteen years, delivering forty lectures on the history of philosophy, forty lectures on the history of art, and forty more on the history of music. "Because his audience was composed mostly of men and women who had never gone beyond elementary schooling," Ariel remarks, "he was compelled to be clear, to humanize his material with vignettes of creative personalities, and to bring it into some connection with current affairs; here was the happy compulsion that forged the order and clarity of his later exposition and style."[117]

By chance, one of his lectures on Plato was attended by Emanuel Haldeman-Julius of Girard, Kansas, who commissioned Durant to write a "blue book" on the subject. This led to a whole series of popular booklets which, rooted in Durant's talks at the Ferrer Center as well as the Labor Temple, formed the basis of *The Story of Philosophy*, a bestseller which sold more than three million copies in nineteen languages.[118]

The success of *The Story of Philosophy* provided Will and Ariel with enough money to embark on their eleven-volume *Story of Civilization*, which took nearly fifty years of research and writing to complete. (The last volume appeared in 1975.) In the course of these years, they became one of America's most successful literary partnerships. In 1935 they moved to California, and in 1943 purchased the two-and-a-half-acre estate in Hollywood Hills which they still occupy and where they recently completed their "dual autobiography." Though their ties to the past had loosened with their growing success, they continued to exchange letters and occasional visits with their old Ferrer School friends. On January 10, 1977, Will and Ariel were awarded the Medal of Freedom by President Gerald Ford at the White House for their contribution to American cultural life. One need not speculate about the reaction of Emma Goldman, had she survived to witness the occasion.

CORA BENNETT STEPHENSON

When Will and Ariel announced their intention of marrying, the Ferrer Association began to search for a new principal for the Day School. The executive board's choice soon fell upon Cora Bennett Stephenson, a well-educated woman of middling years and advanced social views. In 1909 she had published a novel, *The Hand of God*, based on the theory that "the principles of sex-worship underlie all modern religions." Having taught for some years in midwestern public schools, Mrs. Stephenson had, in Leonard Abbott's words, "come to recognize the immeasurable superiority of libertarian over authoritarian methods."[119] A disciple of Eugene Victor Debs, America's foremost socialist leader, she had been discharged from her position in an Illinois public school after protesting against the execution of Ferrer. Moving to Indiana, she began a correspondence with Emma Goldman, who recommended her as Durant's successor.

"Well-combed and well-corseted," Mrs. Stepenson arrived in New York in May 1913 to take up her new assignment. On June 2nd she addressed the third annual dinner of the Ferrer Association, and on the 20th she spoke at a memorial meeting for Voltairine de Cleyre, who had died a year before in Chicago. Around the same time, she plunged headlong into the task of directing the Day School. In pedagogical matters, she followed the theories of G. Stanley Hall, the well-known psychologist and champion of the child-centered school, who exerted a powerful influence upon avant-garde educators of the period. Seldom without a book of Hall's under her arm, she took to heart his dictum that "there is nothing else so worthy of love, reverence, and service as the body and soul of the growing child."[120]

For reasons which will be explained, Mrs. Stephenson remained at the Modern School only one year. Yet during her brief tenure a number of important developments took place. She organized the first Ferrer Summer School in July 1913 and conducted it for ten weeks with a dozen pupils, Eva Bein and Magda Boris among them. "From all accounts," reported *Mother Earth*, "the children are in love with the teacher and her methods." The children spent two of these weeks at an open-air camp in Maplewood, New Jersey, on land donated by Bolton Hall, where they were under the care of a French-born anarchist named Jacques Dubois and his Russian-Jewish wife Fanya.[121]

When the fall semester began, Mrs. Stephenson revived the Sunday School that Will Durant had started on East Twelfth Street for children unable to attend during the week. Its initial teacher was Dr. Solomon Bauch, a Jewish physician, who soon left to establish a new Sunday School in Brooklyn. Yet the experiment was continued, and by the spring of 1914 eighteen pupils were enrolled, nearly all of them girls, whom Bauch's successor, Carl Zigrosser, took on outings to the Metropolitan Museum of Art, the Museum of Natural History, the Children's Museum in Brooklyn, the Bronx and Central Park zoos, and the aquarium at the Battery.

At the same time, Mrs. Stephenson started a kindergarten for children too young to attend the primary class. Assisted by Helen Lund, an individualist anarchist from Chicago, she brought Montessori equipment into use, over the objections of some of the parents, to whom the Montessori method seemed essentially authoritarian. She also introduced a microscope into the primary class, causing a great stir among the pupils, some of whom still recall it with excitement.[122]

As the functions of the school expanded under Mrs. Stephenson's vigorous direction, the need for capable hands to manage its physical plant and nonclassroom affairs made itself felt. Accordingly, in November 1913 Joseph Cohen of the Philadelphia Modern School was invited to fill the position of organizer of the Ferrer Association, combining the duties of custodian and general manager.[123] When Cohen arrived on December 1, 1913 (he remained until the move to Stelton in May 1915), the Day School had twenty-six pupils in attendance, fourteen of them in the primary class and twelve in the kindergarten. Membership in the Ferrer Association continued to expand, and money trickled in from different parts of the country. The school, wrote Leonard Abbott, "enters its third winter season stronger than ever before."[124]

What was the nature of the Modern School curriculum? According to Joseph Cohen's daughter, a pupil in the primary class, the methods of instruction were quite conventional on the whole, with emphasis on reading, arithmetic, and grammar. There was even place for lessons in etiquette, conducted by Mrs. Stephenson, who taught the girls how to use a fan. "There is nothing in the libertarian idea that is antagonistic to genuinely good manners," she believed, and "decorum is one of the things kept in mind by the Modern School." In addition, the pupils spent a good deal of time reading *The Book of Knowledge* and in "poring over the microscope looking at everything we could find." Leonard Abbott would drop in with a gentle word of encouragement, and no project was complete until he had beamed his approval. His habitual "Quite so" made things "seem really quite so and the world quite right."[125]

Yet, however conventional the instruction may have appeared, it was conducted in an atmosphere of freedom and of respect for the individual child that differed sharply from that of the traditional school. Consider the experience of a twelve-year-old student named Maurice Hollod. In the fall of 1913, Maurice was enrolled in P.S. 188 on 106th Street near Madison Avenue when he met a boy in Central Park who attended the Ferrer School. "He told me about the school," Hollod recalls, "and took me over there. He led me upstairs to a classroom. There was a long table with a group of kids around it. In the center was a tall man [Leonard Abbott] peering through a microscope at a drop of blood, explaining to the kids what they were seeing under the 'scope. I became so entranced that I made up my mind on the spot that I'm going to this school. That was it! It opened my eyes to what school could be."

Hollod found Cora Bennett Stephenson "the most lovable person I had ever met. The third day I'm in the school I acted a little smark-alecky. She said to me: 'I don't think you're ready for class yet. I think you want to play. So why don't you go out in the yard today?' She said this calmly, without any hostility. I thought, what kind of school is this where they punish you by letting you play? I played in the yard all day. And the next day too. The day after that I told Mrs. Stephenson that I didn't want to go into the yard again. She said, 'Do you feel ready to sit down and work with the rest of the class?' I said yes. 'All right, come in.' Can you imagine the difference between this type of discipline and that in the public schools of that day, a military type of discipline, a barracks discipline?"[126]

To cite another example, Anna Schwartz decided to send her two children, Marucci and Zack, to the Modern School after Marucci, denied permission to go to the bathroom in her public school, wet her pants and got a severe scolding. "I went to complain to the Principal," recalls Mrs. Schwartz, "a big red-haired Irish woman, who called me a greenhorn and all sorts of names. So I transferred Marucci to the Ferrer School and enrolled little Zack also. The school had a yard in the back, and Zack would climb on the fence to celebrate his freedom." Mrs. Schwartz herself attended the adult lectures in the evening and on Sunday afternoon. "I met Leonard Abbott and Harry Kelly, Alexander Berkman and Emma Goldman. They were people from heaven to me. They were different from the people I grew up with. It was a completely new world."[127]

There was much more to the school besides academic study. The children had a painting and drawing class (with the young William Zorach), they put on plays and operettas, and there were lessons for those who wanted them in violin and piano. Instruction in hygiene was provided by Dr. Liber, who gave a "long and passionate lecture," with a personal demonstration, on how to clean one's teeth. "We looked at the man with undisguised amazement," Emma Cohen recollects. "For anyone his age to be so absorbed in a proceeding so elementary seemed to us remarkable." Dr. Liber also gave a talk on the care of the hair, accompanied by another demonstration. "He hung over a chair, with his head down to get a flow of blood in it and his face turned a lovely purple, then he put both hands into his thick, long mop of hair and pulled hard with appropriate facial expressions."[128]

Under the tutelage of James Morton, the children also studied Esperanto. Learning to write and sing as well as read it, they corresponded with children in other countries and were taken to Esperanto conventions. Then, too, they had various games, play being an important feature of the school. Among their favorites were "Pocahontas" and "Snow White," into which they threw themselves "with unflagging enthusiasm and joy." Beyond this, there were frequent outings and picnics, visits to zoos and museums, to the studios of William Zorach and Manuel Komroff, and to the apartment of Leonard Abbott, where "the rugs, pictures, books, music, made a home richer in texture and color than most of us knew."[129]

When school let out, the children sometimes walked to the offices of *Mother Earth* on 119th Street between Lenox and Fifth Avenues, a dozen blocks away. They were sure of a "warm booming welcome" from Alexander Berkman—"Sasha," as he liked them to call him—who always had time for some boisterous fun, catching the youngsters up and tossing them into the air to their squealing delight. But when Emma Goldman came out everything grew cold. She never said anything, but her austere, unsmiling demeanor frightened them. She was ill at ease in the presence of children. Besides, she was busy with her work and did not like interruptions.[130]

During the 1913-1914 academic year, attendance at the Day School ranged from 94 to 97 percent, a measure of the success of Mrs. Stephenson's administration. To observe the experiment at first hand, visitors came from the University of Jena, the University of Zurich, and the Pedagogical Institute of Frankfurt, from the Out-of-Door School in Buffalo and the Liberal School in Santa Barbara. Public school teachers and settlement house workers also came, not to mention newspapermen, city school inspectors, fire marshals, and detectives.[131]

Adult classes and lectures were continued on a wide range of subjects. Leonard Abbott repeated his evening course on radical literature. Will Durant, now a graduate student at Columbia, came to lecture on the history of philosophy. James Morton continued his lessons in Esperanto, Carl Zigrosser his lessons in English, and Jacques Rudome started a class in French. The art class of Henri and Bellows remained extremely popular, and there were classes in dressmaking and in sexual hygiene, the latter conducted by Dr. Liber. At the Ferrer Dining Club on Saturday nights Lincoln Steffens spoke on the McNamara case, involving the bombing of the Los Angeles Times Building; George Brown of the Philadelphia Modern School spoke on the single-tax colony at Arden, Delaware, of which he was a member; and André Tridon spoke on the New Unionism, analyzing the upsurge of revolutionary syndicalism in Europe and the United States. Sunday afternoon lectures included Leonard Abbott on "Giordano Bruno, the Free Thought Martyr," Elizabeth Gurley Flynn on "The Paterson Strike and After," and a symposium on the Commune of Paris, with Alexander Berkman, Harry Kelly, and Leonard Abbott among the participants. Other speakers that year included Emma Goldman, Clarence Darrow, Manuel Komroff, Hutchins Hapgood, and Hippolyte Havel. "The Ferrer School is doing well," remarked Abbott in March 1914. "Many of our lectures have been packed to the doors."[132]

There were also musical recitals every week, and well-known writers, such as the poet Edwin Markham, read from their works. The tea room remained a popular gathering place for informal discussion, and a library of books on social movements and modern education was built up. To raise funds for these activities, a modest fee was charged for courses and lectures, and the Ferrer Association sponsored a variety of entertainments, including a Masque Ball in April 1914 at the Lenox Casino on 116th Street. Under the auspices of the association, the fourth anniversary of Ferrer's death was commemorated on October 12, 1913, at the Forward Hall on East Broadway. On the list of speakers were Cora Bennett Stephenson, Alexander Berkman, Emma Goldman, and Harry Kelly, as well as Bruce Rogers of the Seattle Modern School, with Leonard Abbott presiding. "The Ferrer School in New York is now firmly based," Abbott declared, "and goes on to larger and more important work. It holds within itself the three germinal ideas of a Day School for Children, a People's University, and a Lecture Forum. Nothing can check its progress. For it grows out of the eternal and unquenchable desire of humanity for Freedom, and it draws its sustenance from the life-blood of a man who died for Freedom."[133]

CHAPTER 4

Rebels and Artists

THE ACADEMY HUMANE

THE FERRER SCHOOL, established in 1911, became an important focus of cultural and social ferment in the years preceding the First World War. In New York City this was a period of extraordinary intellectual brilliance, in which many of the seminal ideas of twentieth-century politics and art were being developed. Anarchism, socialism, syndicalism, revolution, birth control, free love, Cubism, Futurism, Freudianism, feminism, the New Woman, the New Theater, direct action, the general strike—all were intensely discussed at the Modern School. "The place seethed with animation and debate of vital issues," said Harry Kelly, "and no cause was too poor nor too radical or delicate to be denied a hearing." Kelly hoped that similar centers would be opened throughout the country to rally the "free spirits" of every locality.[1]

The Ferrer Center was open every day and evening, Saturday and Sunday included. It was a place where radicals could come to hear lectures on social or literary topics, to discuss the burning questions of the day, to see new plays staged by Moritz Jagendorf's Free Theatre, to listen to concerts by Hyman Rovinsky or the Modern School Trio, to study art with Robert Henri and George Bellows. It was an outlet for men and women of talent, where Man Ray could experiment with camera and brush, Mike Gold read from Shelley and Blake, Sadakichi Hartmann put on finger dances and perfume concerts. It was a place to learn the English language, to study French or Spanish or Esperanto, to dance, drink tea, and talk for hours on end. People gathered there, young and old, from the immediate neighborhood and from distant corners of the city, for classes, lectures, and conversation. "As much as the Day School meant to me, the Center meant more," recalls Maurice Hollod, who was thirteen when he began to attend. "That's where things were happening! I got to know people from all parts of the world and all parts of the radical spectrum. Living three blocks away, I was able to attend many of the evening affairs. I practically lived there. I was home so rarely that mother went to Bill Shatoff and begged him to talk to me, which he did. But there was no keeping me away!"[2]

The roster of Ferrer Center speakers was impressive, including some of the most celebrated intellectuals of the day: Jack London and Edwin Markham, Lincoln Steffens and Upton Sinclair, Margaret Sanger and Elizabeth Gurley Flynn, not to mention such regulars as Leonard Abbott, Harry Kelly, Alexander Berkman, Emma Goldman, Hutchins Hapgood, and Will Durant. From Chicago came Clarence Darrow to hold forth on Voltaire. Theodore Schroeder spoke on anthropology, primitive religion, and phallic worship, André Tridon on Maeterlinck and Rodin, John Weichsel on the history of education, Louis Levine on the general strike. The lectures were invariably followed by lively discussion. Among the subjects threshed out, says Harry Kelly, were "economics, politics, sex, psychology, psychoanalysis, literature, art, drama, the Single Tax, Socialism, Guild Socialism, Anarchism, and Syndicalism."[3]

In addition to the lectures and forums, the Ferrer Association organized balls, picnics, and excursions, and in this way gave a new revolutionary content to traditional social activities. "So much was happening," says Maurice Hollod, "so much was packed into just a few years—that's what's so amazing to me." The Center was "throbbing with activity and vitality," recalls Moritz Jagendorf, the director of its theater group. It was "a seething ocean of thought and activity, everybody working and creating." The teacher of the French class, Jacques Rudome, remembers it as "bustling with life and activity." "There was always something interesting going on," another frequent visitor recalls, "and interesting people to meet." Whatever its limitations, writes Harry Kelly, it was "vital and alive all the time."[4]

For Manuel Komroff, who later became a best-selling novelist and story writer, discovering the Ferrer Center marked a turning point. A "miserable, confused youngster," in his own description, the product of a broken home and plagued by a bad stammer, he had entered Yale to study engineering but had left after two years, in 1912, unsatisfied and without a degree. His life lacked direction and inspiration. One evening he was attending a lecture at the Rand School of Social Science when someone told him about the Ferrer Center. It was then located on East Twelfth Street, and he went over to have a look. "My quest was over," he tells us. "I liked it at once. One felt unfettered, one felt free. Views were freely exchanged between the speaker and the audience, and the air seemed charged with excitement, for the ideas which we explored were in themselves exciting and related to our lives."[5]

During the next five years, Komroff spent as much time as he could at the Ferrer Center, engaged, he tells us, in a "great adventure" which altered the course of his life. "The school was a furnace of ideas to me; it was a college, and much of what I am I owe to this encounter," he later wrote. "It was an 'Academy Humane,' a place where ideas were weighed in the scales of justice." Attending the lectures and discussions, new horizons opened before him. "I heard people speak on different subjects that I never dreamed existed: Joseph McCabe on his thirteen years in an English monastery; Theodore Schroeder on phallic symbols and free speech; Clarence Darrow, whom I introduced several times when Abbott was not there; Will Durant on 'Havelock Ellis, Sex, and Society,' a course of six lectures. After one of the latter, Mrs. Konrad Bercovici got up and said in a thick Jewish accent: 'Mr. Durant, I don't want to ask a question and I don't want to make a discussion, but I myself have personally been in the sexual movement for fifteen years and I can see no progress.' "[6]

A versatile young man, brimming over with enthusiam, Komroff took advantage of the whole range of the Ferrer Center's activities, studying art with Henri and Bellows, staging plays with Moritz Jagendorf, participating in the Ferrer Dining Club, attending symposia and debates. "The Ferrer Center became my whole education," he afterwards remarked. "It taught me everything I know and opened up new worlds. We had wonderful times. Not a nickel, but wonderful times."[7]

Within a short time, Komroff recalls, he was no longer unhappy or confused. He had found direction and a "zest for living." He was excited by the volley of ideas that "broke like bombshells on our open forum." He lost a good deal of his timidity, and even his stammer disappeared, so that before long he himself was a "star speaker" at meetings and banquets, exhibiting, in the words of Carl Zigrosser, "a dramatic sense of the ludicrous which he exposed with a detached and almost regretful air."[8]

With his strong creative impulse and versatile talent, his remarkable breadth of interests and abilities, Komroff became a mainstay of the Center's artistic and cultural program. He wrote experimental plays for the Free Theatre, conducted a course in music appreciation, served as associate editor of *The Modern School* magazine, painted, played the piano, and dabbled in woodcrafts and photography.

For Komroff, as for other young rebels and enthusiasts, these years at the Ferrer Center were the most stimulating of his life. In his novels and stories he made frequent use of what he had learned, "a barrage of ideas, all related to the lonely inner core of man and his freedom at a time when the world was changing and a new race of people was emerging." The experience remained with him forever. "Often I lie awake with the beating of my heart and think of the Center," he told a Modern School reunion in 1974, "and a hundred little thoughts and fragments cross my memory. It was because of this Academy Humane that many of our lives have been wonderfully enriched."[9]

PERSONALITIES

More than anything else, what gave the Ferrer Center its characteristic flavor was the circle of people who gathered there. Political radicals, avant-garde writers and painters, bohemians and feminists, they were men and women of vigorous and combative intelligence, with a wide range of interests and an insatiable desire for conversation, the sharper the better. They were creators and devotees of the arts, propounders and disciples of the "isms," advocates of a life free from the trammels of convention. Some of them—Mike Gold, Man Ray, Lola Ridge—stood at the threshold of celebrity; others—Edwin Markham, Robert Henri, George Bellows—had already achieved it. Most, however, had little claim to artistic distinction, and yet were notable for their vivid personalities or advanced beliefs. There were diet and clothing reformers, health faddists, and hangers-on of every type, including some who came merely to see "all the 'free love' business."[10] Tolstoyans and pacifists who spurned revolutionary activity rubbed shoulders with tough labor activists, Nietzschean supermen, and apostles of terrorism and dynamite.

Among the "disturbers" and "irresponsibles," as their less militant colleagues dubbed them, were "a few who sought to destroy, a few who sought personal gain," while a whole group of "spitoon revolutionists" made its headquarters in the basement.[11] For sheer excitement, at any rate, the Center had scant competition. "Looking at events in retrospect often gives them a romantic glow that they lacked when they took place," wrote Harry Kelly in his memoirs. "Whether it is that which makes it seem so now, or if it was in fact so, it is difficult to tell, but many who were associated with the Ferrer Association have since declared that those who gathered at the center formed the most dynamic group of men and women of its kind ever brought together in this country."[12]

Adding color to the Ferrer Association was the ethnic diversity of its membership, which exceeded three hundred on the eve of the war. The majority were working-class immigrants. Eastern European Jews predominated, but there were Frenchmen, Germans, Italians, Spanish, English, Irish, Russians, Rumanians, and other nationalities, who gave the Center a richly cosmopolitan atmosphere. To these recent arrivals, hungry for education and culture, the Ferrer School was "a genuine people's university, one deeply rooted in the masses," as their English instructor described it.[13]

Most of the teachers, by contrast, were of native, middle-class background. Dissatisfied with the world of their fathers, and repelled by industrial capitalism with its slums and sweatshops and degradation of the human spirit, they had "gone to the people," like the nineteenth-century Russian Populists, in a mission of enlightenment and expiation. Fascinated by the "spirit of the ghetto," they were drawn irresistibly to the vibrant immigrant culture of Harlem and the Lower East Side, so alive and exhilarating alongside the Victorian sobriety of their own family environment. Refugees from middle-class philistinism, they yearned for a new world of passion, diversity, and freedom—free verse, free art, free love, freedom from the drab commercialism of conventional society.

Among the college-educated native Americans who mingled with the Ferrer School immigrants and "thought it a privilege to be their teachers,"[14] the examples of Bayard Boyesen, James Morton, Will Durant, and Cora Bennett Stephenson have been considered. Another case in point was Carl Zigrosser, born in Indianapolis to a comfortable family of non-Jewish Swiss and Austrian background. In 1908, at the age of seventeen, Zigrosser entered Columbia College, where Boyesen, his teacher in freshman English, stimulated his interest in radicalism as well as literature and gave him a copy of Kropotkin's *Memoirs of a Revolutionist*. The book made a powerful impression, and Zigrosser followed it up with *Mutual Aid* and *Fields, Factories and Work-*

shops, with its "early advocacy of the decentralization of industry." A brilliant student, Zigrosser was elected to Phi Beta Kappa and was graduated in three years, having served on the editorial board of the *Columbia Monthly*, together with Randolph Bourne (his future roommate) and Alfred Knopf. The following year he wrote to Kropotkin, asking what he could do to serve humanity. Kropotkin, echoing his famous *Appeal to the Young*, advised him to put his idealism and talents at the disposal of the working classes.[15]

In the Ferrer Center, which he began to frequent in 1913, Zigrosser found the vehicle to implement Kropotkin's advice. An oasis of excitement and nourishment in a desert of complacency, as Zigrosser describes it, the Center had "the potentiality of a genuine people's university." Apart from teaching an English class for adults, Zigrosser took charge of the Sunday School and of the sale of literature at Ferrer Association gatherings. "My identification with the Ferrer Center, however, was based not only on my sympathy for the underdog," he tells us, "but also on my quest for new experience. I had lived a relatively solitary life in the pursuit of knowledge, mostly from books. Now I wanted to know people, all kinds of people in every walk of life. . . . I felt that there was more to society than its upper segment. I wanted to discover 'how the other half lives.' "[16]

Like Will Durant before him, Zigrosser was deeply impressed by the Center's core group—Leonard Abbott, Harry Kelly, Joseph Cohen, Manuel Komroff—who gave their all to the school in spite of the meager resources available to them. "They were not wild-eyed revolutionaries," he remarked, "but were honest, decent, and cooperative in their dealings. They had great respect for literature and the arts, and were gentle souls—intolerant of only one thing, namely social injustice, and then only as individuals and not in association." Cohen he found to be "a tower of strength with his tenacity and common sense," while Kelly was "that rare phenomenon of a practical idealist." Zigrosser was equally impressed by Alexander Berkman, with his "hair-splitting analytical mind," and by Emma Goldman, "with her thick gutteral accent and her powerful bull-like neck." He was disgusted, however, by Emma's then companion, Ben Reitman, "a vulgar and unstable character, no asset to any movement."[17]

A more sympathetic personality was Stewart Kerr, the Scottish-born anarchist who, "silent and incorruptible," kept account of the Modern School finances. Tall, handsome, grey-haired, "of somber spirit, proud integrity, and rare speech," he was a telephone engineer by profession and an intimate of Berkman and Goldman, who admired his "considerate and non-invasive nature." Kerr's soul, says Will Durant, had been "softened and saddened by some youthful Old-World tragedy," yet a volcano "seethed under his tight-lipped self-control." To Zigrosser he almost seemed to have stepped out of the pages of Henry James's *Princess Casamassima*.[18]

Another Ferrer Center standby with a mysterious, almost fictional air was an Englishman named Edward Frederick Mylius, who, in a case that achieved considerable notoriety, had served a year in prison for libeling King George V. After his release, Mylius went to the United States in quest of sanctuary, only to be held on Ellis Island by the immigration authorities, who tried to exclude him as an anarchist and former jailbird. Hearing of his plight, sympathizers at the Ferrer Center mounted a successful protest movement and, securing his release, proceeded to extend him hospitality. "I find all the people here interesting, warm hearted and full of enthusiasm for the new, elevating ideas, which are now dawning in our midst," he wrote in February 1913, having made the Center his home.[19] A few weeks later he joined Hippolyte Havel in editing *The Social War*, "A Revolutionary Weekly Advocate of Free Communism."

Kerr and Mylius were among the many remarkable characters in the Ferrer Center gallery of rebels. Another was Romany Marie, in her colorful gypsy costume, who doubled as waitress in the tea room and usher, ticket-taker, and bursar at entertainments and lectures. A warm, expansive personality and ardent anarchist, she was always "either trying to get someone out of jail or talking about the crew of vultures who ought to be put in," recalls the artist Harry Wickey, a frequent visitor to the Center.[20] She afterward opened her own tea room in Greenwich Village, a gathering place for radicals and bohemians, featuring good food, fortune telling, and gypsy music.

Yet another of the Center's fixtures was John Rompompas, a Greek tobacco importer, who delivered an occasional lecture and financed Hippolyte Havel's *Revolutionary Almanac* under the imprint of the "Rabelais Press." There was also Charles Loring Andrews, the tall, distinguished-looking dentist of Central Park West, bearded and old-fashioned, a figure out of the nineteenth century, who "made you love him even while he was drilling your tooth."[21] And there was Carlo Tresca, the flamboyant Italian militant, attractive and irrespressible, whose broad-brimmed hat and flowing tie fit the conventional image of the European-born anarchist.

Among the most active figures at the Center was Belgian-born Adolf Wolff, with dark hair, dark beard, and intense gaze, whom women found seductive despite his protruding stomach. A militant revolutionary, Wolff was also a "faker and poseur" who never earned a penny, left a trail of debts, and was supported by his girlfriend Vera, who had a house on 113th Street.[22] Having attended Robert Henri's class in art and Leonard Abbott's class in literature, Wolff himself became a sculptor and poet. Every Thursday afternoon he taught art to the Day School children, who modeled with clay and tinkered with mallet and chisel in the yard. He was a strong believer in libertarian education. "The Modern School," he wrote, "is a sort of alchemist's laboratory where the philosopher's stone of education is being evolved. It is the great pedagogic experimental station of the new society. Its efforts should be encouraged, its results scrutinized. . . . We are futurists in education; we are idealists; but we are practical idealists, firmly believing that the dream of today will be the reality of tomorrow. We believe in tomorrow, and the children of the Modern School shall be the men and women of tomorrow."[23]

Wolff's poems, as well as his sculpture, had a crude, unrefined power. Though Komroff thought him a "lousy" poet, his writing frequently appeared in *Mother Earth* and *The Modern School*, of which he was an associate editor. His first collection of poems was dedicated to Leonard Abbott, in whose class they were composed during 1912 and 1913, and was published in Alfred Kreymborg's journal *The Glebe* under the title "Songs, Sighs and Curses." Wolff could not decide how to arrange them, so, leaving it to fate, threw the manuscripts into the air and had them printed in the order in which he picked them up from the floor.[24]

The following year Wolff published in book form a second collection of poetry, *Songs of Rebellion, Songs of Life, Songs of Love*, one of which was addressed to his daughter Esther, a pupil in the Modern School:

May you be a Judith decapitating a Holofernes,
A Joan of Arc leading a people to victory,
A Louise Michel fighting on the barricades,

A Voltairine de Cleyre singing songs of revolt,
An Emma Goldman preaching the gospel of rebellion.

Other poems were devoted to Shelley, Walt Whitman, and William Morris, to Frank Tannenbaum, Arturo Giovannitti, and Elizabeth Gurley Flynn, and to Leonard Abbott's daughter Voltairine, who had died soon after birth. Still another, "Prophetic Vision," contained Wolff's forecast of the millennium:

When the people awaken,
This Moloch will vanish as the smoke in the wind.
When they awaken from the horrible nightmare
Into which they were plunged by the vile conquerors,
Then the Gods and the Laws,
The priests and the lawyers,
The diseases and the superstitions,
The miseries and the crimes,
All these shall vanish from the midst of men,
And henceforth,
The world shall be beautiful
And life shall be good.[25]

Apart from Wolff, no one plunged more enthusiastically into the activities of the Center than Jack Isaacson, a studious, bespectacled anarchist, dubbed "the Rabbi" by his comrades. (Joseph Cohen was "the *Shames*," Alexander Berkman "the Pope," and Emma Goldman "the Red Queen.") Garment worker, locksmith, restaurant worker, Isaacson yearned for the coming of the social revolution ("We hope the day is not far distant when a million I.W.W.'s will make this country safe for human habitation").[26]

Conspicuous among the younger habitués of the Center was David Rosenthal, newsboy, actor, and poet, whose well-modulated voice would become familiar to millions of radio listeners as that of "David Ross," one of America's best-known announcers in the decades between the world wars. His poem "Nan of Nineveh," published in Hippolyte Havel's *Revolt*, a journal printed in the Center's basement, created a sensation:

I am Nan, a whore, the bastard of society's fecund system.
I live in the lonely lagoons of darkness,
Where I lust for food and am food for lust.
Bread—body—bed, Bread—body—bed,
A million times over and over.

And there was seventeen-year-old Hyman Rovinsky—afterwards "Anton" Rovinsky—the "Paderewski" of the group, "rousing us with his piano artistry."[27]

Visitors to the Center represented every shade of the radical spectrum, from pacifism to terrorism, from collectivism to individualism. Bill Shatoff exemplified the anarcho-syndicalist position. Having emigrated from Russia in 1907, when he was twenty, he was to return in 1917 to take part in the Revolution. During his ten years in America, as Emma Goldman notes, he "shared the life of the true proletarian and was always in the thick of the struggle for the betterment of the workers' condition." A hod-carrier in Boston, shoemaker in Lynn, printer in New York, longshoreman in Philadelphia, window-cleaner in Pittsburgh, steelworker in Gary, housepainter in Detroit, and iron-peddler in San Francisco, to mention only some of his numerous jobs, Shatoff was a Jack-of-all-trades who never shrank from physical labor, however unpleasant or difficult. He was also "a splendid organizer, an eloquent speaker, and a man of courage," riding the rails from one end of the country to the other as a lecturer for the I.W.W. and its Slavic counterpart, the Union of Russian Workers in the United States and Canada. Big, jovial, and friendly, dependable in every emergency, he was "filled to the brim with the red blood of life," one of the Center's most dynamic personalities.[28]

At the other end of the spectrum stood the essayist Benjamin De Casseres, part Nietzschean, part Stirnerite, all individualist, descendant of Spinoza and conjurer of the written word: "I am nihilist, anarch, Nazarene-Harlequin, inventor of masks, a vendor of poses, a fantastic who waltzes on the brinks of cataclysmic mutations. My havens are horizons, a shooting star is my anchor; life is my death and the tomb is a dressing-room for my next transsubstantiation. Like the eagle's eye, I have warred against the sun, and I have walked the Zodiaque with feet that spurned their candle-gleam, I am the anonymous tyranny of the Unknown, the Will-to-Sham, a giant of the unbegotten Light crucified here on the calvaries of apprehension." Yet another personality, called "Back to Nature," represented the early incarnation of a hippie, fifty years ahead of his time. "He wore his wavy hair long to his shoulders, had a beard, wore only linen and canvas and went about preaching a return to the natural life and vegetarianism," writes Emma Cohen, who adds that the only attractive thing about him was his whistling, "most liquid and beautiful whistling."[29]

HIPPOLYTE AND SADAKICHI

Of all the striking Ferrer Center personalities, none were more vivid or picturesque than Hippolyte Havel and Sadakichi Hartmann. Drinking companions and kindred spirits, both were anarchists and bohemians and wasted talents. Always in need of money, they were forever sponging off friends and passing acquaintances. With the booty thus obtained, they would walk downtown from 107th Street to Greenwich Village and "never miss a gin mill on the way."[30] Their blatant eccentricity, the sheer improbability of their behavior, sometimes assumed such grotesque proportions as to make it seem that one was watching two great actors in comic roles invented by a dramatic genius. Yet their lives were touched by sadness, and both were to end their days in tragic circumstances.

Havel, in Albert Parry's description, was "an Anarchist bursting with atmosphere."[31] A small, rotund figure with spectacles, goatee, and mustache, his high forehead topped with disorderly black hair streaked with grey, he was one of the most colorful personalities in the movement. He always carried a silver-tipped cane, and his manner and appearance had a distinctly old-world flavor. A friend likened him to a ragged chrysanthemum. Yet he was an imposing character with a long and interesting radical history.

To avoid deportation during the Red Scare, Havel told immigration authorities that he was a native American, born in Chicago in 1871, the year of the great fire, in which many official records were destroyed. When asked his national origin he replied, "Cro-Magnon."[32] In truth, however, Havel was born in 1869, in the Bohemian town of Burowski, of a Czech father and gypsy mother. Educated in Vienna, he became a journalist for the Austrian anarchist press, but was arrested in 1893, after delivering a fiery May Day speech, and served eighteen months in prison. When his term expired, he was deported from Vienna to his native village. A short while later, however, he was again arrested after taking part in a demonstration in Prague. On his release, he tramped through Germany, lecturing and writing for the anarchist movement, then returned to Vienna to visit his family, who had meanwhile moved there, only to be discovered by the authorities and jailed for violating his banishment.[33]

But Havel's adventures were only beginning. Transferred to an insane asylum on the grounds that only a lunatic could disbelieve in government, he had the good fortune to encounter Professor Krafft-Ebing, the well-known psychologist, who was visiting the institution. Krafft-Ebing informed the authorities that they had made a mistake ("he knows more about psychology than I do"). The doctors protested that Havel was an anarchist. "He is saner than any of us," was the professor's reply.

At Krafft-Ebing's insistence, Havel was released from the asylum. Deported again, he journeyed to Zurich and then to Paris, where he resumed his anarchist agitation. His method was to stand on a street corner holding up the bare, stretched ribs of an umbrella without a covering. When a sufficient number had gathered, he would begin to speak: "You may think I am crazy to be holding this open umbrella over my head, but I tell you I am no more ridiculous than is the society you live in." And then he would launch into his discourse on the evils of the world.[34]

From Paris Havel moved to London, where he supported himself by menial labor, such as shining shoes and sweeping floors. There, in 1899, he met Emma Goldman. The pair became lovers, and in 1900 Havel accompanied her to Paris to an international anarchist congress, which was broken up by the police. Returning with her to America, he settled in Chicago and was detained briefly in 1901 during the antianarchist hysteria that followed the assassination of President McKinley. When *Mother Earth* was founded in New York, Havel became Emma Goldman's right-hand man and, though their more intimate association had ended, their friendship never faltered and they continued to work together, at the Ferrer School and *Mother Earth*, until her deportation in 1919.[35]

A man of erudition and of flowing literary style, Havel was at ease in a half-dozen languages and contributed to many anarchist periodicals. He himself edited a number of journals and wrote interesting sketches of Emma Goldman and Voltairine de Cleyre, which appeared as introductions to their collected works. But he never produced a full-length book, and his pamphlet *What's Anarchism?* was a disappointing effort, a far cry from Berkman's *What is Communist Anarchism?*, published around the same time.

Though reputed to have a brilliant mind, Havel could seldom

stick to anything for a protracted length of time. Impatient, irascible, he was "in a perpetual state of vituperative excitement" and, when confronted with sustained argument, would resort to invective and personal abuse. Alcohol, in which he frequently sought refuge, further impaired his intellectual capacities. When he began to drink he at first became effusive, affectionate. ("Hello, little monkey face," he would welcome a friend.) He "vibrated very pleasantly, and his talk was happy and charming." But a drink too many and he exploded with hatred, and his fury against life came pouring out.[36]

Thoroughly drunk, Havel once got up at a Ferrer memorial meeting and started to speak: "We are here to honor the memory of Francisco Ferrer—Francisco, the martyr—Saint or San Francisco, that teeming metropolis on the West Coast," whereupon he was pulled down. On another occasion, according to Manuel Komroff, he urinated in broad daylight on lower Fifth Avenue and was hailed into court for disorderly conduct. "Why did you do it publicly on Fifth Avenue?" asked the judge. "Why didn't you go on a side street?" Havel angrily replied: "You mean, I should do it where the poor people live? No, no, I refuse to do it there. I protest!" Hutchins Hapgood, over Havel's objections, paid the five-dollar fine.[37]

Havel's main claim to distinction was as a colorful bohemian character. He cut a conspicuous figure even among the exotic inhabitants of Greenwich Village, where he and Polly Holladay, an anarchist from Evanston, Illinois, opened a small café on the eve of the First World War. Located at 137 Macdougal Street, Polly's Restaurant catered to the artists and intellectuals who flocked to the Village in those years. Polly, in contrast to Havel, was "staid and quiet and suburban," looking "very madonna-like." Yet she collected about her in her restaurant the "wildest and noisiest horde of young folk in America," presiding over them "with benignant serenity" and seeing to it that "these truants and orphans were properly fed."[38]

Polly's lover and general factotum, Havel was the mainstay of the enterprise, serving as dishwasher, waiter, and cook, a capacity in which he excelled. To the artist William Zorach his cooking was no less than "superb," and Emma Goldman, herself well known for her culinary talents, judged him a "first-class chef." From time to time he would prepare meals at the Dobbs Ferry home of Hutchins Hapgood, who remembered his Hungarian goulash "with particular joy."[39]

With its good food and stimulating atmosphere, Polly's became a haven for the New York literary and political avant-garde. The *Mother Earth* and Ferrer Center crowd patronized the place, as did Havel's writer friends, among them Eugene O'Neill and Theodore Dreiser, as well as Max Eastman and Floyd Dell of *The Masses*. "Havel," Dreiser remarked, "is one of those men who ought to be supported by the community; he is a valuable person for life, but can't take care of himself. If I ever have any money, I'll certainly settle some of it on Hippolyte."[40]

For the time being, however, the restaurant prospered, in spite of Havel's "volcanic outbursts" against the customers, whom he denounced, even as he served them, as "bourgeois pigs." On such occasions, Floyd Dell thought him "formidable in aspect," notwithstanding his diminutive size. ("He was very small," observed Mabel Dodge, "and very obscene in his talk.")[41] An uncompromising revolutionary, Havel had little patience for dinner-table conversation. His heroes were activists like Johann Most and the Haymarket martyrs, Luigi Galleani and Louise Michel, Ravachol and Clément Duval. His own militancy was reflected in the titles of his journals—*The Social War, The Revolutionary Almanac, Revolt*—whose pages bore the aroma of dynamite. In a heated exchange with John Reed, Havel accused him of being a "parlor socialist," to which Reed retorted, "And you're a kitchen anarchist!" Attending editorial meetings of *The Masses*, Havel lost his temper and thundered against the practice of voting on poetry selections. "Bourgeois pigs!" he shouted. "Voting! Voting on poetry! Poetry is something from the soul! You can't vote on poetry!" His protest was long remembered, Max Eastman afterward confessed, "because it contained so much good sense."[42]

Havel, moreover, was a man of "extremely jealous temperament." Though in theory a proponent of free love, his tolerance ended where his own companion was involved, and he made terrible scenes in the restaurant, interfering with business. Polly complained bitterly of these eruptions. But her main grievance, according to Hutchins Hapgood, was that Hippolyte had not committed suicide after vowing repeatedly to do so. "He promised me," she lamented, "over and over again, but he just won't keep his word."[43]

Next to Havel, the most exotic personality at the Ferrer Center was Sadakichi Hartmann. Hartmann's father was a German merchant, his mother a Japanese woman who died soon after childbirth, and Sadakichi, according to Manuel Komroff, "inherited the worst traits of both races."[44] Like Havel, he was an inveterate sponger and drinker ("a tremendous boozehound," to quote Maurice Hollod). Sadakichi in Japanese means "steady luck," or "fortunate if constant." "The moniker means 'Gimme some dough,' " quipped W. C. Fields, who knew him from his Hollywood years. According to John Barrymore, he was "presumably sired by Mephistopheles out of Madame Butterfly."[45]

Born in Nagasaki in 1867, Sadakichi was sent to Germany to be raised in the household of a wealthy Hamburg uncle, "among whose books and art treasures," he would recall, "I spent my childhood, and whom I have to thank for my first appreciation of art."[46] For his education he was sent to a naval academy at Kiel, but he rebelled against the strict military discipline and ran away to Paris, whereupon his father disinherited him and shipped him off to relations in Philadelphia. Arriving in 1882, he worked at a succession of menial jobs while reading in the library at night. When he learned that Walt Whitman lived across the river in Camden, New Jersey, he visited the aging poet and they fried eggs together, recited verses, and discussed literature and art.

Sadakichi emerged as a man of diverse artistic talents, "poet, writer, painter, and a marvelous reader of the poems and stories of Whitman and Poe," as Emma Goldman describes him.[47] He wrote fiction, drama, poetry, essays, and sketches, half a dozen books and hundreds of articles in the fields of painting and photography, including important studies of Japanese and American art. In the 1880s and '90s he was already informing the American public, in a wide range of magazines and newspapers, both in German and English, about Ibsen and the French Symbolists, and introducing Japanese art and literature to women's clubs of Philadelphia, Boston, and New York. He was probably the first person, according to Kenneth Rexroth, to write English haiku ("White petals afloat / On a winding woodland stream / What else is life's dream?").[48] In 1897 he produced the first psychedelic light show, and in 1902 held his first "perfume concert." He also gave lessons in body language, mostly to "young women fascinated by his rakish good looks, restless energy, and courtly manners."[49] Ezra Pound, with whom he corresponded, placed him at the head of the lost legion of American avant-garde writers of the fin-de-siècle era, and Alfred Stieglitz considered him one of the best critics of photography in the United States. (He was a regular contributor to Stieglitz's *Camera Work*, writing as "Sidney Allan" when not under his own name or initials.)

In physique Sadakichi was tall and thin—so thin, a friend remarked, that he "looked as if he only exhaled and never inhaled."[50] Immensely photogenic in spite of his rotting teeth, he was incapable of being photographed badly. Thousands of pictures were taken of him, not one without interest. Attractive to women, he sired a dozen children, most of whom he gave the names of flowers or herbs. In 1891 he married Elizabeth Blanche Walsh, the daughter of an English colonel, who bore him five of his children and served as his secretary for many years. Long after he deserted her in 1910, she still spoke of him with loyalty and affection, once saying: "He was three parts genius and one part devil, and I was in love with all four parts."[51]

"Sadakichi is singular, never plural," Gertrude Stein remarked. Vain, stubborn, eccentric, he was capable of the most outlandish behavior. On one occasion, masquerading as a Japanese prince with an escort of costumed companions, he hoodwinked the City of New York into holding a parade down Broadway.[52] "A grotesque etched in flesh by the drunken Goya of Heaven," wrote Benjamin De Casseres of Sadakichi. "A grinning, obscene gargoyle on the Temple of American Letters. Superman-bum. Half God, half Hooligan; all artist. Anarch, sadist, satyr. A fusion of Japanese and German, the ghastly experiment of an Occidental on the person of an Oriental. Sublime, ridiculous, impossible. A genius of the ateliers, picture studios, ginmills, and East Side lobscouse restaurants. A dancing dervish, with graceful, Gargantuan feet and a mouth like the Cloaca Maxima. A painter out of Hakusai, Manet, Whistler. Result: fantastic realism. A colossal ironist, a suave pessimist, a Dionysiac Wobbly."[53]

In a philosophical sense at least, Sadakichi was also an anarchist. He called on Kropotkin when the Russian prince visited New York in 1897 on his first lecture tour of America. He attended anarchist meetings, mingled in anarchist circles, was friendly with Goldman and Berkman, and contributed to *Mother Earth* and other anarchist publications. Among his pieces was a poem to Ferrer, and Tobias Sigel of the Detroit Modern School was his old friend and physician. Regarding life and art as "the twin flames of revolt," he refused to be herded along by prevailing tastes and standards, and he rejected "stagnant crowd-thinking and mass-meeting morality."[54] Unlike Havel, however, he remained on the periphery of the anarchist movement, a sympathizer rather than an activist, too cynical perhaps to believe in a successful libertarian revolution that would inaugurate the stateless millennium. "I personally do not believe in reform," he wrote to a friend. "Human nature in itself (in all of us) is so beastly and nasty that reform is impossible."[55]

For several years the Ferrer Center was Sadakichi's chief point of contact with the anarchists. "He fell in love with the Ferrer gang," Maurice Hollod recalls, "for they were the very warp and woof of what he stood for." An admirer of Henri and Bellows, he drifted in and out of their art class, "loaded with fire-water and bacchanalic spirits." (On such occasions, of course, work from nude models had to be suspended.)[56]

A gifted reciter and performer, Sadakichi became one of the Center's star attractions. When he opened his mouth to speak, says Manuel Komroff, he was toothless "except for two tusks," but he had "a fine, sonorous voice, which today would be thought too dramatic." Apart from declaiming his own verse, he read from Whitman and Poe and Amy Lowell, from Tolstoy and Ambrose Bierce. He staged shadow pictures and perfume concerts, pantomimes and hand dances. "Nobody danced like Sadakichi," was the general verdict.[57]

The high point, however, arrived when he read from his cycle of symbolist dramas, *Confucius, Buddha, Christ,* and *Mohammed* ("providing Sadakichi doesn't change his mind," the programs warned). When *Christ*, which James Gibbons Huneker pronounced "absolutely the most daring of all decadent productions," was published in Boston in 1893, the work was immediately confiscated and burned, and Sadakichi himself was arrested and spent Christmas week in the Charles Street jail. *Buddha*, published in 1897, was described by Vance Thompson as "strange, gaudy, fantastic—a thing all color and incense; something as gilded and monstrous and uncouth as the temple of Benares."[58] When Sadakichi read from *Christ* at the Ferrer Center in 1915, Maurice Hollod was in the audience. "The first night," he remembers, "limousines pulled up with women in fur coats and lorgnettes, things never seen on 107th Street before! During the intermission he drank a pint of liquor to get primed for the second act. During one particularly obscene segment, the rich ladies all got up and walked out."[59]

Very poor during these years, Sadakichi subsisted on handouts and small sums earned from his articles and sketches. Hutchins Hapgood remembers visiting his apartment one day and "admiring him tremendously because of the way he could quietly sit and work or talk while the children, like flies, dropped all over him. Certainly a man who could accommodate himself as beautifully to the life of the young had something." And yet he could not maintain a secure existence. Unable to discipline his unruly talents, he alternated, as his biographers have noted, between "the Bohemian stance and the role of a serious scholar."[60] He was an important historian of art, observed a pupil of Henri and Bellows, but he was also an opportunist, "a con-man who sought patrons and felt the world owed him something." To Jacques Rudome, who taught French at the Center, he was a "half-baked genius with great promise that blew up in smoke," like one of his perfume concerts.[61]

Radical Centers

It has already been noted that, like the Barcelona Escuela Moderna, the Modern School of New York was a center of political and social radicalism, concerned not only with educational matters but also with such causes as industrial unionism, birth control, and free speech. Emma Cohen compares it to the anarchist club on Jubilee Street in the Whitechapel district of London: "the same high-minded belief in brotherhood and the perfectibility of man, the same passion for culture and the arts, and, alas, the same ambivalence about propaganda by the deed, which brought both to grief."[62]

The Modern School might also be compared to the other New York centers of social, intellectual, and artistic revolt that flourished at the same time, mostly in Greenwich Village, America's leading avant-garde citadel, to which rebels from all over the country flocked with "a pathetic eagerness to participate in the celebrated joys of Bohemian life."[63] A better known if less exciting institution, for example, was the Rand School of Social Science, then on East 19th Street, "a center of socialistic light and learning,"[64] with an even more comprehensive program of adult lectures and classes than its uptown anarchist counterpart. The Liberal Club, located above Polly's Restaurant on Macdougal Street, became another favorite meeting place of radicals and bohemians, as did the Washington Square Book Store next door. At the Hotel Brevoort gathered Emma Goldman, Alexander

Berkman, Hippolyte Havel, Theodore Dreiser, and Benjamin De Casseres, among others, to discuss social and literary topics. And across the street, at 23 Fifth Avenue, was the celebrated salon of Mabel Dodge, which drew as many as a hundred people, writers, artists, and reformers, to debate a wide range of issues.

To these various centers trooped an assortment of artistic and social rebels, earnest and tireless talkers, who discoursed upon anarchism, syndicalism, socialism, feminism, psychology, modern literature, and modern art. "Imagine, then, a stream of human beings," wrote Mabel Dodge of her Wednesday soirées, "passing in and out of those rooms; one stream where many currents mingled together for a little while. Socialists, Trade-Unionists, Anarchists, Suffragists, Poets, Relations, Lawyers, Murderers, 'Old Friends,' Psychoanalysts, I.W.W.'s, Single Taxers, Birth Controlists, Newspapermen, Artists, Modern-Artists, Clubwomen, Woman's-place-is-in-the-home Women, Clergymen, and just plain men, met there and, stammering in an unaccustomed freedom a kind of speech called Free, exchanged a variousness in vocabulary called, in euphemistic optimism, Opinions!"[65]

These were the comparatively innocent days, before the Russian Revolution and America's entry into the war, when future antagonists still dealt with each other in amity, when anarchists, syndicalists, and socialists mingled together on friendly terms. In these years the lines of leftist political thought were not yet sharply drawn, and it was possible for diverse types of radicals to find common ground for discussion. Estranged from the commercialism of middle-class America, they agreed on many of their antipathies—anticapitalism, antimilitarism, antiphilistinism—if not on the remedies to cure them. They did not take a dogmatic or exclusivist stand on either aesthetic or social issues, and, whatever their disagreements, shared a hostility toward the existing order, with its business and money culture, its babbittry and moral hypocrisy.

Yet, for all their pragmatic spirit, they had an unshakable faith in the coming millennium. They imagined themselves at the dawn of an epoch-making revolution, cultural as well as social and political. "There is a light in the sky and a glint on the hills that augurs well for the future," wrote Harry Kelly in 1913. As Margaret Sanger expressed it: "A religion without a name was spreading over the country. The converts were liberals, socialists, anarchists, revolutionists of all schools. They were as fixed in their faith in the coming revolution as ever any Primitive Christian in the immediate establishment of the Kingdom of God. Some could even predict the exact date of its advent."[66] It was a final burst of optimism before the crushing disenchantment of the postwar era, the last phase of a romantic revolutionism that has irretrievably passed into history.

The life of the Ferrer Center, stretching from 1911 to 1918, coincided with this Golden Age of romantic insurgency. Patrons of the Center shuttled back and forth between 107th Street and its downtown equivalents, where plays, poetry readings, and parties were always on the agenda. Speakers at the Liberal Club included such Ferrer Center standbys as Emma Goldman, Alexander Berkman, Margaret Sanger, Hippolyte Havel, Hutchins Hapgood, and Theodore Schroeder, who might be heard at other Village salons as well. One evening at Mabel Dodge's, Emma Goldman, William English Walling, and Big Bill Haywood debated the merits of anarchism, socialism, and syndicalism before an assortment of radicals and liberals, including Hippolyte Havel and Walter Lippmann. "They talk like goddam bourgeois," cried Havel, who called the hostess "my little sister, my little goddam bourgeois capitalist sister." By the same token, Miss Dodge contributed poems to *Mother Earth* and admired Goldman and Berkman (who once tried to kiss her in a taxi). "I wanted these people to think well of me," she confesses. "They were the kind that *counted*. They had authority. Their judgment was somehow true. One did not want their scorn."[67]

The Masses, under the editorship of Max Eastman, emerged as yet another focus for these varying groups, articulating their distinctive spirit of undogmatic rebellion. In its editorial manifesto the journal declared itself to be "A Revolutionary and not a Reform Magazine; a Magazine with a Sense of Humor and No Respect for the Respectable; Frank; Arrogant; Impertinent; searching for the True Causes; a Magazine directed against Rigidity and Dogma where it is found; Printing what is too Naked or True for a Money-making Press; a Magazine whose final Policy is to do as it Pleases and Conciliate Nobody—not even its Readers." *The Masses* opened its pages to anarchists and syndicalists as well as socialists, and some of its leading artists—Robert Henri, George Bellows, John Sloan, Robert Minor, Abraham Walkowitz—were closely associated with the Ferrer Center. Floyd Dell, Eastman's associate editor, was a devotee of Emma Goldman and had been drawn to anarchism by "temperamental sympathies" in his youthful Chicago years.[68]

The Ferrer Center itself attracted men and women of differing political philosophies. "There were Socialists, Anarchists, Single-Taxers, Trade-Unionists, I.W.W.'s, Syndicalists," wrote Arthur Samuels, treasurer of the Ferrer Association from 1913 to 1915. "There were Theologians and Atheists. There were Non-resistants and Direct Actionists." Amid this "mumbo-jumbo of radical elements," as Maurice Hollod describes it, the predominant ideology represented a mixture of anarchism, socialism, and syndicalism. Its unifying aim, in Harry Kelly's words, was "the reconstruction of society upon the basis of freedom and justice. The interpretations of freedom and justice and how to attain them differ, but free expression of opinions and interchange of ideas is the working method. To hold robust opinions without being dogmatic is a good war cry." Leonard Abbott put it as follows: "We fight not to standardize life, but to free it in order that it may find its own manifold expressions. We do not teach dogmas; we try to be fair even to doctrines with which we disagree. But we hope that our children will grow up to be men and women devoted to liberty; ready to fight for liberty; and ready, if need be, to lay down their lives for liberty."[69]

As Abbott's words suggest, the spirit of the Center, while flexible and undoctrinaire, was one of defiance and revolt. The Paris Commune, the greatest urban insurrection of the nineteenth century, was upheld as a model of social revolution and of the coming libertarian order, with its acts of heroism and self-sacrifice and its pioneering measures of reform. In March 1914 Abbott, Kelly, and Berkman conducted a symposium in honor of the Commune's forty-third anniversary. Two months later the centennial of the birth of Bakunin was celebrated under the auspices of the Ferrer Association, with speeches by Kelly, Berkman, Havel, and Shatoff, and music by the Modern School Trio.

At the Center's evening discussions, terrorism and expropriation were the subjects of active debate. It was a time of mounting social unrest, and "one could hear the clunk of *sabots* clambering up the long stairway," said Manuel Komroff. "The great sleeping giant was beginning to stir."[70] A popular drawing by William Balfour-Ker, entitled "From the Depths," captured the prevailing mood by depicting the terror of wealthy revelers in a palace of pleasure as a fist is thrust up through the floor by one of the submerged toilers below.

With such energetic fighters for women's rights as Emma Goldman, Margaret Sanger, and Elizabeth Gurley Flynn, the

Ferrer Center became a platform for feminist propaganda and agitation. Margaret Sanger, who exhorted her sisters to confront the world with "a go-to-hell look in the eyes,"[71] spoke on "The Limitation of Offspring" and organized a series of "Mothers' Meetings" to discuss the question of birth control. Elizabeth Gurley Flynn, companion of Carlo Tresca and the "rebel girl" of Joe Hill's song, lectured on "Syndicalism and Woman." When Margaret Sanger and Emma Goldman were arrested for disseminating birth-control information, the Ferrer Association raised money for their defense.[72]

Among the many other feminists who lectured at the Ferrer Center were Dr. Juliet H. Severance, Fola La Follette, Marie Jenney Howe, Amy Mali Hicks, and Henrietta Rodman. Rodman, a disciple of Charlotte Perkins Gilman (herself a contributor to *The Modern School* magazine), also spoke at the first annual dinner of the Ferrer Association in 1911. "A protestor, a leader of demonstrations and ever-new factions, a blazer of trails," as Albert Parry has described her, she was every inch the emancipated woman, with her bobbed hair, sandals, and "meal-sack" gown. In 1914, while serving on the advisory board of the Ferrer Association, she organized the Feminist Alliance to fight for women's equality. A veteran teacher in the New York City schools, she fought the Board of Education on a dozen fronts, as Gurley Flynn observed, but especially for discriminating against the hiring of married women teachers and for denying women the right to return to their jobs after having children. For these criticisms she was suspended from her own post at Wadleigh High School in December 1914.[73]

In addition to feminism, the men and women of the Ferrer Center threw their energies behind other radical causes of the day. An Anti-Militarist League was formed at the Center in 1914, as war clouds were gathering in Europe. A Mexican Revolutionary Committee as well as Unemployment and Free Speech Committees also found a home beneath its roof. The Center supported the Lawrence strike of 1912, the Paterson strike of 1913, and the Ludlow strike and unemployed movement of 1913-1914. "Not a labor problem in which we were not intensely interested," noted Arthur Samuels, "not a labor struggle but we were actively aiding the strikers to win it."[74] The Center arranged meetings to aid Joseph Ettor and Arturo Giovannitti after their arrest at Lawrence, and was one of the first places they visited after being acquitted. Carlo Tresca, Elizabeth Gurley Flynn, and other Ferrer Center activists took a leading part in the Paterson strike. In the strike pageant at Madison Square Garden in June 1913 Manuel Komroff served as John Reed's chief aid and stage manager. Children from both Lawrence and Paterson received shelter from Ferrer Association members and friends.

In an age of industrial violence, anarcho-syndicalism exerted a powerful appeal among Ferrer Center adherents, with its uncomplicated philosophy of action and uncompromising opposition to capitalism. Two of the first American books on revolutionary syndicalism were written by Ferrer Center regulars, *The New Unionism* by André Tridon and *Syndicalism in France* by Louis Levine. Tridon and Levine also delivered lectures and led discussions on the subject, together with Bill Shatoff, Bill Haywood, Carlo Tresca, and Elizabeth Gurley Flynn. *The Modern School* magazine reported that syndicalists and labor militants were "familiar figures at our center."[75]

In October 1912 some sixty men and women gathered at the Ferrer Center and established a Syndicalist Educational League, with Hippolyte Havel as secretary and Harry Kelly as treasurer, to spread "the idea of Syndicalism, Direct Action, and the General Strike among the organized and unorganized workers of America." Critical of the reformist unions, which were dominated by liberals and moderate socialists, the League maintained that an improvement in working conditions would in no way eliminate the evil of wage slavery. Echoing the preamble to the I.W.W. constitution ("The working class and the employing class have nothing in common"), its program proclaimed that "economic compromises with capital are based on the fundamental fallacy of the identity of interests between master and slave, and are detrimental to the cause of labor." The League was equally opposed to political action, which "serves only to mislead and dupe the workers, robs them of their initiative, and weakens their power of resistance." The business of the League was to educate the workers to the necessity of "effective, revolutionary action" against capitalism and to prepare them "for their mission of taking charge of production and distribution in the future society."[76]

This program, in many respects, was similar to that of the Marxists. For both anarchists and Marxists, the ultimate goal was a libertarian communism in which exploitation, classes, and government would have ceased to exist. Both movements were anticapitalist, antinationalist, and anti-imperialist. Both sought to destroy the bourgeois order.

In other respects, however, there were deep divisions. The Marxists were committed to a firm belief in the superiority of centralization over decentralization and to the indispensability of strong leadership, as opposed to the freewheeling spontaneity of the anarchists. Whatever their points of contact, Marxism and anarchism embodied two rival conceptions of the revolution and of the society that would follow it, the one based on a disciplined political party working toward the centralized direction of social life, the other based on a libertarian belief in a loose association of autonomous organizations in which the means of production would be directly controlled by the workers who used them.

Marxist boasts of propounding a "scientific" socialism were regarded by the anarchists with contempt. Economic determinism was, in Harry Kelly's words, "as fixed and rigid a dogma as the one of the Immaculate Conception."[77] Individual destinies, the anarchists felt, were not governed by economic forces alone, nor preordained by the inexorable course of historical development as foretold by Marx and his disciples, but were settled by a multiplicity of forces, including, besides sheer accident, the initiatives, imaginations, and even the whims of individual men and women.

Manuel Komroff had further objections: "I didn't like Marx; he was so cumbersome! I didn't like his materialist interpretation of history. Nor did I care for his theory that the revolution would come first in advanced industrial countries. And he was autocratic and dogmatic." Marx's philosophy, moreover, said too little about "art, music, craftsmanship, creative imagination of literature. To me these are the things that are important. These are the things that have inspired me ever since I can remember."[78]

Pronouncing Marx "devoid of sympathy and clarity," Komroff turned to the works of Kropotkin, the Russian prince who had abandoned his aristocratic heritage to become the foremost leader and theorist of the anarchist movement. At the recommendation of Harry Kelly, Komroff read *An Appeal to the Young*, in which Kropotkin called on youthful idealists to join the cause of liberation, "the never-ceasing struggle for truth, justice, and equality among the people, whose gratitude you will earn—what nobler career can the youth of all nations desire than this?" Kropotkin's words made a powerful impression. "I was young when I read this pamphlet, and lost in a big, wide world," Komroff recalls. "It served as a compass and gave me direction. This direction changed my whole life." Komroff followed the *Appeal* with three of Kropotkin's full-length works, *Mutual Aid, Fields, Factories and Workshops,* and *Memoirs of a Revolutionist.* "Here we found a civilized socialism which had in it the spirit of freedom and was devoid of dogmatic certainties that soon dissolved into doubts," he remarks. "I loved Kropotkin. I became a philosophical anarchist. But also a pacifist and opposed to terrorism."[79]

Komroff was not alone among his contemporaries to fall under Kropotkin's spell. Kropotkin, after all, was the most venerated figure in the anarchist movement. His personal qualities exerted a strong attraction; and his writings, with their systematic and lucid presentation, had an irresistible charm which won him more than a few converts. All of his books were published in American editions, and his essays appeared and reappeared in left-wing publications, making him the most widely read anarchist writer in America. His portrait was hung in anarchist clubs, and a number of anarchist groups adopted his name.

Among the idealists and rebels of the Ferrer Association, Kropotkin found a particularly eager response. Reading his *Appeal to the Young*, they felt that they were among those "with warm hearts and noble natures" to whom its message was directed. For Elizabeth Gurley Flynn, the *Appeal* "struck home to me personally, as if he were speaking to us there in our shabby poverty-stricken Bronx flat. 'Must you drag on the same weary existence as your father and mother for thirty or forty years? Must you toil your life long to procure for others all the pleasures of well-being, of knowledge, of art, and keep for yourself only the eternal anxiety as to whether you can get a bit of bread?' "[80]

By his writing and personal example, Kropotkin influenced a whole range of figures in American life, anarchist and non-anarchist alike. His vision of a free society appealed to those who were repelled by an increasingly centralized and conformist world. His emphasis on the natural and spontaneous, his criticism of arid ideological dogma, his distrust of bureaucracy and standardization, his faith in voluntary cooperation and mutual aid, attracted an untold number of radicals and reformers. "He was a prominent figure in the realm of learning," wrote Emma Goldman in her memoirs, "recognized as such by the foremost men of the world. But to us he meant much more than that. We saw in him the father of modern anarchism, its revolutionary spokesman and brilliant exponent of its relation to science, philosophy, and progressive thought."[81]

Kropotkin, one could safely say, became the Ferrer Center's chief ideological mentor. In 1912, as we have seen, Will Durant made a pilgrimage to his home at Brighton; and later that year *Mother Earth* devoted a special seventieth birthday issue to him, with tributes by Leonard Abbott, Harry Kelly, Hippolyte Havel, Emma Goldman, and Alexander Berkman, who called him "my teacher and inspiration." For the same occasion, a celebration took place at Carnegie Hall, at which the Ferrer Association was prominently represented. Apart from Will Durant, moreover, Emma Goldman, Leonard Abbott, Harry Kelly, and Hippolyte Havel all visited Kropotkin in England, Sadakichi Hartmann met him in New York, and Carl Zigrosser sought his advice through correspondence. Bayard Boyesen, who had given Zigrosser a copy of Kropotkin's memoirs, spoke of "the enduring quality of their influence."[82]

Kropotkin's attraction extended beyond the anarchist movement to socialists, single-taxers, and other reformers, such as Hutchins Hapgood, Theodore Schroeder, and Bolton Hall. What appealed to them most, perhaps, was his ethical vision, his attacks on wage slavery and the division of labor, with their corrosive effect on human dignity, his quest for a balanced, integrated community, embracing fields as well as factories and manual as well as mental work. "Reading Kropotkin's *Memoirs of a Revolutionist*," Hapgood remarked, "one can detect no element of the egotistical attitude. Kropotkin desired neither self glory nor the destruction of individuals, no matter from what social background they might have been produced. Prominent and gifted as he was, his essential nobility enabled him beautifully to become genuinely assimilated into the revolutionary labor movement of the world."[83]

ART AND ANARCHY

Anarchism, with its spirit of daring and inquiry, its criticism of old standards and values, and its emphasis on individual freedom, innovation, and experiment, has always held a special attraction for artists and writers. It is the natural creed for intellectuals and bohemians who consider themselves aesthetically and socially in the avant-garde and therefore irrevocably opposed to the existing order. Anarchists, moreover, have been less tempted to set rules for artistic creation than other groups, and more inclined to accept art for what it is as it comes from the artist's workshop. Small wonder, then, that painters and sculptors, poets and novelists should have found anarchism a congenial doctrine.

As Hippolyte Havel observed: "A searcher for new expression is actually a rebel, and where do you find a rebel without anarchistic tendencies?"[84]

Thus, many well-known artists and writers have adhered to the anarchist movement or been influenced by anarchist ideas. Artists who have been linked to anarchism in one way or another include Gustave Courbet, Camille Pissarro, and Paul Signac in France, and Robert Henri, George Bellows, and Man Ray in the United States. Among the writers are figures of such stature as Oscar Wilde and George Bernard Shaw, Leo Tolstoy and Franz Kafka, James Joyce and Eugene O'Neill. What drew these and other artistic and literary rebels to anarchism was their conviction that the freedom of the individual was indispensable for the flowering of culture. They believed that a libertarian society would be more favorable to the artist than any other, that art, indeed, depends on the full and free development of individual capacities. Their search for self-development and self-expression, their desire to live and work free from academic and government restrictions, to assert their independence of all conventions and restraints, drove them inevitably along the anarchist path.

Combined with their quest for personal freedom and sense of alienation from existing aesthetic values was an acute social awareness, a sympathy for the sufferings of the poor, which drew them to the anarchist creed. They too were responding to Kropotkin's *Appeal to the Young*, which called on writers and artists to "come and take the side of the oppressed because you know that the beautiful, the sublime, the spirit of life itself are on the side of those who fight for light, for humanity, for justice." "You poets, painters, sculptors, musicians," Kropotkin exhorted, "if you understand your true mission and the very interests of art itself, come with us. Place your pen, your pencil, your chisel, your ideas at the service of the revolution."[85]

Between 1890 and 1920, it is probably no exaggeration to say, anarchism became the favorite doctrine of the literary and artistic avant-garde, in America as well as in Europe. For creative rebels, as Daniel Aaron has noted, anarchism and anarcho-syndicalism had a greater appeal than the more respectable schools of reform; and militants like Emma Goldman and Alexander Berkman, Bill Haywood and Bill Shatoff, were closer to the spirit of artistic rebellion than the bread-and-butter theorists of trade-unionism and social democracy, who seemed tame and colorless beside the advocates of direct action and social revolt. According to Art Young of *The Masses*, "many of the best artists and writers of that period thought of themselves as Anarchists, not as Socialists. They wanted to be at liberty to act as individuals without the restrictions of government, Mrs. Grundy's opinion, or any other frustrating element."[86]

Some of these writers and artists became mere anarchist sympathizers, but others wrote and drew for anarchist publications, while still others became intimately involved in the day-to-day workings of the movement, teaching in Ferrer schools and participating in protests and demonstrations. For all of them, whatever their degree of commitment, aesthetic and social rebellion went hand in hand. "The work of the artist, the composer, the painter, the sculptor, or the writer mirrors the reflex of the various struggles, hopes, and aspirations of our social life," declared Hippolyte Havel. "The creative artist has the deepest appreciation of the tendencies of his time. He is therefore the fittest exponent of new ideals, the coming reconstruction; indeed, he is the prophet of the future social order."[87]

In other words, avant-garde art and radical politics were part of the same revolutionary process. As Hutchins Hapgood put it: "Post-Impressionism is as disturbing in one field as the I.W.W. is in another. It turns up the soil, shakes the old foundations, and leads to new life, whether the programs and ideas have permanent validity or not."[88]

This combination of revolutionary politics and revolutionary art was nowhere more evident than at the Ferrer Center, a place where cultural experimentation mingled with social insurgency in virtually every sphere of activity. To those who frequented the Center, art constituted a revolutionary force, a powerful instrument of change; and what they sought was an upheaval that would be at once political, social, and aesthetic, an overthrow of traditional forms in every area of life. "The Anarchists, be it understood, are not only rebels in the economic field," proclaimed Hippolyte Havel, "but also in the realm of science, literature and art, in short in every endeavor of the human mind. The prevailing views of ethics and morality find in us their most uncompromising opponents. Our mission is not only to change economic conditions but to revolutionize the human mind in every direction."[89]

In their quest for arguments with which to attack the established order, many of the Ferrer School iconoclasts turned to Nietzsche and Ibsen, whose works exposed the shams and hypocrisies of bourgeois life, indeed whose very names represented all that was independent, emancipating, and unconventional in modern thought. Eager for fresh areas of exploration, fresh modes of expression, fresh tools for analyzing the individual and society, they turned also to the teachings of Freud, which further undermined accepted beliefs and provided yet another key to self-understanding and emancipation. Freud's strictures against "civilized" sexual morality, like those of Edward Carpenter and Havelock Ellis, struck a particularly responsive chord. His ideas were eagerly discussed at Ferrer Center meetings, cropping up in the lectures of Will Durant, Theodore Schroeder, and Emma Goldman, who had heard Freud lecture in Vienna in 1896 and again at Clark University in 1909 during his only visit to America. "I was deeply impressed by the lucidity of his mind and the simplicity of his delivery," she later recalled. "Among the array of professors, looking stiff and important in their university caps and gowns, Sigmund Freud, in ordinary attire, unassuming, almost shrinking, stood out as a giant among pygmies."[90] Among the Ferrer Association stalwarts, Dr. Liber was to become a psychiatrist and André Tridon a lay analyst who in 1920 brought out a pirated edition of Freud's *General Introduction to Psychoanalysis*. Tridon, however, dissented from Freud's doctrine of sublimation as "romantic nonsense."[91]

The Ferrer Center emerged as a laboratory of artistic innovation during the years preceding the war. In keeping with their educational theories, its members sought to develop all of their creative abilities, and they tried their hand at photography as well as painting, at drama as well as the dance. Lola Ridge not only wrote poems for *Mother Earth* but designed the cover for one of Emma Goldman's pamphlets. Max Weber (the painter), by the same token, contributed verse as well as woodcuts to *The Modern School* magazine; and Manuel Komroff, Sadakichi Hartmann, and Man Ray all experimented in a variety of art forms. Like Kropotkin and William Morris, they foresaw a central place for art in the future libertarian society, and they sought to make culture accessible to ordinary working people rather than the special preserve of the wealthy and educated. Accordingly, Emma Goldman popularized new literary and dramatic currents, Will Durant the history of ideas. With the same purpose, Leonard Abbott conducted his weekly class in literature, discussing Blake, Shelley, and Byron, Emerson, Thoreau, and Whitman, Nietzsche, Ibsen, and Shaw.

"Every new work of literary value—and also old ones for that matter—was discussed at the center," recalled Arthur Samuels.[92] Of the older writers it was Whitman who had the greatest appeal. Apostle of plebeian democracy and sexual freedom, Whitman had liberated verse from formal conventions, sung of the ordinary worker, called on young Americans to "resist much, obey little," and said "I am for those who have never been mastered." Libertarians of all stripes admired Whitman's expansive spirit and egalitarian values ("I am the sworn poet of every dauntless rebel the world over"). They considered him one of their own, "uncouth, elemental, Anarchistic." Manuel Komroff and William Thurston Brown wrote pamphlets about his work, Voltairine de Cleyre called him a "supremely Anarchist" writer, and once a year Emma Goldman and a troop of Whitman enthusiasts met at the Hotel Brevoort to discuss his work. Whitman's friend and secretary Horace Traubel was a contributor to *The Modern School* magazine, and his daughter Gertrude Traubel taught piano at the 107th Street school. Whitman's poems were frequently reprinted in anarchist periodicals, *Mother Earth* among them. And during the antiradical hysteria of 1919 *The Modern School* devoted a special issue to Whitman, who, said Leonard Abbott, "would have held out his hands to Emma Goldman, Berkman, Haywood, and Debs in their prison cells."[93]

At the Ferrer Center itself, writers of every type abounded. There were novelists and poets, journalists and historians, playwrights and critics, nearly all of whom could be counted on to recite from their works or contribute to *The Modern School* magazine. Among the poets, Lola Ridge and Edwin Markham have been mentioned; but there were many others, including Harry Kemp, the "hobo poet" from Mornington, Ohio, crude and slovenly, who wrote for *Revolt* and *Mother Earth* in addition to *The Modern School*. Journalists were equally numerous, among them Lincoln Steffens, Upton Sinclair, and Charles Edward Russell, not to mention Leonard Abbott and Hutchins Hapgood, whose works treated unorthodox subjects—anarchists, immigrants, labor militants—in an original way. Konrad Bercovici wrote sketches of the Lower East Side and works of fiction, biography, and travel.

It was at the Ferrer Center, furthermore, that young novelists like Manuel Komroff and Mike Gold (then still Irwin Granich) got their start. Gold was one of a number of well-known American Communists—Robert Minor was another—who began their radical careers as anarchists. For in those years, Gold remarked, anarchism was "still a brilliant and fearless" revolutionary movement, with which he was proud to be associated. Hearing of the Ferrer Center in 1914, he went there and "discovered history, poetry, science, and the class struggle." At night he worked as a porter for the Adams Express Company, "but in my mind," he says, "I lived in the idealistic world of Shelley, Blake, Whitman, and Kropotkin."[94]

On the periphery of the movement were such celebrated writers as Eugene O'Neill and Theodore Dreiser, who occasionally attended the Center's lectures and theatrical performances. Dreiser, in addition, contributed an article in a Nietzschean vein to Hippolyte Havel's *Revolt*, published in the Center's basement, calling for a thoroughgoing revaluation of existing values ("Nothing is fixed; All is permitted and possible"). In the 1920s Dreiser penned a sympathetic portrait of Emma Goldman (her life was "the richest of any woman of our century") and encouraged her to write her autobiography: "You are—and will remain—a great force."[95]

THE FREE THEATRE

During the summer of 1914, Moritz A. Jagendorf proposed the establishment of a "Free Theatre" at the Ferrer Center. Anarchists and socialists alike recognized the power of the drama as an instrument of propaganda as well as a vehicle of art, and they were anxious to exploit its possibilities in spreading the gospel of social emancipation. Few media, they felt, had the capacity to stir the emotions and sympathies of the public as did the stage. Emma Goldman, for one, had a passionate love for the theater and herself possessed distinct dramatic talent which manifested itself in her lectures. She served as manager of the Orleneff and Nazimova troupe when it toured the United States in 1905 and 1906, often spoke on the theater, and published a book called *The Social Significance of the Modern Drama*. The stage, as she saw it, was the "strongest force in developing social discontent," and such playwrights as Ibsen, Hauptmann, and Chekhov represented "the social iconoclasts of our time."[96]

Not surprisingly, then, Jagendorf's idea was greeted with enthusiasm, and a small theater was launched at the Center which both antedated and influenced the more famous Washington Square Players and Provincetown Players in Greenwich Village. Jagendorf, the driving force of the enterprise, was a young, energetic dentist who in later years would become a well-known authority on folklore, publishing more than thirty books on the subject. Born in Czernowitz, Austria, in 1888, he grew up with an independent cast of mind and at thirteen was already reading Max Stirner's *Ego and His Own*, the bible of unrestrained individualism. The words "you can do as you wish," he later recalled, "leaped from the page, and I became an anarchist and the bane of my poor mother's life."[97] Two years later, in 1903, Jagendorf emigrated to the United States. Completing high school, he spent a year at Yale studying law but hated it and gave it up. He then enrolled at Columbia where, in 1912, he came across the journal *Mother Earth*. It made a deep impression and he wrote to Emma Goldman, who invited him to come to the Ferrer Center. Thus began an association which ended only with the closing of the Center six years later.

The first production of the Free Theatre was given in the back yard of the school on September 5, 1914. It was a one-act play by Jagendorf himself, dealing with "those who spend their nights on wooden park benches instead of a warm bed." José Rubio, a Spanish anarchist at the Center, took the leading role and "struggled with the English words more valiantly than Don Quixote with the mills." The performance came off with cheers from the audience and catcalls and missiles from the neighbors.[98]

Since the use of the yard depended as much on good weather as on the friendly disposition of the neighbors, Jagendorf decided to move the theater indoors. Assisted by volunteers, including his tiny, doll-like wife Sophie (or "Cupie," as her friends called her), he improvised a small stage in the auditorium on which, week after week, were given performances "of which any little theatre would be proud." The children of the Day School were encouraged to take part, and they staged their own productions under the guidance of Jagendorf, "blasting us with the white fire of his creative drive," while his wife "fluttered about trying to calm and soothe us."[99]

During its first season, in 1914-1915, the Free Theatre put on a variety of plays by American and European writers. Audiences packed the narrow room to see works by Maeterlinck and Galsworthy, O'Casey and Synge, "provocative, interesting, and vital."[100] Jagendorf wrote to Lord Dunsany, who sent plays in manuscript, two of which, satirizing religion and government, had their American premiere at the Center. André Tridon staged a drama by Robert Browning called *Porphyria's Lover*; there was a one-act play by Manuel Komroff that "no one understood except in its maze of falling newspaper streamers"; and in another one-acter, by W. W. Gibson, the characters remained immobile throughout the production. Performances on a larger scale were given at the Lenox Casino on 116th Street and the auditorium of Wanamaker's department store, where audiences ran to several hundred. Marc Epstein, the printer of *Mother Earth*, provided beautiful programs and forgot the cost. It was all immensely gratifying, Jagendorf recalls. "There were pleasure, happy hard work, and humor—which is the way life should be."[101]

Jagendorf's enterprise held a pioneering place in the "little theater" movement which emerged in New York during the war. Links between the Free Theatre and drama groups in Greenwich Village were numerous. Floyd Dell brought his troupe from the Liberal Club to perform at the Ferrer Center, and members of both companies had a role in forming the Washington Square Players, of which Jagendorf briefly served as director. The Provincetown Players, launched in 1916, emerged from the same circles, with Floyd Dell, Hutchins Hapgood, Eugene O'Neill, William Zorach, and Stella Ballantine (Emma Goldman's niece) among the founders. Harry Weinberger, a close friend of Emma and Berkman, became the group's attorney, and M. Eleanor Fitzgerald, Berkman's companion, its manager and most vital figure. Among its first productions were works by Mike Gold and John Reed, as well as Dell and O'Neill, all of whom attended the Ferrer Center.

O'Neill's relationship with anarchism, going back a number of years, merits some discussion. In 1907, a dropout from Princeton, O'Neill was introduced to Benjamin Tucker, America's leading individualist anarchist, by Louis Holladay, whose sister Polly we have already encountered. O'Neill spent many hours in Tucker's bookshop on Sixth Avenue, browsing in all shades of advanced thought, from Tolstoy and Kropotkin to Nietzsche and Shaw, not to mention the works of Tucker himself, which, on O'Neill's own testimony, greatly influenced his "inner self."[102] On one visit he found Tucker in a state of excitement about Stirner's *Ego and His Own*, which he had just published in its first English translation, and O'Neill was deeply impressed by this "veritable breviary of destruction," this "striking and dangerous book," as James Gibbons Huneker called it. He also read Nietzsche's *Thus Spake Zarathustra* and later told Benjamin De Casseres that it "has influenced me more than any book I've read." In addition, O'Neill began to read Emma Goldman's *Mother Earth* and, to his father's chagrin, began to echo her views. According to his biographer, she became "one of O'Neill's idols."[103]

A few years later, when O'Neill became part of the New York bohemian scene, he came to know Goldman personally, as well as Berkman and other anarchists, including Hippolyte Havel, Robert Henri, and Manuel Komroff, who was his editor at Liveright. Among O'Neill's favorite haunts was Polly's Restaurant, and it was there that he got to know Havel, whom he would depict, still denouncing the bourgeoisie ("Capitalist swine! Stupid bourgeois monkeys!") as Hugo Kalmar ("one-time editor of Anarchist periodicals") in *The Iceman Cometh*.[104]

Another of O'Neill's anarchist friends, perhaps the closest of them all, was Terry Carlin, whom he would immortalize as Larry Slade, the "old foolosopher," in *Iceman*. A tall, stooped Irishman with gaunt face, yellow teeth, and disheveled grey hair, Carlin was a prime specimen of the hard-drinking and spellbinding talkers who inhabit the pages of Irish literature.[105] Unkempt, unwashed, but charming, Carlin, like O'Neill, had been a disciple of Benjamin Tucker during the early years of the century and secretary of the Liberty Group in Chicago. Giving up work as a tanner, he became a drifter who maintained himself largely on handouts, sponging off O'Neill, Dreiser, and Hutchins Hapgood, among others. Hapgood, who had known him since his Chicago days and made him the hero of *An Anarchist Woman*, thought him "a man of great intensity and a passionate sense of justice, and capable of great devotion."[106]

Apart from providing the model for Larry Slade, Carlin gave O'Neill the idea for one of the main strands of *Iceman*'s plot when he told him the inside story of the McNamara dynamite case and how Donald Vose, the son of a Home Colony anarchist, had wormed his way into *Mother Earth* and the Ferrer Center and betrayed David Caplan and Matthew Schmidt, who had been involved in the bombing. Vose appears in *Iceman* as Don Parritt (i.e. "stool-pigeon," as Hugo Kalmar brands him in the play), a guilt-racked soul who had informed on his own mother.[107]

O'Neill took Carlin and Havel seriously, as few but their closest friends did. "After Hippolyt'd had a few drinks he would get up in the center of the room and whirl around, while the rest of us laughed," recalled Dorothy Day, then Max Eastman's assistant on *The Masses*. "But not Gene! 'This man's been in every prison in Europe,' he would say. 'He's suffered for what he believes in.'

Gene was very responsive to people who had suffered."[108] For this reason, he had a special sympathy for Berkman, who had spent fourteen years in prison for his assassination attempt on Frick. "As for my fame (God help us!) and your infame," O'Neill wrote Berkman in 1927, "I would be willing to exchange a good deal of mine for a bit of yours. It is not hard to write what one feels as truth. It is damned hard to live it."[109]

O'Neill came to the defense of both Berkman and Goldman during their antidraft agitation of 1917 and sent Goldman a volume of plays after her imprisonment for obstructing the war effort. She had been one of the first to recognize his importance as a modern dramatist, and she afterwards lectured on him in England. Through M. Eleanor Fitzgerald of the Provincetown Players, O'Neill was kept "au courant with the shattering disenchantment in the Soviet Utopia suffered by Berkman and Emma Goldman," writes Isaac Don Levine. Having absorbed Tucker's individualism and hostility to state socialism, he "entertained no illusions about the realities of the Soviet situation and never allowed himself to be drawn into the fashionable pro-Soviet currents that later engulfed most of the American literary world."[110]

ROBERT HENRI

The most popular of the adult activities at the Ferrer Center was the art class conducted by Robert Henri and George Bellows. Henri, a philosopher and writer as well as a painter, was a powerful influence on the development of American art in the twentieth century. He inspired hundreds of talented pupils, organized and encouraged exhibitions of progressive art, and was the leader of the famous group of painters known as The Eight. "When I listen to Henri talk, or read his book," wrote Bellows, referring to *The Art Spirit*, "I say to myself his is one of the finest voices which express the philosophy of modern men in painting."[111]

Born in 1865 of old American stock, Henri, as Van Wyck Brooks remarked, emerged "out of a Bret Harte story of the West," where his father, a land speculator, was also a professional gambler. As a young man, Henri studied art in Philadelphia. Then, in 1889, he went to Paris, returning two years later fired with enthusiasm for avant-garde painting and social ideas. Over the next two decades, in Brooks's words, he became "the arch-radical and high priest of all the rebels against the 'genteel tradition.' "[112] As leader of The Eight, he launched a frontal attack upon established Victorian standards and the entrenched power of academic art. To Henri and his associates the gentility of the academy was a sign of effeteness and decay, of a failure to confront the newer and more vital aspects of American society. "What we need," Henri declared, "is more sense of the wonder of life and less of this business of picture-making."

Breaking with older conventions, The Eight turned to the realistic depiction of urban life. With their illustrator's technique and documentary style, they captured the vigor and dynamism of the city and created a new kind of painting with a new set of characters—peddlers, gypsies, Indians, Negroes, pugilists, immigrants, laborers, and others whose behavior and appearance embodied a freedom from middle-class American proprieties. Relishing the "sheer vitality of struggling against lifeless academicism," as Milton Brown has put it,[113] they confronted the environment on its own terms, with all its angularity and rawness. They found the congested and turbulent life of the slums more exciting than the humdrum existence of the middle classes or the straitlaced formality of the rich. Amid the squalor and poverty they found happiness, laughter, the joy of living. To Henri, the poor and humble were "my people," a world of individual types "through whom the dignity of life is manifest."[114]

The work of these realists represented the first phase of an artistic revolution in early twentieth-century America. In 1908 The Eight held an exhibition at the Macbeth Gallery in New York, and for the next five years they were dominant among the younger generation of artists. Clearly a new force had been liberated in American art. To conservatives and academicians, The Eight and their disciples were a "Revolutionary Gang," a "Black School," the "Ash Can School." But to others, like the critic Giles Edgerton, they were creating an original art by taking account of "our towering, crude, vibrating, nervous, uncertain civilization" and depicting "our East Side polyglot populace."[115]

Henri and his Ash Can circle were philosophically committed to the social revolution and the amelioration of the lot of the poor whom they portrayed in their paintings. Henri always felt a deep sympathy for the downtrodden and exploited. At the root of his philosophy, says Milton Brown, was "an ethical concept of justice."[116] All his thinking and all his activity were motivated by that idea, coupled with an intense faith in the dignity and brotherhood of man, which found expression in his portraits of people of many races and nationalities.

It was this faith in the dignity of the individual that led Henri to distrust the academic establishment and traditional artistic instruction, which, he felt, limited natural growth by imposing fixed standards from above. He opposed tradition, moreover, because it seemed to him a bulwark against progress, perpetuating conditions, both social and aesthetic, that he deemed unjust. To Henri the new meant life and freedom, the old oppression and death. "Every movement, every evidence of search is worthy of consideration," he declared. "Every one who has shown the world the way to beauty, to true culture, has been a rebel, a 'universal' without patriotism, without home, who has found his people everywhere, a man whom all the world recognizes, accepts, whether he speaks through music, painting, words or form."[117]

It was Henri's fervent belief, writes Carl Zigrosser, that only freedom can bring out the best in the individual. Given this conviction, it is not surprising that he should have considered himself an anarchist, a doctrine to which he adhered from the 1890s until his death in 1929. His interest in anarchism was aroused during his student days in Paris, when the movement was at the height of its influence. Becoming a "great reader" of Bakunin, he drew further inspiration from such thinkers as Nietzsche, Ibsen, and Whitman, and concluded in the end that "all government is violence."[118]

Henri made no secret of his anarchist beliefs, though this is an aspect of his life that is not well known or understood. He was outraged by the American government's callous treatment of the Indians and by the attempt by Pinkertons to suppress the Homestead steel strike, in which his future comrade Berkman tried to assassinate Frick. In 1917 Henri was to serve on a committee to prevent Berkman's extradition to California to face charges of complicity with Mooney and Billings in their famous bombing case in San Francisco.[119] At the same time, he championed other radical causes, from birth control to industrial unionism, and when Emma Goldman was imprisoned for "daring to tell the laboring women how to have fewer idiots and scrawny degenerates," Henri fought for her release as a member of the Birth Control Committee, which mounted protests at Union Square, Carnegie Hall, and the Harlem River Casino.[120] Apart from Berkman and Goldman, Henri's friends at the Ferrer Center included Sadakichi Hartmann, whom he had known years before in Philadelphia, and Bill Haywood, who visited his art studio. Both Henri and Bellows served on the advisory board of the Ferrer Association and donated paintings in support of the Lawrence strike of 1912.[121]

How did Henri become associated with the Modern School? Once again, as with Bayard Boyesen, Moritz Jagendorf, and many others, it was Emma Goldman who was responsible. By 1911 Henri had been reading her magazine *Mother Earth* and was curious to hear her speak. "Like many another," he tells us, "I had heard of her as a violent and dangerous agitator, an Anarchist bent on the destruction of the institutions of our civilization and an advocate of chaos." He was determined to see for himself; and in January 1911 he attended one of her lectures. What he found was remote from the stereotype created by the popular press. On the platform stood a "cool, logical and brilliant speaker, appealing to the reason and understanding of her audience." He was overwhelmed with feelings of admiration. "A woman of remarkable address and convincing presence," he confided to his diary. "I had never heard so good a lecture. This is a very great woman." He also liked what she had to say: "Her arguments are for order and for human kindness; and they are undoubtedly destroying to all those institutions of our civilization which not only make possible, but bring about war, labor strife, all kinds of prostitution, and education which does not set the spirit free."[122]

Hungry for more, Henri the very next day read her *Anarchism and Other Essays*, fresh off the presses of the Mother Earth Publishing Association. He pronounced it "a great work by a great and noble woman." For the rest of the year he faithfully attended her lectures and came to regard her as "one of the world's greatest fighters for the freedom and growth of the human spirit."[123]

At one Sunday afternoon lecture Henri mustered the courage to introduce himself. "I enjoy your magazine," he told her, "especially the articles on Whitman. I love Walt, and follow everything that is written about him." Emma recognized her admirer as a kindred spirit, and a friendship developed between them. Afterwards Henri wrote a tribute to her in *Mother Earth* and painted her portrait at his studio in Gramercy Park, while they talked about art, literature, and education. "I learned to know Henri as an exceptional personality, a free and generous nature," she writes in her memoirs. "He was in fact an anarchist in his conception of art and its relation to life."[124]

Toward the end of 1911, Emma Goldman invited Henri to teach an evening art class at the Ferrer School. Welcoming the opportunity to put into practice the libertarian educational principles he had long held, he eagerly accepted. What was more, he interested his friend and former pupil George Bellows in the project. Together, says Emma Goldman, "they helped to create a spirit of freedom in the art class which probably did not exist anywhere else in New York at that time."[125]

Henri's association with the Ferrer Center continued nearly seven years. He taught there virtually throughout its entire existence, coming to East Twelfth Street during the winter of 1911-1912, moving with the school to East 107th Street the following fall, and remaining until it closed in the spring of 1918. His colleague Bellows stayed nearly as long, dividing his enthusiasm between anarchism and socialism until he abandoned them both in 1917 when the war trumpets sounded for America. Of New England pioneer stock, Bellows had grown up in Columbus, Ohio, and was a star infielder for the Ohio State University baseball team. Nobody would have taken him for an artist, with his homespun manner and athlete's physique, yet he left college in 1904 to study with Henri in New York.

Though seventeen years apart in age, master and pupil hit it off at once. Henri encouraged Bellows, as he did all his pupils, not to fret over preliminary plans or sketches but to paint swiftly and forthrightly whatever moved him. Assimilating Henri's teachings, Bellows soon matched him in technical proficiency. He showed a unique gusto and sense of action as well as a "search for the monumental in the realm of the commonplace."[126] He became the most popular of the Ash Can painters, winning public acceptance as the embodiment of such American virtues as bigness, vitality, and rugged individualism. While studying with Henri, Bellows found that his teacher's views on life and society also agreed with his own. The two became intimate friends, and their friendship, unspoiled by jealousy or rivalry, flourished until Bellows' untimely death from a ruptured appendix in 1925.

In their class at the Modern School Henri and Bellows made an extraordinarily effective team. Both were charming men and excellent, inspiring teachers. They taught without pay two evenings a week, alternating with one another. The class was meant primarily for adults, though a few of the older children attended. (Smaller children received art instruction during regular daytime hours from Amy Londoner, Adolf Wolff, and William Zorach.) For the most part, the students did paintings and charcoal drawings, but also sculpture, clay modeling, and woodcuts. A notable feature of the class was drawing from a nude model, to the accompaniment of piano music by Hyman Rovinsky, who improvised by the hour.[127]

Henri and Bellows attracted to their class a large group of young men and women, many of whom have become notable in the history of art in this century. Among those who attended were John Sloan, Rockwell Kent, Man Ray, Max Weber, Abraham Walkowitz, Samuel Halpert, Adolf Wolff, William and Marguerite Zorach, William Gropper, Niles Spencer, Helen West, Martha Gruening, Paul Rohland, Jean Liberté, Andrée Ruellan. Sol Wilson, Robert Brackman, Moses Soyer, Harry Wickey, Ben Benn, Robert Minor, and Kenneth Russell Chamberlain. Another famous pupil, as Henri's diary reveals, was Leon Trotsky, who lived for two months in New York in early 1917, before returning to Russia.[128]

As a teacher, even more than as a painter, Henri was one of the leading influences in twentieth-century American art. He himself, perhaps, never developed into a truly great artist, but a number of his students did, and in this sense he can justly be labeled the father of modern American painting. He had extraordinary personal magnetism as well as a fervor, a passion for communicating his ideas. A tall, lean figure with a sallow face and Eurasian features, he taught, as William Innes Homer notes, "with a quiet, concentrated intensity of speech and gesture, though he could lash out against anything he believed was wrong or unjust."[129] Warm and sympathetic, he could inspire both personal devotion and devotion to art like no other teacher of his time. On this we have the testimony of his pupils, whom he imbued with a self-confidence and spirit of independence which they might otherwise have lacked. "Henri," declared John Sloan, "could make anyone want to be an artist, and in his presence he could make pupils with mere flickerings of talent blossom and do work with considerable vitality." For years, Sloan, when asked where a young man should study art, always said, "with Henri, none other." Rockwell Kent went even further. As an inspirational force, he wrote, Henri was "possibly the most important figure in our cultural history."[130]

With the rest of the Modern School faculty, Henri deplored conventional methods of instruction. "You cannot impose education on anyone," he declared. "The school is not a place where students are fitted into the groove of rule and regulation but where personality and originality of vision is encouraged, and inventive genius in the search for specific expression is stimulated." He therefore championed self-education, and self-education only. "It seems to me," he remarked, "that before a man tries to express anything to the world he must recognize in himself an individual, a new one very distinct from others. Walt Whitman did this, and that is why I think his name so often comes to me. The one great cry of Whitman was for a man to find himself, to understand the fine thing he really is if liberated." The ideal school, Henri felt, was one which stimulated the development of each student as an individual, "recognizing in him a man, another new force; giving him the use of knowledge and experience but never dictating to him what or how he shall do."[131]

And Henri practiced what he preached. His class at the Ferrer School involved no systematic instruction. He did not impose his own style or methods on his pupils. "I have little interest in teaching you what I know," he told them. "I wish to stimulate you to tell me what *you* know." Insofar as he dwelled on technique at all, he emphasized "living line, living form, living color." He also encouraged his students to paint and draw swiftly. "Work with great speed," he said. "Have your energies alert, up and active. Finish as quickly as you can. There is no virtue in delaying." For the most part, however, he merely looked and suggested, cultivating spontaneity and individual initiative. "He does not teach—he guides—and therein lies his success," a pupil remarked. Adolf Wolff said that the sum total of his instruction amounted to the command, "Be thyself."[132]

The recollections of Harry Wickey and Moses Soyer will serve to illustrate Henri's method. Wickey, freshly arrived from the midwest, went to the Ferrer Center in 1914 with a portfolio of his sketches and compositions. Henri looked them over very carefully and put about a dozen aside. "I would be very proud if I were the author of that work," he said. Wickey was thrilled: "I didn't quite believe the statement but received a great deal of encouragement from it nevertheless." For the next six months he continued to study with Henri and Bellows, "and, although I do not recall their ever having given me one piece of technical advice, they did provide an atmosphere that was stimulating to one of my temperament."[133]

Moses Soyer had a similar reaction after a single visit to the class. Henri, uncharacteristically, criticized one of his drawings for its academic and superficial cleverness. Soyer was so struck by Henri's remarks that the whole direction of his artistic development was altered. Returning home, he "elatedly" described the encounter to his brothers Raphael and Isaac, who were also aspiring young artists. They were deeply impressed, Soyer tells us, and "that night the light burned late in our room."[134]

Under the impact of Henri's personality, young artists such as Wickey and Soyer felt a sense of exhilaration, of undergoing a crucial experience, never to be repeated, which would profoundly affect their lives. They learned a great deal from Henri, and not only about art. He discoursed freely on a wide range of subjects, "giving his pupils the equivalent of a liberal education." "Henri was a wonderful teacher," Robert Brackman remembers. "He talked about literature, philosophy, and religion, as well as art. I also heard Emma Goldman lecture on economics. I used to study everything there. That's where I got all my education. It made a big impression on me. It made me think."[135]

Henri, as we have noted, possessed a deep sympathy for the oppressed, and succeeded in communicating it to his students. He influenced their thinking on social and political questions, instilling them with a respect for working people, immigrants, persecuted minorities, and children. "Feel the dignity of the child. Do not feel superior to him, for you are not," he told them, echoing the whole tradition of libertarian education from Godwin to Ferrer. "Henri," Dr. Liber summed it up, "was not only an artist, but a great teacher and a powerful personality. He held the most advanced ideas regarding life in general, social conditions, modern education, and he always gave his views to his students unstintingly."[136]

Nor was this all. To enable members of his class to display their work, Henri organized exhibitions at the Ferrer Center which "attracted large crowds and interested criticism."[137] He also lent the school reproductions of famous paintings to hang on the walls in order to cultivate the love of beautiful things. From time to time he would drop in during the day to see how the children were progressing. "He would talk to us about Paris, about art," recalls Révolte Bercovici. "The man knew color, the man knew life, and I used to get up and dance for him. He was a natural teacher."[138] It was at his instigation that an exhibition of the children's art work was held at the Macdowell Gallery in 1915. That same year he got the children tickets to see Isadora Duncan, whom he passionately admired. ("Isadora dances and fills the universe," he wrote in *The Art Spirit*. "She exceeds all ordinary measure.") The children were entranced. "She opened up a new world of music and light and rhythm to us," Emma Cohen remembers. "We went back to the school and danced and danced."[139]

THE MODERNISTS

In 1908, when The Eight offended conservative taste with their exhibition at the Macbeth Gallery, a second key event occurred in the history of twentieth-century American art: Alfred Stieglitz showed the work of Matisse at his 291 Gallery on Fifth Avenue. The Matisse show was the first to introduce French modernism to the United States, and it inaugurated Stieglitz's long campaign to win acceptance for abstract and expressionist art in this country. At 291 he fought against conservative elements in painting and photography, exhibited the work of foreign and native modernists, and emerged as the leading spokesman for artistic innovation in America. Aside from Henri, there was no more important figure in shaping the direction of twentieth-century American art.

It is interesting to note that Stieglitz, like Henri, was a philosophical anarchist and a supporter of Emma Goldman's *Mother Earth*.[140] He shared Henri's view that artistic individuality is sacred and that a work of art must express the unique personality which created it. Challenging traditional aesthetic standards, he presided, like Henri at the Ferrer Center, over freewheeling intellectual discussions at his 291 studio, which became yet another radical salon where artists and rebels could find congenial minds to thresh out the crucial issues of the day. According to Man Ray, 291 was a unique source of inspiration to the New York avant-garde in the years preceding the war.[141]

Man Ray was among a sizable group of Ferrer Center habitués who were "constant visitors" to 291, attracted by its proprietor's "restless life-breathing personality, his endless quest," as Hutchins Hapgood put it.[142] Hapgood himself was part of this company, as were Hippolyte Havel, Sadakichi Hartmann, Benjamin De Casseres, John Weichsel, Max Weber, Abraham Walkowitz, Samuel Halpert, William Zorach, Ben Benn, Adolf Wolff, and Alfred Kreymborg, several of whom wrote for Stieglitz's *Camera Work*, the staunchest defender of all advanced artistic currents of the day. "Among the bombthrowers I am acquainted with," declared Havel in the journal, "Alfred Stieglitz stands without doubt in the foremost rank. He is a most dangerous agitator, a great disturber of the peace; more than any other man he has helped to undermine old institutions; he has helped to kill venerable beliefs, and to destroy sacred traditions. An iconoclast in the realm of art, he has succeeded in shocking cruelly the moral guardians of classicism. At 291 he has created a social center unique in character, a battlefield for new ideas, where every sinner's confession is accepted at its own value."[143]

So it was that two radical tendencies emerged from the ferment in American art in the years before the war. The earlier was the native school of realists led by Henri, the later the modernist movement emanating from Paris with Stieglitz as its foremost champion. Both tendencies flourished at the Ferrer Center: the realists, who shocked the establishment more by their subjects—mostly scenes from the city slums—than by innovations in technique, and the expressionists, who experimented with new forms and struck out in new directions.

The balance shifted in favor of the latter with the celebrated Armory Show of 1913, which presented a striking selection of the principal European modernists as well as the work of their forerunners, Cézanne, Gauguin, and Van Gogh. Next to these artists, the work of Henri and The Eight, which had once seemed so daring and vital, appeared almost conventional to the youthful avant-garde, awakened to fresh possibilities of artistic creation. The impact of abstraction and expressionism gave rise to a new wave of art by which Henri and his followers were at least partially eclipsed.

Of the Ferrer Center modernists, the most notable were Max Weber, Abraham Walkowitz, Samuel Halpert, and Man Ray. All were of Jewish origin, born in Eastern Europe or in the ghettos of urban America. All had been in the avant-garde even before the Armory Show, which inspired them to undertake further experimentation and helped them find their identities. All but Man Ray had studied in Paris—and he was afterward to spend most of his life there—and they transmitted to their contemporaries the new ideas and approaches of the European avant-garde, mingled with the influence of their own Jewish heritage. All of them experimented in a variety of artistic media. They painted, modeled in clay, did woodcuts, drawings, watercolors, gouaches, pastels, and lithographs, and sculpted in metal and stone. Man Ray tried his hand at photography, and they all dabbled in poetry and criticism. Though despised by conventional critics, though regarded as dangerous subversives, even as madmen, degenerates, or charlatans, these young iconoclasts have since been crowned with success and popularity.

The oldest of the group, Max Weber (he was thirty-one when he began to frequent the Ferrer Center in 1912), was one of the few American Cubists of lasting importance. Holger Cahill rightly calls him "the child of the modern spirit," and according to John Baur, several of his paintings done between 1910 and 1915 "are among the most successful early abstractions produced in this country."[144] Living in Paris during a period of great artistic ferment, Weber was swept off his feet by the painting of Cézanne, Picasso, and Matisse, with whom he studied in 1907 and 1908. Returning to New York awhirl with new ideas, he developed a bold and highly individual artistic style which showed both Cubist and Futurist features. In 1911 he had his first exhibition at Stieglitz's 291 and another at the Murray Hill Gallery the following year. "The first impression, and the one that remains," wrote Hutchins Hapgood of the latter, "is the splendor of the color as a whole. Then, as you look at the paintings in detail, you notice that this man is a serious thinker, that he is struggling with the problems of form."[145] Henri, equally impressed, brought his students to see the show and persuaded the gallery to keep it on an extra week. (Mabel Dodge, it might be noted, bought three of the paintings.)

Weber and Henri became friends, and it was apparently Henri who introduced him to the Ferrer Center. A radical by temperament, Weber found the place very much to his taste and began to take part in its activities. In June 1913 he was a speaker at the third anniversary dinner of the Ferrer Association, along with Alexander Berkman, Harry Kelly, Hippolyte Havel, Hutchins Hapgood, James Morton, and Cora Bennett Stephenson. He contributed poetry and woodcuts to *The Modern School* and published two poems, "The Outcast" and "The Workmass," in Havel's *Revolt*.[146] Throughout the years he never lost his radical sympathies. "I would suggest to the artist and student," he declared in 1937, "to take time off from the life-class and go out among the people who toil in the mills and shops, go to scenes of bridge construction, foundries, excavation. There he will find the energy and heroism of those who create the wealth and wonder of modern times. Let the student look upon the artisan and mechanic as did the Greeks upon their gladiators, discus throwers and wrestlers."[147]

Fascinated by the dynamics of the city, with its lofty skyscrapers and great bridges, Weber, between 1912 and 1916, painted a series of New York scenes to which he applied Cubist and Futurist principles. His work was beginning to acquire a reputation within avant-garde circles, though he was still ignored or treated with contempt by conservative opinion. "Weber," wrote Manuel Komroff in 1915, "was ridiculed, laughed at, starved, excommunicated, censured, refused and annoyed as no man in art has ever been before. But he stood by the new spirit he had brought till it caught fire like a song in a revolution—and what happened then? Why, he was robbed, exploited, fleeced, pulled about, contorted by the imitators and judged by the critics."[148]

Primitivism was another theme that ran through Weber's work, and he steeped himself more deeply than any of his contemporaries in the art of the American Indian, which he studied with great intensity at the Museum of Natural History. In 1919 one of his early woodcuts in the primitivist vein appeared in *The Modern School* magazine, inspired by aboriginal sculptures of North and Central America. After this, he began to produce remarkable vignettes of Jewish life on the Lower East Side, thus returning to a favorite theme of the Henri school which the avant-garde had largely discarded. Weber had come full circle. Yet he did not entirely abandon the modernist approach. Rather he retained all his stylistic elements, old and new, in a unique combination. For the rest of his career, his work continued to breathe the spirit of freedom and experiment which had emerged in his Ferrer School years.

The paintings of Abraham Walkowitz, like those of Max Weber, offered a vision of the world which rejected traditional standards, both social and aesthetic. As *Camera Work* put it, "the spirit which urges men to free themselves from the bonds of obsolete laws and conventions permeates his work." Walkowitz and Weber had met as students in Paris and struck up a friendship which continued after their return to New York. They were frequent companions at the Ferrer Center and at 291, where Walkowitz exhibited his paintings in 1912 and 1915. "He is a true artist," wrote Ben Benn, reviewing the second show for *Revolt*, "whose works have a past, present and future."[149] Walkowitz, like Henri, was fascinated by the dancing of Isadora Duncan, and he became noted for the hundreds of drawings and watercolors he made of her. To Walkowitz, Isadora was the symbol of insurgent modernism, transforming the dance, as he and his colleagues were transforming art, into a medium of ecstatic expression.

The youngest and probably the most famous representative of the Ferrer Center avant-garde was Man Ray, born Emmanuel Rabinowitz in Philadelphia in 1890, the son of Russian-Jewish immigrants, who moved to New York when he was seven. Painter, photographer, film maker, Man Ray was a many-sided artist who set his distinctive stamp upon twentieth-century culture, in Europe as well as in America. All his life he experimented with new artistic media. Impish, witty, irreverent, given to riddles and puns, he became one of the founders of both Dadaism and Surrealism; indeed, he was the only American artist to play a leading role in these two far-reaching movements. He was a clever and versatile innovator, possessed of a sharp and fertile imagination with which he mocked established ideas and values.[150]

Man Ray grew up to be a small, wiry, talkative young man with dark hair and penetrating eyes. Though an avid reader (Thoreau and Whitman were among his favorite writers), and though he won a scholarship in architecture at New York University, he dropped his formal education after high school and worked at various jobs to support himself, living with his parents in Brooklyn. In 1908 he attended the exhibition of The Eight at the Macbeth Gallery and afterward became a regular visitor to the 291 Gallery, where Stieglitz "talked at length about modern art to anyone willing to listen to him."[151] It was there that he became interested in photography and, in all probability, first heard of Henri's art class at the Modern School.

Man Ray began to attend the Ferrer Center in the fall of 1912, just after its move to Harlem. Entering through the basement on his first visit, he discovered an animated crowd in the dining room drinking coffee served by "a small dark woman dressed in gypsy clothes, wearing long gold earrings" (it was Romany Marie). The art class, he was informed, was held on the floor above. Ascending the stairs, he found a nude model on a raised platform, "surrounded by a mixed group of all ages working away in various media: pencil, charcoal, watercolor and oil." The model was extremely attractive, "a magnificent, voluptuous blond with an ivory skin; every movement she made expressed languor and sensuality." His erotic impulses were strongly aroused. Indeed, the whole atmosphere of the place was stimulating. In addition to art, there were classes in literature and philosophy, not to mention a day school for children. "All courses were free," he later recalled. "Some well-known writers and painters volunteered their services as instructors; in fact, everything was free, even love." Everyone he met, students and teachers, was eager to discuss a whole range of subjects, social and political as well as aesthetic. "I went home that night with my head in a whirl, immense possibilities opened before me both in art and love."[152]

During Man Ray's second visit to the art class, a "tall, distinguished-looking man" came in. His face was "sallow and slightly pock-marked, with a thin nose." It was Henri, whose work he already admired for its "bold, slashing strokes and heightened color." Passing around the room from pupil to pupil, Henri made "gentle, encouraging remarks, but never touched the drawings nor criticized adversely." He talked of many things, and "I found his ideas more stimulating than any direct criticism." At another session, Bellows was the instructor. Speaking at length about "initiative and imagination," he selected some of Man Ray's drawings as exhibiting both of these qualities, much to the young man's encouragement.[153]

Among the friends Man Ray made at the Center were Bill Shatoff and Manuel Komroff, Hippolyte Havel and Adolf Wolff (thinly disguised as the sculptor Loupov in his autobiography). Wolff's seven-year-old daughter Esther, a beautiful child with big blue eyes and golden hair, poised and graceful in her movements, posed nude before the art class when a regular model was unavailable.

From December 28, 1912 to January 3, 1913 an exhibition of the students' work was held at the Center, including paintings by Man Ray, Manuel Komroff, Helen West, Ben Benn, and Gilbert Stodola. These were reproduced in the spring 1913 issue of *The Modern School* magazine. The autumn issue contained a woodcut by Man Ray as well as a poem by him, and the following summer he designed two antiwar covers for *Mother Earth*. These remarkable works, which are important for an understanding of Man Ray's artistic development, have escaped the attention of art historians. Produced during his pre-Dada period and showing strong Cubist and post-Impressionist influences, they reflect his emerging liberation from the realist conventions of the Henri school and foreshadow the best of his early modernist works, such as his portrait of Stieglitz and his large canvas of men and horses, *A.D. MCMXIV*. They reflect, too, his early political views: anarchism and antimilitarism. For instance, his August 1914 cover for *Mother Earth* depicts a two-headed monster, labeled "Capitalism" and "Government," devouring the struggling body of "Humanity."

Though Man Ray at this time was still living in Brooklyn, he continued to make the long trip to Harlem to attend the Modern School. "There were always new faces," he remembers, "people dropping in out of curiosity or in sympathy with liberal ideas."[154] One night, while he was sitting and talking in the tea room, a painter, Samuel Halpert, came in. Introduced by Romany Marie, the two young artists became friends. In the spring of 1913 they set out to explore the Palisades across the Hudson River and, at Ridgefield, New Jersey, found a peaceful spot near an orchard with a cluster of cabins and a view of the Jersey meadows, "striped and streaked with the Passaic and Hackensack rivers, lazily rolling away to the horizon."[155] Attracted by the quiet beauty of the place, so rural yet so close to New York, they rented one of the cabins from the old Polish blacksmith who owned them. When summer arrived, Alfred Kreymborg the poet came over with a chess set and mandolin to join them.

Ridgefield provided a welcome relief from the routines of city life, a refuge to work and think. Life in the woods inspired Man Ray with thoughts of Thoreau, and he "hoped some day to liberate myself from the restraints of civilization."[156] One Sunday afternoon Manuel Komroff, Bill Shatoff, Adolf Wolff, and Wolff's former wife, a French beauty named Adon Lacroix, came to visit, together with other Ferrer School friends. Komroff was so enchanted that he too rented a cabin, sharing it with a New York commercial artist, William Tisch.[157] Adon Lacroix also remained, becoming Man Ray's companion. Though she was slender and attractive, with fair hair and grey eyes, her face had a strained expression which Man Ray captures in the portraits he made of her during this period.

Other visitors to Ridgefield included Hippolyte Havel, Max Eastman, and William Carlos Williams, who practiced medicine in nearby Rutherford. Slowly a little artists' colony took shape in this Jersey retreat, where Kreymborg launched two literary reviews, *The Glebe* and *Others*. (The first issue of *The Glebe*, dated September 1913, consisted of Adolf Wolff's "Songs, Sighs and Curses.") In March 1915 Man Ray himself issued what his biographer has aptly called "America's first proto-Dada periodical," *The Ridgefield Gazook*, a single hand-produced sheet, folded to form four pages, in which he parodied Wolff ("Adolf Lupo"), Adon Lacroix ("Adon La+"), Kreymborg ("A. Kreambug"), Havel ("Hipp O'Havel"), Komroff ("Kumoff"), and a Czech anarchist, Joseph Kucera ("Mac Kucera"), who was Voltairine de Cleyre's last lover. Among other satirical devices, Man Ray employed an ink-blot, a blank square, and a drawing of three bombs served up on a tray with knife and fork.[158]

It was at the Ridgefield colony, during the summer of 1915, that Man Ray met Marcel Duchamp, beginning a friendship that lasted until Duchamp's death in 1968. Duchamp, newly arrived in the United States, was already an avant-garde celebrity because of the furor which had greeted his *Nude Descending a Staircase* at the 1913 Armory Show. During the next few years he and Man Ray exchanged views on art and influenced each other in numerous ways. Together with Francis Picabia they comprised the nucleus of a Dadaist school in New York even before the term was invented and the movement officially launched in Zurich in 1916.[159]

Man Ray had been evolving in this direction even before the eventful year of 1913, which saw the Ferrer Center exhibition, the Armory Show, and the formation of the Ridgefield colony. Not yet twenty-three, the "large-eyed, curly-haired dreamer," as Kreymborg depicts him, already had "an enviable record as a daring performer in versatile experiments." As Man Ray himself told Arturo Schwartz, the Armory Show merely served to encourage him "to pursue the way I had already chosen, to confirm my own intentions, as it were. I had a clear, firm will at the time. I knew what I wanted to do."[160] His meeting with Duchamp further accelerated his modernist development, and he quickly emerged as one of the pioneers of abstract art in America.

Until his departure for Paris in 1921, Man Ray remained close friends with Adolf Wolff and the rest of the Ferrer circle. In March 1919 he published a solitary issue of *TNT* with Wolff and Henry S. Reynolds, "a tirade," as he described it, "against industrialists [and] the exploitation of the workers. We were all mixed up with the anarchist group. It was anarchism rather than anything else. Socialism was beginning to come along, and that had a bad name in America too. But we were out-and-out anarchists."[161]

When Man Ray arrived in Paris, he was immediately welcomed as a member of the inner circle, and it was as a representative of the Paris avant-garde in the years between the wars that he secured his place in the history of modern art. Moving from Dadaism to Surrealism, he produced his extraordinary "Rayographs" and a rich variety of important work. He became so French, says Milton Brown, that people forgot he was an American, and so famous as a photographer that they forgot his achievements as a painter, which were considerable. Yet he himself always regarded painting as his first love. And he always remembered with affection his days at the Ferrer Center and Ridgefield, which he evokes in his memoirs published in 1963. In 1976 he died of a lung infection in his Paris studio at the age of eighty-six.[162]

The Modern School MAGAZINE

No discussion of the artistic achievements of the Ferrer movement would be complete without taking *The Modern School* magazine into account. Growing out of the *News Letter* of the Ferrer Association, which appeared in 1910 and 1911, *The Modern School* was one of the so-called "little magazines" which proliferated during the early decades of the century, mounting an attack upon the "genteel tradition" in the arts. Lovingly edited and printed, it became one of the most beautiful cultural journals ever published in America, rich alike in content and design. Launched in 1912, it continued until 1922, surveying the whole range of literary, artistic, and educational ferment of the period. According to Manuel Komroff, it "cut new furrows in a parched land."[163]

The idea of publishing *The Modern School* originated with Lola Ridge, who, in her own words, "started, edited, made up and saw to the printing, circulating and distributing" of the magazine.[164] Her companion, David Lawson, a gentle, soft-spoken young Scot, designed the cover for the first issue, which appeared in February 1912. A few months later, however, not long after the second number appeared, the couple abandoned New York, leaving the journal to other hands. Over the next ten years it was edited in turn by Leonard Abbott, Harry Kelly, William Thurston Brown, Carl Zigrosser, and Frank V. Anderson, with Manuel Komroff and Adolf Wolff as associate editors.

It was under the editorship of Zigrosser, from June 1917 to April 1919, that *The Modern School* reached its zenith, becoming a true work of art and one of the most interesting little reviews in the country. (The printing was done by Joseph Ishill, a latter-day William Morris, of whom more will be said in a later chapter.) "I have tried to make it a beautiful thing," wrote Zigrosser to a friend, "a medium of expression for creative thinkers and artists. It deals with radical ideas in education, and by education I mean every activity that broadens and enhances life."[165]

Zigrosser proved extremely resourceful in recruiting artistic and literary talent. During his editorial tenure, the contributors included the poets Hart Crane, Wallace Stevens, Maxwell Bodenheim, and Witter Byner, artists Rockwell Kent, Max Weber, Man Ray, and Raoul Dufy, and writers Mike Gold, Konrad Bercovici, Rabindranath Tagore, and Padraic Colum. Many of these figures Zigrosser knew personally, for instance Rockwell Kent, who not only contributed woodcuts and drawings but designed the cover and a whole alphabet of decorative initials, some of which are used in this book. Kent also designed the cover of Zigrosser's pamphlet *The Modern School*, which, depicting a boy playing with a dog, became the emblem of the Modern School Association of North America. "You and he are a wonderful combination," wrote Leonard Abbott of Zigrosser and Kent, "and I prophesy that some day bibliographers will search for, and will treasure, the copies of the 'Modern School' that express what you and he are doing together."[166]

For some of its readers, however, *The Modern School* concerned itself too much with literature and art and too little with education. After the Day School moved to Stelton, the colony leader Joseph Cohen complained that "a person can read the magazine every month from cover to cover and not suspect even that we are running a school and having a hard time making ends meet."[167]

Such criticisms had little foundation. Hardly an issue appeared that did not contain extended discussion of educational matters, both practical and theoretical. The magazine carried articles by Charlotte Perkins Gilman, Margaret Naumburg, and Caroline Pratt, and lists of recommended works on education by such writers as Rousseau, Godwin, Stirner, Pestalozzi, Froebel, Fourier, Owen, Maclure, Warren, Alcott, Emerson, Thoreau, Spencer, Proudhon, Bakunin, Kropotkin, Tolstoy, Robin, Faure, and Ferrer, not to mention John Dewey, A. S. Neill, and Bertrand Russell. Furthermore, excerpts from these works appeared regularly under the heading of "Readings in Libertarian Education." During Zigrosser's editorship, the subtitle of the journal was "A Monthly Magazine Devoted to Libertarian Ideas in Education," and Zigrosser himself provided an interview with Marietta Johnson and reviews of Dewey's *Democracy and Education* and

Neill's "Dominie" books. "I wish that unique Scotch schoolmaster, A. S. Neill, were here in America within hailing distance," he wrote. "I should like very much to make his acquaintance."[168]

Of the subjects debated in *The Modern School*, none aroused more controversy than the methods of Maria Montessori, which Leonard Abbott thought had "much in common with those of Francisco Ferrer." To this Manuel Komroff replied with "An Attack on the Montessori Method," finding its religious exercises particularly abhorrent to the libertarian spirit.[169] The debate sharpened in the fall of 1913, when Cora Bennett Stephenson introduced Montessori equipment into the Ferrer kindergarten, provoking a blast from Stewart Kerr, who drew a sharp line between Montessori and Ferrer. Though both condemned the prevailing system of education, Kerr admitted, "the teaching of Ferrer is libertarian, and that of Montessori is authority in subtle disguise."[170]

Worse than Montessori, however, was the system of public education, the chief target of criticism in *The Modern School*. On this all its writers were unanimous. The public school, said Harry Kelly, was "a powerful instrument for the perpetuation of the present social order with all its injustice and inequality." Its curriculum, "mapped out by faculties and crammed down the throats of pupils by dogmatists or mechanics masquerading as teachers," was designed to mold obedient citizens who would submit to the authority of the state and function as loyal workers within the capitalist system. The Modern School, by contrast, encouraged its pupils "to think and act independently" and "to express their individuality in every direction, without losing sight of the principle that the liberty of others must not be invaded." Its teachers were "neither asked nor expected to teach specific social or religious theories" but rather to foster "the libertarian spirit and answer the child truthfully on any questions presented."[171]

Alexander Berkman agreed: "We try in every way to dispense with the stiff formalities that have so long been associated with the schoolroom. The teacher is not enthroned on a lofty platform, with a row of cowering youngsters toeing the mark before him. He sits at a low round table, with its scholars clustered close round him, ready to serve them in any way." Children, Berkman added, must learn "to acquire knowledge for its own sake, instead of working for a material reward or to 'beat' a comrade. As for exams, the ability to answer a series of stereotyped questions is an obviously unfair test of knowledge." The basic principle, he concluded, was "to make the school fit the child, instead of forcing the child to fit the school. The stronger the individual genius, the more it suffers from compulsion of any sort. Nature is the wisest, as she was the first schoolmistress."[172]

Throughout the entire run of the journal, the keynote was freedom in education, with emphasis on individuality and self-development. As Stewart Kerr summed it up: "The Modern School seeks to develop intellectual rebels, and in this lies the chief difference between it and the state-supported school. In ordinary schools individuality and initiative are suspected the moment they appear; in the Modern School they are welcomed as evidence of intellectual vigor. . . . We do what the ordinary schools have never done; we impose no dogma on the child, we treat him, not as one who will enter life when he leaves our hands, but as one who has entered life already. He will leave with his mind free to accept or reject what appeals to his reason; he will not upbraid us for hiding from him facts he would inevitably discover for himself; the memory of the school where he was free to form and express his own opinions regardless of whether these were shared by the teacher or not will stay with him as long as he lives."[173]

CHAPTER 5

Three Anarchists

THE THREE MEN who form the subject of this chapter, Leonard Abbott, Harry Kelly, and Joseph Cohen, were nearly exact contemporaries. All three were born in the same decade, Kelly in 1871, Abbott and Cohen in 1878. All three died in 1953, the year which also marked the demise of the Stelton school, of which they were the principal founders. All three began their radical careers at an early age, sharing a sympathy for the working class, a belief in the dignity of labor, and a hatred of industrial capitalism. All were endowed with intelligence and with an ability to express themselves in effective language, though none can be regarded as an original or imaginative thinker. All had Jewish wives, Abbott and Kelly as well as Cohen; and while they differed in background and temperament, all three became anarchists, and their destinies were bound together by the movement for libertarian education to which they dedicated so much of their energies.

LEONARD ABBOTT

There was little in Leonard Abbott's background to forewarn that he would become an anarchist. Indeed, he was the only one of eight brothers to embark on a radical career, the others pursuing the respectable commercial traditions of the old New England family into which they were born. Their father, Lewis Lowe Abbott, a prosperous metal merchant from Andover, Massachusetts, devout Episcopalian, Yale class of 1866, spent twenty years representing American firms in Liverpool, England, where his son Leonard Dalton Abbott was born on May 20, 1878. Young Leonard attended the fashionable Uppingham School where, discovering the works of Thomas Paine, Peter Kropotkin, and William Morris, he began to stray from the conventional paths on which his conservative upbringing had placed him.[1]

By 1895, when he was only seventeen, Abbott was already attending socialist meetings in Liverpool. He heard the leading socialist orators of the day, among them Keir Hardie, Edward Carpenter, and H. M. Hyndman. At one meeting, Carpenter held forth on "Shelley and the Modern Democratic Movement." After his lecture, he stepped down to a piano and played the accompaniment of his socialist hymn "England Arise," while the audience sang. Young Abbott was enthralled. He was afterwards introduced to Carpenter, read his books, and corresponded with him until Carpenter's death in 1929. Carpenter, he thought, was a very great man, "great as a poet and seer; great as a prose writer; great as a sex radical; and great in the simplicity and beauty of his personality."[2]

Abbott's admiration for Carpenter was exceeded only by his admiration for William Morris. To his regret, he never came to know Morris personally, nor did he hear him speak, but he met his daughter May as well as several of his closest friends, and he corresponded with Morris himself, who sent him an inscribed copy of his *News from Nowhere*, perhaps the greatest libertarian utopia ever written. In 1897, shortly before leaving for America, Abbott visited Peter Kropotkin at Bromley. He came as a total stranger, yet Kropotkin gave him several hours of his time, talking of English trade unions and the cooperative movement, of Belgian workers, French peasants, and Russian serfs, of the beginnings of English socialism, of Owen, Fourier, and Saint-Simon, of Marx and Bakunin, the International and the Paris Commune. Struck by Kropotkin's "sheer humanity and beautiful courtesy," Abbott came away with an admiration for the princely anarchist that never abated.[3]

To his years in England, Abbott later recalled, "I can trace many of the strongest intellectual tendencies of my life." Among these were socialism, anarchism, pacificism, agnosticism, and sexual emancipation. Abbott, a middle-class idealist of a type that was fairly common at the turn of the century, nourished himself upon a wide range of radical and liberal thought. Apart from Carpenter, Morris, Kropotkin, and Tolstoy, he devoured the works of Oscar Wilde, Henry George, Walt Whitman, Percy Bysshe Shelley, Robert Owen, and Karl Marx. "Out of a welter of conflicting counsels," he tells us, "Socialism emerged. I became more and more convinced that the realization of a co-operative commonwealth, the organization of a society on a collectivist basis, was the one object worth striving for." Whoever shared this purpose was for Abbott a kindred spirit, and he grappled him to his soul with hoops of steel. "I love the whole army of revolt," he declared. "My heart goes out to all who have felt the urge of the democratic spirit, and have turned their backs upon capitalism."[4]

When the Abbotts sailed for America in 1897, Leonard was nineteen years old. He was also a confirmed socialist. Determined to strike out on his own, he settled in New York and immersed himself in radical causes, refusing to join the family business or even to enter a university, though his father could easily afford it. In 1898, at the age of twenty, he published his first socialist pamphlet, *The Society of the Future*, a blend of Marx, Kropotkin, and Morris, calling for public ownership of industry and agriculture, for the organization of producers' cooperatives on decentralist lines, for the equality of women and liberty for every individual. "Some of us," he wrote, "are thoroughly dissatisfied with the life of today, its strife, its heartlessness, its artificiality, its shabbiness. We long to cast from our midst forever the black nightmare of poverty; we yearn for fellowship, for rest, for happiness."[5]

For the next ten years Abbott was an important and extremely active figure in the American socialist movement. By 1900, when he was twenty-two, he was a member of the executive committee of the Socialist Party of America. In 1905 he was a founder of the Inter-Collegiate Socialist Society (later called the League for Industrial Democracy) and a member of its executive committee. He was also on the original board of directors of the Rand School of Social Science, established in 1906 as an intellectual center of the socialist movement. His colleagues in these organizations included a number of prominent individuals who were to figure in the Ferrer Association, such as Jack London, Clarence Darrow, and Upton Sinclair, whom Abbott himself converted to socialism in 1902.

From 1901 to 1905, moreover, Abbott served on the editorial board of *The Comrade*, a leading socialist monthly edited by John Spargo and George D. Herron. Notable for its undoctrinaire character, *The Comrade*, anticipating *The Masses* in this respect, dispensed the views of Tolstoy, Henry George, and William Morris along with those of Engels and Marx. Abbott himself was a frequent contributor, writing on Carpenter and Morris as well as on Emerson and Thoreau. A prolific journalist, Abbott published numerous articles and reviews during these years, in both socialist and nonsocialist periodicals. On behalf of the Socialist Party he also produced a number of widely distributed pamphlets; and when George D. Herron married Carrie Rand in an unorthodox "socialist" ceremony (performed by William Thurston

Brown), Abbott was on hand to describe the occasion.[6] From 1899, Abbott was also an associate editor of the *Literary Digest*, which brought him into contact with many of the writers and artists who were afterward associated with the Modern School. In 1905 he took the same position at *Current Literature*, which later changed its name to *Current Opinion*, a post he held until 1925.

Given his standing among the socialists, why Abbott should have shifted to the anarchists is not entirely clear. As a socialist, however, he had always been closer to the libertarian vision of Carpenter and Morris than to the economic determinism of Engels and Marx. Further study of Kropotkin may have played a part in the transition, as did the impact of Ferrer's execution. By 1907, at any rate, Abbott had begun to write for Emma Goldman's *Mother Earth*, contributing an obituary of Ernest Howard Crosby, America's leading disciple of Tolstoy. The following year he contributed an essay on Maxim Gorky, after which he continued his association with the journal until its suppression in 1917.

Abbott had known Emma Goldman since 1903, when he and Ernest Crosby met with her to discuss the plight of Berkman, who had by then been behind bars more than ten years for his attempt on the life of Frick. Abbott was deeply impressed by the force of her personality, by her honesty and physical courage. "E. G. has been one of the strongest influences in my life," he later told a friend. She, in turn, came to regard him as "a wonderfully fine human being."[7] Abbott was similarly impressed by Voltairine de Cleyre, after whom he named his first child, who died in infancy in 1914. He regarded Emma Goldman, Voltairine de Cleyre, and Louise Michel as the "three great anarchist women of modern times." Had his second child been a girl, he said, he would have called her Louise Michel. It was a boy, however, arriving in 1915, and he was named after William Morris. When another girl did appear, after a five-year lapse, she was called Ellen Key for the Swedish libertarian and feminist.[8]

The years after his meeting with Emma Goldman found Abbott drifting closer and closer to the anarchist camp, so that by the time of Ferrer's execution his primary allegiance was to Kropotkin rather than Marx. Yet his view of the world, while deeply influenced by anarchism, was never completely dominated by it. Nor did he ever shed his socialist beliefs. Between the two schools of thought he saw no contradiction. "I find truth in the theories both of Socialism and of Anarchism," he wrote in 1910, "and I do not see how in the long run either can be excluded from a comprehensive social philosophy. Socialism represents altruism. Anarchism represents egoism. Both are necessary. Socialism embodies the revolt of the workers against capitalistic exploitation; it points the way to the next great world-task—the abolition of poverty. Anarchism stands for the right and duty of the individual to express himself freely and completely. Individuality and solidarity ought to go hand in hand."[9]

At the same time, both his anarchism and socialism were tempered by the conservative traditions in which he was reared. "I am both more radical and more conservative, I think, than I have ever been before," he wrote to a friend in 1912. "I understand *both* points of view almost equally well, feel the strength and limitations of both almost equally. Of course my sympathies are overwhelmingly with the radical point of view. Yet whereas in the past years I took the radical attitude impulsively and almost spontaneously, now I am almost painfully conscious of the *two* points of view. I want to feel the radical point of view more ardently than I do."[10]

Abbott's values were too mixed, his view of the world too broad, for him to cleave to any single social or political doctrine. "Life sometimes seems to me like a fabric of many colors—gold, crimson, and gray," he remarked. "It is not completed yet. There are different threads, the different schools of thought, and all are necessary to make the whole."[11] Alive to the complexity of human nature and to the many areas of life in need of reform, he threw his energies into a variety of causes, from free speech and free thought to antimilitarism and population control. In addition to becoming the first president of the Ferrer Association, he served as president of the Thomas Paine National Historical Association as well as of the Free Speech League. He was also chairman of the Free Speech Committee, was active in the Free Thinkers of America, and wrote for *The Truth Seeker* and other rationalist publications. Voltaire, Paine, and Darrow ranked among his chief idols, all "really great men."[12] A lifelong pacifist, he took a prominent part in the anticonscription agitation of 1917 and was for many years a member of the War Resisters League. "I think of him as a rationalist, humanist, pacifist, socialist, and anarchist," Abbott's son remarked. John Sloan, who met Abbott in 1910, found him "an enthusiastic Radical, a socialist and anarchist keenly alive to all the present conditions, active in trying to preserve Free Speech in the United States."[13]

Throughout the Ferrer Center years, from 1911 to 1918, Abbott was a ubiquitous figure. There was scarcely a meeting he did not attend, a cause he did not champion, a journal he did not support, whether financially or by his writing. A charter member of the Ferrer Association, he was not only its first president, as has been noted, but also a speaker at its founding conference and editor of the Ferrer memorial volume published under its imprimatur. For several years, moreover, he conducted a literary class for adults which ranked among the most popular offered at the Center. Not himself a creator of literature (he wrote neither poetry nor fiction), he was, like Will Durant, a "born summarizer and lecturer-popularizer," to quote Carl Zigrosser's description, who could convey "the arguments and opinions of others intelligently and accurately."[14] With his tall figure and resonant voice, he made an ideal chairman at Ferrer Association gatherings, a task he was often called upon to perform. Articulate and obviously sincere, he became the leading spokesman for the organization during its formative period. "Amid a crowd of excitable spirits denouncing Western civilization and demanding a proletarian paradise," recall Will and Ariel Durant, "Leonard never, to our knowledge, uttered one bitter note, never hated, never advocated—though he could forgive—violence. He went his quiet way, teaching less by words than by the example of his patient understanding, tolerance, and goodwill."[15]

Yet, for all his attractive qualities, there was an underlying ambivalence in Abbott's personality. Cordial, smiling, he was at the same time serious and remote. A vein of sadness lay beneath his outward calm and composure. Though not entirely without humor, he was at bottom a melancholy figure, with his long face and sad brown eyes. Conservative in habit and appearance, he avoided alcohol, disliked profanity, and always dressed in formal clothes. He was a "pure man," thought Hutchins Hapgood, "so pure indeed and so shrinking from any kind of real vulgarity and from any false ambition, that some of the rough spirits in the movement continually tried to make him blush, sometimes succeeding. The grossest of these abominable humorists was Ben Reitman, who under the cloak of the revolutionary movement practiced a free speech like that of a vulgar and ribald salesman, and especially liked to heckle Abbott."[16]

As time wore on, and especially after his wife fell seriously ill, Abbott became increasingly taciturn and morose. He looked almost funereal in his plain dark suits. Lacking drive and decision, he was possessed by a wavering, Hamlet-like quality that prevented him from uttering strong opinions. "No matter what anyone said to him," recalls Emma Cohen, "he would answer, 'Quite so, quite so.' That was his favorite phrase." A malicious word was never spoken about him, not even by his political opponents, and he was seldom, if ever, embroiled in polemics or personal debate. He had a horror of bickering and confrontation, and "unless he could persuade through patient reasoning," said Will Durant, "he went away with his sad smile, regretful but as friendly as before. He was incapacitated by nature from quarreling with any man; and I doubt if ever in his life he said no to a request that fell within his physical powers. He suffered with those he saw suffering; every bit of evil that came within his experience found him, like Shelley, all nerves, and cut him to the soul."[17]

Although a lifelong freethinker, Abbott possessed deep-seated spiritual urges. "In regard to religion," he wrote in 1910, "I find myself with the rationalists one moment, with the mystics the next." In later life he described himself as "an agnostic with leanings toward some kind of theism."[18] A friend of Ernest Crosby and George Herron, two of America's leading Christian socialists, he shared many of their values and predispositions. Had he been born a generation or two earlier, he would have been a New England Transcendentalist and Non-Resistant of the Emerson or Garrison type. To a perceptive pupil at the Modern School he had the qualities of a Protestant minister; and Moritz Jagendorf thought him "the first real Christian since St. Francis of Assisi."[19] There was indeed something saintly in his love of nature, birds, and flowers, something Christlike in his lean figure and pale features. The Jewish immigrants with whom he mingled were entranced by this idealistic young gentile who had come to teach them, who devoted himself to their causes, shared their hopes and sufferings, and married one of their daughters.

It was at the Ferrer Center that Abbott met Rose Yuster. She had been born of a Rumanian-Jewish family, all of whom were anarchists, including her mother Esther and her sister Romany Marie. She was "young, beautiful and extremely intelligent," and she and Abbott fell in love.[20] From 1913 to 1915 they lived together in free union, without sanction of government or church. Their first child, Voltairine, was born and died in May 1914; and in April 1915, shortly before the arrival of their son, they decided to get married.

Although Abbott sired three children, his ambivalent nature

extended to the area of sex. At the Ferrer Center he was nicknamed "Sister Abbott," and his letters hint of youthful homosexual attachments. "When I was a young man, homosexualism fascinated me. I have been strongly influenced by four homosexuals of genius (Whitman, Wilde, Carpenter, and Viereck), the last two of whom I have known personally," he wrote in 1935. "From 1906 to 1910 I played with the idea that I was myself homosexual. But later, like many others, I came to the conclusion that my supposed homosexualism was really in large part underdeveloped heterosexualism. Women have been among the major blessings of my life. I have found the normal sexual relationship between man and woman much preferable to any homosexual relationship I have ever known."[21]

Always a champion of sexual freedom, Abbott in 1910 published a defense of homosexuality in *The Free Comrade*, the little journal he edited with J. William Lloyd. In later writings he specifically linked his admiration for Whitman, Carpenter, and Wilde with his interest in homosexuality, calling Carpenter a "homosexual saint" and his *Love's Coming of Age* a "modern classic."[22] With his own combination of male and female impulses, Abbott was what we would now call bisexual, or a heterosexual with strong homosexual leanings, a member of what Carpenter termed the "third" or "intermediate" sex. Unaware of Abbott's sexual ambivalence, Will Durant envied him "his tall figure, his dark brooding eyes, his handsome and sensitive face." Women at the Ferrer Center, says Durant, "gazed up at him with eyes dripping with admiration and devotion; and even the men, some of them hard and cynical, looked upon him as the redeeming angel of the anarchist movement." Abbott, however, failed to take advantage of his attractiveness. "This saint was as handsome and dashing as Don Juan," wrote Durant to Manuel Komroff, "and all the ladies fell in love with him; many a husband in our group was a second choice, taken because Leonard couldn't marry all the girls. With every opportunity to be a Casanova he has led the life of a loyal and devoted husband, and he has given us all an inspiring example of steadiness and honesty."[23]

Harry Kelly

Henry May Kelly—he was always called Harry—was born in St. Charles, Missouri, on January 19, 1871. From his name he was generally assumed to be of Irish descent, which more than once spared him trouble with the police. But this was not the case. His father, Richard Kelly, hailed from Cornwall, on the west coast of England, where his forebears had lived for three hundred years. Emigrating to America in 1835, he prospected for precious metals in the vicinity of Lake Superior, where he made friends with the Indians and lived among them. After this, he entered the coal mining and railroad industries in Pennsylvania. For a time he prospered. But his wife died, he lost the bulk of his fortune, and he moved to Missouri, where he worked as a mine inspector and married Harry's mother, Nancy Jane Stevens, a descendant of the Calverts who had settled in Maryland in the seventeenth century.[24]

When Harry came into the world, his father was still sufficiently well-off to have a thirteen-room house in St. Charles and to support the local Episcopalian church. During the panic of 1873, however, one of the worst in America's history, the Kellys fell on hard times and were forced to move to St. Louis, where Richard Kelly died in poverty when his son was only four. After the fifth grade Harry was compelled to go to work in a grocery store to help support the family. By the time he was fourteen he already felt like an adult and mingled with boys much older than himself.

It was then that he took up the trade of printing, with which he was to be associated for the next thirty-five years. At nineteen he became secretary of the International Typographical Union local in St. Louis and three years later headed its delegation to the Chicago Trades and Labor Assembly. His first clear consciousness of the struggle between capital and labor, he tells us, grew out of the Homestead strike of 1892, in which the resistance of the workers to the Pinkertons called in by Frick excited him "beyond anything in my experience."[25]

Thrown out of work by the panic of 1893, Kelly left St. Louis and rode the rods in hobo fashion, eventually winding up in Boston, where his mother and brother joined him. Here, in 1894, he became an anarchist. Twenty-three and out of a job, he was walking down Washington Street one Sunday evening when his eye was attracted by a green handbill which, blown by the wind, fluttered from a door onto the pavement. Kelly picked it up and saw that it advertised an anarchist speaker from England named C. W. Mowbray, who was about to start his lecture. Others were drifting into the hall, and Kelly went in with them. The meeting changed the course of his life. Mowbray, a large, powerfully built man with dark hair and resonant voice, spoke on the meaning of anarchism, and what he said, thought Kelly, was "interesting, novel and vital." Mowbray was a magnetic speaker, and Kelly was impressed by the ease with which he answered questions, parried criticisms, and "bowled over his opponents."[26]

Greatly stimulated by the lecture, Kelly attended the rest of the series (there were six in all) and joined the study group that was formed at the end. He and Mowbray took to each other, and in no time a warm friendship sprang up between them. By the end of the year Kelly found himself the secretary of an anarchist-communist group created largely through Mowbray's efforts. In addition, he became the secretary of the Union Cooperative Society of Printers, while Mowbray himself held the same post in the Union Cooperative Society of Journeymen Tailors, both of which became affiliated with the Central Labor Union of Boston. Kelly took great pride in his new activity and was delighted with the progress he was making among the workers. "Remember," he wrote in March 1895, "this is BOSTON, the 'Cradle of Liberty,' the home of Wendell Phillips; is it not gratifying?"[27]

Soon after these words were written, however, wanderlust overcame him. In April 1895, Kelly, armed with a steamship ticket, seventeen dollars in cash, and "a large stock of Anglo-Saxon assurance," set sail aboard the *Umbria* for London, "a Mecca for devout revolutionists of those days." He also bore a letter of introduction from Mowbray to John Turner, general secretary of the Shop Assistants' Union, who was fated to become the first person deported from the United States under the anti-anarchist law enacted after the assassination of McKinley. Turner, an active member of the Freedom Group, introduced Kelly to his comrades, among them Peter Kropotkin, who became the greatest influence in Kelly's life.[28]

Kelly remained in England for three and a half months, taking part in a May Day demonstration, visiting his father's birthplace, and becoming the chief link between the anarchist-communist movements in Britain and the United States. When he returned to Boston, he was eager to start a journal to advance the ideas of the anarchist-communist school, a kind of American version of the London *Freedom* founded by Kropotkin and his associates. For this purpose, seventy dollars was raised by holding a raffle in which the prize was a tailor-made suit. Kelly and Mowbray peddled tickets among the Boston unions, in which they were now familiar figures, and bought material for the suit out of the funds collected. James Robb, another anarchist tailor, contributed the skills of his craft by sewing the prize suit.

Out of these efforts *The Rebel* ("A Monthly Journal Devoted to the Exposition of Anarchist Communism") was launched in September 1895. Edited and printed by Kelly, Mowbray, and Robb, together with Henry A. Koch, a Boston hatter, and N. H. Berman, a Russian-Jewish typographer, it featured articles by Kropotkin and Louise Michel as well as by American anarchists like Voltairine de Cleyre, who came to Boston in November 1895 and shared the speakers' platform with Kelly at a Haymarket memorial sponsored by *The Rebel* group. Around this time, Kelly also met Emma Goldman, who describes him as "a young and ardent comrade." Kelly, for his part, thought Voltairine and Emma "the two most notable women it was ever my good fortune to meet. Widely different in racial background, character, temperament, and education, they had two attitudes in common—love of freedom and dauntless physical and moral courage."[29]

A lively as well as intelligently edited journal, *The Rebel* made a distinct impact on the radical and labor movements in Boston. "Educate," ran its motto, "in order to understand our true value as workers; Organize, to overthrow the power of government, capitalism and superstition, and thus pave the way for that bright future when the worker shall have free access to the means of life, and the world shall cease to know misery, poverty and crime." For lack of funds, however, *The Rebel* was compelled to cease publication after only six issues, a great disappointment to Kelly. A few months later he and Mowbray started another journal, called *The Match*, which "sputtered for two numbers and went out."[30]

At this point Kelly was seized again with wanderlust. Leaving Boston, he rode the rails back to St. Louis, lecturing on anarchism whenever the opportunity presented itself. His thirst for travel momentarily assuaged, he spent the greater part of 1897 in New York City, working with a group of fellow anarchists to secure Berkman's release from prison, an effort which failed to bear fruit. In October of that year, Kropotkin arrived in New York on his first lecture tour of the United States. Kelly was on hand to greet him, together with John H. Edelmann, a contributor to the now defunct *Rebel* and editor of his own anarchist paper, *Solidarity*, as well as being a gifted architect and a friend of Louis Sullivan. It was at the Edelmann apartment on East 96th Street that Kropotkin stayed during his visit.[31] Edelmann's wife, Rachelle Krimont, was one of three daughters and a son of East European Jewish immigrants, all of whom were anarchists. Her younger sister Mary was to become Kelly's wife.

By now Kelly was working as a salesman of printing equipment for the American Machine and Foundry Company, and in January 1898 he went to London as its representative. This was his second journey to England, and he remained nearly seven years. Mary Krimont followed him there, forming a companionship that was to endure until her death in 1922. In 1899 their daughter Elsie was born, a "marvelous little girl" who was herself to become active in the Ferrer movement.[32]

Along with his duties for the American Machine and Foundry Company, Kelly found time to engage in a wide range of radical activity. On March 18, 1898, soon after arriving from America, he spoke at an anniversary celebration of the Paris Commune, together with Kropotkin, Louise Michel, and John Turner. In November of the same year he again shared the rostrum with Kropotkin during a Haymarket gathering in Whitechapel. When Emma Goldman and Voltairine de Cleyre came to England in 1899 and 1903, they stayed at Kelly's house, and he acted as chairman at their lectures. Beyond this, he helped with the printing of *Freedom* and was active in the local typographical union, which he joined shortly after his arrival. He also became a regular contributor to *Freedom*, writing mostly on labor issues and developments in the United States. By the same token, he reported on the scene in Britain for American anarchist papers, notably *Free Society*.

During his long stay in England, Kelly completed his anarchist apprenticeship. His mentors, who included Errico Malatesta and Max Nettlau in addition to Kropotkin, were among the most distinguished names in the movement, and under their tutelage he received a thorough grounding in anarchist theory and practice. Afterward, he always prided himself on his friendship with these figures, above all with Kropotkin, which enhanced his standing in the movement. Living in the London suburb of Anerly, he was only a few miles from Kropotkin's house at Bromley. He visited Kropotkin often, and despite the difference in their ages, they became "intimate to a considerable degree."[33] Kelly always remained devoted to Kropotkin, whose writings he introduced to more than a few young comrades at the Ferrer Center. And Kropotkin returned his affection. When Emma Goldman visited the venerable anarchist in Soviet Russia shortly before his death, he asked her to remember him to all his comrades in America, sending "special love to H. K."[34]

In August 1904 Kelly returned to the United States with his wife and five-year-old daughter. Settling in New York, he resumed his work of selling printing equipment while devoting all his spare time to anarchism. In 1905 he organized a protest meeting at the Academy of Music against the Bloody Sunday massacre in St. Petersburg. The following year he helped with the launching of *Mother Earth* and became one of its regular contributors, sometimes signing his articles "Henry May," his first and middle names. As in England, he was a frequent speaker at Haymarket and Paris Commune commemorations; and he maintained his British connection, writing not only for *Freedom* but also for *The Voice of Labour*, an anarcho-syndicalist weekly.

In the fall of 1909, together with Abbott, Berkman, and Goldman, Kelly was in the front ranks of the protest movement against the execution of Ferrer. The following spring he joined his three comrades as a charter member of the Ferrer Association, chairing its founding meeting and editing its monthly bulletin. On January 1, 1911, he took part in the inauguration of the Ferrer Center on St. Mark's Place. Two months later, however, tired of selling printing machinery and always interested in communal experiments, he went to California to join the Aurora Colony, founded near Sacramento by Abe Isaak, a Russian Mennonite turned anarchist, who had edited *Free Society*.

But Kelly could seldom stay long in one place. "Restless" was a common word in his vocabulary, and he forever had the itch to move on. He was at Aurora only three weeks when a telegram arrived from Leonard Abbott inviting him to become organizer of the Ferrer Association, Dr. Luttinger having resigned after only a few weeks in the post. Kelly promptly accepted and returned at once to New York.

Kelly was now forty years old. With his gregarious nature, his experience in the anarchist movement, and his enthusiasm for practical ventures of this sort, he was admirably suited for the job. If he had inherited his father's migratory restlessness, he was also heir to his mother's down-to-earth common sense. In short, he was "that rare phenomenon of a practical idealist," as Carl Zigrosser described him.[35] Open, honest, unaffected, he was at ease with people and very well liked, without the slightest lust for power or urge to dominate. A man of simple tastes and habits, he was never fussy about food or clothes. As a youth he developed a passion for baseball that he retained throughout his long life. "He knew baseball from A to Z," a friend remarked, "and wouldn't miss a game on TV in his later years until his eyesight failed."[36]

Small and slight (he was five feet two inches tall and weighed barely a hundred pounds), with a straw-colored mustache and twinkling blue eyes, Kelly was as gentle as Leonard Abbott and, though only half his friend's size, commanded equal respect because of his warm and sympathetic personality and ability to get things done. Though capable of stubbornness when he felt he was in the right, he had a sense of fun and humor that Abbott largely lacked. All his life he retained the unaffected simplicity of manner to which he owed so much of his popularity, and throughout his years in New York he remained an incurable provincial, homespun and garrulous, speaking, said Manuel Komroff, "horse sense." Komroff recalled a characteristic incident. After one of Kelly's lectures at the Ferrer Center, someone in the audience asked, "If everyone is free to do as he wants, how can an orchestra play one piece? What if I marched down the aisle playing 'Yankee Doodle Dandy' on the piccolo?" "Then we'd take you by the collar and throw you out," was Kelly's reply. "Is there a limit to freedom?" he was asked on another occasion. "Liberty is not unbridled," he answered. "You cannot have all the liberty you can take. Your liberty stops where it begins to interfere with the freedom of others."[37]

Compared with Abbott, Kelly was an uncomplicated personality. His sensibilities were less refined than those of his friend. Yet he was not a whit less intelligent, and he possessed a greater capacity for coping with practical detail. As his English friend John Turner later wrote: "I have felt you were one of the few who had succeeded in applying Anarchist principles to current events. In my opinion that is what is wanted!"[38] Remarkable, too, was the consistency throughout his life of his moral and intellectual attitudes. Freedom, he always believed, might never be fully attained. Yet the struggle was nonetheless worthwhile. Nor was anarchism something merely to dream of for the future. It was a guide to everyday behavior, to be applied in all relations with one's fellow men. Such was Kelly's position for more than half a century.

Kelly himself came as close as anyone to living up to this philosophy. His was an extremely generous nature; and when Mary Krimont bore a son by another man, he took him in and raised him as his own. He adored his daughter Elsie and loved the children of the Modern School. Roger Baldwin remembers him as "the quietest and most non-resistant anarchist you could ever dream of. And his talk about anarchism was the mildest recital of principles that you might read in a book. I have never heard him get excited or even be severely critical of anyone. He had a nice, pleasant manner, calm and cool."[39]

There were times, however, when Kelly thought resistance was necessary. In 1912, for instance, when anarchists and I.W.W.'s were set upon by vigilantes during a free-speech fight in San Diego, he and Berkman and Havel issued a warning: "If the public sentiment of the country and the passive attitude of the press continue to encourage these outrages, we feel that the Anarchists and other social rebels will be forced, as a matter of self-defense, to answer violence with violence." Yet his humanitarian and idealistic outlook shrank from methods which he in theory professed and justified. He himself was never involved in a violent act. In this he was at one with Leonard Abbott. Both, said Manuel Komroff, were "overflowing, generous spirits, and without them the Ferrer Center would not have been so inspiring a place."[40]

JOSEPH COHEN

Joseph Jacob Cohen was born in a Jewish village in Minsk province on August 31, 1878. "My very first recollections," he says in *The House Stood Forlorn*, an account of his youth which he wrote near the end of his life, "are those which impressed upon me that I was born a Jew, a scion of a persecuted race suffering oppression, misery and injustice all through the ages."[41] This awareness of his Jewish heritage, even after he had broken with its religious aspects, contributed much to the development of Cohen's ideas. As an old man he could still remember the pogroms that swept his native district following the assassination of Tsar Alexander II in 1881, when he was not yet three years old. Many Jews were uprooted, and Cohen himself, at the age of five, was taken to the town of Turets, where his maternal grandfather was a blacksmith. Enrolled in a Jewish elementary school, he made such rapid progress that he was sent a few years later to Minsk to study for the rabbinate.

In Minsk, Cohen's life took a new turn, in the direction it was to follow until his death. Falling prey to religious doubts, he was plunged into a state of mental anxiety which resulted in a temporary breakdown. At the same time, he became acquainted with the revolutionary ideas that were spreading through Russia during this period. From early childhood he had been filled with anger at the oppression of the Russian peasantry. This, together with his own sense of persecution as a Jew, gave the impulse to his revolutionary development. He read with excitement the poetry of Nekrasov, with its rebellious spirit and sympathy for the people, and he was stirred by an account of the Paris Commune which he found in a Hebrew-language history of the world. The more the author tried to portray the Communards in a bad light, Cohen recalled, "the more they became attractive to me. I felt a close relationship to their purpose and a personal sympathy for their martyrdom."[42]

When he was seventeen, Cohen became involved in an attempt to organize the Minsk workers into unions. After he was questioned by the police, his family insisted that he return home, and he spent the next few years working as a forester, his father's occupation, acquiring a love for the countryside that was to influence his later development. By this time all thought of following a religious career had been abandoned. Once again Cohen was reading whatever forbidden literature he could lay his hands on, such as Bellamy's *Looking Backward* and a report of the trial of the revolutionaries who were hanged for the assassination of the tsar. It was at this time that Cohen met a girl named Sophie from a neighboring village who was to become his lifelong companion.

In 1898 Cohen was called up for service in the tsarist army, and he spent the next four years in the garrison at Grodno. His military duties were not heavy, however, and he used his spare time to continue his radical education. "They were maturing years," he later remembered. "There was a good library in Grodno. In my off-hours I would haunt the place, utilizing its facilities to the utmost, often smuggling books into the garrison. I read voluminously, had time to observe the social forces at work in the city, and time for reflection. Here were sown some of the seeds of that libertarian philosophy which, flowering later, became the profound motivating force of my life."[43] Cohen also organized a revolutionary group among the soldiers of his artillery unit, and he and his comrades laid plans for seizing the batteries dominating the city in the event of a revolutionary outbreak.

But the outbreak did not come until 1905. By then, having completed his military service, Cohen had emigrated to America and was living in Philadelphia with Sophie, who shared his revolutionary convictions. Employed as a cigarmaker, he studied English with Voltairine de Cleyre, who lived in the Jewish ghetto and was a teacher of the working-class immigrants. "I had the honor and privilege to be her pupil for many years and cherish her memory dearly," Cohen wrote afterward.[44] It was under her influence, for the most part, that he became a convert to anarchism, though he was indebted also to Emma Goldman (after whom he named his daughter) and Alexander Berkman, whose imprisonment had made his name "a kind of talisman, a source of inspiration and encouragement."[45] As with Kelly, however, Kropotkin became Cohen's chief ideological mentor, and in 1906 he published a short-lived anarchist journal whose title *Broyt un Frayhayt* (Bread and Freedom) derived from the Yiddish title of Kropotkin's *Conquest of Bread*.

A strong and able individual, as Kelly describes him,[46] Cohen quickly emerged as a leading figure in the Jewish anarchist movement. Not only was he the driving force of the Radical Library and of the Philadelphia Modern School, but he went on to become a founder of the Stelton Colony, the editor of the *Fraye Arbeter Shtime*, a founder of the Sunrise Colony in Michigan, and the author of four books and countless articles which chronicle these ventures in which he played so central a part. Between December 1913 and May 1915, moreover, he served as the organizer of the Ferrer Association and custodian of the 107th Street school.

Known as "J. J." to his associates, Cohen, like Abbott and Kelly, combined pragmatic with idealistic characteristics. Carl Zigrosser thought him "a tower of strength with his tenacity and common sense." To others he was a "great idealist," yet also a "serious man" who got things done.[47] Of the three figures discussed in this chapter he had the greatest administrative ability. But he was also the least loved. His personality had a sharper edge than that of Abbott or Kelly; he was more assertive and domineering. For all his dedication and integrity, which his worst enemies would not have impugned, he possessed a streak of vanity, intolerance, even arrogance that earned him the reproach of not a few comrades. "He had a good mind," a colleague recalled, "he was capable and respected, but I don't think he was loved. He carried grudges and was intolerant of different opinions. When Cohen had something against a person, he didn't let go. He was very vindictive."[48]

In contrast with Harry Kelly, Cohen was far from being a gregarious individual, nor was there much humor or warmth in his makeup. At parties and gatherings he would sit and read the newspaper, pulling his cap down over his forehead to discourage intrusions. "If you put a glass of tea near him," joked a longtime associate, "it would turn to ice." Severe, aloof, unsentimental, he took pride in the fact that "all my adult life I have been known as one who has never shed a tear, no matter what the occasion." Many found him lacking in compassion. According to his own son, "father loved humanity in the abstract, but not individual people."[49] "Cohen was a difficult man," remarked a member of the *Fraye Arbeter Stime* board. "He sat in the office with a cap over his eyes, writing, smoking cigarettes, but looking at no one and talking to no one who came to visit." Another colleague on the paper found him "so autocratic in the way he conducted meetings, so cold and inflexible," that she ceased to attend. "God help the poor creature," replied Cohen's son-in-law to such charges, "who tries to establish a leadership role in the anarchist movement!"[50]

Abbott, Kelly, Cohen: three men, three temperaments, three personalities. Each had his strengths and limitations. Yet all were indefatigable laborers in the anarchist vineyard, unstintingly devoted to their cause. And each, in his own way, made an essential contribution to the movement for libertarian education in the United States.

CHAPTER 6

Lexington Avenue

ULY 4, 1914, dawned bright and sunny, ideal weather for the Independence Day picnic arranged by Leonard Abbott at his cottage in Westfield, New Jersey, to which the whole Ferrer School crowd had been invited. Jack Isaacson, who was planning to attend, left his apartment on East 103rd Street to buy the morning paper. It was shortly after 9 A.M. As he approached the corner of Lexington Avenue there was a terrific explosion, "a crash like that of a broadside from a battleship," and he saw a piece of a body, a man's arm, fly through the air and fall to the street.[1]

Moritz Jagendorf was also preparing to go to Abbott's picnic when the explosion occurred. He lived with his parents on East 109th Street. "Suddenly," he recalls, "there was a great crash. I rushed out and ran down Lexington Avenue about five or six blocks and saw rubble and smoke. A crowd had gathered, and the police were hustling everyone away. I started home but saw detectives questioning my father—they wanted to talk to me—so I went straight to Abbott's place. He served us corned beef and tongue sandwiches and beer. Everyone was hushed. There was an undercurrent of excitement. No one knew what to say."[2]

The explosion had come from a six-story tenement at 1626 Lexington Avenue, between 103rd and 104th Streets, in a thickly populated immigrant district of Harlem, five blocks from the Ferrer Center, where the noise of the blast was clearly heard. The three upper floors of the tenement were wrecked. The roof was shattered into fragments. Debris showered into the street and over neighboring roofs. The fire escape and ironwork in front of the building were twisted and torn out of place, and ceilings, walls, and stairways of the apartments on the upper floors had tumbled down as if in an earthquake. So great was the force of the explosion that articles of furniture were blown hundreds of feet into the air, some of the wreckage landing on the tops of houses more than a block away. A rain of glass had crashed to the street from hundreds of broken windows.[3]

Four people died in the explosion, three men and a woman, all in the same top-story apartment where the blast originated. Arthur Caron, Charles Berg, and Carl Hanson, three young anarchists in their twenties, had been regular visitors to the Ferrer Center, and Marie Chavez had attended occasional lectures. All were killed instantly. Berg was torn to pieces, and it was his arm that Jack Isaacson saw fall to the street. Inside the apartment were found the badly mutilated bodies of Hanson and Mrs. Chavez. Caron's body was thrown out onto a fire escape. It was still intact, and death was probably due to a fractured skull. Twenty other people were injured, seven of them severely enough to be hospitalized.

The blast had been caused by a large quantity of dynamite that had been accidentally ignited. What had the victims been up to? Had the dynamite been intended for Rockefeller, as the newspaper headlines proclaimed? How did the explosion affect the destinies of the Modern School? To answer these questions one must go back a few months, to February 1914 and the movement of the unemployed.

THE UNEMPLOYED

Throughout the winter of 1913-1914 the United States lay in the grip of depression. Millions were out of work, and there were demonstrations by the unemployed in many cities. In New York the demonstrations took a novel form. On February 27, 1914, a thousand men, led by a twenty-one-year-old anarchist named Frank Tannenbaum, marched to the Old Baptist Tabernacle at 164 Second Avenue and demanded food and shelter. Evening service had barely begun, reported *The New York Times*, when "the tramping of many feet down the church aisle brought it to a sudden close."[4] After an exchange of words between Tannenbaum and church officials, the police appeared and the crowd dispersed.

Tannenbaum, however, was undeterred. On February 28th he led six hundred men to the Labor Temple on East Fourteenth Street, where they were given shelter. This pattern was repeated for the next few nights. On March 1st a band of homeless men, with Tannenbaum again in the lead, assembled in Rutgers Square and tramped through the snow to the First Presbyterian Church on Fifth Avenue between Eleventh and Twelfth Streets, where the pastor gave them money for food and shelter. The following evening they invaded the parish house of St. Mark's Episcopal Church at Second Avenue and Tenth Street, where food and lodgings were provided.[5]

The most active element in this movement was a group of young rebels—anarchists and Wobblies, workers and intellectuals, Irishmen and Jews—who, rebuffed by city and union officials, took matters into their own hands. All were habitués of the Ferrer Center, where the movement had its origins. Tannenbaum, who attended evening classes at the Center and helped out at the offices of *Mother Earth*, was to become a distinguished scholar at Columbia University, one of the nation's leading authorities on Latin America. An immigrant from Austria-Hungary at nine, a runaway Massachusetts farm boy at thirteen, by the age of twenty, in 1913, he was a waiter in a New York restaurant and a labor activist with anarchist and I.W.W. affiliations. "We all loved Frank for his wide-awakeness and his unassuming ways," recalled Emma Goldman. Alexander Berkman considered him "an intelligent and revolutionary worker." To Carlo Tresca he was "young, alert, restless, inspired and inspiring."[6]

Apart from Tannenbaum, the main leaders of the sit-ins were Frank Strawn Hamilton, Charles Robert Plunkett, and Arthur Caron, one of the victims of the Lexington Avenue explosion. Hamilton, from the West Coast, was a friend of Jack London's and the model for the protagonist of one of his novels. Plunkett, a year older than Tannenbaum, had been born in New York of a middle-class Irish family and had been a scholarship student at Cornell. A voracious reader, he devoured all three volumes of *Capital* and the whole of *Principia Mathematica* before discovering the works of Kropotkin, whose *Fields, Factories and Workshops* became "my social bible." During the summer of 1912, after his junior year at Cornell, Plunkett got a job with Thomas Edison in his West Orange, New Jersey, laboratory, making motion pictures of the life histories of insects. When he began to organize the workers of Edison's shop, he was promptly dismissed. Instead of returning to Cornell, he became an organizer for the I.W.W., working in Paterson during the great 1913 strike, then in Allentown and Williamsport, Pennsylvania, and finally in New York. "I always threw myself into things heart and soul," he remarked sixty years later. "I never stopped half way."[7]

Arthur Caron, in his late twenties, had worked in a cotton mill in Fall River, Massachusetts, his home town, before becoming a machinist and engineer. His grandfather had been an Indian chief, and he himself had marked Indian features, with his "high cheek bones and his erect, dignified bearing."[8] Tall, handsome, and strongly built, he was proud of his heritage and referred to it often. His work, which took him to the West Indies and to France as well as through the United States, brought him good wages, but his rebellious, restless spirit would not allow him to settle down to a conventional life. He was "a vibrant fellow," recalls Maurice Hollod, with "boundless energy and great physical courage."[9]

Hatched by Frank Tannenbaum, the idea of occupying the churches—"the menacing gesture of the depths," as Berkman called it—was a form of "direct action," of nonviolent "propaganda by the deed," to dramatize the plight of the jobless. "The whole value of this church-raiding system," as Leonard Abbott told reporters, "lies in its advertising the issue of the unemployed in a way that is compelling and makes everybody think."[10] As such, it was a notable success. John Haynes Holmes of the Church of the Messiah in New York, a future leader of the American Civil Liberties Union, declared that the true meaning of the sit-ins was that they had "forced ninety million people in the United States to acknowledge that there is a question of the unemployed and to ask what can be done about it."[11] Holmes advised his fellow churchmen that it was their Christian duty to help the impoverished men who sought admission rather than to turn them away. And while some churches canceled evening services for fear of a visit from Tannenbaum's bedraggled army, others, whether out of fear or compassion, offered food and shelter or the money to obtain them.

Emboldened by their initial success, Tannenbaum and his associates continued their campaign for several days. "At first things went smoothly," Charles Plunkett recollects. "We went to a few Protestant churches without incident. But then we made the mistake of going to a Catholic church. That brought the police—most of them Irish—crashing down on us."[12] The incident occurred on March 4th at the Church of St. Alphonsus on West Broadway. Heading a band of two hundred unemployed, Tannenbaum together with Caron, Plunkett, and Hamilton requested permission to spend the night. The rector refused and sent for the police. As Carlo Tresca sardonically noted, "the Church of the Carpenter of Jerusalem refused to give aid and comfort to the hungry and unemployed carpenters, shoemakers, garment workers of New York." The men had begun to leave when a photographer from *The New York World* took their picture with a faulty flash bulb which exploded with a pop. Fearing gunshots, both police and unemployed panicked and a minor riot ensued. The police sealed off the church and arrested 189 men and one woman, Gussie Miller of the Ferrer School.[13]

Charged with inciting to riot, Tannenbaum was tried, convicted, and sentenced by City Magistrate John A.L. Campbell to the maximum penalty of one year in prison plus a five-hundred dollar fine. Eight others, Caron and Plunkett among them, received lesser sentences, and the rest were released. Tannenbaum, on being convicted, bitterly denounced "the judge, the jury, and all the instruments of the law." Society, he declared, was ready to forgive every offense but that of "preaching a new gospel. *That's* my crime. I was going about telling people that the jobless must be housed and fed, and for that I got locked up." To Alexander Berkman, who had been present at the St. Alphonsus occupation, Tannenbaum was a victim of "class justice," but his raids had accomplished "more in tearing off the mask of religious hypocrisy than the years-long propaganda of freethinkers."[14]

Tannenbaum's fine was paid by the Ferrer Association, the *Fraye Arbeter Shtime*, and the Labor Defense Committee, organized at the apartment of Mary Heaton Vorse three weeks before the St. Alphonsus arrests. But he was made to serve out his one-year term on Blackwell's Island, where *The Modern School* magazine reported him to be studying hard so as to emerge from prison "better equipped than before to play his part in the social struggle."[15] During Tannenbaum's confinement, Adolf Wolff dedicated the following poem to him, which Maurice Hollod, nearly sixty years later, recited to me from memory with great emotion:

Degraded in the convict's stripes,
He chafes behind the prison bars,
And breathes the dungeon stench.

Arrayed in sacerdotal garb,
The priest is celebrating mass,
Preaching to men the word of God.

The potentate upon the bench,
Wrapped in judiciary gown, he sits,
A judge of fellow-men.

Yet would I rather be—
The dirt on the feet of a Tannenbaum
Than the soul
Of such a judge—of such a priest.[16]

The arrest of Tannenbaum and his confederates did not call a halt to the movement of the unemployed. On the contrary, the tempo of agitation was increased. Over the next three months, open-air demonstrations, among the greatest ever held in New York, took place in the public squares of lower Manhattan, at which thousands of jobless men and women applauded the speeches of avowed anarchists, denouncing capitalism and government. Night after night marches, occupations, and rallies were staged to dramatize the plight of the unemployed and to protest the iniquities of the existing order. At the same time, the city was circularized with leaflets explaining the causes of unemployment and suggesting measures of relief. New York, wrote Charles Plunkett, was witnessing a period of anarchist activity "unequalled in this country since the stirring days of 1886 in Chicago." "Hunger," said Plunkett, "had become articulate. Misery had found its voice!"[17]

To coordinate the demonstrations, a number of organizations sprang into being during the early months of 1914. Most important were the Labor Defense Committee, founded by Elizabeth Gurley Flynn, Carlo Tresca, Bill Haywood, and others at Mary Heaton Vorse's apartment on East Eleventh Street; the I.W.W. Unemployed Union of New York, with headquarters and reading room on East Fourth Street; and the Conference of the Unemployed, formed at the Ferrer Center with Joseph Cohen as secretary. If the movement had an overall strategist, it was Alexander Berkman, who moved from center to center providing guidance, inspiration, and organizational talent. Next to Berkman, the leading activists, after their release from prison, were Arthur Caron, Charles Plunkett, and Frank Strawn Hamilton, "all of them boys of education and attainment who had thrown their lot with the workers."[18]

On Saturday, March 21st, at Berkman's suggestion, the Conference of the Unemployed held the first of a series of mass meetings in Union Square. The principal address was delivered by Emma Goldman, described by Carlo Tresca, who shared the platform with her, as "the most colorful and brilliant woman speaker I have ever known," greater even than his companion Gurley

Flynn.[19] Two decades before, under similar circumstances, Goldman had spent a year on Blackwell's Island after exhorting a crowd of unemployed in Union Square to "demonstrate before the palaces of the rich; demand work. If they do not give you work, demand bread. If they deny you both, take bread. It is your sacred right!" Now her message was the same. "Go to the churches," she declared, "go to the hotels and restaurants, go to the bakeshops and tell them that they must give you something to keep you from starving." Berkman and Tresca spoke along the same lines, asserting the right of the unemployed to satisfy their hunger by any means and working the crowd up to a high pitch of excitement.[20]

The meeting concluded with a parade up Fifth Avenue, "a march of the disinherited," as Berkman described it, "whose very appearance was a challenge to the guilty conscience of the exploiters and well-fed idlers." With a large black banner waving at the head, embroidered in red letters with the Italian word "Demolizione," one thousand jobless marched all the way to the Ferrer Center, from Fourteenth Street to 107th Street, where they were treated to food and cigarettes and where those who needed it were given lodgings for the night. As they marched, reported *The New York Times*, they sang revolutionary songs, "punctuated with maledictions upon the homes of the rich that they passed." At the corner of 84th Street, added the *Times*, a limousine found itself blocked by the procession, and Becky Edelsohn, a young anarchist firebrand, spat at the passengers within.[21] For the first time in American history, Berkman remarked, did the black flag of hunger and misery "flutter a menacing defiance in the face of parasitic contentment and self-righteous arrogance."[22]

Two weeks later, on Saturday, April 4th, a second large rally took place in Union Square under the auspices of the Conference of the Unemployed. Black flags, inscribed with "Hunger," "Bread or Revolution," and "Tannenbaum Shall Be Free," proclaimed the purpose of the assembly. But the fight of the unemployed also became a fight for free speech, as the police used the occasion to avenge themselves for the successful demonstration of March 21st by a show of brutality equaled, in Berkman's words, "only by Russian Cossacks of the Red Sunday days." "The cops were mostly Irish," observed Charles Plunkett, himself of Irish descent, "all brutal, and hated everyone who was not Irish, especially Italians and Jews."[23] Led by a mounted detachment, they swooped down on the crowd, wielding their clubs left and right in an effort to break up the meeting. "I was sick at heart last night," wrote Lincoln Steffens the following day. "I was in Union Square yesterday, and saw the unemployed clubbed. I've seen such things for twenty years now, but I can't get used to it. It lifts my stomach every time I see a policeman take his night stick in both his hands and bring it down with all his might on a human being's skull. And then, when he does it, the crowd come about me and ask me if I won't make a complaint against the cop and have him fired! As if I could!"[24]

Many of the demonstrators were injured, including the sculptor Adolf Wolff, who was struck by a policeman and then arrested. Dublin-born Joe O'Carroll, an activist in the movement from the beginning and dubbed "Wild Joe" O'Carroll by the police, was singled out for special treatment in spite of his Irish nationality. Followed from the square by detectives, he was set upon without warning and beaten so severely about the head that he never completely recovered from his injuries. According to eyewitnesses, he might have been clubbed to death but for the intervention of Becky Edelsohn, who threw her arms about him, protecting him with her own body until the clubbing had ceased. Even so, the bleeding was so profuse that an ambulance surgeon from Bellevue Hospital had to take five stitches in O'Carroll's scalp. "I saw O'Carroll covered with blood," a witness declared. "Police and plain clothes men were all around him clubbing and blackjacking him. I saw Becky Edelsohn standing over Joe trying to shield him. I tried to get to her but the police pushed me back. They kicked Joe up Fourth Avenue toward Sixteenth Street, clubbing him. They were clubbing Art Caron. They banged him on the back of the head and kicked him in the calf of his legs. He was all wuzzy. He screamed, 'For Christ's sake, stop hitting me.' "[25]

Caron's affidavit picks up from there: "I was taken to an automobile that was waiting and in it I saw Joe O'Carroll sitting beside Officer No. 744. There were other plain clothes men on the running board and some in front. I was thrown into the automobile and as I stumbled in, No. 744 said, 'You bastard, we've got you now,' and struck me in the face. I fell to my knees and with my head in Joe's lap. I tried to get up and I got another crash in the face, crushing in the right side of my nose, and then I was struck again on the back of the head. I don't know who hit me then. As I went down I remember Joe O'Carroll reached down and patted my cheek and said, 'Poor Caron, poor boy! Jesus! You're getting it awful.' The next thing I knew I was dragged out of the automobile and into the police station. When we got inside we were given a shove and told to go over and sit on a bench by one wall. I was made to sit at one end and O'Carroll at the other. The plain clothes men then discussed what charges they should bring against us. One of them pointed to O'Carroll and said, 'That's O'Carroll: we'll charge him with striking an officer and resisting arrest.' Officer No. 744 pointed to me and said, 'What'll we charge that big bastard with?' The other fellow said, 'Charge the —— with trying to take him away from the police and yelling, 'Kill the bastards!' Officer No. 744 said, 'What do you think of the job I did on that big —— ?' to another officer and pointing at me. Then they made us wash the blood from our faces and necks and hands. They took away O'Carroll's collar which was soaked with blood. Then they took us before the desk and made charges against us, with one of the police officers who was in the lead, dancing and saying merrily, 'We got 'em.' "[26]

To justify the assaults on O'Carroll and Caron, the police charged both men with disorderly conduct and resisting arrest. But the signs of brutality were so overwhelming that the trial magistrate not only discharged the defendants on the ground that they had been arrested without justification, but also criticized the offending officers for interfering with the right of free speech, going so far as to advise counsel for the defense to bring suit against them for assault. Treated for a broken nose and other injuries, Caron, sporting a black eye, emerged from the hospital in time to attend the next demonstration, held in Union Square on April 11th. O'Carroll, however, remained in the hospital until the end of the month, facing the prospect of further operations on his scalp and teeth.[27]

LUDLOW

In the midst of the unemployment agitation, an incident occurred in Colorado which brought matters to a climax. Since the summer of 1913, the Colorado Fuel and Iron Company, in which John D. Rockefeller, Jr., held a controlling interest, had been struck by its workers, most of whom were immigrants from southern and eastern Europe. What the miners were demanding, for the most part, were rights to which they were entitled under existing Colorado statutes, limiting the length of the working day, requiring adequate safety precautions, payment of wages in cash instead of scrip, and freedom to organize without being harassed or blacklisted. The operators, who had been ignoring these statutes for years, refused to deal with union representatives. Instead, they began laying in arms and hiring private guards, who were deputized by local sheriffs and thus given official powers.[28]

In September 1913 armed patrols evicted miners from the company-owned hovels in which they and their families lived, compelling them to move to a tent colony set up by the union at Ludlow. Guards and workers clashed frequently as the strike dragged on. On October 7, 1913, guards attacked the tent colony, killing a miner and wounding a small boy. At Walensburg several days later they fired into a meeting, killing three. The next day a guard was killed when miners fired on the "Death Special," an armed locomotive, forcing it to retreat. At this point the Colorado governor sent in the National Guard to impose order. The strikers at first welcomed them as preferable to the private army of the employers, but the troops proceeded to harass and arrest miners and to molest their wives and daughters. Before long they joined in the efforts of the company to crush the strike.

The historians of the Ludlow strike, George McGovern and Leonard Guttridge, call it "the most ferocious conflict in the history of American labor and industry."[29] It was without doubt one of the most flagrant examples of the use of armed force, both public and private, by an employer against organized labor. To John D. Rockefeller, Jr., the central issue was that of the open shop. "We would rather that the unfortunate conditions should continue," he declared, "and that we should lose all the millions invested, than that American workmen should be deprived of their right, under the Constitution, to work for whom they please. That is the great principle at stake. It is a national issue." President Woodrow Wilson himself wrote that he was "deeply disappointed" by the refusal of management to confer with the miners, yet Rockefeller, called before a Congressional committee, stood firm on his position. Asked why he refused to travel to Colorado to mediate the dispute, he replied: "We have gotten the best men obtainable and are relying on their judgment." In any case, he added, he was guarding a cherished principle by opposing organized labor. "And you will do that if it costs all your property and kills all your employees?" one Congressman asked. "It is a great principle," he replied.[30]

A few weeks later, the strike reached its tragic climax. On April 20, 1914, a detachment of National Guardsmen attacked the Ludlow tent colony with rifles and machine guns, killing five miners and a boy. They then poured oil on the tents and set them ablaze. Eleven children and two women were smothered to death. Three prisoners, including a Greek-born leader of the strike, were savagely beaten and then murdered. "It was," Howard Zinn has noted, "the culminating act of perhaps the most violent struggle between corporate power and laboring men in American history."[31] The strikers retaliated by attacking mines throughout the area. By April 29th, when President Wilson sent in federal troops, seventy-four had been killed on both sides. On December 30, 1914, the miners gave up and called off the strike.

The Ludlow Massacre, as the episode of April 20th became known throughout the nation, marked a turning point in the history of the Rockefeller family, an experience it was never to forget. The smoldering encampment and charred bodies of the miners' families would haunt the Rockefeller clan for half a century, until the name of Attica, where Rockefeller's son Nelson similarly refused to go to mediate the trouble, could take its place. "Mr. Rockefeller," remarked *The New York World* on April 27, 1914, "recently testified that he was willing to sink his entire investment in Colorado rather than yield to the demand of his employees that they be permitted to organize. He has not sunk and he does not intend to sink his entire investment, but he has debauched an American commonwealth, and the blood of women and children is on the hands of his barbarous agents, private and public."[32]

Demonstrations against the Ludlow butchery were not long in coming. Shortly after the incident, silent protestors took up vigil at Rockefeller's New York City residence. On April 28th Upton Sinclair drafted a "solemn warning" to Rockefeller. "I intend this night," he wrote, "to indict you upon a charge of murder before the people of this country."[33] The following week Sinclair led a "silent mourning" parade in front of Rockefeller's office in the Standard Oil Building at 26 Broadway, with Arthur Caron and Leonard Abbott among the marchers, who, dressed in black or wearing black armbands, anticipated the guerrilla theater demonstrations against the Vietnam War.

At one point, a young militant named Marie Ganz managed to enter the Standard Oil Building and make her way upstairs to Rockefeller's office, threatening to shoot him "like a dog" for the Colorado murders, but his doors were locked against her and she was carried off to jail. The protests, however, continued. On May

10th the Reverend Bouck White, pastor of the "Church of the Social Revolution," led a small group (including Arthur Caron and Carlo Tresca) to the Calvary Baptist Church, of which the Rockefellers were members, and challenged the minister to debate the Ludlow affair. As one of the intruders, an anarchist named Milo Woolman, attempted to read verse 24 of the 19th chapter of Matthew ("And again I say unto you, it is easier for a camel to go through the eye of a needle, than for a rich man to enter into the kingdom of God"), the police arrived and arrested him and Reverend White. Brought before Magistrate Campbell, who had tried the St. Alphonsus case, they were condemned to the maximum penalty of six months' imprisonment.[34]

As the Ludlow protests merged with the movement for the unemployed, it was the anarchists, headed by Berkman, who once again assumed the lead. Nightly meetings were held in various parts of the city, with mass rallies in Union Square every Saturday afternoon. At one of these rallies Carlo Tresca made an impassioned speech in Italian, his heart "burning with hatred" against those responsible for the Ludlow killings. Mentioning the name of an Italian victim, he tells us, "tears came to my eyes and my voice was trembling; and in my closing remarks I asked the Italians present the name of the murderer. A roar of angry voices answered: 'Rockefeller! Rockefeller!' Others in the audience joined the chant, 'Rockefeller! Rockefeller!' And then the angry voices of Italians, 'Vendetta! Vendetta!' " As Tresca descended the platform, Caron came up and shook his hand, saying "You made a touching speech, Carlo!" Caron was tense and turned away, murmuring, "We must avenge them. We must."[35]

The anarchist press was likewise calling for vengeance. Denouncing Rockefeller as a "blackhearted plutocrat whose soft, flabby hands carry no standard but that of greed," Margaret Sanger's *Woman Rebel* called on all radicals to "remember Ludlow! Remember the men and women and children who were sacrificed in order that John D. Rockefeller, Jr., might continue his noble career of charity and philanthropy as a supporter of the Christian faith."[36] "What are the American workingmen going to do?" asked *Mother Earth* in its May 1914 issue. "Are they going to pallaver, petition and resolutionize? Or will they show that they still have a little manhood in them, that they will defend themselves and their organizations against murder and destruction? This is no time for theorizing, for fine spun argument and phrases. With machine guns trained upon the strikers, the best answer is—*dynamite*." A month later, in June 1914, *Mother Earth* again called for militant action, including a general strike of all American workers, lamenting that the Ludlow murders were "so far unavenged."

Rockefeller, his life in danger, had meanwhile retreated to the security of Pocantico Hills, the family estate near Tarrytown, some thirty miles north of New York City, where the gates were locked against intruders and guards patrolled around the clock. On May 30th, however, a dozen Ferrer Center anarchists, among them Caron, Plunkett, Jack Isaacson, and Becky Edelsohn, went to Tarrytown and tried to start a meeting in Fountain Square, the recognized outdoor forum of the village. Their aim was to call Rockefeller to account for the Colorado bloodshed. One by one they attempted to speak, but each in turn was arrested. Then the whole group was locked up in the Tarrytown jail, charged with disorderly conduct, blocking traffic, and endangering the public health.

The idea of carrying the protest to Rockefeller's back yard had originated with Alexander Berkman, the chief strategist of the campaign. "Berkman," according to Leonard Abbott, "inspired the entire fight and was in the thick of it."[37] The following day, a Sunday, Berkman himself led a second group to Tarrytown and tried to speak in Fountain Square, only to be roughed up by the police, who arrested three of his companions. The same evening a band of twenty more, mostly Italian and Spanish anarchists, arrived to reinforce Berkman's group, but were pummeled and pushed about by the police and finally driven out of town.

Undaunted, Berkman vowed to continue the struggle. "We are going to defy Rockefeller, the mayor, and the city magistrate," he declared, "and will carry on our agitation and hold meetings no matter who is opposed to us or what machinery is used against us." Over the next few weeks Tarrytown remained the scene of repeated skirmishes between the authorities and the protestors, who invaded Rockefeller's bailiwick, as Will Durant put it, to "bring to his own guarded ears, to the walls and fences that shut him in from the poverty and suffering of the world, the story of what his menials were doing with the slaves he had never seen."[38]

On June 3rd, for instance, Romany Marie Yuster and a committee of Ferrer Center women distributed 5,000 handbills throughout the village, demanding the right to free speech. And on June 22nd a company of forty, including Romany Marie and

Berkman, together with Caron, Plunkett, and Becky Edelsohn, who had been released on bail and were awaiting trial for their arrest on May 30th, went again to Tarrytown in an effort to hold a meeting, this time on land adjacent to the Croton Aqueduct and belonging to the City of New York. A crowd of hostile villagers gathered to hurl insults and missiles. When Caron attempted to speak, a stone struck him full in the mouth, and the blood flowed so profusely that it was difficult to staunch it. When the meeting ended and the anarchists tried to return to the railroad station, the police, who had done nothing to quell the disorder, joined the crowd in assaulting the speakers, clubbing them even as they boarded the train. To Caron, Berkman, and their associates, this was the last straw. Never again would they attempt to demonstrate peacefully in Tarrytown. Denied the right of free speech, they began to contemplate other methods of protest. "Some cherished thoughts of revenge," wrote Leonard Abbott, "and some may have decided to take revenge."[39]

DYNAMITE

Between June 22nd and July 4th a conspiracy was hatched at the Ferrer Center to blow up Rockefeller's mansion. Among the parties to the conspiracy were Arthur Caron, Carl Hanson, and Charles Berg, all of them victims of the Lexington Avenue explosion. Caron, as we have seen, had played a key role in the movement of the unemployed, speaking at open-air meetings and taking part in the occupation of churches, being one of the men who were arrested with Frank Tannenbaum at the Church of St. Alphonsus. During the subsequent weeks spent in prison, he was, said Leonard Abbott, the "soul" of the group, "energizing and inspiring his comrades and holding them up to what he conceived to be a spirit worthy of revolutionists."[40] Caron's release from jail found him once more in the thick of the fight. When Joe O'Carroll was set upon by the police in Union Square, Caron rushed to his defense and was severely beaten. Released from jail for the second time, he was appalled by the news of the massacre at Ludlow. It "ran through his consciousness like a flame," and he threw himself into every effort to fasten the responsibility on the Rockefellers, taking part with Upton Sinclair in his "silent mourning" at 26 Broadway, invading the Calvary Baptist Church with Bouck White, and finally carrying the protest to Tarrytown, where he was stoned as he tried to speak.

For weeks Caron brooded over the bloodshed in Colorado, the assaults by the company guards and the burning of women and children in their tents. He brooded over the failure of the workers to take reprisals. With the suppression of free speech in Tarrytown and the harassment and arrest of his comrades, his indignation rose to fever pitch. "I shall avenge myself!" he cried after being injured on June 22nd. "I knew Caron well," Carlo Tresca later wrote. "I already suspected what he was up to and what the consequences might be." A few days before the explosion, Moritz Jagendorf ran into Caron at the Ferrer Center. "Let's have a cup of coffee," Jagendorf suggested. "No, Moritz," was Caron's reply, "I'm too busy with something very important." "He had a set face," Jagendorf remembers, "very tense. They were working at it—they must have been working at it—from the way he looked and spoke."[41]

Caron's chief accomplices, Carl Hanson and Charles Berg, were Latvians by birth and seasoned revolutionaries, though only in their early twenties. Born in the province of Kurland in 1891, Berg, at fourteen, took part in the 1905 Revolution as a member of the Forest Brethren, a guerrilla band operating in the Baltic region and consisting of anarchists and other uncompromising insurgents.[42] When the group dispersed, Berg continued his revolutionary activity by helping to transport guns and ammunition across the Russian border. For several years thereafter, he worked as a merchant seaman, as did Carl Hanson, a fellow Latvian and revolutionary. The two met in Hamburg and became close friends, making several voyages on the same ship and coming to New York together in 1911, where both found work as carpenters and joined the Latvian Anarchist Group. When a Latvian branch of the Anarchist Red Cross was organized in December 1913, Berg and Hanson were founding members, together with Hanson's half-sister Louise Berger, in whose apartment the explosion occurred. A "quiet, reserved man who made the impression of a distinct and strong personality," Berg joined the Conference of the Unemployed at the Ferrer Center, becoming its assistant treasurer. On May 30th he was arrested with Caron at Tarrytown, and he was also among the group of demonstrators who returned on June 22nd to continue the fight for free speech. Hanson, meanwhile, had been fired from his job as a construction worker on a new Long Island bridge for distributing anarchist literature among his workmates.[43]

Apart from Caron, Hanson, and Berg, who volunteered to carry out the actual bombing, the plot involved several other Ferrer Center militants, among them Louise Berger, Becky Edelsohn, and Charles Plunkett. The chief strategist, however, was Alexander Berkman, older and more experienced than the others and possessed of exceptional organizational abilities. Of Berkman it is generally believed that he had shed his faith in terrorist violence after spending fourteen years in prison for shooting Frick. The facts, however, are otherwise. "Speaking for myself," he wrote to Bolton Hall in 1907, barely a year after his release from jail, "I may say that the fear of the law would not for a moment deter me from advocating anything I believe in. I do not believe in violence, per se. Theoretically speaking, as an Anarchist, I am opposed to violence. I neither advocate it, nor condemn it, when it is the mere explosion of long suppressed misery. If the psychologic moment should arise when I would consider a certain act of violence necessary, I should not advocate it, but execute it myself."[44]

The following year Berkman defended a fellow anarchist who had exploded a bomb in Union Square after the police had broken up a rally of the unemployed with severe clubbings and beatings, a foretaste of 1914. "The bomb," declared Berkman in *Mother Earth*, "is the echo of your cannon, trained upon our starving brothers; it is the cry of the wounded striker; 'tis the voice of hungry women and children; the shriek of those maimed and torn in your industrial slaughter houses; it is the dull thud of the policeman's club upon a defenseless head; 'tis the shadow of the crisis, the rumbling of suppressed earthquake—it is manhood's lightning out of an atmosphere of degradation and misery that king, president and plutocrat have heaped upon humanity. The bomb is the ghost of your past crimes."[45]

To Berkman, in other words, acts of terrorism were the inevitable reply to the much greater violence—war, execution, torture, repression—perpetrated by government and capital against the workers. The greatest bombthrowers were not the isolated individuals driven to desperation, but the military machine of every government—the soldiers, militias, police, firing squads, hangmen. The most immoral acts were committed not by the lonely assassins, but by the captains of industry, the Rockefellers and Fricks, who presided over economic establishments at great remove from the consequences of their crimes. They never thought of themselves as criminals, nor were ever punished as such. On the contrary, they sat on boards of charitable organizations, taught at Sunday schools, accepted honorary degrees from universities, and attended fashionable clubs and churches.

Such was Berkman's position. And for the rest of his life it remained basically unaltered. "He was unrepentant," writes Will Durant, who met him at the Ferrer School in 1912, "and still believed that when other avenues of social protest were blocked by the power of wealth, the oppressed were justified in resorting to violence." In 1914, says Emma Goldman, he was "the revolutionist of old, with the same fanatical belief in the Cause." In 1920 Emma was still referring to Sasha's "conspiratory imagination." And in 1933, three years before his death by his own hand, Berkman himself confided to a friend: "I have grown older since 1892, and I have gained experience. But neither my character nor my views have changed in any fundamental manner. Nor my temperament and revolutionary logic. I believe today, as I believed in 1892, in the justification and *necessity* (under certain circumstances) of revolutionary action, collective as well as individual."[46] Leonard Abbott well understood this aspect of Berkman's character. "He has been one of the strongest influences in my life," he wrote after his friend's suicide, "and at times dominated me, but of course I never accepted his violent doctrines. I liked him *in spite of* his violence, rather than because of it. He was of the type of Michael Bakunin. I am more of the type of Elisée Reclus."[47]

Under the right circumstances, then, or at the appropriate "psychologic moment," as he put it, Berkman regarded terrorism as indispensable. In July 1914 such a moment had arrived. After the repression of the unemployed in Union Square, the slaughter of the miners at Ludlow, the smothering of free speech at Tarrytown, the time was ripe to act. "I am sick of appeals to legality," Berkman declared in *Mother Earth*, "sick of the hope for class justice. It is high time to begin to fight Satan with his own hell fire. An eye for an eye; a tooth for a tooth!"[48] In Berkman's mind, Ludlow, with its Pinkertons and militia and killing of workers, was a repetition of Homestead, and Rockefeller another Frick. Although twenty-two years had since elapsed, all the indignation came rushing back, and all the determination to retaliate.

One recalls that Berkman, in 1892, had tried, unsuccessfully, to construct bombs in a New York tenement to be used against Frick. This time the bomb making was left to others, Berkman limiting himself to the organization of the enterprise, a task at which he excelled. His precise role remains unclear. That he knew the details of the conspiracy is evident from his outline for an autobiography, drafted in 1932, a chapter of which was to recount "the inside story of some explosions."[49] His direct involvement, while harder to prove, is either hinted at or attested to by several of his anarchist comrades. After the explosion, reporters asked Carlo Tresca if Berkman had had a hand in it. "Now, boys, you're pushing me too far," Tresca replied, clearly implying that he had. "Was Berkman involved?" said Moritz Jagendorf when I put the question to him years later. "Well, he was very straightforward, practical, a man of action and of organizing strength. I honestly feel that Berkman was involved, that he helped at least with the planning." The wife of Jack Isaacson went further. "Berkman," she flatly declared, "was the mastermind of the plot."[50]

The most important testimony, however, comes from Charles Plunkett, himself a party to the conspiracy, if not one of its central figures. In *Mother Earth* of July 1914 Plunkett as much as admitted the aim of the group: " 'My conscience acquits me,' said young Rockefeller. We replaced his conscience; we became his Nemesis. His well-oiled conscience acquitted him; but we, the militant workers, have convicted him and passed judgment from his own Bible—'A life for a life.' "[51] As to Berkman's complicity, Plunkett leaves little room for doubt. "Only a few people were involved," he told me in 1975. "Caron, Hanson, and Berg, of course. Louise Berger, Hanson's half-sister, knew about it. It was her apartment, and she left it just minutes before the explosion. I knew about it too, and in fact had spent the previous night—the night of July 2nd—in the apartment. Becky Edelsohn knew about it. And Alexander Berkman. It was Berkman who organized it, though the others were to carry it out, as he was still on probation for his attempt on Frick. He was the only older man in the group, the only one with experience. Emma Goldman was not involved—in fact she was away on a lecture tour at the time. Berkman still believed in the necessity of violence."[52]

After the June 22nd demonstration at Tarrytown, Berkman and his comrades began to discuss reprisals. They met on a number of occasions, the last time at the Ferrer Center on July 3rd, the night before the explosion. Maurice Hollod and several other teenage boys from the school stood guard to make sure that no one interrupted the deliberations. "Berkman was upstairs," Hollod recalls, "with Caron, Hanson, and Berg. In fact, he was the central figure. There had been a number of earlier meetings, and Berkman had attended them all. He hadn't gotten rid of his 'propaganda by the deed' mentality. Around 1 A.M. the men came downstairs. I was wearing a button that said 'GENERAL STRIKE.' Berg saw the button and asked me if he could wear it at a meeting the following day. That was the last I saw of them, because the explosion occurred in the morning."[53]

Immediately after the meeting, it appears, Caron, Hanson, and Berg went up to Tarrytown with a bomb they had constructed. That it was to be planted at Rockefeller's house at Pocantico Hills is beyond dispute, though the details of the plot remain obscure. Apparently the conspirators were unaware that Rockefeller had already gone to his summer home at Seal Harbor, Maine, so that had their plan succeeded he would not have been among the victims, who would have consisted mainly of the servants and staff of the mansion, ordinary workers like themselves. The scheme, in any event, did not come off. Whether the explosive failed to detonate, or whether Caron, Hanson, and Berg were unable to penetrate the heavily guarded estate is still a mystery. At any rate, they were compelled to return to New York with their mission unaccomplished.[54]

What happened from this point on is largely a matter for conjecture. For several months past, it appears, Caron, Hanson, and Berg had been accumulating a supply of dynamite, either to be smuggled into Russia for use by revolutionary groups or to be used in connection with the unemployed agitation in New York. The dynamite, some of which had been stolen from the site of the Lexington Avenue subway, then under construction, had been stored in Louise Berger's apartment, to which the three men now repaired. Their intention, as far as can be determined, was to make another try at Rockefeller later in the morning. At 9 A.M. Louise Berger left the apartment and went to Berkman at the office of *Mother Earth* on 119th Street, possibly to inform him that the device had been adjusted and was ready for use. At 9:16, while she was talking to Berkman, the explosion occurred. "It was the bomb for Rockefeller that set it all off," lamented Plunkett years later. "I'll never know why they brought the damn thing back!"[55]

The effects of the explosion have already been described. Caron, Hanson, and Berg were instantly killed, together with Marie Chavez, who had not been involved in the conspiracy but merely rented a room in the apartment and occasionally attended Ferrer Center lectures. One other person was in the apartment, a young

Wobbly named Michael Murphy. Asleep when the blast occurred, Murphy had a miraculous escape when his bed fell through the floor to the apartment below. Dazed but uninjured, he staggered into the street, where a policeman gave him his coat. Murphy managed to slip away and went to the office of *Mother Earth*, where Berkman at once sent him, accompanied by Plunkett, to Abbott's picnic in New Jersey. From there he was taken to Philadelphia by members of the Radical Library whom Joseph Cohen had summoned by telephone. After lying low for a while, he was sent to England by way of Canada. More than twenty years later, he wrote to Cohen asking if it was safe to come back. "Dad gave such a double-take when he read that," Emma Cohen remembers, "and figured that if he had to ask such a question after all that time he had better stay put. So he answered no."[56]

By the time Murphy arrived at Westfield, Berkman was already being questioned by the police, who suspected him of complicity in the bomb plot. Berkman denied any knowledge of the affair, though he acknowledged Caron, Hanson, and Berg as acquaintances. When asked about the July 3rd meeting at the Ferrer Center, he said it had been merely to discuss the defense of the Tarrytown demonstrators, who were shortly to stand trial. The police, unconvinced, put a constant tail on Berkman in an effort to link him with the explosion. One day, shortly after the incident, Maurice Hollod saw Berkman on the street and ran over to greet him. "Berkman was a lovable character," Hollod reminisces. "He loved children. He was an impeccable dresser in a light grey suit with panama hat and cane, mustache and glasses. I ran instinctively to him. He stopped me and quietly told me to go home. I was crushed. But he later explained that he was being followed and didn't want me hurt."[57]

In addition to Berkman, the police questioned Louise Berger, Marie Ganz, and other Ferrer Center militants, but could get nothing out of them. Women detectives offered ten-year-old Emma Cohen ice cream and "tried to wheedle information out of me," but she too remained silent.[58] The Ferrer School and *Mother Earth* were put under continuous surveillance, and policemen raided the Bresci group on 106th Street and roughed up its members, all to no avail. No evidence was uncovered to implicate anyone else in the conspiracy, or indeed to prove that a conspiracy had existed.

Some radicals, however, were sufficiently intimidated to disclaim all connection with the alleged dynamiters. Speaking for the I.W.W., Joseph Ettor denied that Caron had been a member of his organization, which did "not approve of dynamiting or setting off bombs." Carlo Tresca, infuriated by this cowardly display, insisted that Caron had indeed belonged to the I.W.W. Unemployed Union, formed in New York the previous winter, and expressed his admiration for Caron's courage, "because it shows that he was not the man who can be trampled upon with impunity."[59] In a letter to Mary Heaton Vorse, Tresca's companion, Elizabeth Gurley Flynn, complained that "everybody is busy here repudiating the poor boys although no connection has actually been established between them and the bomb dynamite." Even if the charges were true, she added, "the terrible treatment Caron received at the hands of the police, plus his personal suffering, is responsible for his psychology." Gurley Flynn speculated that the explosion had been the work of the police or of Rockefeller's agents, bent on removing the most troublesome protestors. Her suspicions focused on "this mysterious figure called Murphy who drifted in a few days ago, claimed he was in the apartment yet was the only one not killed and has now disappeared completely. How easy it would be for a detective to pose as a down and out, work on their sympathy and leave incriminating evidence in their apartment, possibly not intending it to explode, but preparing for a raid!"[60]

At the Ferrer Center itself there were some who feared that the incident might damage the school's reputation. *The Modern School* magazine pointed out that Caron, Hanson, and Berg had not been dues-paying members of the Ferrer Association, yet acknowledged that they had been frequent visitors to the Center and "participated in the discussions and social life, the same as all others who come there." Leonard Abbott wrote to Rose Pastor Stokes in a similar vein: "Needless to say, the Association, as an Association, had nothing to do with the Lexington Avenue affair. Caron, Berg and Hanson, the boys who were killed, were not even members of the Association, tho they came to the School occasionally and I knew them all. Whatever they did, they did on their own initiative and without consultation with others."[61]

The majority of anarchists, however, hastened to defend their fallen comrades, hailing them as martyrs to the cause of the oppressed. Mike Gold and Adolf Wolff dedicated poems to their memory, and their deaths were lamented in the Russian organ of the Anarchist Red Cross, which printed a black box with the names of Berg and Hanson, who had been active members. *The Woman Rebel*, praising their courage and defiance, declared that it was time "to accept and exult in every act of revolt against oppression, to encourage and create in ourselves that spirit of rebellion which shall lead us to understand and look at the social situation without flinching or quavering or running to cover when any crisis arises."[62]

No one defended Caron, Hanson, and Berg with greater vehemence than Alexander Berkman. On July 6th Berkman proposed that the three men be given a public funeral, with a procession through the streets of the city to be followed by memorial speeches over their coffins in Union Square. Big Bill Haywood, the Wobbly leader, tried to dissuade Berkman, fearing "another eleventh of November," referring to the Haymarket affair of the 1880s.[63] The procession, in any case, was forbidden by the police, and on Wednesday, July 8th, the bodies of Caron, Hanson, and Berg were cremated quietly in Queens in the presence of a small group of mourners, including Berg's brother, Hanson's half-sister (Louise Berger), and Caron's mother and sister, who came from Fall River for the ceremony.

Not one to let such a moment slip by unnoticed, Berkman set about arranging a mass memorial demonstration to pay tribute to the three men and assess the significance of their deaths. On Saturday, July 11th, a crowd of fifteen to twenty thousand assembled in Union Square in a gathering described by *Mother Earth* as "the most impressive of its kind ever held in America."[64] Among the organizations represented were the Ferrer Association, the Mother Earth Publishing Association, the Anti-Militarist League, and Jewish, Italian, and Spanish anarchist groups from Philadelphia, Trenton, Paterson, Newark, Hoboken, and Albany, as well as New York. The demonstrators wore red and black armbands and red flowers in their lapels. Placards and banners carried such pronouncements as "We Mourn Our Comrades," "You Did Not Die in Vain," and "Capitalism the Evil, Anarchism the Remedy." A band played Chopin's funeral march, the *Marseillaise*, the *Internationale*, and selections from David Edelstadt's revolutionary songs. The crowd joined in, and strains of song carried far across the square. It was an intensely emotional occasion.

From the speakers' platform, bedecked with an array of banners, wreaths, and flowers, Berkman opened the meeting with a eulogy to Caron, Hanson, and Berg, "martyrs to the cause of humanity," who had proved that "there are still men in the labor movement who will not stand quietly by when they themselves and other workers are persecuted, oppressed and maltreated." Alluding to the explosion that had taken their lives, Berkman declared: "I want to go on record as saying that I hope our comrades had themselves prepared the bomb, intending to use it upon the enemy. Why do I say this? Because I believe, and firmly believe, that the oppression of labor in this country, the persecution of the radical elements especially, has reached a point where nothing but determined resistance will do any good. And I believe with all my heart in resistance to tyranny on every and all occasions. It was a great American who said that the tree of liberty must be watered now and then by the blood of tyrants. That holds good today as it did a hundred years ago. When workers are shot down for demanding better conditions of living, when their women and children are slaughtered and burned alive, then I say that it is time for labor to quit talking and begin to act." Berkman ended by proclaiming Caron, Hanson, and Berg harbingers of the social revolution, "determined to show an example to labor by resisting to the full extent of their ability the exploitation, the oppression and the persecution of the capitalist class. As such I acclaim them the conscious, brave and determined spokesmen of the working class, and I call upon you, friends and fellow workers, for three cheers for our dead comrades."[65]

Berkman was followed by Leonard Abbott, who placed the Lexington Avenue incident against the background of the mounting social conflict of the times: "the fight to overthrow the horrors of Russian autocracy; the struggle of the unemployed in New York to get work, food and shelter; the death-cries of miners and their women and children massacred by the hired gunmen of capitalists in Colorado; the throttled voices of men and women who tried to tell of these things in Tarrytown and to call the richest man in the world to account for his crimes—all are related to these friends of ours who died so terrible a death last week." Had Caron, Hanson, and Berg been allowed the normal avenues of protest, Abbott said, "they would still be living men. The real danger lies always in suppression, not expression." Abbott laid their deaths at the door of the capitalist system: "If men of generous and ardent minds are driven to the manufacture of dynamite bombs as a remedy for the wrongs under which they suffer, there must be something fundamentally wrong with our social system. And there IS something fundamentally wrong, as every serious man admits. A society in which extreme luxury and extreme poverty are the normal condition; in which hundreds of thousands of men seek, but cannot find, employment; in which the most industrious are often the poorest; in which we see every day suicides caused by poverty; in which we see prostitution flaring at every street corner—stands self-condemned and carries within itself the germs of every kind of pathological expression."

The next speaker, Becky Edelsohn, pursued the same tack, demanding to know "why it is that in the twentieth century men, sensitive men and women, can be so goaded by oppression that they are forced to retaliate with violence." The press talks of the violence committed by our comrades, she said. "But consider: every day that the capitalist system is in existence, it is perpetuated by violence; and that is the only way that it manages to hold its own. They talk about violence! What about the massacre in Ludlow? What about the Triangle fire? What about the thousands and thousands of victims in the factories who are daily crippled and maimed or killed in explosions in the subway, railways and mines? Talk about violence! What about the thousands of boys who are enlisted in the armies, sent to murder or be murdered before they realize the significance of joining the army? Talk about violence! Where are the Rockefellers, who are guilty of the slaughter committed in Ludlow? Why doesn't the prostitute press talk about *their* violence? Because they are kept by just these Rockefellers and the rest of the rotten fellows that uphold this capitalist system. Oh, don't let us hear any more twaddle about violence. All the violence that has been committed by the labor movement since the dawn of history wouldn't equal one day of violence committed by the capitalist class in power."

In the most militant speech of the day, Charles Plunkett quoted the defiant words of the Haymarket anarchist Louis Lingg: "If you attack us with cannon, we will attack you with dynamite." While mourning the death of his comrades, Plunkett rejoiced that the social revolution was still alive, indeed "more alive than ever." "I cannot answer for others," he declared. "I can speak only for myself; as for me, I am for violence. Not only defensive violence, but offensive violence. I don't believe in waiting until we are attacked. We have done that too long. It is time for labor to learn to strike the first blow." Echoing the words of Louis Lingg,

Plunkett concluded as follows: "They have guns, they have cannon, they have soldiers, they have discipline, they have armies—and we have dynamite. To oppression, to exploitation, to tyranny, to jails, to clubs, guns, armies and navies, there is but one reply: dynamite!"[66]

For all the violent rhetoric, the meeting passed off without incident. The next day, July 12th, an urn containing the ashes of Caron, Hanson, and Berg was put on display at the Mother Earth Publishing Association on East 119th Street. Thousands of visitors filed through the offices and into the garden, where a kind of altar, a small stand draped in black and red, had been erected, upon which the urn reposed. The fence surrounding the garden was hung with the banners and placards used in the previous day's demonstration. Wreaths and crimson blossoms completed the picture.

The urn, bearing the inscription "Killed, July 4, 1914, Caron, Hanson, Berg," took the shape of a pyramid, with a clenched fist bursting from the apex, evoking Balfour-Ker's drawing "From the Depths," with its worker's fist breaking through a ballroom floor to menace the wealthy above. The urn exerted a powerful and strangely hypnotic effect and was vividly remembered decades later by those who had seen it. Its creator, Adolf Wolff, explained the symbolism of the design: "It conveys three meanings. By the pyramid is indicated the present unjust gradation of society into classes, with the masses on the bottom and the privileged classes towering above them to the apex, where the clenched fist, symbolical of the social revolution, indicates the impending vengeance of those free spirits who refuse to be bound by the present social system and rise above it, threatening its destruction. The urn further symbolizes the strength and endurance of the revolution, having its foundation in so solid a base. A third suggestion is that of a mountain in course of eruption, the crude, misshapen stem fist indicating the lava of human indignation which is about to belch forth and carry destruction to the volcano which has given it birth."[67]

From *Mother Earth* the urn was taken to the Ferrer Center and displayed in the auditorium. A few years later, when the Center was preparing to close, it was removed to the Stelton Colony. A memorial meeting was held, with Leonard Abbott reciting a brief eulogy, after which the ashes were scattered to the winds blowing across an open field. For a long while thereafter, according to

Harry Kelly, the bronze fist with the hollow pyramid beneath served "the peaceful function of a bell to call children to school and adults to meetings."[68]

THE HUTCHINSONS

The Lexington Avenue tragedy had immediate and severe repercussions within the Modern School. In the wake of the explosion, police spies infiltrated the adult lectures and meetings in an effort to sniff out conspiracy. Hitherto ignored by the press, the school fell prey to snooping reporters, eager for stories of sedition. Overnight, like the Barcelona Escuela Moderna, it acquired a reputation as a bomb factory, a hotbed of incendiarism and subversion. For a time, noted Leonard Abbott, it appeared that the whole venture might go up "in a blaze of sensation," sparked by the Lexington Avenue incident.[69]

With each passing week the situation continued to deteriorate. Appalled by the explosion, Alden Freeman withdrew his financial support. Since the rent and salaries had come largely from his monthly contributions, the school faced the prospect of bankruptcy. Freeman, moreover, quit the advisory board of the Ferrer Association, as did Upton Sinclair, J. G. Phelps Stokes, and several other socialists and liberals, ending the alliance between revolutionaries and reformers on which the association had been founded. The most serious defection, apart from Freeman's, was that of Cora Bennett Stephenson, who resigned as principal of the Day School after a single year in the job. With only a few weeks remaining before the start of the new semester, the association began a frantic search for a replacement. By a stroke of good fortune, its efforts were successful, and the school, during what proved to be its final year in New York, found itself in the capable hands of Robert and Delia Hutchinson.

The Hutchinsons were a remarkable couple. Like Bayard Boyesen, Hutchins Hapgood, and Carl Zigrosser, they were well-to-do college-bred people whose social conscience led them to contribute their services to the underprivileged. From a family of Philadelphia lawyers, Bobby Hutchinson, "an ardent young gentleman of leisure," in Joseph Cohen's description,[70] was educated at Harvard, then taught for two years at the Berkshire School before returning to Harvard for graduate study. Deedee was a Radcliffe girl whose maternal and paternal grandfathers were Henry Wadsworth Longfellow and Richard Henry Dana, who himself had taught at Bronson Alcott's pioneering Temple School in Boston. (Another ancestor, Charles Dana, had taught at the school of the Brook Farm community.) One of Deedee's brothers, Henry Wadsworth Longfellow Dana, was to be discharged from the Columbia University faculty by Nicholas Murray Butler for opposing America's entry into the war, and was later active on behalf of Sacco and Vanzetti. Deedee, a hygiene and diet enthusiast, dropped out of Radcliffe in order to train as a nurse at Johns Hopkins, and wrote a book about the "natural" approach to child care, which she was to practice with her own offspring and teach to the pupils of the Modern School.[71]

Married in June 1913, Bobby, then twenty-five, and Deedee, twenty-three, spent their honeymoon on a trip around the world, highlighted by an eight-month visit to New Zealand. There they studied the socialist system at first hand. In a book based on their experience, they concluded that state socialism was in reality a species of state capitalism, though they were to name their first child Tregear, after the New Zealand socialist leader.[72] Their trip cut short by the outbreak of the war, they returned to the United States and went almost directly to the Ferrer School, of which Bobby became the third principal in as many years, succeeding Will Durant and Cora Bennett Stephenson.

Under the direction of the Hutchinsons, the school gained a new lease on life. Outgoing and genial, Bobby was a tall, thin, and good-looking young man, "all angles and crinkly," as one pupil remembered him, but with a friendly smile. Deedee was "more solid, brisk and positive," and very attractive. In her unconventional dress and short tunic, and with her short hair held back by a headband, she seemed to Carl Zigrosser "the incarnation of a pagan goddess." The children were at once enamored of this attractive upper-class couple, with their stories of the far-off places they had visited and the strange ways of life they had seen, though to inhabitants of the Harlem ghetto Deedee's tales of Boston society life—"teas and dowagers, dances and Harvard football games"—were as exotic as Bobby's descriptions of Egypt.[73]

The new school year opened on September 15, 1914. To celebrate the occasion a luncheon was held at which the speakers were Bobby Hutchinson, Joseph Cohen, and Gussie Miller, with Leonard Abbott in the chair. Alexander Berkman arrived during the course of the festivities and "spoke informally to the children,"[79] who afterward settled down to work. For all the recent troubles, 1914-1915 proved to be an exciting year, one of the most successful in the school's history. "We were taken to the theater and movies," recalls Magda Boris, "including the first documentary about penguins at the North Pole. Robert Henri, a friend of Isadora Duncan's, got us tickets for her dancing and for Sophocles' *Oedipus*, staged by her brother Raymond. We saw Maeterlinck's *Blue Bird*, which we ourselves produced at Stelton a few years later."[75]

Seeing Isadora Duncan was a particularly memorable experience. The children sat in the orchestra of the Metropolitan Opera House, "where the strong conflicting smells of the fine ladies distracted us," wrote Emma Cohen, "so that we could hardly pay attention to the performance. She opened up a new world of music and light and rhythm to us. We went back to the school and danced and danced," especially the ten-year-old daughter of George Brown and Mary Hansen, about whom Henrietta Rodman composed a poem:

Heloise Hansen hyphen Brown,
Never stands up when she can sit down,
Never sits down when she can be dancin',
Heloise Brown hyphen Hansen.[76]

Bobby Hutchinson, who at Harvard had played in productions of the Hasty Pudding Society, taught the children the more traditional forms of dancing, humming Mendelssohn's *Spring Song* and repeating "Down and up, and one, two, three" as he moved across the floor, "so long and thin," says Magda Boris, "that he was funny."[77] Under Bobby's supervision, the children produced their own magazine, a small mimeographed affair containing stories, poems, and illustrations, the first of a long series of children's magazines that was to continue at Stelton and Mohegan.

Well acquainted with the history of libertarian education, on which he wrote a series of articles for *The Modern School*,[78] Bobby experimented with different methods of instruction and had a mind open to new ideas. On one point, however, he was emphatic: the importance of individual initiative and self-development. Hailing Pestalozzi's dictum, "It is life that educates," he interpreted it to mean that education consists in one's own experiences and cannot be obtained at second hand. "Education should be libertarian," he insisted, "that is, the child should not be forced to do what it has no desire to do," but should be encouraged to pursue its own interests and to work in its own way. The teacher, accordingly, should merely observe and encourage, without intruding too much, lest the healthy spontaneity of learning be disrupted. Nor must the motive of the pupil be "reward or fear of punishment," but only "the joy of doing the thing."[79]

In keeping with this approach, the children of the Modern School were permitted to work at their own pace, "always in their own way." They selected their own projects, purchased their own supplies, and even (under Deedee's supervision) prepared and served their own lunch in the dining room downstairs. "We were always building or planning something," recalls Emma Cohen, "and our school life was very zestful." By her own choice, she herself read astronomy with Bobby throughout the school year, an experience she found "terribly exciting."[80]

Play occupied an important part of the school day. A favorite game was "Robin Hood and His Merry Men," in which, as Emma Cohen remembers, "the triumph of the young over the old, the poor over the rich, the spirit of the wild free life of the woods over the forces of law and order all satisfied and enriched us." The pupils also played a game called "Hospital," in which Deedee, a trained nurse, coached them on the symptoms and treatment of illness. "We all became very glib in describing and diagnosing ailments and learned much about first aid," says Emma Cohen, "and it was unusually good fun." Deedee, moreover, brought a life-size celluloid doll to school and taught the children how to bathe and care for a baby (she herself was pregnant at the time). She also took the girls upstairs for a talk about sex, but as soon as it was over they ran right out into the yard and told the boys all about it. "No one," Emma Cohen remembers, "ever sequestered us for any purpose after that."[81]

As in the past, the children went on frequent excursions and outings. They haunted the Museum of Natural History and the Metropolitan Museum of Art, visited a newspaper plant and various factories, including the Sunshine Biscuit Company, where they sampled the products in such quantity that many returned sick. ("What a clucking among the mothers when Bobby brought us back that day!") During the course of the year the teaching staff increased from two to four, and a number of visiting instructors (including Temma Camitta and Gertrude Traubel from Philadelphia) assisted in the work. New classes were added in cello, singing, and other subjects.

For the adults too it was an active year, in spite of accumulating troubles. The roster of visiting lecturers included such distinguished names as Clarence Darrow of Chicago and Joseph

McCabe of London, in addition to Edwin Markham, Lincoln Steffens, Hutchins Hapgood, Theodore Schroeder, and such regulars as Leonard Abbott, Harry Kelly, and Will Durant. Hundreds crowded the small auditorium to hear them and to hear Margaret Sanger on "The Limitation of Offspring" and Elizabeth Gurley Flynn on "Syndicalism and Woman," not to mention Hippolyte Havel, who delivered a series of ten lectures on anarchism. There was also a rich variety of evening courses—in art, English, drama, mathematics, Esperanto, singing—so that Abbott urged Rose Pastor Stokes to visit ("Things are really moving here") and Joseph Cohen called the season "the most successful in the history of the School."[82] Among the special events was the fourth annual ball of the Ferrer Association, held at the Harlem Casino on 116th Street, and a meeting to commemorate the fifth anniversary of Ferrer's execution, held in the Forward Hall on East Broadway, with Bill Shatoff, Harry Kelly, and Alexander Berkman as featured speakers.

For all this vitality, however, the problems created by the July 4th explosion refused to disappear. The most serious was the financial crisis resulting from the withdrawal of Alden Freeman's support. Though Bobby Hutchinson relinquished his salary and money continued to come in from sympathetic labor unions and branches of the Workmen's Circle, it was not enough to meet expenses. To replenish the association's coffers a number of expedients were adopted. A modest rise in tuition went into effect, and Jagendorf's Free Theatre put on plays by Galsworthy and Lord Dunsany as benefit performances for the school. In December 1914 a Christmas bazaar, organized by Rose Abbott and Minna Lowensohn, brought thousands of visitors to the Center and hundreds of dollars to its treasury. And in April 1915 a debate on "Social Revolution versus Social Reform" took place between Emma Goldman and Dr. I. A Hourwich, a well-known socialist physician, which netted additional funds. Despite repeated appeals, however, an endowment sufficient to assure a continuous income failed to materialize.

Another serious problem was the growing number of spies and provocateurs who infested the Center. Shortly after the explosion, two new faces made their appearance at association meetings. "Both became very active and always delivered revolutionary, inflammatory speeches," Isidore Wisotsky recalled. "They were strong proponents of violence, bombs and dynamite."[83] One of the spies, whose name was Spivak,[84] was exposed when he neglected to place a stamp on the envelope containing one of his reports. Mailed on stationery of the Modern School, the letter was returned to 107th Street. Abbott, noticing the words "Burns Detective Agency" on the envelope, opened it and at once informed Berkman, who saw to it that Spivak did not return. The second newcomer, Amedeo Polignani, was a detective with the Police Department Bomb Squad. Joining the Bresci group on East 106th Street, a few blocks from the Center, he proceeded to entrap two young members, Frank Abarno and Carmine Carbone, into a dynamite conspiracy. On October 13, 1914, the anniversary of Ferrer's execution, Abarno and Carbone planted bombs in St. Patrick's Cathedral and in the Church of St. Alphonsus, which exploded with minor damage. The men were arrested afterward and condemned to six to twelve years in Sing Sing prison.[85]

Apart from Spivak and Polignani, several other double agents were uncovered, among them David Sullivan, who spoke at the Union Square memorial for Caron, Hanson, and Berg, took part in the Tarrytown protests (for which he spent thirty days in jail!), and acted in Jagendorf's theater group before his identity came to light. To gain entry into the Center's inner circle, yet another agent, Max Potocki, made love to Minna Lowensohn until his wife found out and exposed him. Potocki had already aroused suspicion when he came to Jagendorf for dental work. While drilling his teeth Jagendorf brushed against him and felt a gun in his hip pocket. "What scoundrels they were," Jagendorf recollects, "talking with us, laughing with us, sharing our ideals, our hopes, our excitement—or at least pretending to!"[86]

The severe financial straits in which the school found itself, combined with the presence of police spies and the general atmosphere of anxiety and suspicion, led a growing number of Ferrer Association members, above all Harry Kelly, to consider a change of location for the enterprise. During the summer of 1914, shortly after the explosion and when the destiny of the school hung in the balance, Kelly had spent his vacation at Fellowship Farm, a socialist colony in Stelton, New Jersey, some thirty miles south of New York, where his companion Mary Krimont had a shack on the property of the colony's secretary, Robert Graham. Aware of the association's plight, Graham suggested to Kelly that it buy the adjoining farm, then sell enough land as individual plots to cover the cost, leaving the old buildings and a few acres of ground for the school.

The suggestion took root. On his return to New York, Kelly

pursued the idea with Leonard Abbott and Joseph Cohen. Cohen, reminded of "the boundless fields and meadows in the old country" where he had spent his own childhood, was particularly enthusiastic.[87] On September 24, 1914, a meeting was called at the Ferrer Center to consider the establishment of a colony within commuting distance of New York. Those who favored the project argued that, removed from "the distracting elements of the city," the pupils of the Day School would be "in a more receptive mood" to learn. "Children," they insisted, "require brightness and joy and they can best receive that far, and yet not too far, from 'the madding crowd.' " On the premise that "the country would provide better soil for the development of Ferrer's ideas of education," a Ferrer Colony Association, with Kelly as chairman and Abbott as treasurer, was formed to look into the purchase of land.[88]

A search then began for a quiet rural location where the New York experiment might be continued in the kind of natural setting of which libertarians had always dreamed. By early 1915 the adults at the Ferrer Center were "all talking colony." Bobby Hutchinson, putting the situation to pedagogical use, had the children divide the auditorium into plots with chalk lines. "We laid out roads and community holdings and built orange crate houses," Emma Cohen recalls. "We built our own community and played 'colony' till the spring, when we moved out to Stelton to begin to live the game we had played."[89]

After examining a number of alternative sites, the Colony Association decided on the spot originally suggested by Robert Graham, adjacent to Fellowship Farm. The initial purchase of land, known as the First Tract, consisted of sixty-eight acres, fifty of which were sold to members at one hundred and fifty dollars an acre, nine acres being set aside for the school. The remainder was taken up by roads and waste land. The association took formal possession of the property on March 15, 1915. Meanwhile, the desire to live close to nature, the proximity of the site to the city, and the favorable terms on which the land could be acquired attracted many prospective buyers, and all the plots were quickly sold. On April 13th a banquet was held in Beethoven Hall on East Fifth Street to celebrate the signing of the deeds, with speeches by Harry Kelly, Leonard Abbott, and Joseph Cohen, as well as by Bobby Hutchinson, Hippolyte Havel, Hutchins Hapgood, and Saul Yanovsky. Preparations were started to move the school the following month. A new chapter in the history of the Ferrer movement was about to begin.

AFTERMATH

After the departure of the Day School, which took place in May 1915, the Ferrer Center remained in existence for three more years, continuing to provide a forum for revolutionary ideas until the spring of 1918, when it was driven out of business by the antiradical hysteria that followed America's entry into the war. During these years, the evening and weekend lectures and adult courses went on much as before. An Anarchist Forum was held every Sunday at 8 P.M., with discussions conducted by Abbott, Kelly, Havel, and Gussie Miller, "the type," according to *The Woman Rebel*, "who can be depended upon in the class struggle—the Rebel type."[90] Beginning in January 1916, the basement of the Center became the headquarters of a circle of anarchist militants known as the Group Revolt, which launched a weekly journal called *Revolt* ("the Stormy Petrel of the Labor Movement") and sponsored meetings to commemorate the Paris Commune and other events on the anarchist calendar.[91]

To replace Joseph Cohen as custodian, a veteran anarchist named Lydia Landau came to live at the Center and, with her teenage daughters Sophie and Eva, cleaned, cooked, and kept the place in order. Bill Shatoff, who also lived at the Center, took over Cohen's job as organizer of the Ferrer Association. Although no attempt was made to start a new Day School, the Sunday School was revived under Dr. Solomon Bauch, with the usual picnics, outings, and visits to zoos and museums. To provide for rent and upkeep, an admission fee was charged for some of the lectures and the former classrooms on the second floor were rented out as apartments. Yet without more substantial resources it was hard to make ends meet. By the summer of 1916, as Abbott wrote Carl Zigrosser, the Center was "struggling for its very existence."[92]

The final crisis occurred after the United States entered the war in April 1917. As a center of antimilitarist propaganda, 63 East 107th Street came under the surveillance of federal and local authorities. "Police were there every night," recalls Maurice Hollod, "arresting and harassing the boys." The Lusk Committee, formed by the New York State legislature to investigate seditious activity, charged that Ferrer School children had been taken "at the most impressionable age" and taught an "utter disregard for our laws, and imbued with the idea that a state of anarchy was the true blissful state." That such an institution should have been allowed to exist for almost ten years, the committee complained, was "not a very high compliment to the City of New York."[93]

The magazine *Revolt*, which had taken a strong antiwar stand, had already been banned from the mails in 1916, and now *Mother Earth* and *The Blast* were also suppressed and Emma Goldman and Alexander Berkman imprisoned for agitating against conscription. In an effort to secure their release, Leonard Abbott, Pryns Hopkins, and Dr. C. L. Andrews formed a League for the Amnesty of Political Prisoners. But to no avail. In December 1919, after serving two years in federal prison, Berkman and Goldman were deported to Soviet Russia, along with hundreds of militants of various stripes, some of whom had been associated with the Ferrer Center. Other Ferrer members, including Bill Shatoff and Louise Berger, had meanwhile returned to Russia of their own volition to fight for the Revolution.

In April 1918, deprived of its most active supporters and under mounting pressure from the government, the Ferrer Center was forced to close.[94] For another year, from October 1918 to June 1919, the Ferrer Association continued to offer lectures in a rented hall on Madison Avenue, before completely suspending operations. Thus ended a vital phase in the history of the Modern School. In after years, an anarchist branch of the Workmen's Circle named itself the Ferrer Center branch in honor of the educational experiment which had flourished in New York between 1911 and 1918. After the Second World War the building at 63 East 107th Street, which had served as the Center's quarters for most of its seven and a half years, was torn down to make way for a low-income housing project.

Part II
Stelton

Chapter 7

The Early Years

Pioneers

On Sunday, May 16, 1915, the Modern School moved from New York to Stelton. The weather was unpropitious, for it rained all day and the air was raw and chilly. Arriving at Stelton station on the early morning train, more than a hundred adults and children marched a mile and half in the downpour and reached the colony soaked to the skin. Their spirits, however, were not dampened, as Alexis Ferm remarked, "for when were pioneers deterred from their endeavors by the hardships imposed by nature!"[1]

Except for Alexander Berkman and Emma Goldman, who were both on lecture tours, nearly all the key figures of the Ferrer movement were present for the opening ceremonies, held in the unfinished children's dormitory. Against a background of posters from Ferrer's original Escuela Moderna, sent for the occasion by Margaret Sanger (then on tour of Spain and Europe), Leonard Abbott, Harry Kelly, Joseph Cohen, Will Durant, and Bobby Hutchinson addressed the inaugural gathering, after which Carl Zigrosser planted two lilac trees on the lawn in front of the farmhouse. Thus began the longest experiment in anarchist education and communal living in American history.[2]

When the ceremonies were over, most of the visitors departed, leaving six adults and thirty-two children to face the hardships of country life, to which few of them were accustomed. The colony, consisting of sixty-eight acres of land, an old farmhouse without modern conveniences, an old ramshackle barn, and the uncompleted dormitory, presented a bleak appearance, accentuated by the flat terrain and rainy weather, which continued for the rest of the month. The soil was poor, Stelton being situated along the clay belt running from Perth Amboy to Trenton. There was no adequate water supply or source of heat for the winter, and visitors were disappointed "not to see rolling hills or more picturesque views." As Joseph Cohen admitted, "we selected a homesite without knowing anything about the requirements of soil, drainage, shade, bathing facilities and all the other things that make life in the country pleasant and attractive."[3]

The first settlers lived in tents and tar-paper shacks until more permanent dwellings could be erected. "We had to work for our living, build our own homes, lay out our own streets and plant our own trees," Cohen recalls. Mosquitoes kept the colonists awake at night. On the eve of the dedication, moreover, the ceiling of the farmhouse collapsed, and a group of volunteer carpenters and painters from Brownsville had to make hasty repairs. As one of the children describes it: "the nearest telephone was a mile away. There was no electricity and no central heating. We had outhouses for many years and unreliable running water. Dirt roads became impassable during the spring. It was all very primitive."[4]

The initial months were the hardest, but with effort and perseverance most of the difficulties were overcome. Bit by bit, trees and gardens were planted, heating and water facilities installed, shacks and tents replaced by permanent houses. The old farmhouse was refurbished and the barn transformed to include a library and stage. On July 4, 1915, a Second Tract of forty acres was acquired. Before the year was over a Third Tract of thirty-two acres was added, making a total of 140 acres. At the same time, the number of colonists mounted, so that by 1919 about one hundred families had land at Stelton, of which between twenty and thirty lived there all year round.[5]

For the writer Mike Gold, who spent four months at the colony, Stelton was "a strange exotic jewel of radicalism placed in this dull setting, a scarlet rose of revolution blooming in this cabbage patch, a Thought, an Idea, a Hope, balancing its existence in the great Jersey void."[6] Within the interstices of American society, the colonists sought an alternative to an economic and social system that they regarded as morally monstrous and unjust. They sought to recapture a more natural life unspoiled by urban and industrial blight, to create a freer world in which they would direct their own affairs in accordance with libertarian values. "They wish," as Mike Gold put it, "to become free workers—gentle, creative, loving, truthful men and women, toiling shoulder to shoulder in a community of friends, envying no one, commanding no one, taking no thought of the morrow and of the individual self, living according to that divinest of rules for the conduct of life, 'From each according to his ability, to each according to his need.' "[7]

If such was their object, they fell short of achieving it. For one thing, the economy at Stelton was neither collectivist nor self-sufficient. Rather, it was closely tied to the economy of the outside world. Nearly all of the residents were wage-earners who commuted to jobs in New York (a few worked in New Brunswick and Philadelphia), mostly in the garment industry, though there were carpenters, painters, plumbers, electricians, cigarmakers, and workers in other trades. To supplement their income, a number of colonists engaged in small farming, principally poultry raising, and a number of cooperatives were started—a cooperative grocery, cooperative jitney service, cooperative credit union, cooperative ice-delivery, and cooperative garment shop. These, however, remained a peripheral if not unimportant feature of the Stelton economy.

What was more, only the land set aside for the school was communal property. The rest was owned by the individual members in one- or two-acre plots, on which they built private homes. This, combined with the voluntaristic and relatively unstructured pattern of life, proved to be a source of stability which enabled the colony to survive more than three decades, lapsing ultimately into a residential settlement of more or less like-minded inhabitants.

There was yet another respect in which the colony fell short of its ideals. Stelton, like all similar experiments, had its share of personal quarrels and rivalries, so that Mike Gold could speak of the "intensely human scandals, rumors and jealousies thick as mosquitoes and about as plentiful as in any other close-knit community." Sex was a major cause, "for when men and women are in close proximity and haven't much else to do," wrote Harry Kelly, "it is a common circumstance for them to fall in love with one another's husbands and wives." Beyond this, friction developed between parents and staff over educational policy, and political and social questions were also hotly disputed. "Anarchism," lamented Kelly, "is an ideal to strive for but it requires patience and fortitude in an uncanny degree to live it."[8]

There was one point, however, on which the colonists were unanimous: the school was to be the most important feature of the settlement, the center of its life and main reason for its existence. "The one thing that tied them together was the school," remarked Joseph Cohen's son-in-law. "In other matters they largely went their own way." As Harry Kelly put it, "we built a community around a school, something which had never been done before so far as we know. Communities always come first and schools after, but we reversed the order and today the school dominates the community instead of being an incidental part of it."[9]

Like the colony as a whole, however, the school faced serious problems in the early months. Bobby and Deedee Hutchinson, who continued as principal and teacher, came from New York with the initial group and built a small cottage to live in. But in July, after less than two months, they abruptly resigned to start their own school at Stony Ford, New York. They had wanted, it seems, to have the children placed entirely upon their own responsibility, without interference from the parents. But in a community like Stelton, where adults lived on the premises and were determined to have a voice in running the school, this proved to be impossible. So Bobby and Deedee decided to start their own institution within a more isolated setting. Helen Lund, who had conducted the kindergarten at 107th Street and had accompanied the Hutchinsons to Stelton, departed with them, as did a number of the children, creating hard feelings among the colonists that never completely abated.[10]

STONY FORD

As the site for their school the Hutchinsons purchased a large farm of 137 acres near Stony Ford station, situated in a dairy region of New York state some fifty miles north of the city. Bordered on one side by the Wallkill River, the farm was far more picturesque than the one at Stelton, with woods and rolling hills and a brook running into the river. The old-fashioned Dutch farmhouse, with its large stone fireplace, was remodeled for the school and an open-air children's dormitory added. Across from the house stood a big barn in which workshops were installed.

In contrast to impoverished Stelton, considerable sums went into renovating the place. Deedee's brother Richard, a professional architect, designed a new wing to the house which was larger than the original structure and which contained the children's dining room, the Hutchinsons' living quarters, and a nursery for their new baby, Tregear (later renamed Peter).[11] The house was brilliantly lit in the evening, and neighboring farms called it "The Light House." Adjacent to the new wing stood the dormitory, overlooking the river.

The central idea of the school, as the Hutchinsons' daughter describes it, was "to develop the human being as well as to teach classroom subjects; to develop a sense of responsibility and awareness of others, and of appropriate behavior towards others." The pupils, accordingly, had to perform various chores, such as cleaning house, making the beds, cooking, clearing table, washing dishes, and taking in the milk, the tasks being rotated every week among groups of three children. If the dishes were not washed, then the next meal was eaten off dirty dishes, and "you can imagine that the rest of the students had something to say to those who were on dishwashing duty that day! The same was true of making beds. They soon found it was more comfortable to sleep in clean sheets and in beds that had been aired and made up properly."[12] Each week a group of children would be responsible for getting supplies, and Bobby drove them into Middletown in his Model-T Ford.

Health was another important concern, including plenty of fresh air and exercise. "We slept in a dormitory with the back and sides sheltered but the front open," recalls Eva Bein, who accompanied the Hutchinsons from Stelton. "They would put us in sleeping bags tied at the neck, then put us in bed." The dormitory was left open all year round, even in winter. "But we had plenty of quilts and blankets," says Marucci Schwartz. "We loved it!"[13]

For exercise there was hiking, swimming, and a variety of games. "We had a wonderful deep brook that made gurgling noises," Marucci recalls. "The Hutchinsons put a dam in and that made a swimming pool for us. But the dam had to be broken up because it flooded the farmers' pasture land." The children swam naked and "could go swimming in winter too if we liked," says Eva Bein, who acquired a passion for the sport that was to make her a national champion. Floating down the river on makeshift rafts was another favorite recreation, and Deedee's brother, H.W.L. Dana, once came up from Columbia and "took us for an overnight outing—we slept outdoors on a hill—and taught us all about the stars."[14]

Deedee taught nursing and baby care, and "there was an attempt to have you not feel ashamed of your body," another pupil remembers. When the children asked questions about sex, the Hutchinsons told them, even the youngest, what they knew of conception and birth. "The child's mind is clean and pure," they declared. "It has no evil association about things, and if these facts come to it in a simple and beautiful way and are referred to perfectly freely, but always with respect and reverence, the child will grow to think of them with respect and reverence."[15]

Bobby and Deedee were vegetarians and believed in eating

only two meals a day. "We ate Protose and Notose (mostly nuts and beans, I think) and all sorts of Kellogg's cereals which they would buy at Macy's and have shipped up to Stony Ford, and bread without yeast," Eva Bein recollects. "And they always emphasized that we shouldn't overeat." In their two daily meals, served at 10:45 A.M. and 5 P.M., the children had whole-wheat bread, coconut milk, honey, nuts, fruits, and vegetables, but no meat, white bread, cane sugar, tea, or coffee. "The ideas of that school were so strong," says Eva Bein, "and I held on so hard, that when I came home I couldn't touch a morsel of breakfast. To this day, in fact, I have never enjoyed breakfast."[16]

There were fifteen pupils at Stony Ford, ranging in age from six to fourteen. Nearly all had attended the Modern School at New York or Stelton, or both. The staff, apart from Bobby and Deedee, consisted of Helen Lund, Anna Schwartz (whose children Màrucci and Zack were among the pupils), and a man named Hugo who came from time to time to give piano lessons.[17] Emphasis in the classroom was on individuality and self-reliance. Learning, declared the Hutchinsons, must begin with "the inclinations of the child." Though suggestions might be put before him, "his interest is the starting point and gives the impetus."[18] There were no punishments or rewards, apart from the natural pleasure of doing a thing well. Each pupil chose his own course of study and proceeded at his own speed, without timetables or examinations. Thus when Valentine Levine wanted to learn about Russian history, Bobby ordered a textbook and the two of them read it together.[19] The pupils called the teachers by their first names, and there was a high degree of mutual respect and affection. "There was a leisurely feeling about the place," Eva Bein remembers. "We never felt pressed, rushed, harassed. I don't remember anybody raising his voice at Stony Ford. There was no hostility in their voices. Those were my happiest years."[20]

The stress on individual initiative did not, however, preclude working in groups. On the contrary, there was a whole range of collective projects centering on different geographical areas and historical periods. "We worked for weeks making Dutch shoes, skates, and windmills—everything to do with Holland—we had to touch and feel and smell and become acquainted with everything about it; and then we read a story. We went through *The Dutch Twins*, *The Spanish Twins*, and so on," recalls Eva Bein. Valentine Levine remembers a project on the history of the

Crusades: "We made an enormous clay model of Europe and the Mediterranean area on the living room floor. It was very creative." Marucci Schwartz recalls a similar project dealing with Greece: "We drew a big map of Greece on the floor—we were all on our hands and knees doing it. We were doing a play at the same time that had to do with Greek history and that we ourselves made up. So we were learning theater, geography, history, reading, and writing at one stroke."[21]

Handicrafts and play were also important aspects of the curriculum. The children worked in the garden and carpentry shop and had a dog, a cow, and a horse in their care. They had lessons in piano, singing, and dancing, and produced a little magazine called *The Wallkill*, containing their own poems, articles, and stories. They also studied current events. When H.W.L. Dana was dismissed from Columbia for his antiwar activities, Bobby and Deedee told the children all about it. "They used to discuss these things with us," says Eva Bein, "things you would think pertinent only to adults. We discussed everything together and were always told just what was taking place. They really respected us as people."[22]

The Stony Ford experiment was apparently successful. Joseph Cohen's assertion that it "caused a great deal of suffering to the children and adults"[23] is not borne out by the evidence. Yet in May 1918 the school disbanded, after only three years of operation. What brought about its demise? One problem was that, try as they might, the Hutchinsons could not escape the intrusions of parents, which had caused them to abandon Stelton. "Delia and I used to say that our great advantage in being out here was that the parents did not come to bother us," wrote Bobby to Carl Zigrosser in 1917. "But alas it is not so even here, and I have a nightmare that if we installed a school on the further banks of the river Styx we would too often see, as the sun went down, a boatload of parents, all sprouting horns and waving at their progeny from up the water."[24]

But there was another, more personal, reason for the closing of Stony Ford. Bobby fell in love with another woman, "and the breakup of the marriage," as Anna Schwartz put it, "led to the breakup of the school."[25] Moving to Mamaroneck, Bobby and Deedee remained together for a few more months before going their separate ways. Deedee was deeply hurt and never got over it. Bobby, after a short while, left the new girl and eventually married a sister of the actress Eva Le Gallienne. He died in London in 1975. Deedee, who never remarried, lives alone on the west coast in her eighty-ninth year.

When the Hutchinsons broke the news to their pupils, the children were devastated. "I cried," recalls Eva Bein, "and all the other children cried. I liked Stelton, but Stony Ford was the best experience I had as a child. I loved it, and many of the ideas I hold to this day were conceived and nurtured there. I'm very conscious of my health, of exercise, of the love of learning. As a teacher I always had great rapport with my students. I think it helped a great deal in my life. They were more conscious of food than other people. Now it's quite common to eat whole-wheat bread and the like, but then it was new. I never ate a frankfurter or drank tea or ate penny candy. In fact, I was a vegetarian until eighteen, and that all started at Stony Ford."

For nine-year-old Eva the transition to public school had fearful results. "After the New York Ferrer School, Stelton, and Stony Ford," she recalls, "public school was a traumatic experience. Susan Dubois, my good friend, was sent to Ethical Culture, and that would have been much better. Public school was conventional and rigid. The teacher once told me that if I came late again I shouldn't bother coming to school. I once made a blotch with the pen-point on the paper and the teacher slapped me in the face. I was a good reader, but I knew very little math. I didn't seem to fit. They called me the 'wild Indian.' I had a Dutch haircut with short bangs and looked different from the other girls, and I wore the oldest rags for clothes. I was very fidgety because I wasn't accustomed to sitting still in the classroom all the time. And maybe I spoke out, as we all did at Stony Ford and Stelton. I got the most horrible headaches at that school and would cry all day, and sometimes even fainted, which I had never done at the other schools. It was extremely hard to adjust, though after the first year I had no difficulties."[26]

The Stelton School

When the Hutchinsons left Stelton in July 1915, the Ferrer Association, for the fifth time in five years, faced the task of hiring a new principal. Within a few weeks, a suitable replacement was found in the person of Henry T. Schnittkind, a twenty-seven-year-old Harvard Ph.D., who had written children's books and taught at Socialist Sunday Schools in Boston. Schnittkind was a pacifist as well as a socialist, and his antiwar play *Shambles* was among the first to be produced by the Stelton children. He came to the colony, to quote his own words, "flushed with the dreams and enthusiasms of a young man as yet unacquainted with life." A brilliant teacher, he quickly won the confidence of his pupils and established a relationship of mutual respect, he tells us, "where neither assumed an air of superior intelligence, but where each was ready to learn from the other."[27] "He taught us the most unbelievable word games," Emma Cohen recalls. "He taught us Dickens, he taught us algebra. He was a classics scholar and an extraordinary teacher. Years later, when I went to high school, I could still recall his algebra and that made it very easy for me. I think he was the most gifted teacher I ever met. He enjoyed every bit of it, and we enjoyed every bit of it."[28]

It was Schnittkind's hope that the school would become "a testing laboratory for a new world."[29] But his tenure was too brief for him to realize this ambition. After a few weeks it became clear that his wife Sarah, a city-bred girl of twenty, could not endure the trials of pioneer life. And so the couple departed at Thanksgiving. Returning to Boston, Schnittkind became an editor with Stratford Publishers and a prolific popularizer of social and literary ideas. Under the name of Henry Thomas, he compiled a series of "Living Biographies" of famous writers, painters, philosophers, scientists, women, rulers, and religious leaders, as well as anthologies of stories and poems. But his few months at Stelton, he later declared, "stand out as the most beautiful experience in my life. It was a painful experience, too, but beauty is always the more intense because of the pain associated with it, especially in retrospect."[30]

To fill in as acting principal, Joseph Cohen induced Abe Grosner of the Philadelphia Modern School to interrupt his doctoral studies at the University of Pennsylvania and come to Stelton until a permanent replacement could be secured. Over the next few months, as Leonard Abbott wrote, the school waged "a terrific struggle for existence." Matters, however, took a brighter turn when William Thurston Brown, the peripatetic founder of Modern Schools, agreed to assume the director's mantle. Brown, then fifty-five years old, arrived from Chicago in the spring of 1916, the fourth principal in Stelton's initial year. With his companion Elsie Pratt, who assisted him in his administrative and teaching duties, he occupied the house built by the Hutchinsons and began to inject new vigor into the school's activities. Like his predecessors, he believed that an individualized education must replace the "goose-step system" of the public schools. Eschewing rote and repetition, he sought to educate the children in what he called the "processes of life," relating what they were taught to "actual work and play." Stelton, he believed, was "the most important educational experiment in America." Indeed, "with its back toward musty tradition and its face toward freedom and the future," it was "the educational hope of the world."[31]

Though his gifts did not match those of Henry Schnittkind, Brown was a diligent and animated teacher, and the children soon came to like him. "We went to his house," Ray Miller recalls, "made fudge and popped corn. He read us Dickens and Mark Twain and laughed so hard he had to stop reading, and we all just sat there and watched him laugh. I still remember how he enjoyed that book!" He also told stories from early American history, "and it was all perfectly real and wonderful."[32]

During his three and a half years as principal, Brown made no attempt to alter the school's fundamental direction. Education continued along the lines laid down in New York. There was no segregation of the sexes either in the boarding house or the school. Attendance was voluntary. The children came and went as they pleased, pursuing what interested them, ignoring the rest. There was no discipline, no punishment, no formal curriculum. Above all, the methods of public and parochial education were avoided. "The ordinary schools with their uniform curriculum attempt to impose the same interests on all," as Carl Zigrosser wrote. "The Modern School, accepting the dictum that the impulse for genuine culture must come from within, makes the pivot of the curriculum the interest of each individual child."[33]

A central assumption of the colonists was that the anarchist ideal of a free society without formal authority or economic oppression would be realized through the education of a generation of children uncorrupted by the commercialism and selfishness of the capitalist system and undisturbed by political repression and indoctrination in religion or government as taught in traditional schools. "We claim for the Modern School," wrote Harry Kelly, "that the hope of the future lies in the ability of the rising generation to think and act independently without regard to the prejudices of the past." As Joseph Cohen put it: "The intrinsic value of the School could best be described in negative terms: it did not teach any dogmatism; it did not stuff the heads of the children with superficial cramming; it did not attempt to make good patriots of them to any particular nation, and so on and so forth. This in itself was, of course, an accomplishment and a great gain in those hysterical war-days. In a great measure it satisfied me and others among the parents and active members. We were pleased to see our children enjoying their youth in a free and unrestricted atmosphere."[34]

As in New York, much effort was devoted to experiment and improvisation. The colonists, with few exceptions, knew little of pedagogical theory. Even Leonard Abbott, for all his erudition, had little acquaintance with the pioneers of libertarian education. "I have never read Froebel carefully," he later admitted, "but I intend to do so; and I intend also to study Pestalozzi." The influence of Ferrer himself had begun to fade. Something of his teachings was still recalled from the early flood of literature issued after his death, but by now he had become little more than a name or symbol. "One heard little about Ferrer's educational theories," Ray Miller recalls, "though a good deal about his martyrdom."[35]

Given the school's new location in the country, an outdoor education was more the rule than ever, featuring hiking, swimming, and a variety of games and sports. "We had our own vegetable garden, lived close to nature and to the soil," Ray Miller remembers. "Boys and girls swam together, nude, to be natural and avoid hangups. I felt the anarchists were the only people with the right attitude towards life. Personal relationships were the most important thing. People were allowed to develop their own potentialities. You didn't live according to rigid rules, but could do what you wanted, as long as you didn't interfere with the rights of other people." Swimming was done in the little brook that bisected the colony. In 1918 the colonists dammed the brook, creating John's Pond, which not only served as a swimming hole but also "yielded an endless supply of deep blue modeling clay and magnificent cattails."[36]

In conformity with the principle of integral education, due emphasis was laid on handicrafts as well as books. Thus a French anarchist named Jules Scarceriaux came from Trenton to teach pottery and brickmaking, and Joseph Ishill started a class in printing. Under the guidance of Hugo Gellert, moreover, the children produced strikingly original art work. "We want more men like Thoreau, Kropotkin, and William Morris," wrote Harry Kelly in *The Modern School*, "men who can weave carpets, write poetry or prose, cut type, print books and do a hundred other things; have a knowledge of science and a love of nature, an individuality that refuses to be crushed to the dead level of its surroundings, with a love of mankind so strong that their talents and time are devoted to making a larger and freer life for all."[37]

Beyond their regular teachers, the children came into contact with many fascinating adults among the parents and visitors. They went on outings to the Jersey seashore and to Leonard Abbott's cottage at Westfield. Supervised by John Edelman and Hugo Gellert, they put on plays and entertainments, the first productions being *The Pratie Pot* by Edmund McKenna and *The Idol's Eye* by Lord Dunsany. When five-year-old Leo Kolodny arrived at Stelton in 1916, he saw *A Midsummer Night's Dream* performed in the glade next to the soccer field. "It was like going into a fairy land," he recalls. From time to time Bernard Sexton, director of the Little School in the Woods at Greenwich, Connecticut, came down and taught Indian lore to the children, including a "caribou dance" and games "to which we came running no matter what else we were doing."[38] "The children!" exclaimed Mike Gold. "They are everywhere one turns in the colony, dotting the place with color so that one comes upon them with joy as upon blue flowers under corn rows. The whole green tract is their school, and they absorb that universal education that comes to man only through all his five senses, and that he misses if he reads only books and knows only abstractions."[39]

Yet if the balance favored crafts and play, academic study was not neglected. William Thurston Brown launched a special effort to prepare the older children for high school, "in order to placate the doubts of some parents who feared that their children might not be able to face the requirements of a 'practical world,' " as Alexis Ferm sardonically put it.[40] In the autumn of 1917 the first two pupils—Ray Miller and Emma Cohen—entered high school at New Brunswick and made a brilliant showing, leading their class in all subjects. Emma was graduated as valedictorian (Ray had meanwhile moved to New York) and went on to study at Radcliffe, eventually becoming a child psychologist.[41] This pattern continued in later years, though some of the children got into trouble for challenging the teachers in class, a habit acquired and indeed encouraged at the colony.[42]

Stelton was no ordinary school. The doors were open all year round and there were no holidays or vacations. Play and work, education and life were inextricably intertwined. School was not something that started at 9 and ended at 3. It began when the children got up and finished when they went to bed. The strain this produced on the teachers is not hard to imagine, and many were forced to drop out. Those who remained had unusual stamina or dedication to sustain them. For the children, in a majority of cases, Stelton proved a highly stimulating educational experience. Ray Miller's evaluation is typical: "We did everything ourselves—we were gardeners, we were typesetters, we were cooks—we did everything with our own two hands. Instead of merely reading *A Midsummer Night's Dream*, we put on the play, and put it on outdoors. The grownups got involved too. I never avoided taking part in anything, whereas in high school everything seemed a chore, even though I always got good marks. The only thing I liked was French. I went through four years of high school but didn't make a single real friend. In Stelton everyone was my friend. And I went to grammar school for six years in Philadelphia before coming to Stelton, yet I can't remember anything we did or any of the teachers, except that they read the Bible to us every morning and that three Civil War veterans visited school one day. I read at home avidly, but school was a blank. On the other hand, I remember a great deal about Stelton. Stelton was not only a school but a community; it wasn't just education—it was living."[43]

JOSEPH ISHILL

Of all the teachers at Stelton during its early years, none made a deeper impression on the colonists or played a more important role in the anarchist movement than the printer Joseph Ishill. Ishill, whom Rudolf Rocker called "one of the most extraordinary men I have met in my life," was one of a cluster of Rumanian Jews—the Libers, the Bercovicis, the Yusters—involved in the Modern School experiment. Born Joseph Ishileanu in 1888, he was the son of a small farmer who lived near Botoşani in the Rumanian province of Moldavia. The father, in his younger years, had been employed as a bookkeeper on the estate of a Rumanian landowner, but had left to farm on his own. There were few Jews at that time to whom the Rumanian government granted permission to live in the countryside, but Ishill's father was a war veteran and had the right to choose his place of residence. Acquiring a plot of land in the village of Cristeşti, he settled down to raise a family, eking out a precarious existence from the soil.[44]

Here Joseph Ishill was born. Growing up in the country, he developed an intense love of nature that never abated. "I would walk through the denseness of the forests," he later recalled, "or the open spaces of the fields, and with full breath absorb the enchanted panorama of green with its undulating background of blue mountains."[45] Rumania, however, was a bulwark of anti-Semitism, and young Ishill was often taunted with "Jew, be off to Palestine!" His sympathy for the outcast and insulted, like that of Joseph Cohen, derived in part from his Jewish heritage, for which he had suffered as a child. In addition, he remembers, "the fate of the downtrodden and exploited peasant class lent a tragic tone to the exquisite beauty of the land. And I felt stirring within me the fine roots of a wider beauty: love of mankind—love for those silent sufferers. I saw an entire caste, by far the greater portion of humanity, sunk in misery and bleeding from the wounds inflicted upon it by centuries of barbaric traditions."[46]

Ishill's compassion for living things expressed itself in yet another form. As a young boy he saw a group of lambs being led to slaughter, and they cried so pitifully that he vowed never again to eat the flesh of any animal. He kept this vow for the rest of his life, avoiding not only beef but also fish and fowl, his diet consisting wholly of vegetables, fruit, and dairy and wheat products.[47]

At the age of fourteen Ishill was apprenticed to a printer in Botoşani. He quickly developed a passion for the craft which never left him. "I felt as if the very printer's ink were penetrating my veins and irredeemably tinging the color of my desires," he afterward wrote. "I began to see a world of realizable dreams. I had found my vocation."[48] It was at this time, too, that Ishill's lifelong interest in literature was awakened. For his own amusement he wrote essays and did translations from Yiddish and German, and in 1907 he started a small Rumanian-language periodical called *The Wandering Jew*, of which only a few numbers appeared. In the same year he wrote his *Balkan Episodes*, a record of the personal encounters of his youth.

After the demise of his journal, Ishill went on the tramp, wandering for several months about the country before settling in Bucharest. There he fell under the influence of the most prominent Rumanian anarchist of the time, Panait Muşoiu, who published *The Review of Ideas*. Drawn into the circle which gathered about Muşoiu's journal, Ishill acquired a knowledge of anarchist literature and of the activities of the movement throughout Europe. Among the works he now read, Thoreau's *Civil Disobedi-*

ence struck a particularly responsive chord, providing "the initial impulse in the direction of the loftiest ideals, like snow-crowned peaks tinged with the purest sunlight and coloring all my thoughts."[49]

Thus Ishill was already an anarchist when he emigrated to America in 1909. One of the last acts he performed in his native country was to take part in a protest meeting in Bucharest against the death sentence imposed on Ferrer, which was broken up by the police and university students, who behaved like "ordinary hoodlums."[50] Shortly thereafter, the twenty-one-year-old printer left Rumania, never to return. On November 30, 1909, he arrived in the United States, where he was to develop the unique field of work which occupied him throughout his adult years.

Finding employment as a typesetter in New York City, Ishill began to attend anarchist meetings, as he had done in Bucharest. Anarchism in America had reached its zenith, and Ishill was deeply interested in all phases of the movement. He cleaved to no specific tendency or group, but was an eclectic thinker who drew inspiration from the whole range of libertarian thought, individualist and collectivist alike. From 1910 he attended the lectures of Emma Goldman, and he became a frequent visitor to the Ferrer Center after its opening in 1911.[51]

Ishill came to Stelton in the spring of 1915, shortly after the colony was founded. "Everything seemed so fantastically strange," he later wrote, "and yet so pleasantly colorful—the bursting of the buds, new life, new hope." With his own hands he built a one-room cottage, from foundation to roof, and became one of the colony's most valued members. Installing an old hand press in a corner of the farmhouse, he instructed the children in the rudiments of his craft, which became one of their favorite activities. "Joseph Ishill taught us printing," said Magda Boris more than half a century later, "and I still remember how to set up type." Emma Cohen thought him nothing less than "an artistic genius."[52]

Under Ishill's supervision, the children published a small monthly magazine, *The Path of Joy*, which they themselves wrote, set up, and printed.[53] On the same hand press Ishill printed *The Modern School*, making it, in the words of William Thurston Brown, "the most artistic magazine in the entire radical movement."[54] For teacher and pupils, the print shop became a "beehive of activity," editorial office, composing room, and press room all in one.

On Thanksgiving Day 1916, Ishill attended a ball in New York for the benefit of the Stelton school. There he met Rose Florence Freeman, a gifted lyrical poet, whose work was praised by Lola Ridge, J. William Lloyd, and Havelock Ellis. A Harvard critic, Dr. Isaac Goldberg, described her as "a feminine Walt Whitman." The couple fell in love and decided to get married. Rose returned with Ishill to Stelton, becoming his lifelong companion and co-worker and a contributor to his various publications.[55]

It was in Stelton that Ishill began the long series of private editions that was to occupy him for the rest of his life. The first of these, Oscar Wilde's *Ballad of Reading Gaol*, appeared in 1916 with a special preface by Frank Harris. This was followed by *Iris-Heart*, a booklet of poems by J. William Lloyd, and by two collections of his wife's poetry, *Rain Among the Bamboos*, written in a Japanese style inspired by Lafcadio Hearn, and *Petals Blown Adrift*, so named because she would throw the pages of verse out of the window of their Stelton home—"Little Nirvana," she had christened it—and he would catch them as they flew about in the garden.[56]

Like the majority of his fellow colonists, Ishill earned his living in New York, where he worked as a typesetter in commercial printing establishments. In January 1918, to be closer to his place of employment, he and Rose left Stelton and moved to an apartment in the Bronx. Missing the countryside, however, they remained only eight months. In September 1918 they bought from Bolton Hall a three-room bungalow in Berkeley Heights, New Jersey, perched on the edge of a woods and bordered by the picturesque Watchung Mountains, which reminded Ishill of Rumania.[57] Over the next few years Ishill added several rooms and built a basement in which he installed his printing equipment. Here he and his wife remained for more than four decades and raised three children, Anatole, Oriole, and Crystal.

It was here too that Ishill performed the work that won him a place in the history of fine printing. Still employed in New York, he devoted his evenings and free days to his own press, on which he produced many exquisite specimens of the printer's art, "books of the rarest beauty and inspiration," as Leonard Abbott called them.[58] Living two hours distant from the city, he had to leave early every morning and return mostly after dark. It was then that his real life would begin. "The highlight of his day," says his daughter, "was his homecoming, and the long walk from the station, laden with the fresh fruit and vegetables he carried home from the city together with the evening papers." After dinner he would set to work. "Far from the rumble of the Metropolis," he mused, "and with sadly inefficient equipment, the writer has endeavored to do what he considers his spiritual duty. To this quiet spot of earth and sky he returns exhausted with the day's work, and when the wheels and arms took their nightly rest, he began to set and print these pages."[59]

For more than forty years Ishill's small press in Berkeley Heights produced gems of the typographer's art, little known to the general public but admired by connoisseurs of printing and by those who shared his anarchist ideals. One of his chief aims was to make available libertarian works whose publication through the usual commercial channels was unfeasible. He produced some 250 books and pamphlets, all of his own choice, seldom printing more than 200 copies of any work, often much fewer. These small editions were generally not sold but distributed as gifts to friends and libraries around the world. The authors in most cases—Peter Kropotkin, Benjamin Tucker, Havelock Ellis, Elie and Elisée Reclus—were personal acquaintances or correspondents, as were several of the well-known artists—Louis Moreau, Maurice Duvalet, Frans Masereel, John Buckland Wright—whose woodcuts and engravings adorn the books.[60] "Believe me," wrote Alexander Berkman to Ishill, "I admire your devotion to this good cause, and your wonderful energy and perseverance in compiling, setting, publishing and binding such wonderful products of your art, and all in your few hours after a day's hard toil to earn a living. It is a most exceptional and admirable work."[61]

At first, Ishill called his enterprise the Free Spirit Press. In 1926, however, it became the Oriole Press, so named because of the family of orioles nesting in the old tool shed at Stelton where he found the abandoned "Favorite" press on which some of his best work was produced. Ishill was deeply influenced by William Morris, for whom his admiration was boundless. (Even his small, beautiful handwriting resembled Morris's calligraphic script.)[62] He had a Morris chair in his library, and on his desk were a bust of Tolstoy, an inkwell from Benjamin Tucker, and an antique folder with letters from correspondents throughout the world. Later he moved the library out of the house and into the garage he converted and called his "Thoreau Library," which was surrounded by dense foliage.[63]

The Oriole Press was a one-man operation of which Ishill was typographer, printer, compositor, pressman, and sole proprietor.

Apart from his wife's editorial assistance, he himself performed all the labor, without outside help, from the most complex and demanding to the simplest mechanical details. He was always filled with a passion to create, and he derived incalculable pleasure from his work. All his labors were performed with the same meticulous care, each work set in special type and embellished with attractive designs.

Such private endeavors gain their vitality from their founder's artistic talents and social convictions, and Ishill's intense dedication to his craft and his ideals is stamped on every work he produced. "One by one," he wrote, "the pages were set up and printed by a single pair of hands, and the first crow of the neighbor's cock, indicating the passing of midnight, was the signal for me to 'lay off' for the night. In spite of handicaps, however, I never felt really fatigued at my work. There was always nervous energy to eke out the physical, and I felt a certain exaltation in the thought that if I *was* burning the candle at both ends, it was for a social cause. I felt what almost every other individual would feel in a society differently constituted from the present one: I was doing the work I loved—doing it with enthusiasm, if not physical strength, unimpaired."[64]

In addition to the numerous books and pamphlets that he turned out with such skill over the years, Ishill also published several magazines and anthologies. Between 1919 and 1921 he and his wife edited a small literary review, *The Free Spirit*, of which five numbers were issued and whose contributors included Leonard Abbott and Will Durant. In 1925 he published, jointly with Hippolyte Havel at Stelton, *Open Vistas*, of which six numbers appeared. And in the 1930s he put together two thick volumes of *Free Vistas: An Anthology of Life and Letters*, a treasure trove of libertarian philosophy, literature, and history, with illustrations by Raoul Dufy, Maurice Duvalet, and other prominent artists.

It requires, as Rudolf Rocker noted, "a great deal of inner strength" to live one's life according to so severe a moral code and regimen of work. In Berkeley Heights, said Rocker, who visited there in 1926, Ishill had his own little world which he "ruled as a magician of the graphic art." Aloof, remote, introspective, he was a "solitary," as Rocker called him. A neighbor remembers him as "a withdrawn man, hard to get to know," and his son thought him "stubborn, strong-willed, unbending."[65] He was "by nature somewhat of a recluse," Ishill himself admitted. As such, he felt a special kinship with Thoreau, who had revealed a path to life "free from external intrusions." A member of the Thoreau Society, he made a pilgrimage to Walden Pond, which provided a kind of "mystical experience." Driven by a passion for his craft, he devoted himself almost exclusively to the task which absorbed him so deeply. "He shows," as Rocker put it, "what one man alone is capable of achieving when he possesses creative faculties and great will power."[66]

Ishill performed yet another valuable service as a collector of anarchist literature. Throughout his life he corresponded with prominent anarchists and libertarians and, with the instincts of a scholar, preserved their letters and manuscripts. In 1960 he sold the bulk of his collection to Harvard University which, as a result, houses one of the richest libertarian archives in the United States. This pleased Ishill greatly. Largely self-taught, he had had only a few years of formal education in Rumania before embarking on his apprenticeship. "At last I am going to Harvard," he was now able to jest.[67]

In 1964 Ishill was invited by the University of Florida to become its printer in residence. Accepting, he moved with his wife to Gainesville to take up the post. Before long, however, they began to miss their little home in New Jersey, where they had lived for more than forty years. After a few months, they decided to return. Ishill was now nearing the end of his eighth decade. The countless hours spent at his press had taken their toll. He was easily fatigued. Yet on March 14, 1966, he set off on foot to deliver a talk in the Berkeley Heights public library. On the way home he fell suddenly ill. With his last strength he managed to reach his house. Grasping his wife's hand, he whispered: "Rose, don't be afraid." Then he collapsed and died.[68]

THE DICKS

Of the eighty-odd pupils who attended the Stelton school during the first year of William Thurston Brown's administration, between forty and fifty lived with their parents, who had built houses in the colony. For the rest, children of broken homes or of parents unable to care for them, the old farmhouse was converted into a boarding house, next to which an open-air dormitory had been constructed. The children slept on bunks with straw mattresses. There was no indoor toilet or furnace either in the house or dormitory. Ray Miller remembers waking up on winter mornings "with my hair frozen to the pillow." Water for washing had to be heated on a slow-burning kerosene stove, and the children kept warm "by exercise or with the aid of bonfires" lighted nearby.[69]

Until heat could be installed, meals were eaten by pupils and staff huddled in overcoats and blankets. As in Stony Ford, the children cleaned the dining room, set the tables, and helped with the cooking. Here too they were subjected to the dietary whims of the adults, which involved abstention from meat and cooking vegetables in their jackets to preserve their iron content. When Anyuta Krimont took charge, "we ate only nuts and raisins for a while," Ray Miller recalls. According to another pupil, "we were told to chew our food at great length. Also, the fruit had to be soft, so we threw oranges, tomatoes, bananas against the wall to make them soft. The diet was largely vegetarian, and many of the parents were vegetarians." The children, Joseph Cohen complained, talked more "about elements, starches, acids and body poisons than about games." Cohen marveled at the sturdiness of the children in the face of these "ridiculous" experiments. It was the fresh country air, he conjectured, that saved them from the "fancies of their caretakers." During these early years, there was only one fatality, when Margaret Sanger's daughter Peggy came down with pneumonia and had to be removed to a hospital in New York, where she died in November 1915. Her mother, who had just returned from Europe, suffered a nervous breakdown. "The joy in the fulness of life went out of it then," she later wrote, "and has never quite returned."[70]

For the first two years the children of the boarding house were placed in the care of an assortment of adult volunteers, differing widely in age, background, and temperament. Mary Hansen, who had been Voltairine de Cleyre's closest friend in Philadelphia, was a quiet and lovable personality as well as a talented storyteller and poet. "She had no mean qualities, no jealousies and so far as I could tell no hatreds," Alexis Ferm remembered. "If the majority of people had her state of mind, there would be no wars, no jostling for position, no 'grab while the grabbing is good.' "[71]

Her fellow volunteers included Sophie Cohen, Anyuta Krimont, Anna Schwartz, and Jacques Dubois. As part-time helpers, however, they were inadequate to the tasks of maintaining the boarding house in proper order. What was required was a permanent staff to manage affairs on a continuing basis. With the arrival of Jim and Nellie Dick in the spring of 1917 this need was finally met. Both had been ardent proponents of libertarian education in England, where they had founded Modern Schools in Liverpool and London. Well versed in the aims of the Ferrer movement, they were at the same time experienced in dealing with children (Ray Miller found them "warm, friendly, and easy going") and therefore admirably qualified to assume direction of the boarding house and, soon afterward, to join the teaching staff of the school. From 1924 to 1928 they were to operate the boarding house and school at Lake Mohegan, after which they returned to Stelton as co-principals before starting their own Modern School at Lakewood, New Jersey, which continued for twenty-five years, closing in 1958. For a full half-century, then, they played important roles in the movement for libertarian education on both sides of the Atlantic.

The companionship of Jim and Nellie, the handsome young Briton and the pretty immigrant girl, has the trappings of a story-book romance. The son of Scottish parents (his father was a policeman), James Hugh Dick was born in Liverpool on October 7, 1882. As a young man he became a tea-taster and the manager of a grocery store. He was also a teetotaler and played in a temperance band, having himself wrestled with the temptations of alcohol. Attending classes at the University of Liverpool, he met Lorenzo Portet, Ferrer's comrade and literary executor, who was a teacher of Spanish. The two became friends, and when Ferrer himself visited Liverpool in 1907 Portet introduced them.[72]

For Jim it was a memorable occasion, and it made a deep impression. In the fall of 1908, inspired by his encounter with Ferrer, he opened a Modern School in Boswell Street, Liverpool, which affiliated itself with the International League for the Rational Education of Children, founded earlier that year. "To break down national prejudice," Jim declared, "and that patriotic piffle which is inculcated into the children of our present-day schools is, to my mind, the finest propaganda we can do to ensure the solidarity of the workers of all nations."[73]

By the end of the year, the Liverpool Communist School—in fact an anarchist undertaking—was a "marked success," with twenty-six pupils in attendance. To raise funds, a social was held in January 1909 at which the children sang revolutionary songs, concluding with the *Internationale* in French. By springtime the number of pupils had risen to thirty-eight, and the term ended on a strong note. The summer, however, witnessed the Tragic Week in Barcelona, and when the school reopened in September Ferrer was in prison awaiting trial, his life hanging in the balance. His case was discussed with the children, and a message of protest was sent to the Spanish embassy in London. After Ferrer's execution, Jim Dick accompanied Portet to Barcelona to settle Ferrer's estate. On his return to Liverpool, the school changed its name to the International Modern School and issued a pamphlet entitled *The Martyrdom of Francisco Ferrer*.[74]

During the 1909-1910 year, the International Modern School had some forty children in regular attendance. It also sponsored an International Club for adults, for whom lectures were arranged in Spanish and French as well as English, to accommodate visiting sailors and students. A favorite speaker was Mat Kavanagh, an eloquent Liverpool anarchist and a teacher in the school, who gave a talk on William Morris and addressed a November 11th meeting in memory of the Haymarket martyrs.

In spite of financial difficulties, the school was able to reopen in the fall of 1910 with a full program of adult and children's activities, including classes in French and Spanish and protests against the death sentence pronounced on Kotoku and his comrades in Tokyo. In January 1911, however, amid the hysteria following the Houndsditch affair, in which a band of alleged anarchists were involved in a shoot-out with the London police, the school was evicted from its quarters and compelled to suspend operations. Not long afterward, it moved to a new location, but the distance proved too great for most of the pupils, and in May 1911 the school was closed.[75] Some months later Jim Dick left to attend Ruskin College at Oxford and the Central Labour College in London, returning periodically to Liverpool to continue his radical activities.

It was a year after the closing of the Liverpool Modern School that Nellie launched a similar venture in London. Born Naomi Ploschansky in Kiev on May 25, 1893, she had been brought to England as a child and raised in the Whitechapel district of London, where her father, a baker and cap-maker, was active in the anarchist movement. Nellie's was by no means the first libertarian school in London. Back in 1891 an International School had been organized by the celebrated French anarchist Louise Michel, who, according to a contemporary source, taught her pupils "to disrespect their Gods and Laws and masters."[76] Around the turn of the century a similar school was started at the Whiteway Colony, the British counterpart of Stelton, while a few years later another sprang up at the Jubilee Street Club in Mile End, where

1. Leonard Abbott around 1905

2. Joseph Cohen around 1950

3(top): Workshop at Camp Germinal, Pennsylvania, around 1926. 4(bottom): Cora Bennett Stephenson with children of New York Modern School, 63 East 107th Street, Fall 1913

5. William Thurston Brown

6. Harry Kelly, New Rochelle, New York, 1945

7. The Detroit Modern School, 1914, teacher Yetta Bienenfeld (note portrait of Ferrer)

8. Will Durant and pupils of the New York Modern School, 104 East Twelfth Street, 1912. Magda Boris is seated, third from left; *middle row*: Révolte Bercovici, Amour Liber, Ruth ?, Gorky Bercovici

SADAKICHI AT THE FERRER CENTRE

SADAKICHI
TRYING HARD TO BE
A GREAT MAN, WENT
FRYING EGGS WITH THE GREAT WHITMAN
LB

SUNDAY, NOVEMBER 14, 1915

Eight-thirty P. M.

Donated by Guido Bruno.

9. Announcement of reading by Sadakichi Hartmann at Ferrer Center, November 14, 1915, caricature by Lillian Bonham Hartmann

Programme

(Providing Sadakichi doesn't change his mind).

In the Land of Poe

"The Tell-Tale Heart."

Eight Years with Walt Whitman

"The Open Road."

The Story of My Own Life

"Nancy Pennington."

Sadakichi Hartmann, author of "Christ," "Buddha," and "The Whistler Book," will read at the Ferrer Centre, 63 East 107th Street, on Sunday Evening, November 14th. After an introductory talk he will give selections from his favorite author, Edgar Allan Poe and from his fellow-journeyman for years, Walt Whitman.

ADMISSION, TWENTY-FIVE CENTS

10. Cover by Man Ray for *Mother Earth*, September 1914

11. Cover by Adolf Wolff for *Mother Earth*, July 1914, showing his urn for the Lexington Avenue victims

12(top): Picnic at Leonard Abbott's cottage, Westfield, New Jersey, July 4, 1914, on day of Lexington Avenue explosion. *Standing*: Leonard Abbott (extreme left), Rose Yuster, Esther Yuster, Harry Kelly, Adolf Wolff (tenth from left with dark hair and beard), Dr. C. L. Andrews (older man with beard, next to Wolff), Manuel Komroff (center, smiling, with mustache), J. William Lloyd (with white beard), Arthur Samuels (dark hair, next to Lloyd), Donald Vose (at rear, with blond crew cut), Alden Freeman (grey hair and glasses), Ida ("Puck") Kaufman (Ariel Durant) (next to Freeman, in white blouse), Will Durant (crouching next to Ida, with arm around her sister); *seated*: Minna Lowensohn (fourth from left, slightly to rear, with hand touching cheek), Sophie Cohen (next to Minna Lowensohn), Joseph Cohen (holding son), Emma Cohen, K. D. Marchand (Romany Marie's husband, behind Emma Cohen), Romany Marie Yuster (with pearl necklace), Fanya Dubois (buttons on blouse), Helen Rudome (next to Fanya Dubois), Hyman Rovinsky (extreme right). 13(bottom): Dormitory and Living House, Stelton, 1915

14(top): Little Isadora Duncans, Stelton, 1915. 15(bottom): Joseph Ishill at his printing press, Berkeley Heights, New Jersey

16. Cover design by Rockwell Kent, 1917; became emblem of Modern School Association of North America

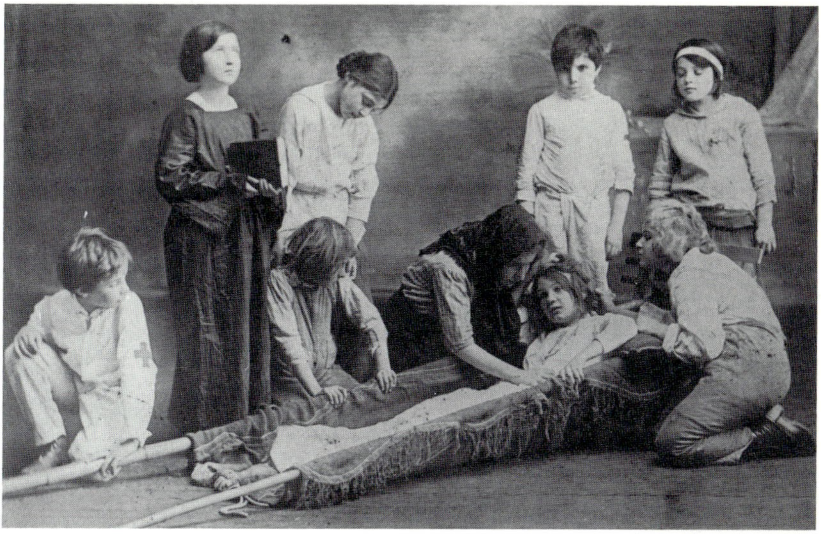

17(top): Stelton children's theater. Heloise Hansen Brown is the patient, with Magda Boris (third from left) grasping stretcher. 18(bottom): Edgar Tafel (left) leading the Stelton children's orchestra, early 1920s

19. Staff meeting at Stelton. *Standing*: Mary Hansen, John Edelman, Hugo Gellert, Joseph Cohen, Sherwood Trask; *seated*: Elizabeth Ferm, Bill Pogrebysky, Harry Kelly, Elsie Kelly, Paul Scott, Alexis Ferm, Mary Stechbardt, James Dick

20. Elizabeth Ferm in the 1930s

21. Alexis Ferm, Fairhope, Alabama, 1958

22. Hippolyte Havel at Stelton, 1935

23. Sadakichi Hartmann in California, 1940

Kropotkin, Malatesta, and Rocker were frequent visitors. Nellie herself often accompanied her father to the Club and, when the school suspended operations, decided to start one of her own.

Her International Modern School (also known as the Ferrer Sunday School) opened at New King's Hall, Whitechapel, in June 1912.[77] It was an immediate success. By the end of the year it had one hundred children in attendance, ranging in age from five to middle teens—almost as old as the teacher herself. In the spring of 1913 Nellie moved the school to her father's house at 146 Stepney Green. "We had some wonderful gatherings there," she recalls. "There was a room downstairs with sliding doors. We opened these doors and the kids came running in. I taught them songs from a book called *Chants of Labour*. The rabbis told the parents not to send their children to 'that anarchist school.' But we would have dances and entertainments, and they kept on coming."[78]

On May 1, 1913, Nellie took her pupils to a May Day demonstration at the Victoria Embankment. While distributing antimilitarist leaflets, she noticed the banner of the Central Labour College in the crowd. She went up and asked for Jim Dick, who had been writing a children's column in the Liverpool *Voice of Labour* which he signed "Uncle Jim," giving her the impression that he was an older man. She had heard that he was attending the college and wanted to invite him to speak at her school. "I saw a young man with grey hair," she recalls, "who looked gentler than the rest, and I asked him if Jim Dick was there. 'I'm Jim Dick,' he said with a bow."

Jim was a fine-looking, well-knit young man of thirty, with piercing blue eyes, prominent cheekbones, and prematurely grey hair; Nellie was a vivacious, rosy-cheeked girl of nineteen. They made a striking couple as they walked along the embankment and through the streets to Hyde Park, where Nellie's father and a group of fellow anarchists were holding forth. That evening Nellie recited a poem by Voltairine de Cleyre at the Jubilee Street Club, and Jim came to listen. It was his first encounter with Jewish anarchists, among whom he would spend the rest of his life. A few days later an actor named Sam Goldenberg asked Mrs. Ploschansky, "How would you like Nellie to marry a *sheygets*?" Nellie demanded to know what he meant. "I saw you talking to him at Hyde Park gate, and I knew he was the one."[79]

Jim, of course, readily agreed to speak at Nellie's school. Over the next few weeks, moreover, he brought several of his colleagues from the Central Labour College to address the pupils, among them Will Lawther, a former Durham miner who later became a Labour M.P. and was knighted.[80] By the fall of 1913 Jim had joined Nellie as co-director, and the ensuing year was perhaps the most active in the school's history. A Welsh miner named Griff Maddocks spoke on the causes and cure of explosions in the collieries. There was a visit from Bonar Law, who recited "The Ballad of Reading Gaol." Kropotkin came and played and danced with the children ("I was scared to death he'd have a heart attack," Nellie recalls). The children read William Morris's *News from Nowhere* and started a magazine called *The Modern School*. Miss Roche conducted a class in Esperanto, a cricket team was formed, and there were picnics and boating on the Thames. On October 13, 1913, the school held a meeting to commemorate the fourth anniversary of Ferrer's execution. A message of greeting was read from Lorenzo Portet in Barcelona, and Tarrida del Mármol, a leading Spanish anarchist in London, spoke to the children about Ferrer and his work.[81]

In December 1914 the International Modern School moved to its final location, 24 Green Street, Cambridge Road, East. Here Jim and Nellie began to live as man and wife, though without the sanction of state or church. By now Great Britain had gone to war and the authorities were cracking down on antimilitarist groups. The office of the London *Freedom* was raided, *The Voice of Labour* was suppressed, and anarchist clubs and meeting places were forced to close. The German-born Rudolf Rocker found himself interned as an "enemy alien," and many anarchists were imprisoned for agitating against the draft. Those who refused to register were compelled to go into hiding. A few, like Fred Dunn, the editor of *The Voice of Labour*, took refuge in the United States.[82]

The International Modern School had its share of trouble from the authorities. "Once we had a garden party which was raided by the police—there was a spy in our group—who arrested everybody without a registration card," Nellie recollects. "A Conservative paper in London—*John Bull*, I believe—had a center-page article about our school which said that Jim was related to Lenin and I to Trotsky (I was a Jew and he was not) and that we dressed our children in little white aprons and were teaching them to make love and revolution."[83]

In 1916 Jim and Nellie were legally married so that he could avoid conscription. When married men became eligible for the draft, they decided to go to America. Embarking in January 1917, their first thought was to see the Ferrer School, which they had heard so much about and which paralleled their own endeavors in Britain. "When we reached New York," says Nellie, "we immediately got in touch with the comrades. We went to the Ferrer Center and the office of *Mother Earth*. It was Harry Kelly who suggested that we come to Stelton and take charge of the boarding house."

Arriving at Stelton in March 1917, the Dicks were met at the railroad station by Fred Dunn, who had preceded them by several months. Taken to the colony, they found their work cut out for them. The boarding house had been neglected and needed cleaning and repairs. "The place was a mess," Nellie remembers, "and the children themselves needed a scrubbing. So we set to work at once. I played 'Lords and Ladies' with the children to teach them manners. I read them modern poetry before bedtime, which they didn't understand but loved the sounds and rhythms of the words. I kept house and did a little teaching, and Jim taught basketry and metal work." With Fred Dunn, Jim organized a cooperative jitney service to the railroad station. He also taught the girls ballroom dancing. "Jimmy Dick was a marvelous dancer," Ray Miller recalls. "He would put on his dancing pumps for Saturday night dances, and we were very impressed." Emma Cohen remembers being taught to tango by Pryns Hopkins, "but dancing the waltz with Jim Dick was one of the greatest experiences of my life!"[84]

For their services, Jim and Nellie each received a salary of $6.50 a week, which they often spent taking their charges to the movies and for ice cream in New Brunswick. "Once when they played *The Star-Spangled Banner* in the theater the kids refused to stand, and we got into a big argument with the manager," Nellie recalls. It was a hint of troubles to come. The Red Scare was on the horizon.

TIME OF TROUBLES

In getting the boarding house into shape, the Dicks were assisted by a young Chinese anarchist from Canton, Gray Wu, who served as cook and general handyman and was the "best and ablest worker the boarding house ever had." Quiet, intelligent, modest, Wu was "an earnest student of Laotze," a "philosophical type."[85] Before coming to Stelton, he had been studying under John Dewey at Columbia and working in a Chinese restaurant, from which he was dismissed after organizing a strike. Threatened with deportation, he took refuge at the colony. "Gray Wu was one of those I loved best," Magda Boris recalls. "He gave me Tolstoy's *What Is To Be Done*? He took us to New York to Chinatown and bought us Chinese slippers."[86] Leaving Stelton during the 1920s, Wu returned to China and eventually became a dean of Peking University. He was killed in a Japanese air raid during the 1930s.

Wu typified the ethnic diversity of the colony's membership. Although East European Jews predominated, there were Italians, Spaniards, Frenchmen, and a sprinkling of other nationalities, not to speak of native Americans, who were conspicuous among the staff. There was also a contingent of Englishmen, most of whom—Jim Dick, Fred Dunn, Bill Stevens, Harry Clements—were conscientious objectors who had fled to the States to avoid military service. The majority of the colonists were anarchists, though other radicals constituted a sizable group. Most came from New York and Philadelphia and had been active in the Modern Schools of these cities.

From its beginning in 1915, the membership of the colony grew steadily. By 1920 the number of year-round inhabitants—parents, children, and staff—approached 150. Summertime brought an influx of vacationers, which nearly doubled the Stelton population. On weekends, furthermore, crowds of visitors descended on the colony from New York, Philadelphia, and other cities to take part in discussions and entertainments. Every Saturday evening the whole community, visitors included, gathered around a bonfire to sing in the languages of the countries from which they originated. Guitars and balalaikas accompanied Russian, Yiddish, Italian, Spanish, French, German, Rumanian, Hungarian, Scottish, English, and American songs. John Reed, Robert Minor, Emma Goldman, and Roger Baldwin all visited the colony during these early years, as did Max Eastman, Art Young, and John Dewey.

As the colony grew, adult activities expanded. Lecturers held forth on a variety of subjects, and William Thurston Brown conducted a class in "Dynamic Sociology," following an outline by Lester F. Ward. Colonists from adjacent Fellowship Farm often joined in these activities. One evening Daniel De Leon's son Solon came over with a telescope to lead an outdoor star-gazing session.[87]

Every year, there were two weekend events which drew hundreds of visitors to the colony. The first, held on Decoration Day weekend in May, was to celebrate the anniversary of the school's removal to Stelton. The second was the annual convention of the Modern School Association of North America, meeting on the Labor Day weekend in September. The Decoration Day weekends were launched in 1916 with a concert and ball on Friday, May 26th, followed by an educational conference on the 27th and 28th. Emma Goldman, visiting Stelton for the first time, was the featured speaker, together with William Thurston Brown, making his debut as principal of the school, and Harry Kelly, who appealed for financial contributions. In succeeding years the Decoration Day gathering was marked by bazaars, art exhibitions, and poetry readings, as well as by plays, musicales, and dances.

On June 15, 1916, shortly after the first anniversary celebration, a special meeting was convened of delegates from New York, Philadelphia, Newark, Paterson, and New Brunswick. It was at this meeting that the Modern School Association of North America came into being as the successor to the Francisco Ferrer Association, which maintained a fading existence until the closing of the New York Center in 1918. To administer the affairs of the Modern School Association, a board of managers of twelve persons was elected, including Harry Kelly as chairman, Leonard Abbott as secretary, Anyuta Krimont as treasurer, and Joseph Cohen, Mary Hansen, Stewart Kerr, and Dr. C. L. Andrews among the members.

Thereafter, the Modern School Association of North America held an annual convention every Labor Day weekend, delegates attending not only from New York, Philadelphia, and New Brunswick, but also from Newark, Passaic, and Paterson, and even Baltimore and Washington, D.C. At the second convention, held on September 2 and 3, 1917, teaching methods was the theme of discussion. Louis C. Fraina (later known as Lewis Corey) drew loud applause when he argued that education must be tailored to the needs of each pupil. "A child," he said, "lives in a world of feeling, of imagination, of action. He loves to dance and play. Don't kill the spirit of joy in the child!"[88] To crown the system of Modern Schools, Jim Dick proposed the creation of a Workers' College, remarking that the years he himself had spent at the Central Labour College in London had been among the happiest of his life. While endorsed by Harry Kelly and Manuel Komroff, the Workers' College never materialized, although such enterprises as Commonwealth College in Arkansas and Brookwood Labor College in New York had links with the Modern School Association.

By September 1918, when the third convention took place, the Modern School Association could boast some two hundred members around the country, more than fifty of whom lived at Stelton. The thirty-five delegates to the convention took part in the dedication of the swimming hole, listened to musical recitals, and watched a performance of Maeterlinck's *Blue Bird* by the children as well as dramatic presentations by the adults in English, Russian, and Yiddish. Earlier that year, the Modern School Association had sponsored a series of conferences on libertarian educational experiments at the Sunwise Turn Book Store in New York, where William Thurston Brown spoke on Stelton, Bobby Hutchinson on Stony Ford, Pryns Hopkins on Boy Land, and Marietta Johnson on the Organic School, while Charlotte Perkins Gilman delivered a talk "Concerning Children."[89]

One of the main purposes of these gatherings was to raise money for the Modern School. During the first years, no tuition was charged and board was kept low in order to make the school accessible to children of working-class parents, some of whom could not pay even the small amount required. As a result, money to run the school had to be obtained from other sources. Some assistance was provided by labor organizations—the International Ladies' Garment Workers' Union, the Amalgamated Clothing Workers Union, the Workmen's Circle—and by well-to-do sympathizers such as Pryns Hopkins and Dr. Michael Cohn. But it was seldom enough to meet expenses. Consequently, various fund-raising projects were undertaken, ranging from costume balls and entertainments to benefit performances by the Stelton Players, who went on tour to New York, Philadelphia, Newark, and New Brunswick with Maeterlinck's *Blue Bird* and Henry Schnittkind's antiwar play *Shambles*. "At times," said Ray Miller, "life took on the aspect of a traveling stock company during those days. When funds were low we trooped the neighboring towns while Uncle Will harangued the public and we children tried to charm them, with our singing and dancing, into parting with a few coins to keep our school alive."[90]

At this point in our narrative a few words must be said about Pryns Hopkins, who succeeded Alden Freeman as the school's leading benefactor.[91] Like Freeman, Hopkins was of old New England lineage—his ancestors came over on the *Mayflower*, and Stephen Hopkins signed the Declaration of Independence—and the heir to a substantial fortune. (His father had been married to Ruth Singer of the sewing-machine family, who died in childbirth, leaving a large block of Singer Manufacturing Company stock.) Again like Alden Freeman, Hopkins was attracted to the Ferrer movement by Emma Goldman. Graduating from Yale in 1906, he attended Columbia University Teachers College, taking an M.A. in educational psychology under Edward L. Thorndike, J. M. Cattell, and John Dewey. He also began to attend anarchist gatherings, meeting Alexander Berkman and Emma Goldman. Emma's lectures, he later recalled, "profoundly changed my outlook on life." Under her influence he read Tolstoy, Kropotkin, and Ibsen, and through her he met Margaret Sanger and his lifelong friend Roger Baldwin. "Emma made pacifists and individualists of us both," he remarked, "though neither of us accepted wholly her creed of Anarchism." Nor could he accept the theories of Marxism, which seemed authoritarian and doctrinaire. Drawn instead to the writings of Robert Owen and William Morris, he became a libertarian socialist, and when he later journeyed to England, he joined the Fabian Society. He also visited Kropotkin at Brighton, bearing a letter of introduction from Emma Goldman, who remained his "socio-intellectual mother," having awakened him to "the contemporary world of struggling human beings."[92]

An early supporter of the Ferrer Association, Hopkins believed in "a schooling which respects the freedom of a child to do as he likes, short of imperiling the equal freedom of others or his own safety."[93] In 1912, using his Teachers College training and his private fortune, he started a school of his own at Santa Barbara, California. Called Boy Land, it lasted until 1918 and had thirty-five students at its peak. A far cry from the austerity of Stelton, Boy Land boasted a fully equipped gymnasium, an indoor swimming pool, and a professional stage for plays. Hopkins spared no expense to install the most up-to-date devices, including a miniature railroad with a gasoline-powered locomotive and flat cars built by the pupils in their shop. The most dramatic feature of the school, however, was a concrete map of the world, a Phillips projection 400 feet long and 200 feet wide, with all continents and major islands represented. There were mountains and even volcanoes, which the pupils caused to smoke by building fires with greenwood in the openings. One can imagine the intense pleasure derived by the children from reducing the whole earth to a single area of play. "The boys greatly enjoyed this," Hopkins recalled, "as also the sensation of navigating the seas on home-made rafts, or swimming across the 'oceans' from port to port."[94]

The map aroused considerable interest in educational circles, and geography teachers from U.C.L.A. came up to work with the students. When Hopkins described the map in his lectures on the school, it made a tremendous impression. "It was like a dream," recalled Joseph Freeman, the communist writer, who had heard Hopkins speak as a boy. "The children were free; nobody bullied or beat them; they had their own workshops in which they built furniture, their own small trains which they operated themselves and in which they went places; and they studied geography not from dull textbooks but from a huge relief map of the world built on a lake. Around this world they traveled in small boats which they learned to run, and listened to 'guides' tell them about various countries. How different from our own dingy school with its army drill, its police department, its dusty classrooms, its harsh discipline, its whacking with the ruler, its wretched nights of homework. If only we had been brought up that way. That's what Prince Hopkins said: if all the children of this world were trained in the freedom of his school, if the natural instincts of the child, uncorrupted by the conventional discipline, were given free play, we would have a race of men and women that could build a new, beautiful life on this earth."[95]

The school, however, got into trouble when Hopkins, an ardent pacifist, denounced America's participation in the war. When he addressed an I.W.W. meeting in Los Angeles in 1918, he was arrested for violating the Espionage Act. Boy Land was raided in a search for evidence and was soon forced to close. Hopkins sent two of his ablest teachers, Inez Termaat and Marie Travis, to Stelton, which he himself had visited on several occasions. After the war, he went to England and took his Ph.D. at the University of London, where he lectured on psychology. In 1926 he started a libertarian school at Chateau de Bures near Paris, which had a map in concrete like the one at Boy Land. Emma Goldman visited the school in 1931 and saw the children put on *Androcles and the Lion* by George Bernard Shaw.[96]

The arrival at Stelton of Inez Termaat and Marie Travis came at an opportune moment. For money was not the only problem that the school confronted. The shortage of qualified teachers was another. Most of the teachers were amateurs, without special training or experience. Some, it is true, possessed a natural gift for teaching, and what they lacked in formal preparation they made up for in enthusiasm, warmth, and sympathetic understanding. Above all, they had none of the puritanical severity so often encountered in public and parochial schools. Yet there was a vagueness about their methods and goals. "Hardly any of us know what we mean when we talk about 'libertarian' education and the 'Free Society' of the future," confided Leonard Abbott to Lola Ridge. Even worse was the exhausting schedule, seven days a week all year round, which caused a heavy turnover of personnel. "The teachers at Stelton gave everything they had," remarked Nellie Dick. "That's why they didn't last long. The children sucked them dry like a lemon, and then they left."[97]

The war created further problems. Kropotkin's support of the Allies touched off bitter polemics among anarchists over whether to follow his example or to remain true to their antipatriotic and antimilitarist heritage. The majority parted company with their mentor and issued an International Manifesto Against the War, whose signatories included Leonard Abbott, Harry Kelly, Joseph Cohen, Alexander Berkman, Emma Goldman, Hippolyte Havel, Bill Shatoff, and Fred Dunn. The war, as they saw it, was a capitalist struggle for power and profit with the masses serving as cannon fodder, so that it was absurd to regard a victory for either side as preferable. In early 1917, Berkman, Goldman, and Abbott organized the No-Conscription League and held a series of mass rallies against compulsory military service.[98] Adolf Wolff, by contrast, though one of the Ferrer movement's most militant rebels, became a super-patriot after the invasion of his native Belgium and defended the Allied cause, proclaiming that Goldman and her associates should be "hanged from the nearest lamppost."[99]

America's entry into the conflict in April 1917 further complicated the situation. More than a few who had hitherto opposed the war now passed to the other side. William Thurston Brown, a partisan of Woodrow Wilson, not only defended the draft but offered his services to the government. When Bayard Boyesen came out in support of the war effort, he was rebuked by Emma Goldman. "Really, Bayard, the claim of this country to make the world safe for democracy must make Satan laugh," she wrote amid a flurry of government repressions which saw the closing of *Mother Earth* and the arrest of herself and other dissenters.[100]

Harry Kelly was another who turned "strongly prowar," said Leonard Abbott, who himself remained a staunch pacifist and, with Joseph Cohen, rejected the war "in principle and in toto." Though opposed to compulsory conscription, Kelly argued that a

German victory would be "a terrible calamity" for the progress of freedom. "I feel and felt the German military machine had to be crushed," he wrote in 1919. Of Kropotkin's and Benjamin Tucker's prowar stand he later declared: "their instincts and judgment were sound and even prophetic when they called for the defeat of Germany in 1914-18, in spite of their warm feelings for the German people."[101]

The outbreak of the Russian Revolution elicited a more uniform reaction. Nearly all American radicals—anarchists, socialists, I.W.W.'s—joined the chorus of praise not only for the overthrow of the autocracy, but also for the accession to power of the Bolsheviks, though some were later to change their minds about the latter. The Revolution, wrote Joseph Cohen, spread "enthusiasm and hope all through the world." Every gathering at Stelton was "a demonstration for Russia and the final emancipation of mankind."[102] To Alexander Berkman the Revolution was "unquestionably the greatest event of modern times." "Never since the dawn of time," Berkman rhapsodized, "has the world been pregnant with the mighty spirit that is now rocking Russia in the throes of a new birth—a new life, a new humanity, a new international. It is the Messiah come, the Social Revolution."[103] Emma Goldman hailed "Lenin, Trotsky and the other heroic figures who hold the world in awe by their personality, their prophetic vision and their intense revolutionary spirit." The Bolsheviks, she declared, "are translating into reality the very things many people have been dreaming about, hoping for, planning and discussing in private and public. They are building a new social order which is to come out of the chaos and conflicts now confronting them."[104]

The creation in Russia of what was believed to be a workers' republic, opposed to exploitation and war, was an inspiration to nearly everyone on the left. For Leonard Abbott, Lenin and Trotsky were "prophets of a new dispensation, architects of a new social order," their assumption of power "a challenge to the very idea of government and a prophecy of the Free Society." The real significance of the Revolution, he added, "lies in the fact that Russia is lifting high the torch of liberty at a time when America is lowering that same torch. America is *betraying* liberty at the very moment that Russia is glorifying it."[105]

Enthusiasm for the Revolution carried a number of Modern School activists of Russian birth—Bill Shatoff was a notable example—back to their native land. On March 2, 1918, Berkman's companion, M. Eleanor Fitzgerald, cabled Shatoff in Petrograd: "Mother Earth group with our lives and our last cent are with you in your fight." The same day Abbott sent a cable to Trotsky: "Ferrer Association is with you to the death. Are forming Red Guards to help you defend the Revolution."[106] Mike Gold and Hugo Gellert were among the hundreds of young men who joined the Red Guards, only to be denied permission to leave the country by the State Department, which advised them that if they wanted to fight they should enlist in the army.[107]

Amid the antiradical hysteria touched off by the Russian Revolution, the Ferrer movement became the object of government persecution. In 1918 the New York Ferrer Center was forced to close, and during the Red Scare of 1919-1920 a number of Ferrer Association stalwarts were deported, Emma Goldman and Alexander Berkman being the most notable examples, while others, like Jack Isaacson were driven underground. "The recent raids have disorganized things," wrote Harry Kelly in January 1920, "as many of the boys have been arrested and are being deported."[108] Around this time, Attorney-General Palmer sent agents to Stelton to question the colonists, and one afternoon a group of vigilantes calling themselves Home Guards rode over from New Brunswick to ferret out subversives. Finding a red flag on the water tower, they demanded that it be taken down. As it was a working day, only a few men were present at the colony, so that resistance was impossible. Nevertheless, the colonists refused to comply, and the intruders had to climb the tower themselves to remove the offending banner.[109]

Apart from this, there was no outside interference in the colony's affairs, although the neighbors of surrounding Middlesex County regarded it as a nest of atheists, insurrectionists, and libertines with over-indulged offspring reared in an atmosphere of unbridled promiscuity on a diet of vegetables and nuts. Nellie Dick once got a lift to New Brunswick from a man who asked her if she came from "that free-love colony where a bell rings at midnight and everyone changes partners." Another resident, when asked by a delivery man if free love was practiced at the colony, replied: "Isn't all true love free?"[110]

At the height of these tensions, Stelton lost its principal when William Thurston Brown resigned after three and a half years at the school. In 1918-1919 Brown went on a cross-country lecture tour on behalf of the Modern School Association of North America, arousing public interest, soliciting funds, and attracting new members. While in Los Angeles he organized a branch of the Association and, succumbing to the lures of southern California, agreed to head a day school there as soon as it could be established. When the Walt Whitman School opened in the fall of 1919, Brown left Stelton to become its director.

"The first proletarian school in the West," as the Walt Whitman School styled itself, was located at 517 South Boyle Avenue, in the immigrant quarter of Los Angeles, and catered mostly to Jewish and Mexican pupils of radical parents. (Among the pupils was the grandson of Ricardo Flores Magón, the foremost Mexican anarchist, then in federal prison at Leavenworth, Kansas.)[111] Assisting William Thurston Brown were his wife Elsie Pratt and a number of well-known Los Angeles anarchists, including Thomas H. Bell, Joseph Spivak, and Jules Scarceriaux, who had taught pottery at Stelton in 1917. The educational advisor was Professor Paul Jordan Smith, book critic of *The Los Angeles Times*. From Pryns Hopkins's Boy Land, now closed, came a whole scientific museum, including books, specimens, and equipment. Tom Bell, a tall, red-bearded Scotsman, summed up the aims of the school: "Education does not mean stuffing into a child's head a lot of information, a great deal of it inapplicable to the child's life; but is rather what the word meant originally, the 'drawing out,' the unfolding of the child's personality, the encouragement of its own powers so as to develop its observation, its self-reliance, and to produce a man or woman bold alike in thought and action."[112]

Although the Walt Whitman School survived until 1924, Brown, following his usual pattern, left after two years to devote himself to other pursuits. At first a sharp critic of the Bolsheviks, he now became secretary of the Friends of Soviet Russia and a passionate defender of its policies. "I myself regard the movement which is now coordinating itself carefully with the constructive work being done by the advance guard in Russia as far and away the sanest and most valuable movement in the whole history of the labor struggle," he wrote to a Wobbly friend in 1922. A year later he considered studying agriculture and the Russian language and going to aid the Soviet regime because "the constructive work now going on in Russia is incomparably the most important and valuable that is being done anywhere on this planet." In spite of mounting criticism of the Bolshevik dictatorship on the part of his anarchist friends, Brown remained a staunch supporter of the Soviet experiment, even after Stalin's rise to power. "I've never found clear thinking among 'anarchists,'" he wrote, "though I still have very dear friends among them."[113] After teaching for several years at a boys' school in Menlo Park, California, Brown died in 1938 at the age of seventy-seven.

When Brown left Stelton in November 1919, John W. Edelman filled in as acting principal while the Modern School Association looked for a permanent replacement. Born in Belleville, New Jersey, in 1893, Edelman (originally Edelmann) was Harry Kelly's nephew, being the son of Mary Krimont's sister Rachelle and her husband John H. Edelmann, a prominent American anarchist and architect who died in 1900 when the boy was seven years old. Taken to England by his mother, John and his sister Sonia grew up at the Whiteway Colony, the British equivalent of Stelton, which had a school of the Ferrer type. A precocious youth, he became at fourteen the youngest branch secretary of the Independent Labour Party. Enrolling at the London School of Economics, he developed a talent for journalism and became a reporter for labor newspapers and an organizer of textile workers before returning to America in 1916 and settling at Stelton, where he directed the children's theater group with the aid of Hugo Gellert.

Though only twenty-six when he replaced Brown, Edelman proved a capable and vigorous administrator. During his year as acting principal, according to Leonard Abbott, he performed "Herculean labors" at the colony,[114] aided by his wife Kate Van Eaton and a staff consisting of Jim and Nellie Dick, Sherwood Trask, Hugo Gellert, and Harry Kelly's daughter Elsie. In later years he was to resume his labor activities, organizing hosiery factories in Massachusetts, Pennsylvania, and New Jersey, editing trade-union publications, and eventually heading the C.I.O. Regional Division in Philadelphia and then the Washington office of the Textile Workers' Union of America until his retirement in 1963. Once proposed by Walter Reuther as Assistant Secretary of Labor, he served on the Task Force on the Aging Poor under the Kennedy and Johnson administrations and as president of the National Council of Senior Citizens until his death from cancer in 1971, a veteran of more than half a century in the labor movement.[115]

The most notable achievement of Edelman's brief tenure as acting principal was the erection of a schoolhouse, which was to serve the colony until its demise in the 1950s. Since 1915, classes had been held in a variety of places, including private homes, the old barn, and outdoors when weather permitted. In the spring of 1919, however, while William Thurston Brown was still director, a surprise gift of 10,000 rubles ($726) was received from Bill Shatoff, now an official in the Bolshevik administration.[116] This sum enabled the colonists to draw up plans for a school building and to begin to acquire materials for its construction. On June 29, 1919, the cornerstone of the schoolhouse was laid.

After this initial burst of activity, however, construction ground to a halt. For one thing, Brown announced his intention to leave; for another, additional funds were required to proceed. Thus the fourth Labor Day convention, held in September 1919, found the cornerstone "lying lonesome, where it had been buried on June 29th."[117] When the question of raising money was taken up by the delegates, a visitor from Philadelphia urged the colonists to pitch in and build the school themselves. The next day the whole assembly came out and started digging trenches and laying the foundation, supervised by an expert mason named Hans Koch, who was later to work for Frank Lloyd Wright. A call went out for builders, carpenters, painters, electricians, plumbers. Dozens of volunteers came from New York, Philadelphia, and other cities to spend weekends digging, hammering, and sawing. In the evenings they would build a bonfire and sing songs in Russian, Italian, and Yiddish, and a group of Russians played balalaikas and danced the *kazachok*. To pay for building materials, Harry Kelly canvassed labor and radical organizations, with excellent results.

By the end of the year the work was largely completed. On January 11, 1920, the schoolhouse opened its doors. The following month a dinner was held in New York to celebrate the occasion, bringing together not only new friends of the school, but such pioneers of the Ferrer movement as Bayard Boyesen, Hippolyte Havel, Hutchins Hapgood, Stewart Kerr, Dr. C. L. Andrews, and Lola Ridge, who read from her poems. Members of the Stelton staff—John Edelman, Elsie Kelly, Jim Dick—were on hand to describe their work, and addresses were delivered by Harry Kelly, Harry Weinberger, Anna Strunsky Walling, and Dr. Cecile Greil. Robert Minor sent greetings from Chicago, and about two hundred dollars was collected for the school.[118]

Stelton had acquired a schoolhouse for its children. Still lacking was a permanent director. But this too would shortly be remedied. The arrival in May 1920 of Elizabeth and Alexis Ferm, two of the most impressive figures ever to associate themselves with the Ferrer movement, marked a turning point in the history of the school. Stelton entered upon a new phase that was to continue for the next five years.

CHAPTER 8

Elizabeth and Alexis Ferm

THE FERMS—Aunty and Uncle, as they were affectionately called—were among the earliest pioneers of libertarian education in the United States. In October 1901, at the same time as Ferrer in Barcelona, they started a free school in New Rochelle, moving to Brooklyn and then to the Lower East Side, before ending up at Stelton in 1920. Both—and especially Elizabeth—were strong personalities who left a deep imprint on the Ferrer movement, in which they were involved for nearly thirty years. Their arrival at Stelton signaled a new departure for the school, which embarked on its most creative—and controversial—period. During their tenure, the Modern School became one of the most radical experiments ever to take place in the history of American education. Who then were the Ferms? What were their educational precepts? In what sense did they, as Joseph Cohen put it, turn "a new leaf in the history of the school"?[1] To answer these questions, one must look back to nineteenth-century America, in which their lives, ideas, and characters took shape.

AUNTY FERM

The daughter of pioneering Irish farmers, Mary Elizabeth Byrne was born in the midwestern town of Galva, Illinois, on December 9, 1857, three and a half years before the Civil War. When Elizabeth was six, her father suddenly died, and her mother took the children to live at their grandmother's home in Montreal. By then the Civil War had reached its climax, and Elizabeth remembers that she was on the street in Montreal when the news came that "President Lincoln had been shot and that she ran in to tell her mother about it."[2]

Elizabeth received her first education in private schools in Montreal and later in a convent at Lachine, where she learned French and piano in addition to her regular subjects. She acquired a deep love for music, and playing the piano remained one of her greatest pleasures for the rest of her life.[3] As a child she was deeply religious, and her mother thought she might become a nun. At the convent, however, a severe discipline was imposed from which Elizabeth instinctively recoiled. Like Voltairine de Cleyre, who was educated in similar circumstances, she had to struggle very hard to maintain her individuality and spirit of independence. Afterward, while teaching in a Brooklyn kindergarten, she revolted against the rules and regulations which, she was convinced, robbed the pupils of their creativity and self-expression.

In 1877, before her twentieth birthday, Elizabeth was married to an older man named Martin Battle. Shortly afterward, they moved from Montreal to New York to open a book store on Third Avenue. Battle, it turned out, had rigid ideas concerning wifely submission. But his strong-willed bride refused to bow to his authority. When he locked her in the house one Sunday, she threatened him with a hatchet until he opened the door and let her out. Soon after this, she left him and moved in with friends until her mother came down from Montreal to be with her, buying a house in Brooklyn, where they lived for several years.[4]

Elizabeth, who had resumed studying the piano, was graduated from the New York Conservatory of Music in June 1885 and supported herself by giving lessons. At about this time, she became a chorister of St. Stephen's Roman Catholic Church on East 29th Street, presided over by Father Edward McGlynn. An ardent reformer, McGlynn championed the cause of labor and, against the wishes of Archbishop Corrigan, established an orphanage for the poor. He was also an Irish nationalist and was linked with the single-tax movement through the Irish Land League, which favored reforms similar to those advanced in Henry George's *Progress and Poverty*. In defiance of Corrigan, McGlynn spoke in favor of George's candidacy for mayor of New York in 1886, for which he was suspended from the pulpit.[5]

Under the influence of Father McGlynn, Elizabeth embraced both Irish nationalism and the single tax, joining Henry George's Anti-Poverty Society in May 1887. When McGlynn was excommunicated two months later, she herself left the church and plunged into a variety of progressive causes, from spiritualism and theosophy to temperance and women's rights, going to Washington as a delegate to the National Woman Suffrage Association when Susan B. Anthony and Elizabeth Cady Stanton were its leaders. She never returned to the church, though for the rest of her life she retained the religious quality which had marked her since early childhood when she attended the convent near Montreal.

In the midst of this activity Elizabeth found her life's calling. In 1887 she entered the training school attached to the Free Kindergarten of All Soul's Church, whose pastor, R. Heber Newton, was a friend of Henry George and Father McGlynn.[6] Graduating in June 1889, she secured a position at the Brooklyn Guild Kindergarten, where she remained for eight years, serving as director from 1890. There she began to put into practice what she had learned in training school, based largely on the theories of Froebel, which emphasized self-activity and creativity. *The Education of Man* became her bible, and she quoted it in all her writings, applying its methods and ideas throughout her long career. "I accept the declaration of Froebel that the tendency of every thing is to unfold its essence," she was later to proclaim. Exalting diversity and individuality over conformity and standardization, she insisted that every life is unique, so that education "cannot be reduced to a system." The educator to be avoided was the one who endeavored to "leave an impression on the child." For education was not pedagogy, not the imparting of facts from without. Rather it was "the development of self-knowledge, self-consciousness through spontaneous self-activity." Her own method was to allow the children to develop as distinct individuals at their own speed and in the directions of their choice. "Education," she declared, following Froebel, "has to do with unfolding, revealing and objectifying the inner life, the interior qualities of the individual," enabling him to "realize himself physically, mentally and spiritually, as an entity, as a complete whole." Thus conceived, it would allow every child to fulfill its unique destiny "as a self-conscious being, self-determining, self-directing, self-revealing."[7]

When Elizabeth first arrived at the Brooklyn Guild, she had begun by employing orthodox methods of instruction. Discovering, however, that the children were not taking any initiative but were merely following her directions, she reread *The Education of Man*. Suddenly Froebel's notions of self-activity took on new meaning. She wondered what would happen if the children were left on their own responsibility, so she began to let them choose their own wools, cubes, and other Froebel "gifts." The sewing cards, moreover, which had been pricked to make exact forms, were changed to the soda cracker type so that the children could sew pictures according to their own designs.

The results were remarkable. The pupils originated many new designs that were more beautiful and interesting than those which had been made for them. "The variety," comments Alexis Ferm, "showed the individuality of the children and verified the statement made by Froebel that each individual is unique and complete in himself. The outer manifestation became a representation of the inner need of the individual, instead of mere copying of the kindergartner's instructions." Learning from her experiment, Elizabeth gradually dropped one restriction after another until the children were given freedom in all their work and play. There was a "constant loosening of the reins," as Alexis Ferm put it, so that "instead of followers and imitators, the little ones became creators under freedom."[8]

Following Froebel's teachings, play became a central feature of the Guild curriculum. Froebel had emphasized the creative value of play and its importance in the natural development of the child. "Play is the purest, most spiritual activity of man at this stage, and, at the same time, typical of human life as a whole—of the inner hidden natural life in man and all things," he had written. "The plays of childhood are the germinal leaves of all later life; for the whole man is developed and shown in these, in his tenderest dispositions, in his innermost tendencies."[9]

For Elizabeth, as for Froebel himself, the Froebel playthings, or "gifts," had a deep-seated mystical significance. Always in primary colors, the balls, blocks, cylinders, oblongs, and prisms became the stock-in-trade of her teaching, along with the sewing cards, wools, and paints, providing for the children's play while also sharpening their dexterity and creativity. "When infant, child, youth, or man plays, the floodgates are opened, the spirit of man is released," she later wrote. "Once the play spirit is aroused in man, it should stay with him through his whole earthly experience."[10]

Music, singing, and dancing also played an important role. It was Elizabeth's habit to open morning activities by having the children place their chairs in a circle so all could sing songs and tell stories in a kind of communal rite, a practice she was to continue for the rest of her career. Like her use of the Indian totem pole, like her belief in fairies and leprechauns, morning assembly reflected something fundamental in Elizabeth's nature. It was part of her unique appeal and gave an added dimension to her stature as the prophet of a new educational system.

From all accounts Elizabeth was an arresting personality. Tall, slender, and beautiful, with golden hair and large blue eyes, she cut an extraordinary figure. By the mid-1890s she was arousing audiences in New York and Brooklyn with her provocative talks on education. Hans Koch, who heard her for the first time at the Harlem Liberal Alliance, has left a vivid description: "Her face radiated the warmth of her generous heart, the features were well formed and revealed strength, the eyes were living and showed sometimes the glint of the fanatic, her voice was firm and positive and she spoke a language almost of her own coinage. She was one of those rare beings you see but once and they stay with you forever."[11]

UNCLE FERM

Twelve years younger than Elizabeth Byrne, Alexis Constantine Ferm was born in Halmstad, Sweden, on February 18, 1870, the son of a shoemaker who emigrated to the United States when the boy was two. Settling in Brooklyn, the family eked out a shabby existence, and Alexis had to leave school at fourteen, taking a job in F. Loesser & Co. Dry Goods Store at $1.50 a week.[12] Efficient and reliable, he rose from stock clerk to office manager, a post he held until 1893, when he left to manage a country store in upstate New York. He soon returned to the city, however, and obtained a job in the advertising department of *The New York Times* at $8 a week. Within a year he was promoted to assistant manager, earning $25 a week, a considerable salary in those days. After two years at the *Times*, he moved to *The Brooklyn Daily Eagle*, then to William Randolph Hearst's *New York Journal*, where he remained until 1899.[13] By that time he had met Elizabeth Battle and his life had begun to take a new direction.

What kind of man was Alexis? Like his future mate, he had been attracted to several of the reform movements—temperance, theosophy, the single tax—which proliferated in New York during the 1880s and '90s. Though compelled to leave school as a boy, he had always been a voracious reader, especially of history and biography, and Longfellow was "my boyhood poet." Among his favorite prose writers were Emerson and Thoreau, with their message of self-reliance and individual development. Hungry for education, young Alexis attended classes at the YMCA and would walk across the Brooklyn Bridge to hear Dr. W. M. Salter and other speakers at the Ethical Society in Manhattan. At one point he thought he would some day become an Ethical teacher, and by the age of seventeen he was participating in debates in the Chautauqua Circle for Study on capitalism and women's suffrage.[14]

Gradually his political philosophy took shape. A rugged individualist of the nineteenth-century type, he deplored the development of corporate industrialism and of strongly centralized government. Together with many other reformers of his generation, he was attracted by the self-sufficient, noncommercial aspects of American life, the lost Jeffersonian ideal of autonomous communities and every man his own master, which had fallen victim to centralized economic and political power. Influenced by Tolstoy and Thoreau as well as Jefferson, his was a backward-looking vision of an idealized rural past inhabited by sturdy artisans and homesteaders who lived in harmony with nature, joined by the ties of voluntary cooperation. Throughout his life he felt nostalgia for a simpler era before the emergence of large-scale industry and government. Like Tolstoy and Thoreau, a friend remarked, he strove for "simplicity in life." A nature-lover and vegetarian, he hated warfare and killing and remained a lifelong pacifist and nonresistant. He regarded Ernest Howard Crosby, Tolstoy's leading American disciple, as "one of the finest men I ever met."[15]

It is not surprising that these predispositions should have led Alexis Ferm to the doctrines of anarchism and the single tax. When a friend gave him a pamphlet on Henry George, he at once became a convert, convinced that the single tax would destroy monopoly, eliminate poverty, and make land available once more to the small independent farmer. "If the land were taxed according to its *rental value*," he later wrote, "there would not be the unfairness of a man holding a piece of land out of use, waiting for a rise to draw in that which he has not earned, for it would not pay him to hold it without putting it to use."[16] Joining the Single Tax Club of Brooklyn, Alexis became a faithful proponent of the Georgeite creed, contributing to single-tax publications, attending single-tax conventions, and numbering single-taxers among his closest friends. At one time or another, he and Elizabeth lived at all three principal single-tax colonies in the United States, Arden, Delaware, Free Acres, New Jersey, and Fairhope, Alabama, where he spent the last years of his life.

At the same time, Alexis became an adherent of the individualist wing of the anarchist movement, of which Josiah Warren and Benjamin Tucker were the leading exponents. Together with Thoreau, Henry George, and Ernest Crosby, he counted Warren and Tucker among the men he most keenly admired.[17] And like both Tucker and Thoreau, he carried the Jeffersonian dictum, "That government is best which governs least," to its ultimate conclusion: "That government is best which governs not at all." "I do not know of any time that I have felt so strongly that I shall miss someone as I do at this time when you are going away," he wrote to Tucker in 1908, on the eve of the latter's departure for Europe. "Your steadfast devotion to the work that you have set yourself to do and your uncompromising honesty is equalled by only one person that I know, and she is my daily companion."[18] Alexis was also an admirer of Kropotkin, though he rejected his belief in social revolution and in communal property. In March 1901, when Kropotkin came to America on his second lecture tour, Alexis attended his meeting at the Grand Central Palace in New York and helped sell anarchist literature in the lobby.[19]

For Tucker as for Henry George, monopoly was the principal *bête noire*, the source of injustice and exploitation; and Alexis, who shared this opinion, sought to combine their anarchist and single-tax philosophies into a unified doctrine. "Many years ago," he wrote in 1963, "when Tucker was still running his 'Unique' book store on Sixth Avenue and had his printing press in the Parker Building on Fourth Avenue, and Fred Schulder was traveling around the country selling Tucker's [edition of] 'The Ego and His Own' and other books, Fred Schulder and I sat up until 2 o'clock one night discussing the problem and decided to call ourselves Single Tax Anarchists."[20] We may accept this label as an accurate summation of Alexis's social philosophy, to which he adhered for the rest of his life. Nor was the combination unique; in the Ferrer movement alone it was shared by such figures as Bolton Hall, Konrad Bercovici, and Dr. Liber.

Another facet of Alexis Ferm's philosophy must be noted at this point, if only because it led to his meeting with Elizabeth Byrne Battle. While sharply critical of organized religion, he had long been interested in its ethical and spiritualistic aspects. Thus in 1893 he went to hear Annie Besant, the English theosophist, when she spoke at Chickering Hall on Fifth Avenue. Impressed by her lecture ("Mrs. Besant can fill the very soul with food," he wrote in his diary), he immersed himself in theosophical literature and became one of the founders of the Brooklyn Theosophical Society. Before long, he was in demand as a speaker before theosophical groups in New Jersey as well as New York.

On February 18, 1897, his twenty-seventh birthday, Alexis addressed the Brooklyn Theosophical Society on "The Child in the Light of Theosophy." A member of the group, Mrs. Thaddeus Hyatt, happened to be Elizabeth Battle's assistant at the Guild Kindergarten, and, thinking the subject might interest her, invited her to attend.[21] After the lecture, Alexis and Elizabeth were introduced, and they talked for a while. Alexis was a fine-looking man, 5′9″ in height, whose slender frame made him appear taller. Though twelve years his senior, Elizabeth looked much younger than her years and, at thirty-nine, her beauty was undiminished. In short, they made a handsome couple. And as fellow single-taxers and reformers, they found they had a good deal in common. Both were interested in temperance, women's rights, and spiritualism. Both were of northern European immigrant stock and of farmer-artisan background. They were immediately drawn to each other. It was the beginning of a lifelong companionship.

Over the next few months Alexis and Elizabeth saw each other more and more often. When she spoke to him of her school, he found that it awakened an interest in education the depths of which he had not previously realized. Working at the *Journal* in the evening, he started going to her kindergarten during the day, observing her methods and helping with the children. He also began to study Froebel and found himself sharing his views. Little by little his energies were shifting from his work at the newspaper to his work at the school. He was gradually discovering his vocation.

"Many great things have happened in my life since my last birthday anniversary," Alexis confided to his diary a year after his first meeting with Elizabeth. "Particularly in my relations to Mrs. Battle, which have taken on such a form as I might have hoped but could hardly have expected."[22] The couple had fallen in love. In September 1898 they were married, Martin Battle having died a few months before. Their partnership, marked by an intense mutual devotion, had begun. From that moment their thoughts were turned to the possibility of opening their own school.

THE CHILDREN'S PLAYHOUSE

Shortly before her second marriage, Elizabeth resigned her position at the Brooklyn Guild Kindergarten. For eight years she had served as its director, and it was there that her pedagogical genius first flowered. But her unorthodox methods had made her the center of controversy. She was repeatedly accused of allowing too much freedom in the classroom and even of making anarchists of the pupils. Her direct, almost imperious manner offended some, particularly those with money and influence, who felt that their views should be respected even when not adopted. Yet Elizabeth would brook no interference. Convinced of the rightness of her methods, she refused to make concessions.

In the spring of 1898, matters came to a head. A Miss Buttrick, who contributed a thousand dollars a year to the work of the school, threatened to withhold further donations unless Mrs. Battle reduced the noise and freedom of the children and adopted a more formal system of teaching. Although a friend offered to supply the thousand dollars, the board of the Guild asked Elizabeth to modify her approach. That, for her, was sufficient reason to resign. The mothers in her Mothers' Club, which was the largest in the city, resolved to go on strike on her behalf, but she persuaded them not to do so. It was time, she felt, to depart.[23]

Soon after their marriage, Elizabeth and Alexis decided to start a school of their own. Two wealthy admirers—a Miss Otis of Philadelphia and Mrs. J. Stanwood Menken of Brooklyn—offered to provide financial support. Miss Otis, however, who had four adopted daughters of school age, persuaded the Ferms to wait until she could dispose of her Philadelphia house, as she wanted her girls to attend.

As it turned out, it was not until three years later that the Ferms were able to launch their experiment. In the meantime, Elizabeth returned to teaching the piano and Alexis left the *Journal* to work for the United States Battery Company, where he remained until plans for the school became settled. This took place on July 1, 1901, when the Ferms found a suitable house in New Rochelle, New York, with a house next door for Miss Otis and another nearby for Mrs. Menken's brother-in-law, S. L. Lawson, and his family. A fourth building, a block away, was rented as a boarding house for the children who did not live in the neighborhood and was christened the Living House by the Ferms.

The Children's Neighborhood Playhouse and Workshop—called the Children's Playhouse for short—opened on October 1, 1901, with ten pupils ranging in age from three to nine (two more would enroll a bit later). Among them were Mrs. Menken's nephew, John Howard Lawson, and Miss Otis's four daughters, Miriam, Allah, Laura, and Edith. Edith, then aged nine, became an accomplished cellist and a teacher at the Henry Street Settlement on the Lower East Side. John Howard Lawson, aged seven, became a well-known playwright, noted for his experiments in Expressionism and proletarian drama. One of the "Hollywood Ten" screen writers who were blacklisted by the motion-picture industry at the time of the McCarthy hysteria, he was jailed in 1948 for refusing to tell the House Committee on Un-American Activities whether or not he was a communist.[24]

The children, as a rule, went to school seven days a week, from 8 in the morning to 4 in the afternoon. Attendance, however, was not mandatory, and the pupils were free to come and go as they pleased. Nor were they subjected to punishment, corporal or otherwise. "Fear and obedience," Elizabeth declared, "could make slaves and hypocrites, but not independent men and women."[25] Applying Froebelian techniques, the Ferms sought to cultivate self-reliance and self-development and to bring out the creative potential of the pupils by exposing them to play materials (notably the Froebel "gifts") designed to attract their natural interest in color, form, and harmony. Uncle and Aunty, as they henceforth came to be called, both loved music and set a high value on its educational function, assigning it a central place in the curriculum. Uncle started a carpentry shop and a vegetable garden, in which he communicated to the children his love for handicrafts and nature.

There was no charge for tuition at the Children's Playhouse, as the Ferms "did not want money to enter into the question of attendance."[26] Funds for rent and materials were supplied by Miss Otis and Mrs. Menken, while the Ferms donated their services without pay. When the school opened, Alexis was thirty-one and Elizabeth forty-three, and they had been married for three years ("our relationship has grown closer and closer each day," Alexis recorded in his diary). Both were vegetarians, and lived on fruits and nuts while doing all the painting and papering to get the

Playhouse into shape.[27] To provide for their personal needs and also to help support the school, Uncle learned the trade of mechanical dentistry from a black friend, Dr. Frank Davenport, and then divided his time between the Playhouse and his job, spending mornings with the children and leaving at noon for the dental laboratory in New York where he worked.[28]

Before the end of the first year, however, the school received a setback when Mrs. S. L. Lawson died, and Mr. Lawson decided to send his son to a boarding school in Yonkers. Meanwhile, Dr. Thaddeus Hyatt of Brooklyn, whose wife had brought the Ferms together, came up to New Rochelle to see if he could not induce them to move to his neighborhood of Dyker Heights, so that his little boy could attend the school. By now the Ferms were themselves eager to return to Brooklyn, and, with the encouragement of Miss Otis, they began to look for new quarters.

In October 1902, after a year at New Rochelle, the Ferms rented a house in Dyker Heights and opened a new Children's Playhouse with some fifteen pupils, including the four Otis girls and Kenneth Hyatt. A year later the school moved to a nearby house bought for it by Miss Otis and containing a carpentry shop and spacious playrooms. For children who were boarding at the school, a second house was acquired across the street and managed by a Mr. and Mrs. Potter.

Until 1906 these buildings remained the premises of the Ferms' educational experiment, and it was here that their pioneering methods began to attract attention in libertarian circles, drawing such visitors as Emma Goldman, Leonard Abbott, Ernest Howard Crosby, and Bolton Hall. Abbott found the Ferms "a remarkable couple" and considered Elizabeth "a genius in her own way," although he could not accept all her ideas.[29] As for Emma Goldman, who spent an evening at the school sitting on the floor and singing Russian and Jewish songs to the children, the Ferms were "the first Americans I met whose ideas on education were akin to mine; but while I merely advocated the need of a new approach to the child, the Ferms translated their ideas into practice. In the Playhouse, as their school was called, the children of the neighborhood were bound by neither rules nor textbooks. They were free to go or come and to learn from observation and experience. I knew no one else who so well understood child psychology as Elizabeth and who was so capable of bringing out the best in the young. She and Alexis considered themselves single-taxers, but in reality they were anarchists in their views and lives. It was a great treat to visit their home, which was also the school, and to witness the beautiful relationship that existed between them and the children."[30]

During these years at Dyker Heights, the Ferms plunged into the radical intellectual life of New York City, mingling with theosophists and freethinkers, single-taxers and Tolstoyans, and anarchists of both the individualist and collectivist schools. They attended the Civic Club and the Sunrise Club, taking an active part in lectures and discussions. For several years Alexis served as president of the Manhattan Liberal Club, where both Emma Goldman and Clarence Darrow lectured under his chairmanship. He also presided at the Harlem Liberal Alliance when Alexander Berkman spoke on anarchist communism. The Ferms themselves addressed anarchist and secularist groups and contributed to such publications as *Free Society* and *Mother Earth*.

Their main effort, however, was devoted to running the Children's Playhouse, a task of considerable proportions. As in New Rochelle, the pupils came seven days a week, from early morning to late afternoon, and there was no imposed discipline or punishment. Freedom was the overriding principle. "Not absolute freedom," Alexis explained, "but as much freedom as is possible, in the condition of growth for the individual."[31] The Ferms, noted Ernest Crosby, who visited the school and included a chapter on it in his book *Tolstoy as a Schoolmaster*, "do not believe in letting the children ride rough-shod over them, and if the invasion of their own rights were pronounced enough they would interfere in any way that they deemed necessary." But they interpreted "their own rights" meagerly, Crosby added, and had "no objection to the invasion of their ear-drums by noises of all kinds." Indeed, the tumult was so great, said Crosby, that "it was hardly necessary for me to ask which house it was, for the sounds of romping were evident enough in the street."[32]

The first aim of the Ferms, as in New Rochelle, was the cultivation of initiative and self-expression. They deplored all external interference from parents or teachers. "The child who has been subjected to direction," Elizabeth argued, "is always non-creative, restless, exacting and capricious. He has been trained to look to others for help." She drew a sharp line, as we have seen, between pedagogy and education, between making the child into something and allowing him to realize his own potential. "The educator's endeavor should be directed towards the development of self-dependence in the child," she explained. "The test of an educator's value must be found in the degree [to which] the child is freed from reliance and dependence on the educator."[33]

Alexis emphatically agreed. "Education means development from within," he quoted his wife as saying in one of her talks. "Pedagogy means filling up from without. Education is the path to discovery, to knowledge. Pedagogy is the path to the discovered, to information." "Your teachers," he wrote to a former pupil, "are only human beings like yourself. What you will *know* must come from your own experience, not from the experience of your teachers or your mother or father."[34]

For similar reasons, the Ferms did not teach reading at Dyker Heights. They believed that by compelling children to read too early, by cramming them with facts and information, conventional schools stifled their initiative and creativity. The Ferms, it seems, in violation of their own libertarian tenets, even discouraged spontaneous urges to read on the part of the pupils. "*You* don't really want to read that," Aunty told one child. "Your *mother* wants you to!" According to Ernest Crosby, "Mrs. F. laughed at the ordinary method: 'I see a cat. Do you see a cat?' People do not talk that way. Why, then, should they learn to read that way? I inquired what she would do in case a child showed too great a fondness for books, and neglected outdoor exercise in consequence. She said that she had not yet met such an abnormal boy or girl, and that only unnatural conditions could produce them." Parents, Aunty was convinced, were suffering from a "pseudo-intellectual obsession" which caused them to overestimate the value of reading. "I am inclined to think, that if we read less we might think more deeply, be more receptive to simple truths. We might even attain more leisure to appreciate things which live and develop in the outdoors."[35]

The Ferms were equally troubled by the tendency of parents to view education as a means to some end, a preparation for some future goal, rather than as something important in itself. "Always the child is to be educated for society, for life, for his country, for a cause, for his church," Alexis complained. "When will it be that he will be educated for his own sake, for what it will mean to him?"[36] Childhood, the Ferms believed, was not a mere preliminary to the maturer years of life, but was important in its own terms. Nor was education a matter of a set interval of time. It was a lifelong process. Every day, every moment counted. The individual never ceased to grow, to develop.

Dyker Heights, then, was viewed as an end in itself. It was not,

Elizabeth emphasized, preparation for high school or for a job. "Just a playhouse and a workshop for the neighborhood," nothing more, nothing less.[37] Many years later, Alexis jotted down what he felt a parent ought to want from a school:

> To help my child to think for himself.
> Not to interfere with his growth towards freedom.
> Not to regiment him in any way.
> To try to understand my child's idiosyncracies.
> To let him feel that "freedom" is not only a word.
> To help him to *grow* according to his inner need.
> To help him to understand (or know) honesty from pretense.
> To make a condition where the child may use his own judgment in order to develop judgment.
> In the process of teaching that the teacher shall teach only, not think for the child.
> That the teacher shall be a passive follower of the child, but strong in his or her own integrity.[38]

Throughout Uncle's long career, this credo would never vary.

Underscoring freedom and spontaneity in learning, the Ferms abandoned all "formulas, plans, projects, assignments," as well as grades, exams, and compulsory work. Play and crafts occupied the center of the Dyker Heights curriculum. "We were always on swings, rings, or trapeze," Eva Brandes recalls. Uncle, as in New Rochelle, taught the children carpentry and gardening, and they worked with blocks, wool, beads, and other Froebel "gifts." Even three-year-old Leon tried his hand at woodworking, Uncle was pleased to note, "using chisel, saw and hammer."[39] Many of the children were fond of drawing and took "the greatest pride in each other's work, boasting of it almost as if it were their own," Ernest Crosby observed. The children, added Crosby, enjoyed having stories read to them. "They pick up reading in connection with these stories, trying to find their favorite stories for themselves in the book, following the reading, and gradually learning to recognize now this word and now that."[40] They also learned arithmetic, geography, and history in conjunction with the problems of actual life, conducting, for example, a debate on the Russo-Japanese War after its outbreak in 1904.

Another favorite activity was the performance of skits and plays with such names as "The Bold Bank Robbery," "A Vaudeville Show," "A Scene from the Civil War," and "The Troubles of a Millionaire." On January 13, 1906, the Ferms took the children to see *Peter Pan*, with Maude Adams in the starring role. "Aunty talked of fairies and leprechauns," Eva Brandes remembers, "which made us all the more excited about the play. We had a big picture on the wall of Maude Adams as Peter Pan. After seeing her perform, we put on the play ourselves, over and over."[41]

So enthralled were the children that the Ferms invited Miss Adams to visit the school, "but she couldn't make it and sent a dancing instructor instead." Dancing and music, which Elizabeth considered "one of the potent factors in the development of the individual," continued to occupy an important place throughout the life of the school, which boasted a grand piano on which Aunty accompanied morning assembly as well as the various children's entertainments. After being taken to the opera, the boys and girls put on their own version of Wagner's *Niebelungen* cycle, with painted cardboard scenery and self-made costumes.

And yet there was something wanting in the Ferms' treatment of their charges. For all their belief in kindness and sympathy, they failed to give the pupils the love they needed. "The Ferms were interesting and good people," Eva Brandes remembers, "but neither was particularly affectionate, which was an important thing to be lacking in with children." Eva found some of the affection she craved in Miss Otis, "a kind, soft person," who not only gave the children tenderness but prepared a special dish for them every week to supplement their austere diet and let them have a large slab of ice cream for dessert.

Of the two Ferms, Elizabeth was the dominant partner. She had the greater intensity, the more powerful personality, and the more inflexible ideas. "Aunty Ferm was strong-willed, cranky, very prudish," says Eva Brandes. "Not Uncle, who was always decent, soft-spoken, easy to approach. She was lovely and worked very hard, but she was too sharp." Even worse were her deeply ingrained prejudices, which manifested themselves on frequent occasions. "She once asked us when we were born," Eva recalls. "I said July. She said: 'Anyone born in July is lazy.' I was very hurt. And I can feel it to this day."[42]

Elizabeth could never free herself from such prejudices, which were bound up with her mystical nature. They remained a permanent part of her makeup and often reacted upon her pupils, especially where sex was concerned. Elizabeth's attitude toward sex was deeply rooted in the Victorian and Catholic morality in which she was reared. She labeled premarital sex as "unhealthy indulgence" and condemned masturbation as "self-abuse." One day the children were hiding in a closet during play when she rushed in and warned them against masturbating ("it was very bad, and we would lose our minds").

In Elizabeth's ideas about sex there were elements not only of Victorian puritanism but of what can only be termed outright cruelty, elements which she was unable to control but from which she suffered remorse. She once washed a boy's mouth out with soap for using foul language, and while the children were on an overnight trip in the country she hit another boy for looking in at the girls in the outhouse. "She was deeply upset by sex," recalls Eva Brandes. "When she caught Walter peeking in at the girls she made a terrible scene. She hit him so. We were all terribly frightened. And then she cried, and that made things even worse."[43]

This last incident occurred at Newfoundland, New Jersey, where, in May 1906, the Ferms bought land as a retreat with a loan from Mrs. Menken and took the children there for outings. During the summer of that year, Aunty and Uncle conducted a camp school on the property. The children lived in tents and were expected to work to the best of their ability. They all made their own straw beds, swept out the tents, tidied up the grounds, and fetched water. Each child contributed $1.50 a week for food. Elizabeth did the cooking, while the girls made desserts from apples and berries gathered by the boys; but anyone who did not do his share of work could not expect a piece of pie.[44]

The summer camp at Newfoundland marked the end of the Dyker Heights experiment. After four years in their comfortable Brooklyn surroundings, the Ferms decided to move to a working-class neighborhood, as they had originally intended. Another reason for leaving Dyker Heights, and perhaps the more critical reason, was the friction that had developed between Elizabeth and some of the parents over the conduct of the school. Returning from New Jersey at the end of the summer, the Ferms moved to an apartment on East 31st Street in Manhattan, where they were to live for the next seven years.

In the fall of 1906 Elizabeth was walking through the Lower East Side on her way to Alexis's dental laboratory when she noticed an empty store in a tenement on Madison Street which she thought might be a good place to open a school. Alexis had his doubts, but she managed to persuade him. Mrs. Menken offered to stand the expense of rent and materials, and a new Neighborhood Playhouse and Workshop was launched, perhaps the first "storefront" school in an American ghetto, anticipating by more than half a century the hundreds of similar ventures of the 1960s and '70s.

The pupils at Madison Street, children of Jewish, Italian, and Irish immigrants, included Hyperion, Gorky, and Révolte Bercovici,[45] who were later to attend the Ferrer School on East Twelfth Street. Konrad Bercovici, who had recently arrived from Rumania and Paris, remembers the school as the only ray of light in a bleak existence. Mrs. Ferm, tall and beautiful, was as "patient as an angel." Her husband came in the afternoons after his work at the laboratory. In one of the rooms he had installed a workbench and lathe where he "gathered the older boys about him to teach them to work and to instill in them the joy and pride of work." The store was otherwise empty, except for a few chairs and a piano. Yet all by themselves the Ferms "did more for the morale of the neighborhood than all the settlement institutions put together."[46]

For the next seven years the Ferms conducted their Madison Street Neighborhood Playhouse, meanwhile continuing their activities in libertarian circles. Elizabeth, throwing herself into the cause of Irish independence, joined the Gaelic Society and Sinn Fein, and Irish exiles, including young Eamon de Valera, visited the Ferms' apartment. Among their closest friends during this period were John and Abby Coryell, who lived in the same building and who became the first teachers at the Ferrer Day School. When the Coryells left, Emma Goldman invited the Ferms to take their place, and they came over to have a look. But Elizabeth was upset to find anticlerical pictures on the walls, including a portrait of Ferrer himself, and she and Alexis apparently thought the parents too vociferous and meddlesome to allow them to run the school without interference. At any rate, they declined the offer.

By 1913, however, the Ferms were ready for a change. Seven years of hard work in the ghetto had taken their toll. Elizabeth was exhausted, and Alexis had begun to develop headaches owing to the frequent inhalation of nitric acid fumes used in the work of dental prosthesis. If they hoped to recover their health, they would have to change their mode of living. After considering various alternatives, they decided to take up farming, and bought a little farm in Hampton, Connecticut, where they scratched out a living for the next seven years, until invited to come to Stelton. Their new occupation suited them. Elizabeth had a farming background, Alexis was a good gardener and handyman, and both were spartan in their tastes, diet, and work habits. While Alexis did the planting and cultivating, Elizabeth helped with the chickens and shucked the corn.

Not that they had isolated themselves completely from their former existence. Friends, including the Coryells and Trasks, visited from New York. They kept abreast of new educational developments. Elizabeth set on paper the ideas she had been evolving since the 1890s, which appeared as a series of articles in *The Modern School* magazine as well as in pamphlet form as *The Spirit of Freedom in Education*, beautifully printed by Joseph Ishill with initial letters by Rockwell Kent. In early 1920, finally, Harry Kelly came up from Stelton to try to induce them to end their self-imposed exile and to take over the boarding house at the colony. Alexis again had his doubts. But Kelly promised them a "free hand," and Elizabeth could not resist. "A workers' school! A poor school! A neglected school!" she told a friend. "Ah! It was a call. And we never missed a call yet."[47]

STELTON

After a hurried trip to Stelton, Elizabeth returned to Connecticut and told Alexis that there were children in need of care. Without further debate, they accepted Kelly's proposal. Selling their farm, they drove to New Jersey in a horse-drawn buggy, with their luggage on the back seat. The trip took a week, and it was hard to find livery stables on the way, most having been converted into garages. Arriving after dark on April 20, 1920, they found the boarding house empty, the children being away in New York with John Edelman giving a play to raise money for the school. But Gray Wu was on hand to greet them and to help them get settled for the night.[48]

The next morning the Ferms examined their new surroundings. To their dismay, the boarding house was in "a state of chaos," with the grounds outside "looking like a dump for ashes." Though Alexis was now fifty and Elizabeth sixty-two, they at once settled down to work, cleaning, painting, refurbishing. Alexis, a skilled carpenter, made new furniture, while Elizabeth rose every morning at 5 to tidy up and get breakfast ready with the help of the older children. Meanwhile, they rechristened the structure the Living House, as its counterparts had been called at New Rochelle and Dyker Heights, "so the children would not get the impression of merely boarding. We wished the children to feel that it was their home."[49]

When the Ferms agreed to come to Stelton, the understanding was that they would be responsible for the boarding house only, in which they had been promised a free hand. Not long after their arrival, however, Elizabeth noticed that the younger children of the colony, at least those who lived with their parents, had no center of activity and seemed to be wandering about aimlessly, as if lost for something to do. In late May or early June, with materials supplied by the parents, she opened a kindergarten in the old barn, using Froebel techniques and playthings—colored wool, beads, lace, peg boards, blocks, design cards—as in the past. Thereupon the children "naturally and eagerly went to work."[50]

Impressed by the success of the kindergarten, the board of management, headed by Joseph Cohen, became convinced that "here, at last, we had found the right people to introduce the proper method of libertarian education at our School,"[51] which had been without a permanent director since William Thurston Brown's departure the previous year. Before the summer was over, the Ferms, while remaining in charge of the Living House, were asked to become co-principals of the school as well.

Alexis and Elizabeth demurred. For one thing, they had their hands full with the Living House alone, which required constant attention to maintain in proper order. For another, as Uncle asserted, they preferred doing educational work where "we would have complete care and control of the children," undisturbed by outside interference, whether from parents or the board of management. Such was the case with the Living House, which remained their exclusive preserve "for twenty-four hours of the day."[52] At the school, by contrast, there would be a large number of "day" children, that is children who lived at home and were subject to the influence of their parents, in whose judgment the Ferms placed little confidence. The Ferms wanted nothing less than total control over the children's environment, lest the true process of education be compromised.

The Ferms were hesitant for yet another reason, perhaps the most important of all. Under William Thurston Brown and John Edelman, the curriculum of the school had become heavily academic, aiming to prepare the students to enter high school, a goal for which the Ferms had only contempt. Apart from Hugo Gellert's art class, there was little left in the way of manual or "creative" work, as the Ferms termed it. In May 1920, two weeks after their arrival, the Ferms had already expressed their disappointment before the board: "Alexis Ferm declared that he was very little interested in the academic side of the school. What he wanted to know was: How the children acquired responsibility in household work and in other activities? Judging from what he had seen since his arrival at Stelton, the children were somewhat deficient in responsibility. He also raised the question: Why no shop and manual training? He wanted to see the whole capacity of the child developed. He thought that too much emphasis had been laid on book-work, and that too little attention had been given to the home, the manual-training shop, etc. Mrs. Ferm supported this attitude."[53]

Cohen, however, promised them freedom to change the curriculum as they saw fit and to provide whatever materials were needed to carry out their program. Under these conditions, they agreed to take over, provided that the annual convention of the Modern School Association went along and was willing "to give us full control of the work."[54] Over the Labor Day weekend in September 1920, the matter was brought before the membership and debated "from eight p.m. to two a.m. without pause," a portent of troubles to come. Yet when the vote was taken, the Ferms won unanimous approval as co-principals. More than that, their approach to education received strong endorsement. The convention, as Cohen put it, decided "to revolutionize the whole procedure, abandon the preparatory work and formal academic instruction, basing the School and development of the children on manual work and creative activity."[55]

The Ferms took charge of the school on October 1, 1920. Until that time, Abe Bluestein recalls, the curriculum had been "largely academic." But Aunty and Uncle "reshaped it entirely." According to another pupil, "the whole philosophy of the school changed dramatically." The program, centered almost exclusively on crafts and play, was "innovative, even revolutionary." Printing, weaving, carpentry, basket-making, pottery, leather crafts, metal work, not to mention singing, dancing, and sports, became "the primary activities for teachers and pupils, academics being relegated to a back seat in the curriculum."[56]

To accommodate this new approach, the Ferms completely altered the way in which the schoolhouse was employed. One classroom was converted into a carpentry shop, another into a print shop, still another into a metal-working shop, installed by the children themselves under Uncle's supervision. Later on, a sewing and weaving room was added. Only one room, the library, was retained for what the Ferms deprecatingly called "abstract" work, with Jim Dick in charge, offering English, arithmetic, and other academic subjects. "We took breaks by sitting around the floor and reading Shakespeare," James Dick, Jr., recalls. "It was fun, and we never realized it was 'classics'—that we were 'learning' something." Activities were continually changing in accordance with the children's and teachers' inclinations. "What we do this year may be different from what we may do the next," Uncle declared. "Some activities may be dropped and others added. Experimentation is constantly in the air. We live the experimental life."[57]

The auditorium was used for the kindergarten and for morning assembly, which became a regular feature of the school. When the first assembly was opened, Elizabeth suggested to the parents that they join in the circle, holding hands with the children while singing the good-morning song and other songs ("Pretty little dandelion / Growing in the grass / With your hair of shining gold / Merry little lass"), which Elizabeth accompanied on the piano. After the singing, Aunty played for "interpretive dancing," in which some of the mothers took part. "Not many of the boys had the nerve to try," Alexis recalls, "but the girls did some interesting dancing."[58]

Morning assembly, which had the character of an animistic nature rite and which Aunty considered the essential "spirit of the school," was enjoyed by the whole community, children, parents, and staff. Jim Dick, for one, never missed it, for it was "the time when all the children are fresh and bubbling over with life." It was good, he said, "to see our kids romping down to 'school' every morning, fresh and beautiful as the pansies now in bloom in our garden. What a glorious sight for the gods! They are now ready to dance with the daffodils or sing their merry songs. Aunty touches the magic keyboard and off they go, singing and dancing as every full-blooded kid should do at the flush of dawn. Then a song of the sun and of the great brown earth, of the caterpillar and its wonderful transformation into the butterfly, and of those pussy-willows down by the brook. You should hear those kids ask the pussy-willows to sit down by the fire as other pussies do, and our wee bairns who take sides with the pussies of the brook singing in reply, 'Oh, no; we couldn't and we wouldn't do that! We belong to the fairy folk and we are their pussy cats.' And they certainly mean it, too. Then more dancing and singing as into a shell we crawl, then off to our various kinds of art and craft we go. So the story of the morning begins. We have shaken the sleep out of our eyes and learned the lesson of the fields in song."[59]

After morning assembly, the children went off to a variety of activities of their own choosing, from arts and crafts to gardening and athletics. Frequently there were hiking and camping to keep them fit and in touch with nature. "The school room of the 'great outside' is even more important than any room in the school building," Uncle Ferm remarked. Whether indoors or out, an atmosphere of freedom prevailed. "We went each day and did exactly what we wanted to do," Abe Bluestein remembers. "This could mean playing all day or periods of frenzied activity in the weaving shop or the carpentry shop or the printing shop." James Dick, Jr., has a similar recollection: "We had no grades, no marks, no compulsion to get to class. We called the teachers by their first names. They were friends rather than superiors, and all were equal in the school. We had weekly meetings where the children voted equally with the teachers. It was a place of freedom and joy."[60]

Not all the teachers were happy about these changes. Yet, as Laurence Veysey has noted, they responded to the powerful impact of the Ferms' personalities by cooperating fully in executing them.[61] Hugo Gellert continued his art instruction, assisted by his talented young protégé Bill Pogrebysky, who took charge after Gellert left in 1922. The children took to art "as ducks to water," Gellert recollects. "We had a great big table with different colors in one-quart jars. Little three-year-olds would say, 'Please pass the magenta.' When their work was exhibited at the Civic Club in New York, Alfred Stieglitz came and said to me, 'What did you do to them? Every one is a genius!' "[62]

Basketry, a popular activity, was taught by Jim Dick, Sherwood Trask, Kate Van Eaton, and Anna Koch-Riedel. Mrs. Koch-Riedel, who also taught sewing and gardening, went down to the single-tax colony at Arden, Delaware, to take lessons in hand weaving from a Miss Rhodes, an expert in the craft, after which she took charge of weaving instruction at Stelton, herself becoming "a true artist." Her husband, Hans Koch, from whom she was now separated, taught woodworking and metal crafts. An expert builder (he had overseen construction of the schoolhouse), he later worked with Frank Lloyd Wright at Taliesin West. A native of Hatzfeld, an enclave of German culture in the Banat district of Hungary, Koch was "a very intelligent man and an ardent anarchist," who had edited a series of antiauthoritarian journals in New York between 1907 and 1912, when he became acquainted with the Ferms.[63] To Koch, Stelton was the hope of the future, producing human beings who were "unfettered, free, creative, constructive."[64]

The printing teacher was Paul Scott, a former agitator and tramp, "who among a thousand other adventures," Mike Gold tells us, "was once run out of Mexico with Benjamin De Casseres for publishing a revolutionary labor paper Porfirio Díaz didn't like."[65] Under Scott's gentle guidance *The Voice of the Children* was born, written, set, and printed by the pupils, with wood and linoleum cuts notable for their freshness and originality. Scott found so much joy in working with these creative youngsters that he was to look back on his years at Stelton as "the most satisfactory period of my life."[66]

Another highly regarded teacher was Sherwood Trask, a Dartmouth graduate from the midwest, who offered history and geography as well as basketry and took the children hiking and camping. Harry Clements, a member of the English contingent, taught leather crafts, shoe repairing, and sandal making. A Jack-of-all-trades, he also built hand looms for the children and offered them instruction in agriculture. Another Englishman on the staff, William Bridge, arrived in 1923 from Grinnell College with his daughters Pauline and Joan. (Joan was to become the mother of the folk-singer Joan Baez.) Bridge left a few years later to join the speech department at Hunter College, but was dismissed for having an affair with one of his students. In 1930 he opened the Floral Hill School at Chatham, New Jersey, which seems to have been modeled after Stelton, offering, according to its prospectus, "a simple life without frills, but giving every opportunity to the children *to learn through living*. It is not a school for robots or slaves or child-parasites: but children whose parents seek freedom in sane growth. It is a school for individual development through creative activity."[67]

Music instruction at Stelton was provided by Frances Goldenthal, a graduate of the Damrosch Institute and proficient in both violin and piano, and by Suzanne Hotkine, a girl of eighteen who, having emigrated from Paris, also offered lessons in French. Of Russian-Jewish parentage, Suzanne had read the works of Kropotkin, and when someone told her about Stelton she decided to pay it a visit. "I came for a day, stayed for a year, and it became part of me forever," she recalls.[68]

Such were the activities at Stelton and the teachers who conducted them. Only a few had professional training, such as Lillian Rifkin, who came in 1923 for a year after being educated at Teachers College under Dewey and Kilpatrick and teaching at the Organic School at Fairhope. Yet their accomplishments were remarkable. As Agnes de Lima wrote: "Visitors to the school have been astonished that children without formal instruction or no instruction should achieve such frequently fine results in painting, in mural decor, in rug weaving, in clay and pottery, no less than in ordinary academic subjects, and the humbler crafts of printing, shoe-making, and forge work."[69]

The adults, too, enjoyed a varied program of activities, including lectures, conferences, and entertainments. Among the visitors during these years were Helen Keller, Paul Robeson, Ammon Hennacy, Caroline Pratt, and Isadora Duncan's brother Raymond. From time to time communal dinners were held for the benefit of the school, and on Sunday evenings there were singing and dancing accompanied by Aunty Ferm at the piano. The Ferms arranged weekly parents' meetings for discussion of educational problems, and Elizabeth started a class to explain "the meaning of the creative activity, initiative and self-activity of Froebel's principles." Not only were these sessions well attended but the mothers took notes, asked questions, and wrote small essays on the subjects discussed. "I still have my notes," says Dora Keyser. "I think I got more out of the school than the children!"[70]

Harry Kelly's fiftieth birthday, falling in January 1921, became the occasion of a special celebration, attended by two hundred comrades and friends. "Harry," declared Mike Gold, "has been true as the north star; he never lost faith, though on his devoted head has beaten many a storm; he is the mainspring of the group at Stelton."[71] Addressing the assembly, Kelly compared the Stelton adventure to analogous experiments of the past: "Perhaps this community will grow large and unwieldy and the charming intimacy now prevailing will pass away, or again, like Brook Farm, it may die and leave a fragrant memory. If it does, we believe the same tribute paid Brook Farm will be paid the Ferrer Colony: that none who have lived here during the past six stormy years will ever admit it was a failure."[72]

Politically, anarchism remained the dominant ideology at the colony and Kropotkin the chief theoretical mentor. After Kropotkin's death in 1921, the new Stelton library, erected next to the schoolhouse, was dedicated in his memory, while a Kropotkin

Publishing Society was formed in New York by such leaders of the Modern School Association as Leonard Abbott, Harry Kelly, Joseph Cohen, John Edelman, Bolton Hall, and Elizabeth Gurley Flynn.[73] In 1923, Joseph Ishill published a beautiful memorial volume to Kropotkin under the imprint of his Free Spirit Press. Every November 11th Haymarket memorials were held at the colony, and anarchist conferences continued to meet regularly, drawing delegates from all over the northeast. In addition, a number of anarchist periodicals were published at Stelton, most notably *The Road to Freedom*, launched in 1924, the first important English anarchist journal in the United States since the suppression of *Mother Earth* in 1917, with contributions by Berkman, Goldman, Abbott, Kelly, and many other figures prominent in the movement. Its editor was Hippolyte Havel, "that battered hoary paladin of 100 per cent Communism," as Mike Gold called him, who moved into the Kropotkin Library, his home for the next twenty-five years.[74]

During the 1920s, the number of communists at the colony multiplied, and a group of Young Pioneers was organized, with their white shirts and red ties and hosannas to Soviet Russia. Yet, if tensions between communists and anarchists inevitably increased, they never reached the breaking point as at Mohegan. Indeed, as Harry Kelly wrote to Elizabeth Gurley Flynn, Stelton was "one of the very few places, if not the only one, where anarchists and communists, as well as others not so violently opposed to each other, have been able to work together."[75]

A controversy of greater proportions emerged in another quarter. As the months and years passed, dissatisfaction with the Ferms and their methods mounted sharply. Many of the colonists, whether anarchist or communist, felt that social and political questions should have a place in the curriculum, from which the Ferms had rigorously excluded them. Education, the militants argued, was not merely an instrument of self-development but also a lever of social transformation, a means of altering social foundations. Abe Bluestein, regarded by some as "a young Bakunin," found the school "derelict in training revolutionists, in preparing us to overthrow the capitalist system." Others wished to see the pupils imbued with the spirit of proletarian solidarity "since the founders of the school were class-conscious workers," to which Aunty replied that "the savior of the world will not be the class-conscious worker but the creative artist."[76] Revolution, the Ferms were convinced, would in any case merely replace one tyranny with another, as the experience of Soviet Russia had shown.

Education, as the Ferms conceived it, had nothing in common with propaganda or indoctrination. Children, rather, must be left to develop in freedom, to find their own identity unhindered by the prejudices of adults. On December 8, 1924, a debate took place at Stelton on the question "Should Anarchism Be Taught to the Children?," Hippolyte Havel arguing in favor, Alexis Ferm against. "To become a radical, an anarchist, a free man," Uncle declared, was "a matter of inner experience," of "personal growth." To establish "anarchist schools," he argued on another occasion, was "to follow in the footsteps of the church, the Communists, and all the reactionaries. . . . All that the adults can do for the education of the young is to foster the spirit of freedom in the schools and to establish schools where freedom of the child in his growth will be the paramount idea. The moment you label a children's school 'Anarchist' it no longer stands for freedom. Just think it over."[77]

In January 1925 Uncle engaged in a similar debate at the Rand School on the question "Has Propaganda Any Value in Education?" His opponent was Scott Nearing, the socialist economist whose dismissal from the University of Pennsylvania in 1915 had become a *cause célèbre* in the history of academic freedom. Nearing, a fellow-traveler who believed that Soviet Russia was "the world's largest, and most important, educational laboratory," upheld the role of propaganda in the classroom, a view which Uncle vigorously opposed. For the remainder of his career Uncle continued to argue against propaganda or indoctrination in the school. "Education is never Anarchism, Socialism, Single Taxism, Republicanism nor any other ism," he wrote in 1940. It loses its true character "the minute it becomes the work of some group calling themselves by the name of some philosophy-ending-ism."[78]

On a related issue, there were some who criticized the Ferms for their single-minded preoccupation with Froebel, to the neglect of Ferrer and other socially oriented theorists. "I think it is a bit strange that the name of Ferrer was not even once mentioned in 'Freedom in Education,' " wrote Leonard Abbott to Alexis, referring to Elizabeth's book.[79] To Elizabeth, with her Catholic background, Ferrer was an uncongenial figure. Uncle, by contrast, quoted Ferrer's essay *The Modern School* when it coincided with his own views ("Education is not worthy of the name unless it is stripped of all dogmatism and unless it leaves to the child the direction of its powers and is content to support them in their manifestations"), and in 1959 he wrote an article about Ferrer for the *Fraye Arbeter Shtime* on the centennial of his birth. After the advent of the Ferms, however, Ferrer was seldom mentioned at the school, which, to all intents and purposes, became a new Froebelian playhouse and workshop. During their tenure at Stelton, it may be worth noting, the Ferms took an active part in the Progressive Education Association, speaking at its conventions, serving on its committees, and contributing to its journal. (Alexis addressed the 1922 convention in Boston and the 1925 convention in Philadelphia.) The association, for its part, kept abreast of developments at Stelton, and *The Voice of the Children* was distributed to all member schools.

For all their rejection of dogma, for all their defense of spontaneity and self-determination, the Ferms were imposing a specific educational philosophy upon the children. Their aversion to academic instruction, their faith in Froebelian methods, their refusal to compromise the principles to which they adhered with such tenacious conviction, clashed sharply with the slogan of "Freedom in Education" which they trumpeted throughout their writings. "Both were extraordinarily gifted," remarked Emma Cohen, "but both had a kind of anti-intellectualism and distrust of theories, except for those of people they accepted, like Froebel. Aunty expounded all sorts of Froebelian principles that were way out—though absolutely real to her—and had nothing to do with anything." Yet the children were expected to observe them. "Aunty was very rigid," Ray Miller remembers. "She lived by a great many rules and regulations and expected other people to conform to her ideas." According to Wanda Swieda, "Aunty was opinionated and self-assured. She thought whatever she preached was gospel, and was intolerant of differing views."[80]

Beyond all this, there were still other causes of friction. For one thing, the Ferms favored the children of the Living House—their "own" children—over the children who lived with their parents. For the Living House children, to whom they became surrogate parents, they developed a special attachment, accentuated, one imagines, by their lack of offspring of their own. This attachment, not unnaturally, aroused the envy and resentment of the children who lived at home. "We felt a little left out of things," as one of them put it.[81]

Another source of friction was rooted in Aunty's personality.

An admirer of independence and backbone, she "hated every form of human weakness" and was "an extremely harsh disciplinarian," even where the very young were concerned. If a child wet his bed, for example, she made him sleep in the damp sheets. And her attitude toward cursing and masturbation has already been noted. "I think she was well meaning," says Hugo Gellert, "but she had a dictatorial streak. Some of the children didn't take to her, while they all liked Uncle. Yet she would have done anything for the kids. She was honest and hard-working and thought she was doing the right thing."[82]

Determined to protect her charges from outside intruders, Aunty once drove off two newspapermen who had come to the colony to take pictures. She "swooped down like an eagle, with her poncho belts flying, and scooped up both tripods in one grasp and broke both cameras," Ellen Brooke remembers. Yet her aloof and sometimes forbidding manner, her sudden shifts of mood and periods of extreme nervous tension, inspired fear in more than a few of the children, to say nothing of the adults. In many ways, Uncle was equally unbending, but his was a gentler and more considerate nature, and he "always had a twinkle in his eye which was very welcome when things became desperate with Aunty," Pauline Bridge remarked. "There were differences in their character," said Anna Schwartz, "which I think had mainly to do with her early life and Catholic background. She was always proud of that—of her Irish name—Elizabeth Byrne Battle Ferm!"[83]

Suzanne Hotkine, who came to know Aunty better than most, has left a vivid impression: "In the school Aunty insisted on rainbow colors—primary colors—as with the Froebel 'gifts.' It brought out the positive side of people, of life, she said. No other colors were allowed. There was something mystical about this, as with Froebel himself, but it was very beautiful. Her mysticism was very powerful. She was still full of religion, full of the convent from which she had come. She had a horror of sex. She was puritanical, with a repressed sexual drive and a strange attitude towards men. She was far stronger than Uncle, a bigger person, more complex, more profound than he was. Greater, but harder too. If a child came to school without a shirt, even on a hot day, she would send him home. And she objected to nudity in the colony—even at swimming—and tried to stop it. She was a fiery Irish woman who would brook no interference from anyone and looked down on the colonists as somehow inferior. She had a deep-seated anti-Semitic streak, stemming from her Irish

Catholic upbringing. Despite her break with the church, she was still a Catholic, and Catholicism meant a great deal to her."

"Yet at the same time," Suzanne continues, "she had a broad outlook, a wide scope. Of the two she was the visionary. It was *she* who inspired *him*. She had two pairs of eyes. She didn't mix much with the colonists, yet knew what was going on in every household. She was very Irish. She recited Gaelic poetry, sang Gaelic songs, marched in St. Patrick's Day parades. She was a twisted genius. She spoke French fairly well (from her years in Canada) and played the piano with verve, especially Beethoven. Her playing, though lacking technically, had a spiritual greatness about it. We played duets for hours—Haydn, Beethoven, Mozart. Uncle too loved music. I played 'The Moonlight Sonata' for him on his 101st birthday, and the tears streamed down his face. He was softer, sweeter than she, but she was the heart of the educational experiment."[84]

DEPARTURE

What proved the Ferms' undoing was their hostility toward academic education. "Metaphysical" or "abstract" training, as Alexis termed it, was to them no education at all and placed an alien burden on youthful minds. Whether directly or indirectly, the Ferms discouraged the children from spending their time with books. Jim Dick was supposed to sit in the library every morning and wait for children who might seek instruction in reading and arithmetic. "At first there were a great many who went in," Alexis recalled, "since many had had nothing else but abstract work and did not know what else to do. But gradually as they became interested in other activities they forgot to go to Jim's class and after a while Jim was left very much to himself."[85]

Many of the parents, perhaps a majority, were never convinced of the wisdom of the new course introduced by the Ferms. No one questioned the desirability of crafts or play, of nature walks or learning by doing. But for many these were not enough. As their children grew older, parents began to worry about their backwardness in academic subjects. They were concerned lest the children should grow up unequipped to cope with life as it really was. Moreover, as Laurence Veysey has noted, "the Ferms' curriculum in effect idealized the simple, sturdy way of life of the craftsman; the immigrants, on the other hand, were all too familiar with that life under unfavorable conditions and admired the intellectual skills that would enable their children to enter into far more interesting careers."[86] Why not give equal encouragement to reading and writing? they asked. Would this not be more in keeping with the principle of developing all aspects of the child's personality? Some parents were reduced to smuggling books into the home for their children to read after school. The question of academic work became a source of increasing bitterness. Discussions at meetings became more and more heated. A growing number of children were withdrawn and placed in other schools.

Under mounting attack from the parents, Uncle Ferm defended his position. "The complaint from most of our parents has been that we have not given as much attention to abstract work as we have to manual or art work and that, therefore, we have not given the children a chance to get it if they wanted it. This in spite of the fact that we have had some classes and that the children were at liberty to ask questions whenever they felt like it or were in need of information," he wrote. "At all events there is no doubt in my mind that most of the time spent in the arithmetic class or English class is lost time, unless the children seem to have some specific calling for it."[87]

"The greatest bugaboo in our midst," Uncle declared on another occasion, "is the fear that our children may not learn to read and to count their money. But our parents do not seem to notice when our children lack coordination or ability to use their hands, have poor control of their bodies and become knock-kneed and flabby." To be able to read and write, he added, "does not spell freedom or intelligence, nor development of strength, nor creative ability, nor a sense of fairness, nor good judgment, nor bigness of heart, nor fine temperament." By being tied down to books, rather, "we are prevented from soaring or from looking within ourselves when we are young and should be dreaming of the things that we would be." Uncle lamented that so many parents should want their children "to compete with the children of the conservative world" and should believe in "medals, degrees, high marks and rewards for surpassing others in competitions."[88]

The Ferms were not lacking for defenders, including some, like Leonard Abbott, who did not endorse all of their methods. "The voice of the Ferms," wrote Abbott, "is the clearest voice, in its statement of educational principles, that has ever come out of Stelton. This remarkable couple have given the School a meaning and a dignity that it never had before."[89] Besides, as the Ferms themselves contended, academics were far from being totally neglected. English, for example, was taught at various times by Jim Dick, Paul Scott, Lillian Rifkin, and William Bridge, not to mention French by Suzanne Hotkine and German by Anna Riedel. There was also instruction in history, geography, and mathematics, though usually tied in with "practical" work. Stelton children, as Harry Kelly pointed out, continued to do "exceedingly well" in high school; and in an examination at the local public school, Uncle Ferm noted, they were "several years ahead of their age in literataure."[90]

The strongest support, however, came from the children themselves. In retrospect, at least, the great majority looked back on their years with the Ferms as intensely creative and enriching. "From the Modern School I learned to rely on myself to develop the capacities I had in me," Pauline Bridge recollected. "I learned simplicity of living, self-discipline, most of all I learned the joy of living a creative life. These are the kind of lessons that one never forgets." Her sister Joan had similar memories. "There was one school she was sent to which she loved," wrote Joan Baez of her mother. "They left her alone there, and she could sit by a brook and not go to class."[91] Not all the children, of course, were as happy as Pauline and Joan, but their experience was not untypical.

A few, who were to achieve prominence in later life, attributed their success to the colony. It was at Stelton that Ethel Butler, a dancer with the Martha Graham troupe, discovered her life's vocation. At her first morning assembly she found herself in "a high state of ecstatic joy and more sure of myself as an integral part of humanity than ever before." She vowed that, whatever obstacles might present themselves, she would become a professional dancer.[92] And one of the boys, Edgar Tafel, built such interesting structures with the Froebel "gifts" that Aunty predicted he would become an architect. In his second year at Columbia he decided to enter Frank Lloyd Wright's school at Taliesin, Wisconsin, and he afterward assisted Wright in designing the famous Johnson Building in Racine and other structures, and became a leading architect in New York. His years at the school, he believes, had been crucial to his imaginative development.

In 1947 Uncle Ferm sent Edgar pictures of the designs he had made while at Stelton.[93] Like Tolstoy, Uncle remained deeply interested in his former pupils. He was eager to know where they were and what they were doing and how their lives were turning out. He remembered their names and what they had been like at the school, and held them in affection for the rest of his life. "You know," he wrote to Gilbert and Victoria Aronoff at the end of 1941, "that we wish you a better and a spiritually more profitable New Year. By 'spiritual' we mean your inner self, that part of you that no one can put his finger on; that part that refers to your thought, your likes and dislikes, your loves and hatreds, your wishes and dreams. And may those dreams be radiant for a more beautiful world. The physical world is already beautiful. Even the storms are beautiful."[94]

In 1925 the Ferms decided to leave Stelton. For more than five years they had directed the school and the Living House. They had cleaned and cooked and repaired. They had kept the dormitory in order. They had overseen the daily life of the children and taken part in adult evening socials. Above all, they had conducted a vital educational experiment. But in the process, according to Harry Kelly, they had come to think of the school as their own. "Your business is to raise money," Elizabeth told the board of management, "and leave the school to us." It was the old story, said Kelly, "of the people against the individual. The Ferms did not want any interference, and the people who created the school and suffered for it wanted a voice in it. Both were wrong and both right."[95]

None could dispute that the Ferms had given their heart and soul to their efforts. After the first year, in fact, Aunty was so worn out that she had to go to the Arden Colony for several months of recuperation, Uncle visiting her on weekends.[96] By 1925 she was in her sixty-eighth year. Uncle was fifty-five. On top of all the work, he noted, the "constant fault-finding" was intolerable. "We thought we had had enough criticism and wanted to have a little time to think for ourselves and to give the folks of the school an opportunity to work out their own salvation."[97]

So the Ferms tendered their resignation. And with their departure, as Suzanne Hotkine put it, the "magic" was gone from the school. Nor were they the only ones to leave. Sherwood Trask had already departed in 1922. After a brief stint at the Organic School, he traveled to Europe, visited A. S. Neill's international school at Hellerau, near Dresden, and then completed his teaching career at the progressive Walden School in New York. But his memories of the colony remained vivid. "I have never ceased to be thankful," he wrote to Leonard Abbott in 1940, "that you men took me in at Stelton which (chicken-coop that it was) had *the real thing*." Stelton, he said, was "life, raw and real."[98]

In addition to Trask, Hugo Gellert also left in 1922, Paul Scott in 1924, Anna Riedel in 1925. Hans Koch left to join Frank Lloyd Wright in Arizona, Suzanne Hotkine to attend Juilliard, John Edelman to organize unions in Pennsylvania. Fred Dunn, after a dispute with Harry Kelly, became an organizer for the Consumer Cooperative Housing Association in New York City, where he died prematurely in 1925. In 1923 Kelly himself left to found the Mohegan Colony, to which the Dicks likewise moved in 1924. In 1925 Joseph Cohen returned to Philadelphia and started Camp Germinal. Leonard Abbott dropped out to take care of his wife, who had fallen ill with multiple sclerosis.

By the mid-1920s, then, the heyday of Stelton was over. Meanwhile, however, a new colony had sprung up on Lake Mohegan, New York, with a Modern School of its own that endured for nearly two decades.

Chapter 9

Mohegan

A New Colony

T THE BEGINNING of 1923, Harry Kelly, whose passion for starting colonies rivaled William Thurston Brown's passion for starting schools, learned of a tract of land for sale in upper Westchester County, about forty-five miles from New York City. The property, fronting on Lake Mohegan, occupied 450 acres a few miles east of Peekskill. Once the estate of General John Paulding of the Continental Army, who in a well-known episode of the American Revolution had aided in the capture of Major André, it now belonged to the Baron de Hirsch Fund, which for several decades had sponsored Jewish agricultural colonies in different parts of the world. The property included a farmhouse of nineteen rooms and three bathrooms, with steam heat, electric lighting, and running water. There was also a large barn and a well in working order. Kelly could not resist. "It looks like a colony," he exclaimed.[1]

On February 27, 1923, a meeting was held at the Civic Club in New York to discuss the formation of a community "based on the broadest liberal or libertarian principles." A group, known as the Mohegan Colony Association, was organized to purchase the land, with Kelly as president, Moritz Jagendorf as treasurer, and Arnold Krimont (Mary Krimont's younger brother) as general manager. In short order an agreement was reached with the Baron de Hirsch Fund. The land was transferred to the Kelly group, then sold in one-acre plots. The plots could not be subdivided, and no colonist could hold more than three acres.[2]

By the middle of March, Kelly was "up to my eyes" in work, as he wrote to the anarchist historian Max Nettlau. "I am in hopes that we will have a town of 1000 people within two years and the social organization based on Anarchist principles."[3] The following month the Mohegan Colony Association renamed itself the Mohegan Modern School Association and drew up a constitution, in which the object of the group was set forth: "The education of our children is stunted and corrupted by a public system which has for its aim the raising of a patriotic generation of workers who will fit into the existing capitalist system. We are organizing this settlement in the hope that we may free ourselves and our children from at least some of the diseases of city life; to give free rein to our thoughts and ideals; to offer our children a libertarian education which will fit them to be fighters for a better world."[4]

By the end of 1923, some twenty-five families had come to Lake Mohegan with the dream, as one settler put it, of "establishing a community with intellectual freedom and where the ordinary working man would have an opportunity for a better way of life."[5] As in Stelton, most of the founding members came up on weekends and lived in tents while permanent homes were being built. A number, however, moved into the old farmhouse and lived on a cooperative basis, with Hippolyte Havel serving as cook until he left for Stelton in 1924. The rest moved into their own dwellings before the end of the same year, and the farmhouse was converted into a residence for boarding children, christened the Living House as at Stelton.

As time went by, roads were built, a school was started, a post office established (known as Crompond, New York), a modern water system installed, and the lakefront transformed into a handsome beach, which, together with a park and forest reserve, was maintained by the Mohegan residents. Lewis Mumford, an admirer of William Morris and Peter Kropotkin and the author of a widely acclaimed study of utopias, helped plan the layout of the community,[6] which had about three hundred families by the end of the decade.

Mohegan had several advantages over Stelton, from which many of its settlers originated. The most obvious was physical beauty. In contrast to Stelton's drab surroundings, Mohegan was located in a hilly, wooded area with a 2,000-foot frontage on the lake. The economic level of its membership was a cut above that at Stelton. In general, Mohegan projected a more prosperous, more middle-class image, with professionals and even businessmen quite common among its inhabitants. It started fewer cooperative ventures than Stelton and lacked its distinctive pioneer spirit. Whereas Stelton had been forged at the height of the anarchist movement, in the crucible of war and revolution, Mohegan took shape during a period of "normalcy" when the movement was in decline. Thus its anarchist character was less pronounced.

And yet the two colonies had much in common. As in Stelton, Mohegan residents lived in private homes on one-, two-, or three-acre plots, and in most cases commuted to work in New York City. Anarchists, during the early years at least, constituted a large majority, but there were growing numbers of communists, socialists, and liberals. About 90 percent were East European Jews, with small groups of Italians, Frenchmen, Englishmen, and Russians, as well as a few Germans, Spaniards, and Finns. Many of the non-Jewish males—Bill Stevens, Pat Bannister, Jim Dick, André Miroy, Henri Dupré, Jacques Dubois, Vasili Dodokin, Sasha Gromm, Ferrero Conde, Valerio Isca—had Jewish wives. "There was no racial or ethnic friction at Mohegan," one of the teachers recalls. "It was almost like an extended family, a European village, a kind of community that the young generation of today misses. Ages, too, mixed more readily, without the hostility or stratification of today."[7]

Both by occupation and personality it was a varied and interesting group. Among the French members were two chefs, a jeweler, a garage mechanic, and a translator of film subtitles. The Finns were mostly carpenters and builders, including Gus Alonen, who had been jailed during the Red Scare for publishing an anarcho-syndicalist paper. One of the Russians, Vasili Dodokin, built "orgone" boxes for the psychoanalyst Wilhelm Reich. And a Jewish engineer named Bern Dibner built up what *The New York Times* called "one of the most extensive and important private collections of instruments, manuscripts and books, documenting the history of science and technology."[8]

As in Stelton, many of the colonists were health and food faddists, some of them devotees of Dr. E. K. Stretch, a New Jersey chiropractor and physical therapist who held extreme dietary views, including a powerful aversion to starch. Lydia Landau, who had been Joseph Cohen's successor as custodian of the Ferrer Center and whose daughters had attended the Dyker Heights Children's Playhouse, was one of Stretch's most ardent disciples. When Hitler invaded Poland she composed a little jingle: "The soldiers march, Because of starch."[9]

Mohegan, like Stelton, boasted a wide range of adult activities. Many of the colonists were amateur or professional musicians, and they put on frequent concerts, especially during the summer, when cultural events of various kinds were held every weekend, often in connection with fund-raising efforts. In June and July of 1933, for example, a series of six recitals was performed by the Arion String Quartet, including the well-known violist Milton Katims. The following year a Summer Institute on Social, Economic, and Political Problems was organized, with presentations by Sidney Hook, V. F. Calverton, George Counts, A. J. Muste, and Scott Nearing. In addition, a regular Friday evening forum brought in such speakers as Norman Thomas, Roger Baldwin, Manuel Komroff, Arturo Giovannitti, Ralph Borsodi, and Isaac Don Levine. Every spring, as in Stelton, an educational conference took place, featuring lectures, discussions, dramatic entertainment, and exhibitions of adult and children's art work. In October 1927 Harry Kelly arranged a benefit for the Kropotkin Museum in Moscow; and beyond all this there were teas, picnics, community dinners, bazaars, May Day festivals, dances, and marionette shows. Visitors over the years included Mike Gold, Paul Robeson, Alexander Schapiro, Angelica Balabanoff, and Lucy Parsons.

Both Mohegan and Stelton were involved in political causes, most notably the Sacco-Vanzetti case in the 1920s and the Spanish Civil War in the 1930s. One Spanish anarchist from Mohegan, César Vega by name, went to join the fight against Franco, only to be seized when his boat landed and immediately shot. During the affair of Sacco and Vanzetti, rallies were held at the two colonies to raise funds for their defense. Leonard Abbott, who chaired meetings and wrote articles on their behalf, called their execution "one of the blackest crimes of the twentieth century." Harry Kelly was reminded of the Haymarket tragedy of 1887. "The Sacco-Vanzetti murder practically broke my heart," he wrote to Emma Goldman. "Things have not changed . . . one iota in 40 years unless for the worse."[10] From France, Alexander Berkman lamented that in all the United States there was no "avenging hand" to take retribution. "Has no conscience in America," he wrote to Leonard Abbott, "been sufficiently outraged by this fearful double and cold-blooded murder to forget 'purposefulness' and danger and for once give expression to one's torturing indignation and resentment?" It was, he thought, "a sad commentary upon human nature."[11]

Yet, if no avenger came forward, virtually the entire Ferrer movement, past as well as present, threw itself into the campaign to save the two anarchists. Some, including Abbott and Havel, visited the condemned men in prison. Others served on defense committees and agitated for a reprieve. Lola Ridge, Polly Holladay, Mike Gold, and John Howard Lawson were arrested for picketing the Massachusetts State House, together with Dorothy Parker, Katherine Anne Porter, and Edna St. Vincent Millay.

Lola Ridge's "Three Men Die" remains among the most powerful works of literature inspired by the execution, and Mike Gold condemned the New England aristocracy as "flamed up into a last orgy of revenge" and "insane with fear and hatred of new America."[12]

THE MOHEGAN SCHOOL

As at Stelton, the school stood at the center of the Mohegan experiment. Started in 1924, it was directed for the next four years by Jim and Nellie Dick, who were also in charge of the Living House, a name they appropriated from the Ferms. Where the Ferms were American reformers, however, spiritualist, Froebelian, and anticollectivist in outlook, the Dicks were European revolutionaries, materialist, Ferrerist, and pro-Soviet. Yet they had many similar ideas on education. "The old, painful and weather-beaten method of religiously sticking noses into books, the bending and forging of immature minds into certain established forms with 'chalk and talk' will always come into conflict with the new method now emphasized by the more advanced schools of thought, that of self-expression of the child in arts and crafts and life unfolding in natural surroundings," declared Jim Dick in 1926. "Children will express themselves with spontaneity and originality if not subjected to the rigidity and discipline of the school-room. . . . Freedom is the star, and to that we hitch our wagon."[13]

Under the Dicks, more than a few of the techniques introduced by the Ferms at Stelton were transferred to the new colony. Not only was the boarding house baptized the Living House, but each day began with morning assembly, children, teachers, and parents gathering in a great circle to dance and to sing songs to nature. "Forty-year-old women with big hips and dressed in shorts went out and made like fairies," a teacher recalls. "It was funny, yet very beautiful. It had a complete loveliness about it. It developed a close relationship between pupils, teachers, and colonists."[14]

The rest of the day, as at Stelton, was spent largely in crafts and play. "Academics" were relegated to the library, pupils being free to attend or not. "We never force any book knowledge," wrote Jim Dick in 1927. "We stimulate such, which comes through the seeking of the child. Our teachers are not taskmasters; they are in personal touch and sympathetic relation with the children. The teachers do not impress *their* individuality upon the child; they try to discover that of the child and develop it. We do not predispose the children in favor of any creed, system or theory; we leave this for the time when their own reason and inclinations enable them to choose for themselves. Nothing in our school is screwed in or nailed down; the children feel free to change the furniture or leave their seats. The school rooms are part of a home and not a factory. We have no 'home work.' Our children learn every hour of the day by DOING things, instead of cramming facts. At present we have textile weaving, basket making, metal work, clay modeling, carpentry, nature studies, drawing, painting, music, dancing and academic studies in our curriculum. The children are left free to choose or neglect any of them. The parents are asked not to scold the children for any of these neglected subjects, but to consult the teacher. We want EXPRESSION and not REPRESSION. What the child learns through liking is of permanent value to it; what it learns through force is worthless in after life. We try to make the place in which the child is to acquire knowledge—THE SCHOOL—a happy hunting ground for it where it will feel as you do when relaxing for recreation or pleasure. We believe that in educating the child in the atmosphere of freedom we are creating an INDIVIDUAL—a person who in the future will be capable of asserting himself."[15]

Needless to add, there were no rewards or punishments at the Mohegan Modern School, and competition among the children was avoided. "Trying to force the success of a pupil generally succeeds in robbing him of the most essential qualities that he ought to possess," Jim Dick declared, "his physique, power of concentration and perseverance. Formal lessons are not the main thing in their little lives."[16] Replying to a questionnaire distributed by the Progressive Education Association in 1927, Jim Dick wrote as follows:

1. *Do you give marks at all?* No.

2. *Do you give tests and examinations?* No.

3. *Do you let the children know their marks?* —

4. *If you do not give marks, how do you arrive at a grade standing?* By studying each individual child.

5. *Do you keep for purposes of promotion an office record of the child's academic rating or some approximate percentage scale?* No.

6. *Do you send such records to the parents?* We discuss with the individual parent about the child's development.

7. *Do you have grades based on academic standing?* No.

8. *Do you promote from grade to grade only on the basis of academic standing?* No.

9. *Do you use standard tests and if so how often?* No.[17]

Such was Dick's approach at the Mohegan School. A vivid glimpse into his methods and personality may be obtained from a letter he wrote to A. S. Neill in 1928, during his final months at the colony. The full text reads as follows:

Dear Neill:

I have just received a copy of the "New Era" containing your report of "Summerhill" and I cannot refrain from writing to you about the similarity of your methods (or lack of 'em) with ours at the Mohegan School.

For *many* years I have made up my mind to compliment you on your books and the various articles I have been fortunate to read. Your present article (with slight variations) might have been written about our school here. Problem children we have in galore only to find that it is the problem parents that is the seat of the trouble. We have had "thieves" and "vagabonds" from families of "respectability," but with a dose of freedom and a hale-fellow-well-met attitude they soon develop into something like social being. I am beginning to think that it is not the problem child but the problem parent in the majority of occasions and I take the liberty of asking you to start a school for problem parents. I feel sure that we should get to the seat of the parent problem (I nearly typed "pants").

The kids around this joint (as the Yanks would have it) salute me with "Big Jim" and the rest of the teachers by their first or second names. How they just love to call me names, if I should get on my high horse and tell them just "where to get off" (another Yankeeism). One little tot of some five summers, together with several more of his years, were discussing the future professions they would take up. One said I am going to be a doctor, another a dentist, another a professor. Said my hero "I'm going to be a donkey." "But why a donkey" said another. "Well," said this kid, "even a donkey can kick a professor in the pants."

Your remarks about your tools etc. are so true about my own troubles. You give your kids a big barn to play in and don't put your nose inside and see the effect. You will find more junk in that barn than you would see around a shipwrecker's yard. You talk of getting a blacksmith to build a house, that is a solution. I certainly maintain that we are somewhat to blame for all this destruction. How in the name of the gods can we expect kids to fit into an adult house?

I must not bore you with too much of this, but it is seldom one gets hold of teachers with some common sense ideas about kids and their education. I have a friend named Sherwood Trask who visited your school some three years ago. He told me that I ought to know you because of this similarity of ideas. Well being of Scottish parents myself you can guess how shy I might be. I was born in England, alas for my prestige, and have been here ten years. One day I will go back to the land of my birth, but one gets so wrapt up in school ties that it is hard to break.

The kids of this school wish to convey their greetings to your gang as they were all interested in your little story in April's "New Era." "Gee," they said, "ain't it like our school."

Yours very sincerely,
Jas. H. Dick[18]

For reasons which will be explained below, the Dicks left Mohegan in 1928 and returned to Stelton, where they remained until 1933. After their departure, the character of the school changed considerably. The number of non-anarchist residents—liberals, socialists, communists—had been growing, and the colony was losing whatever ideological homogeneity it had formerly possessed. The more prosperous colonists tended to favor a progressive rather than a libertarian education for their children. After a new stone schoolhouse was completed in 1928 (under Gus Alonen's supervision) the curriculum took on a more structured and less spontaneous aspect. The children were divided into three groups, aged four to six, seven to nine, and ten and over. Reading and arithmetic were introduced in the middle group, which also had work units on Eskimo and Indian life. For the latter exercise, the children ate Indian food outdoors and slept in a tepee with an Indian garden.[19]

While play and crafts remained important, increasing attention was paid to academic subjects, which had previously been neglected. Ferrer and Froebel were all but forgotten. "We knew little of Ferrer's theories," says Dorothy Rick, who taught at Mohegan during the 1930s. "Many colonists had not even *heard* of Ferrer. I *had* studied Dewey, but not much theory was involved here. By the mid-thiritities it was a progressive rather than a 'Modern' school. Reading was taught when the children were ready for it. 'Projects' were a big thing—what they're trying to do now in most regular schools. We studied Egypt as a unit, not its geography, history, and the like separately. We had an Indian project. The children made trips to New York and painted a mural of the city."[20]

As at Stelton, the majority of pupils were happy with their school experience. Those who went on to Peekskill High School performed well and were "unusually creative," according to the superintendent of the school district.[21] Some did well in later life. Iris Miroy earned a doctorate in biology at Harvard. Pauline Mont became a professor of engineering at the University of Michigan. Her cousin Daniel Bell, who spent several summers at Mohegan, became a distinguished sociologist. "They didn't feel they were being held in," says Dorothy Rick. "They didn't look upon it the way most children look on school. Yet there was enough structure so that they did not feel at loose ends."[22]

Another teacher, Ben Lieberman, remembers the unusual tolerance the pupils showed toward one another. "A striking thing," he recalls, "is that there was very little victimization of one child by the rest. Kids were kinder, more generous, than in ordinary schools. One child was a Mongoloid but was never persecuted. Kids who would have been the butt of jokes and persecution in public school—big, clumsy, odd—were liked and treated well. For some, of course, it was not a happy time. But most liked the school. By and large, I would say, the results differed little from what is obtained in other schools, except that the children emerged a bit more human, a bit less prejudiced, easier to talk to, gentler."[23]

George Seldes and Rudolf Rocker

In addition to Harry Kelly and Hippolyte Havel, a number of prominent anarchists lived at the Mohegan Colony during its thirty-odd years of existence. The principal figure during the 1920s was George Sergius Seldes, whose lifelong interest in communitarian experiments resembled that of Kelly and Joseph Cohen. Born near the city of Kiev in 1860, Seldes was twenty-one years old when Tsar Alexander II fell victim to a revolutionist's bomb. The wave of anti-Semitism that followed drove many Russian Jews to emigrate. George Seldes was among them. Joining the Am Olam movement, which held that the salvation of the Jewish people lay in a return to farming as a way of life, he helped found the Alliance Colony in southern New Jersey in 1882, becoming its postmaster and justice of the peace. The failure of the colony, according to his son, was the disappointment of Seldes' life. Thereafter he always dreamed of establishing a successful community in America, which had a long history of utopian experiments. Mohegan was his last attempt to do so.[24]

Seldes, like Alexis Ferm, became both an anarchist and a single-taxer. In 1886, while working as a librarian in New York City, he volunteered his services for Henry George's mayoral campaign, embracing the single-tax philosophy, to which he cleaved for the rest of his life. His first son, George Henry Seldes, was named after Henry George and became a well-known political journalist. A second son, Gilbert, likewise turned his hand to writing, becoming managing editor of *The Dial* and a specialist in the popular arts. He ended his career as Dean of the Graduate School of Communications at the University of Pennsylvania. (Gilbert's daughter is the talented actress, Marian Seldes.)

By the 1890s George Seldes the elder had added Kropotkinian anarchism and Tolstoyan pacifism to his list of ideological allegiances. From both Kropotkin and Tolstoy he sought advice on how to organize a libertarian community, and for several years he corresponded with them on a variety of social questions. With Kropotkin he discussed the concept of mutual aid, which he hoped to make the guiding principle of a new colony. Before the First World War, while Seldes was operating a drug store in Pittsburgh, all the letters were burned by a cleaning woman who needed paper to start a fire.[25]

Between his residence in New York and in Pittsburgh, to which he moved in 1907 and where his visitors included Emma Goldman and Sadakichi Hartmann,[26] Seldes worked in a drug store in Philadelphia while studying law at night. Although he never completed his legal training, he managed to save enough money to open his own pharmacy, where discussions on anarchism and other subjects were held in the back room. In 1906, when Maxim Gorky was visiting the United States with his common-law wife, the leading hotel in Philadelphia, the Bellevue-Stratford, threw them out into the street, and they came straight to Seldes' pharmacy for help.[27]

Throughout his years in Philadelphia and Pittsburgh, Seldes never ceased to contemplate the formation of a utopian community, of which he had dreamed since the days of his youth. In 1923 a new opportunity arrived when Harry Kelly organized the Mohegan Colony Association to purchase the site near Peekskill. By then Seldes was again living in New York City. The previous year he and Kelly had tried to start a Modern School in the Bronx, but had been forced to give it up for lack of support. Now, at the age of sixty-two, Seldes threw all his energies into the creation of the Mohegan Colony. He himself became one of the first settlers and, by dint of his idealism and hard work, a source of inspiration to the rest.

Scholarly, erudite, philosophical, Seldes became the sage of the Mohegan venture. According to the president of the Mohegan Modern School Association, he had "opinions galore on every subject."[28] An accomplished linguist, with a mastery of Russian, French, German, Yiddish, and Hebrew in addition to English, he "understood the philosophy of anarchism," said Harry Kelly, "as well as it is possible for any mortal man to understand it and he added to his vast learning a tender love for humanity and human freedom, a genial temperament and an optimism that came as a tonic to many a depressed comrade seeking solace in his company."[29] He had read Thoreau and Emerson as well as Kropotkin and Tolstoy, and Proudhon's "property is theft" was one of his favorite quotations. (The first words he taught his sons in French were "la propriété, c'est le vol!") "Once we moved books into the garage and lightning struck and they were all burned up," a former colonist recalls. "He came in and picked up the remains and put the pages together. 'You should always cherish books,' he told us."[30]

"During the long years we knew each other," wrote Harry Kelly of George Seldes, "I never knew, or met anyone else who knew him to waver in the slightest degree in his devotion to his ideals nor doubt for a moment that they would some day be realized."[31] Kelly, however, was mistaken. For while his ideals remained intact, Seldes, by the mid-1920s, had become deeply discouraged over the constant bickering among his fellow colonists. "I have been all my life near great and small men in the movement," he wrote his son in 1925, "and the pygmies shrank to ants while the giants shrank into pygmies. Now, outside of my still firm and absolute faith in ideals, which will probably 'go down with me,' I have [lost] all hope of reconstructing anything or anybody."[32]

In the six years that were left to him, Seldes saw matters grow worse. At the end of the 1920s he suffered a great blow when a majority of the colonists were defeated by a minority of communists who, according to his son, "alone had organized and planned and intrigued and finally taken over the machinery of the government."[33] Seldes' lifelong vision of communal harmony had been irreparably shattered. Weakened both morally and physically, he fell gravely ill and had to be taken to a hospital in New York City. There he died on February 7, 1931, in his seventy-first year.

The passing of George Seldes left an intellectual and moral vacuum at Mohegan that remained unfilled until the arrival of Rudolf Rocker in 1937. One of the greatest orators of the movement, Rocker, although himself a gentile, had been the apostle of anarchism to the Jewish workers of London in the decades preceding the war. The story of how he came to Whitechapel and became a Yiddish writer and editor is one of the most fascinating of that period.[34] A German by birth and upbringing, he had not so much as met a Jew until he was eighteen. Yet he settled among the Jews, took one of their daughters for his wife, learned to speak, read, and write their language, and shared in their poverty and suffering.

Orator, editor, writer, Rocker placed the highest value on the education of the workers, adults as well as children, and was deeply influenced by the ideas of Ferrer, about whom he often wrote and lectured. (His older son, Rudolf Jr., taught at the Dicks' Modern School in Whitechapel and later founded his own short-lived school in Canada.) Alexander Berkman thought Rocker "one of our very finest men and comrades." His companion, Milly Witkop, was also "a beautiful character,"[35] and their deep, abiding affection was one of the great love stories in the history of the anarchist movement.

Rocker spent the war years in a British prison camp, having been interned as an "enemy alien" despite his continuing opposition to German authoritarianism and regimentation. After the war he returned to his native country. There he became the driving force of the German anarchist movement and principal founder of the International Working Men's Association, the so-called Berlin or Anarcho-Syndicalist International, established in 1922. When Hitler came to power in January 1933, Rocker and his wife had to flee for their lives. Escaping to Switzerland on the last train out of Berlin, they became part of the great wave of refugees from Nazi oppression that enriched American life over the next generation.

Rocker spent the last twenty-five years of his life in the United States, speaking and writing for libertarian causes. Arriving in New York in September 1933, he undertook a number of coast-to-coast lecture tours, contributed countless articles to anarchist publications in many languages, and produced a series of books that made a permanent contribution to anarchist philosophy and history. His *Nationalism and Culture*, a powerful indictment of the state, was hailed by Albert Einstein as an "extraordinarily original and illuminating work," while Bertrand Russell called it "an important contribution to political philosophy, both on account of its penetrating and widely informative analysis of many famous writers, and on account of the brilliant criticism of state-worship, the prevailing and most noxious superstition of our time."[36]

Rocker settled at Mohegan in 1937, renting a cottage from the anarchist bookseller Leon Kramer. He was later given his own house by the anarchists of the colony, to whom he was a venerable figure. While he took little part in the social or administrative life of the community, he was its dominant intellectual leader for the next twenty years. His death in 1958 marked not only the passing of the last great anarchist with an international reputation. It also sounded the knell of the Mohegan experiment, the last of the major anarchist colonies in the United States.

THOREAUVIAN ANARCHISTS

The teachers at Mohegan were a mixed lot, as in other schools, including Stelton. "Some were marvelous, some absolutely awful," one mother recalls.[37] Some were professionally trained, others rank amateurs at their tasks. In a few cases, such as Jacques Dubois who taught carpentry and André Longchamp who taught French, their association with the movement went back to the Ferrer Center in New York. Zack Schwartz had been a pupil at 107th Street, at Stelton, and at Stony Ford. Frances Goldenthal came from Stelton to teach violin and piano. And John

Scott had taught both at Stelton and the Walt Whitman School in Los Angeles.

Scott, who styled himself a "Thoreauvian anarchist" and owned first editions of all of Thoreau's works, combined pedagogical talent and experience with personal magnetism and charm. Brought up in the Ozark Mountains, where his father, a Civil War veteran, sold charcoal, he had his first three years of education in an old-fashioned one-room schoolhouse. A brilliant pupil, he finished high school in two years and was graduated Phi Beta Kappa from the University of Missouri, going on to earn a Ph.D. in sociology. After teaching at Kansas State University for several years, Scott went to California and joined the staff of the Walt Whitman School. In 1926, two years after Walt Whitman closed, he came to Stelton to fill in for the Ferms, who had recently departed, and to start a youth movement in which teenagers and young adults might learn to make a living from the soil. Before this scheme could be implemented, however, the restless Scott moved up to Mohegan, where he taught on and off for the next three years, dropping out for several months "to secure a rest and a change."[38]

As a disciple of Thoreau, Scott was a strong individualist with a deep love of nature, a subject he taught with great proficiency at the Manumit School as well as at Stelton and Mohegan. Yet, for all his individualism, he had known Eugene Victor Debs and joined the Socialist Party during his early years in the middle west. His first son, interestingly enough, was named Marx Scott. But he broke with the socialists during the First World War and remained an individualist and pacifist for the rest of his life. In 1930, when a second son arrived, Scott called him Jon Thoreau. "A son named Marx, then seventeen years later another named Thoreau—that's an interesting evolution!" Scott's companion remarked.[39]

In his complex and protean character, Scott reminds one of Elizabeth Ferm, with whom he shared a mystical bent, harboring "a vague pantheism and a theory of dreams—that after death you went on living in your former dream world." In sexual matters, however, he and Aunty were worlds apart. For Scott was a strong believer in "free love and multiple loves." And, a ruggedly handsome man in his forties, he put his beliefs into practice, "a Don Juan with six women on the string at one time," according to a Mohegan colleague.[40]

Such at least was the situation before Jo Ann Wheeler arrived at the colony in May 1929 to become a member of the staff. An attractive young woman of twenty-three, she had taught for four years in a one-room schoolhouse in upstate New York and had taken summer courses at Teachers College. During Christmas vacation one year, she was visiting her parents at Reading, Pennsylvania, when she met John and Kate Edelman, who were working there as union organizers. They told her about Stelton and Mohegan and gave her a copy of Elizabeth Ferm's *Spirit of Freedom in Education*, which came as "something of a revelation."[41]

When invited to Mohegan by Dr. Barkas, a successor to the Dicks as principal of the school, Jo Ann eagerly accepted. "That was in 1929," she recalls, "an important year for me. I met John Scott and I met the Ferms. John was working partly at Manumit and partly at Mohegan, as the nature teacher. I worked in the Living House, a hard job that taxed my strength, but I liked it. I also taught the children piano. Barkas was a well-meaning man, tall and lean with a loping walk, who lent himself to caricature. But 'well-meaning' is about all I can say for him. The Ferms were far more interesting. They came up from their place at Newfoundland, I think, and led a discussion group on education. I was very much taken with them, though a little daunted by Aunty's spirit. She was so full of spirit, so full of fire. Uncle was much easier-going. That's why they made such a good team, I guess. I was deeply influenced by the Ferms and completely devoted to them. Their idea of creative development, of development from within rather than the child as a receptacle for information poured into him by others, was a confirmation of what I was aiming at. The philosophy of the individual and of growth from within was something I could wholeheartedly accept."[42]

Jo Ann was equally taken with John Scott—and he with her. "I had known many conventional men at Craryville," she recalls, "and I was considered queer or fast because I didn't want to stay with the same boy after one or two dates, as the town expected. I was a young girl, and the older women in the colony must have been hurt. John was visiting me and also Anna Schwartz, Lillian Buck, and Celia Bushwick."[43]

In the fall of 1929, Scotty and Jo Ann left Mohegan for Stelton, where they taught for a year before moving to the Wheeler family farm at Craryville, New York, where their two children, Jon Thoreau and Shelley, were born. As self-proclaimed "Thoreauvian anarchists," they were going back to the land, to till the soil and to publish a little journal whose title, *Mother Earth*, was borrowed from Emma Goldman's magazine of two decades before.

The aim of the new *Mother Earth*—"A libertarian Farm Paper Devoted to the Life of Thoreauvian Anarchy," in the words of its subtitle—was to attack "the money power" and promote "decentralization of population, simplification of life, and the love of mother earth."[44] "We no longer use our hands to fashion a simple useful serene livelihood from the materials that lie about us," complained Jo Ann in words that sound quite up-to-date four decades later. "We have forsaken self reliance and lost the deep satisfaction that hand craft gives, to worship at the shrine of a cold impersonal science. We have sacrificed the joys of creativeness for bodily comfort. The atrophied appendages we call hands will soon be fit for nothing but to press a button. Scant use to bemoan the fate of wage slaves while thing slaves remain."[45]

At the same time, Jo Ann arrived at a new view of education that anticipated the "de-schooling" theorists of the 1970s. Libertarian schools, she conceded, with their emphasis on freedom and creative work and on learning by doing, were far superior to conventional schools, but "schools of any kind are unnecessary for the sort of education that we consider desirable." That education, she explained, was to take place in a rural, family environment (such as her own Craryville farm) and in "natural circumstances" over which no external controls are imposed.[46] "How can we be men—whole upright individuals—how can we be ourselves as we are born to be, when from childhood on we are cramped and warped to fit a ready-made world; when we are taught unthinking obedience to authority, and conformity to accepted patterns of thought and action; when every free impulse and every original action is punished as rebellion?" she wrote in a Thoreau centennial symposium. "When Mother knows best and Father knows best and Teacher knows best and the State knows best and God knows best—'God knows' how we *know* anything at all."[47]

Jo Ann and Scotty continued to pursue their Thoreauvian existence until 1934, when they returned to Stelton. By now their liaison was dissolving. Scotty was twenty-six years older than Jo Ann, and "a family with two obstreperous children was more than he could take." Toward the end of the year he left for Camp Germinal, Pennsylvania, where the following spring he tried to organize an "Educational Commune," the first step in "the larger University of the Free Life."[48]

Nothing, however, came of his efforts, apart from the planting of a vegetable garden and some field crops. Captivated by the doctrines of the Social Credit movement, Scotty moved to New York (which he now took to calling "Jew York") and started a magazine called *Money*, in which he published the notorious Protocols of Zion and sought to expose a Jewish conspiracy to control the world financial system.

Scott's new line, not surprisingly, provoked the ire of his former comrades, many of whom were Jewish. "That was his blind spot," says Jo Ann, who insists that he was never an anti-Semite. "He was politically naive and could be taken in by anyone who was willing to work with him."[49] In 1948 Scott ran for president of the United States on the Greenback ticket, a survival from the previous century. In the last years of his life he became a Quaker, a member of the Taconic Meeting. He died in November 1953 at the age of seventy-four. Jo Ann remained at Stelton a dozen years, not leaving until 1946. Marrying a classical musician, she works for a literary agency in New York, returning occasionally to Craryville where she and Scott conducted their experiment in Thoreauvian living more than forty years ago. Unswervingly loyal to the Ferms, she continues to cherish their memory and, when the opportunity arises, to spread the gospel of free education to a new generation of reformers.

BREAKUP

Like virtually every other communitarian experiment in American history, the Mohegan Colony fell prey to personal bickering and factional disputes. As early as 1925, only two years after the formation of the community, George Seldes took note of the problem. "It involves neither principle nor ideals," he observed. "They concern some details, mostly unimportant, in administering colony finances and the friction is caused in an inane effort to hold power—something in the nature of the Republican or Democratic parties; no essential issues, no differences in platforms, no change in the country's affairs; merely a sparring for power!"[50]

While only a foretaste of what was to come, the quarreling was bad enough to discourage even such optimists as Harry Kelly, who with Seldes was the main founder of the colony. "How easy it was all these years to talk and talk Anarchism and to write articles about the solidarity of mankind etc., and how different it is when one tries to practice it," he wrote to Alexander Berkman in 1925. "I suppose partly from habit I will go on until I die, but the cowardice, fanaticism and general contemptibility of the average man is really beyond belief." Berkman provided little encouragement. Indeed he wondered whether maintaining the community was worth the effort and agony. "I myself," he said, "have little faith in colonies. You cannot build the new society that way. And generally those experiments with colonies end disastrously."[51]

Yet Kelly refused to despair. Unlike Berkman, he continued to regard colonies as the most appropriate setting for educational experiments and "a means of propaganda for an Anarchist mode of life," as he told a conference at Stelton in July 1925.[52] Indeed, though disappointed with Mohegan, he soon started two new ventures at the village of Croton-on-Hudson, some thirty miles above New York, in an area as beautiful as Mohegan, with stunning views of the Hudson River and the surrounding Westchester hills. The first, a summer colony called Belle Terre, was established in 1925, with a large house for community meetings and cabins for individual members.[53] In 1926 a year-round settlement, the Mount Airy Colony, was launched, with homes on quarter-acre plots and five-and-a-half acres set aside for a Modern School. The school, however, was never built, nor did a genuine colony materialize, though a number of anarchist families lived there into the 1970s. As for Belle Terre, it too survived for several years but never got beyond the summer-camp stage.[54]

Owing to this rapid succession of land deals, Kelly acquired the reputation in some circles of being a "real-estate man," a description he deeply resented. (On his 1927 passport he listed his occupation as "educator.") He gained little if any profit from his ventures and, far from being a land speculator, as his critics maintained, was merely a compulsive organizer of colonies. "Man cannot live alone," he wrote toward the end of his life, "even if he is an individualist such as myself, and I for one have never desired it."[55] But once a colony was on its feet, the itch to move on overcame him, and he would begin to contemplate a new project.

In the meantime, matters at Mohegan were going from bad to worse. In 1927 Arnold Krimont, general manager of the Mohegan Modern School Association since its inception, was accused of siphoning off funds for his personal use. ("I always knew that Arnold is crooked," was Emma Goldman's comment on hearing the news.) A series of lawsuits resulted, sharpening tensions among the members. It was a heavy blow to Kelly, who acknowledged the truth of the charges against his brother-in-law. "My life has for good or evil been tied up with Anarchism for over 30 years," he lamented, "but I get so tired and discouraged over the stupidities of the mass in general and over our comrades in particular. I would gladly retire if it could be done quietly and decently."[56]

As if all this were not enough, Kelly became embroiled in a bitter controversy with Jim and Nellie Dick, which ended in their departure from the colony. The origins of the controversy remain clouded, but the Dicks, it appears, were determined to have their own way in running the school and resented interference from the board of directors, of which Kelly was chairman. Kelly might have been surprised by their attitude had he not been through a similar dispute with the Ferms at Stelton. "I foresaw that you would one day unconsciously grow to think of the school as *your* school," he wrote Jim and Nellie, "just as the Ferms grew to think of the Stelton school as *their* school." "Vanity, vanity, all is vanity," he lamented, "and that even with Anarchists."[57]

The Dicks were deeply hurt by these accusations. "It is getting kinda late in the day for such as you, Harry, to question my power," wrote Jim at the outset of the controversy. ". . . You and your erstwhile board almost compelled me to take over the school and make something of it, and I am willing to bet, dollars to dough-nuts, that there would have been no school in Mohegan Colony (such as you required) had not Nellie and I weathered thru these last three winters. If anybody ought to know the difficulty of getting this kind of school over the Mohegan Colonists it ought to be you. I do not want POWER, Harry, for with it comes responsibility, but I cannot conceive your school at Mohegan Colony materializing as *you* and I think it ought to without a person in charge who is the embodiment of the principles of libertarian education. You can name that person what you like but that is my opinion and I fear you are going to find [I am right] in the near future."[58]

Their conflict with the board of directors left the Dicks severely disenchanted. "My ideas are dying," said Jim. "I guess they are dying hard, but they are dying alright—and I feel that the day is not far distant when the Babbitts will 'get me yet,' like many of our comrades gone before." To Tom Keell, editor of the London *Freedom*, Jim denounced the whole Mohegan board, and especially its "dominant high mogul" Kelly, "dabbling in real estate, looking for some society to recognize his services to humanity and pension him off or send him to Italy to study art. . . . Suffice it to say I have never been subjected to such a scurrilous attack as from my erstwhile friend and comrade. No chance have I to retaliate. He has sent the news to England. He did the same to Fred Dunn, and then came to shed tears over his corpse."[59]

In the spring of 1928 the Dicks, having resigned the previous year only to be persuaded to remain, were unceremoniously dismissed. Amid mutual recriminations and accusations, they departed for Stelton. "Our treatment by the Mohegan Board hurt us very badly," Nellie recalls. "We were there from 1924 to 1928. We built up the Living House until we had fifty kids. We became well known in progressive educational circles. Visitors came to see our school. Jim spoke at the Progressive Education Association conventions in Boston and Baltimore. Yet the board decided to replace us as principals. They claimed that Jim didn't know how to raise money for the new school building. They wanted somebody who could go out and make speeches, and we weren't interested in that sort of thing."[60]

After the departure of the Dicks, the Mohegan School passed through a series of rapidly changing administrations. Between 1928 and 1936 no less than four new principals—Winfield Woodings, B. W. Barkas, Betty A. Davis, and Lallah Blanpied—came and went. "I had a terrible time up there," recalls Mrs. Blanpied, "very disillusioning. I had previously swallowed the anarchist philosophy hook, bait, and sinker. I had read Kropotkin and Dewey and was familiar with Froebel, Ferrer, and Pestalozzi. But the parents constantly interfered with the teaching and administration. Political differences also had an adverse effect on the school. I commuted from New Rochelle, attended all the meetings, got worn out, sick, and quit."[61]

The financial crisis caused by the Depression contributed to the weakening of the school. Money was a constant problem. The 1930s saw a growing rift between those (especially the anarchists) who strove to maintain a libertarian education completely independent of the state and those who argued for a progressive education with government support. Moderates like Bern Dibner wanted to incorporate the school into the state system and thus receive equipment and financial assistance. Eventually the latter view prevailed. But by then the school was in rapid decline. In 1941, after seventeen stormy years, it closed its doors.

The colony itself survived another fifteen to twenty years. But it was not a happy period. Tensions mounted as the number of non-anarchists grew and the communists, through the device of packing meetings of the Mohegan Modern School Association, tried to take control of the administration. As in Stelton, a group of Young Pioneers was organized. They sang the *Internationale* and marched around the colony shouting "One, two, three, Pioneers are we, Fighting for the working class, Against the bourgeoisie!"[62]

As the strength of the communists increased, an anticommunist faction took shape, consisting of anarchists aided by a few liberals and socialists. As a conciliatory gesture to their allies, a few of the anarchists, among them Harry Kelly, adopted the label "libertarian socialist," for which Hippolyte Havel denounced them as "ersatz Anarchists."[63] A particularly determined group of anarchists, including Helen Rudome, Eva Brandes, and Anita Miroy, fought the communists tooth and nail. "At first our admissions committee kept out the Communists and the well-to-do," Eva Brandes recollects. "But gradually they came in, and the colony began to change. Far more than at Stelton, the Communists were responsible for the breakup of the colony. But the liberals too shared the blame. They were not committed to genuine libertarian ideas or to libertarian education. They wanted a middle-class progressive school with a professional staff. The anarchists were too weak or apathetic to resist these incursions. We had to drag them to election meetings to vote." Jacques Rudome agreed. "What ruined Mohegan," he declared, "was letting in outsiders who had nothing in common with anarchism and didn't belong. Eventually they became a majority and took over and ran things in their own way. The early years were the best."[64]

Needless to say, no Popular Front emerged at Mohegan before the Second World War. On the contrary, with Stalin's great purge and the bitterness of the Spanish Civil War, a polarization occurred, pitting communists and fellow-travelers against anarchists and democratic socialists. It was like trying "to mix oil and water," the latter group declared. The result was "a house divided against itself which cannot continue."[65]

With the outbreak of World War II, tensions between communists and anarchists eased as both groups bent their energies toward the defeat of fascism.[66] During the Cold War that followed, however, hostilities flared out of control. Vito Marcantonio, a communist Congressman from New York City, was prevented by the anarchists from speaking at the colony. Fist fights erupted at meetings, and Rudolf Rocker and William Z. Foster, who was living at Mohegan at the time, would pass each other on the road without uttering a word of greeting. Some anarchists went so far as to cooperate with the FBI by providing information about their rivals.

A climax occurred with the notorious Peekskill Riot of 1949, which sealed the community's fate. In August of that year, the communists made arrangements for an open-air concert at the Mohegan lakefront, with Paul Robeson as the featured performer. When the news got around, local red-baiters were determined to stop it. As Harry Kelly once remarked, Mohegan stood next to "the most Babbitt community in the country," and during a Sacco-Vanzetti meeting in the 1920s members of the local Ku Klux Klan had burned a cross opposite the community.[68] Now, some twenty-five years later, bands of hoodlums drove through the colony looking for communists and attacked a group of visitors who were viewing the proposed concert site. "It was a reign of terror," Eva Brandes recalls.

The concert, after being postponed, was rescheduled for September 4th, and the sponsors, anticipating further trouble, imported guards from New York who patrolled the area with clubs and baseball bats. The concert went on as planned. But afterward, for miles along the road to New York City, cars were attacked by police and vigilantes who threw rocks, beat members of the departing audience, and shouted anticommunist, anti-Negro, and anti-Semitic epithets. "It was a traumatic experience," says Eva Brandes, "and the final blow to the colony."

The next day, September 5, 1949, an anti-Red slate, including Joseph Brandes, Helen Rudome, and Joseph Aronstam, won control of the board of directors of the Mohegan Modern School Association by the largest vote ever cast in the history of the colony. In the ensuing months a Mohegan Civic Association, a coalition of anarchists, liberals, and socialists, was formed to prevent "the domination of our community by a well disciplined group whose sole purpose is to utilize every opportunity to further its aims without regard to the interests and well being of the rest of us."[69]

But the disputes had taken their toll. Hatred and mistrust never abated. By the end of the 1950s, its members aging and their children growing up and moving away, the colony had lost its distinctive identity and was being transformed into a politically mixed residential community. "It was prosperity," says Juan Anido, "that led to Mohegan's dissolution. At first it was a working-class community, but it became more and more middle class. I sold my house—the smallest in the colony, I think—in 1965. There had been happy times and sad times, but all in all they were good years and I'm glad I was there. The younger generation doesn't seem to want to accept responsibility. They want something made to order. And that's what they are getting and probably will continue to get in the future. With anarchism the individual has to think for himself and to realize that he must accept responsibility in order to be himself. It's too bad. The fruit was wonderful, the flowers were beautiful, but the tree refused to grow."[70]

Today only a handful of former colonists remain. Mohegan, says Eva Brandes' sister, has become "just another middle-class suburban community, with IBM junior executives and New York City commuters of every political persuasion. Their houses are all decorated at Christmas. When I saw a man reading *The Daily News*, I knew the colony was finished."[71]

CHAPTER 10

The Declining Years

THE DICKS

AFTER LEAVING Mohegan in June 1928, Jim and Nellie Dick returned to Stelton, where for the next five years they served as co-principals of the school and resumed their old job of running the Living House. The colonists, wrote Jim to the Ferms, had agreed to refrain from interfering. "They are evidently heart-sick of the floundering about that has existed since you both left. There is quite a young element here growing up and making themselves felt, so while I have some of our old pupils by my side, and the softening down of factional disputes, I have accepted it in good faith and thrown myself into the work."[1]

Jim had his work cut out for him. "The place was in a horrible condition," he wrote to Tom Keell, "demoralized to the extreme."[2] His first task was to renovate the Living House, which had fallen into disrepair. When this was done, he fixed up and painted the schoolhouse. Then he plunged into teaching the children, with the same energy and methods as in the past. "We learned weaving and basketry," a pupil recalls. "The older kids built a canoe in shop and tried to harpoon fish." *The Voice of the Children* was revived, and "we learned some reading and writing by setting type for our stories. Jim Dick read Shakespeare to seven-year-olds. He loved Shakespeare. There was never any feeling of being in a 'class.' "[3] To this familiar fare a new element was added. Movies, borrowed from the Museum of Natural History in New York, were shown every week, portraying construction and manufacture as well as plant and animal life.

A month after returning to Stelton, Jim wrote the following letter to A. S. Neill, with whom he had kept up his correspondence:

The Stelton Modern School
July 4th, 1928 (Der Tag we
Yanks beat the British)

Dear Dominie Neill,

I nearly stole that word Dominie for myself, but alas, the

Yankee kids would soon add the adjective DUMB, the alliteration is too easy.

Thanks for your letter. I thought perhaps you had "given me the gate" (Ask your Yankee kids to translate this letter).

This is to let you know that I have transferred my effects and affections to the school above. You will perhaps recollect that Sherwood Trask was here for some time, before he took his trip to Europe. We worked together here, and I went to Peekskill, N.Y.

The Ferms left here three years ago, after a hullabaloo over the too much insistence by the folk here for academics. During the three years there has been chaos and confusion, and as I got into hot water for the same thing in Mohegan School, so the sequence is that the people here repented and asked me to reorganize the school as of old. (There's nowt so queer as folk.) Here I am with a gurruntee of five years immunity. I accepted the challenge (as the school was in a dilapidated condition) and am here on my old stamping ground working like a horse.

Some of the kids came along with me and believe me they are getting to know what pioneering means. "Our middle name is PAINT." They are getting an education with a vengeance.

The other day a couple of [public] school teachers happened along to see the school and in the course of the conversation asked about the usual question "discipline." Well, I said, I guess I understand what you mean, and perhaps to illustrate the point, an incident occurred yesterday when one of my kids was up a ladder painting the school. I was looking over the job and chanced to remark to him—Say kid what's the great idea? D'ye call that a decent job? For gards sake make it slick and do it snappy. He replies—For crying out loud whatya think I am, a painter? Gee whiz some particular guy you are, get up and do it yourself if you don't like it, I resign forthwith from my position. The look of astonishment at this was wonderful to behold.

Shall be happy to read your new book when it sees the light. My endeavors as a pith prospectus writer pale along side of your snappy book writing, and I am envious of your story telling proclivities. (We shall form a mutual admiration society.) I have just finished another folder for this school, differing slightly from the last. I will let you have one when printed. Please send me yours.

Sherwood has a house near by but lives and works in New

York City. He is at present at the Walden School, N.Y.C. I will certainly tell him of your inquiry.

Hope you will travel West one day, as I hope to travel East to view the old countree folk and the schools (particularly yours).

Kind regards to the kids.

Best wishes,
James H. Dick

Through much hard work on the part of the Dicks, the school was restored to a healthy state. By the fall of 1929 some sixty children were enrolled, compared to between forty and fifty the previous year. Things were back "in ship-shape condition," Jim could report, "the kids are happy, and work goes on with a swing and all is well."[4] Money was now the chief concern. The Depression having descended over the country, sources of support were drying up. But the school managed to keep its head above water as contributions filtered in from anarchist and labor organizations. A typical donor was the International Anarchist Group of Detroit, composed of Jewish, Russian, Italian, and Spanish members. "You can tell your Spanish comrades," wrote Jim to its secretary, "that the writer of this letter had the personal pleasure of meeting Ferrer and was along with his successor Señor Portet in his endeavor to recover the schools of Barcelona, but alas it did not materialize owing to clerics and the iron hoof of the government." Jim added that he saw Stelton as a tribute to Ferrer's memory, "fully appreciating the fact that there is something irrepressible in life striving for liberty of thought, action, individual and society."[5]

Thanks to the labors of the Dicks, a full range of adult activities was also restored at the colony. Visitors included Isadora Duncan's daughter Irma with her troupe, the black leader Adam Clayton Powell, and John Louis Horn, professor of education at Mills College in Oakland, California, who was greatly impressed by what he saw. The spring and fall educational conferences were once again well attended, with A. J. Muste of Brookwood Labor College and Dr. B. W. Barkas of Mohegan among the participants, together with John Scott, William Bridge, Abe Grosner, and Alexis and Elizabeth Ferm, not to mention Jim and Nellie Dick themselves. Anarchist forums were held in the Kropotkin Library with such speakers as Joseph Cohen, Hans Koch, and Sam Dolgoff. The Dicks, moreover, invited Mike Gold to give a talk on new educational endeavors in the Soviet Union, for which

Jim and Nellie felt strong sympathy. "I understand," wrote Jim to Gold, "that we are known in Russia as of the same ilk in our scholastic efforts."[6]

In the fall of 1930 Nellie left for a prolonged visit to her homeland, to which her parents had returned after the Revolution. Her sister Dora took charge of the Living House in her absence, and Jim remained behind to run the school. The following summer Jim sailed for England to meet Nellie on her return from Russia. While there, he saw his old Central Labour College and anarchist comrades, including Will Lawther and Tom Keell, with whom he had kept in touch since emigrating to America. He also visited the Summerhill School at Leiston, Suffolk, and made the acquaintance of A. S. Neill, who had been urging him to come. "Your 'Voice' comes regularly," Neill had written, "and is much praised here. It is a real value in young art." "Just roll up when it is convenient to you," he told Jim before his departure. "I am always on the premises. I am quite excited about meeting you."[7]

In October 1932, like Harry Kelly a decade before, Jim Dick celebrated his fiftieth birthday with a party arranged by his Stelton colleagues. It was attended by friends from throughout the area. Only Mike Gold was unable to come. "Sorry I couldn't get in for the 50th anniversary of the whitehaired cockney christ," he wrote. "I have a bum knee and a busted auto."[8]

By now the Dicks had completed four years in charge of the school and Living House. Despite all promises to the contrary, they had met with considerable interference from the parents, though nothing to compare with their experience at Mohegan. At any rate, like the Hutchinsons and the Ferms before them, they made up their minds to leave. "I have a keen desire to start a school of my own," Jim had written to Tom Keell, "without interference or likely interference. Ferrer had the ideal way—sole control, with sympathetic personalities about him—this way and this way only would give me the satisfaction I crave."[9]

The Dicks left Stelton for the second and last time in June 1933. In October they opened a new Modern School at 115 Carey Street, Lakewood, New Jersey, which endured for the next twenty-five years. "We didn't follow theories much," Nellie recalls, "but experimented on our own, except that we remembered that Ferrer was a rebel, that he was shot, and that he believed in giving children a wider scope. We had children from nursery age—three or four—through the primary grades. After that they went on to Lakewood High School or went home. It differed from

Stelton in that it was in a city rather than in the country, and we had a bit more academic structure. We were a household of ourselves, a huge family affair. The children who came to board were from broken homes or couldn't stand the air in New York (asthma, allergies, and the like). Most were from New York and a few from Philadelphia, but some came to day school from Lakewood."[10]

During a typical year, between thirty and forty children attended the Lakewood Modern School, a few of whom had been at Stelton. Nearly all were of working-class parents, who came out on weekends to see them. "We believed in freedom of education," Nellie remembers. "The children were never forced to attend class. If the kids got rowdy, Jim would simply walk out. As in Stelton, the worst punishment was to tell a child he couldn't go to school. I handled the nursery and kindergarten and housekeeping, while Jim had the grades. Many of the kids went on to become doctors, lawyers, scientists—and I still keep in touch with them. The children were happy. It was not just a school, but a home, a big family, and when we sold the place the kids cried."[11]

During the summer months, the Dicks ran a Modern School Camp, first at Montrose, New York, for one year, then at Carmel, New York, until about 1943, and finally at Stroudsburg, Pennsylvania, for a year or two. After that, they stayed at Lakewood and had their camp there.

A great majority of the former pupils have pleasant and enthusiastic memories of the time they spent at Lakewood. One pupil recalls how she came to love Shakespeare from Jim Dick's classes, as well as Greek mythology, Gilbert and Sullivan, and *Cyrano de Bergerac*—so much so that she named her daughter Roxanne after the heroine of the play. Nine and ten year olds could recite Shakespeare's sonnets, and they knew all the lines when Jim and Nellie took them to a Shakespeare play in New York.[12]

In June 1953, after Julius and Ethel Rosenberg were executed for conducting espionage for the Soviet Union, their two small sons were staying at Toms River, New Jersey, not far from Lakewood. A friend asked the Dicks if they would take the boys in, and Nellie agreed, in spite of opposition from colleagues and comrades. "If I had said no I could never have lived it down," she later recalled. "They stayed for the summer. My son, little Jim, was the only one who backed me up. The rest said, 'Why do you want to stick your neck out?' "[13]

In 1958 the Lakewood school closed, the last of the Modern Schools in America. By then Jim was in his seventy-sixth year, and Nellie was sixty-five. Not long afterwards, they moved to Miami, Florida, where Jim died in 1965. Nellie, at eighty-six, survives, an active participant in the local Senior Citizens' movement. "My views on education have remained essentially the same," she said, looking back over sixty years in the movement, "just being human to the children. When children are treated with respect and are given responsibility, they will be happy. We were interested in the children. We were concerned with their lives, their whole beings, and with their happiness. But you can't attribute the child's successes or failures to school alone. You must know his whole background and how he grew up. A few years ago, the former Stelton children had a reunion at little Jim's house on Long Island and the question was asked, 'What was it about Stelton and the other schools that stays with us so much, that makes us feel as we do about them?' Love? Freedom? I thought of it later, and it struck me that the answer was security, the security of the family, of being part of one big close-knit family, which they had lacked before they came to the school. That's what they had, the feeling of security, of a family, of home."[14]

THE FERMS

After the Ferms left Stelton in 1925, the school carried on for three years in an increasingly disorganized state before the Dicks finally came to the rescue. In early 1926, John Scott took over for several months before moving to Mohegan. That autumn Abe Goldman, a Polish-born anarchist, Esperantist, and vegetarian, who had been one of the first teachers in the Workmen's Circle schools, was appointed principal, only to resign after a single year.[15] During 1927-1928, the school was closed for the first time in its history, "and weeds and grass instead of children got busy in the garden of the Living House."[16] However, a Work and Play Center was set up in one of the residents' homes, run by Bill Pogrebysky, Anna Schwartz, Dora Keyser, and Sally Axelrod, so that the children were never left completely on their own. Finally, the Dicks arrived in June 1928 and managed to get the school back on its feet. But, though it survived until 1953, it was never again what it had been during its initial decade.

The Ferms, meanwhile, had been leading a busy life. After their departure, they lived briefly at Free Acres, the single-tax colony in Berkeley Heights, before moving to their cabin at Newfoundland. In August 1926 Uncle gave a course of lectures on "Child Education" at the Belle Terre summer camp in Croton. In the spring of 1927 he taught a class of twelve to fourteen year olds at the Country Day School in Caldwell, New Jersey, a progressive institution.[17] He and Elizabeth attended the single-tax convention of that year, and in 1929 they went to Mohegan to conduct a discussion group on education.

Nor was this all. For four summers, beginning in 1929, Uncle directed the Pioneer Youth Camp at Rifton, New York, sponsored by the National Association of Child Development, whose aim was "to encourage activities which will stimulate the critical and creative faculties of children, will liberate their minds from dogma and fear, and will help each one to become a force for the reconstruction of society."[18] During the same period, he conducted an education column in *The Road to Freedom*, lectured at Commonwealth College in Arkansas (whose director, William E. Zeuch, had been a principal of the Organic School), and served on the board of directors of Manumit, an experimental school for workers' children at Pawling, New York, with A. J. Muste as chairman.[19] In 1932-1933 Uncle filled in as director of the school for the entire year.

Nor had the Ferms severed all ties with Stelton. Between 1928 and 1933 they attended its spring and fall educational conferences, though Uncle declined Jim Dick's invitation to be the main speaker. "I really do think that it will be better for you and the school if you can get someone who has not been regularly attached to the school to do the speaking," he wrote. "I remember years ago when I was interested in the Manhattan Liberal Club where we used to hold weekly meetings for lectures and discussion and where I used to take part in the discussion very often, one evening when I was walking to the platform to say something Elizabeth heard someone in the rear say 'there goes that long-haired Ferm again.' And so some of the members are likely to feel, even if they do not say it, 'there's Uncle talking again.' "[20]

And yet when the Dicks departed for Lakewood, the Ferms agreed to return as co-principals. Undeterred by advanced age (Elizabeth was seventy-five, Alexis sixty-three) or by unpleasant recollections of the past, they were eager to get back to work. On October 1, 1933, after an absence of eight years, they resumed their former position, applying the same techniques and principles which had aroused such controversy before. Aunty had aged, to be sure, but she had not mellowed. Her prejudices were as deeply ingrained as ever. "At morning assembly I was once lost in thought and stood apart from the rest," recalls Ben Lieberman, who taught at Stelton after Mohegan. "Aunty came over and poked me in the chest with a finger. 'You're a dead tree,' she said."[21]

Nor had the Ferms modified their educational philosophy. "We are more concerned about their creative ability, self-activity and initiative," said Uncle of his pupils, "than we are with their ability to mumble off a lot of stuff that they may need to properly pass into something that they do not want but that others think they ought to have."[22] "I do not claim that my methods are the best nor that someone else may not do better," he told the president of the Modern School Association of North America. "I do not fight for our own ways of doing things, but the question of human development thru experience and creative work is another matter. All that I have seen and read has not changed me, not because I am stubborn, but because my mind's eye sees education that way. . . . But all this is talk. We'll go on as far as we can in what we're trying to [do] and we will live in the hope that someone will be inspired to carry it on after us in spite of opposition and indifference. Some day it must be recognized."[23]

Yet not even the Ferms, for all their dedication, could reverse the decline into which the school had fallen since their departure. As a working-class community, Stelton was hard hit by the Depression. A growing number of parents were unable to pay their fees. More and more pupils were withdrawn from the school, so that by 1938 only thirty were in regular attendance.[24] While money continued to trickle in from radical groups and from individual benefactors like Pryns Hopkins, it was insufficient to meet expenses, so that entertainments and bazaars had to be arranged, both in Stelton and New York. Every year, for example, a "Daybreak Costume Ball" was held at Webster Hall on East Eleventh Street, a block or two from the site of the first Ferrer Day School in the city. The Stelton Players continued to put on benefit performances, and Anton Rovinsky (the "Paderewski" of the Ferrer Center) gave a piano recital to raise funds.

These expedients, however, were barely enough to keep the school from closing. During the mid-thirties, when the need for revenue became acute, the Living House had to be sold as a private residence and the children placed in homes of individual members. Yet the work of the colony went on. In 1936 the

Kropotkin Group sponsored an Anarchist Summer School, with seminars on the history of the American labor movement, the history of the international anarchist movement, schools of anarchist thought, anarchist influences in art and literature, child education, the philosophy of history, current trends in the labor movement, the dictatorship of the proletariat, and the anarchist position in the modern world.[25] In 1939 the annual Labor Day convention marked the thirtieth anniversary of Ferrer's execution with "a review of his life, his work and the principles for which he made the ultimate sacrifice." Among the speakers were Harry Kelly, Joseph Cohen, James Dick, and Rudolf Rocker.[26]

The following year the twenty-fifth anniversary of the colony was celebrated by a dinner at the Hotel Diplomat in New York, with Leonard Abbott presiding and recitals by Ray Miller, soprano, and Clara Freedman, pianist. Just three days earlier, on May 14, 1940, Emma Goldman had died in Toronto, and the dinner served also as a tribute to her memory.[27] To many of the participants the colony itself seemed to be fading. But, as Alexis Ferm pointed out, "when a work continues for twenty-five years in the face of opposition and misunderstanding there must be some vital spark that inspires the workers."[28]

The coming of the Second World War heralded what Anna Schwartz called "the final ruin of the school."[29] In 1940 the U.S. War Department bought land adjacent to the colony for the Camp Kilmer embarkation center. Over the next few years the coming and going of thousands of soldiers changed the whole atmosphere of the area. "The soldiers," wrote Harry Kelly to Leonard Abbott, "march through the colony and have sham battles so it is quite military."[30] Worse than this, hearing about the "free-love" colony next door, soldiers came looking for "action." Previously, women and children had gone about the community without fear for their safety. Nor had the colonists been in the habit of locking their doors. Now everything changed as homes were broken into and women and even children were molested. Residents began to move away, taking their boys and girls out of the school. By 1948 enrollment had dwindled to fifteen, mostly of kindergarten age.

The death of Elizabeth Ferm came as another blow. In 1934 Aunty had suffered a mild stroke, which affected her speech slightly. But she had made a complete recovery. During the summer of 1937 she suffered another mild stroke and had to give up work at the school. She was then in her eightieth year. With Uncle's help, she could still attend to the housework, but in June

1942 she suffered yet another stroke, which left her bedridden. In November 1942 she had a fourth stroke. With careful treatment she was able to make herself understood and could sit up in a chair. In this condition she carried on until April 12, 1944, when she died from an internal hemorrhage.[31]

At the cremation ceremony, Jo Ann Wheeler read from Aunty's writings, children sang her morning assembly songs, and eulogies were delivered by Harry Kelly and other leaders of the movement. On Decoration Day of 1944 a memorial meeting was held for her at Stelton. Letters of sympathy poured in from all over the country. Abby Coryell, the first teacher in the New York Modern School and an old friend of the Ferms, was among the many who expressed their condolences. Another was Sherwood Trask. "Elizabeth was such a powerful force," he wrote to Uncle, "that it must have been a mighty and creative struggle at all times in your life." Joseph Cohen compared their educational experiment to that of Bronson Alcott a century before.[32] In 1946, at the annual convention of the Modern School Association of North America, a committee was formed to publish Elizabeth's writings. The book, called *Freedom in Education*, appeared in 1949 and became a sacred text of the movement.

After Aunty's death, Uncle continued as principal for four more years. In 1948 he retired and moved to Fairhope, the single-tax colony in Alabama, where he spent the remaining twenty-three years of his life. "There are a great lot of 'nut' down here besides myself," he wrote to Dora Keyser. "There is a group of Peacemakers, a group of Theosophists, a group studying Dianetics, an art group, studying art. Miss Winifred Duncan, an author and sculptress who is teaching the sculpture group, asked me to pose for my head, which I promptly refused. I'm not a model."[33]

For his own part, Uncle remained faithful to the individualist and single-tax ideas which he had nurtured since his youth. He continued to quote from *Progress and Poverty* and Jefferson's maxim that the least government is the best government. A believer in self-reliance, he was opposed to the income tax and to welfare, and applied for social security only at the age of ninety-eight so as not to burden friends with his support. He wrote letters on education to *The Henry George Newsletter* and asked Sally Axelrod to send a copy of *Freedom in Education* to the Henry George Library in New York. "I do feel that I'd like to help the single tax people," he told Dora Keyser in 1959, "for they are trying to teach the people that what they earn for their work belongs to them and not to the government or the church or to anyone else that we are not interested in. The Henry George people come the nearest to placing before the people the idea that somehow we shall be able to use the land and that it should not be monopolized by a few or by anyone. Of course I can give only a few dollars but 'every mickle makes a muckle' as the Scotch say."[34]

Another cause to which he contributed was that of racial equality. A lifelong defender of the Negro, he gave what he could to civil rights organizations and was a strong supporter of Martin Luther King.[35] For criticizing the local White Citizens' Council in P. D. East's *The Petal Paper*, he received threatening letters and broken windows, but remained unintimidated.

His love of music and of nature also remained powerful to the end. He listened to radio broadcasts of the New York Philharmonic, subscribed to *Natural History* magazine, and pasted bird stickers on the envelopes of his letters. In 1962 he bought a record by Joan Baez, whose mother had been his pupil at Stelton. "Joan has an interesting voice—and pleasant and she knows how to sing her songs," was his judgment, and he was pleased when several years later the elder Joan Baez sent him more of her daughter's recordings.[36]

Not one to remain idle, Uncle engaged in a whole range of activities, from writing movie reviews for *The Fairhope Courier* and articles for *The Green Revolution* to fixing old toys for indigent children and building bookshelves for the public library. Toward the end of 1948 he began, singlehandedly, to build his own house, a task he completed with the pride of workmanship which he had always sought to instill in his pupils. "I can't understand this harping on old age at 69-76," he wrote when he was 100. "There should be no talk about old age before the age of 90. At 79 I built my own hollow-tile house, mixing the cement and climbing the ladder with cement to build not only the walls but the fireplace of brick. Some people get the idea that when they reach 60 or 65 they are old."[37]

Uncle's chief passion, however, remained education. From time to time he would look in at the Organic School to see the children at work or play. He watched them conduct a Halloween party and went to see their outdoor folk dancing, which he enjoyed very much, though he could not refrain from noting that his own school at Stelton had been the only one with "interpretive dancing." On another occasion, he visited the school with Suzanne

Hotkine, and "she had the children dancing to her music, a sonata of Beethoven's."[38]

In February 1961 Uncle read A. S. Neill's *Summerhill*, sent to him by Anna Schwartz, and was so impressed that he gave a talk on it at the Fairhope library. "If you want to read something really radical in education you should read 'Summerhill' by A. S. Neill," he wrote a friend shortly afterward. And he began a correspondence with Neill himself, which unfortunately has not been preserved. Uncle also read *The Lives of Children* by George Dennison, which he found "a very interesting book." "I happened to have an extra copy of Elizabeth's book," he wrote to Jo Ann Wheeler, "so I mailed it to him ℅ Random House. His philosophy is like our own."[39]

As the years passed, however, Uncle became increasingly pessimistic. In a letter to Leonard Abbott he scorned the "howling ignorant crowd, the crowd that put Sacco and Vanzetti to death, that deported the radicals in the Palmer days, that lynch the colored man in the south and that dragged Garrison thru the streets of Boston at the end of a rope."[40] "Are we to continue to be directed, animated automatons or may we become self-directed human beings?" he had asked while still at Stelton. "It is true that it is hard to picture a small effort like ours ever making any impression on the world, yet how is it that many of the public schools are taking up activity programs, work that we did over forty years ago? An impression must have been made somewhere. Then, what will happen after this terrible craze has passed, since they are now entirely regimenting the boys and girls for war work? After the war they are counting on the boys and girls being ready to do mechanical work to be of use in a regimented society. I fear freedom will have gone by the board. You will be expected to be a mere cog in the big cogwheel of society."[41]

A decade later, Uncle was still lamenting the domination of government everywhere, the crowds looking for heroes to worship, forgetting their own individual capacities. He quoted Shelley:

> Man who man would be
> Must rule the empire of himself: in it
> Must be supreme, establishing his throne
> On vanquished will, quelling the anarchy
> Of hopes and fears, being himself alone.[42]

He was convinced, as the end drew near, that he was "leaving the world worse than I found it."

In February 1970 the Fairhope community threw a party on Uncle's hundredth birthday. Soon afterwards he broke his hip in an accident and was confined to a local nursing home. It was there that Suzanne Hotkine visited him on his 101st birthday and played *The Moonlight Sonata* and saw the tears run down his face. The following May, a month before his death, she wrote him the following letter:

Friday, May 14 '71

Dearest Uncle,

I had quite an experience this morning. I felt I had to tell you about it.

It was a beautiful day and the flowers seemed to be smiling at me—in their full glory. Where we live, in the West Bronx, we still have the good fortune to see trees and flowers around our homes—particularly in our little street. As I was stepping into our car for the week-end marketing I spotted the little dandelions in the grass—and I found myself singing the song that Aunty used in the assembly:

Pretty little dandelion—
Growing in the grass—
With your hair of shining gold
Merry little lass.

When your pretty hair turns white
Pray what will you do?
Will you make a hundred more—
Just as nice as you?

Do you remember that song which the children and Aunty sang with such tenderness and feeling? . . . As I was singing it I had a very moving, strange experience. It was as though I was truly back there, in Stelton, 1924-25. I really became transported and *completely* there. The song had a new, very deep beauty and I felt your presence, and Aunty's, as though I could touch you. And I was overwhelmed by the greatness of your work—of the magnificent spiritual, creative environment you had created for all of us, fortunate ones, who had the blessing to be brought into it. How could we ever thank you adequately!!? How could you ever measure the seeds of beauty and truth and creativeness that you implanted in us—so many of us.

Isn't it indeed like the magic of the dandelion who could make "a hundred more"? Think of it—through my work with you, I alone have brought so much joy to all my pupils—several hundred at least—have been influenced creatively and inspired. And you, with Aunty, have made an incalculable number of inspired people—by being the forerunners of creative education in this country—and perhaps in the world. Your seeds are actively spreading, and spreading. So often I come across articles, and books on modern education—which are just about beginning to catch up somewhat on what you knew and practiced these many, many years ago—they still have a long way to go to catch up to you. But they will eventually get there—after passing through the fires. But you—and Aunty—had the *vision*—the heavenly truth of education and human development *before* anyone. For this truth you gave of yourselves unstintingly.

That is why all of us who have experienced your and Aunty's work—all of us consider you among the *greats* of this world.

Like the golden, beautiful, modest dandelion, you have the magic and the power of eternal life.

Your work will persist and persist and bless the world.

Your presence will *never fade away from all of us* who knew your greatness—and your beauty.

Thank you, again and again for all you did for me—and the others—and please accept our deepest love, and more than that we cannot adequately express,

Suzanne

THE MOVEMENT

"Now that Elizabeth Ferm is dead," wrote Leonard Abbott in 1949, "and Alexis Ferm has retired from teaching, I doubt if the school has any real future. There is no one to take the place of the Ferms."[43] Alexis had resigned the previous year at the annual convention of the Modern School Association, which only eighteen members attended, a measure of the movement's decline. Uncle's assistant, Anna Schwartz, was elected to succeed him. One of the colony's original settlers, she had also been at the Ferrer Center, Stony Ford, and Mohegan. Her children, Marucci and Zack, had attended the schools at New York, Stony Ford, and Stelton, and Zack had taught at Stelton and Mohegan. It is not surprising, then, that she should have followed in the footsteps of her predecessors. "The child," she summed up her method, "unfolds and develops into a self-sufficient individual thru freedom, thru unhindered expression in creative activity."[44]

By the time Anna Schwartz took charge, however, the school had become a mere kindergarten for children aged three to seven. And only a handful of pupils were enrolled. The school was on its last legs. "Parents of today," she lamented, "are a great deal more conservative than parents of the past were. Oh, it is all so complicated. We want to keep the school alive, but it is so very hard to do so."[45]

Not long before the school expired, it was suddenly brought back to its roots. In August 1949 Anna Schwartz received a letter from Ferrer's granddaughter, Olga. She was living in New York and had just learned about the school. "It was so marvelous to discover The Modern School of Stelton and to hear about you," she wrote.[46] Soon afterward, Leonard Abbott brought her out for a visit. Delighted, she asked Anna Schwartz to send her mother, living in Paris, a copy of *Freedom in Education*. It brought an excited response. "My emotion was great learning of all your efforts," wrote Sol Ferrer, "and will be glad to make your work known here abroad." Stelton, she added, was "following the tradition of the Barcelona model."[47]

That same year, the fortieth anniversary of Ferrer's execution, saw the last annual meeting of the Modern School Association of North America. Harry Kelly attended. "I enjoyed being there and seeing the folks," he said, "but the glory has departed. Not more than twenty people and perhaps even less were at the convention."[48] Four years later, in 1953, the school was permanently closed. In February 1955, thirty-five years after it was built, the schoolhouse was destroyed by fire. On December 18, 1955, the first steps were taken to disband the Modern School Association and to distribute its remaining assets. The process was completed at a meeting in the Bronx on May 21, 1961, at which the association was formally dissolved.[49]

Thus ended the movement inspired by the martyrdom of Ferrer half a century before. What had brought about its demise? Aside from the impact of the Depression, the rift between the anarchists and communists had played a part. Ever since the 1920s, American radicals had been bitterly divided. The shared goals and spirit of comradeship of the Ferrer Center era had given place to factionalism and a hardening of political lines. "In the old days," one anarchist observed, "Socialists, I.W.W.'s, Anarchists, etc. somehow were friends in spite of their differences. Now all who are not Communists are reactionaries, yellow renegades, fascists. That was the golden age we lived in compared to the problems and complex situations we face today."[50]

Since the 1920s, furthermore, the anarchist movement had fallen into disarray. With the Palmer raids many of the most active leaders had been silenced by imprisonment or deportation. At the same time, the older generation was dying out, and with it the classic era of anarchism in which the Ferrer movement had taken shape and from which it drew its sustenance and inspiration. By the mid-1920s Harry Kelly had already found "an absence of that idealism that was prevalent before the war," and Hippolyte Havel believed that there was "no Anarchist movement, and for that matter no radical movement in the United States at all." As Theodore Schroeder put it in 1931, "much of the pre-war cock-suredness is gone. With some persons, practically the whole of their theories for social betterment has been abandoned, or even reversed."[51]

As for the younger generation, born and bred in the United States, assimilation into American society was accompanied by a reduction of ideological intensity. Many became professionals and entered the mainstream of American life. As Uncle Ferm noted, one could hardly expect the school to outweigh "the home, the disagreements of the parents, the impact of the commercial world with its foolish fashions, the feeling of not wanting to be left out in the cold when the crowd is going one way and they happen to be going another."[52]

Ben Lieberman offered a similar explanation: "Why did the colonies break up? Chiefly because the world was too much with us. Try as we might, we could not divorce ourselves from it, could not build utopia and the 'new man.' Nobody knows how, and too few among us appreciate the extent of man's quarrelsomeness. Before the First World War radicals of different stripes could still argue about their differences, could still have their different groups and theories and yet agree about a common enemy, capitalism, and be friends—could even start colonies together. But after the war and the Russian Revolution, this became more and more difficult. Earlier, if an anarchist got into trouble, the socialists would come to his defense; all rallied to Haymarket and Johann Most, for example. But with the Russian Revolution came an event which forced you to put up or shut up. And between patriots and internationalists no peace or compromise was possible. Bitter quarrels divided them for life."

"I am convinced," Lieberman added, "that the First World War was a great watershed of the modern period. The result of this split in the radical ranks was an irreconcilable legacy of bitterness and enmity, a line of blood drawn between them. Charges of 'traitor,' 'renegade' were continuous. All this poisoned the colonies. The Ferrer Center would hide anarchists, pacifists, conscientious objectors, and socialists. Even after the war some cooperation was possible. Things still hadn't gotten that hot. The decisive split occurred during the 1930s with the emergence of Stalin and Hitler. With Stalin something happened of a special nature that divided radicals irrevocably. Thus the main reason for the decline of the colonies was political not educational. All those politics tore both colonies apart. Not even the Popular Front could heal the breach. Most anarchists, syndicalists, Trotskyists refused to accept it. Besides, the damage was already done; totalitarianism was already entrenched. All these issues deeply affected the colonists, who took their politics very seriously. Block voting occurred on every question, however trivial, including school questions. Teachers and students were caught in the middle. Quarrels made community life difficult, and ultimately impossible. People weren't talking to one another. Fist fights occasionally broke out. The outside world kept impinging on the colonies. There was no way to avoid the goddam world!"[53]

It remains to describe the fate of the participants in the Modern School movement, at least of those who have not yet been accounted for. Of the Ferrer Center artists, Man Ray moved to Paris and achieved world fame as a painter and photographer. He died there in 1976 in his eighty-seventh year.[54] Adolf Wolff, by contrast, sank into obscurity. In the fall of 1914 he spent thirty days on Blackwell's Island for his role in the Union Square and Tarrytown demonstrations. "I do earnestly hope," he wrote to Alfred Stieglitz from his cell, "that all the rotten, filthy, corrupt prisons will be wiped away and the system that necessitates prisons will vanish from the face of the earth while the spirit of '291' will grow and multiply, for it is the spirit of freedom, of self-expression, of art, of life in the highest and deepest."[55] Shortly afterward, however, Wolff became an "hysterical patriot" and called for the deportation of his antiwar friends. Abandoning his art, he attended chiropractor school but did not establish a practice. Instead, he was supported by his girlfriend Vera, a designer with a house in Harlem. He died, forgotten, in 1944.[56]

Several others at the Center went on to distinguish themselves in American letters. "Durant, Konrad Bercovici, Lola Ridge, and Manuel Komroff are the four most successful writers who have sprung from the old Ferrer group thus far," wrote Leonard Abbott to Emma Goldman in 1930.[57] Lola Ridge had left New York in 1912 with her companion David Lawson, not returning until 1917. By then the Modern School had moved to Stelton and the Ferrer Center was breathing its last, so that she could not have resumed her former role in the movement even had she been inclined to do so. As it was, she limited her activity to contributing a few poems to *The Modern School* magazine ("To the Free Children," "To Alexander Berkman 'In Solitary,'" "To Abe Bluestein," "Will Shakespeare Sees the Children of the Ferrer Modern School Playing A Midsummer Night's Dream") and to reading from her work before the opening celebration of the Stelton schoolhouse. She also recited poems to Alexander Berkman and Emma Goldman at a farewell dinner on the eve of their deportation ("Only time / standing well off / shall measure your circumference and height," she wrote of Emma). In after years she kept in touch with Emma and Sasha in Western Europe. "I have not forgotten you, dear Lola," wrote Sasha on Christmas Day of 1927.[58]

It was only with the appearance of *The Ghetto and Other Poems* in 1918 that Lola Ridge's reputation was established. Though forty-five years old and a veteran at her craft, she was hailed as an important new talent. In 1927 she went to Boston to demonstrate for Sacco and Vanzetti and was arrested with Mike Gold, Polly Holladay, and other Ferrer Center comrades for picketing the Massachusetts State House. After an execution-night vigil, she returned to New York and began *Firehead*, a powerful epic inspired by the tragedy. Often in frail health, she contracted tuberculosis in the 1930s. Yet she lived to be seventy-seven, dying in her Brooklyn home in 1941.[59]

Next to Lola Ridge, Manuel Komroff was perhaps the most talented of the many Ferrer Center writers, and both, said Leonard Abbott in 1929, were "covering themselves with literary glory."[60] During the Ferrer Center years Komroff had served his apprenticeship as art critic for *The New York Call* and editorial writer for *The Daily Garment News*. In 1917, as a correspondent for *The*

New York World, he went to Russia to report on the Revolution. Editing *The Russian Daily News* in Petrograd, where he stayed with Bill Shatoff, he witnessed the Bolshevik seizure of power, after which he left for the Far East by way of the Trans-Siberian Railroad. In Shanghai he worked on *The China Press* for several months before returning to the United States and joining the publishing firm of Boni & Liveright as editor of The Modern Library series, later taken over by Random House.

A born story-teller, Komroff began the series of books—*The Grace of Lambs* (1925), *The Juggler's Kiss* (1927), *Coronet* (1929), *Two Thieves* (1931)—that made him famous. It is unlikely that he will be remembered as one of the leading writers of his generation, yet he wrote in an easy, natural style that had widespread appeal. He was immensely prolific, with more than 50 books and 150 short stories to his credit, and also dabbled in painting and photography, becoming a member of an important camera group, The Third Eye.

Komroff attributed at least part of his success to the Ferrer Center, which had opened new horizons in his life. In his novels and stories, he tells us, he made good use of what he had learned there. Stelton, however, he held in low regard. "My visit out there two years ago has had such a terrible effect that I am still not recovered," he wrote Leonard Abbott in 1940. "Such sordid squalor I have never believed possible. The shanty towns built on the river's edge in the very low of our existence presented a better appearance and some were even neat and trim. If Stelton is the result of 20 years of building by idealists then I say, Gessus No! I doubt if the look of the thing can be matched anywhere in America. I think one would have to go to the center of priest ridden Ireland to match the Stelton hugger-mugger." Komroff preferred the pleasant surroundings of Woodstock, New York, where he spent the last years of his life. He was working on his autobiography, "A Story-Teller's World," at the time of his death from cancer in 1974.[61]

One of Komroff's closest friends at the Ferrer Center had been the director of the Free Theatre, Moritz Jagendorf. While pursuing his dental practice, Jagendorf became a well-known folklorist, the author and editor of dozens of books on the subject. Another friend, David Rosenthal, became a celebrated radio announcer who entertained millions of listeners "with fervent readings of his own and other poems." In 1969 the Poetry Society of America gave him the Christopher Morley award for light verse for his "Elegy for an Overworked Undertaker." When I telephoned him in 1973, he called the Ferrer Center a "juvenile episode" in his life and refused to talk about it. He died of a heart attack in 1975 at the age of eighty-four.[62]

Still others drifted away from the movement and, as Dr. Liber said of Margaret Sanger, "forgot the working class." By 1939, when Hutchins Hapgood published his memoirs, Mrs. Sanger was "a pillar of society, though she got her ideas from the leaders of the lowly and despised."[63] She died in New York in 1966. More than a few made their mark as scholars, journalists, and teachers. Carl Zigrosser, for one, dropped out of Columbia graduate school in 1917 to work for Frederick Keppel, a New York dealer in prints. In 1919 he opened his own establishment, the Weyhe Gallery, with which he remained associated for more than two decades, becoming a noted authority on the graphic arts. From 1941 to 1963 Zigrosser served as curator of prints and rare books at the Philadelphia Museum of Art, besides being associated with the Whitney Museum of American Art and the Museum of Modern Art in New York. A Guggenheim Fellow, he published a number of highly regarded books on painting and prints. His beautifully produced autobiography, *My Own Shall Come to Me*, is a valuable source of information on the Ferrer movement in its early years. Shortly before his death in Switzerland in 1975, he contributed the foreword to a catalogue of Rockwell Kent's prints, published by the University of Chicago Press.[64]

The Ferrer Center produced a second museum curator in its Esperanto teacher, James F. Morton. In 1924 Morton moved from New York to Paterson, New Jersey, and the next year became curator of the Paterson Museum, a post which he held for the rest of his life. Maintaining his interest in Esperanto (he was vice-president of the Esperanto Association of North America), he also composed cryptograms and word puzzles and was a familiar figure in the National Puzzlers' League and the Riddlers' Club. Morton, wrote Theodore Schroeder to Emma Goldman in 1928, was "getting very fat in body and *mind*, but just as enthusiastic about the exhibition of a large vocabulary."[65] Morton also loved walking and went for long walks through the city and in the surrounding woods and quarries, where he collected rocks and minerals for the museum. Walking along the road in October 1941, he was struck and killed by a passing automobile. He had been on his way to a meeting of the Paterson Chaucer Guild, of which he was a founder.[66]

Frank Tannenbaum and Charles Plunkett, one would have thought, would be less likely to pursue a scholarly career than Zigrosser or Morton, having been among the most militant Ferrer Center activists during the crisis of 1914. Yet both earned doctorates at Columbia University and became highly respected academicians. Tannenbaum, after his release from Blackwell's Island for leading the church occupations, got a job at *The Masses* and enrolled at Columbia to study history and political science. Elected to Phi Beta Kappa, he was graduated with highest honors and was on his way to becoming a noted authority on Latin America. In 1925 he was still a socialist but of a more moderate bent than before, for "the social problem," he said, "is not a Gordian knot that can be cut by one sweep of the sword."[67]

Plunkett, it will be recalled, had been a party to the Lexington Avenue conspiracy. After the explosion, he lay low for a while at the artists' colony in Ridgefield before enrolling at Columbia like Tannenbaum. By 1925 he was married to Becky Edelsohn and an instructor in biology at New York University. "I know now the futility of the methods we employed and the defects of our thinking," he confessed. "I suppose it may all be attributed to emotionalism of the young and to general restlessness." With people like Plunkett in mind, Emma Goldman inveighed against the young hotheads at the Ferrer Center who had done "a world of harm and then recanted all they had pretended to be."[68] Advancing through the ranks, Plunkett became chairman of the NYU biology department and author of a standard biology textbook. He and Becky Edelsohn lived together for nine years and had a son, who is now a professor at a large midwestern university. Becky Edelsohn moved to California where she took her own life in 1971. Plunkett, long since retired from the university, lives quietly in rural New Jersey.

Of Plunkett's fellow Lexington Avenue conspirators, Louise Berger returned to Russia in 1917 and took part in the Revolution. She died in the great typhus epidemic which swept the country in 1920-1921.[69] Bill Shatoff, too, returned to Russia and cast his lot with the Bolsheviks, although he did not join the Communist Party. Lenin, he was convinced, was resolved to inaugurate anarchy by "withering away the state" the moment he got hold of it. Saturated with "that peculiarly American driving force and energy," Shatoff played a leading role in the movement for workers' control in Petrograd and was one of four anarchist members of the Military Revolutionary Committee which, headed by Trotsky, engineered the October seizure of power.[70]

During the Civil War against the Whites, Shatoff served Lenin's government with the same resourcefulness that he had displayed at the time of the October insurrection. As chief of security in Petrograd and an officer of the Tenth Red Army in 1919, he threw his energies into the defense of the old capital against the advance of General Yudenich. The following year he was summoned to Siberia to become minister of transportation in the Far Eastern Republic. Several years later he was again sent east, this time to supervise construction of the Turkestan-Siberian Railroad. Lenin included him among the many anarchists who were "becoming the most dedicated supporters of Soviet power."[71] Harry Kelly had a different reaction. "Bill Shatoff," he wrote to Max Nettlau, "of whom you have probably heard as the Anarchist Chief of Police of Petrograd, was organizer one year at our Ferrer Center and I feel sure if I could see Bill now he would say the latter job was more difficult than the former."[72]

Nor did Shatoff forget the Ferrer movement. It was his gift of 10,000 rubles, it will be recalled, that started construction of the Stelton schoolhouse in 1919. And when Emma Goldman and Alexander Berkman arrived in Petrograd in 1920, Shatoff was on hand to greet them. While critical of some of the methods of the Bolsheviks, Shatoff insisted that it was necessary to work with them. "Now I just want to tell you," he said, "that the Communist State in action is exactly what we anarchists have always claimed it would be—a tightly centralized power still more strengthened by the dangers of the Revolution. Under such conditions, one cannot do as one wills. One does not just hop on a train and go, or even ride the bumpers, as I used to do in the United States. One needs permission. But don't get the idea that I miss my American 'blessings'. Me for Russia, the Revolution, and its glorious future."[73]

During construction of the Turkestan-Siberian Railroad, Shatoff was regarded with "childlike adulation" throughout Central Asia. His English, reported Eugene Lyons, who met him in 1930, "brimmed over with juicy Americanisms ten or fifteen years out of date." America was still fresh in his mind, and he asked Lyons about Carlo Tresca, Elizabeth Gurley Flynn, and his other old anarchist and Wobbly comrades. When Nellie Dick was in Russia in 1931, she visited Shatoff in Moscow. Wearing all his medals and decorations, he told her he was still an anarchist "even though I worked with the Communists." On a second visit, in 1933, Nellie again went to his apartment but this time was not allowed in.[74] His services to the regime notwithstanding, Shatoff was arrested in 1937, at the height of the Great Purge, and shot the following year.

In 1920, when Shatoff defended Bolshevik repressions as necessary expedients in a life-and-death struggle, Emma Goldman and Alexander Berkman accepted his analysis and appealed to all progressive forces in the West to work to lift the Allied blockade, the chief cause, as they saw it, of Russia's "terrible hunger and suffering."[75] Before long, however, they changed their minds. They were stunned by the wholesale arrests of Russian anarchists, the dispersal of Makhno's army in the Ukraine, and the conversion of local soviets into mere rubber stamps for a new bureaucracy. The Bolsheviks, they concluded, while ruling in the name of the workers, were in fact destroying the popular initiative and self-reliance on which the success of the Revolution depended. The final blow came with the crushing of the Kronstadt rising in March 1921, which to Berkman marked "the beginning of a new tyranny."[76]

Shortly before Kronstadt, the anarchists had suffered another setback when Kropotkin, who had returned to Russia in 1917, died of pneumonia. His funeral became a political demonstration in which the black flag of anarchy was paraded through Moscow for the last time. Two weeks later, the Kronstadt rebellion broke out and a new wave of political arrests swept the country, scattering the remaining anarchist organizations. At the end of the year, their illusions shattered, Berkman and Goldman decided to emigrate. After a brief sojourn in Stockholm, they settled in Berlin, from which Emma wrote to Stewart Kerr about their experience, citing Shatoff as an example of "the corrupting influence of power."[77]

From Germany, Berkman and Goldman moved to France, where they lived out the rest of their lives. In their letters to America, they often inquired about the Modern Schools, in which they maintained an active interest. In 1923 Emma visited A. S. Neill's school at Hellerau, and in 1931 Pryns Hopkins' school near Paris. Berkman, under constant threat of expulsion by the French government, earned a precarious living by translating, editing, and occasional ghost-writing, which had to be supplemented by gifts from his comrades and friends. By the early thirties his health had begun to fail, and his letters often complained of depression and fatigue. In early 1936 he underwent two operations for a prostate condition, which left him in chronic pain. Finally, in June 1936, suffering from his illness and unwilling to exist on the generosity of others, he shot himself to death in his Nice apartment. He died just three weeks before the outbreak of the Spanish Revolution, which, as Emma Goldman suggested, might have revived his spirits and given him a new lease on life.

Emma herself, however, had only four more years to live. From 1936 to 1939 she placed herself at the disposal of her Spanish comrades, whose defeat dealt her a crushing blow. In May 1940, a month short of her seventy-first birthday, she collapsed and died in Toronto while on a lecture tour. Her body was removed to Chicago and buried in the Waldheim Cemetery, near the graves of Voltairine de Cleyre and the Haymarket martyrs.

"If it was Emma's wish to rest at Waldheim I am glad she is there," wrote Sadakichi Hartmann to Ben Reitman, Emma's erstwhile lover. "I am not so particular—any Potter's Field or the ocean are sufficient for me."[78] To relieve his chronic asthma, which grew worse as the years went by, Sadakichi had moved to the drier climate of southern California during the early 1920s, settling in the town of Beaumont. Trying his hand as a motion-picture script writer, he became attached to John Barrymore's Hollywood circle and acted in Douglas Fairbanks' 1923 film *The Thief of Baghdad*, playing the Chinese magician. He also gave poetry readings, as in the past, and wrote *The Last Thirty Days of Christ*, a book highly praised by Ezra Pound. It took him only four months to complete it. Living in the desert, he wrote Ben Reitman, "I had no library to go to, had no reference or any books with me except a ponderous old bible that I found in one of the deserted cottages in the foothills."[79]

From 1938 until his death in 1944, Sadakichi lived in a shack he had built on the Morongo Indian Reservation in Banning, on the edge of the desert southeast of Los Angeles, with funds supplied by Ezra Pound and others, as he himself, always in need of cash, was "as poor as a poet can be."[80] During the Second World War, the FBI inquired into his German-Japanese background, despite the fact that he had come to the United States in 1882 and been a citizen since 1894. The harassment never ceased, as reports filtered in to the authorities that Sadakichi was making periodic climbs to the top of Mount Jacinto to signal Japanese planes with a lantern.[81] Under these scarcely favorable conditions, Sadakichi began to work on his autobiography. He died in November 1944 in St. Petersburg, Florida, where he had gone to consult family records at the home of his eldest daughter.

Sadder yet was the fate of Hippolyte Havel, Hartmann's old drinking companion. After several months as cook at Mohegan, Havel had come to Stelton in 1924 to edit *The Road to Freedom*. Moving into the Kropotkin Library, next door to the schoolhouse, he lived there the rest of his life, "rereading some books and periodicals and sardonically laughing at the repetition of historical events." "The situation is pretty bad," he wrote in 1927, "and, I am afraid, is getting worse. Reaction everywhere and the apathy of the workers prevents any worthwhile action. Still, we oldtimers have to 'carry on.' "[82]

In February 1929 a dinner was held in New York to celebrate Havel's sixtieth birthday. One of the few surviving "knights of idealism," as a Stelton neighbor described him, he remained a colorful bohemian character, with his beard and beret and walking stick, a sponger and drinker to the end, relying on handouts from old comrades. "It is hell to think that after a life of struggle a man like Hippolyte must depend upon the few measly crumbs that are thrown at him now and then," wrote Jacques Rudome in 1930. But such was Havel's lot. At one point he was so broke that he did not have a stamp with which to mail a letter. "Couldn't you try to collect a few grands for me," he asked Rudome. "The charity league of this dump is split in about 100 cliques and all try to save the starving miners and send toys to children in Sovetia. No chance for poor me."[83]

As the years passed, Havel grew increasingly irascible, abusing friends in public, either drunk or sober. His hatred of Bolshevism never abated. "A Delegation of Stalinists came here and invited me to join their united front," he wrote Rudome in 1935. "You can imagine what answer I gave them. Mine old ex-comrade Mike Gold was their spokesman. What a joke life is." In large part because of his drinking, Havel's health was in rapid decline. "I am going to the clinic today to have my kidneys examined," he told Rudome in 1934. "Can't even make a stew out of them." Nevertheless, he continued to make periodic trips to Greenwich Village, returning drunk and broke, and someone in the colony had to pay the bus driver his fare.[84]

In 1934 Havel made his last lecture tour around the country, stopping at the University of Michigan in Ann Arbor to deposit material with the Labadie Collection. "I have him registered—his big hat and cane and all!" wrote Agnes Inglis, the curator, to Joseph Ishill. A few years later Havel began to work on his memoirs but made little headway, owing to illness and "great mental stress."[85] The bottle remained his only comfort. Once, while drinking heavily, he took a gift of money from the International Group in Detroit and one by one tossed the bills on the road, shouting "Capitalism! Avarice! Fraud! Deception!" as a friend followed behind gathering them up. In a drunken stupor, moreover, he fell off a platform near the school and broke his leg. In his last years, according to Anna Schwartz, he was "very ill and often bitter, for he was practically forgotten by his friends."[86] He ended his days raving mad in the Marlboro Psychiatric Hospital of New Jersey, where he died in 1950.

One by one the old guard was dying and, as Alexander Berkman had noted the year before his own death, "there are almost none of the younger generation to take its place, or at least to do the work that must be done if the world is ever to see a better day."[87] Hans Koch died in Los Angeles in 1948. Anna Riedel, who had gone to teach crafts at Antioch Preparatory School in Ohio, lost her sight toward the end and became known as "the blind weaver." Mary Hansen died at her Stelton home in 1952. Bill Pogrebysky went to Russia in the 1930s and was killed at the front during World War II. His wife, Rose Frumkin, a former Stelton pupil, died in Moscow in 1972.[88]

We have still to account for Leonard Abbott, Harry Kelly, and Joseph Cohen, the central figures of the movement. Before doing so, however, the destinies of Pryns Hopkins and Jack Isaacson are worth recording. Hopkins, after running his school in France for a half-dozen years, worked at the Psychological Laboratory of London University before returning to the United States to teach at Clairmont College in California. He had once been a great enthusiast for libertarian education, wrote Leonard Abbott to Anna Schwartz, "but time seems to have tamed him, as it has tamed all of us."[89] His interest in political prisoners, however, remained undiminished, and he served on the advisory board of Amnesty International until 1972, when he died in Santa Barbara, where he had launched his Boy Land experiment sixty years before.

Of all the characters in our story, Jack Isaacson of the Ferrer Center met the most tragic end. Ordered deported to Russia during the Red Scare, he went underground for the rest of his days, using the surname of his companion, Gussie Denenberg. After spending some years in Chicago, they moved to Washington,

D.C., where Jack opened a little grocery store with a pot-belly stove by which he would read when not waiting on customers. At the end of the Second World War, Gussie applied for her citizenship papers. The FBI, conducting a routine check, discovered her husband's identity. "They hounded him, you know," Maurice Hollod recalls. "He was a very gentle, sensitive human being. I knew of no man who gave of himself as much as Jack. They don't make them that way any more. Finally, he said, 'If you want to deport me, then deport me.' 'Oh, no, Mr. Denenberg, we don't want to deport you,' they replied. Yet they kept on hounding him, questioning him every other week, until he broke down. One evening in April 1946 I saw him at someone's house and he looked unusually cheerful, as if some heavy weight had been lifted from his shoulders. He was smiling, talking animatedly. But from time to time he would rub his neck with his fingers. That bothered me, so when I was ready to leave I went up to him and said, 'It's good to see you in such good spirits, Jack, but why do you keep rubbing your throat?' At that his eyes opened wide. He reared back, then he fled from the house. He hanged himself in his grocery the following morning."[90]

ABBOTT, KELLY, AND COHEN

After the closing of the Ferrer Center in 1918, Leonard Abbott's life had little happiness. He became a lonely man, dogged by misfortune. In 1920 his wife Rose contracted multiple sclerosis, which left her incurably paralyzed. Abbott devoted all his free time to her needs. He sat with her, read to her, got friends to come to visit her. His own life became increasingly secluded. He withdrew from all radical activities. After the excitement of his youth, life seemed dull and dispiriting. "Those old days, with all their intensity, their enthusiasms, seem very far away today," he lamented. "What an anti-climax life becomes for so many of us!"[91]

Since 1905 Abbott had been an associate editor of *Current Literature* and its successor *Current Opinion*. In 1925, however, *Current Opinion* merged with *Literary Digest*, and Abbott found himself out of a job. He was forced to sell his cottage at Westfield, New Jersey, where so many Modern School gatherings had been held. Literary odd jobs, on which he now had to rely for a living, brought him "indifferent success." He fell prey to fits of depression. "I have never been so melancholy," he confided to Emma Goldman. "I knew that life was bad, but I didn't know it was as bad as *this*! Yet I feel ashamed to put on paper even so much. Self-pity is the weakest and least attractive of moods, and, in a sense, it can be trodden under foot. If only I had faith in *something*, I might pick myself up even yet. But what is there? I have never, in twenty-five years, known the radical movement here so weak and anemic as it is now."[92]

With the prosecution of Sacco and Vanzetti, however, Abbott's radicalism gained a new lease on life, and he engaged in a brief but vigorous period of activity, throwing all his energies into their defense. His son recalls his "concern over their fate and his hopes for a last-minute reprieve down to the hour of their execution."[93] Apart from his writings and speeches on their behalf, Abbott went to Massachusetts and visited the condemned men in prison. A month before the execution, he and Dr. Cohn took part in the last demonstrations "and watched, together, the unfolding of this terrific drama." "I am actually dizzy with reading and thinking about the case," he wrote on the eve of their death. "I am alternately shocked, depressed, inspired. I have never been through anything like it, psychologically." To Alexander Berkman he pronounced it "the most heinous crime that America has committed since the Chicago affair."[94]

The Sacco-Vanzetti case was Abbott's last active period in the radical movement. After 1927 he sank back into his former despondency. "I am in a very depressed mood, and keep out of everything," he wrote to Berkman, "but perhaps some day the tide will turn and I will recover some of my old zest for life."[95] The tide, however, did not turn. "I am obsessed by a sense of futility of all that I have done or have tried to do," he wrote to Joseph Cohen. "I feel as if I have been chasing phantoms for thirty-five years. Hippolyte Havel says that the Anarchist movement is weaker now than it was thirty years ago but that he is not discouraged. I say the same thing, and I add that I *am* discouraged."[96]

After ten years of suffering, Rose Abbott died on December 21, 1930. She had endured her illness with a fortitude that never deserted her, sustained by the memories of happier days. As Harry Kelly noted, "she was able to look upon a youth when she was strong and took an active part in the life that swirled around the Ferrer Center."[97] Her death, to be sure, lifted some of the weight from Abbott's shoulders. Yet Emma Goldman's belief that had he not been so handicapped by Rose's illness he would have become "a much greater force, both in the movement and in the literary sense" was mistaken, as Abbott himself was aware. He remained, by his own admission, a "troubled spirit." "I am not so sure that the terrible experience through which I passed with Rose has made me the skeptic and Hamlet that I am," he wrote to Emma. "I was a skeptic and Hamlet before I ever set eyes on Rose; but I admit that what I went through with her accentuated my pessimism. She became the perfect symbol of my disillusionment."[98]

What he needed, he told Emma, was a cause to believe in and a woman to love. "I have, so to speak, the skeleton of each, the possibility of each, without having the reality of either." Regarding the first, anarchism had become a fading dream; as for the second, his blossoming friendship with Anna Strunsky Walling, though it gave him more than a little comfort, remained platonic. He never remarried, nor were there further women in his life. As for his writing, he could not lift himself out of his Oblomov-like lethargy. He contemplated a study of Whitman and a book about the anarchists, their lives and teachings. But nothing came of either of these projects.

In 1929, on the other hand, he had managed to secure a regular position, becoming an editor of the *Encyclopedia of Social Sciences*. The task occupied him until 1934, when the enterprise was completed. Then once again he was out of work. It was not long, however, before a new opportunity presented itself. In 1935 the director of the Federal Writers' Project, Henry G. Alsberg, offered him the post of research editor of a multivolume American National Guide, "a kind of glorified Baedeker," as Abbott describes it.[99] Alsberg, who as a newspaper correspondent in Russia had been friendly with Alexander Berkman and Emma Goldman and had attended Kropotkin's funeral, invited a number of anarchists to join his staff, and Abbott, with his extensive editorial experience, was among them.

Abbott gratefully accepted, and from 1935 to 1939 he worked at the Federal Writers' Project headquarters in Washington. "It has been a fruitful and vivid experience," he wrote to Anna Strunsky Walling after two years on the job. "I am curiously alone, but my solitude is something that I myself have willed. I have withdrawn from people rather than people have withdrawn from me."[100] With his stiff and serious demeanor, Abbott had never been easy to know on more than a casual basis, not even during his earlier years. But now his isolation was complete. As a member of the staff later wrote, he "loomed like a specter as he sat, year after year, in a corner of the Washington office searching for errors in the material sent in from the states. His ghostly quietness, which matched the pallid texture of his skin, seemed to embarrass his younger colleagues, and they hardly ever spoke to him."[101]

Abbott's assignment with the Federal Writers' Project was completed in 1939. After four years in Washington, he was back in New York and again out of a job. Casting about for a position, he wrote to the president of the New School, Alvin Johnson, about the possibility of a lectureship, but without result. Though his family annuity provided a small income, such were his financial straits that he was reduced to applying for a loan from the League for Mutual Aid, of which, founded by Harry Kelly and Roger Baldwin in 1920, he himself was a charter member. The loan, though granted, totaled only one hundred dollars spread out over ten months, so that true relief did not come until 1942, when his old Stelton friend Henry Schnittkind invited him to help with the "Masterworks" series that he was editing for Doubleday.[102]

By 1951, however, when the Doubleday project was completed, Abbott was once more in financial difficulties. He was forced to dip into the capital of the trust fund from which he derived his only income. However frugally he lived in his small Greenwich Village apartment, he could barely make ends meet. "Poor Leonard," wrote Harry Kelly to Joseph Cohen, "his life has not been too happy."[103] The last bright moment, perhaps, had occurred back in 1940, when a banquet was held in his honor at Town Hall, attended by all his old Modern School comrades. Abbott, for all his melancholy and isolation, looked back with pride upon his role in the Ferrer movement. "I regard the founding of the Ferrer School as the most important accomplishment of my life," he told Anna Schwartz in 1949, "and I am far from indifferent to the persistence and idealism which has kept the school going all these years. 'Long live the Modern School!' "[104]

At the same time, paradoxically, he remained ambivalent toward libertarian education. "I think that I understand what libertarian education means, and I am not sure that I accept it entirely," he confided to Haldeman-Julius. "If libertarian education means that a child is wiser than its elders, I certainly do *not* accept that! If libertarian education means that a child should be encouraged to develop along the lines of its own authentic character, I certainly *do* accept that. But surely a child needs *control and guidance* as well as self-expression."[105] It is significant, in this connection, that Abbott did not send his own children to the Modern School. "I never went to the Stelton school," his son remarked, "which I suppose is a measure of my father's mixed feelings about the enterprise."[106] Nor, it might be added, did Abbott himself live at either Stelton or Mohegan, though he was a frequent visitor to both colonies.

Old age found Abbott in an increasingly reflective mood. "It has taken me sixty years to realize that social and religious radicalism is a *luxury*," he mused. "My definition of happiness: To feel that one is on the *ascending curve*. To feel that strength—especially psychic strength—is increasing, not decreasing. To feel that one has the strength to do what one wants to do. All this may have something—a great deal!—to do with what people call mysticism. Only, in my case, I do not associate it consciously with 'Godism,' prayer, or anything like that. It seems to come, unsummoned, from the unconscious. All that is necessary is to be in a receptive mood. This is Emerson's doctrine, isn't it? The weather of the soul."[107]

Yet he never completely discarded his former ideals. "I have *not* abandoned my radicalism," he wrote to an old associate on *Current Opinion*. "But I am an extremely disillusioned radical!" In 1947 he described his political evolution as changing from a socialist to "a socialist in sympathy with anarchism. I should now call myself a libertarian socialist. In military affairs I am a pacifist, in religion, a freethinker." Abbott remained a pacifist even during World War II, though he detested Hitler and considered anti-Semitism "one of the most disgusting things in the world." For him socialism had regained its former priority; he had never been as deeply committed to anarchism as Harry Kelly or Joseph Cohen. "I see things as they are," he wrote to Anna Strunsky Walling, "and cannot live as exclusively as they do in faith and fantasy."[108]

In 1952 Abbott found that he was suffering from cancer. Like Alexander Berkman, he thought of ending his own life. An elder brother had taken this course many years before. But he saw it through to the end, dying on March 19, 1953, in his seventy-fifth year. His body was cremated and the ashes scattered over Hemlock Grove, a wooded area in the Bronx where he had liked to stroll in happier times. Eulogies were delivered by Konrad Bercovici, Manuel Komroff, and Anna Strunsky Walling. But his epitaph had already been written by Will Durant in a letter of 1940 to Komroff: "He has never said a word because it might make him popular or successful; and thru a thousand adventures with ideas he has maintained, without obstinacy, fanaticism, or intolerance, the philosophy that won him in his youth. He has made the most vital sacrifices to be true to his beliefs and his friends."[109]

While it cannot be said that Harry Kelly escaped the wave of disillusionment which engulfed so many anarchists of his generation, compared to Leonard Abbott he was a model of steadfastness and cheer. "I know of no one who has pursued his goal with greater singleness of purpose than Harry Kelly," wrote Theodore Schroeder in 1939, "no one who in the midst of insurmountable difficulties, has always maintained his poise and sense of humor."[110] Always friendly and smiling, Kelly gave the appearance of undiminished optimism. Yet he too was having doubts. "Anarchism as we saw it and still see it in our mind's eye is a long way off," he had written to Max Nettlau as early as 1919, "that is a society based on voluntary agreement. I advocate it because it must one day prevail and it must be advocated, but it will not be in my time or in your time. I have lived and worked with the workers in unions and voluntary organizations for thirty years now and I feel that they are far too underdeveloped socially to work together along pure Anarchist lines. . . . As I say, the idea must be preached and lived as far as we can live it, but I cannot pretend to myself it is close at hand."[111]

By the mid-1920s Kelly's opinion on this score had not changed. "Authorities under new forms with other names have taken the place of the old ones, and it will require the intellect and audacity of a Bakunin to destroy this many headed monster," he wrote to Nettlau. "I have had considerable experience with the working class in my life, and while I hope I am tolerant or even charitable I certainly do not expect our ideas will be ushered in by them." On the contrary, "the mass of men are indifferent to anything."[112] In a letter to Alexander Berkman, Kelly supported this contention by pointing to the forthcoming Scopes trial in Tennessee. Correctly predicting its outcome, he wrote: "It will surely be a scream, for the trial will probably be held in a baseball park and have many elements of a circus, in which case Bryan will win in so far as having the man convicted. I would hate to have my life or liberty at stake with a southern mob listening to Bryan roaring and raving. Who in hell said there was progress?"[113]

Yet his faltering faith in the masses did not keep Kelly from applying his energies on their behalf. In 1920, with Roger Baldwin and Elizabeth Gurley Flynn, he was instrumental in creating the League for Mutual Aid, which provided interest-free loans to individuals affiliated with labor and libertarian causes. The name of the organization was inspired by Kropotkin's famous book, *Mutual Aid*, which Kelly and the others considered a kind of bible. During the 1940s, looking back over fifty years of radical activity, Kelly regarded the League for Mutual Aid and the Stelton Colony as the two most worthwhile endeavors with which he had been associated.[114]

In 1921, the year after the establishment of the League for Mutual Aid, Kelly traveled to Berlin as a delegate to a worldwide anarcho-syndicalist conference which laid the groundwork for the Berlin International. The driving force behind the conference was Rudolf Rocker, Kelly's old comrade in London, and the two had a warm reunion. From Berlin Kelly went to Stockholm to see Alexander Berkman and Emma Goldman, who had just left Soviet Russia. He then went to Vienna to see Max Nettlau, like Rocker a comrade from his London years. The remainder of his itinerary included Rome, Paris, and London, where he spoke at the Jubilee Street Club in Whitechapel. He also visited the Whiteway Colony in the Cotswolds, where Mary Krimont's sister Rachelle was still living. Returning to New York, Kelly found Mary herself gravely ill. She died on May 2, 1922, within days of his arrival.

In 1925 Kelly took a second wife, Leah Lowensohn, who had taught at the Modern Sunday School on 107th Street and whose sister Minna had been one of the Ferrer Association's most dedicated workers. Together with Leah, he embarked on his second journey to Europe that year, again visiting comrades and friends. He made two further trips, in 1927 and 1931, when he saw Alexander Berkman and Errico Malatesta for the last time. Malatesta, in his late seventies, had been living in Rome under house arrest, a prisoner of the Mussolini dictatorship. Kelly found "his mind as keen as ever, even though his body was bent and his heart full of sorrow at the conditions surrounding him."[115]

By now, having entered his seventh decade, Kelly himself had become a kind of elder statesman of the anarchist movement, receiving letters from young idealists all over the world, among them a group in China who wanted to open a Modern School.[116] In 1933 and 1934 he edited an anarchist journal called *Freedom*, together with Moritz Jagendorf and Louis Raymond, who still lives at Stelton, one of the few remaining residents of the community. Kelly, however, had lost his faith in revolution as a means of renovating society. "I am forever telling our comrades that I am much less concerned with talking about revolution than I am about what kind of society we want and should want to build," he wrote Nettlau in 1933. "Science and technological development are bringing the downfall of capitalism, and it is for us to prepare men's minds for a new society based upon freedom."[117]

Like Abbott, Kelly took to using the label "libertarian socialist" as a substitute for "anarchist," drawing the fire of militants like Hippolyte Havel who upheld "anarchist" as a "badge of honor." Like Abbott, too, Kelly almost went to work for the government during this period. In need of a job, he was interviewed by Harry Hopkins for a post with the Tennessee Valley Authority. When he listed his politics as "anarchist," Hopkins suggested that this might offend the President. But Kelly refused to adopt a euphemism, not even "libertarian socialist." "I've been an anarchist all my life," he said.[118]

In 1939, once again like Abbott, Kelly was honored with a testimonial dinner at the Hotel Brevoort, attended by Abbott, Durant, Komroff, and many other old friends. By now Kelly's mood alternated between hope and despair. In spite of all the setbacks, his passion for starting colonies had not abated. With so many of his aging comrades going south, he began to organize a settlement in central Florida and got as far as making a down payment on a tract of land before the deal fell through. His chief hopes now lay in education. But with "the press, radio, church and all forces against us," he remarked to Nettlau, prospects were not encouraging. "Preaching freedom and tolerance, comradeship etc. All very good my dear Nettlau but when one newspaper can spread a lie to 500,000 readers how can we catch up with them?" At times, he said, it seemed that the anarchists were "just another religious sect preaching ethics in an unethical world. The love of liberty has existed so many centuries perhaps it will continue in another form, but just now the world is mad and authority is the dominant idea. . . . A sense of humor is the only thing that keeps me out of the lunatic asylum."[119]

With the coming of the Second World War, despair gained the upper hand. "I never expected to see such wanton cruelty and disregard of human rights as we have now all over the world and feeling unable to do anything about it," he confessed. Fifty years before, Spencer had spoken of "The Coming Slavery." Now, said Kelly, it was "actually here and spreading like some fungus growth until it threatens to engulf all mankind." History, he concluded, had shown that "when the lion and the lamb lie down together it has usually been with the lamb inside the lion."[120]

How would it all end? The odds, felt Kelly, seemed "in favor of a complete breakdown of even this poor civilization and a return to methods of the cave men." In the meantime, he wrote to Jacques Rudome, "we should see each other as often as we can and in that association insist that not all men are beasts or crooked swine." Beyond that, he declared, the forces of darkness must be opposed with every available means. "Pacifism," he told Abbott, "is a luxury that only people who believe in a hereafter can afford to indulge in. My anarchism has always been based upon self-defense, and as I see it to preach pacifism is to make success easier and more assured a Nazi victory."[121]

To add to his despair, Kelly's most cherished friends were passing away. One by one he saw them into the grave. The first had been George Seldes back in 1931. In 1933 came the turn of Dr. C. L. Andrews, "one of our oldest and best loved comrades." In the succeeding years, Kelly mourned the deaths of many others, including Alexander Berkman, Emma Goldman, and Lola Ridge. "The news of Emma's passing has upset me," he wrote to Abbott in 1940, "and coming in the midst of the slaughter in Europe—and the outlook—has made me very sad." When Lola Ridge died the following year, he sent condolences to her companion: "Poor Lola, she deserved far greater recognition than she received, but we still starve poets, don't we? Lola's passing reminds me that the dreams we had and hopes cherished thirty years ago were beautiful things while they lasted, but honestly I cannot say they were more than hopes and dreams." Three months later, he read of James Morton's death in *The New York Times*: "So many old friends are dying or being killed I begin to feel lonely."[122]

Kelly himself still had a dozen more years to live. He spent the time quietly, in New Rochelle, where his wife was a school librarian. When friends came to visit he liked to take them to the Thomas Paine memorial house erected by William van der Weyde, the first secretary of the Ferrer Association, for it "always reminds me of the libertarian movement," he wrote to Abbott. With Abbott and Komroff, meanwhile, Kelly organized a monthly dining club called The Skeptics, attended by Moritz Jagendorf, Carlo Tresca, Robert Allerton Parker, and other old associates. His main task, however, was to work on his autobiography, which he had begun but put aside in the 1920s. "I am getting melancholy thinking and writing about these friends of long ago," he said in 1948. But the manuscript was soon completed and, though it remains unpublished, it constitutes a valuable source for the history of anarchism and the Modern School.[123]

In January 1951 Kelly celebrated his eightieth birthday. "Yes, I am now an octogenarian," he remarked, "four score and still around if a little battered and buffeted in the struggle for human freedom." By now, however, he was totally blind, reduced to "reading" books on records and unable to pursue his favorite pastime of watching baseball on television.[124] Kelly died on May 27, 1953, two months after Abbott. He was buried in Chicago's Waldheim Cemetery near Emma Goldman and Voltairine de Cleyre. His epitaph reads: "He shared his life with humanity."[125]

The last of the trio, Joseph Cohen, died the same year as his comrades. Cohen, it will be recalled, had left Stelton in 1925, after the departure of the Ferms, and organized Camp Germinal in Pennsylvania with his former colleagues of the Radical Library. Since 1923, moreover, he had been serving as editor of the *Fraye Arbeter Shtime*, the leading Jewish anarchist newspaper, a post in which he continued until 1932. He also founded a second summer camp on Lake Mohegan, called Camp Sharon, which he operated until he resigned from the *Fraye Arbeter Shtime* to found the Sunrise Co-operative Farm Community in Michigan.

Like Harry Kelly, Cohen could not shed his dream of establishing a true libertarian community based on voluntary cooperation and mutual aid. Perhaps, in such a community, he saw a way back to the lost idealized age of his childhood, when the world seemed a happier place. Be that as it may, in 1933 the Sunrise Colony began a stormy existence which ended seven years later amid bitterness and recrimination. This is not the place for a detailed history of the community, which has little connection with the Ferrer movement, although some of its members had been at Stelton and Mohegan.[126] Suffice it to say that Cohen, the principal leader of the enterprise, became the focus of controversy and abuse. In 1938 he finally left and returned to Stelton after an absence of thirteen years. By this time, a friend recalls, Cohen looked like "an old bird of prey, hawk nose, hunched shoulders, glasses, owlish look. You could almost feel the wings." To gain a livelihood, he and his wife Sophie raised chickens until her death in 1944.[127]

For the previous two decades, Cohen, like Abbott and Kelly, had been evolving a more moderate and pragmatic philosophy than the one he had professed in his youth. "I feel at times that our attitude towards the State ought to be revised," he told Max Nettlau in 1923. "In the first place there are certain forms of management and regulation absolutely necessary and beneficial in present day society which will undoubtedly remain even in the freest of future societies. Ignoring local government, questions of education, sanitation, and even protection against abuse did not do our movement any good. Then comes the fundamental question of Revolutionary periods. The outstanding fact of the Russian Revolution is that our comrades—the best of them—did not know what to do or suggest to the masses."[128]

It was not that Cohen had abandoned his ultimate ideal. Yet anarchists, he had come to believe, were obliged to modify their views in the light of experience. Old concepts and vocabularies were out-of-date. "The perpetual talk about struggle; the great emphasis on conflict and cataclysm; the bitter antagonism between the socialists of the various schools—Anarchism included—where do all these things lead us to? If we, the very small advanced minority, treat each other like beasts and educate our followers to do the same—what can we expect of the bulk of humanity that will not reach our mental attitude in another hundred years?"[129]

Cohen, accordingly, called for cooperation with other socialists so as to "realize part of our aims at least—more freedom for the individual and less power for the state." "I have lived and worked in the movement long enough," he wrote in 1929, "to realize that no single idea, movement or group of people will ever carry the day, socially speaking, to such an extent as to have its whole program adopted by the whole of the human race. The differences of opinion are too great, the struggle too strenuous to hope for a miracle [that] everybody could begin to think alike and act like a decent human being. We are very far from it. All we can do is to popularize our ideas, spread them as far as we can and at the same time deepen our understanding and conviction to the best of our ability."[130]

Returning to this theme in the 1930s, Cohen advised his anarchist comrades in Spain to join in a coalition against fascism. "Work hand in hand with the liberal parties," he wrote the Iberian Anarchist Federation in Barcelona, "with the Republicans, the Democrats and with the Social Democrats who are not too fanatical about the State. See to it that the government should not take to itself too much power, should not interfere with the liberties of the people, and trust to the people to find their way, in time, to greater Freedom and the utter abolishment of Government. This may sound as a repudiation of our Anarchist principles and a bad compromise with those who believe in the State; in my humble opinion it is nothing of the kind. It is merely a practical step, bringing us nearer towards the full realization of our principles, and the step is fully in line with our fundamental ideals. We cannot hope to convert the whole population in a short while, and we surely cannot dare to force our opinions on others."[131]

A year or two after the death of his wife, Cohen remarried and embarked with his new companion on a series of travels which took them to Mexico and to the west coast, where they spent the summer of 1948 at Home Colony. A year later they moved to Paris, where Cohen edited a Yiddish anarchist paper called *Fraye Gedank* (Free Thought). He also set to work on his memoirs. But his weeks and months were so filled with activity that he never had time to complete more than the small volume, *A House Stood Forlorn*, dealing with his early years in Russia. During this period, Cohen visited Israel and traveled widely in Europe, including a trip to Czechoslovakia. George Woodcock, the Canadian writer, encountered him in Paris in 1951, "frail, worn by his hard and energetic life, but extraordinarily alert and full of interest in the world around him."[132]

Shortly after this, Cohen returned to the United States and settled in New York. In 1952 he visited Harry Kelly at New Rochelle. He had not seen his friend for several years, and they spent a pleasant afternoon talking over old times. "We have traveled a long way side by side," Cohen wrote to Kelly a bit later, "nearly forty years now as far as I can recollect, and while we did not see eye to eye [on] some of the serious occurrences which happened in our time, it did not affect our relation and the high esteem we felt for each other. Our attachment was, and remains pure, unselfish and unpretentious. I feel a great satisfaction at the thought of having had the privilege of counting you among the few intimate friends it was my good fortune to meet in this world."[133]

Seven months later, Kelly was dead, having survived Leonard Abbott by only two months. Cohen himself died four months after Kelly, on September 28, 1953. The same year saw the closing of the Stelton Modern School, which all three had deemed their greatest achievement.

CHAPTER 11

Conclusion

THE MODERN SCHOOL ASSOCIATION of North America was disbanded between 1955 and 1961. This occurred on the eve of a remarkable resurgence of interest in anarchist thought and activity. The social ferment of the 1960s, which accompanied the civil rights movement and the Vietnam War, saw a revival of radical experimentation on a wide scale. The ideas of libertarian education emerged again with renewed vitality. Shortly after the publication in 1960 of a compendium of A. S. Neill's writings, *Summerhill: A Radical Approach to Child-Rearing*, a tide of enthusiasm for the Summerhill idea swelled across the country. In New York City a Summerhill Society was organized by Neill's American publisher, Harold Hart, together with such collaborators as Paul Goodman and James Dick, Jr., the son of Jim and Nellie, now a Long Island pediatrician. Moreover, *Summerhill* was followed by a whole series of books on similar lines, by Goodman himself and many others.

In the mid-1960s this educational movement gathered momentum with the appearance of "free schools" of every type. Many of these schools, usually without being aware of it, harked back to the libertarian experiments of the past, not least to those of the Ferrer movement. Like the Modern Schools, they featured active methods of learning, pupil participation in decisions, informal relations between pupils and teachers, and the cultivation of manual skills. They sought to reshape the curriculum so as to encourage creative development, individual study, independent habits of mind, and self-reliance. They rejected the authoritarianism of the conventional classroom, the preoccupation with order and discipline, the invidious competition for marks and prizes, the pressures for standardization and conformity. Their central concern was with the self-realization of the child, the development of all his abilities and talents, in an atmosphere of spontaneity and freedom.

In the majority of cases, these ventures were undertaken with little or no consciousness of the libertarian tradition that preceded them. Yet a few direct links can be established with the Modern Schools. The younger James Dick, it has been noted, was a founder of the Summerhill Society. And Paul Goodman, an active anarchist since the 1940s, was acquainted with the Stelton experiment, at least in its general outlines. Furthermore, several Stelton teachers and pupils went on to join the staffs of private and public schools, bringing their libertarian preconceptions with them. And a number of Stelton alumni themselves established libertarian schools in different parts of the country, such as the Walden School in Berkeley, California, and the Open Door School in Charlottesville, North Carolina.

Indirect influences are more difficult to determine. Back in the 1930s members of the Modern School Association were already beginning to speculate about the impact of their enterprise upon the rest of the educational world. "How much influence it has had on the radical and progressive movements in education we have no exact means of knowing," declared a Modern School circular in 1934, "but we do know that many of the ideas first advocated and practiced by us are now urged and practiced by educators everywhere."[1] The same might also be said of the 1960s and '70s. Through its former teachers and pupils, through its books, brochures, and journals, above all through the record of its educational ventures, the Ferrer movement continued to make an impression in advanced pedagogical circles.

To preserve the legacy of the movement as well as to perpetuate its ideas, a group of former teachers and pupils met in 1973 and established the Friends of the Modern School. In September of that year, the new organization held its first annual conference at Rutgers University, a stone's throw from the defunct Stelton Colony. Since that time, Rutgers has become the repository of the Ferrer movement archives, and hundreds of pupils and teachers, colonists and friends have attended the Friends of the Modern School reunions, among them Nellie Dick and her son and the children and grandchildren of Leonard Abbott, Harry Kelly, and Joseph Cohen. From all over the country the alumni of the New York and Philadelphia Modern Schools, of Stelton, Stony Ford, Mohegan, and Lakewood, have gathered each year to deposit photographs, letters, notebooks, and art work in the Rutgers collection and to take part in lectures and symposia on the different phases of their movement.

"No matter how our paths may have diverged," said Jo Ann Wheeler at the 1975 meeting, "no matter how some of us may have learned outward conformity, one thing emerges from the three reunions we have had so far. Once one has been touched by the Modern School experience, one is never the same again. Inwardly, at least, we have been marked for life."[2] To what extent is this true? In what ways are the Ferrer graduates different from those of ordinary schools? Have they shown a greater capacity for self-reliance in adult life? Do they make better parents or neighbors? Are they more decent and humane, more compassionate toward their fellow men and women? Do they lead richer or happier lives? If so, to what extent is this due to the type of education they received?

Such questions are exceedingly difficult to answer. Yet certain observations may be hazarded, however tentative or impressionistic. It would appear that few of the students became "famous" or "important" or made an unusual mark in the world of business, science, or the arts, though the proportion of those who did is perhaps greater than that for conventional schools. By material standards, they were not much more successful than the population as a whole. For most of them, however, fame and wealth were beside the point. " 'Success,' " one alumna declared, "is not what it's supposed to be all about, but rather what kind of people we are and what we can contribute to society whether we are doctors, teachers, parents, ditch diggers, house painters or picture painters, and that the measure of a person's worth is what that person is, not what degrees he or she has earned."[3]

What then of their personal qualities? Back in 1940, John and Kate Edelman noted that graduates of the Modern School seemed "more interesting than the average run of their contemporaries," that they had kept "a certain freshness of outlook, a measure of self-confidence, a degree of versatility" which distinguished them from the products of traditional education.[4] On the whole, judging from my own encounters with Modern School alumni, this seems a valid observation. What is more, the great majority appear to have carried away a strong cooperative and libertarian ethic, a spirit of mutual aid and individual sovereignty, which has remained with them throughout their adult years, regardless of their politics or occupations.

To say this, however, is not to ignore the deficiencies of libertarian education, at least as it was practiced in the Modern Schools. According to its own theorists, from Godwin to Ferrer, children vary widely in their capacities and needs. It follows that no single method of education will be ideal for all pupils. For some, self-direction, freedom of choice, a minimum of supervision and guidance constitute the best approach. Others, however, will thrive best with greater direction and structure.

According to Ferrer and his precursors, moreover, all aspects of the child's development should be encouraged, intellectual as well as physical and moral. Yet the hostility exhibited toward academic learning, above all by the Ferms, did violence to this principle. Was not forbidding the children to read at all just as dogmatic and arbitrary as compelling them to read before they were ready? Should not a truly "integrated" education include books as well as games and crafts? Are they not, indeed, complementary rather than contradictory? Surely more attention to the basics would have benefited at least some of the Modern School children, if not all.

Notwithstanding these strictures, however, the achievements of the Ferrer Schools are impressive. It is true that their libertarian goals were not fully realized. Yet in terms of devotion to principle, of the development of an alternative method of education that repudiated dogma and repression, they were a notable success. "We make no claim to saving the world," wrote Harry Kelly in 1921. "We are but trying to save our own 'souls.' . . . If we have not reached the promised land, we have at least stumbled into one of its by-paths, and that is something."[5]

Notes

The locations of letters and other unpublished sources are given in the Bibliography under Archival Materials.

Preface

1. Leonard D. Abbott to Anna Strunsky Walling, February 27, 1938, Walling Papers.

Chapter 1

1. James Joll, *The Anarchists*, London, 1964, p. 233. See also Sol Ferrer, *La vie et l'oeuvre de Francisco Ferrer*, Paris, 1962.
2. *The Truth Seeker*, October 16, 1915.
3. Emma Goldman, *Anarchism and Other Essays*, New York, 1911, p. 148.
4. J. Martel, "Ferrer's Experimental School as a Symbol of Modern Progressive Educational Movement," Ph.D. dissertation, New York University, 1933, p. 51.
5. Jean Grave, *Enseignement bourgeois et enseignement libertaire*, Paris, 1900.
6. Goldman, *Anarchism and Other Essays*, p. 149.
7. *Liberty*, October 6, 1894.
8. Caleb Keenan, "A Libertarian School," *Freedom* (London), September 1897.
9. *Les Temps Nouveaux*, September 11-17, 1897, quoted in Stephen Leberstein, "Revolutionary Education: French Libertarian Theory and Experiments, 1895-1915," Ph.D. dissertation, University of Wisconsin, 1972, p. 165.
10. Yvonne Turin, *L'Education et l'école en Espagne de 1874 à 1902*, Paris, 1959, p. 317, quoted in Joll, *The Anarchists*, p. 234.
11. Joan Connelly Ullman, *The Tragic Week: A Study of Anticlericalism in Spain, 1875-1912*, Cambridge, Mass., 1968, p. 34.

12. *Ibid*., p. 95. See also Rudolf Rocker, "Precursors of Ferrer in Spain," in *Modern School of Stelton: Twenty-Fifth Anniversary, 1915-1940*, Stelton, N.J., 1940, pp. 5-6; and Clara E. Lida, "Educación anarquista en la España del ochocientos," *Revista de Occidente*, XCVII (1971), 33-47.

13. G. P. Maximoff, ed., *The Political Philosophy of Bakunin*, New York, 1953, p. 333.

14. Francisco Ferrer, *The Origin and Ideals of the Modern School*, London, 1913, p. 64; Emma Goldman, *Living My Life*, New York, 1931, p. 458.

15. Ferrer, *The Origin and Ideals of the Modern School*, p. 44.

16. William Godwin, *Enquiry Concerning Political Justice*, in *Patterns of Anarchy*, ed. by Leonard I. Krimerman and Lewis Perry, Garden City, N.Y., 1966, pp. 434-35.

17. Ferrer, *The Origin and Ideals of the Modern School*, pp. 52, 56. See also Joel Spring, *A Primer of Libertarian Education*, New York, 1975, pp. 22-23.

18. Ferrer, *The Origin and Ideals of the Modern School*, pp. 49-51.

19. Education, wrote Bakunin, must have "no other aim than that of freedom." Maximoff, ed., *The Political Philosophy of Bakunin*, pp. 332-33.

20. James L. Axtell, ed., *The Educational Writings of John Locke*, Cambridge, 1968, pp. 64-65.

21. *Patterns of Anarchy*, ed. Krimerman and Perry, p. 431.

22. George Woodcock, *Anarchism*, Cleveland, 1962, p. 90.

23. Friedrich Froebel, *The Education of Man*, New York, 1887, p. 13. It is interesting to note that the French anarchist Proudhon, while living in exile in Brussels, moved his home in order that his children might attend a kindergarten run on Froebelian principles.

24. David Zeldin, *The Educational Ideas of Charles Fourier (1772-1837)*, London, 1969, p. 38.

25. Max Stirner, *The False Principle of Our Education*, Colorado Springs, Colo., 1967, p. 23.

26. Peter Kropotkin, *Fields, Factories, and Workshops*, revised edn., London, 1913, p. 382.

27. Ernest J. Simmons, *Leo Tolstoy*, Boston, 1946, p. 195; *Tolstoy on Education*, Chicago, 1967, pp. 16-31; Henri Troyat, *Tolstoy*, New York, 1969, p. 274.

28. Stirner, *The False Principle of Our Education*, p. 11.

29. David Fleisher, *William Godwin: A Study in Liberalism*, London, 1951, p. 32.

30. Quoted in George B. Lockwood, *The New Harmony Movement, 1818-1848*, New York, 1905, p. 225.

31. *Tolstoy on Education*, pp. 231-37.

32. Stirner, *The False Principle of Our Education*, p. 7.

33. *Patterns of Anarchy*, ed. Krimerman and Perry, p. 425; Fleisher, *William Godwin*, p. 16.

34. *Patterns of Anarchy*, p. 412.

35. Simmons, *Leo Tolstoy*, p. 209.

36. Sam Dolgoff, ed., *Bakunin on Anarchy*, New York, 1972, pp. 373-74.

37. Lockwood, *The New Harmony Movement*, p. 225; Froebel, *The Education of Man*, p. 14.

38. Arthur E. Bestor, *Backwoods Utopias*, 2nd edn., Philadelphia, 1970, p. 136; Kropotkin, *Fields, Factories and Workshops*, p. 382.

39. Stewart Edwards, ed., *Selected Writings of Pierre-Joseph Proudhon*, Garden City, N.Y., 1969, pp. 80-87.

40. Karl Marx, *Capital*, Moscow, 1957, p. 483; M. Bakunin, *Oeuvres*, 6 vols., Paris, 1895-1913, V, 131-36.

41. Dolgoff, ed., *Bakunin on Anarchy*, p. 373.

42. Stewart Edwards, *The Paris Commune, 1871*, London, 1971, p. 275.

43. *Les Temps Nouveaux*, April 16-22, 1898.

44. *L'Ecole Renovée*, April 15, 1908; *Mother Earth*, August 1908.

45. Michael Bakunin, *God and the State*, New York, 1970, p. 32.

46. L. H. Berens, *The Digger Movement in the Days of the Commonwealth*, London, 1906, p. 275; Charles Fourier, *Design for Utopia*, New York, 1971, p. 73.

47. Bakunin, *Oeuvres*, V, 144-45.

48. Rudolf Rocker, *The London Years,* London, 1956, p. 198; *Freedom* (San Francisco), November 1910.

49. Ferrer, *The Origin and Ideals of the Modern School*, p. 87; William Archer, *The Life, Trial, and Death of Francisco Ferrer*, London, 1911, p. 60. For additional data on equipment, enrollment, and teaching methods, see Martel, "Ferrer's Experimental School," pp. 102-62.

50. Ferrer, *The Origin and Ideals of the Modern School*, pp. 43-44.

51. *Ibid*., pp. 50-51; *The Agitator*, October 15, 1911.

52. Ferrer, *The Origin and Ideals of the Modern School*, p. 55; Leonard D. Abbott, ed., *Francisco Ferrer: His Life, Work and Martyrdom*, New York, 1910, p. 78.

53. Ferrer, *The Origin and Ideals of the Modern School*, p. 53.

54. *Ibid*., pp. 71-72.

55. Dolgoff, ed., *Bakunin on Anarchy*, p. 334.

56. Leberstein, "Revolutionary Education," p. 129.

57. *Modern School of Stelton*, p. 4; Carolyn P. Boyd, "The Anarchists and Education in Spain, 1868-1909," *The Journal of Modern History*, XLVIII (December 1976), 171-72.

58. Ferrer, *The Origin and Ideals of the Modern School*, p. 62. A fable with an anarchist moral, *Nono*, translated from the French by Anselmo Lorenzo, compares a libertarian paradise called Autonomia with the capitalist system represented by a neighboring kingdom whose motto is "Money is superior to right."

59. Launched on October 30, 1901, the *Boletín* was distinguished by its artistic covers, a sample of which is beautifully reproduced in Domenico Tarizzo, ed., *L'Anarchia*, Milan, 1976, p. 229.

60. Ferrer, *The Origin and Ideals of the Modern School*, p. 52.

61. Quoted in Boyd, "The Anarchists and Education in Spain," p. 147.

62. Dolgoff, ed., *Bakunin on Anarchy*, pp. 94-95.

63. Ferrer, *The Origin and Ideals of the Modern School*, p. 65.

64. Goldman, *Anarchism and Other Essays*, p. 155.

65. Raymond Carr, *Spain: 1808-1939*, Oxford, 1966, p. 442; Joseph McCabe, introduction to Ferrer's *Origin and Ideals of the Modern School*, pp. xi, xiv; E. A. Vizetelly, *The Anarchists*, London, 1911, p. 274.

66. William C. Owen in *Why?* (Tacoma), March 1913.

67. Goldman, *Anarchism and Other Essays*, p. 160.

68. Quoted in Boyd, "The Anarchists and Education in Spain," p. 158.

69. Goldman, *Living My Life*, p. 458; Turin, *L'Education et l'école en Espagne*, p. 320; Carr, *Spain*, p. 468.

70. Jean Maitron, *Le Mouvement anarchiste en France*, 2 vols., Paris, 1975, I, 411-13; J. Romero Maura, "Terrorism in Barcelona and Its Impact on Spanish Politics, 1904-1909," *Past and Present*, No. 41 (December 1968), 144. See also "Facts About the Ferrer Case," *Freedom* (London), June 1907; and Charles Malato, "Mateo Morral," *Mother Earth*, October 1907. Whether Morral was Ferrer's rival for the love of Soledad Villafranca, as is sometimes asserted, has not been clearly established.

71. Quoted in Boyd, "The Anarchists and Education in Spain," p. 155, from *El Corazón de Jesús* of Bilbao.

72. Goldman, *Living My Life*, p. 458.

73. Maura, "Terrorism in Barcelona," p. 142.

74. On the eve of his execution in 1909, Ferrer was preparing illustrated Spanish editions of Reclus's *Man and the Earth* and Kropotkin's *Great French Revolution*, which did not appear in print.

75. *L'Ecole Renovée*, April 15, 1909. An English translation appeared in Emma Goldman's *Mother Earth*, July 1910.

76. *Freedom* (London), August 1908.

77. Emma Goldman, " 'La Ruche' (The Beehive)," *Mother Earth*, November 1907.

78. The fullest study in English is Ullman, *The Tragic Week*. See also J. Romero Maura, *"La rosa del fuego"—republicanos y anarquistas*, Barcelona, 1975.

79. Quoted in Gerald Brenan, *The Spanish Labyrinth*, Cambridge, 1943, p. 35.

80. Ferrer to Alfred Naquet, October 4, 1909, *Mother Earth*, November 1909.

81. Voltairine de Cleyre, *Selected Works*, New York, 1914, p. 298.

82. Goldman, *Anarchism and Other Essays*, p. 165.

83. Abbott, ed., *Francisco Ferrer*, p. 55; *The Agitator*, October 15, 1911.

84. Ferrer, *La vie et l'oeuvre de Francisco Ferrer*, p. 195. See also T. P. Park, "The European Reaction to the Execution of Francisco Ferrer," Ph.D. dissertation, University of Virginia, 1970; and Luis Simarro y Lacabra, *El proceso Ferrer y la opinión europea*, Madrid, 1910.

85. Leonard D. Abbott, "Monuments to Francisco Ferrer," *The Modern School*, February 1912; *The Road to Freedom*, November 1, 1926.

CHAPTER 2

1. Arthur Samuels in *Modern School of Stelton*, p. 29.

2. Goldman, *Living My Life*, p. 456.

3. Emma Goldman to Ben L. Reitman, October 13, 1909, Reitman Papers.

4. *The Firebrand* (Mount Juliet, Tenn.), October 30, 1909.

5. *Mother Earth*, June 1910; Abbott, ed., *Francisco Ferrer*.

6. Abbott, ed., *Francisco Ferrer*; de Cleyre, *Selected Works*, pp. 297-320.

7. Leonard D. Abbott to Albert Mordell, November 20, 1909, Mordell Papers.

8. The date of June 12, 1910, given by Harry Kelly in "A Short History of the Francisco Ferrer Association," *The Modern School*, Autumn 1913, and repeated in most subsequent accounts, is incorrect.

9. Leonard D. Abbott to Rudolf Grossmann, July 19, 1910, Ramus Archive.

10. "The Organization of the American Ferrer Association," in Abbott, ed., *Francisco Ferrer*; Francisco Ferrer Association leaflet, June 1910, Ramus Archive; Kelly, "A Short History of the Francisco Ferrer Association."

11. *Mother Earth*, June 1910.

12. Max Eastman, *Enjoyment of Living*, New York, 1948, p. 423.

13. Floyd Dell, *Women as World Builders*, Chicago, 1913, p. 60.

14. *Mother Earth*, March and June 1910, July 1911.

15. *Free Society*, September 24, 1899.

16. Interview with Roger N. Baldwin, New York City, January 29, 1974; Richard Drinnon, *Rebel in Paradise*, Chicago, 1961, p. 88. Twenty-five years later, Baldwin shared the platform with Emma Goldman and John Dewey when she lectured in New York in 1934.

17. Goldman, *Anarchism and Other Essays*, p. 35; Goldman, *Living My Life*, pp. 408-409.

18. *Mother Earth*, November 1910.

19. See Leon Harris, *Upton Sinclair*, New York, 1975, pp. 58, 253.

20. See Alden Freeman *et al.*, *The Fight for Free Speech*, East Orange, N.J., 1909.

21. Eastman, *Enjoyment of Living*, p. 467; Goldman, *Living My Life*, p. 484.

22. Hutchins Hapgood, *A Victorian in the Modern World*, New York, 1939, p. 279.

23. Konrad Bercovici, *It's the Gypsy in Me*, New York, 1941, pp. 68-69.

24. Goldman, *Living My Life*, p. 348. Hall succeeded Dr. Foote as treasurer of the Ferrer Association when the latter fell ill in 1911.

25. Kelly, "A Short History of the Francisco Ferrer Association"; *Modern School of Stelton*, p. 7.

26. Hapgood, *A Victorian in the Modern World*, pp. 277-78.

27. W. M. van der Weyde, "Thomas Paine: Anarchist," *Mother Earth*, July 1910.

28. *The Modern School*, Winter 1912-1913.

29. Joseph McCabe, *The Martyrdom of Ferrer*, London, 1909; Archer, *The Life, Trial, and Death of Francisco Ferrer*. McCabe was also the translator of *The Origin and Ideals of the Modern School*.

30. De Cleyre, *Selected Works*, pp. 297-320; *Mother Earth*, November 1910; *The Agitator*, November 15, 1910.

31. See their letter of September 20, 1910, in the Labadie Collection.

32. John R. Coryell, "Ferrer," *Mother Earth*, November 1911.

33. William Thurston Brown, *Prospectus of the Modern School Established at Salt Lake City*, Salt Lake City, 1910.

34. Lockwood, *The New Harmony Movement*, p. 225.

35. Mark Holloway, *Heavens on Earth*, 2nd edn., New York, 1966, p. 114; Lillian Symes and Travers Clement, *Rebel America*, New York, 1934, p. 18.

36. Bestor, *Backwoods Utopias*, p. 149; David Harris, *Socialist Origins in the United States*, Assen, 1966, p. 68; J.F.C. Harrison, *Quest for the New Moral World*, New York, 1969, p. 38.

37. Will S. Monroe, *History of the Pestalozzian Movement in the United States*, Syracuse, 1907, p. 12. At his agricultural school in Alicante, Spain, Maclure applied the formula of "physical labor . . . combined with moral and intellectual culture."

38. *Ibid*., pp. 85, 102.

39. *Ibid*., p. 89.

40. *Ibid*., pp. 87-88, 103.

41. William Bailie, *Josiah Warren: The First American Anarchist*, Boston, 1906, pp. 30-34.

42. James J. Martin, *Men Against the State*, revised edn., Colorado Springs, Colo., 1970, pp. 30-35.

43. Josiah Warren, *Modern Education*, Modern Times, Long Island, 1861; *The Peaceful Revolutionist*, April 5, 1833.

44. Morris Hillquit, *History of Socialism in the United States*, New York, 1910, p. 97; Lindsay Swift, *Brook Farm*, New York, 1900, p. 69. In 1847 the Brook Farm journal, *The Harbinger*, printed a series of articles on "Integral Education" by John S. Dwight.

45. John A. Collins *et al*., *The Social Pioneer*, Boston, 1844, p. 89. In

1856 another little-known American anarchist, James Arrington Clay, called in similar terms for an equal and integral education: "The whole man, physical, intellectual and spiritual, must be trained in harmony, else we may ever expect the continuance of the same discord which now prevails." Clay, *A Voice from the Prison*, Boston, 1856, p. 259.

46. Interview with Jo Ann Wheeler Burbank, New York City, January 12, 1973.

47. Odell Shepard, *Pedlar's Progress: The Life of Bronson Alcott*, Boston, 1938, p. 125; Shepard, ed., *The Journals of Bronson Alcott*, Boston, 1938, pp. 18, 27.

48. Monroe, *History of the Pestalozzian Movement*, p. 149; F. B. Sanborn and W. T. Harris, *A. Bronson Alcott*, 2 vols., Boston, 1893, I, 182-85.

49. Howard Mumford Jones, ed., *Emerson on Education*, New York, 1966, p. 211; Emma Goldman, "The Social Importance of the Modern School," *Red Emma Speaks*, ed. by Alix Kates Shulman, New York, 1972, p. 117.

50. Jones, ed., *Emerson on Education,* pp. 216-17, 225-26.

51. Walter R. Harding, *A Thoreau Handbook*, New York, 1959, pp. 158-59.

52. Arthur P. Dudden, *Joseph Fels and the Single-Tax Movement*, Philadelphia, 1971, p. 109; Marietta Johnson, *Thirty Years With an Idea*, Fairhope, Ala., 1974, pp. 16-17; Paul and Blanche Alyea, *Fairhope: 1894-1954*, Birmingham, Ala., 1956, p. 155.

53. Quoted in Lawrence A. Cremin, *The Transformation of the School*, New York, 1961, pp. 150-51.

54. Interview with Emma Cohen Gilbert, White Plains, N.Y., September 23, 1974; *Souvenir Program of Concert and Ball Arranged by the Modern School Association and Radical Library, May 26, 1916*, Stelton, N.J., 1916.

55. Interview with Morris Beresin, Philadelphia, November 28, 1971.

56. Interview with Richard Gilbert, White Plains, N.Y., September 23, 1974.

57. Interviews with Ellis Grosner, Atlantic City, N.J., July 3, 1972; and Emma Cohen Gilbert, September 23, 1974. On the Philadelphia Modern School see also Joseph J. Cohen, *Di yidish-anarkhistishe bavegung in Amerike*, Philadelphia, 1945, pp. 387-90; Cohen, "The Workmen's Circle, Philadelphia," *Freedom* (London), July 1911; and Abe Brandschein to Bolton Hall, January 26, 1912, Hall Papers, New York Public Library.

58. *Germinal* was adopted by Rudolf Rocker as the title of a Yiddish anarchist journal that he edited in London, where many of the Philadelphia anarchists had lived before coming to the United States. Ferrer's house near Barcelona, it might be noted, was called "Mas Germinal."

59. Emma Goldman, *Voltairine de Cleyre*, Berkeley Heights, N.J.,

1932, p. 41. See also Paul Avrich, *An American Anarchist: The Life of Voltairine de Cleyre*, Princeton, 1978.

60. De Cleyre, *Selected Works*, pp. 321-41.

61. Interview with Gussie Denenberg, Washington, D.C., March 20, 1973.

62. See Dr. Rudolf von Liebich, "A Ferrer School for Chicago," *Mother Earth*, September 1914; and William Thurston Brown's letter in *The Truth Seeker*, May 8, 1915. Von Liebich wrote the music for the well-known I.W.W. song "We Have Fed You All for a Thousand Years." See Joyce L. Kornbluh, ed., *Rebel Voices: An I.W.W. Anthology*, Ann Arbor, 1964, p. 29.

63. William Thurston Brown, "How I Became a Socialist," *The Comrade*, May 1903. His pamphlets included *After Capitalism What?* (1899) and *Axe at the Root* (1901), published by Charles H. Kerr of Chicago.

64. *Mother Earth*, May 1910. On Brown's dismissal see *The Socialist Spirit*, June 1902, with interesting photographs.

65. See, for example, "Shall We Be Free?" and "The Springs and Possibilities of Character," *Free Society*, June 29, 1902, and May 31, 1903.

66. Emma Goldman, "The Power of the Ideal," *Mother Earth*, May 1912.

67. Quoted in Gibbs M. Smith, *Joe Hill*, Salt Lake City, 1969, p. 90.

68. *Ibid.*, p. 179.

69. Quoted in Harvey O'Connor, *Revolution in Seattle*, New York, 1964, pp. 160-61.

70. *The Free Comrade*, September-October 1911.

71. Brown's assistant at the Portland Modern School was the anarchist and feminist poet Louise Olivereau, whose arrest for antimilitarist agitation in 1917 became a *cause célèbre* on the west coast.

72. *The Modern School*, March 1, 1914. See also Solomon Bauch, *Whose Fault?*, New York, 1908.

73. *The Detroit News*, March 14, 1914.

74. William Thurston Brown, *The Walt Whitman School*, Los Angeles, 1922.

75. Mildred Rebac to Joseph J. Cohen, March 6, 1922, Cohen Papers; *The William Morris School*, San Francisco, n.d., Bell Papers.

76. Emma Goldman, "On the Trail," *Mother Earth*, July 1911.

77. *The Modern School*, October-November-December 1921; Harry Kelly to Max Nettlau, September 8 and December 25, 1922, Nettlau Archive. Insufficient funds appears to have played a part.

78. Henry David, *The History of the Haymarket Affair*, New York, 1936, p. 100.

79. William T. Holmes, "Our Chicago Letter," *The Alarm*, August 18, 1888.

80. Jane Addams to Mary Linn [Blaisdell], March 13, 1889, Hull House.

81. Quoted in Ira Kipnis, *The American Socialist Movement, 1897-1912*, New York, 1952, pp. 256-57.

82. See D. A. Klagin's account in *Erkenntnis und Befreiung* (Vienna), October 11, 1925.

83. *L'Era Nuova*, February 19, 1916; *The Modern School*, November 1918; Hugo Rolland (Erasmo Abate) to Paul Avrich, August 28, 1975.

84. *Espoir* (Toulouse), February 24, 1974.

85. Interview with Radium LaVene, Los Angeles, June 22, 1974.

86. Jay Fox, "Civilization, a Gilded Lie," *The Agitator*, February 1, 1912.

87. *Discontent*, November 28, 1900; Stewart Holbrook, "Anarchists at Home," *The American Scholar*, xv (Autumn 1946), 429.

88. Quoted in Charles P. LeWarne, *Utopias on Puget Sound, 1885-1915*, Seattle, 1975, p. 202; *Discontent*, December 7, 1898.

89. Leonard D. Abbott, "The Fourth Anniversary of Ferrer's Death," *Mother Earth*, October 1913.

90. *Why?* (Tacoma), January and February 1913. This journal had for its mottoes: "Accursed Be Man Who Silenced Child's First Inquiry For He Laid Foundation of All Tyrannies" and "No Consecrated Absurdity Would Have Stood Its Ground If Man Had Not Silenced Child's Objections."

91. Bruce Calvert, *Rational Education*, Griffith, Ind., 1911, pp. 10ff.

CHAPTER 3

1. *Mother Earth*, July 1911.

2. Carl Zigrosser, *My Own Shall Come to Me*, Haarlem, 1971, p. 64.

3. Hapgood, *A Victorian in the Modern World*, pp. 281-82; Mabel Dodge Luhan, *Movers and Shakers*, New York, 1936, p. 138. It is interesting to note that Boyesen's elder brother had signed a petition for clemency on behalf of the Haymarket anarchists, executed in 1887.

4. Goldman, *Living My Life*, p. 475.

5. Zigrosser, *My Own Shall Come to Me*, p. 64.

6. Bruce St. John, ed., *John Sloan's New York Scene: Notes and Correspondence, 1906-1913*, New York, 1965, p. 463; interview with Gussie Denenberg, March 20, 1973.

7. Leonard D. Abbott, "The Work of the Ferrer Association," in Bayard Boyesen, *The Modern School in New York*, New York, 1911, p. 7.

8. Dr. Foote died the following year. A memorial meeting in New York, on December 22, 1912, was addressed by Theodore Schroeder, Bolton Hall, James F. Morton, Leonard Abbott, and William Thurston Brown, among others. See *Edward Bond Foote: Biographical Notes and Appreciatives*, New York, 1913; and *Mother Earth*, November 1912.

9. Harry Kelly, "American Notes," *Freedom* (London), November 1899.

10. Among Morton's many pamphlets and articles was *The Truth About Francisco Ferrer*, New York, 1913.

11. Leonard D. Abbott, "The Ideal of Libertarian Education," *Mother Earth*, June 1911.

12. Interview with Gussie Denenberg, March 20, 1973; Arthur Samuels in *Modern School of Stelton*, p. 29.

13. *Mother Earth*, November 1910.

14. Bayard Boyesen, *Prospectus of the Francisco Ferrer Association of New York*, New York, 1911, pp. 1-2.

15. *Mother Earth*, June 1911.

16. Alden Freeman to Emma Goldman, July 11, 1911, Goldman Papers, New York Public Library.

17. Harry Kelly to John Nicholas Beffel, October 2, 1947, Beffel Papers. The church, at 110 East Twelfth Street, is still standing but the school building was demolished for a parking lot. A photograph of it appears on the cover of Boyesen's *Modern School in New York*.

18. Rion Bercovici, "A Radical Childhood," *Scribner's Magazine*, August 1932, pp. 102-103; interview with Révolte Bercovici, New York City, September 29, 1977.

19. B. Liber in *Modern School of Stelton*, p. 8; *Mother Earth*, October 1911.

20. Boyesen, *The Modern School in New York*, pp. 1-2.

21. *Ibid.*, pp. 4-5.

22. *Ibid.*, pp. 3, 6.

23. Goldman, *Living My Life*, p. 336.

24. Russell M. Coryell, "The Birth of Nick Carter," *The Bookman*, July 1929, p. 500. See also Quentin Reynolds, *The Fiction Factory*, New York, 1955, pp. 61-63.

25. Harry Kelly, "Roll Back the Years: Odyssey of a Libertarian," unpublished autobiography, 17:5. Around this time, Coryell was publishing his own short-lived monthly, *The Wide Way*.

26. Rion Bercovici, "A Radical Childhood," p. 102; *Mother Earth*, October 1911.

27. John R. Coryell, "Ferrer," *Mother Earth*, November 1911.

28. Interviews with Dr. Amour Liber, Bronx, N.Y., April 17, 1973; and Mollie Albert, Bronx, N.Y., October 7, 1972.

29. B. Liber, *A Doctor's Apprenticeship*, New York, 1956, p. 245; *Freedom* (Stelton), October-November 1919.

30. *The Modern School*, February 1912.

31. Quoted in *The Agitator*, January 15, 1912.

32. Will and Ariel Durant, *A Dual Autobiography*, New York, 1977, p. 40.

33. Konrad Bercovici, *It's the Gypsy in Me*, p. 65.

34. Rion Bercovici, "A Radical Childhood," p. 102; Konrad Bercovici,

"The Emancipation of the Child," *The Modern School*, February 1912. A fourth Bercovici child, Mirel, was to marry Leonard Abbott's son Morris.

35. Interview with Magda Boris Schoenwetter, Brooklyn, N.Y., January 5, 1973.

36. *The Woman Rebel*, March 1914; Justin Kaplan, *Lincoln Steffens*, New York, 1974, p. 201.

37. Margaret Sanger, *An Autobiography*, New York, 1938, p. 75.

38. Kelly, "Roll Back the Years," 20:11; interviews with Révolte Bercovici, September 29, 1977; and Amour Liber, April 17, 1973.

39. Talk at Third Conference of the Friends of the Modern School, Rutgers University, September 27, 1975.

40. *Mother Earth*, October 1912.

41. *The Modern School*, February 1912.

42. Will Durant interviewed by James Day, January 14, 1974, PBS-TV, Los Angeles; *The New York Times*, May 26, 1976; Durant, *Transition*, New York, 1927, p. 135; Durant, *A Dual Autobiography*, p. 36.

43. Durant, *A Dual Autobiography*, p. 40; Durant, *Transition*, pp. 152-53.

44. Durant, *Transition*, p. 120.

45. Durant, *A Dual Autobiography*, p. 37.

46. Durant, *Transition*, p. 188. This autobiographical novel presents a fictionalized account of Durant's years in the Ferrer movement, with the Ferrer Association thinly disguised as the "Freedom Association," Leonard Dalton Abbott as "Ronald Dalton," Alden Freeman as "Henry Alden," Konrad Bercovici as "Radkon Vicoberci," and so on.

47. *Ibid*., p. 167.

48. Interview with David Lawson, Brooklyn, N.Y., November 17, 1977; David Lawson to Paul Avrich, February 22, 1978; Sanger, *An Autobiography*, p. 74; *The Modern School*, January 1919; Durant, *A Dual Autobiography*, pp. 40-41; Durant, *Socialism and Anarchism*, New York, 1914, p. 1.

49. Durant, *Transition*, pp. 196, 200.

50. *Ibid*.; Durant, *Socialism and Anarchism*, pp. 17, 23.

51. Durant, *Transition*, pp. 183-87, 196.

52. Will Durant, *The Ferrer Modern School*, New York, 1912, p. 4.

53. *Ibid*., pp. 2-3.

54. *Ibid*., p. 5. See also Will Durant, "The Political and Philosophical Basis of Educational Theory," *The Modern School*, October and November-December 1916.

55. Durant, *The Ferrer Modern School*, p. 8.

56. Durant, *Transition*, pp. 183-87; Durant, *Socialism and Anarchism*, p. 1.

57. Rion Bercovici, "A Radical Childhood," p. 102.

58. Durant, *The Ferrer Modern School*, pp. 4, 7.

59. Interviews with Révolte Bercovici, September 29, 1977; and Amour Liber, April 17, 1973.

60. Liber, *A Doctor's Apprenticeship*, p. 486.

61. Lola Ridge to Harold Loeb, February 1922, Loeb Papers; telephone interview with Dr. Grant Sanger, Mount Kisco, N.Y., September 27, 1977; Sanger, *An Autobiography*, p. 75.

62. Joseph J. Cohen and Alexis C. Ferm, *The Modern School of Stelton*, Stelton, N.J., 1925, p. 62; *Mother Earth*, October 1912.

63. Durant, *The Ferrer Modern School*, p. 6.

64. *Ibid.*, p. 4.

65. *Ibid.*, p. 7; Durant, *Transition*, pp. 197-98.

66. Durant, *Transition*, p. 199.

67. Sanger, *An Autobiography*, p. 75.

68. *The Modern School*, February and April 1912.

69. Rion Bercovici, "A Radical Childhood," pp. 102-103.

70. Harry Kelly, "The Francisco Ferrer Association and Syndicalism," *Freedom* (London), August 1912; *The Modern School*, Autumn 1913.

71. *The Modern School*, February 1912.

72. Rion Bercovici, "A Radical Childhood," p. 103.

73. *The Modern School*, Autumn 1913.

74. Kelly, "Roll Back the Years," 20:15.

75. Cohen and Ferm, *The Modern School of Stelton*, p. 61.

76. Lola Ridge to Harold Loeb, February 1922, Loeb Papers; Joseph J. Cohen, "The Difficulties of the Modern School," *The Modern School*, September 1, 1914.

77. Voltairine de Cleyre to Joseph J. Cohen, August 22, 1910, Cohen Papers.

78. De Cleyre to Cohen, April 13, 1911, Cohen Papers.

79. Kelly, "Roll Back the Years," 19:7.

80. Paul Luttinger, *The Burning Question: Rational Education of the Proletariat*, New York, 1913, pp. 28-40. Lola Ridge maintained that Luttinger himself had "got things and people into an awful snarl." Ridge to Loeb, February 1922.

81. Bayard Boyesen to Hutchins Hapgood, August 2, 1913, Hapgood Papers.

82. Leonard D. Abbott to Lola Ridge, February 24, 1920, Ridge Papers.

83. Emma Goldman to Bayard Boyesen, June 5, 1925, Goldman Archive. See also Hapgood, *A Victorian in the Modern World*, pp. 505-506; and Zigrosser, *My Own Shall Come to Me*, pp. 64-68.

84. Durant, *The Ferrer Modern School*, p. 6.

85. Durant, *Transition*, pp. 214-15.

86. Letter from London, September 16, 1912, *Mother Earth*, October 1912.

87. *Ibid.*; Durant, *A Dual Autobiography*, p. 69; Durant, "An Afternoon with Kropotkin," in Joseph Ishill, ed., *Peter Kropotkin*, Berkeley

Heights, N.J., 1923, pp. 89-90. Kropotkin's admonitions did not prevent Durant from visiting Havelock Ellis, whose radical sexual theories he had incorporated in his Ferrer School lectures.

88. *Mother Earth*, October 1912.

89. Amour received no formal schooling until he was enrolled in Townsend Harris High School. He afterward attended Cornell University. Following in his father's footsteps, he became a physician and eventually chief pathologist at the Bronx Veterans Hospital, where I interviewed him in 1973.

90. Will Durant, "Problems En Route," *The Modern School,* Spring 1913.

91. Interview with Eva Bein, New York City, January 13, 1973.

92. Interview with Benjamin G. Benno, New York City, September 24, 1972.

93. Durant, "Problems En Route."

94. Interview with Magda Boris Schoenwetter, January 5, 1973.

95. Durant, "Problems En Route."

96. *Mother Earth*, October 1913.

97. *Modern School of Stelton*, pp. 22-23. Ferrer himself, like many of his anarchist comrades, had been an ardent Esperantist and had attended an Esperanto Congress in Barcelona shortly before his trial and execution.

98. Zigrosser, *My Own Shall Come to Me*, p. 72. According to Zigrosser, "the procedure in the class was very free and flexible. No routine whatever was established and everything that was done was taken up by mutual agreement between the teacher and the pupils." *The Modern School*, July 1, 1914.

99. Talk at Third Conference of Friends of the Modern School, Rutgers University, September 27, 1975.

100. Durant, *Transition*, p. 240.

101. Durant, "Problems En Route."

102. Interview by James Day, January 14, 1974. In *A Dual Autobiography* (p. 23) Ariel mistakenly identifies the woman as Cora Bennett Stephenson, who did not come to the school till the following year.

103. Durant, *Transition*, p. 241; interviewed by James Day, January 14, 1974.

104. Durant, *A Dual Autobiography*, p. 26; Man Ray, *Self-Portrait*, Boston, 1963, p. 23.

105. Interviews with Eva Brandes, Bronx, N.Y., January 12, 1972; and Eva Bein, January 13, 1973.

106. Durant, *A Dual Autobiography*, p. 23; Durant, *Transition,* pp. 241-42.

107. Durant, *A Dual Autobiography*, pp. 27, 45-46.

108. Durant, *Transition*, pp. 246-47.

109. *Ibid.*; Durant, *A Dual Autobiography*, pp. 51-52.

110. Interview by James Day, January 14, 1974; interview with Manuel Komroff, Woodstock, N.Y., September 29, 1972.

111. *Columbia Reports*, Summer 1974; Durant, *Transition*, pp. 290-92.

112. *Modern School of Stelton*, p. 23; Durant, *Transition*, pp. 263-64.

113. Interview by James Day, January 14, 1974; *The New York Times*, May 26, 1974.

114. Emma Goldman to Joseph Ishill, December 29, 1927, Goldman Archive.

115. Durant, foreword to *Transition*.

116. Interview with Will and Ariel Durant, *Modern Maturity*, August-September 1972; Durant, *A Dual Autobiography*, pp. 72-73.

117. Durant, *A Dual Autobiography*, p. 59.

118. Interview by James Day, January 14, 1974; *The New York Times*, November 6, 1975. Emma Goldman found the book "superficial stuff that any truckman can read." Goldman to Rudolf Rocker, December 4, 1934, Rocker Archive.

119. *Mother Earth*, October 1913.

120. *Modern School of Stelton*, p. 22; Cremin, *The Transformation of the School*, p. 103.

121. *Mother Earth*, July 1913; interview with Jacques Dubois, Lake Mohegan, N.Y., September 19, 1972.

122. Interviews with Nora Horn, Lake Mohegan, N.Y., September 19, 1972; and Emma Cohen Gilbert, September 23, 1974.

123. During the 1913-1914 school year, Leonard Abbott remained president of the Ferrer Association, Arthur Samuels served as treasurer, and Stewart Kerr as secretary. The advisory board consisted of Alexander Berkman, Emma Goldman, Bayard Boyesen, Alden Freeman, Dr. C. L. Andrews, Hutchins Hapgood, Jack London, Upton Sinclair, J. G. Phelps Stokes, and Rose Pastor Stokes.

124. *The Modern School*, January 1, 1914; *Mother Earth*, October 1913.

125. Cora Bennett Stephenson, "Parents and the Modern School," *The Modern School*, Autumn 1913; *Modern School of Stelton*, pp. 22-23; interview with Mary Schwartz Rappaport, Brooklyn, N.Y., January 5, 1973.

126. Interview with Maurice Hollod, North Miami, Florida, December 20, 1972.

127. Interview with Anna Schwartz, Palo Alto, Calif., June 17, 1974.

128. *Modern School of Stelton*, p. 22.

129. *Ibid.*, pp. 22-23.

130. *Ibid.*, p. 23; interviews with Nora Horn, September 19, 1972; and Magda Boris Schoenwetter, January 5, 1973.

131. Report of the Modern School for 1913-1914, *The Modern School*, July 1, 1914.

132. Leonard D. Abbott to Albert Mordell, March 2, 1914, Mordell Papers.

133. Abbott, "The Fourth Anniversary of Ferrer's Death," *Mother Earth*, October 1913.

CHAPTER 4

1. Kelly, "Roll Back the Years," 21:8; *The Modern School*, April-May-June 1920.

2. Interview with Maurice Hollod, December 20, 1972.

3. Kelly, "Roll Back the Years," 21:7. Other lecturers at the East 107th Street Center included Hippolyte Havel, Charles Edward Russell, Joseph McCabe, Charles T. Sprading, William Thurston Brown, Ben Reitman, Saul Yanovsky, Frank Tannenbaum, Carlos Wupperman, William English Walling, and Harry Kemp.

4. Interviews with Maurice Hollod, December 20, 1972; Moritz Jagendorf, New York City, April 14 and May 28, 1973; Jacques Rudome, New York City, February 10, 1972; Henry Fruchter, New York City, May 1, 1972; Kelly, "Roll Back the Years," 21:8.

5. Interview with Manuel Komroff, September 29, 1972; Komroff, "Homage to the Modern School," tape, 1974.

6. Interview with Manuel Komroff, September 29, 1972. Cf. Symes and Clement, *Rebel America*, p. 279.

7. Interview with Manuel Komroff, September 29, 1972.

8. Zigrosser, *My Own Shall Come to Me*, p. 70.

9. Komroff, "Homage to the Modern School."

10. Interview with Eva Brandes, September 9, 1974.

11. *Modern School of Stelton*, p. 29; Cohen and Ferm, *The Modern School of Stelton*, p. 23.

12. Kelly, "Roll Back the Years," 21:2.

13. Carl Zigrosser, "The English Class," *The Modern School*, July 1, 1914.

14. Laurence Veysey, *The Communal Experience*, New York, 1973, p. 85.

15. *Ibid.*, pp. 95-97; Zigrosser, *My Own Shall Come to Me*, pp. 68-69.

16. Zigrosser, *My Own Shall Come to Me*, pp. 72-78.

17. *Ibid.*, p. 73.

18. *Ibid.*; Durant, *A Dual Autobiography*, pp. 27, 40; Durant, *Transition*, p. 189; Goldman, *Living My Life*, p. 546.

19. Edward F. Mylius to Bolton Hall, February 28, 1913, Hall Papers, New York Public Library. See also "The Case of Edward F. Mylius," *Mother Earth*, January 1913; and E. F. Mylius, "Stepping-Stones Towards the New Social Order," *The Modern School*, Spring 1913.

20. Harry Wickey, *Thus Far: The Growth of an American Artist*, New York, 1941, pp. 46-47.

21. Durant, *A Dual Autobiography*, p. 40.

22. Interviews with Manuel Komroff, September 29, 1972; and Moritz Jagendorf, May 28, 1973.

23. Adolf Wolff, "The Modern School," *The Modern School*, Spring 1913.

24. *The Glebe*, Spring 1913.

25. Adolf Wolff, *Songs of Rebellion, Songs of Life, Songs of Love*, New York, 1914, p. 15.

26. *The Social War*, December 1917.

27. *Revolt*, February 19, 1916; Durant, *A Dual Autobiography*, p. 26.

28. Goldman, *Living My Life*, p. 595; Komroff, "Homage to the Modern School"; interview with Manuel Komroff, September 29, 1972.

29. Benjamin De Casseres, "Pierrot-Parabrahma," *Revolt*, February 12, 1916; *Modern School of Stelton*, p. 23.

30. Interviews with Jacques Rudome, April 5, 1972; and Maurice Hollod, December 20, 1972.

31. Albert Parry, *Garrets and Pretenders*, New York, 1933, p. 271.

32. Interviews with Valerio Isca, New York City, November 25, 1972; and Hugo Rolland, Elmhurst, N.Y., October 11, 1971.

33. *L'Adunata dei Refrattari*, May 13, 1950.

34. Kelly, "Roll Back the Years," 17:5; Zigrosser, *My Own Shall Come to Me*, p. 74.

35. See Goldman, *Living My Life*, pp. 258ff.

36. Hapgood, *A Victorian in the Modern World*, pp. 198, 328; Louis Sheaffer, *O'Neill: Son and Playwright*, Boston, 1968, p. 329.

37. Zigrosser, *My Own Shall Come to Me*, p. 74; interview with Manuel Komroff, September 29, 1972.

38. Floyd Dell, *Love in Greenwich Village*, New York, 1926, p. 23; Dell, *Homecoming*, New York, 1933, p. 247.

39. Goldman, *Living My Life*, p. 278; William Zorach, *Art Is My Life*, Cleveland, 1967, p. 45; Hapgood, *A Victorian in the Modern World*, p. 327.

40. Hapgood, *A Victorian in the Modern World*, pp. 359-60.

41. Dell, *Love in Greenwich Village*, p. 23; Luhan, *Movers and Shakers*, p. 41.

42. Parry, *Garrets and Pretenders*, p. 289; Art Young, *On My Way*, New York, 1928, p. 281; Eastman, *Enjoyment of Living*, p. 439.

43. Hapgood, *A Victorian in the Modern World*, p. 318.

44. Interview with Manuel Komroff, September 29, 1972.

45. Gene Fowler, *Minutes of the Last Meeting*, New York, 1954, p. 51.

46. Sadakichi Hartmann, dedication to *A History of American Art*, 2 vols., Boston, 1902.

47. Goldman, *Living My Life*, p. 474.

48. Kenneth Rexroth, foreword to Sadakichi Hartmann, *White Chrysanthemums,* New York, 1971, p. ix; *Sadakichi Hartmann Newsletter*, Winter 1972.

49. Harry Lawton and George Knox, introduction to Sadakichi Hartmann, *Buddha, Confucius, Christ*, New York, 1971, p. xxii.

50. Fowler, *Minutes of the Last Meeting*, p. 20.

51. Lawton and Knox, introduction to *Buddha, Confucius, Christ*, p. xxvii.

52. Fowler, *Minutes of the Last Meeting*, p. 10; Lawton and Knox, introduction to *White Chrysanthemums*, p. xxii.

53. Benjamin De Casseres, "Five Portraits in Galvanized Iron," *The American Mercury*, December 1926.

54. Goldman, *Living My Life*, p. 395; Lawton and Knox, introduction to *White Chrysanthemums*, p. xxv.

55. Sadakichi Hartmann to Leopold Fleischmann, March 8, 1924, Hartmann Papers, University of California, Riverside.

56. Interview with Maurice Hollod, December 20, 1972; Wickey, *Thus Far*, p. 47.

57. Interviews with Manuel Komroff, September 29, 1972; and Charles Plunkett, Long Valley, N.J., June 4, 1975; Magda Boris Schoenwetter talk to Friends of the Modern School, Rutgers University, September 27, 1975.

58. Lawton and Knox, introduction to *White Chrysanthemums*, pp. xix-xx. See also Sadakichi Hartmann to Ben L. Reitman, October 19, 1941, Abbott Papers.

59. Interview with Maurice Hollod, December 20, 1972.

60. Hapgood, *A Victorian in the Modern World*, p. 330; Lawton and Knox, introduction to *White Chrysanthemums*, p. xxii.

61. Interviews with Benjamin G. Benno, September 24, 1972; and Jacques Rudome, February 10, 1972.

62. Emma Cohen Gilbert to Paul Avrich, April 6, 1975.

63. Dell, *Homecoming*, pp. 324-26.

64. Symes and Clement, *Rebel America*, p. 278. In 1917 the Rand School moved to 7 East 15th Street.

65. Luhan, *Movers and Shakers*, p. 83.

66. *The Modern School*, Autumn 1913; Sanger, *An Autobiography*, p. 69.

67. Luhan, *Movers and Shakers*, pp. 58, 89-90.

68. Dell, *Homecoming*, p. 183.

69. *Modern School of Stelton*, p. 29; *The Modern School*, Autumn 1913 and May 1916.

70. Komroff, "Homage to the Modern School."

71. *The Woman Rebel*, March 1914.

72. Margaret Sanger's pamphlet *Family Limitation* was clandestinely printed by Bill Shatoff, and Gilbert E. Roe was retained to defend her in court, but she left for Europe and her case never came to trial.

73. Parry, *Garrets and Pretenders*, p. 270; Elizabeth Gurley Flynn, *Rebel Girl: An Autobiography*, New York, 1973, p. 172; *Mother Earth,* January 1915.

74. *Modern School of Stelton*, p. 29.

75. *The Modern School*, Winter 1912-1913. Leonard Abbott wrote in *Mother Earth* (October 1913) that I.W.W. leaders like Haywood and Gurley Flynn "have always been welcome visitors at 63 East 107th Street."

76. *Mother Earth*, November 1912.

77. *The Modern School*, May 1916. According to Theodore Schroeder, the doctrine of economic determinism offered "only the superficial and partial formulation of complex biological and psychologial necessities." "A Psychologist's Social Credo," November 24, 1931, Sunrise Colony Archives.

78. Interview with Manuel Komroff, September 29, 1972; Komroff to Paul Avrich, September 30, 1972.

79. Peter Kropotkin, "An Appeal to the Young," *Kropotkin's Revolutionary Pamphlets*, ed. by Roger N. Baldwin, New York, 1927, p. 279; Manuel Komroff to Paul Avrich, November 2, 1972.

80. Flynn, *Rebel Girl*, p. 48.

81. Goldman, *Living My Life*, p. 509.

82. Bayard Boyesen, "Peter Kropotkin," *The Road to Freedom*, February 1927.

83. Hapgood, *A Victorian in the Modern World*, p. 313.

84. *Camera Work*, July 1914.

85. *Kropotkin's Revolutionary Pamphlets*, pp. 273, 278.

86. Art Young, *Life and Times*, New York, 1939, pp. 387-88.

87. Hippolyte Havel, "Art and the Social Life," *Open Vistas*, March-April 1925.

88. *Camera Work*, April-July 1913.

89. *The Social War*, I:1, 1913.

90. Goldman, *Living My Life*, p. 455. See also *Mother Earth*, September 1909.

91. André Tridon, *Psychoanalysis and Behavior*, New York, 1920, pp. 239-51. See also Nathan G. Hale, Jr., *Freud and the Americans*, New York, 1971, p. 327.

92. *Modern School of Stelton*, p. 29.

93. *Free Society*, November 23, 1902; de Cleyre, *Selected Works*, p. 152; Leonard D. Abbott, "Whitman as Revolutionary," *The Modern School,* April-May 1919.

94. *Mike Gold: A Literary Anthology*, ed. by Michael Folsom, New York, 1972, pp. 209-10. Gold read poetry at the Ferrer Center literary forum and contributed to *Revolt* and *The Modern School*.

95. Theodore Dreiser, "Change," *Revolt*, February 5, 1916; Dreiser to Emma Goldman, September 29, 1926, Goldman Archive.

96. Goldman, *Anarchism and Other Essays*, pp. 242, 271; Goldman, *The Social Significance of the Modern Drama*, Boston, 1914, p. 7.

97. Interview with Moritz Jagendorf, April 14, 1972.

98. Moritz Jagendorf in *Modern School of Stelton,* p. 19; Jagendorf, "The Free Theatre," *The Modern School*, September 1, 1914.

99. *Modern School of Stelton*, pp. 19, 22.

100. Komroff, "Homage to the Modern School."

101. *Modern School of Stelton*, p. 20; Ann U. Abrams, "The Ferrer Center," *New York History*, July 1978, pp. 318-19.

102. Quoted in Sheaffer, *O'Neill*, p. 102. Tucker also had a strong influence on Shaw and James Joyce, a subject which I hope to treat on another occasion.

103. Sheaffer, *O'Neill*, pp. 106, 122-23; Arthur and Barbara Gelb, *O'Neill*, New York, 1962, pp. 119-20.

104. According to Leonard Abbott, O'Neill "used to read and write some of his first plays, before becoming famous, in the tavern of Romany Marie (Rose's sister) in Greenwich Village." Abbott to Dr. Michael A. Cohn, February 15, 1928, Cohn Papers.

105. See Sheaffer, *O'Neill*, pp. 335-36.

106. Hapgood, *A Victorian in the Modern World*, p. 200.

107. See Carlin's letters on Vose in Havel's *Revolt*, January 22 and February 19, 1916. It might be noted that another anarchist, Christine Ell (sometime lover of E. F. Mylius), figures in O'Neill's *Anna Christie* and other plays.

108. Quoted in Sheaffer, *O'Neill*, p. 404. O'Neill's first published work appears to have been an unsigned poem in *Mother Earth*, May 1911. See Winifred Frazer, "A Lost Poem by Eugene O'Neill," *The Eugene O'Neill Newsletter*, May 1979, pp. 4-6.

109. Eugene O'Neill to Alexander Berkman, January 29, 1927, Berkman Archive. Berkman translated O'Neill's *Lazarus Laughed* into Russian for the Moscow Art Theater.

110. Isaac Don Levine, *Eyewitness to History*, New York, 1973, p. 86.

111. In Robert Henri, *The Art Spirit*, 1930 edn., p. ii.

112. Van Wyck Brooks, *John Sloan*, New York, 1955, pp. 17, 42-43.

113. Milton W. Brown, *American Painting: From the Armory Show to the Depression,* Princeton, 1955, p. 5.

114. Robert Henri, *The Art Spirit*, New York, 1923, p. 141.

115. Quoted in John I. H. Baur, *Revolution and Tradition in Modern American Art*, Cambridge, Mass., 1959, p. 15.

116. Brown, *American Painting*, p. 10.

117. Henri, *The Art Spirit*, p.103; Henri, "An Artist's Social Maxims," *The Road to Freedom*, November 1924.

118. Carl Zigrosser, "Henri and Manship," *The Little Review*, October

1915; William Innes Homer, *Robert Henri and His Circle*, Ithaca, N.Y., 1969, pp. 180-81.

119. *Mother Earth*, August 1917. The other members of the committee were Leonard Abbott, Harry Kelly, Bayard Boyesen, Margaret Sanger, M. Eleanor Fitzgerald, and Dr. Michael Cohn.

120. *Mother Earth*, July 1916; Goldman, *Living My Life*, p. 569. On the eve of her arrest, Henri attended a banquet for Emma Goldman at the Hotel Brevoort, along with Bellows, John Sloan, Robert Minor, and John Cowper Powys.

121. Hapgood, *A Victorian in the Modern World*, p. 295; Charles H. Morgan, *George Bellows*, New York, 1965, p. 154.

122. Henri diary, January 29, 1911, quoted in Homer, *Robert Henri and His Circle*, p. 180; Robert Henri, "An Appreciation by an Artist," *Mother Earth*, March 1915.

123. Henri diary, January 30, 1911, quoted in Homer, *Robert Henri and His Circle*, p. 180; *Mother Earth*, March 1915.

124. Goldman, *Living My Life*, pp. 528-29. Apart from Emma Goldman, Henri also did portraits of Puck Durant and Mother Yuster.

125. *Ibid*. According to Harry Kelly, it was Henri himself who offered to start the class, and "we jumped at that offer." "Roll Back the Years," 20:14.

126. Homer, *Robert Henri and His Circle*, p. 199; Brown, *American Painting*, p. 33.

127. Zigrosser, *My Own Shall Come to Me*, p. 72; interviews with Benjamin G. Benno, September 24, 1972; and Manuel Komroff, September 29, 1972. Among the models were Becky Edelsohn, Puck Durant, and Eureka Marchand, Romany Marie's sister-in-law.

128. Homer, *Robert Henri and His Circle,* p. 174. Trotsky arrived in New York on January 13th and departed on March 27th. He found it a "city of prose and fantasy, of capitalist automatism, its streets a triumph of cubism, its moral philosophy that of the dollar. New York impressed one tremendously because, more than any other city in the world, it is the fullest expression of our modern age." Leon Trotsky, *My Life*, New York, 1930, p. 270.

129. Homer, *Robert Henri and His Circle*, p. 158. "Henri spoke with hypnotic effect," recalls Manuel Komroff, "sort of Chinese looking with his high cheekbones." Interview, September 29, 1972.

130. Brooks, *John Sloan*, pp. 19, 43; Rockwell Kent, *It's Me, O Lord: The Autobiography of Rockwell Kent*, New York, 1955, p. 81.

131. Henri, *The Art Spirit*, pp. 134, 255, 281; Homer, *Robert Henri and His Circle*, p. 160.

132. Henri, *The Art Spirit*, pp. 6, 11, 17; Walter Yarrow and Louis Bouche, eds., *Robert Henri: His Life and Works*, New York, 1921, p. 28; *The Modern School*, Spring 1913.

133. Wickey, *Thus Far*, p. 47; Carl Zigrosser, *The Artist in America*, New York, 1942, pp. 73-74.

134. Zigrosser, *The Artist in America*, pp. 58-59. Henri, another of his pupils remarked, had "the priceless gift of stirring the imagination of his pupils—of making them excited about their work." Helen Appleton Read, "Word Painter: Robert Henri (1865-1929)," in *Great Teachers*, ed. by Houston Peterson, New Brunswick, N.J., 1946, p. 320.

135. Telephone interview with Robert Brackman, Mystic, Conn., October 27, 1977. "In the Henri art class I heard Walt Whitman for the first time unblushingly discussed in a mixed gathering." Helen Appleton Read in *Great Teachers*, pp. 320-21.

136. Liber, *A Doctor's Apprenticeship*, p. 502. Manuel Komroff spoke of "the noble world of ideas and aesthetic ideals that he built up for us." Komroff to Mrs. Robert Henri, July 15, 1929, Henri Papers, Yale University.

137. Leonard Abbott in *Mother Earth*, October 1913.

138. Interview with Révolte Bercovici, September 29, 1977.

139. *Modern School of Stelton*, p. 23.

140. See William Innes Homer, *Alfred Stieglitz and the American Avant-Garde*, Boston, 1977, p. 78; and Emma Goldman to Stieglitz, April 11, 1912, Stieglitz Papers.

141. Ray, *Self-Portrait*, pp. 18-20.

142. Hapgood, *A Victorian in the Modern World*, pp. 336-37.

143. *Camera Work*, July 1914.

144. Holger Cahill, *Max Weber*, New York, 1930, p. 1; Baur, *Revolution and Tradition in Modern American Art*, p. 48.

145. Quoted in Lloyd Goodrich, *Max Weber*, New York, 1949, p. 27.

146. *Mother Earth*, May 1913; *Revolt*, January 1 and February 19, 1916: "I am in anger, / I hate— / A wandering outcast I am. / I sorrow, / I wander, / My heart with silence is locked, / And without tears I weep." Weber also published a volume of "cubist poems" in 1914.

147. Quoted in Goodrich, *Max Weber*, p. 46.

148. Quoted in Alfred Werner, *Max Weber*, New York, 1975, p. 43, from *The New York Call*, of which Komroff was then art critic.

149. *Camera Work*, January 1913; *Revolt*, February 19, 1916.

150. The fullest and most satisfactory study of Man Ray and his work is Arturo Schwarz, *Man Ray: The Rigour of Imagination*, London, 1977. See also Roland Penrose, *Man Ray*, London, 1975; Ray, *Self-Portrait*; and Hilton Kramer, "Man Ray: Faithful Disciple," *The New York Times*, January 12, 1975.

151. Ray, *Self-Portrait*, p. 18.

152. *Ibid.*, pp. 21-22. Actually the courses were not free, but a small tuition was imposed. During 1912-1913, for instance, rates were: art, $2 for 12 classes, $1.10 for 6, 20 cents for 1; literature, $1.50, 80 cents, 15 cents; Esperanto, $1.10, 60 cents, 15 cents.

153. *Ibid.* pp. 22-23.

154. *Ibid.*, p. 23.

155. Alfred Kreymborg, *Troubador: An Autobiography*, New York, 1925, p. 200.

156. Ray, *Self-Portrait*, p. 31.

157. Interview with Manuel Komroff, September 29, 1972. The cabins were in the Grantwood, or Edgewater Heights, district of Ridgefield, which has since lost its rural character.

158. *The Ridgefield Gazook*, dated March 31, 1915, is reproduced in Schwarz, *Man Ray*, p. 22. *Others* included poems by Kreymborg, Man Ray, Adolf Wolff, Adon Lacroix, Lola Ridge, Bayard Boyesen, Benjamin De Casseres, and William Carlos Williams (not to mention Wallace Stevens, T. S. Eliot, Amy Lowell, Carl Sandburg, and Maxwell Bodenheim), and art work by Samuel Halpert and William and Marguerite Zorach.

159. See Dickran Tashjian, *Skyscraper Primitives: Dada and the American Avant-Garde, 1910-1925*, Middletown, Conn., 1975; and Carl Belz, "Man Ray and New York Dada," *The Art Journal*, XXIII (Spring 1964), 207-208.

160. Kreymborg, *Troubador*, p. 201; Schwarz, *Man Ray*, pp. 25-26.

161. Schwarz, *Man Ray*, p. 49.

162. Brown, *American Painting*, p. 105; *The New York Times*, November 19, 1976.

163. Komroff, "Homage to the Modern School."

164. Lola Ridge to Harold Loeb, February 1922, Loeb Papers.

165. Carl Zigrosser to John Cotton Dana, n.d., Zigrosser Papers.

166. Kent, *It's Me, O Lord*, p. 353; Leonard Abbott to Anna Schwartz, March 20, 1952, Rutgers University; Abbott to Zigrosser, December 27, 1918, Zigrosser Papers. Kent's initials were exhibited in the Butler Library of Columbia University in 1972. Other covers of *The Modern School* were designed by David Lawson and Helen West.

167. Joseph Cohen to Carl Zigrosser, January 25, 1918, Zigrosser Papers.

168. *The Modern School,* September 1917. Yet in 1951 Teachers College of Columbia University discarded its set of *The Modern School* as containing "old educational themes now out of date."

169. *The Modern School*, February 1912 and Winter 1912-1913.

170. Stewart Kerr, "Ferrer and Montessori," *ibid.*, Autumn 1913.

171. *Ibid.*, Winter 1912-1913 and Autumn 1913.

172. *Ibid.*, Winter 1912-1913.

173. *Ibid.*, June 1, 1914.

CHAPTER 5

1. Clarence C. Abbott to Leonard D. Abbott, October 29, 1951; Leonard Abbott to M. Scheer, March 11, 1952, Abbott Papers. See also John Nicholas Beffel, "Tsum undenk fun Leonard Abbott," *Fraye Arbeter Shtime*, May 22, 1953.

2. Leonard D. Abbott, "Edward Carpenter, A Radical Genius," *The Road to Freedom*, September 1931.

3. Leonard D. Abbott, "An Intellectual Giant," *Mother Earth*, December 1912.

4. Leonard D. Abbott, "How I Became A Socialist," *The Comrade*, October 1903.

5. Leonard D. Abbott, *The Society of the Future*, Girard, Kans., 1898, p. 4.

6. Leonard D. Abbott, *A Socialistic Wedding*, New York, 1901. In addition to *The Comrade*, Abbott and Brown were both contributors to *The Socialist Spirit*, published in Chicago from 1901 to 1903. Among Abbott's other early writings were "The Socialist Movement in Mass," *The Outlook*, February 17, 1901, and *The Root of the Social Problem*, New York, 1904.

7. Leonard Abbott to Jeanne Levey, January 11, 1950, Abbott Papers; Emma Goldman to Minna Lowensohn, January 22, 1925, Lowensohn Papers.

8. *The American Freeman*, July 1949; Leonard Abbott to Rose Pastor Stokes, May 19, 1915, Stokes Papers, Tamiment Library; interview with William Morris Abbott, New York City, January 14, 1972.

9. *The Free Comrade*, July 1910. Abbott was co-editor of this journal with his friend J. William Lloyd, a prolific poet and former individualist anarchist of the Benjamin Tucker school who now called himself a "free socialist," a label that equally suited Abbott. The two men were longtime neighbors at Westfield, New Jersey, where Abbott had a summer cottage.

10. Leonard Abbott to Albert Mordell, April 14, 1912, Mordell Papers.

11. *The Free Comrade*, July 1910.

12. Leonard Abbott to Sherman D. Wakefield, June 14, 1948, Abbott Papers.

13. Interview with William Morris Abbott, January 14, 1972; *John Sloan's New York Scene*, p. 432.

14. Zigrosser, *My Own Shall Come to Me*, pp. 69-70

15. Durant, *A Dual Autobiography*, p. 40.

16. Hapgood, *A Victorian in the Modern World*, pp. 282-83.

17. Interview with Emma Cohen Gilbert, September 23, 1974; Durant, *Transition*, pp. 190-91.

18. *The Free Comrade*, July 1910; Leonard Abbott to Stella Smith, October 8, 1951, Abbott Papers.

19. Interviews with Ray Miller Shedlovsky, New York City, October 14, 1972; and Moritz Jagendorf, April 14, 1972. Emma Goldman and Will Durant also called him a "saint."

20. Harry Kelly in *The Road to Freedom*, April 1931.

21. Leonard Abbott to Thomas H. Bell, March 23, 1935, Bell Papers. By Viereck he meant the writer George Sylvester Viereck, a fellow editor

at *Current Literature* and afterward editor of *The International*, to which Abbott was a frequent contributor. For a time, according to Laurence Veysey, the two young men had a "homoerotic relationship." *The Communal Experience*, p. 89.

22. *The Road to Freedom*, March 1926 and September 1931.

23. Durant, *Transition*, pp. 190-91; Will Durant to Manuel Komroff, January 25, 1940, Abbott Papers.

24. Harry Kelly to Emma Goldman, July 23, 1929, Goldman Archive; Kelly, "Roll Back the Years," Chapter 1. See also John Nicholas Beffel, "Tsum undenk fun Harry Kelly," *Fraye Arbeter Shtime*, July 3, 1953; and Rudolf Rocker, "Harry Kelly un zayn verk," *ibid.*, July 17-August 28, 1953.

25. Kelly, "Roll Back the Years," 2:3; Kelly to Max Nettlau, December 23, 1920, Nettlau Archive.

26. Harry Kelly, "An Anarchist in the Making," *Mother Earth*, April 1913.

27. Letter to the editor, dated March 14, 1895; *The Firebrand*, April 7, 1895. See also Kelly, "A Letter from Boston," *Solidarity*, April 1, 1895.

28. *Mother Earth*, April 1913; Kelly, "Roll Back the Years," 5:1; Kelly to Joseph Cohen, October 18, 1943, Cohen Papers.

29. Goldman, *Living My Life*, p. 178; Kelly, "Roll Back the Years," 6:4.

30. *The Rebel*, September 20, 1895; *Mother Earth*, April 1913. See also Kelly, "Kill the Editor," *Revolt*, January 15, 1916.

31. See Paul Avrich, "Kropotkin in America," *International Review of Social History*, 1980, Part 1.

32. Interview with Mollie Albert, October 7, 1972.

33. *Centennial Expressions on Peter Kropotkin, 1842-1942*, Los Angeles, 1942, p. 28.

34. Emma Goldman to Stella Ballantine, November 4, 1920, Wald Papers, Columbia University.

35. Zigrosser, *My Own Shall Come to Me*, p. 73.

36. Interview with Lallah Blanpied, New Rochelle, N.Y., April 7, 1972.

37. Interview with Manuel Komroff, September 29, 1972; Komroff, "Homage to the Modern School."

38. John Turner to Harry Kelly, July 31, 1933, Kelly Papers.

39. Interview with Roger N. Baldwin, January 29, 1974.

40. Komroff, "Homage to the Modern School."

41. Joseph J. Cohen, *The House Stood Forlorn*, Paris, 1954, p. 17.

42. Introduction to Cohen, *In Quest of Heaven*, New York, 1957.

43. Cohen, *The House Stood Forlorn*, p. 174.

44. Joseph Cohen to Max Nettlau, May 17, 1932, Nettlau Archive.

45. Cohen, *Di yidish-anarkhistishe bavegung*, p. 194.

46. Harry Kelly to Max Nettlau, March 29, 1921, Nettlau Archive.

47. Zigrosser, *My Own Shall Come to Me*, p. 73; interviews with Eva Brandes, January 12, 1972; Shaindel Ostroff, Bronx, N.Y., September 28,

1972; Ray Miller Shedlovsky, October 14, 1972; and Sonya Deanin, Farmingdale, N.Y., September 18, 1974.

48. Interview with Abraham Blecher, Miami Beach, Fla., December 16, 1972.

49. Interview with Philip Trupin, Nutley, N.J., May 31, 1972; Cohen, *The House Stood Forlorn*, p. 79; interview with E. V. Conason, White Plains, N.Y., September 23, 1974.

50. Interviews with Morris Gamberg, Bronx, N.Y., February 2, 1974; Hilda Adel, Croton-on-Hudson, N.Y., April 14, 1973; and Richard Gilbert, September 23, 1974.

CHAPTER 6

1. Interview with Gussie Denenberg (Isaacson's wife), March 20, 1973.

2. Interview with Moritz Jagendorf, May 28, 1973.

3. "The Lexington Avenue Explosion," *Mother Earth*, July 1914; *The New York Times*, July 5, 1914.

4. *The New York Times*, February 28, 1914.

5. *Ibid.*, March 2 and 3, 1914.

6. Goldman, *Living My Life*, p. 523; Alexander Berkman, "Tannenbaum Before Pilate," *Mother Earth*, April 1914; Carlo Tresca, "The Unemployed and the IWW," *Retort*, June 1944.

7. Interview with Charles Plunkett, June 4, 1975.

8. Marie Ganz, *Rebels: Into Anarchy—and Out Again*, New York, 1920, p. 167. There is a good photograph of Caron on the front page of *The New York Times*, July 5, 1914.

9. Interview with Maurice Hollod, December 20, 1972; *Mother Earth*, July 1914.

10. Alexander Berkman, "The Movement of the Unemployed," *Mother Earth*, March 1914; *The New York World*, March 23, 1914.

11. Quoted in Paul T. Ringenbach, *Tramps and Reformers, 1873-1916*, Westport, Conn., 1973, p. 163.

12. Interview with Charles Plunkett, June 4, 1975.

13. *Retort*, June 1944; *The New York Times*, March 5, 1914.

14. *The New York Call*, March 28, 1914; *Mother Earth*, April 1914.

15. *The Modern School*, January 1915.

16. Interview with Maurice Hollod, December 20, 1972; Wolff, *Songs of Rebellion*, p. 31.

17. Charles Robert Plunkett, "Dynamite!" *Mother Earth*, July 1914.

18. Mary Heaton Vorse, *A Footnote to Folly*, New York, 1935, p. 58. Emma Goldman calls Berkman the "active spirit of the movement," its "organizing and directing influence." *Living My Life*, pp. 523-25.

19. Carlo Tresca, unpublished autobiography, p. 292, Tresca Papers.

20. Goldman, *Living My Life*, p. 123; *The New York Times*, March 22, 1914. "Yesterday at Union Square," wrote Lincoln Steffens on March

22nd, "I got the cops to stand by and let Emma Goldman, Berkman, and others urge to looting of stores and then lead 1,000 men up Fifth Avenue." Quoted in Kaplan, *Lincoln Steffens*, p. 205.

21. *The New York Times*, March 22, 1914. This incident is confirmed by Maurice Hollod, who took part in the march.

22. Berkman, "The Movement of the Unemployed."

23. *Mother Earth*, April 1914; interview with Charles Plunkett, June 4, 1975. David Lawson agrees that the police in those days were a particularly "rough kind." Lawson to Paul Avrich, February 22, 1978.

24. Quoted in Kaplan, *Lincoln Steffens*, p. 205.

25. *The New York Times*, April 5, 1914; Vorse, *A Footnote to Folly*, p. 71.

26. Vorse, *A Footnote to Folly*, pp. 71-72.

27. Joe O'Carroll to Mary Heaton Vorse, May 6, 1914, Vorse Papers.

28. The fullest history of the Ludlow strike is *The Great Coalfield War* by George McGovern and Leonard F. Guttridge, Boston, 1972. See also Howard Zinn, "The Ludlow Massacre," in *The Politics of History*, Boston, 1970, pp. 79-105; Samuel Yellen, *American Labor Struggles*, New York, 1936; Richard Hofstadter and Michael Wallace, eds., *American Violence*, New York, 1970; and Harry Kelly, "The Miners' War in Colorado," *Freedom* (London), June 1914.

29. McGovern and Guttridge, *The Great Coalfield War*, p. vii.

30. *Ibid*., p. 135; Zinn, "The Ludlow Massacre," pp. 100-101; Yellen, *American Labor Struggles*, p. 221.

31. Zinn, "The Ludlow Massacre," p. 79.

32. Raymond B. Fosdick, *John D. Rockefeller, Jr.*, New York, 1956, p. 167; Art Young, *Life and Times*, p. 218. See also Peter Collier and David Horowitz, *The Rockefellers*, New York, 1976.

33. Quoted in Harris, *Upton Sinclair*, p. 144.

34. The stenographic minutes of the trial, preserved in the Municipal Archives and Records Center, New York City, reveal Judge Campbell's extreme bias against the defendants, as does his letter to Mayor John Purroy Mitchel advising against a reduction of sentence. Bombs were later planted in Campbell's office in the Tombs in reprisal for his handling of the Tannenbaum and White cases, but they failed to go off.

35. Tresca, unpublished autobiography, p. 296.

36. *The Woman Rebel*, May 1914.

37. Leonard D. Abbott, "The Courage and Faith of Alexander Berkman," *The Road to Freedom*, December 1930.

38. Julian F. Jaffe, *Crusade Against Radicalism*, Port Washington, N.Y., 1972, p. 43; Durant, *Transition*, p. 201.

39. Leonard D. Abbott, "The Fight in Tarrytown and Its Tragic Outcome," *Mother Earth*, July 1914. See also *The New York Call*, June 23, 1914.

40. *Mother Earth*, July 1914.

41. Tresca, unpublished autobiography, pp. 302-306; interview with Moritz Jagendorf, May 28, 1973.

42. See Paul Avrich, *The Russian Anarchists*, Princeton, 1967, p. 63.

43. *Mother Earth*, July 1914.

44. Alexander Berkman to Bolton Hall, April 16, 1907, Goldman Archive.

45. Alexander Berkman, "Violence and Anarchism," *Mother Earth*, April 1908.

46. Durant, *A Dual Autobiography*, p. 25; Goldman, *Living My Life*, pp. 540, 830; Alexander Berkman to Mollie Steimer, July 14, 1933, in *Nowhere at Home: Letters from Exile of Emma Goldman and Alexander Berkman*, ed. by Richard and Anna Maria Drinnon, New York, 1975, pp. 104-105.

47. Leonard Abbott to Anna Strunsky Walling, July 3, 1936, Abbott Papers.

48. *Mother Earth*, August 1914.

49. *Nowhere at Home*, p. xxvii.

50. Interviews with Moritz Jagendorf, May 28, 1973; and Gussie Denenberg, March 20, 1973.

51. *Mother Earth*, July 1914.

52. Interview with Charles Plunkett, June 4, 1975.

53. Interview with Maurice Hollod, December 20, 1972. Also present at the July 3rd meeting were Becky Edelsohn, Charles Plunkett, Louise Berger, Michael Murphy, Harry Wilkes, Adolf Aufricht, Maurice Rudome, Frank Mandese, Louis Pastorella, and Joseph Secunda, all of whom had taken part in the Tarrytown demonstrations. Mandese, Pastorella, and Secunda were members of the Bresci group at 301 E. 106th Street as well as frequenters of the Ferrer Center. According to the head of the New York Police Department Bomb Squad, Mandese was arrested on July 4th "in uncomfortable proximity to the estate and person of John D. Rockefeller." Thomas J. Tunney, *Throttled! The Detection of the German and Anarchist Bomb Plotters*, Boston, 1919, p. 42.

54. Interviews with Charles Plunkett, June 4, 1975; and Gussie Denenberg, March 20, 1973. See also Cohen, *Di yidish-anarkhistishe bavegung*, p. 311.

55. Interviews with Charles Plunkett, June 4, 1975; Gussie Denenberg, March 20, 1973; and Jacques Rudome, February 10, 1972.

56. Interview with Emma Cohen Gilbert, September 23, 1974.

57. *Mother Earth*, July 1914; interview with Maurice Hollod, December 20, 1972.

58. Interview with Emma Cohen Gilbert, September 23, 1974.

59. *Mother Earth*, July 1914.

60. Elizabeth Gurley Flynn to Mary Heaton Vorse, July 5, 1914, Vorse Papers.

61. *The Modern School*, August 1, 1914; Leonard Abbott to Rose Pastor Stokes, July 17, 1914, Tamiment Library.

62. Irwin Granich [Mike Gold], "Three Whose Hatred Killed Them," *The Masses*, August 1914; Adolf Wolff, "To Our Martyred Dead: Arthur Caron, Charles Berg and Carl Hanson," *Mother Earth*, July 1914; *Golos Ssyl'nykh i Zakliuchennykh Russkikh Anarkhistov*, October 1914; *The Woman Rebel*, July 1914.

63. Quoted in Joseph R. Conlin, *Big Bill Haywood and the Radical Union Movement*, Syracuse, 1969, p. 101.

64. *Mother Earth*, July 1914.

65. *Ibid.*

66. *Ibid.*

67. *Ibid.*

68. Kelly, "Roll Back the Years," 23:9.

69. In Cohen and Ferm, *The Modern School of Stelton*, p. 121.

70. *Ibid.*, p. 63.

71. H.W.L. Dana, *The Dana Saga*, Cambridge, Mass., 1941; Ann Hutchinson Guest to Paul Avrich, July 29, 1975. See also *The Modern School*, October 1, 1914.

72. Robert H. Hutchinson, *The "Socialism" of New Zealand*, New York, 1916. The chapters on "Woman Suffrage" and "Social Legislation" were mostly the work of Delia.

73. Zigrosser, *My Own Shall Come to Me,* p. 83; *Modern School of Stelton*, p. 23.

74. *The Modern School*, October 1, 1914.

75. Talk at Friends of Modern School conference, Rutgers University, September 27, 1975.

76. Recited to me by Magda Boris Schoenwetter, Janaury 5, 1973.

77. Friends of Modern School, September 27, 1975; interview with Mary Schwartz Rappaport, January 5, 1973.

78. "Ideals in Education" (October 1, 1914), "Herbert Spencer and the Modern School" (February-March 1915), "Froebel and the Modern School" (April 1915), "Pestalozzi, Herbart and the Modern School" (May 1915), "Montessori and the Modern School" (June 1915), "Francisco Ferrer and the Modern School" (July-August 1915), "Rousseau and the Modern School" (September 1915).

79. Hutchinson, "Ideals in Education."

80. Cohen and Ferm, *The Modern School of Stelton*, p. 63; *Modern School of Stelton*, p. 23.

81. *Modern School of Stelton*, pp. 23-24; interviews with Magda Boris Schoenwetter, January 5, 1973; and Mary Schwartz Rappaport, January 5, 1973.

82. Leonard Abbott to Rose Pastor Stokes, January 13, 1915, Tamiment Library; Cohen and Ferm, *The Modern School of Stelton*, p. 25.

83. Isidore Wisotsky, "Such a Life," manuscript, Labadie Collection, p.

178. An anarchist and Wobbly, Wisotsky was one of the young men arrested with Frank Tannenbaum at the Church of St. Alphonsus. During the 1960s he served as editor of the *Fraye Arbeter Shtime*.

84. Not to be confused with Joseph Spivak, a lifelong anarchist of unblemished dedication, who died in 1971.

85. Interview with Maurice Hollod, December 20, 1972; *Mother Earth*, December 1914 and May 1915; *The Modern School*, May 1915.

86. Interview with Moritz Jagendorf, May 28, 1973.

87. Cohen and Ferm, *The Modern School of Stelton*, p. 45.

88. *The Modern School*, November 1914; *Mother Earth*, December 1914.

89. *Modern School of Stelton*, p. 24.

90. *The Woman Rebel*, March 1914.

91. *Revolt* was edited by Hippolyte Havel, with Jack Isaacson as secretary and Gussie Miller as treasurer. Among its contributors were Leonard Abbott, Harry Kelly, Adolf Wolff, Robert Minor, Max Weber, Harry Kemp, Theodore Dreiser, Mike Gold, Benjamin De Casseres, Terry Carlin, Jay Fox, Bill Haywood, Moritz Jagendorf, Hutchins Hapgood, Neith Boyce, and Margaret Sanger.

92. Leonard Abbott to Carl Zigrosser, August 25, 1916, Zigrosser Papers.

93. *Revolutionary Radicalism*, 4 vols., Albany, 1920, II, 1447.

94. Leonard Abbott to Albert Mordell, April 11, 1918, Mordell Papers: Abbott to Professor Donald Drew Egbert, September 29, 1951, Abbott Papers.

CHAPTER 7

1. Alexis C. Ferm, "A Sketch of the Life of the Modern School," manuscript, Rutgers University.

2. "The Opening of the Ferrer School at Stelton," *Mother Earth*, June 1915; Cohen and Ferm, *The Modern School of Stelton*, pp. 9-10. See also Terry Perlin, "Anarchism in New Jersey: The Ferrer Colony at Stelton," *New Jersey History*, Fall 1971, pp. 133-48; and Veysey, *The Communal Experience*, pp. 115ff.

3. *Mother Earth*, June 1915; *Modern School of Stelton*, p. 10.

4. Interview with Abe Bluestein, New York City, December 9, 1972.

5. Harry Kelly to Max Nettlau, October 1, 1919, Nettlau Archive.

6. Mike Gold, "A Little Bit of Millennium," *The Liberator*, March 1921.

7. *Ibid*.

8. *Ibid*., Kelly, "Roll Back the Years," 26:3, Kelly to Max Nettlau, January 8, 1920, Nettlau Archive.

9. Interview with Richard Gilbert, September 23, 1974; Harry Kelly, "The 25th Anniversary of the Freie Arbeiter Stimme," manuscript, Rutgers University.

10. Cohen and Ferm, *The Modern School of Stelton*, p. 13; interview with Anna Schwartz, June 17, 1974.

11. A second son, Bertrand (after Bertrand Russell), was born at Stony Ford in June 1917 and a daughter, Ann, in New York City in November 1918.

12. Ann Hutchinson Guest to Paul Avrich, July 29, 1975.

13. Interviews with Eva Bein, January 13, 1973; and Mary Schwartz Rappaport, January 5, 1973.

14. Interview with Eva Bein, January 13, 1973.

15. Telephone interview with Val R. Lorwin, January 27, 1973; Robert H. and Delia D. Hutchinson, "Stony Ford," *Experimental Schools*, 1917, No. 5, pp. 7ff.

16. Interview with Eva Bein, January 13, 1973.

17. In addition to Marucci and Zack Schwartz and Eva Bein, the pupils were Valentine Rogin-Levine (son of Rose Rogin and Louis Levine, the Ferrer Center historian of syndicalism), Susan Dubois, Virginia Horton, Nora Huebsch, Meyer Richman, Abie Herben, Ben Hegel, Marie and Bruno Albasi, and Jessie, Rosy, and Barney Mendelson.

18. Robert and Delia Hutchinson, "Stony Ford."

19. Telephone interview with Val R. Lorwin, January 27, 1973. Pursuing this interest, the boy went on to become a distinguished economic historian, specializing, like his father, in the French labor movement.

20. Interview with Eva Bein, January 13, 1973.

21. *Ibid.*; interviews with Val R. Lorwin, January 27, 1973; and Mary Schwartz Rappaport, January 5, 1973.

22. Interview with Eva Bein, January 13, 1973, who possesses the only surviving copy of *The Wallkill*.

23. Cohen and Ferm, *The Modern School of Stelton,* p. 64.

24. Robert H. Hutchinson to Carl Zigrosser, August 21, 1917, Zigrosser Papers.

25. Interview with Anna Schwartz, June 17, 1974.

26. Interview with Eva Bein, January 13, 1973.

27. *Modern School of Stelton*, p. 16; Cohen and Ferm, *The Modern School of Stelton*, p. 15.

28. Interview with Emma Cohen Gilbert, September 23, 1974. Her high opinion of Schnittkind's teaching abilities was shared by other pupils, including Ray Miller and Magda Boris.

29. *Modern School of Stelton*, p. 16.

30. Cohen and Ferm, *The Modern School of Stelton*, pp. 14-15.

31. William Thurston Brown, *Education for Constructive Democracy*, Stelton, N.J., 1918, pp. 26-32; Brown, *Citizenship and Education*, Stelton, 1917, p. 31; Brown, *The Most Important Educational Experiment in America*, Stelton, n.d. [1917 or 1918], pp. 3, 27. See also his article "The 'Why' of the Modern School," *Slate*, April 1917.

32. Interviews with Ray Miller Shedlovsky, October 14, 1972; and Emma Cohen Gilbert, September 23, 1974.

33. Carl Zigrosser, *The Modern School*, Stelton, 1917, p. 6.

34. Cohen and Ferm, *The Modern School of Stelton*, pp. 67, 116.

35. Leonard Abbott to Alexis Ferm, September 6, 1949, Abbott Papers; interview with Ray Miller Shedlovsky, October 14, 1972.

36. Bob Kenner, "Childhood Memories," *Exit 9* (New Brunswick, N.J.), March 1974.

37. *The Modern School*, October 1917.

38. Friends of the Modern School, Rutgers University, September 27, 1975. For Sexton's description of the Caribou Dance, see *The Modern School*, April 1921.

39. *The Liberator*, March 1921.

40. Ferm, "A Sketch of the Life of the Modern School."

41. Her valedictory address was printed in *The Modern School*, Summer 1921.

42. Cf. Ralph Waldo Emerson: "if the boy stops you in your speech, cries out that you are wrong and sets you right, hug him." *Emerson on Education*, pp. 226-27.

43. Interview with Ray Miller Shedlovsky, October 14, 1972.

44. Joseph Ishill, "Biographical Notes," Rocker Archive; Rudolf Rocker in Ishill, ed., *The Oriole Press: A Bibliography*, Berkeley Heights, N.J., 1953; *Correspondencia selecta de Joseph Ishill*, ed. by V. Muñoz, Mexico City, 1967.

45. Joseph Ishill in *Testimonial to Rudolf Rocker*, Los Angeles, 1944, p. 39.

46. Joseph Ishill, "Reflections of a Proletarian," in *Elisée and Elie Reclus*, Berkeley Heights, N.J., 1927, p. xi.

47. Crystal Ishill Mendelsohn, "Tsum undenk fun mayn foter Yoysf Ishill," *Fraye Arbeter Shtime*, November 1976.

48. *Elisée and Elie Reclus*, p. xii.

49. Joseph Ishill in *Thoreau, "The Cosmic Yankee"*, Los Angeles, 1946, p. 3. A Rumanian translation of *Civil Disobedience* appeared in 1897.

50. *Modern School of Stelton*, p. 14.

51. Joseph Ishill to Emma Goldman, November 22, 1931, Goldman Archive.

52. *Modern School of Stelton*, p. 14; interviews with Magda Boris Schoenwetter, January 5, 1973; and Emma Cohen Gilbert, September 23, 1974.

53. This magazine appeared in 1916 with Ray Miller as editor, Emma Cohen associate editor, Heloise Hansen Brown treasurer, and Walter Krimont circulation manager.

54. William Thurston Brown to Max Metzkow, May 1, 1917, Ishill Papers, Harvard University.

55. *The Oriole Press: A Few Comments*, Berkeley Heights, N.J., 1950, p. 16; Rose Freeman-Ishill, "Tsu Yoysf Ishills 10tn yortsayt," *Fraye Arbeter Shtime*, October 1976; Joseph Ishill to Max Nettlau, August 5, 1921, Nettlau Archive. Ishill had had a previous wife, Sophie Somer, a relative of the Libers and Bercovicis, who died shortly after their marriage.

56. Written in Stelton in 1917, *Petals Blown Adrift* was published in New York the following year.

57. The single-tax colony of Free Acres, of which Hall was a founder, was located in another part of Berkeley Heights.

58. Leonard Abbott to Rose Freeman-Ishill, August 4, 1951, Abbott Papers.

59. *Fraye Arbeter Shtime*, November 1976; Ishill, foreword to *Peter Kropotkin*.

60. Extensive collections of Ishill's work are to be found in the New York Public Library, the libraries of Rutgers University, Harvard University, the University of Florida, the Labadie Collection of the University of Michigan, the International Institute of Social History, and the public library of Berkeley Heights, New Jersey. See Crystal Ishill Mendelsohn, "A Complete Checklist of the Publications of Joseph Ishill and His Oriole Press," *The American Book Collector*, xxv, September 1974-February 1975.

61. Alexander Berkman to Joseph Ishill, February 28, 1928, Berkman Archive. See also Emma Goldman to C.E.S. Wood, November 2, 1932, Goldman Archive.

62. Berkman thought that Ishill's work "possessed the spirit of William Morris." Berkman to Emma Goldman, September 15, 1933, Goldman Archive; Berkman to Max Metzkow, April 14, 1934, Labadie Collection.

63. Mendelsohn, "Tsum undenk fun mayn foter Yoysf Ishill."

64. *Elisée and Elie Reclus*, pp. xii-xiii.

65. Interviews with Jacob Endin, Berkeley Heights, N.J., February 13, 1973; and Anatole Freeman Ishill, Staten Island, N.Y., September 23, 1975.

66. *Modern School of Stelton*, p. 14; *Thoreau, "The Cosmic Yankee"*, p. 3; *The Oriole Press: A Bibliography*, p. xvi.

67. Mendelsohn, "Tsum undenk fun mayn foter Yoysf Ishill."

68. Freeman-Ishill, "Tsu Yoysf Ishills 10tn yortsayt."

69. Interview with Ray Miller Shedlovsky, October 14, 1972; Cohen and Ferm, *The Modern School of Stelton*, pp. 27-28,

70. Interview with Ray Miller Shedlovsky, October 14, 1972; Harry Friedman, talk at Friends of Modern School, Rutgers University, September 27, 1975; Cohen and Ferm, *The Modern School of Stelton*, p. 53; Singer, *An Autobiography*, p. 182.

71. Alexis Ferm to Gladys Hourwich, March 31, 1952, Rutgers University.

72. "Ferrer in Liverpool," *The Voice of Labour*, (London), August 24, 1907; James H. Dick, "Recollections of Lorenzo Portet," *The Modern School*, June-July 1917.

73. *Freedom* (London), November 1908 and February 1909. Dick's regular reports on the school in this journal are signed "Dick James" or "J.H.D."

74. *Ibid.*, November 1909; Rudolf Rocker, *In Shturem*, Buenos Aires, 1952, p. 362. For Dick's anarchist activities in Liverpool, see Bob Holton, *British Syndicalism, 1900-1914*, London, 1977, pp. 47, 59-60.

75. *Freedom*, February and May 1911. The International Club survived until September 1911.

76. *The Sheffield Anarchist*, November 1, 1891.

77. *Freedom*, June 1912. Around the same time, another Ferrer Sunday School was started on Charlotte Street in Soho, where Malatesta spoke on "Ferrer and the Modern School Movement" on September 8, 1912.

78. Interview with Nellie Dick, Miami, Fla., December 17, 1972.

79. *Ibid.*

80. *Ibid.*; *Freedom*, June and August 1913. On the Central Labour College see William W. Craik, *The Central Labour College, 1909-29*, London, 1964.

81. Interview with Nellie Dick, Oyster Bay, N.Y., September 16, 1974; *Freedom*, October and November 1913. Two years later, on October 12, 1915, Portet wrote the following message to Jim Dick on a postal card depicting the Ferrer monument in Brussels: "Remember the 13 October 1909." Dick Papers.

82. *Freedom*, December 1914.

83. Interview with Nellie Dick, December 17, 1972; Nellie Dick, talk at Second Conference of Friends of Modern School, Rutgers University, September 28, 1974.

84. Interviews with Ray Miller Shedlovsky, October 14, 1972; and Emma Cohen Gilbert, September 23, 1974.

85. Cohen and Ferm, *The Modern School of Stelton*, p. 41; Ferm, "A Sketch of the Life of the Modern School"; interview with Gussie Denenberg, December 29, 1976.

86. Interview with Magda Boris Schoenwetter, January 5, 1973. See also Gray Wu, "The Self-Activity of the Child," *The Modern School*, October-November-December 1921.

87. Cohen and Ferm, *The Modern School of Stelton*, pp. 34, 58; telephone interview with Solon De Leon, Long Island City, N.Y., March 31, 1974.

88. Cohen and Ferm, *The Modern School of Stelton*, p. 37.

89. *The Modern School*, February 1918. Around the same time, the Modern School Association held a series of after-dinner discussions in Greenwich Village on the theme of "Social Reconstruction After the

War," the participants including Leonard Abbott, Harry Kelly, Pryns Hopkins, Will Durant, Elizabeth Gurley Flynn, Louis Fraina, Bouck White, Harry Weinberger, Bolton Hall, Theodore Schroeder, and Gilbert E. Roe.

90. *Modern School of Stelton*, p. 27.

91. Leonard Abbott to Lola Ridge, February 24, 1920, Ridge Papers.

92. Pryns Hopkins, *Both Hands Before the Fire*, Penobscot, Maine, 1962, pp. 39-45; *Centennial Expressions on Peter Kropotkin*, p. 38.

93. *Modern School of Stelton*, p. 8.

94. Hopkins, *Both Hands Before the Fire*, p. 60. There is a photograph of the children playing on the map, following page 82. On Boy Land see also *The Germ* (1913) and *The Dawn* (1914), edited by Hopkins with his associate Sydney Greenbie.

95. Joseph Freeman, *An American Testament*, New York, 1936, pp. 46-47.

96. Emma Goldman to Alexander Berkman, December 18, 1931, Goldman Archive.

97. Leonard Abbott to Lola Ridge, February 24, 1920, Ridge Papers; Friends of Modern School, Rutgers University, September 28, 1974.

98. Other active members were Rose Yuster Abbott, Mother Yuster, M. Eleanor Fitzgerald, Carlo Tresca, Elizabeth Gurley Flynn, Robert H. Hutchinson, Louis Fraina, and Stella Comyn Ballantine.

99. *Freedom*, March 1915; interview with Gussie Denenberg, December 29, 1976.

100. Emma Goldman to Bayard Boyesen, August 8, 1917, Goldman Papers, New York Public Library.

101. Leonard Abbott to Emma Goldman, December 28, 1929, Goldman Archive; Harry Kelly to Max Nettlau, October 1, 1919, Nettlau Archive; Kelly, "Roll Back the Years," 49:3.

102. Cohen and Ferm, *The Modern School of Stelton*, p. 38.

103. *The Blast*, May 1, 1917; *Mother Earth Bulletin*, October 1917.

104. Emma Goldman, *The Truth About the Boylsheviki* (sic), New York, 1918, pp. 5, 10.

105. Leonard D. Abbott, "The Triumph of Revolutionary Principles in Russia," *The Social War Bulletin*, February 1918.

106. *Revolutionary Radicalism*, I, 846-47. Trotsky, it will be recalled, was an alumnus of Henri's art class at the Ferrer Center.

107. *Mike Gold: A Literary Anthology*, p. 210.

108. Harry Kelly to Max Nettlau, January 8, 1920, Nettlau Archive.

109. *Modern School of Stelton*, pp. 11-12.

110. Interviews with Nellie Dick, December 17, 1972; and Wanda Swieda, Lake Mohegan, N.Y., January 20, 1972.

111. See Paul Avrich, ed., "Prison Letters of Ricardo Flores Magón to Lilly Sarnoff," *International Review of Social History*, XXII (1977), 402-403.

112. Thomas H. Bell, "The Walt Whitman School," manuscript, Bell Papers. See also *The Modern School*, April 1921; and William Thurston Brown, *The Walt Whitman School*, Los Angeles, 1922.

113. William Thurston Brown to Nicholas Steelink, February 10, 1922, January 3, 1923, and June 7, 1931, Steelink Papers.

114. Leonard Abbott to Lola Ridge, February 24, 1920, Ridge Papers.

115. See John W. Edelman, *Labor Lobbyist*, New York, 1974.

116. Harry Kelly to Elizabeth Gurley Flynn, January 18, 1926, Kelly Papers.

117. Cohen and Ferm, *The Modern School of Stelton*, p. 40.

118. *The Modern School*, January-February-March 1920; Leonard Abbott to Lola Ridge, February 24, 1920, Ridge Papers.

CHAPTER 8

1. Cohen and Ferm, *The Modern School of Stelton*, p. 42.

2. Alexis Ferm, "A Biographical Note," in Elizabeth Byrne Ferm, *Freedom in Education*, New York, 1949. The fullest treatment of the Ferms is Arthur Mark, "Two Libertarian Educators: Elizabeth Byrne Ferm and Alexis Constantine Ferm (1857-1971)," Doctor of Education dissertation, Teachers College, Columbia University, 1973.

3. Bach and Beethoven were her favorite composers. Alexis Ferm to Dora Keyser, August 4, 1944, Keyser Papers.

4. Alexis Ferm, "A Biographical Note"; Veysey, *The Communal Experience*, p. 136.

5. See Stephen Bell, *Rebel, Priest and Prophet: A Biography of Dr. Edward McGlynn*, New York, 1937.

6. Heber Newton was a single-taxer with strong Tolstoyan leanings. See his "Political, Economic, and Religious Causes of Anarchism," *The Arena*, XXVII (1902), 113-25.

7. Elizabeth Byrne Ferm, "Activity and Passivity of the Educator," *Mother Earth*, March 1907; Ferm, *Freedom in Education*, pp. 4-9, 22-26.

8. Alexis Ferm, "A Biographical Note," p. 193; Alexis Ferm, "Elizabeth Byrne Ferm," *Why?* (New York), April-May 1944.

9. Froebel, *The Education of Man*, p. 55.

10. Elizabeth Byrne Ferm, *The Spirit of Freedom in Education*, Stelton, N.J., 1919, pp. 45, 50.

11. Hans Koch, "Elizabeth Byrne Ferm," *The Roman Forum* (Los Angeles), November 1944. Cf. Nellie Dick: "I once heard her lecture in New York and I was enthralled. When she spoke I was transfixed. She was charming and beautiful, and there was fire when she spoke." Interview, December 17, 1972.

12. "Diary of Alexis Constantine Ferm," November 14, 1896. See also his autobiographical manuscript, "Sven: The Ordinary Life of an Ordinary Boy," in which "everything is true except the name of the boy."

Alexis Ferm to Jo Ann Wheeler Burbank, April 8, 1970, Rutgers University.

13. "Diary of Alexis Constantine Ferm," April 20, 1894; *Baldwin County Press Register* (Alabama), April 2, 1970.

14. Alexis Ferm to Jo Ann Wheeler Burbank, May 10, 1970, Rutgers University; Alexis Ferm to Suzanne Hotkine Avins, December 11, 1943, Avins Papers.

15. Lilly Raymond, "In Memory—to 'Uncle,'" *Miscellaneous Poems*, Stelton, N.J., 1971; Alexis Ferm to Dora Keyser, August 4, 1944, Keyser Papers.

16. Alexis Ferm to Suzanne Hotkine, November 7, 1927, Avins Papers.

17. Alexis Ferm to Gladys Hourwich, March 31, 1952, Rutgers University.

18. Alexis Ferm to Benjamin R. Tucker, December 18, 1908, Tucker Papers. Ferm's name appears on the subscription list of Tucker's *Liberty*, preserved with the Tucker Papers.

19. Alexis Ferm to Sasha Hourwich, May 23, 1951, Rutgers University.

20. Alexis Ferm to Sally Axelrod, August 12, 1963, Rutgers University.

21. Alexis Ferm to Aurora Greenhouse, July 9, 1961, Rutgers University.

22. "Diary of Alexis Constantine Ferm," February 18, 1898.

23. Alexis Ferm, "Elizabeth Byrne Ferm," manuscript; Alexis Ferm, "Elizabeth Byrne Ferm," *Why?*, April-May 1944.

24. Alexis Ferm to Jo Ann Wheeler Burbank, October 11, 1968; *The New York Times*, August 14, 1977.

25. Elizabeth Byrne Ferm, "The Rod and the Child," *Free Society*, May 1, 1904.

26. Alexis Ferm, "A Biographical Note," p. 195.

27. "Diary of Alexis Constantine Ferm," February 18, 1899; Alexis Ferm to Sasha Hourwich, March 15, 1953, Rutgers University.

28. "Diary of Alexis Constantine Ferm," February 18, 1902; *Baldwin County Press Register*, April 2, 1970. On the train, he tells us, he found time to read some of his favorite literature, including Benjamin Tucker's *Instead of a Book*.

29. Leonard Abbott to Pryns Hopkins, March 26, 1952; Abbott to Professor J. Salwyn Schapiro, March 11, 1952, Abbott Papers.

30. Goldman, *Living My Life*, pp. 335-36.

31. Alexis C. Ferm, *The Problem of Education*, Stelton, N.J., 1934, p. 23.

32. Ernest Howard Crosby, *Tolstoy as a Schoolmaster*, Chicago, 1904, pp. 54-60. Tolstoy himself was familiar with the Ferms' experiment, having read Crosby's book with admiration. Tolstoy to Crosby, April 25,

1906, *Tolstoy's Letters*, ed. by R. F. Christian, 2 vols., New York, 1978, II, 658.

33. *The Modern School*, May 1922; Elizabeth Ferm, *Freedom in Education*, pp. 94, 103.

34. Alexis C. Ferm, "Thoreau and Modern Education," in *Thoreau, "The Cosmic Yankee,"* p. 19; Alexis Ferm to Frances Swieda, October 18, 1954, Rutgers University.

35. Interview with Eva Brandes, January 7, 1972; Crosby, *Tolstoy as a Schoolmaster*, p. 58; Ferm, *Freedom in Education*, p. 165.

36. *The Road to Freedom*, January 1931. Compare the following remark made in 1978 by Jane Sharaf, director of the Solebury School in New Hope, Pennsylvania: "Instead of helping students discover who they are, well-meaning educators have urged them to make something of themselves. Often, traditional methods of education have little to do with nourishing individual growth and personal creativity." *The New York Times*, June 10, 1978.

37. *The Road to Freedom*, November 1929. Paul Luttinger criticized this "ultra-radical" approach to education as "not teaching" but "simply watching the children." *The Burning Question*, p. 18.

38. Alexis Ferm to Sally Axelrod, May 14, 1948, Rutgers University.

39. Alexis C. Ferm, "Diary of the Playhouse Children," March 6, 1906, Rutgers University.

40. Crosby, *Tolstoy as a Schoolmaster*, pp. 56-58.

41. Interview with Eva Brandes, Dyker Heights, September 9, 1974.

42. Interview with Eva Brandes, January 7, 1972.

43. Interview with Eva Brandes, June 12, 1972. It is perhaps significant in this connection that the Ferms never had children of their own.

44. Alexis Ferm, "Elizabeth Byrne Ferm," manuscript. The following year Alexis built a cabin at Newfoundland for weekends, summers, and holidays.

45. Alexis Ferm to Leonard Abbott, September 18, 1942, Abbott Papers.

46. Bercovici, *It's the Gypsy in Me*, p. 65.

47. Koch, "Elizabeth Byrne Ferm."

48. Alexis Ferm, "A Sketch of the Life of the Modern School"; *Modern School of Stelton*, p. 30.

49. Alexis Ferm, "A Biographical Note," p. 198.

50. *Ibid.*, p. 199.

51. Cohen and Ferm, *The Modern School of Stelton*, p. 68.

52. Alexis Ferm, "A Biographical Note," p. 198; *Modern School of Stelton*, p. 30.

53. Cohen and Ferm, *The Modern School of Stelton*, p. 42.

54. *Ibid.*, p. 75.

55. *Ibid.*, p. 68.

56. *Ibid.*; Abe Bluestein and Leo Kolodny, Friends of Modern School, Rutgers University, September 28, 1974.

57. Friends of Modern School, September 28, 1974; Alexis C. Ferm, "Activities at the Modern School," in Elizabeth Byrne Ferm, *The Spirit of Freedom in Education*, p. 60.

58. Alexis Ferm, "A Biographical Note," p. 201.

59. *The Modern School*, Summer 1921. At a Stelton reunion at Rutgers fifty years later, the whole assembly burst into the "dandelion" song when it was mentioned by a speaker.

60. Alexis Ferm, "Activities at the Modern School," p. 58; interview with Abe Bluestein, December 9, 1972; Friends of Modern School, September 28, 1974.

61. Veysey, *The Communal Experience*, p. 141.

62. Interview with Hugo Gellert, Freehold, N.J., December 28, 1972.

63. *Das Freie Wort*, 1907; *Der Anti-Autoritär*, 1911; *Der Strom*, 1910-1912. *Der Strom* (October 15, 1910) includes an article by Elizabeth Ferm on "Legislation and Education" ("Gesetzgebung und Erziehung").

64. Koch, "Elizabeth Byrne Ferm."

65. *The Liberator*, March 1921.

66. *Modern School of Stelton*, pp. 13-14. Other children's magazines produced at Stelton, in addition to *The Path of Joy* (1916), were *Us Kids* (1920), *The Gossiper* (1920), *The Chatter-Box* (1920), *The Stelton Appendix* (1923), *Bavardage* (c. 1931-1932), *The Stelton Outlook* (1932-1933), *The Child Says* (c. 1938-1939), and *New Moon* (1945). Still others were *Little Pages, Our World*, and *The Folio*, whose dates I have not been able to determine.

67. *The Road to Freedom*, January 1931.

68. Interview with Suzanne Hotkine Avins, Bronx, N.Y., March 5, 1973. In 1924 Suzanne organized a small orchestra among the pupils.

69. Agnes de Lima, *Our Enemy, the Child*, New York, 1926, p. 239.

70. Alexis Ferm, "A Biographical Note," p. 201; interview with Dora Keyser, Los Angeles, June 24, 1974.

71. *The Liberator*, March 1921.

72. *The Modern School*, April 1921.

73. See James H. Dick, "Kropotkin Memorial Library at Stelton, New Jersey," *Freedom* (London), October 1922. The other members of the Kropotkin Publishing Society were Roger Baldwin, Dr. Michael Cohn, M. Eleanor Fitzgerald, Albert Jay Nock, Stella Ballantine, and Mary Krimont.

74. In 1919 Harry Kelly and Leonard Abbott published a short-lived monthly at Stelton called *Freedom* ("A Journal of Constructive Anarchism"), and in 1921 appeared *Action* ("Official Organ of the Group of Action of Ferrer Colony"), edited by Marion Trask, Anna Riedel, and Mary Stechbardt.

75. Harry Kelly to Elizabeth Gurley Flynn, January 18, 1926, Kelly Papers.

76. Friends of Modern School, Rutgers University, September 28, 1974; *The Road to Freedom*, February 1931.

77. *The Road to Freedom*, January 1925; *Freedom* (New York), January 1, 1933.

78. Scott Nearing and Alexis C. Ferm, *Has Propaganda Any Value in Education?*, Stelton, 1925; *Man!*, January 1940.

79. Leonard Abbott to Alexis Ferm, September 6, 1949, Abbott Papers.

80. Interviews with Emma Cohen Gilbert, September 23, 1974; Ray Miller Shedlovsky, October 14, 1972; and Wanda Swieda, Woodside, N.Y., January 11, 1972.

81. Interview with Clara Freedman Solomon, Forest Hills, N.Y., June 2, 1973.

82. *Modern School of Stelton*, p. 26; interviews with Siegfried Rolland, Elmhurst, N.Y., June 3, 1973; and Hugo Gellert, December 28, 1972.

83. Friends of Modern School, Rutgers University, September 28, 1974; *Modern School of Stelton*, p. 26; interview with Anna Schwartz, June 17, 1974.

84. Interview with Suzanne Hotkine Avins, March 5, 1973.

85. Alexis Ferm, "A Sketch of the Life of the Modern School." Uncle's aversion to academic training ran deep. When Suzanne Hotkine enrolled at the Juilliard School, he wrote to her as follows: "Well, I do hope that your work at the institute will not kill out your creative instinct, as so much 'Institute' work does, especially among the art schools. I hope you will learn more and more how to expand your creativeness, for if you do not you will be disappointed in the end. And after all—what is the whole of training for if not to help our self-expression? Mostly self-expression gets lost in the shuffle. It gets covered over with training." Alexis Ferm to Suzanne Hotkine, June 2, 1927, Avins Papers.

86. Veysey, *The Communal Experience*, p. 154.

87. Cohen and Ferm, *The Modern School of Stelton*, pp. 86-87.

88. *The Modern School: An Experiment in Libertarian Education*, Stelton, N.J., 1948, p. 11; Alexis Ferm, *The Problem of Education*, p. 10; *Man!*, April 1940.

89. Cohen and Ferm, *The Modern School of Stelton*, p. 121.

90. Harry Kelly to Elizabeth Gurley Flynn, January 18, 1926, Kelly Papers. Alexis Ferm, "A Sketch of the Life of the Modern School."

91. Joan Baez, *Daybreak*, New York, 1968, p. 26.

92. *Modern School of Stelton*, pp. 24-25.

93. Alexis Ferm to Edgar Tafel, September 17, 1947, Rutgers University.

94. Alexis Ferm to Gilbert and Victoria Aronoff, December 28, 1941, Rutgers University.

95. Harry Kelly to James and Nellie Dick, January 3 and May 3, 1928, Dick Papers; Kelly to Elizabeth Gurley Flynn, January 19, 1926, Kelly Papers.

96. Alexis Ferm, "A Sketch of the Life of the Modern School"; Alexis Ferm to Sally Axelrod, October 31, 1959, Rutgers University.

97. Alexis Ferm to Sally Axelrod, July 16, 1968; Ferm, "A Sketch of the Life of the Modern School, " Rutgers University.

98. Sherwood Trask to Leonard Abbott, March 23, 1940, Abbott Papers; *Modern School of Stelton*, p. 19.

CHAPTER 9

1. Harry Kelly to Max Nettlau, February 25 and June 13, 1923, Nettlau Archive; Kelly, "Roll Back the Years," 37:1.

2. Harry Kelly to Lola Ridge, February 27, 1923, Ridge Papers; *About Mohegan Colony*, Crompond, N.Y., 1923, Mohegan Archives. The trustees included Manuel Komroff, Harry Weinberger, George Seldes, Marc Epstein, Minna Lowensohn, and Henry Fruchter.

3. Harry Kelly to Max Nettlau, March 14, 1923, Nettlau Archive.

4. Harry Kelly, "On the Constitution," *Colony News*, August 23, 1935.

5. Eva Brandes, quoted in *The Patent Trader*, Westchester County, September 30, 1964.

6. Minutes of meeting of Mohegan Modern School Association, October 2, 1923, Nettlau Archive. See also Lewis Mumford, *Findings and Keepings: Analects for an Autobiography*, New York, 1975, p. 81.

7. Interview with Ben Lieberman, New York City, April 28, 1972.

8. *The New York Times*, January 6, 1975. Dibner deeded the collection to the Smithsonian Institution.

9. Interview with Fermin Rocker, New York City, January 26, 1972.

10. *The Road to Freedom*, October 1927; Harry Kelly to Emma Goldman, November 23, 1927, Goldman Archive

11. Alexander Berkman to Leonard Abbott, October 12, 1927, Berkman Archive.

12. Mike Gold, "Lynchers in Frock Coats," *The New Masses*, September 1927.

13. James H. Dick, "Report of the Activities of the Modern School," 1926, Mohegan Archives.

14. Interview with Ben Lieberman, April 28, 1972.

15. James Dick to Dear Comrade, June 1927, Mohegan Archives.

16. Dick, "Report of the Activities of the Modern School."

17. Mohegan Archives. Dick, it might be added, addressed the 1926 Progressive Education Association convention on the Modern School.

18. James Dick to A. S. Neill, March 30, 1928, Dick Papers.

19. *Colony News*, July 1, 1933.

20. Interview with Dorothy Rick, Lake Mohegan, N.Y., September 19, 1972.

21. *Colony News*, May 27, 1932.

22. Interview with Dorothy Rick, September 19, 1972.

23. Interview with Ben Lieberman, April 28, 1972.

24. George H. Seldes, "Anarkhistishe kolonies fun mayn foter George Seldes," *Fraye Arbeter Shtime*, March 1976. See also *ibid.*, May and June 1977.

25. George H. Seldes, *Tell the Truth and Run*, New York, 1953, p. xv; telephone interview with George H. Seldes, Windsor, Vt., February 16, 1973.

26. See George H. Seldes in *Sadakichi Hartmann Newsletter*, Winter 1971.

27. Seldes, *Tell the Truth*, p. xix.

28. Interview with Henry Fruchter, New York City, May 1, 1972.

29. *The Road to Freedom*, April 1931.

30. Interview with Jo Ann Wheeler Burbank, January 12, 1973.

31. *The Road to Freedom*, April 1931.

32. George S. Seldes to George H. Seldes, June 17, 1925, Seldes Papers.

33. Seldes, *Tell the Truth*, p. xxii.

34. See Rocker, *The London Years*; and William J. Fishman, *East End Jewish Radicals, 1875-1914*, London, 1975.

35. Alexander Berkman to Dr. Michael Cohn, February 13, 1933, Berkman Archive.

36. *Testimonial to Rudolf Rocker*, pp. 43-46.

37. Interview with Nora Horn, September 19, 1972.

38. Interviews with Jo Ann Wheeler Burbank, January 12, 1973; and Lallah Blanpied, April 7, 1972; Harry Kelly to Elizabeth Gurley Flynn, February 18, 1926, Kelly Papers; John G. Scott to board of directors, May 1, 1928, Mohegan Archives.

39. Interview with Jo Ann Wheeler Burbank, January 12, 1973. Scott passed on his devotion to nature to Jon Thoreau, who is now an ecologist at the State University of New York in Albany.

40. *Ibid.*; interview with Ben Lieberman, April 28, 1972.

41. *Modern School of Stelton*, p. 20.

42. Interview with Jo Ann Wheeler Burbank, January 12, 1973.

43. *Ibid.*

44. *Mother Earth,* April 1933. The last number (October-November-December 1934) was published at Stelton.

45. *Man!*, April 1933.

46. *Ibid.*, August-September 1933.

47. *Thoreau, "The Cosmic Yankee"*, p. 18.

48. *Man!*, June 1935; John G. Scott to Jacques Rudome, n.d. [1935], Rudome Papers.

49. Interview with Jo Ann Wheeler Burbank, January 12, 1973.

50. George S. Seldes to Minna Lowensohn, June 25, 1925, Lowensohn Papers.

51. Harry Kelly to Alexander Berkman, June 9, 1925, Berkman Archive; Berkman to Minna Lowensohn, September 3, 1925, Lowensohn Papers.

52. *The Road to Freedom*, August 1925.

53. In 1926 the Road to Freedom Group held a summer camp at Belle Terre, with lectures by Kelly, Stephen Naft (Siegfried Nacht), Patrick Quinlan, M. J. Olgin, Carlo Tresca, A. J. Muste, and V. F. Calverton.

54. Harry Kelly to Max Nettlau, July 20, 1925, Nettlau Archive; interview with Hilda Adel, Mt. Airy, April 14, 1973.

55. Harry Kelly to Helen Rudome, May 3, 1950, Rudome Papers.

56. Emma Goldman to Alexander Berkman, December 23, 1927, Berkman Archive; Harry Kelly to Emma Goldman, November 23, 1927, Goldman Archive.

57. Harry Kelly to James and Nellie Dick, May 31, 1928, Dick Papers.

58. James Dick to Harry Kelly, January 21, 1927, Dick Papers.

59. James Dick to Thomas H. Keell, November 2, 1929, Dick Papers.

60. Interview with Nellie Dick, December 26, 1972. For some, the Dicks were simply not up to the task of directing the school. "I have not much faith in the future of the Mohegan School," wrote Leonard Abbott, "unless they can get a stronger man than Jim Dick as principal." Abbott to Dr. Michael Cohn, October 30, 1927, Cohn Papers.

61. Interview with Lallah Blanpied, April 7, 1972.

62. Interview with Hilda Brandes, Lake Mohegan, N.Y., January 20, 1972.

63. *Vanguard*, November 1938; *Man!*, December 1938.

64. Interviews with Eva Brandes, January 17, 1972; and Jacques Rudome, February 10, 1972.

65. Letter to Members and Friends, 1935, Mohegan Archives.

66. Appendix to Marcus Graham, *The Issues in the Present War*, London, 1943, p. 30.

67. Telephone interview with Harry Crone, February 6, 1972. Another resident of the colony was the communist dissident Benjamin Gitlow, Foster's running-mate in the 1932 presidential elections.

68. *Colony News*, August 23, 1935; interview with Eva Brandes, January 12, 1972.

69. Mohegan Civic Association declaration, Mohegan Archives.

70. Interview with Juan Anido, New York City, December 7, 1974.

71. Interview with Lydia Miller, New York City, February 12, 1972.

CHAPTER 10

1. James Dick to Alexis Ferm, June 19, 1928, Dick Papers.
2. James Dick to Thomas H. Keell, November 2, 1929, Dick Papers.

3. Interview with Beatrice Markowitz, New York City, September 12, 1972.

4. James Dick to Thomas H. Keell, November 2, 1929, Dick Papers.

5. James Dick to Herman Carter, August 6, 1929, Dick Papers.

6. James Dick to Mike Gold, July 4, 1928, Dick Papers.

7. A. S. Neill to James Dick, April 11 and June 30, 1931, Dick Papers. Unfortunately no account of their meeting has been preserved.

8. Mike Gold to James Dick, n.d. [October 1932], Dick Papers.

9. James Dick to Thomas H. Keell, November 2, 1929, Dick Papers.

10. Interview with Nellie Dick, Lakewood, N.J., December 26, 1972.

11. *Ibid.*

12. Third Conference of Friends of Modern School, Rutgers University, September 27, 1975; interviews with Nellie Dick, December 26, 1972; and Beatrice Markowitz, September 12, 1972. A former pupil at Stelton, Miss Markowitz taught arts and crafts at Lakewood and helped Nellie in the nursery.

13. Interview with Nellie Dick, December 26, 1972.

14. *Ibid.*

15. During the 1930s Goldman ran a short-lived Weekend Modern School in New York City. He died in 1971. See J. Lifshitz, "A. L. Goldman—Ayner fun di ershte Arbeter-Ring lerers," *Kultur un Lebn*, March-April 1971.

16. Alexis Ferm, "A Sketch of the Life of the Modern School."

17. *The Road to Freedom*, August 15, 1926; Alexis Ferm to Suzanne Hotkine, August 28, 1926, and June 2, 1927, Avins Papers.

18. De Lima, *Our Enemy, the Child*, p. 245.

19. Other members of the board, together with Ferm and Muste, were Norman Thomas, Rexford G. Tugwell, Fannia Cohen of the ILGWU, William Heard Kilpatrick of Teachers College, and Harry Overstreet.

20. Alexis Ferm to James Dick, August 23, 1928, Dick Papers.

21. Interview with Ben Lieberman, April 28, 1972.

22. Alexis Ferm to parent, April 15, 1940, Rutgers University.

23. Alexis Ferm to John Aronoff, February 28, 1938, Rutgers University.

24. Report to annual convention, September 1938, Rutgers University.

25. Program of the Anarchist Sunday School, July 10-26, 1936, Nomad Archive.

26. *Challenge*, September 2, 1939.

27. A separate memorial meeting for Emma Goldman was held in Town Hall on May 31, 1940. The speakers included Harry Kelly, Rudolf Rocker, Harry Weinberger, Roger Baldwin, and Norman Thomas, with Leonard Abbott presiding.

28. *Man!*, April 1940. After the dinner a twenty-fifth anniversary booklet was issued, with reminiscences by Hippolyte Havel, Carl Zigrosser, Joseph Cohen, Joseph Ishill, Henry Schnittkind, Dr. Liber, Pryns Hopkins, Theodore Schroeder, Moritz Jagendorf, Alexis Ferm, James

Dick, Arthur Samuels, Harry Weinberger, Rudolf Rocker, Sherwood Trask, John and Kate Edelman, Jo Ann Wheeler, Ray Miller, Emma Cohen, Marucci Schwartz, Zachary Schwartz, Minna Lowensohn, Anna Koch-Riedel, Pauline Bridge Henderson, and Lilly Sarnoff.

29. Interview with Anna Schwartz, June 17, 1974.

30. Harry Kelly to Leonard Abbott, September 8, 1942, Abbott Papers.

31. Alexis Ferm, "A Biographical Note," pp. 202-203.

32. Sherwood Trask to Alexis Ferm, May 27, 1944; Joseph Cohen to Alexis Ferm, April 23, 1944, Ishill Papers, Gainesville.

33. Alexis Ferm to Dora Keyser, December 2, 1951, Keyser Papers.

34. Alexis Ferm to Dora Keyser, December 13, 1959, Keyser Papers.

35. Alexis Ferm to Aurora Greenhouse, August 6, 1968, Rutgers University.

36. Alexis Ferm to Sally Axelrod, July 22, 1962; Mrs. Al Baez to Nathan Marer, February 26, 1967, Rutgers University.

37. Letter to a senior citizens' group, Rutgers University.

38. Alexis Ferm, diary, October 31, 1948; Alexis Ferm to Sally Axelrod, May 10, 1957, Rutgers University; Alexis Ferm to Dora Keyser, December 5, 1967, Keyser Papers.

39. Alexis Ferm to Sally Axelrod, April 5, 1961; Alexis Ferm to Aurora Greenhouse, July 23, 1961; Alexis Ferm to Jo Ann Wheeler Burbank, November 28, 1969, Rutgers University.

40. Alexis Ferm to Leonard Abbott, September 18, 1942, Abbott Papers.

41. *The Voice of the Children*, n.d.; Alexis Ferm to Dora Keyser, January 5, 1944, Keyser Papers.

42. Alexis Ferm to Dora Keyser, New Year's Day 1955, Keyser Papers.

43. Leonard Abbott to E. Haldeman-Julius, July 16, 1949, Abbott Papers.

44. Anna Schwartz, "A Day at the School," *The Modern School: An Experiment*, p. 7.

45. Anna Schwartz to Leonard Abbott, June 7, 1951, Abbott Papers.

46. Olga Ferrer to Anna Schwartz, August 2, 1949, Rutgers University.

47. Sol Ferrer to Anna Schwartz, September 14, 1949, Rutgers University; Sol Ferrer, *La vie et l'oeuvre de Francisco Ferrer*, p. 200.

48. Harry Kelly to Jacques and Helen Rudome, September 6, 1949, Rudome Papers.

49. The minutes of the meetings of December 18, 1955, and May 21, 1961, are to be found in the Spivak Papers, New York City. Anna Schwartz moved to California, where she died in 1978, aged 92.

50. Lillian Kisliuk Dinowitzer to Agnes Inglis, June 17, 1947, Labadie Collection. Between the wars Mrs. Dinowitzer ran a libertarian nursery and kindergarten in Washington, D.C.

51. Harry Kelly, "The 25th Anniversary of the Freie Arbeiter

Stimme"; Hippolyte Havel in minutes of the Road to Freedom conference, New York City, October 12-14, 1928, Nettlau Archive; Theodore Schroeder, "A Psychologist's Credo."

52. Quoted in Veysey, *The Communal Experience*, p. 176.

53. Interview with Ben Lieberman, April 28, 1972.

54. *The New York Times*, November 9, 1976.

55. *Camera Work*, dated July 1914 but published in Janaury 1915. See also Wolff's poem "Weeds" in *Others*, edited by Alfred Kreymborg, 1915.

56. Interviews with Maurice Hollod, December 20, 1972; and Gussie Denenberg, March 20, 1973.

57. Leonard Abbott to Emma Goldman, February 2, 1930, Goldman Archive.

58. Lola Ridge, *Sun-Up and Other Poems*, New York, 1920; Berkman to Ridge, December 25, 1927, Ridge Papers.

59. *The New York Times*, May 21, 1941.

60. Leonard Abbott to Emma Goldman, December 28, 1929, Goldman Archive.

61. Manuel Komroff to Leonard Abbott, March 25, 1940, Abbott Papers; *The New York Times*, December 11, 1974.

62. *The New York Times*, November 14, 1975.

63. Liber, *A Doctor's Apprenticeship*, p. 355; Hapgood, *A Victorian in the Modern World*, p. 280.

64. *The New York Times*, November 27, 1975; Dan Bourne Jones, *The Prints of Rockwell Kent*, Chicago, 1975. Zigrosser had compiled the first such list in *Rockwellkentiana*, New York, 1933.

65. Theodore Schroeder to Emma Goldman, October 24, 1928, Goldman Papers, New York Public Library.

66. *The Boys' Herald*, Point Pleasant, N.J., October 1941, organ of the National Amateur Press Association, of which Morton was a lifelong member and one-time president.

67. Frank Tannenbaum, "The Blackwell's Island Hell," *The Masses*, June 1915; *Collier's*, January 10, 1925.

68. *Collier's*, January 10, 1925; Emma Goldman to Alexander Berkman, May 14, 1929, in *Nowhere at Home*, pp. 148-49.

69. Alexander Berkman to Pauline H. Turkel, September 6, 1921, Tamiment Library; Mollie Steimer to Paul Avrich, April 18, 1975.

70. Avrich, *The Russian Anarchists*, pp. 137ff; Eugene Lyons, *Assignment in Utopia*, New York, 1937, p. 310.

71. Avrich, *The Russian Anarchists*, p. 197.

72. Harry Kelly to Max Nettlau, December 23, 1920, Nettlau Archive.

73. Emma Goldman, *My Disillusionment in Russia*, London, 1925, p. 6; Goldman, *Living My Life*, p. 729.

74. Lyons, *Assignment in Utopia*, pp. 309-10; interview with Nellie Dick, December 17, 1972.

75. Alexander Berkman and Emma Goldman to M. Eleanor Fitzgerald and Stella Ballantine, February 28, 1920, Goldman Archive.

76. Alexander Berkman to Hudson Hawley, June 12, 1932, Berkman Archive; Paul Avrich, *Kronstadt 1921*, Princeton, 1970.

77. Emma Goldman to Stewart Kerr, February 12, 1933, Goldman Papers, New York Public Library.

78. Sadakichi Hartmann to Ben Reitmam, June 2, 1940, Abbott Papers.

79. Sadakichi Hartmann to Ben Reitman, October 19, 1941, Abbott Papers.

80. *Ibid*.

81. *Life and Times of Sadakichi Hartmann*, p. 7.

82. Louis G. Raymond to Agnes Inglis, August 20, 1943; Hippolyte Havel to Agnes Inglis, May 4, 1927, Labadie Collection.

83. Jacques Rudome to James Dick, n.d. [1930], Dick Papers; Hippolyte Havel to Jacques Rudome, August 20, 1932, Rudome Papers.

84. Hippolyte Havel to Jacques Rudome, May 18, 1934, and April 5, 1935; Kenner, "Childhood Memories."

85. Agnes Inglis to Joseph Ishill, June 3, 1934, Ishill Papers, Harvard University; Hippolyte Havel to Agnes Inglis, September 1, 1943, Labadie Collection.

86. Interview with Louis G. Raymond, Stelton, N.J., December 5, 1971; Anna Schwartz to Agnes Inglis, August 24, 1951, Labadie Collection,

87. Alexander Berkman to Rudolf Grossmann, August 21, 1935, Ramus Archive.

88. Their son, a Soviet artist and book designer like his father, visited the United States in 1977 and attended the Fifth Conference of the Friends of the Modern School at Rutgers University.

89. Leonard Abbott to Anna Schwartz, June 11, 1951, Rutgers University.

90. Interviews with Maurice Hollod, December 20, 1972; and Eva Brandes, April 4, 1972; Rudolf Rocker to Max Nomad, April 26, 1946, Nomad Archive.

91. Leonard Abbott to Alexander Berkman, March 30, 1930, Berkman Archive; Abbott to Anna Strunsky Walling, September 1, 1925, Abbott Papers.

92. Leonard Abbott to Thomas H. Bell, August 14, 1928, Bell Papers; Abbott to Emma Goldman, June 13, 1925, Goldman Archive.

93. William Morris Abbott to Paul Avrich, November 5, 1971.

94. Leonard Abbott to Dr. Michael Cohn, August 21, 1927, Cohn Papers; Abbott to Berkman, November 6, 1927, Berkman Archive.

95. Leonard Abbott to Alexander Berkman, March 2, 1930, Berkman Archive.

96. Leonard Abbott to Joseph Cohen, September 27, 1931, Sunrise Archives. In a letter to Anna Strunsky Walling (September 18, 1933)

Abbott wondered how far one used words like "anarchism" and "socialism" as mere pegs "to hang our emotions on."

97. *The Road to Freedom*, April 1931.

98. Emma Goldman to Joseph Ishill, December 29, 1927; Leonard Abbott to Emma Goldman, February 22, 1932, Goldman Archive.

99. Leonard Abbott to Thomas H. Bell, September 23, 1935, Bell Papers.

100. Leonard Abbott to Anna Strunsky Walling, September 11, 1937, Walling Papers.

101. Jerre Mangione, *The Dream and the Deal: The Federal Writers' Project, 1935-1943*, Boston, 1972, p. 62.

102. Henry T. Schnittkind to Leonard Abbott, September 19, 1942, Abbott Papers. Abbott edited two volumes in the series, *Masters of Government* (1947) and *Masters of Economics* (1948).

103. Harry Kelly to Joseph Cohen, December 1, 1944, Cohen Papers.

104. Leonard Abbott to Anna Schwartz, October 4, 1949, Abbott Papers.

105. Leonard Abbott to E. Haldeman-Julius, July 16, 1949, Walling Papers.

106. Interview with William Morris Abbott, January 14, 1972.

107. Leonard Abbott, handwritten notes, March 19, 1951, and October 26, 1952, Abbott Papers.

108. Leonard Abbott to Alexander Harvey, April 2, 1951; Abbott to Mr. Harper, February 22, 1947, Abbott Papers; Abbott to Anna Strunsky Walling, n.d., Walling Papers.

109. Will Durant to Manuel Komroff, January 25, 1940, Abbott Papers.

110. Theodore Schroeder to Marc Epstein, n.d. [May 1939], Kelly Papers.

111. Harry Kelly to Max Nettlau, October 6, 1919, Nettlau Archive.

112. Harry Kelly to Max Nettlau, October 21, 1925, and May 4, 1926, Nettlau Archive.

113. Harry Kelly to Alexander Berkman, June 9, 1925, Berkman Archive.

114. Kelly, "Roll Back the Years," 32:3. The League for Mutual Aid was dissolved in 1971, after half a century of activity.

115. Harry Kelly to Jacques Rudome, April 15, 1932, Rudome Papers.

116. These letters, along with the rest of Kelly's papers, were unfortunately lost in the mid-1970s.

117. Harry Kelly to Max Nettlau, November 15, 1933, Nettlau Archive.

118. *Man!*, December 1938; interview with Lallah Blanpied, April 7, 1972.

119. Harry Kelly to Max Nettlau, June 18, 1932, September 18, 1935, and May 27, 1937, Nettlau Archive.

120. Harry Kelly to Max Nettlau, July 18, 1939, Nettlau Archive; *Fraye Arbeter Shtime*, November 11, 1937.

121. Harry Kelly to Jacques Rudome, February 3, 1940, Rudome Papers; Kelly to Abbott, October 9, 1941, Abbott Papers.

122. *Freedom* (New York), September 1933; Kelly to Abbott, May 27, 1940, and October 8, 1941, Abbott Papers; Kelly to David Lawson, July 11, 1941, Ridge Papers.

123. Harry Kelly to Leonard Abbott, September 18, 1941, Abbott Papers; Kelly to John Nicholas Beffel, February 10, 1948, Beffel Papers.

124. Harry Kelly to Senya and Mollie Fleshin, January 23, 1951, Fleshin Archive; Anna Schwartz to Leonard Abbott, June 22, 1951, Abbott Papers.

125. A plaque to Kelly remains on the building of the Mohegan Modern School, of which he was the principal founder. His wife Leah died in 1977.

126. Cohen himself produced an interesting account: *In Quest of Heaven: The Story of the Sunrise Co-operative Farm Community*.

127. Interview with Johanna Boetz, New York City, December 4, 1972. Cohen's history of the Jewish anarchist movement in America, published in 1945, is dedicated to Sophie's memory.

128. Joseph Cohen to Max Nettlau, July 9, 1923, Nettlau Archive.

129. Joseph Cohen to Max Nettlau, July 29, 1929, Nettlau Archive.

130. *Ibid.*; Cohen to Nettlau, August 30, 1923, Nettlau Archive.

131. Joseph Cohen to the Iberian Anarchist Federation (FAI), February 23, 1937, Sunrise Archives.

132. Introduction to *In Quest of Heaven*, p. xiv.

133. Joseph Cohen to Harry Kelly, October 23, 1952, Kelly Papers.

CHAPTER 11

1. "The Ferrer Modern School," *Freedom* (New York), June 1934.

2. Third Conference of Friends of Modern School, Rutgers University, September 27, 1975.

3. Voltairine Winokour Garst to Reunion Committee of the Friends of the Modern School, December 1, 1976, Rutgers University.

4. *Modern School of Stelton*, p. 21.

5. Harry Kelly, "The Seventh Anniversary of the Stelton School," *The Modern School*, Summer 1921.

Bibliography

ARCHIVAL MATERIALS

The Modern School Collection, Rutgers University. The principal repository for materials on the Modern Schools. Includes the papers of the Modern School Association of North America and of Alexis and Elizabeth Ferm, together with a wealth of correspondence, photographs, brochures, pamphlets, books, and a nearly complete set of *The Modern School* magazine.

The International Institute of Social History, Amsterdam. Houses the foremost collection of anarchist materials in the world, with considerable holdings relating to the Ferrer movement. Citations in the notes from the Berkman, Fleshin, Goldman, Nettlau, Nomad, Ramus, and Rocker archives refer to this collection.

The Labadie Collection, University of Michigan. The best collection of anarchist literature in the United States, containing an immense quantity of printed and manuscript sources, many of them bearing upon the history of the Modern Schools.

Other Libraries and Archives. The papers of Joseph Cohen are preserved in the Bund Archives of the Jewish Labor Movement, New York. The New York Public Library has papers of Emma Goldman not available in the International Institute of Social History, as well as the papers of Benjamin Tucker and fragments of the papers of Carlo Tresca, Sadakichi Hartmann, and Bolton Hall. The bulk of the Hartmann papers are to be found at the University of California, Riverside, and further Bolton Hall materials are housed in the New-York Historical Society. The YIVO Institute of Jewish Research, New York, contains the papers of Dr. Michael A. Cohn and of Abraham L. Goldman as well as relevant printed materials. The Municipal Archive and Records Center of New York City has documents relating to the unemployment crisis of 1913-1914.

An important source for materials on the Ferrer movement, as well as on the anarchist movement as a whole, is the Joseph Ishill collection at Harvard University, supplemented by Ishill's papers at the University of Florida, Gainesville. Yale University houses the papers of Hutchins Hapgood, Robert Henri, and Alfred Stieglitz. Columbia University possesses partial collections of the papers of Theodore Schroeder, Robert Minor, and Rockwell Kent. The papers of Carl Zigrosser and Albert Mordell are in the library of the University of Pennsylvania.

Additional materials are to be found among the papers of Mary Heaton Vorse, John Nicholas Beffel, and Nicholas Steelink, housed in the Archives of Labor History and Urban Affairs at Wayne State University, Detroit; the Margaret Sanger Papers in the Library of Congress; the Jane Addams collection at Hull House, Chicago; the Dana Family Papers, Radcliffe College; the Lola Ridge Papers, Smith College (plus a valuable letter from Lola Ridge to Harold Loeb, dated February 1922, in the Loeb Papers, Princeton University); the Anna Strunsky Walling Papers at the Huntington Library, San Marino, California; and the Ben L. Reitman Papers, University of Illinois, Chicago Circle.

Other institutions with pertinent sources are the Tamiment Library of New York University; the Baskette Collection, University of Illinois, Urbana; the State Historical Society of Wisconsin, Madison; and the Centre International de Recherches sur l'Anarchisme, Geneva.

Private Collections. The most important are the Leonard Abbott Papers, the Harry Kelly Papers (now lost), the Seldes Family Papers, the Minna Lowensohn Papers, the Jacques and Helen Rudome Papers, the Suzanne Hotkine Avins Papers, and the Mohegan Colony Archives, all in New York City, and the James and Nellie Dick Papers, Oyster Bay, Long Island. The Dora Keyser Papers and the Thomas H. Bell Papers are located in Los Angeles, and the Sunrise Colony Papers in Fort Lauderdale, Florida.

Books, Pamphlets, and Articles

Aaron, Daniel. *Writers on the Left*. New York, Harcourt, Brace, 1961.

Abbott, Leonard D. *Ernest Howard Crosby: A Valuation and a Tribute*. Westwood, Mass., the Ariel Press, 1907.

———, ed. *Francisco Ferrer: His Life, Work and Martyrdom*. New York, Francisco Ferrer Association, 1910.

———, ed. *London's Essays of Revolt*. New York, Vanguard, 1926.

———, ed. *Masterworks of Economics: Digests of Ten Great Classics*. Garden City, N.Y., Doubleday, 1948.

———, ed. *Masterworks of Government: Digests of Thirteen Great Classics*. Garden City, N.Y., Doubleday, 1947.

———. *The Root of the Social Problem*. New York, Socialistic Cooperative Publishing Association, 1904.

———. *A Socialistic Wedding: Being the Account of the Marriage of George D. Herron and Carrie Rand*. New York, Knickerbocker Press, n.d. [1901].

———. *The Society of the Future*. Girard, Kans., J. A. Wayland, 1898.

———. *Sociology and Political Economy*. New York, The Current Literature Publishing Co., 1909.

——— and William Thurston Brown, eds. *The Detroit Francisco Ferrer Modern School*. New York, Herold Press, 1912. I have not been able to locate a copy of this pamphlet.

Abrams, Ann U. "The Ferrer Center: New York's Unique Meeting of Anarchism and the Arts," *New York History*, LIX (July 1978), 306-25.

Adamic, Louis. *Dynamite: The Story of Class Violence in America*. Revised edn., New York, Harper, 1935.

Adams, Graham. *Age of Industrial Violence, 1910-15*. New York, Columbia University Press, 1966.

Addresses in Memory of Ernest Howard Crosby (1856-1907). New York, E. H. Crosby Memorial Committee, 1907.

Alexander Berkman: Rebel and Anarchist. New York, Alexander Berkman Memorial Committee and Jewish Anarchist Federation, 1936.

Alexander Berkman: Sixtieth Birthday Celebration. New York, Marstin Press, 1930.

Alyea, Paul E. and Blanche R. *Fairhope, 1894-1954: The Story of a Single Tax Colony*. Birmingham, Ala., University of Alabama Press, 1956.

Archer, William. *The Life, Trial, and Death of Francisco Ferrer*. London, Chapman & Hall, 1911.

Avrich, Paul. *An American Anarchist: The Life of Voltairine de Cleyre*. Princeton, Princeton University Press, 1978.

———, ed. *The Anarchists in the Russian Revolution*. Ithaca, Cornell University Press, 1973.

———. *Kronstadt 1921*. Princeton, Princeton University Press, 1970.

———. "Kropotkin in America," *International Review of Social History*, 1980, Part 1.

———, ed. "Prison Letters of Ricardo Flores Magón to Lilly Sarnoff," *International Review of Social History*, XXII (1977), 379-422.

———. *The Russian Anarchists*. Princeton, Princeton University Press, 1967.

Axtell, James, L., ed. *The Educational Writings of John Locke*. Cambridge, Cambridge University Press, 1968.

Baez, Joan. *Daybreak*. New York, Dial, 1968.

Bailie, William. *Josiah Warren: The First American Anarchist*. Boston, Small, Maynard, & Co., 1906.

Bakunin, Michael. *God and the State*. New York, Dover Publications, 1970.

———. *Oeuvres*. 6 vols., Paris, 1895-1913.

Bauch, Solomon. *Whose Fault?* New York, S. Bauch, 1908.

Baudouin, Charles. *Tolstoy: The Teacher*. London, Kegan Paul, 1923.

Baur, John I. H. *Revolution and Tradition in Modern American Art*. Cambridge, Mass., Harvard University Press, 1959.

Baxendall, Rosalyn Froud. "Elizabeth Gurley Flynn: The Early Years," *Radical America*, VIII (1975), 97-115.

Beecher, Jonathan and Richard Bienvenu, eds. *The Utopian Vision of Charles Fourier*. Boston, Beacon Press, 1971.

Bek-Gran, Robert. *Apologia pro Vita Mia*. Dresden, the Author, 1926.

———. *Vom Wesen der Anarchie*. Nürnberg, "Der Bund," 1920.

Bell, Stephen. *Rebel, Priest and Prophet: A Biography of Dr. Edward McGlynn*. New York, Devin-Adair, 1937.

Bell, Thomas H. *Edward Carpenter: The English Tolstoi*. Los Angeles, Libertarian Group, 1932.

Belz, Carl. "Man Ray and New York Dada," *The Art Journal*, XXIII (Spring 1964), 207-13.

Bercovici, Konrad. *It's the Gypsy in Me*. New York, Prentice-Hall, 1941.

Bercovici, Rion. "A Radical Childhood," *Scribner's Magazine*, XCII (August 1932), 102-106.

Berens, L. H. *The Digger Movement in the Days of the Commonwealth*. London, Simpkin, Marshall, 1906.

Berkman, Alexander. *The "Anti-Climax": The Concluding Chapter of My Russian Diary "The Bolshevik Myth"*. Berlin, Maurer & Dimmick, 1925.

———. *The Bolshevik Myth (Diary 1920-22)*. New York, Boni & Liveright, 1925.

———. *The Kronstadt Rebellion*. Berlin, "Der Syndikalist," 1922.

———. *Now and After: The ABC of Communist Anarchism*. New York, Vanguard, 1929.

———. *Prison Memoirs of an Anarchist*. New York, Mother Earth Publishing Association, 1912.

———, ed. *The Russian Revolution and the Communist Party*. Berlin, "Der Syndikalist," 1922.

———. *The Russian Tragedy (A Review and an Outlook)*. Berlin, "Der Syndikalist," 1922.

——— and Emma Goldman. *Anarchism on Trial: Speeches of Alexander Berkman and Emma Goldman before the United States District Court in the City of New York, July 1917*. New York, Mother Earth Publishing Association, 1917.

——— and Emma Goldman. *Deportation: Its Meaning and Menace*. Introduction by Robert Minor. New York, League for the Amnesty of Political Prisoners, 1919.

Bestor, Arthur E. *Backwoods Utopias: The Sectarian Origins and the Owenite Phase of Communitarian Socialism in America, 1663-1829*. 2nd edn., Philadelphia, University of Pennsylvania Press, 1970.

———, ed. *Education and Reform at New Harmony: Correspondence of William Maclure and Marie Duclos Fretageot, 1820-1833*. Indianapolis, Indiana Historical Society, 1948.

Bluestein, Abe. *Forgotten Men, What Now?* Bronx, N.Y., Libertarian Publishers, n.d. [1935].

Boswell, Peyton, Jr. *George Bellows*. New York, Crown, 1942.

Boyd, Carolyn P. "The Anarchists and Education in Spain, 1868-1909," *The Journal of Modern History*, XLVIII (December 1976), 125-72.

Boyesen, Bayard, *The Marsh: A Poem*. Boston, R. G. Badger, 1905.

———. *The Modern School in New York*. New York, Francisco Ferrer Association, n.d. [1911].

———. *Prospectus of the Francisco Ferrer Association of New York*. New York, n.d. [1911].

Braider, Donald. *George Bellows and the Ashcan School of Painting*. Garden City, N.Y., Doubleday, 1971.

Brenan, Gerald. *The Spanish Labyrinth*. Cambridge, Cambridge University Press, 1943.

Brissenden, Paul F. *The I.W.W.: A Study of American Syndicalism*. New York, Columbia University Press, 1919.

Brock, Peter. *Pacifism in the United States: From the Colonial Era to the First World War*. Princeton, Princeton University Press, 1968.

Brooks, John G. *American Syndicalism: The I.W.W.* New York, Macmillan, 1913.

Brooks, Van Wyck. *John Sloan: A Painter's Life*. New York, Dutton, 1955.

Brown, Milton W. *American Painting: From the Armory Show to the Depression*. Princeton, Princeton University Press, 1955.

Brown, William Thurston. *After Capitalism, What?* Chicago, Charles H. Kerr & Co., 1900.

———. *The Axe at the Root*. Chicago, Charles H. Kerr, 1901.

———. *Citizenship and Education*. Stelton, N.J., Ferrer Colony, n.d. [1917].

———. *Education for Constructive Democracy*. Stelton, N.J., Ferrer Colony, n.d. [1918].

———. *The Education for Tomorrow's Men and Women: The Purpose, Plan and Needs of the Modern School*. Los Angeles, Walt Whitman School, 1922.

———. *How Capitalism Has Hypnotized Society*. Chicago, Charles H. Kerr, 1912.

———. *Love's Freedom and Fulfilment*. Portland, Ore., The Modern School, n.d.

———. *The Modern School*. Salt Lake City, The Modern School, 1911. I have not been able to find this pamphlet.

———. *The Moral Basis of the Demand for Free Divorce*. Portland, Ore., The Modern School, n.d.

———. *The Most Important Educational Experiment in America*. Stelton, N.J., Ferrer Colony, n.d. [1917 or 1918].

———. *The Need of Religion as a Means of Knowing the Real Value of Things*. Salt Lake City, N. S. Dresser, n.d. [1910?].

———. "The Proposals of Socialism and Anarchism Compared." n.p., n.d., mimeographed.

Brown, William Thurston. *Prospectus of the Modern School Established at Salt Lake City*. Salt Lake City, The Modern School, 1910.

———. *The Real Menace of Bolshevism: A Plea for 100% Americanism*. Los Angeles, International Printing Co., 1919.

———. *The Relation of Religion to Social Ethics*. Chicago, Charles H. Kerr, 1901.

———. *The Revolutionary Proletariat*. Chicago, Industrial Workers of the World, n.d.

———. *Walt Whitman: Poet of the Human Whole*. Portland, Ore., The Modern School, 1912.

———. *The Walt Whitman School*. Los Angeles, Walt Whitman School, n.d. [1922].

———. *What Socialism Means as a Philosophy and as a Movement*. Portland, Ore., The Modern School, n.d. [1911 or 1912].

———. *Will You Have War or Peace?* n.p., n.d. [Chicago, Industrial Workers of the World, 1912?].

Bruno, Guido. *Anarchists*. New York, the Author, n.d. [1914 or 1915].

Bucci, John A. "Philosophical Anarchism and Education." Ph.D. dissertation, Boston University, 1974.

Burgess, Charles O. "The Educational State in America: Selected Views on Learning as the Key to Utopia, 1800-1924." Ph.D. dissertation, University of Wisconsin, 1962.

———. "William Maclure and Education for a Good Society," *History of Education Quarterly*, III (June 1963), 58-76.

By Myself: I'm a Book! An Oral History of the Immigrant Jewish Experience in America. Waltham, Mass., American Jewish Historical Society, 1972.

Cahill, Holger. *Max Weber*. New York, The Downtown Gallery, 1930.

Cahn, William. *A Pictorial History of American Labor*. New York, Crown, 1972.

Calvert, Bruce. *Emma Goldman and the Police*. n.p., n.d.

———. *Rational Education*. Griffith, Ind., Open Road Press, 1911.

———. *Thirty Years on the Open Road with Bruce Calvert*. New York, Greenberg, 1941.

Carr, Raymond. *Spain: 1808-1939*. Oxford, Oxford University Press, 1966.

Centennial Expressions on Peter Kropotkin, 1842-1942. Los Angeles, Rocker Publications Committee, 1942.

Chafee, Zechariah. *Free Speech in the United States*. Cambridge, Mass., Harvard University Press, 1942.

Chamberlain, Lawrence H. *Loyalty and Legislative Action: A Survey of Activity by the New York State Legislature, 1919-1949*. Ithaca, N.Y., Cornell University Press, 1951.

Churchill, Allen. *The Improper Bohemians*. New York, Dutton, 1959.

Claghorn, Kate H. *The Immigrant's Day in Court*. New York, Harper, 1923.

Clark, Jane P. *Deportation of Aliens from the United States to Europe*. New York, Columbia University Press, 1931.

Clay, James Arrington. *A Voice from the Prison*. Boston, B. Marsh, 1856.

Coben, Stanley, *A. Mitchell Palmer: Politician*. New York, Columbia University Press, 1963.

Cohen, Joseph J. *The House Stood Forlorn*. Paris, "E.P.," 1954.

———. *In Quest of Heaven: The Story of the Sunrise Co-operative Farm Community*. New York, Sunrise History Publishing Committee, 1957.

———. *Der Urshprung fun gloybn*. Tel Aviv, Fraye Gedank, 1950.

———. *Di yidish-anarkhistishe bavegung in Amerike*. Philadelphia, Radical Library, 1945.

——— and Alexis C. Ferm. *The Modern School of Stelton*. Stelton, N.J., the Modern School Association of North America, 1925.

Cohn, Michael A. *Some Questions and an Appeal*. New York, Independent Sacco-Vanzetti Committee, n.d. [1927].

———. *Two Worlds: An Imaginary Speech Delivered by Bartolomeo Vanzetti before Judge Webster Thayer*. New York, Independent Sacco-Vanzetti Committee, 1927.

Collier, Peter and David Horowitz. *The Rockefellers: An American Dynasty*. New York, Holt, Rinehart and Winston, 1976.

Collins, John A. *et al., The Social Pioneer, and Herald of Progress*. Boston, J. P. Mendum, 1844.

Conlin, Joseph R. *Big Bill Haywood and the Radical Union Movement*. Syracuse, Syracuse University Press, 1969.

Coryell, John R. *Love and Passion*. New York, Corwill, 1907?

———. *Making of Revolution*. New York, Corwill, 1908.

———. *The Rent Strike*. New York, Corwill, n.d.

———. *Sex Union and Parenthood, and What Is Seduction?* New York, Mother Earth Publishing Association, n.d.

Coryell, Russell M. "The Birth of Nick Carter," *The Bookman*, LXIX (July 1929), 495-502.

Craik, William W. *The Central Labour College, 1909-29*. London, Lawrence & Wishart, 1964.

Cremin, Lawrence A. *The Transformation of the School: Progressivism in American Education, 1876-1957*. New York, Knopf, 1961.

Crosby, Ernest Howard. *Edward Carpenter: Poet and Prophet*. Philadelphia, The Conservator, 1901.

———. *Tolstoy as a Schoolmaster*. Chicago, The Hammersmark Publishing Co., 1904.

Curti, Merle. *The Social Ideas of American Educators*. New York, Scribner's, 1935.

Dana, H.W.L. *The Dana Saga: Three Generations of the Dana Family in Cambridge*. Cambridge, Mass., The Cambridge Historical Society, 1941.

David, Henry. *The History of the Haymarket Affair*. New York, Farrar & Rinehart, 1936.

De Casseres, Benjamin. *Forty Immortals*. New York, J. Lawren, 1926.

———. *Mirrors of New York*. New York, J. Lawren, 1925.

———. *Works*. 3 vols., New York, the Author, 1936-1939.

De Cleyre, Voltairine. *Selected Works of Voltairine de Cleyre*. New York, Mother Earth Publishing Association, 1914.

Degalvès, Manuel. *L'Education et la liberté*. Paris, Bibliothèque de la Critique, 1900.

De Lima, Agnes. *Our Enemy, the Child*. New York, New Republic, Inc., 1926.

Dell, Floyd. *Homecoming*. New York, Farrar & Rinehart, 1933.

———. *Love in Greenwich Village*. New York, Doran, 1926.

———. *Women as World Builders*. Chicago, Forbes, 1913.

Dennison, George. *The Lives of Children: The Story of the First Street School*. New York, Random House, 1969.

Deutsch, Helen and Stella Hanau. *The Provincetown: A Story of the Theatre*. New York, Farrar & Rinehart, 1931.

Diggins, John P. *The American Left in the Twentieth Century*. New York, Harcourt, Brace, 1973.

Dolgoff, Sam, ed. *Bakunin on Anarchy*. New York, Knopf, 1972.

Draper, Theodore. *American Communism and Soviet Russia*. New York, Viking, 1960.

———. *The Roots of American Communism*. New York, Viking, 1957.

Drinnon, Richard. *Rebel in Paradise: A Biography of Emma Goldman*. Chicago, University of Chicago Press, 1961.

——— and Anna Maria Drinnon, eds. *Nowhere at Home: Letters from Exile of Emma Goldman and Alexander Berkman*. New York, Schocken Books, 1975.

Dubin, Barbara H. "A Critical Report of the Social and Educational Theories of Josiah Warren and His Individualist School of Anarchism." Ph.D. dissertation, University of Illinois, 1973.

Dubofsky, Melvyn. *We Shall Be All: A History of the Industrial Workers of the World*. Chicago, Quandrangle, 1969.

Dudden, Arthur P. *Joseph Fels and the Single-Tax Movement*. Philadelphia, Temple University Press, 1971.

Durant, William J. *The Ferrer Modern School*. New York, Francisco Ferrer Association, n.d. [1912].

———. *Socialism and Anarchism*. New York, Albert & Charles Boni, 1914.

———. *Transition: A Sentimental Story of One Mind and One Era*. New York, Simon & Schuster, 1927.

——— and Ariel Durant. *A Dual Autobiography*. New York, Simon & Schuster, 1977.

Dykhuizen, George. *The Life and Mind of John Dewey*. Carbondale, Ill. Southern Illinois University Press, 1973.

Eastman, Max. *Enjoyment of Living*. New York, Harper, 1948.
———. *Love and Revolution*. New York, Random House, 1964.
Edelman, John W. *Labor Lobbyist: The Autobiography of John W. Edelman*. Ed. by Joseph Carter. New York, Bobbs-Merrill, 1974.
Edward Bond Foote: Biographical Notes and Appreciatives. New York, Free Speech League, 1913.
Edwards, Stewart. *The Paris Commune, 1871*. London, Eyre & Spottiswood, 1971.
———, ed. *Selected Writings of Pierre-Joseph Proudhon*. Garden City, N.Y., Anchor Books, 1969.
Egbert, Donald Drew. *Social Radicalism and the Arts: Western Europe: A Cultural History from the French Revolution to 1968*. New York, Knopf, 1970.
——— and Stow Persons, eds. *Socialism and American Life*. 2 vols., Princeton, Princeton University Press, 1952.
Eggers, George W. *George Bellows*. New York, Whitney Museum, 1931.
Faure, Sébastien. *La Ruche: son but, son organisation, sa portée sociale*. Rambouillet, La Ruche, 1914.
Ferm, Alexis C. *The Problem of Education*. Stelton, N.J., The Modern School, 1934.
Ferm, Elizabeth Byrne. *Freedom in Education*. New York, Lear Publishers, 1949.
———. *The Spirit of Freedom in Education*. Stelton, N.J., The Modern School, 1919.
Ferrer y Guardia, Francisco. *The Modern School*. New York, Mother Earth Publishing Association, n.d. [1909].
———. *The Origin and Ideals of the Modern School*. London, Watts, 1913.
Ferrer, Sol. *Le véritable Francisco Ferrer*. Paris, L'Ecran du Monde, 1948.
———. *La vie et l'oeuvre de Francisco Ferrer: Un martyr au XXe siècle*. Paris, Librairie Fischbacher, 1962.
Fishman, William J. *East End Jewish Radicals, 1875-1914*. London, Duckworth, 1975.
Fleisher, David. *William Godwin: A Study in Liberalism*. London, Allen & Unwin, 1951.
Flexner, Eleanor. *Century of Struggle: The Women's Rights Movement in the United States*. Cambridge, Mass., Harvard University Press, 1959.
Flynn, Elizabeth Gurley. *The Rebel Girl, An Autobiography: My First Life (1906-1926)*. New York, International Publishers, 1973.
Fosdick, Raymond B. *John D. Rockefeller, Jr.: A Portrait*. New York, Harper, 1956.
Fourier, Charles. *Design for Utopia*. New York, Schocken Books, 1971.
Fowler, Gene. *Minutes of the Last Meeting*. New York, Viking, 1954.
Frazer, Winifred L. *E. G. and E.G.O.: Emma Goldman and "The Iceman Cometh."* Gainesville, Fla., University Presses of Florida, 1974.

Freeman, Alden *et al. The Fight for Free Speech: A Supplement to "Law-Breaking by the Police"*. East Orange, N.J., Record Printers, 1909.

———. *The Suppression of Free Speech in New York and New Jersey: Law-Breaking by the Police at Lexington Hall, May 23, 1909*. East Orange, N.J., Record Printers, 1909.

Freeman, Joseph. *An American Testament*. New York, Farrar & Rinehart, 1936.

Freeman-Ishill, Rose. *Collected Works*. 8 vols., Berkeley Heights, N.J., The Oriole Press, 1962.

———. *Petals Blown Adrift*. New York, Joseph Ishill, 1918.

———. *Rain Among the Bamboos*. Stelton, N.J., J. Ishill, 1917.

Fried, Albert. ed. *Socialism in America*. Garden City, N.Y., Anchor Books, 1970.

Froebel, Friedrich. *The Education of Man*. New York, Appleton, 1887.

Frost, Richard H. *The Mooney Case*. Stanford, Stanford University Press, 1968.

Galcerán-Ferrer, Francisco. *In difesa di Francesco Ferrer*. Barre, Vt., Gruppo di Anarchici, 1910.

Ganz, Marie. *Rebels: Into Anarchy–and Out Again*. New York, Dodd, Mead, 1920.

Gelb, Arthur and Barbara. *O'Neill*. New York, Harper, 1962.

Giffin, Frederick C. *Six Who Protested Radical Opposition to the First World War*. Port Washington, N.Y., Kennikat Press, 1977.

Gilbert, James B. *Writers and Partisans: A History of Literary Radicalism in America*. New York, Wiley, 1968.

Giroud, Gabriel. *Cempuis: Education intégrale*. Paris, Schleicher, 1900.

———. *Paul Robin: sa vie, ses idées, son action*. Paris, G. Mignolet et Storz, 1937.

Gold, Michael [real name Irwin Granich]. *Mike Gold: A Literary Anthology*. Edited by Michael Folsom. New York, International Publishers, 1972.

Goldberg, Harold J. "Goldman and Berkman View the Bolshevik Regime," *Slavonic and East European Review*, LIII (April 1975), 272-76.

Goldman, Emma. *Anarchism and Other Essays*. New York, Mother Earth Publishing Association, 1911.

———. *The Crushing of the Russian Revolution*. London, Freedom Press, 1922.

———. *Living My Life*. New York, Knopf, 1931.

———. *My Disillusionment in Russia*. London, C. W. Daniel, 1925.

———. *The Social Significance of the Modern Drama*. Boston, R. G. Badger, 1914.

———. *The Truth About the Boylsheviki* (sic). New York, Mother Earth Publishing Association, 1918.

———. *Voltairine de Cleyre*. Berkeley Heights, N.J., The Oriole Press, 1932.

——— and Alexander Berkman. *A Fragment of the Prison Experiences of Emma Goldman and Alexander Berkman*. New York, Stella Comyn, 1919.

Goodman, Paul. *Compulsory Mis-Education*. New York, Horizon, 1964.

———. *Growing Up Absurd*. New York, Random House, 1960.

Goodrich, Lloyd. *Max Weber*. New York, The Whitney Museum of American Art, 1949.

Gordon, Linda. *Woman's Body, Woman's Right: A Social History of Birth Control in America*. New York, Grossman Publishers, 1976.

Graham, Marcus, ed. *An Anthology of Revolutionary Poetry*. New York, M. Graham, 1929.

———. *The Issues of the Present War*. London, Freedom Press, 1943.

———, ed. *Man! An Anthology of Anarchist Ideas, Essays, Poetry and Commentaries*. London, Cienfuegos Press, 1974.

Graham, Patricia A. *Progressive Education: From Arcady to Academe*. New York, Teachers College Press, 1967.

Graubard, Allen. *Free the Children: Radical Reform and the Free School Movement*. New York, Pantheon, 1973.

Grave, Jean. *Enseignement bourgeois et enseignement libertaire*. Paris, Les Temps Nouveaux, 1900.

Green, Jonathan, ed. *Camera Work: A Critical Anthology*. Millerton, N.Y., 1973.

Gumbert, Edgar B. and Joel H. Spring. *The Superschool and the Superstate: A History of American Education in the Twentieth Century, 1918-1970*. New York, Wiley, 1974.

Hale, Nathan G., Jr. *Freud and the Americans: The Beginnings of Psychoanalysis in the United States, 1876-1917*. New York, Oxford University Press, 1971.

Hall, Bolton. *Equitable Taxation: Six Essays*. New York, Crowell, 1892.

———. *Three Acres and Liberty*. Revised edn., New York, Macmillan, 1918.

Hapgood, Hutchins. *An Anarchist Woman*. New York, Duffield, 1909.

———. *The Spirit of Labor*. New York, Duffield, 1907.

———. *The Spirit of the Ghetto*. New York, Funk & Wagnalls, 1902.

———. *A Victorian in the Modern World*. New York, Harcourt, Brace, 1939.

Harding, Walter, R. *A Thoreau Handbook*. New York, New York University Press, 1959.

Harris, David. *Socialist Origins in the United States: American Forerunners of Marx, 1817-1832*. Assen, The Netherlands, Van Gorcum, 1966.

Harris, Leon. *Upton Sinclair: American Rebel*. New York, Crowell, 1975.

Harrison, J.F.C. *Quest for the New Moral World: Robert Owen and the Owenites in Britain and America*. New York, Scribner, 1969.

Hartmann, Sadakichi. *Buddha, Confucius, Christ: Three Prophetic*

Plays. Edited by Harry Lawton and George Knox. New York, Herder & Herder, 1971.

———. *A History of American Art*. 2 vols., Boston, L. C. Page, 1902.

———. *Passport to Immortality*. Beaumont, Calif., the Author, 1927.

———. *The Valiant Knights of Daguerre*. Edited by Harry Lawton and George Knox. Berkeley, University of California Press, 1978.

———. *White Chrysanthemums: Literary Fragments and Pronouncements*. Edited by George Knox and Harry Lawton. New York, Herder & Herder, 1971.

Havel, Hippolyte. *Bakunin, May 30, 1814-July 1, 1876*. New York, Centenary Commemoration Committee, 1914.

———. *Harry Kelly: An Appreciation*. Stelton, N.J., Ferrer Colony, 1921.

———, ed. *The Revolutionary Almanac, 1914*. New York, The Rabelais Press, 1914.

———. *What's Anarchism?* Chicago, Free Society Group, 1932.

Haywood, William D. *Bill Haywood's Book: The Autobiography of William D. Haywood*. New York, International Publishers, 1929.

Hemmings, Ray. *Children's Freedom: A. S. Neill and the Evolution of the Summerhill Idea*. London, Allen & Unwin, 1972.

Henri, Robert. *The Art Spirit*. Philadelphia, Lippincott, 1923.

Hillquit, Morris. *History of Socialism in the United States*. New York, Funk & Wagnalls, 1910.

Hofstadter, Richard and Michael Wallace, eds. *American Violence: A Documentary History*. New York, Knopf, 1970.

Holbrook, Stewart. "Anarchists at Home," *The American Scholar*, xv (Autumn 1946), 425-38.

Holloway, Mark. *Heavens on Earth: Utopian Communities in America, 1680-1880*. 2nd edn., New York, Dover Publications, 1966.

Holton, Bob. *British Syndicalism, 1900-1914*. London, Pluto Press, 1977.

Homer, William Innes. *Alfred Stieglitz and the American Avant-Garde*. Boston, Little, Brown, 1977.

———. *Robert Henri and His Circle*. Ithaca, N.Y., Cornell University Press, 1969.

Hopkins, Pryns. *Both Hands Before the Fire*. Penobscot, Maine, Traversity Press, 1962.

———. *Philosophy of Helpfullness* (sic). Minneapolis, Pioneer Printers, n.d.

Hutchinson, Robert H. *The "Socialism" of New Zealand*. New York, New Review Publishing Association, 1916.

Inklings of Activities of Children at the Modern School. Stelton, N.J., The Modern School, 1937.

Ishill, Joseph, ed. *The Centenary of Walt Whitman's "Leaves of Grass," 1855-1955*. Berkeley Heights, N.J., The Oriole Press, 1955.

———. *Correspondencia selecta de Joseph Ishill*. Edited by Vladimiro Muñoz. Mexico City, Ediciones Tierra y Libertad, 1967.

———, ed. *Elisée and Elie Reclus: In Memoriam*. Berkeley Heights, N.J., The Oriole Press, 1927.

———. *Emma Goldman: A Challenging Rebel*. Berkeley Heights, N.J., The Oriole Press, 1957.

———, ed. *Free Vistas: An Anthology of Life and Letters*. 2 vols., Berkeley Heights, N.J., The Oriole Press, 1933-1937.

———, ed. *Havelock Ellis: In Appreciation*. Berkeley Heights, N.J., The Oriole Press, 1929.

———, ed. *The Oriole Press: A Bibliography*. Berkeley Heights, N.J., The Oriole Press, 1953.

———. *The Oriole Press: A Few Comments on the Typographical Publications*. Berkeley Heights, N.J., The Oriole Press, 1950.

———, ed. *Peter Kropotkin: The Rebel, Thinker and Humanitarian*. Berkeley Heights, N.J., Free Spirit Press, 1923.

———. *Theodore Schroeder: An Evolutionary Psychologist*. Berkeley Heights, N.J., The Oriole Press, 1964.

Jaffe, Julian F. *Crusade Against Radicalism: New York During the Red Scare, 1914-1924*. Port Washington, N.Y., Kennikat Press, 1972.

Johnson, Marietta. *Thirty Years With an Idea*. Fairhope, Ala., The Organic School/University of Alabama Press, 1974.

Joll, James. *The Anarchists*. London, Eyre & Spottiswood, 1964.

Jones, Howard Mumford, ed. *Emerson on Education*. New York, Teachers College Press, 1966.

Kaplan, Justin. *Lincoln Steffens: A Biography*. New York, Simon & Schuster, 1974.

Kelly, Harry. *The Ferrer Modern School*. Stelton, N.J., Modern School Association of North America, 1920.

———. "Roll Back the Years: Odyssey of a Libertarian." Edited by John Nicholas Beffel. Unpublished autobiography, Tamiment Library.

Kemp, Harry. *Tramping on Life: An Autobiographical Narrative*. New York, Boni & Liveright, 1922.

Kennedy, David M. *Birth Control in America: The Career of Margaret Sanger*. New Haven, Yale University Press, 1970.

Kent, Rockwell. *It's Me, O Lord: The Autobiography of Rockwell Kent*. New York, Dodd, Mead, 1955.

Kipnis, Ira. *The American Socialist Movement, 1897-1912*. New York, Columbia University Press, 1952.

Koch, Hans. "Elizabeth Byrne Ferm," *The Roman Forum* (Los Angeles), November 1944.

———. *Und sing mein Lied: Gedichte von Hans Koch*. n.p., Friedrich Zwins, 1947.

Koch, Raymond and Charlotte. *Educational Commune: The Story of Commonwealth College*. New York, Schocken Books, 1972.

Komroff, Manuel. *Big City, Little Boy*. New York, Wyn, 1953.

Komroff, Manuel. *Walt Whitman: The Singer and the Chains.* Brooklyn, Long Island University, 1966.

Kornbluh, Joyce L., ed. *Rebel Voices: An I.W.W. Anthology.* Ann Arbor, University of Michigan Press, 1964.

Kreymborg, Alfred. *Troubador: An Autobiography.* New York, Liveright, 1925.

Krimerman, Leonard I. and Lewis Perry, eds. *Patterns of Anarchy.* Garden City, N.Y., Anchor Books, 1966.

Kropotkin, Peter. *Fields, Factories and Workshops.* Revised edn., London, Nelson, 1913.

———. *Kropotkin's Revolutionary Pamphlets.* Edited by Roger N. Baldwin. New York, Vanguard Press, 1927.

Lang, Lucy Robins. *Tomorrow Is Beautiful.* New York, Macmillan, 1948.

Lawrence, Evelyn M., ed. *Friedrich Froebel and English Education.* New York, Philosophical Library, 1953.

Leberstein, Stephen. "Revolutionary Education: French Libertarian Theory and Experiments, 1895-1915." Ph.D. dissertation, University of Wisconsin, 1972.

Levine, Isaac Don. *Eyewitness to History.* New York, Hawthorn, 1973.

Levine, Louis. *Syndicalism in France.* New York, Columbia University Press, 1914.

LeWarne, Charles P. *Utopias on Puget Sound, 1885-1915.* Seattle, University of Washington Press, 1975.

Liber, Benzion. *The Child at Home.* New York, Rational Living, 1922.

———. *A Doctor's Apprenticeship: Autobiographical Sketches.* New York, Rational Living, 1956.

———. *A Glance into People's Lives.* New York, Rational Living, 1954.

Lida, Clara E. "Educación anarquista en la España del ochocientos," *Revista del Occidente*, XCII (1971), 33-47.

The Life and Times of Sadakichi Hartmann, 1867-1944. Exhibition catalogue published by the University Library, University of California, Riverside, 1970.

Lilley, Irene M., ed. *Friedrich Froebel: A Selection from His Writings.* Cambridge, Cambridge University Press, 1967.

A Little of Our Work. Peekskill, N.Y., Mohegan Modern School, 1931.

Lloyd, J. William. *Fantasies of the Strange.* Berkeley Heights, N.J, The Oriole Press, 1940.

———. *Iris-Heart.* Stelton, N.J., Joseph Ishill, 1917.

———. *Life's Beautiful Battle.* Westfield, N.J., The Lloyd Group, 1910.

———. *The Red Heart in a White World.* Westfield, N.J., the Author, 1898.

Lockwood, George B. *The New Harmony Movement, 1818-1848.* New York, Appleton, 1905.

Luhan, Mabel Dodge. *Movers and Shakers.* New York, Harcourt, Brace, 1936.

Luttinger, Paul. *The Burning Question: Rational Education of the Proletariat.* New York, Rational Educational League, 1913.

Lynn, Kenneth S. "The Rebels of Greenwich Village," in *Perspectives in American History,* VIII (1974), 335-77.

Lyons, Eugene. *Assignment in Utopia*. New York, Harcourt, Brace, 1937.

McCabe, Joseph. *The Martyrdom of Ferrer*. London, Watts, 1909.

Macdonald, George E. *Fifty Years of Freethought*. 2 vols., New York, The Truth Seeker, 1929-1931.

McGovern, George and Leonard F. Guttridge. *The Great Coalfield War*. Boston, Houghton Mifflin, 1972.

Maddaloni, Arnold. *Schroeder: The Public Excuser*. Stamford, Conn., the Author, 1936.

Madison, Charles A. *Critics and Crusaders: A Century of American Protest*. 2nd edn., New York, Frederick Ungar, 1959.

Maitron, Jean. *Le mouvement anarchiste en France*. 2 vols., Paris, Maspero, 1975.

Mangione, Jerre. *The Dream and the Deal: The Federal Writers' Project, 1935-1943*. Boston, Little, Brown, 1972.

Marcaccio, Michael D. *The Hapgoods: Three Earnest Brothers*. Charlottesville, University Press of Virginia, 1977.

Marchand, C. Roland. *The American Peace Movement and Social Reform, 1898-1918*. Princeton, Princeton University Press, 1972.

Mark, Arthur. "Two Libertarian Educators: Elizabeth Byrne Ferm and Alexis Constantine Ferm (1857-1971)." Doctor of Education dissertation, Teachers College, Columbia University, 1973.

Martel, J. "Ferrer's Experimental School as a Symbol of Modern Progressive Educational Movement." Ph.D. dissertation, New York University, 1933.

Martin, Alberto, Vladimiro Muñoz, and Federica Montseny. *Breve historia del movimiento anarquista en Estados Unidos de America del Norte*. Toulouse, Ediciones Cultura Obrera, 1973.

Martin, James J. *Men Against the State: The Expositors of Individualist Anarchism in America, 1827-1908*. Revised Edn., Colorado Springs, Colo., Ralph Myles, 1970.

Marx, Karl. *Capital*. Moscow, Foreign Languages Publishing House, 1957.

Maximoff, G. P., ed. *The Political Philosophy of Bakunin: Scientific Anarchism*. Glencoe, Ill., The Free Press, 1953.

May, Henry F. *The End of American Innocence*. New York, Knopf, 1959.

Mendelsohn, Crystal Ishill. "A Complete Checklist of the Publications of Joseph Ishill and His Oriole Press," *The American Book Collector,* XXV (September 1974-February 1975).

Miller, Sally M. *The Radical Immigrant*. New York, Twayne, 1974.

The Modern School: An Experiment in Libertarian Education. Stelton, N.J., The Modern School, n.d. [1948].

Modern School of Stelton: Twenty-Fifth Anniversary, 1915-1940. Stelton, N.J., The Modern School, 1940.

Monroe, Will S. *History of the Pestalozzian Movement in the United States*. Syracuse, C. W. Bardeen, 1907.

Morgan, Charles H. *George Bellows: Painter of America*. New York, Reynal, 1965.

Morton, James F., Jr. *The Curse of Race Prejudice*. New York, the Author, 1906.

———. *The Philosophy of the Single Tax*. New York, the Author, n.d.

———. *The Truth About Francisco Ferrer*. New York, The Truth Seeker, 1913.

Muñoz, Vladimiro. *Alexis C. Ferm, 1870-1972*. Calgary, Alberta, Ediciones La Escuela Moderna de Calgary, 1975.

Murray, Robert K. *Red Scare: A Study in National Hysteria, 1919-1920*. Minneapolis, University of Minnesota Press, 1955.

Nearing, Scott and Alexis C. Ferm. *Has Propaganda Any Value in Education?* Stelton, N.J., The Modern School, 1925.

Neill, A. S. *The Dominie Books of A. S. Neill: "A Dominie's Log," "A Dominie in Doubt," "A Dominie Dismissed."* New York, Hart Publishing Co., 1975.

———. *Summerhill: A Radical Approach to Child-Rearing*. New York, Hart, 1960.

Newton, R. Heber. "Political, Economic, and Religious Causes of Anarchism," *The Arena*, XXVII (1902), 113-25.

Norman, Dorothy. *Alfred Stieglitz: An American Seer*. New York, Random House, 1973.

North, Joseph. *Robert Minor: Artist and Crusader*. New York, International Publishers, 1956.

O'Connor, Harvey. *Revolution in Seattle*. New York, Monthly Review Press, 1964.

Omaggio alla memoria imperitura di Carlo Tresca. New York, Il Martello, 1943.

O'Neill, William L., ed. *Echoes of Revolt: The Masses, 1911-1917*. Chicago, Quadrangle, 1966.

The Paintings of George Bellows. New York, Knopf, 1929.

Panunzio, Constantine M. *The Deportation Cases of 1919-1920*. New York, Federal Council of Churches of Christ, 1921.

Park, Tidu Peter. "The European Reaction to the Execution of Francisco Ferrer." Ph.D. dissertation, University of Virginia, 1970.

Parker, Robert Allerton. *A Yankee Saint: John Humphrey Noyes and the Oneida Community*. New York, Putnam, 1935.

Parry, Albert. *Garrets and Pretenders: A History of Bohemianism in America*. Revised edn., New York, Dover Publications, 1960.

Penrose, Roland. *Man Ray*. London, Thames & Hudson, 1975.

Perlin, Terry M. "Anarchism in New Jersey: The Ferrer Colony at Stelton," *New Jersey History*, Fall 1971, pp. 133-48.

———. "Anarchist-Communism in America, 1890-1914." Ph.D. dissertation, Brandeis University, 1970.

Perry, Lewis C. *Radical Abolitionism: Anarchy and the Government of God in Antislavery Thought*. Ithaca, N.Y., Cornell University Press, 1973.

Peterson, Horace C. and Gilbert C. Fite. *Opponents of War, 1917-1918*. Madison, University of Wisconsin Press, 1957.

Pollin, Burton R. *Education and Enlightenment in the Works of William Godwin*. New York, Las Americas Publishing Co., 1962.

Poole, Dave. "Francisco Ferrer: An Introduction," *The Cienfuegos Press Anarchist Review*, I:3 (Autumn 1977), 59-60.

Post, Louis F. *The Deportation Delirium of Nineteen-Twenty*. Chicago, Charles H. Kerr, 1923.

Pousette-Dart, Nathaniel, ed. *Robert Henri*. New York, Stokes, 1922.

Preston, William, Jr. *Aliens and Dissenters: Federal Repression of Radicals, 1903-1933*. Cambridge, Mass., Harvard University Press, 1963.

Quint, Howard H. *The Forging of American Socialism*. Columbia, S.C., University of South Carolina Press, 1953.

R—skii, M. [probably Maksim Raevskii]. *Frantsisko Ferrer i ego novaia shkola*. Petrograd, Golos Truda, 1920.

Radoslavljevich, Paul R. "The Spirit of Tolstoy's Experimental School," *School and Society*, XXIX (February 9 and 16, 1929), 175-83, 208-15.

Ramus, Pierre [Rudolf Grossmann]. *Francisco Ferrer (10 Januar 1859-13 Oktober 1909): Sein Leben und sein Werk*. Vienna, Erkenntnis und Befreiung, 1921.

Ransom, Will. *Private Presses and Their Books*. New York, Bowker, 1929.

The Rational Education of Children. New York, Francisco Ferrer Association, 1910.

Ray, Man. *Self-Portrait*. Boston, Little, Brown, 1963.

Raymond, Lilly. *Miscellaneous Poems*. Stelton, N.J., the Author, 1971.

Read, Helen Appleton. *Robert Henri*. New York, Whitney Museum, 1931.

——— and Margery Ryerson. "Word Painter: Robert Henri (1865-1929)," in *Great Teachers*, ed. by Houston Peterson. New Brunswick, N.J., Rutgers University Press, 1946.

Read, Herbert. *Education Through Art*. 3rd edn., London, Faber, 1964.

Reed, James. *From Private Vice to Public Virtue: The Birth Control Movement and American Society Since 1830*. New York, Basic Books, 1978.

Reichert, William O. *Partisans of Freedom: A Study in American Anarchism*. Bowling Green, Ohio, Bowling Green University Popular Press, 1976.

Renshaw, Patrick. *The Wobblies: The Story of Syndicalism in the United States*. Garden City, N.Y., Anchor Books, 1967.

Resnick, Nat. *Manuel Komroff: In Memoriam, September 7, 1890-December 10, 1974*. Woodstock, N.Y., Xanadu Press, 1975.

Revolutionary Radicalism: Its History, Purpose and Tactics. 4 vols., Albany, J. B. Lyon, 1920.

Reynolds, Quentin. *The Fiction Factory*. New York, Random House, 1955.

Riasanovsky, Nicholas V. *The Teaching of Charles Fourier*. Berkeley, University of California Press, 1969.

Richmond, William K. *The Free School*. London, Methuen, 1972.

Ridge, Lola. *Dance of Fire*. New York, Smith & Haas, 1935.

———. *Firehead*. New York, Payson & Clarke, 1929.

———. *The Ghetto and Other Poems*. New York, B. W. Huebsch, 1918.

———. *Red Flag*. New York, Viking, 1927.

———. *Sun-up and Other Poems*. New York, B. W. Huebsch, 1920.

Ringenbach, Paul T. *Tramps and Reformers, 1873-1916: The Discovery of Unemployment in New York*. Westport, Conn., Greenwood Press, 1973.

Rischin, Moses. *The Promised City: New York's Jews, 1870-1914*. Cambridge, Mass., Harvard University Press, 1962.

Robert Henri and Five of His Pupils. New York, Century Association, 1946.

Rocker, Rudolf. *Anarcho-Syndicalism: Theory and Practice*. Revised edn., Indore, India, Modern Publishers, 1947.

———. *Francisco Ferrer un di fraye ertsihung fun der yugend*. London, Arbeter Fraynd, 1910.

———. *In Shturem*. Buenos Aires, London Group "Freie Arbeiter Stimme," 1952.

———. *The London Years*. London, Robert Anscombe, 1956.

———. *Milly Witkop-Rocker*. Berkeley Heights, N.J., The Oriole Press, 1956.

———. *Nationalism and Culture*. Los Angeles, Rocker Publications Committee, 1937.

———. *Pioneers of American Freedom*. Los Angeles, Rocker Publications Committee, 1949.

Romero Maura, Joaquín. *"La rosa del fuego"—republicanos y anarquistas*. Barcelona, Ediciones Grijalbo, 1975.

———. "Terrorism in Barcelona and Its Impact on Spanish Politics, 1904-1909," *Past and Present*, No. 41, December 1968, pp. 130-83.

Russell, Charles Edward. *These Shifting Scenes*. New York, Hodder & Stoughton, 1914.

Sacco, Nicola and Bartolomeo Vanzetti. *The Letters of Sacco and Vanzetti*. Edited by Marion Denman Frankfurter and Gardner Jackson. New York, Viking, 1928.

St. John, Bruce, ed. *John Sloan's New York Scene: Notes and Correspondence, 1906-1913*. New York, Harper & Row, 1965.

Sanborn, F. B. and William T. Harris. *A. Bronson Alcott: His Life and Philosophy*. 2 vols., Boston, Roberts, 1893.

Sanger, Margaret H. *An Autobiography*. New York, Norton, 1938.

Sangro y Ros de Olano, Pedro. *La sombra de Ferrer: de la semana trágica a la guerra europea*. Madrid, Sobrinos de la Sucesors de M. Minuesa de los Rios, Miguel Servet, 1917.

Sankey-Jones, Nancy E. *Bibliography of Theodore Schroeder on the Psychology of Religion and the Erotogenetic Interpretation of Mysticism*. Cos Cob, Conn., the Author, 1934.

———. *Theodore Schroeder on Free Speech: A Bibliography*. New York, Free Speech League, 1919.

Schnapper, M. B. *American Labor: A Pictorial Social History*. Washington, D.C., Public Affairs Press, 1972.

Schnittkind, Henry T. *Shambles: A Sketch of the Present War*. Stelton, N.J., Ferrer Colony, n.d., [1916]. Preface by Leonard D. Abbott.

Schroeder, Theodore A. *Constitutional Free Speech Defined and Defended*. New York, Free Speech League, 1919.

———. *The Criminal Anarchy Law; and On Suppressing the Advocacy of Crime*. New York, Mother Earth Publishing Association, 1907.

———. *Erotogenesis of Religion: A Bibliography*. New York, Guido Bruno, 1916.

———. *Free Press Anthology*. New York, Free Speech League, 1909.

———. *Free Speech Bibliography*. New York, H. W. Wilson, 1922.

———. *Free Speech for Radicals*. New York, Free Speech League, 1912.

Schuster, Eunice M. *Native American Anarchism: A Study of Left-Wing American Individualism*. Northampton, Mass., Smith College, 1932.

Schwarz, Arturo. *Man Ray: The Rigour of Imagination*. London, Thames & Hudson, 1977.

Scrivener, Michael. "The Anarchist Aesthetic," *Black Rose* (Boston), I (Spring 1979), 7-21.

Sears, Hal D. *The Sex Radicals: Free Love in High Victorian America*. Lawrence, The Regents Press of Kansas, 1977.

Seldes, George H. *Tell the Truth and Run*. New York, Greenberg, 1953.

Seventy-Fifth Birthday Anniversary Celebration of Rudolph Rocker. Chicago, Rudolph Rocker 75th Jubilee Committee, 1948.

Shannon, David A. *The Socialist Party of America*. New York, Macmillan, 1955.

Shaw, Nellie. *Whiteway: A Colony in the Cotswolds*. London, C. W. Daniel, 1935.

Sheaffer, Louis. *O'Neill: Son and Playwright*. Boston, Little, Brown, 1968.

Shepard, Odell, ed. *The Journals of Bronson Alcott*. Boston, Little, Brown, 1938.

———. *Pedlar's Progress: The Life of Bronson Alcott*. Boston, Little, Brown, 1938.

Shulman, Alix Kates, ed. *Red Emma Speaks: Selected Writings and Speeches by Emma Goldman.* New York, Random House, 1972.

———. *To the Barricades: The Anarchist Life of Emma Goldman.* New York, Crowell, 1971.

Silber, Kate. *Pestalozzi: The Man and His Work.* London, Routledge, 1960.

Silverman, Henry J., ed. *American Radical Thought: The Libertarian Tradition.* Lexington, Mass., D. C. Heath, 1970.

Simarro y Lacabra, Luis. *El proceso Ferrer y la opinión europea.* Madrid, "El Socialista," 1910.

Simmons, Ernest J. *Leo Tolstoy.* Boston, Little, Brown, 1946.

Simon, Brian. *Education and the Labour Movement, 1870-1920.* London, Lawrence & Wishart, 1965.

Smith, Gibbs M. *Joe Hill.* Salt Lake City, University of Utah Press, 1969.

Sochen, June. *The New Woman: Feminism in Greenwich Village, 1910-1920.* New York, Quadrangle, 1972.

Sprading, Charles T. *Liberty and the Great Libertarians.* Los Angeles, the Author, 1913.

Spring, Joel H. "Anarchism and Education: the Dissenting Tradition," *Libertarian Analysis,* I (December 1971), 30-42.

———. *Education and the Rise of the Corporate State.* Boston, Beacon Press, 1972.

———. *A Primer of Libertarian Education.* New York, Free Life Editions, 1975.

Steffens, Lincoln. *The Autobiography of Lincoln Steffens.* New York, The Literary Guild, 1931.

Stephenson, Cora Bennett. *The Hand of God.* Boston, Ball Publishing Co., 1909.

Stirner, Max. *The Ego and His Own.* New York, Benjamin R. Tucker, 1907.

———. *The False Principle of Our Education.* Colorado Springs, Colo., Ralph Myles, 1967.

Summerhill: For and Against. New York, Hart, 1970.

Swift, Lindsay. *Brook Farm: Its Members, Scholars, and Visitors.* New York, Macmillan, 1900.

Symes, Lillian and Travers Clement. *Rebel America: The Story of Social Revolt in the United States.* New York, Harper, 1934.

Tancredi, Libero [Massimo Rocca] and Cosimo Carmas. *La Scuola Moderna.* New York, Biblioteca "Novatore," No. 2, 1910.

Tarizzo, Domenico. *L'Anarchia.* Milan, Mondadori, 1976.

Tashjian, Dickran. *Skyscraper Primitives: Dada and the American Avant-Garde, 1910-1925.* Middletown, Conn., Wesleyan University Press, 1975.

Testimonial to Rudolf Rocker, 1873-1943. Los Angeles, Rocker Publications Committee, n.d. [1944].

Thomas, Edith. *Louise Michel, ou la Velléda de l'anarchie*. Paris, Gallimard, 1971.

Thompson, Fred and Patrick Murfin, eds. *The I.W.W.: Its First Seventy Years (1905-1975)*. Chicago, Industrial Workers of the World, 1976.

Thoreau, "The Cosmic Yankee". Los Angeles, Rocker Publications Committee, 1946.

Tien, Joseleyne S. "The Educational Theories of American Socialists, 1900-1920." Ph.D. dissertation, Michigan State University, 1972.

Tolstoy, L. N. *Tolstoy on Education*. Chicago, University of Chicago Press, 1967.

Tridon, André. *The New Unionism*. New York, B. W. Huebsch, 1913.

———. *Psychoanalysis and Behavior*. New York, Knopf, 1920.

Troyat, Henri. *Tolstoy*. New York, Dell, 1969.

Tucker, Benjamin R. *Instead of a Book*. New York, B. R. Tucker, 1893.

———. *State Socialism and Anarchism*. New York, B. R. Tucker, 1899.

———. *Why I Am an Anarchist*. Berkeley Heights, N.J., The Oriole Press, 1934.

Tunney, Thomas J. *Throttled! The Detection of the German and Anarchist Bomb Plotters*. Boston, Small, Maynard, 1919.

Turin, Yvonne. *L'Education et l'école en Espagne de 1874 à 1902*. Paris, Presses Universitaires de France, 1959.

Ullman, Joan Connelly. *The Tragic Week: A Study of Anticlericalism in Spain, 1875-1912*. Cambridge, Mass., Harvard University Press, 1968.

Vanzetti, Bartolomeo. *Two Worlds: An Imaginary Speech Delivered before Judge Webster Thayer*. Ed. by Michael A. Cohn. Foreword by Leonard D. Abbott. New York, Independent Sacco-Vanzetti Committee, 1927.

Vaughn, W. H. "Toward an Anarchistic Theory of Education: A Systematic Examination of the Educational Thought of Paul Goodman." Ph.D. dissertation, University of Kentucky, 1970.

Veysey, Laurence. *The Communal Experience: Anarchist and Mystical Counter-Cultures in America*. New York, Harper, 1973.

Vizetelly, E. A. *The Anarchists: Their Faith and Their Record*. London, John Lane, 1911.

Vorse, Mary Heaton. *A Footnote to Folly*. New York, Farrar & Rinehart, 1935.

Warren, Josiah. *Equitable Commerce*. New Harmony, Ind., J. Warren, 1846.

———. *Modern Education*. Modern Times, L.I., J. Warren, 1861.

———. *Practical Details in Equitable Commerce*. New York, Fowler & Wells, 1854.

———. *True Civilization*. Boston, J. Warren, 1863.

Warren, Sidney. *American Freethought, 1860-1914*. New York, Columbia University Press, 1943.

Werner, Alfred. *Max Weber*. New York, Harry N. Abrams, 1975.

Wertheim, Arthur F. *The New York Little Renaissance: Iconoclasm, Modernism, and Nationalism in American Culture, 1908-1917*. New York, New York University Press, 1976.

Wickey, Harry. *Thus Far: The Growth of an American Artist*. New York, American Artists Group, 1941.

Wills, W. David. *Homer Lane: A Biography*. London, Allen & Unwin, 1964.

Willson, Lawrence. "Thoreau on Education," *History of Education Quarterly*, II (March 1962), 19-29.

Wisotsky, Isidore. "Such a Life." Unpublished autobiography, Labadie Collection.

Wolff, Adolf. *Songs of Rebellion, Songs of Life, Songs of Love*. New York, Albert & Charles Boni, 1914.

Woodcock, George. *Anarchism: A History of Libertarian Ideas and Movements*. Cleveland and New York, World Publishing Co., 1962.

Yarrow, William and Louis Bouche, eds. *Robert Henri: His Life and Works*. New York, Boni & Liveright, 1921.

Yellen, Samuel. *American Labor Struggles*. New York, Harcourt, Brace, 1936.

Young, Art. *Art Young: His Life and Times*. Ed. by John Nicholas Beffel. New York, Sheridan House, 1939.

———. *On My Way*. New York, Liveright, 1928.

Young, Arthur N. *The Single Tax Movement in the United States*. Princeton, Princeton University Press, 1916.

Zeldin, David. *The Educational Ideas of Charles Fourier (1772-1837)*. London, Frank Cass, 1969.

Zigrosser, Carl. *The Artist in America*. New York, Knopf, 1942.

———. *The Modern School*. Stelton, N.J., Ferrer Colony, 1917.

———. *My Own Shall Come to Me*. Haarlem, J. Enschedé en Zonen, 1971.

Zinn, Howard. *The Politics of History*. Boston, Beacon Press, 1970.

Zorach, William. *Art Is My Life*. Cleveland, World, 1967.

PERIODICALS

Action. Stelton, N.J., 1921. Edited by Marion Trask, Anna Koch-Riedel, and Mary Stechbardt.

L'Adunata dei Refrattari. New York, 1922-1971. Edited by Max Sartin.

The Agitator. Home, Wash., 1910-1912. Edited by Jay Fox.

The Alarm. Chicago, New York, 1884-1889. Edited by Albert R. Parsons and Dyer D. Lum.

Der Anti-Autoritär. New York, 1911. Edited by Hans Koch.

The Blast. San Francisco, New York, 1916-1917. Edited by Alexander Berkman.

Boletín de la Escuela Moderna. Barcelona, 1901-1907. Edited by Francisco Ferrer.

Broyt un Frayhayt. Philadelphia, 1906. Edited by Joseph J. Cohen.

Camera Work. New York, 1903-1917. Edited by Alfred Stieglitz.

Challenge. New York, 1938-1939. Edited by Abe Bluestein.

Colony News. Lake Mohegan, N.Y., 1930-1935. Published by the Mohegan Colony Board.

The Comrade. New York, 1901-1905. Edited by John Spargo and George D. Herron.

La Cronaca Sovversiva. Barre, Vt., Lynn, Mass., 1903-1919. Edited by Luigi Galleani.

Cultura Obrera. New York, 1912-1927. Edited by Pedro Esteve.

The Dawn. Santa Barbara, Calif., 1914. Edited by Pryns Hopkins.

The Demonstrator. Home, Wash., 1903-1908. Edited by James F. Morton, Jr.

Discontent. Home, Wash., 1898-1902. Edited by Charles L. Govan *et al.*

L'Ecole Renovée. Brussels, Paris, 1908-1909. Edited by Francisco Ferrer.

L'Era Nuova. Paterson, N.J., 1908-1917.

La Escuela Moderna. Calgary, Alberta, 1963-1969. Edited by Luigi Maida and Félix Alvarez Ferreras.

Everyman. Los Angeles, 1913-1919. Edited by Luke North.

The Firebrand. Portland, Ore., 1895-1897. Edited by Henry Addis, Abe Isaak, and A. J. Pope.

The Firebrand. Mount Juliet, Tenn., Sweden, Tex., 1902-1910. Edited by Ross Winn.

The Flame. Boston, 1916. Edited by Van K. Allison.

The Free Comrade. Wellesley, Mass., 1900-1902, 1910-1912. Edited by J. William Lloyd and Leonard D. Abbott.

Free Society. San Francisco, Chicago, New York, 1897-1904. Edited by Abe Isaak.

The Free Spirit. New York, Berkeley Heights, N.J., 1919-1921. Edited by Joseph Ishill and Rose Freeman-Ishill.

Freedom. London, 1886-1927. Edited by Peter Kropotkin *et al.*

Freedom. San Francisco, 1910-1911. Edited by Eric B. Morton.

Freedom. Stelton, N.J., 1919. Edited by Harry Kelly and Leonard D. Abbott.

Freedom. New York, 1933-1934. Edited by Harry Kelly, Louis G. Raymond, and Moritz Jagendorf.

Freie Arbeiter Stimme [Fraye Arbeter Shtime]. New York, 1890-1977. Edited by Saul Yanovsky, Joseph Cohen *et al.*

Das Freie Wort. New York, 1907. Edited by Hans Koch.

Gegen den Strom. New York, 1938-1939. Edited by Robert Bek-Gran.

The Germ. Santa Barbara, Calif., 1913. Edited by Pryns Hopkins.

Germinal. Paterson, N.J., 1899-1902. Edited by Michel Dumas.

The Glebe. Ridgefield, N.J., 1913-1915. Edited by Alfred Kreymborg.

Golos Ssyl'nykh i Zakliuchennykh Russkikh Anarkhistov. New York, 1913-1914. Organ of the Anarchist Red Cross in New York.

Golos Truda. New York, 1911-1917. Edited by M. Raevsky *et al.*

The International. New York, 1908-1918. Edited by George Sylvester Viereck.

The Liberator. New York, 1918-1924. Edited by Max Eastman.

Liberty. Boston, New York, 1881-1908. Edited by Benjamin R. Tucker.

Looking Forward! Stelton, N.J., 1937-1938. Published by the Stelton Anarchist Youth Group.

Loyal Citizen Sovereignty. Boston, 1922-1923. Edited by James F. Morton, Jr.

Man! San Francisco, Los Angeles, 1933-1940. Edited by Marcus Graham.

Il Martello. New York, 1916-1946. Edited by Carlo Tresca.

The Masses. New York, 1911-1917. Edited by Max Eastman.

The Match. Boston, 1896. Edited by Harry Kelly.

The Match! Tucson, Ariz., 1969-1977. Edited by Fred Woodworth.

The Modern School. New York, Ridgefield, Stelton, 1912-1922. Edited by Carl Zigrosser *et al.*

Mother Earth. New York, 1906-1918. Edited by Emma Goldman and Alexander Berkman.

Mother Earth. Craryville, N.Y., Stelton, N.J., 1933-1934. Edited by John G. Scott and Jo Ann Wheeler.

The Needle. San Francisco, 1956. Edited by David Koven.

New Trends. New York, 1945-1946. Edited by Alexander Schapiro.

Open Vistas. Stelton, N.J., 1925. Edited by Hippolyte Havel and Joseph Ishill.

Others. Ridgefield, N.J., New York, 1915-1919. Edited by Alfred Kreymborg.

The Peaceful Revolutionist. Cincinnati, Utopia, Ohio, 1833, 1848. Edited by Josiah Warren.

Politics. New York, 1944-1949. Edited by Dwight Macdonald.

The Rebel. Boston, 1895-1896. Edited by Harry Kelly *et al.*

Resistance. New York, 1947-1954. Edited by David Thoreau Wieck.

Retort. Bearsville, N.Y., 1942-1951. Edited by Holley Cantine, Jr., and Dachine Rainer.

Revolt. New York, 1916. Edited by Hippolyte Havel.

The Ridgefield Gazook. Ridgefield, N.J., 1915. Edited by Man Ray.

The Road to Freedom. Stelton, N.J., New York, 1924-1932. Edited by Hippolyte Havel and Walter Starrett.

Sadakichi Hartmann Newsletter. Riverside, Calif., 1970- . Edited by Harry Lawton and George Knox.

Slate. New York, 1917. Edited by Jess Perlman.

The Social War. New York, 1913. Edited by Hippolyte Havel and Edward F. Mylius.

The Social War. Chicago. 1917-1918. Edited by Randolph Miller and William Judin.
The Social War Bulletin. Chicago, 1918.
The Socialist Spirit. Chicago, 1901-1903. Edited by Frederick H. Wentworth.
Solidarity. New York, 1892-1898. Edited by F. S. Merlino and John H. Edelmann.
Der Strom. New York, 1910-1912. Edited by Hans Koch.
The Stylus. New York, 1909-1910. Edited by Sadakichi Hartmann.
TNT. New York, 1919. Edited by Man Ray and Henry S. Reynolds.
Les Temps Nouveaux. Paris, 1895-1914. Edited by Jean Grave.
The Truth Seeker. New York, 1873-1922. Edited by D. M. Bennett, E. M. Macdonald, and G. E. Macdonald.
Vanguard. New York, 1932-1939. Published by the Vanguard Group.
Views & Comments. New York, 1955-1965. Edited by Sam Weiner.
The Voice of Labour. London, 1907. Edited by Alfred Marsh.
The Voice of Labour. Liverpool, 1913.
The Voice of Labour. London, 1914-1916. Edited by Fred Dunn.
The Voice of the Children, Stelton, N.J., 1929-1935. Edited by the Children of the Modern School.
Why? Tacoma, Wash., 1913-1914. Edited by Eugene Travaglio *et al*.
Why? New York, 1943-1947.
The Wide Way. New York, 1907-1908. Edited by John R. Coryell.
The Woman Rebel. New York, 1914. Edited by Margaret H. Sanger.

Index

This book has been composed and printed by
Princeton University Press

Designed by Laury A. Egan

Edited by Judith May

Typography: VIP Century Schoolbook

Paper: Warren's Olde Style

Chapter initial illustrations by
Rockwell Kent
for *The Modern School* magazine